ROBINSON CRUSOE

AN AUTHORITATIVE TEXT

CONTEXTS

CRITICISM

SECOND EDITION

A NORTON CRITICAL EDITION

Daniel Defoe

ROBINSON CRUSOE

AN AUTHORITATIVE TEXT

CONTEXTS

CRITICISM

SECOND EDITION

Edited by

MICHAEL SHINAGEL

HARVARD UNIVERSITY

W • W • NORTON & COMPANY • *New York* • *London*

To my students
in Harvard College and
Harvard Extension School

Copyright © 1994, 1975 by W. W. Norton & Company, Inc.

Printed in the United States of America

The text of this book is composed in Electra
with the display set in Bernhard Modern.
Composition by PennSet, Inc.
Manufacturing by Courier, Westford.
Book design by Antonina Krass.

Library of Congress Cataloging-in-Publication Data
Defoe, Daniel, 1661?–1731.
Robinson Crusoe : an authoritative text, backgrounds and sources,
criticism / Daniel Defoe ; edited by Michael Shinagel. — 2nd ed.
        p.   cm. — (A Norton critical edition)
        Includes bibliographical references (p.   )
1. Survival after airplane accidents, shipwrecks, etc.—Fiction.
2. Defoe, Daniel, 1661?–1731. Robinson Crusoe.   I. Shinagel,
                Michael.   II. Title.
                PR3403.A1   1994
        823'.5—dc20   93-12217

ISBN 0-393-96452-3

W. W. Norton & Company, Inc., 500 Fifth Avenue, New York, N.Y. 10110
W. W. Norton & Company Ltd., 10 Coptic Street, London WC1A 1PU

7 8 9 0

Contents

Twentieth-Century Criticism

Preface

In preparing this Norton Critical Edition of *Robinson Crusoe*, I have
tried to make available to readers an authoritative text based on Defoe's
first edition. Although Defoe was a writer of genius who, as Pope remarked, "wrote a vast many things," he took no special pains to polish
his manuscripts or to see them carefully through the press. *Robinson
Crusoe* poses complex problems to an editor that are commented on in
the Note on the Text. To insure that the text is both faithful to the
original edition and free from obvious printer's errors, I have collated
all six of the authorized editions published by William Taylor in 1719
and annotated the text to assist the reader with textual problems, obscure
words and idioms, variant spellings, and biblical allusions.

The source of Defoe's novel has commonly been held to be the
account of Alexander Selkirk, a Scottish sailor who was put ashore on
the island of Juan Fernandez in 1704 and survived a solitary life for four
years and four months until his rescue in 1709. In the section on
contexts, I have included popular contemporary accounts of marooned
men, notably Selkirk, that were published by William Dampier, Edward
Cooke, Woodes Rogers, and Richard Steele, all of which were readily
accessible to Defoe prior to his writing the novel. But to attribute the
genesis of *Robinson Crusoe* solely to Selkirk is to overlook what Defoe
strongly suggests in the prefaces to his succeeding two volumes on Crusoe: namely, that the story has elements of allegorical autobiography. I
have, therefore, included sections on autobiography and the Puritan
emblematic tradition to provide the reader with information that invites
other insightful approaches to the novel.

The success and influence of *Robinson Crusoe* is perhaps most strik-
ingly to be seen by the assembled comments of various literary and
political figures in the eighteenth and nineteenth centuries. Obviously
every educated person read the novel, and just as obviously they were
all profoundly impressed by it. Some, like Rousseau, were inspired by
it to "return to Nature"; others, like Marx, regarded it as a meretricious
model of economic independence. As critical tastes and society changed
during the two centuries following its publication, the high reputation
of *Robinson Crusoe* remained constant. It underwent literally hundreds
of editions and was translated into many languages.

The section on twentieth-century criticism of *Robinson Crusoe* presents fourteen critical evaluations, including favorable appraisals by two such influential modern novelists as Virginia Woolf and James Joyce. In the last thirty-five years, Defoe has become the subject of serious scholarly study, and numerous books and articles on him have been published. The selected bibliography is designed to provide the reader with the necessary information to pursue the study of Defoe and *Robinson Crusoe* in greater depth and detail.

The idea of first preparing a Norton Critical Edition of *Robinson Crusoe* occurred to me a number of years ago, and I am grateful to Professor M. H. Abrams of Cornell University for encouraging me to pursue this project. Peter W. Phelps of Norton revived my hopes and my interest; he and Susan Bourla assisted me, with their good counsel and good cheer, to complete the first edition with all deliberate speed. I am also indebted to Professors Ian Watt of Stanford University, Maximillian E. Novak of UCLA, George A. Starr of the University of California at Berkeley, J. Paul Hunter of the University of Chicago, Joseph Prescott of Wayne State University, Edward Kelly of SUNY College at Oneonta, and the late John Robert Moore for their cooperation and support. I have benefited from the professional services and resources of the Schaffer Library of Union College, the Widener and Houghton Libraries of Harvard University, the British Museum, and the Rare Book Room of the Boston Public Library.

In preparing this second edition I am grateful to Carol Bemis of Norton for expert editorial support and to Professors John Bender of Stanford University, Leopold Damrosch, Jr., of Harvard University, Carol Houlihan Flynn of Tufts University, Michael McKeon of Rutgers University, and John J. Richetti of the University of Pennsylvania for their scholarly cooperation in abridging their essays for this edition. I am pleased to acknowledge the cheerful and expert secretarial support of my assistant, Linda Hime, in the preparation of the revised manuscript.

MICHAEL SHINAGEL

The Text of
ROBINSON CRUSOE

THE
L I F E
AND
Strange Surprizing
ADVENTURES
OF
ROBINSON CRUSOE,
Of *YORK*, Mariner:

Who lived Eight and Twenty Years,
all alone in an un-inhabited Ifland on the
Coaft of A M E R I C A, near the Mouth of
the Great River of O R O O N O Q U E;

Having been caft on Shore by Shipwreck, wherein all the Men perifhed but himfelf.

W I T H

An Account how he was at laft as ftrangely deliver'd by P Y R A T E S.

Written by Himfelf.

L O N D O N:
Printed for W. T A Y L O R at the *Ship* in *Pater-Nofter-*
Row. MDCCXIX.

Title page of the first edition. By permission of the Houghton Library,
Harvard University.

The Preface

If ever the Story of any private Man's Adventures in the World were worth making Publick, and were acceptable when Publish'd, the Editor of this Account thinks this will be so.

The Wonders of this Man's Life exceed all that (he thinks) is to be found extant; the Life of one Man being scarce capable of a greater Variety.

The Story is told with Modesty, with Seriousness, and with a religious Application of Events to the Uses to which wise Men always apply them (*viz.*) to the Instruction of others by this Example, and to justify and honour the Wisdom of Providence in all the Variety of our Circumstances, let them happen how they will.

The Editor believes the thing to be a just History of Fact; neither is there any Appearance of Fiction in it: And whoever thinks, because all such things are dispatch'd,[1] that the Improvement of it, as well to the Diversion, as to the Instruction of the Reader, will be the same; and as such, he thinks, without farther Compliment to the World, he does them a great Service in the Publication.

---

1. The first and second editions read "*dispatch'd*"; subsequent editions read "*disputed*." The meaning is that such works are read cursorily, and, therefore, it matters little to the entertainment or instruction of the reader if the story be truth or fiction.

The Life and Adventures of Robinson Crusoe, &c.

I was born in the Year 1632, in the City of *York*, of a good Family, tho' not of that Country, my Father being a Foreigner of *Bremen*, who settled first at *Hull:* He got a good Estate by Merchandise, and leaving off his Trade, lived afterward at *York*, from whence he had married my Mother, whose Relations were named *Robinson*, a very good Family in that Country, and from whom I was called *Robinson Kreutznaer*; but by the usual Corruption of Words in *England*, we are now called, nay we call our selves, and write our Name *Crusoe*, and so my Companions always call'd me.

I had two elder Brothers, one of which was Lieutenant Collonel to an *English* Regiment of Foot in *Flanders*, formerly commanded by the famous Coll. *Lockhart*,[2] and was killed at the Battle near *Dunkirk* against the *Spaniards:* What became of my second Brother I never knew any more than my Father or Mother did know what was become of me.

Being the third Son of the Family, and not bred to any Trade, my Head began to be fill'd very early with rambling Thoughts: My Father, who was very ancient, had given me a competent Share of Learning, as far as House-Education, and a Country Free-School generally goes, and design'd me for the Law; but I would be satisfied with nothing but going to Sea, and my Inclination to this led me so strongly against the Will, nay the Commands of my Father, and against all the Entreaties and Perswasions of my Mother and other Friends, that there seem'd to be something fatal in that Propension of Nature tending directly to the Life of Misery which was to befal me.

My Father, a wise and grave Man, gave me serious and excellent Counsel against what he foresaw was my Design. He call'd me one Morning into his Chamber, where he was confined by the Gout, and expostulated very warmly with me upon this Subject: He ask'd me what Reasons more than a meer wandring Inclination I had for leaving my Father's House and my native Country, where I might be well introduced, and had a Prospect of raising my Fortune by Application and Industry, with a Life of Ease and Pleasure. He told me it was for Men

2. Sir William Lockhart (1621–76) captured Dunkirk from the Spanish in 1658.

of desperate Fortunes on one Hand, or of aspiring, superior Fortunes on the other, who went abroad upon Adventures, to rise by Enterprize, and make themselves famous in Undertakings of a Nature out of the common Road; that these things were all either too far above me, or too far below me; that mine was the middle State, or what might be called the upper Station of *Low Life*, which he had found by long Experience was the best State in the World, the most suited to human Happiness, not exposed to the Miseries and Hardships, the Labour and Sufferings of the mechanick[3] Part of Mankind, and not embarass'd with the Pride, Luxury, Ambition and Envy of the upper Part of Mankind. He told me, I might judge of the Happiness of this State, by this one thing, *viz.* That this was the State of Life which all other People envied, that Kings have frequently lamented the miserable Consequences of being born to great things, and wish'd they had been placed in the Middle of the two Extremes, between the Mean and the Great; that the wise Man gave his Testimony to this as the just Standard of true Felicity, when he prayed to have neither Poverty or Riches.[4]

He bid me observe it, and I should always find, that the Calamities of Life were shared among the upper and lower Part of Mankind; but that the middle Station had the fewest Disasters, and was not expos'd to so many Vicissitudes as the higher or lower Part of Mankind; nay, they were not subjected to so many Distempers and Uneasinesses either of Body or Mind, as those were who, by vicious Living, Luxury and Extravagancies on one Hand, or by hard Labour, Want of Necessaries, and mean or insufficient Diet on the other Hand, bring Distempers upon themselves by the natural Consequences of their Way of Living; *That* the middle Station of Life was calculated for all kind of Vertues and all kinds of Enjoyments; that Peace and Plenty were the Handmaids of a middle Fortune; that Temperance, Moderation, Quietness, Health, Society, all agreeable Diversions, and all desirable Pleasures, were the Blessings attending the middle Station of Life; that this Way Men went silently and smoothly thro' the World, and comfortably out of it, not embarass'd with the Labours of the Hands or of the Head, not sold to the Life of Slavery for daily Bread, or harrast with perplex'd Circumstances, which rob the Soul of Peace, and the Body of Rest; not enrag'd with the Passion of Envy, or secret burning Lust of Ambition for great things; but in easy Circumstances sliding gently thro' the World, and sensibly tasting the Sweets of living, without the bitter feeling that they are happy, and learning by every Day's Experience to know it more sensibly.

After this, he press'd me earnestly, and in the most affectionate manner, not to play the young Man, not to precipitate my self into Miseries which Nature and the Station of Life I was born in, seem'd to have

3. Pertaining to manual labor.
4. Solomon. Proverbs 30.8.

provided against; that I was under no Necessity of seeking my Bread; that he would do well for me, and endeavour to enter me fairly into the Station of Life which he had been just recommending to me; and that if I was not very easy and happy in the World, it must be my meer Fate[5] or Fault that must hinder it, and that he should have nothing to answer for, having thus discharg'd his Duty in warning me against Measures which he knew would be to my Hurt: In a word, that as he would do very kind things for me if I would stay and settle at Home as he directed, so he would not have so much Hand in my Misfortunes, as to give me any Encouragement to go away: And to close all, he told me I had my elder Brother for an Example, to whom he had used the same earnest Perswasions to keep him from going into the Low Country Wars, but could not prevail, his young Desires prompting him to run into the Army where he was kill'd; and tho' he said he would not cease to pray for me, yet he would venture to say to me, that if I did take this foolish Step, God would not bless me, and I would have Leisure hereafter to reflect upon having neglected his Counsel when there might be none to assist in my Recovery.

I observed in this last Part of his Discourse, which was truly Prophetick, tho' I suppose my Father did not know it to be so himself; I say, I observed the Tears run down his Face very plentifully, and especially when he spoke of my Brother who was kill'd; and that when he spoke of my having Leisure to repent, and none to assist me, he was so mov'd, that he broke off the Discourse, and told me, his Heart was so full he could say no more to me.

I was sincerely affected with this Discourse, as indeed who could be otherwise; and I resolv'd not to think of going abroad any more, but to settle at home according to my Father's Desire. But alas! a few Days wore it all off; and in short, to prevent any of my Father's farther Importunities, in a few Weeks after, I resolv'd to run quite away from him. However, I did not act so hastily neither as my first Heat of Resolution prompted, but I took my Mother, at a time when I thought her a little pleasanter than ordinary, and told her, that my Thoughts were so entirely bent upon seeing the World, that I should never settle to any thing with Resolution enough to go through with it, and my Father had better give me his Consent than force me to go without it; that I was now Eighteen Years old, which was too late to go Apprentice to a Trade, or Clerk to an Attorney; that I was sure if I did, I should never serve out my time, and I should certainly run away from my Master before my Time was out, and go to Sea; and if she would speak to my Father to let me go but one Voyage abroad, if I came home again and did not like it, I would go no more, and I would promise by a double Diligence to recover that Time I had lost.

This put my Mother into a great Passion: She told me, she knew it

5. Entirely or fully my Fate.

would be to no Purpose to speak to my Father upon any such Subject; that he knew too well what was my Interest to give his Consent to any thing so much for my Hurt, and that she wondered how I could think of any such thing after such a Discourse as I had had with my Father, and such kind and tender Expressions as she knew my Father had us'd to me; and that in short, if I would ruine my self there was no Help for me; but I might depend I should never have their Consent to it: That for her Part she would not have so much Hand in my Destruction; and I should never have it to say, that my Mother was willing when my Father was not.

Tho' my Mother refused to move[6] it to my Father, yet as I have heard afterwards, she reported all the Discourse to him, and that my Father, after shewing a great Concern at it, said to her with a Sigh, That Boy might be happy if he would stay at home, but if he goes abroad he will be the miserablest Wretch that was ever born: I can give no Consent to it.

It was not till almost a Year after this that I broke loose, tho' in the mean time I continued obstinately deaf to all Proposals of settling to Business, and frequently expostulating with my Father and Mother, about their being so positively determin'd against what they knew my Inclinations prompted me to. But being one Day at *Hull*, where I went casually, and without any Purpose of making an Elopement that time; but I say, being there, and one of my Companions being going by Sea to *London*, in his Father's Ship, and prompting me to go with them, with the common Allurement of Seafaring Men, *viz.* That it should cost me nothing for my Passage, I consulted neither Father or Mother any more, nor so much as sent them Word of it; but leaving them to hear of it as they might, without asking God's Blessing, or my Father's, without any Consideration of Circumstances or Consequences, and in an ill Hour, God knows, On the first of *September* 1651 I went on Board a Ship bound for *London*; never any young Adventurer's Misfortunes, I believe, began sooner, or continued longer than mine. The Ship was no sooner gotten out of the *Humber*, but the Wind began to blow, and the Winds[7] to rise in a most frightful manner; and as I had never been at Sea before, I was most inexpressibly s ck in Body, and terrif'd in my Mind: I began now seriously to reflect upon what I had done, and how justly I was overtaken by the Judgment of Heaven for my wicked leaving my Father's House, and abandoning my Duty; all the good Counsel of my Parents, my Father's Tears and my Mother's Entreaties came now fresh into my Mind; and my Conscience, which was not yet come to the Pitch of Hardness to which it has been since, reproach'd me with the Contempt of Advice, and the Breach of my Duty to God and my Father.

All this while the Storm encreas'd, and the Sea, which I had never

6. Propose.
7. Changed to "Sea" in the fourth and fifth editions.

been upon before, went very high, tho' nothing like what I have seen many times since; no, nor like what I saw a few Days after: But it was enough to affect me then, who was but a young Sailor, and had never known any thing of the matter. I expected every Wave would have swallowed us up, and that every time the Ship fell down, as I thought, in the Trough or Hollow of the Sea, we should never rise more; and in this Agony of Mind, I made many Vows and Resolutions, that if it would please God here to spare my Life this one Voyage, if ever I got once my Foot upon dry Land again, I would go directly home to my Father, and never set it into a Ship again while I liv'd; that I would take his Advice, and never run my self into such Miseries as these any more. Now I saw plainly the Goodness of his Observations about the middle Station of Life, how easy, how comfortably he had liv'd all his Days, and never had been expos'd to Tempests at Sea, or Troubles on Shore; and I resolv'd that I would, like a true repenting Prodigal,[8] go home to my Father.

These wise and sober Thoughts continued all the while the Storm continued, and indeed some time after; but the next Day the Wind was abated and the Sea calmer, and I began to be a little inur'd to it: However I was very grave for all that Day, being also a little Sea sick still; but towards Night the Weather clear'd up, the Wind was quite over, and a charming fine Evening follow'd; the Sun went down perfectly clear and rose so the next Morning; and having little or no Wind and a smooth Sea, the Sun shining upon it, the Sight was, as I thought, the most delightful that ever I saw.

I had slept well in the Night, and was now no more Sea sick but very chearful, looking with Wonder upon the Sea that was so rough and terrible the Day before, and could be so calm and so pleasant in so little time after. And now least my good Resolutions should continue, my Companion, who had indeed entic'd me away, comes to me, *Well Bob*, says he, clapping me on the Shoulder, *How do you do after it? I warrant you were frighted, wa'n't you, last Night, when it blew but a Cap full of Wind? A Cap full d'you call it?* said I, *'twas a terrible Storm: A Storm, you Fool you*, replies he, *do you call that a Storm, why it was nothing at all; give us but a good Ship and Sea Room, and we think nothing of such a Squall of Wind as that; but you're but a fresh Water Sailor*, Bob; *come let us make a Bowl of Punch and we'll forget all that, d'ye see what charming Weather 'tis now.* To make short this sad Part of my Story, we went the old way of all Sailors, the Punch was made, and I was made drunk with it, and in that one Night's Wickedness I drowned all my Repentance, all my Reflections upon my past Conduct, and all my Resolutions for my future. In a word, as the Sea was returned to its Smoothness of Surface and settled Calmness by the Abatement of

8. Luke 15.11ff.

that Storm, so the Hurry of my Thoughts being over, my Fears and Apprehensions of being swallow'd up by the Sea being forgotten, and the Current of my former Desires return'd, I entirely forgot the Vows and Promises that I made in my Distress. I found indeed some Intervals of Reflection, and the serious Thoughts did, as it were endeavour to return again sometimes, but I shook them off, and rouz'd my self from them as it were from a Distemper, and applying my self to Drink and Company, soon master'd the Return of those Fits, for so I call'd them, and I had in five or six Days got as compleat a Victory over Conscience as any young Fellow that resolv'd not to be troubled with it, could desire: But I was to have another Trial for it still; and Providence, as in such Cases generally it does, resolv'd to leave me entirely without Excuse. For if I would not take this for a Deliverance, the next was to be such a one as the worst and most harden'd Wretch among us would confess both the Danger and the Mercy.

The sixth Day of our being at Sea we came into *Yarmouth* Roads; the Wind having been contrary, and the Weather calm, we had made but little Way since the Storm. Here we were obliged to come to an Anchor, and here we lay, the Wind continuing contrary, *viz.* at Southwest, for seven or eight Days, during which time a great many Ships from *Newcastle* came into the same Roads, as the common Harbour where the Ships might wait for a Wind for the River.

We had not however rid here so long, but should have Tided it up the River, but that the Wind blew too fresh; and after we had lain four or five Days, blew very hard. However, the Roads being reckoned as good as a Harbour, the Anchorage good, and our Ground-Tackle very strong, our Men were unconcerned, and not in the least apprehensive of Danger, but spent the Time in Rest and Mirth, after the manner of the Sea; but the eighth Day in the Morning, the Wind increased, and we had all Hands at Work to strike our Top-Masts, and make every thing snug and close, that the Ship might ride as easy as possible. By Noon the Sea went very high indeed, and our Ship rid *Forecastle in*,[9] shipp'd several Seas, and we thought once or twice our Anchor had come home;[1] upon which our Master order'd out the Sheet Anchor; so that we rode with two Anchors a-Head, and the Cables vered out to the better End.[2]

By this Time it blew a terrible Storm indeed, and now I began to see Terror and Amazement in the Faces even of the Seamen themselves. The Master, tho' vigilant to the Business of preserving the Ship, yet as he went in and out of his Cabbin by me, I could hear him softly to himself say several times, *Lord be merciful to us, we shall be all lost, we shall be all undone*; and the like. During these first Hurries, I was

9. Rode with the bow underwater.
1. Anchor had come loose.
2. Bitter end or utmost length.

stupid,[3] lying still in my Cabbin, which was in the Steerage, and cannot describe my Temper: I could ill re-assume the first Penitence, which I had so apparently trampled upon, and harden'd my self against: I thought the Bitterness of Death had been past, and that this would be nothing too like the first. But when the Master himself came by me, as I said just now, and said we should all be lost, I was dreadfully frighted: I got up out of my Cabbin, and look'd out; but such a dismal Sight I never saw: The Sea went Mountains high, and broke upon us every three or four Minutes: when I could look about, I could see nothing but Distress round us: Two Ships that rid near us we found had cut their Masts by the Board, being deep loaden; and our Men cry'd out, that a Ship which rid about a Mile a-Head of us was foundered. Two more Ships being driven from their Anchors, were run out of the Roads to Sea at all Adventures,[4] and that with not a Mast standing. The light Ships fared the best, as not so much labouring in the Sea; but two or three of them drove, and came close by us, running away with only their Sprit-sail out before the Wind.

Towards Evening the Mate and Boat-Swain[5] begg'd the Master of our Ship to let them cut away the Foremast, which he was very unwilling to: But the Boat-Swain protesting to him, that if he did not, the Ship would founder, he consented; and when they had cut away the Foremast, the Main-Mast stood so loose, and shook the Ship so much, they were obliged to cut her away also, and make a clear Deck.

Any one may judge what a Condition I must be in at all this, who was but a young Sailor, and who had been in such a Fright before at but a little. But if I can express at this Distance the Thoughts I had about me at that time, I was in tenfold more Horror of Mind upon Account of my former Convictions, and the having returned from them to the Resolutions I had wickedly taken at first, than I was at Death it self; and these added to the Terror of the Storm, put me into such a Condition, that I can by no Words describe it. But the worst was not come yet, the Storm continued with such Fury, that the Seamen themselves acknowledged they had never known a worse. We had a good Ship, but she was deep loaden, and wallowed in the Sea, that the Seamen every now and then cried out, she would founder. It was my Advantage in one respect, that I did not know what they meant by Founder, till I enquir'd. However, the Storm was so violent, that I saw what is not often seen, the Master, the Boat-Swain, and some others more sensible than the rest, at their Prayers, and expecting every Moment when the Ship would go to the Bottom. In the Middle of the Night and under all the rest of our Distresses, one of the Men that had been down on Purpose to see, cried out we had sprung a Leak; another said there was

3. In a state of stupor.
4. At all risks.
5. Officer in charge of the rigging, cables, and anchor.

four Foot Water in the Hold. Then all Hands were called to the Pump.
At that very Word my Heart, as I thought, died within me, and I fell
backwards upon the Side of my Bed where I sat, into the Cabbin.
However, the Men roused me, and told me, that I that was able to do
nothing before, was as well able to pump as another; at which I stirr'd
up, and went to the Pump and work'd very heartily. While this was
doing, the Master seeing some light Colliers,[6] who not able to ride out
the Storm, were oblig'd to slip and run away to Sea, and would come
near us, ordered to fire a Gun as a Signal of Distress. I who knew nothing
what that meant, was so surprised, that I thought the Ship had broke,
or some dreadful thing had happen'd. In a word, I was so surprised,
that I fell down in a Swoon. As this was a time when every Body had
his own Life to think of, no Body minded me, or what was become of
me; but another Man stept up to the Pump, and thrusting me aside with
his Foot, let me lye, thinking I had been dead; and it was a great while
before I came to my self.

   We work'd on, but the Water encreasing in the Hold, it was apparent
that the Ship would founder, and tho' the Storm began to abate a little,
yet as it was not possible she could swim till we might run into a Port,
so the Master continued firing Guns for Help; and a light Ship who had
rid it out just a Head of us ventured a Boat out to help us. It was with
the utmost Hazard the Boat came near us, but it was impossible for us
to get on Board, or for the Boat to lie near the Ship Side, till at last the
Men rowing very heartily, and venturing their Lives to save ours, our
Men cast them a Rope over the Stern with a Buoy to it, and then vered
it out a great Length, which they after great Labour and Hazard took
hold of, and we hall'd[7] them close under our Stern and got all into their
Boat. It was to no Purpose for them or us after we were in the Boat to
think of reaching to their own Ship, so all agreed to let her drive and
only to pull her in towards Shore as much as we could, and our Master
promised them, That if the Boat was stav'd upon Shore he would make
it good to their Master, so partly rowing and partly driving, our Boat
went away to the Norward sloaping towards the Shore almost as far as
Winterton Ness.[8]

   We were not much more than a quarter of an Hour out of our Ship
but we saw her sink, and then I understood for the first time what was
meant by a Ship foundering in the Sea; I must acknowledge I had hardly
Eyes to look up when the Seamen told me she was sinking; for from
that Moment they rather put me into the Boat than that I might be said
to go in, my Heart was as it were dead within me, partly with Fright,
partly with Horror of Mind and the Thoughts of what was yet before
me.

6. Coal barges.
7. Hauled.
8. Promontory on the coast of Norfolk.

While we were in this Condition, the Men yet labouring at the Oar to bring the Boat near the Shore, we could see, when our Boat mounting the Waves, we were able to see the Shore, a great many People running along the shore to assist us when we should come near, but we made but slow way towards the Shore, nor were we able to reach the Shore, till being past the Light-House at *Winterton*, the Shore falls off to the Westward towards *Cromer*, and so the Land broke off a little the Violence of the Wind: Here we got in, and tho' not without much Difficulty got all safe on Shore, and walk'd afterwards on Foot to *Yarmouth*, where, as unfortunate Men, we were used with great Humanity as well by the Magistrates of the Town, who assign'd us good Quarters, as by particular Merchants and Owners of Ships, and had Money given us sufficient to carry us either to *London* or back to *Hull*, as we thought fit.

Had I now had the Sense to have gone back to *Hull*, and have gone home, I had been happy, and my Father, an Emblem of our Blessed Saviour's Parable,[9] had even kill'd the fatted Calf for me; for hearing the ship I went away in was cast away in *Yarmouth* Road, it was a great while before he had any Assurance that I was not drown'd.

But my ill Fate push'd me on now with an Obstinacy that nothing could resist; and tho' I had several times loud Calls from my Reason and my more composed Judgment to go home, yet I had no Power to do it. I know not what to call this, nor will I urge, that it is a secret overruling Decree that hurries us on to be the Instruments of our own Destruction, even tho' it be before us, and that we rush upon it with our Eyes open. Certainly nothing but some such decreed unavoidable Misery attending, and which it was impossible for me to escape, could have push'd me forward against the calm Reasonings and Perswasions of my most retired Thoughts, and against two such visible Instructions as I had met with in my first Attempt.

My Comrade, who had help'd to harden me before, and who was the Master's Son, was now less forward than I; the first time he spoke to me after we were at *Yarmouth*, which was not till two or three Days, for we were separated in the Town to several Quarters; I say, the first time he saw me, it appear'd his Tone was alter'd, and looking very melancholy and shaking his Head, ask'd me how I did, and telling his Father who I was, and how I had come this Voyage only for a Trial in order to go farther abroad; his Father turning to me with a very grave and concern'd Tone, *Young Man*, says he, *you ought never to go to Sea any more, you ought to take this for a plain and visible Token that you are not to be a Seafaring Man.* Why, Sir, said I, will you go to Sea no more? *That is another Case*, said he, *it is my Calling, and therefore my Duty; but as you made this Voyage for a Trial, you see what a Taste Heaven has given you of what you are to expect if you persist; perhaps this is all befallen us on your Account, like* Jonah[1] *in the Ship of* Tarshish.

9. Luke 15.23.
1. Jonah 1.1ff.

Pray, continues he, *what are you? and on what Account did you go to Sea?* Upon that I told him some of my Story; at the End of which he burst out with a strange kind of Passion, What had I done, says he, that such an unhappy Wretch should come into my Ship? I would not set my Foot in the same Ship with thee again for a Thousand Pounds. This indeed was, as I said, an Excursion of his Spirits which were yet agitated by the Sense of his Loss, and was farther than he could have Authority to go. However he afterwards talk'd very gravely to me, exhorted me to go back to my Father, and not tempt Providence to my Ruine; told me I might see a visible Hand of Heaven against me, *And young Man*, said he, *depend upon it, if you do not go back, whereever you go, you will meet with nothing but Disasters and Disappointments till your Father's Words are fulfilled upon you.*

We parted soon after; for I made him little Answer, and I saw him no more; which way he went, I know not. As for me, having some Money in my Pocket, I travelled to *London* by Land; and there, as well as on the Road, had many Struggles with my self, what Course of Life I should take, and whether I should go Home, or go to Sea.

As to going Home, Shame opposed the best Motions that offered to my Thoughts; and it immediately occurr'd to me how I should be laugh'd at among the Neighbours, and should be asham'd to see, not my Father and Mother only, but even every Body else; from whence I have since often observed, how incongruous and irrational the common Temper of Mankind is, especially of Youth, to that Reason which ought to guide them in such Cases, *viz.* That they are not asham'd to sin, and yet are asham'd to repent; not asham'd of the Action for which they ought justly to be esteemed Fools, but are asham'd of the returning, which only can make them be esteem'd wise Men.

In this State of Life however I remained some time, uncertain what Measures to take, and what Course of Life to lead. An irresistible Reluctance continu'd to going Home; and as I stay'd a while, the Remembrance of the Distress I had been in wore off; and as that abated, the little Motion I had in my Desires to a Return wore off with it, till at last I quite lay'd aside the Thoughts of it, and lookt[2] out for a Voyage.

That evil Influence which carryed me first away from my Father's House, that hurried me into the wild and indigested Notion of raising my Fortune; and that imprest those Conceits so forcibly upon me, as to make me deaf to all good Advice, and to the Entreaties and even Command of my Father; I say the same Influence, whatever it was, presented the most unfortunate of all Enterprises to my View; and I went on board a Vessel bound to the Coast of *Africa*; or, as our Sailors vulgarly call it, a Voyage to *Guinea*.

It was my great Misfortune that in all these Adventures I did not ship my self as a Sailor; whereby, tho' I might indeed have workt a little

---

2. Common spelling for *look'd* in the first edition. Defoe frequently employed a shorthand that replaced the final *-ed* of a word with a *t*—e.g., "reacht," "fisht."

harder than ordinary, yet at the same time I had learn'd the Duty and Office of a Fore-mast Man; and in time might have quallified my self for a Mate or Lieutenant, if not for a Master: But as it was always my Fate to choose for the worse, so I did here; for having Money in my Pocket, and good Cloaths[3] upon my Back, I would always go on board in the Habit of a Gentleman; and so I neither had any Business in the Ship, or learn'd to do any.

It was my Lot first of all to fall into pretty good Company in *London*, which does not always happen to such loose and unguided young Fellows as I then was; the Devil generally not omitting to lay some Snare for them very early: But it was not so with me, I first fell acquainted with the Master of a Ship who had been on the Coast of *Guinea*; and who having had very good Success there, was resolved to go again; and who taking a Fancy to my Conversation, which was not at all disagreeable at that time, hearing me say I had a mind to see the World, told me if I wou'd go the Voyage with him I should be at no Expence; I should be his Mess-mate and his Companion, and if I could carry any thing with me, I should have all the Advantage of it that the Trade would admit; and perhaps I might meet some Encouragement.

I embrac'd the Offer, and entring into a strict Friendship with this Captain, who was an honest and plain-dealing Man, I went the Voyage with him, and carried a small Adventure with me, which by the disinterested Honesty of my Friend the Captain, I increased very considerably; for I carried about 40 *l*. in such Toys and Trifles as the Captain directed me to buy. This 40 *l*. I had mustered together by the Assistance of some of my Relations whom I corresponded with, and who, I believe, got my Father, or at least my Mother, to contribute so much as that to my first Adventure.

This was the only Voyage which I may say was successful in all my Adventures, and which I owe to the Integrity and Honesty of my Friend the Captain, under whom also I got a competent Knowledge of the Mathematicks and the Rules of Navigation, learn'd how to keep an Account of the Ship's Course, take an Observation; and in short, to understand some things that were needful to be understood by a Sailor: For, as he took Delight to introduce me, I took Delight to learn; and, in a word, this Voyage made me both a Sailor and a Merchant: for I brought home *L*. 5. 9 *Ounces* of Gold Dust for my Adventure, which yielded me in *London* at my Return, almost 300 *l*. and this fill'd me with those aspiring Thoughts which have since so compleated my Ruin.

Yet even in this Voyage I had my Misfortunes too; particularly, that I was continually sick, being thrown into a violent Calenture[4] by the excessive Heat of the Climate; our principal Trading being upon the

---

3. Spelling for *clothes* throughout most of the text.
4. A tropical disease accompanied by high fever and delirium (from the Spanish *calentura*, "fever").

Coast, from the Latitude of 15 Degrees, North even to the Line it self.

I was now set up for a *Guiney* Trader; and my Friend, to my great Misfortune, dying soon after his Arrival, I resolved to go the same Voyage again, and I embark'd in the same Vessel with one who was his Mate in the former Voyage, and had now got the Command of the Ship. This was the unhappiest Voyage that ever Man made; for tho' I did not carry quite 100 *l.* of my new gain'd Wealth, so that I had 200 left, and which I lodg'd with my Friend's Widow, who was very just to me, yet I fell into Terrible Misfortunes in this Voyage; and the first was this, *viz.* Our Ship making her Course towards the *Canary* Islands, or rather between those Islands and the *African* Shore, was surprised in the Grey of the Morning, by a *Turkish* Rover of *Sallee*,[5] who gave Chase to us with all the Sail she could make. We crowded also as much Canvass as our Yards would spread, or our Masts carry, to have got clear; but finding the Pirate gain'd upon us, and would certainly come up with us in a few Hours, we prepar'd to fight, our Ship having 12 Guns, and the Rogue 18. About three in the Afternoon he came up with us, and bringing to by Mistake, just athwart our Quarter, instead of athwart our Stern, as he intended, we brought 8 of our Guns to bear on that Side, and pour'd in a Broadside upon him, which made him sheer off again, after returning our Fire, and pouring in also his small Shot from near 200 Men which he had on Board. However, we had not a Man touch'd, all our Men keeping close. He prepar'd to attack us again, and we to defend our selves; but laying us on Board the next time upon our other Quarter, he entred 60 Men upon our Decks, who immediately fell to cutting and hacking the Decks and Rigging. We ply'd them with Small-Shot, Half-Pikes, Powder-Chests, and such like, and clear'd our Deck of them twice. However, to cut short this melancholly Part of our Story, our Ship being disabled, and three of our Men kill'd, and eight wounded, we were obliged to yield, and were carry'd all Prisoners into *Sallee*, a Port belonging to the *Moors*.

The Usage I had there was not so dreadful as at first I apprehended, nor was I carried up the Country to the Emperor's Court, as the rest of our Men were, but was kept by the Captain of the Rover, as his proper Prize, and made his Slave, being young and nimble, and fit for his Business. At this surprising Change of my Circumstances from a Merchant to a miserable Slave, I was perfectly overwhelmed; and now I look'd back upon my Father's prophetick Discourse to me, that I should be miserable, and have none to relieve me, which I thought was now so effectually brought to pass, that it could not be worse; that now the Hand of Heaven had overtaken me, and I was undone without Redemption. But alas! this was but a Taste of the Misery I was to go thro', as will appear in the Sequel of this Story.

5. Seaport of Morocco and once a notorious pirate base.

As my new Patron or Master had taken me Home to his House, so I was in hopes that he would take me with him when he went to Sea again, believing that it would some time or other be his Fate to be taken by a *Spanish* or *Portugal* Man of War; and that then I should be set at Liberty. But this Hope of mine was soon taken away; for when he went to Sea, he left me on Shoar[6] to look after his little Garden, and do the common Drudgery of Slaves about his House; and when he came home again from his Cruise, he order'd me to lye in the Cabbin to look after the Ship.

Here I meditated nothing but my Escape; and what Method I might take to effect it, but found no Way that had the least Probability in it: Nothing presented to make the Supposition of it rational; for I had no Body to communicate it to, that would embark with me; no Fellow-Slave, no *Englishman*, *Irishman*, or *Scotsman* there but my self; so that for two Years, tho' I often pleased my self with the Imagination, yet I never had the least encouraging Prospect of putting it in Practice.

After about two Years an odd Circumstance presented it self, which put the old Thought of making some Attempt for my Liberty, again in my Head: My Patron lying at Home longer than usual, without fitting out his Ship, which, as I heard, was for want of Money; he used constantly, once or twice a Week, sometimes oftener, if the Weather was fair, to take the Ship's Pinnace,[7] and go out into the Road a-fishing; and as he always took me and a young *Maresco*[8] with him to row the Boat, we made him very merry, and I prov'd very dexterous in catching Fish; insomuch that sometimes he would send me with a *Moor*, one of his Kinsmen, and the Youth the *Maresco*, as they call'd him, to catch a Dish of Fish for him.

It happen'd one time, that going a fishing in a stark calm Morning, a Fog rose so thick, that tho' we were not half a League from the Shoar, we lost Sight of it; and rowing we knew not wither or which way, we labour'd all Day and all the next Night, and when the Morning came we found we had pull'd off to Sea instead of pulling in for the Shoar; and that we were at least two Leagues from the Shoar: However we got well in again, tho' with a great deal of Labour, and some Danger; for the Wind began to blow pretty fresh in the morning; but particularly we were all very hungry.

But our Patron warn'd by this Disaster, resolved to take more Care of himself for the future; and having lying by him the Longboat of our *English* Ship they had taken, he resolved he would not go a fishing any more without a Compass and some Provision; so he ordered the Carpenter of his Ship, who also was an *English* Slave, to build a little State-

---

6. Corrected to "Shore" in the second and subsequent editions, but "Shoar" throughout most of the first-edition text.
7. Tender.
8. Probably a misprint for "*Moresco*," Spanish for "Moor."

room or Cabin in the middle of the Long Boat, like that of a Barge, with a Place to stand behind it to steer and hale[9] home the Main-sheet; and Room before for a hand or two to stand and work the Sails; she sail'd with that we call a Shoulder of Mutton Sail;[1] and the Boom gib'd over the Top of the Cabbin, which lay very snug and low, and had in it Room for him to lye, with a Slave or two, and a Table to eat on, with some small Lockers to put in some Bottles of such Liquor as he thought fit to drink; particularly his Bread, Rice and Coffee.

We went frequently out with this Boat a fishing, and as I was most dextrous to catch fish for him, he never went without me: It happen'd that he had appointed to go out in this Boat, either for Pleasure or for Fish, with two or three *Moors* of some Distinction in that Place, and for whom he had provided extraordinarily; and had therefore sent on board the Boat over Night, a larger Store of Provisions than ordinary; and had order'd me to get ready three Fuzees[2] with Powder and Shot, which were on board his Ship; for that they design'd some Sport of Fowling as well as Fishing.

I got all things ready as he had directed, and waited the next Morning with the Boat, washed clean, her Antient and Pendants[3] out, and every thing to accomodate his Guests; when by and by my Patron came on board alone, and told me his Guests had put off going, upon some Business that fell out, and order'd me with the Man and Boy, as usual, to go out with the Boat and catch them some Fish, for that his Friends were to sup at his House; and commanded that as soon as I had got some Fish I should bring it home to his House; all which I prepar'd to do.

This Moment my former Notions of Deliverance darted into my Thoughts, for now I found I was like to have a little Ship at my Command; and my Master being gone, I prepar'd to furnish my self, not for a fishing Business but for a Voyage; tho' I knew not, neither did I so much as consider whither I should steer; for any where to get out of that Place was my Way.

My first Contrivance was to make a Pretence to speak to this *Moor*, to get something for our Subsistance on board; for I told him we must not presume to eat of our Patron's Bread; he said, that was true; so he brought a large Basket of Rusk or Bisket of their kind, and three Jarrs with fresh Water into the Boat; I knew where my Patron's Case of Bottles stood, which it was evident by the make were taken out of some *English* Prize; and I convey'd them into the Boat while the *Moor* was on Shoar, as if they had been there before, for our Master: I convey'd also a great Lump of Bees-Wax into the Boat, which weighed above half a Hundred

9. Haul.
1. Triangular sail that resembles a shoulder of mutton.
2. Light muskets.
3. Ensign and pennants.

Weight, with a Parcel of Twine or Thread, a Hatchet, a Saw and a
Hammer, all which were of great Use to us afterwards; especially the
Wax to make Candles. Another Trick I try'd upon him, which he
innocently came into also; his Name was *Ismael*, who they call *Muly*
or *Moely*, so I call'd to him, *Moley* said I, our Patron's Guns are on
board the Boat, can you not get a little Powder and Shot, it may be we
may kill some *Alcamies* (a Fowl like our *Curlieus* [4]) for our selves, for
I know he keeps the Gunner's Stores in the Ship? Yes, *says he*, I'll bring
some, and accordingly he brought a great Leather Pouch which held
about a Pound and half of Powder, or rather more; and another with
Shot, that had five or six Pound, with some Bullets; and put all into the
Boat: At the same time I had found some Powder of my Master's in the
Great Cabbin, with which I fill'd one of the large Bottles in the Case,
which was almost empty; pouring what was in it into another: and thus
furnished with every thing needful, we sail'd out of the Port to fish: The
Castle which is at the Entrance of the Port knew who we were, and
took no Notice of us; and we were not above a Mile out of the Port
before we hal'd in our Sail, and set us down to fish: The Wind blew
from the N.NE. which was contrary to my Desire; for had it blown
southerly I had been sure to have made the Coast of *Spain*, and at least
reacht to the Bay of *Cadiz*; but my Resolutions were, blow which way
it would, I would be gone from that horrid Place where I was, and leave
the rest to Fate.

After we had fisht some time and catcht nothing, for when I had Fish
on my Hook, I would not pull them up, that he might not see them; I
said to the *Moor*, this will not do, our Master will not be thus serv'd,
we must stand farther off: He thinking no harm agreed, and being in
the Head of the Boat set the Sails; and as I had the Helm I run the Boat
out near a League farther, and then brought her too as if I would fish;
when giving the Boy the Helm, I stept forward to where the *Moor* was,
and making as if I stoopt for something behind him, I took him by
Surprize with my Arm under his Twist, [5] and tost him clear over-board
into the Sea; he rise [6] immediately, for he swam like a Cork, and call'd
to me, begg'd to be taken in, told me he would go all over the World
with me; he swam so strong after the Boat that he would have reacht
me very quickly, there being but little Wind; upon which I stept into
the Cabbin and fetching one of the Fowling-pieces, I presented it at
him, and told him, I had done him no hurt, and if he would be quiet
I would do him none; but said I, you swim well enough to reach to the
Shoar, and the Sea is calm, make the best of your Way to Shoar and I
will do you no harm, but if you come near the Boat I'll shoot you thro'

---

4. Curlews, a species of large birds with long legs and a long, curved bill, common in Europe
and America.
5. Crotch.
6. Changed to "rose" in the sixth edition.

the Head; for I am resolved to have my Liberty; so he turn'd himself about and swam for the Shoar, and I make no doubt but he reacht it with Ease, for he was an Excellent Swimmer.

I could ha' been content to ha' taken this *Moor* with me, and ha' drown'd the Boy, but there was no venturing to trust him: When he was gone I turn'd to the Boy, who they call'd *Xury*, and said to him, *Xury*, if you will be faithful to me I'll make you a great Man, but if you will not stroak your Face to be true to me, *that is, swear by* Mahomet *and his Father's Beard*, I must throw you into the Sea too; the Boy smil'd in my Face and spoke so innocently that I could not mistrust him; and swore to be faithful to me, and go all over the World with me.

While I was in View of the *Moor* that was swimming, I stood out directly to Sea with the Boat, rather stretching to Windward, that they might think me gone towards the *Straits*-mouth[7] (as indeed any one that had been in their Wits must ha' been supposed to do) for who would ha' suppos'd we were saild on to the southward to the truly *Barbarian* Coast, where whole Nations of Negroes were sure to surround us with their Canoes, and destroy us; where we could ne'er once go on shoar but we should be devour'd by savage Beasts, or more merciless Savages of humane[8] kind.

But as soon as it grew dusk in the Evening, I chang'd my Course, and steer'd directly South and by East, bending my Course a little toward the East, that I might keep in with the Shoar; and having a fair fresh Gale of Wind, and a smooth quiet Sea, I made such Sail that I believe by the next Day at Three a Clock in the Afternoon, when I first made the Land, I could not be less than 150 Miles South of *Sallee*; quite beyond the Emperor of *Morocco's* Dominions, or indeed of any other King thereabouts, for we saw no People.

Yet such was the Fright I had taken at the *Moors*, and the dreadful Apprehensions I had of falling into their Hands, that I would not stop, or go on Shoar, or come to an Anchor; the Wind continuing fair, 'till I had sail'd in that manner five Days: And then the Wind shifting to the southward, I concluded also that if any of our Vessels were in Chase of me, they also would now give over; so I ventur'd to make to the Coast, and came to an Anchor in the Mouth of a little River, I knew not what, or where; neither what Latitude, what Country, what Nations, or what River: I neither saw, or desir'd to see any People, the principal thing I wanted was fresh Water: We came into this Creek in the Evening, resolving to swim on shoar as soon as it was dark, and discover[9] the Country; but as soon as it was quite dark, we heard such dreadful Noises

7. Straits of Gibraltar.
8. Spelling for *human* throughout the first edition; corrected in the second and subsequent editions.
9. Explore.

of the Barking, Roaring, and Howling of Wild Creatures, of we know not what Kinds, that the poor Boy was ready to die with Fear, and beg'd of me not to go on shoar till Day; well Xury said I, then I won't, but it may be we may see Men by Day, who will be as bad to us as those Lyons; *then we give them the shoot Gun* says Xury laughing, *make them run wey;* such *English* Xury spoke by conversing among us Slaves, however I was glad to see the Boy so cheerful, and I gave him a Dram (out of our Patron's Case of Bottles) to chear him up: After all, Xury's Advice was good, and I took it, we dropt our little Anchor and lay still all Night; I say still, for we slept none! for in two or three Hours we saw vast great Creatures (we knew not what to call them) of many sorts, come down to the Sea-shoar and run into the Water, wallowing and washing themselves for the Pleasure of cooling themselves; and they made such hideous Howlings and Yellings, that I never indeed heard the like.

Xury was dreadfully frighted, and indeed so was I too; but we were both more frighted when we heard one of these mighty Creatures come swimming towards our Boat, we could not see him, but we might hear him by his blowing to be a monstrous, huge and furious Beast; Xury said it was a Lyon, and it might be so for ought I know; but poor Xury cryed to me to weigh the Anchor and row away; no says I, Xury, we can slip our Cable with the Buoy to it and go off to Sea, they cannot follow us far; I had no sooner said so, but I perceiv'd the Creature (whatever it was) within Two Oars Length, which something surprized me; however I immediately stept to the Cabbin-door, and taking up my Gun fir'd at him, upon which he immediately turn'd about and swam towards the Shoar again.

But it is impossible to describe the horrible Noises, and hideous Cryes and Howlings, that were raised as well upon the Edge of the Shoar, as higher within the Country; upon the Noise or Report of the Gun, a Thing I have some Reason to believe those Creatures had never heard before: This Convinc'd me that there was no going on Shoar for us in the Night upon that Coast, and how to venture on Shoar in the Day was another Question too; for to have fallen into the Hands of any of the Savages, had been as bad as to have fallen into the Hands of Lyons and Tygers; at least we were equally apprehensive of the Danger of it.

Be that as it would, we were oblig'd to go on Shoar somewhere or other for Water, for we had not a Pint left in the Boat; when or where to get it was the Point: Xury said, if I would let him go on Shoar with one of the Jarrs, he would find if there was any Water and bring some to me. I ask'd him why he would go? why I should not go and he stay in the Boat? The Boy answer'd with so much Affection that made me love him ever after. Says he, *If wild Mans come, they eat me, you go wey.* Well, Xury, said I, we will both go, and if the wild Mans come we will kill them, they shall Eat neither of us; so I gave Xury a piece of Rusk-bread to Eat and a Dram out of our Patron's Case of Bottles which I mentioned before; and we hal'd the Boat in as near the Shoar as we thought was proper, and so waded on Shoar, carrying nothing but our Arms and two Jarrs for Water.

I did not care to go out of Sight of the Boat, fearing the coming of Canoes with *Savages* down the River; but the Boy seeing a low Place about a Mile up the Country rambled to it; and by and by I saw him come running towards me, I thought he was pursued by some Savage, or frighted with some Wild Beast, and I run forward towards him to help him, but when I came nearer to him, I saw something hanging over his Shoulders which was a Creature that he had shot, like a Hare but different in Colour, and longer Legs, however we were very glad of it, and it was very good Meat; but the great Joy that poor *Xury* came with, was to tell me he had found good Water and seen no wild Mans.

But we found afterwards that we need not take such Pains for Water, for a little higher up the Creek where we were, we found the Water fresh when the Tide was out, which flowed but a little way up; so we filled our Jarrs and feasted on the Hare we had killed, and prepared to go on our Way, having seen no Foot-steps of any humane Creature in that part of the Country.

As I had been one Voyage to this Coast before, I knew very well that the Islands of the *Canaries*, and the *Cape de Verd* Islands also, lay not far off from the Coast. But as I had no Instruments to take an Observation to know what Latitude we were in, and did not exactly know, or at least remember what Latitude they were in; I knew not where to look for them, or when to stand off to Sea towards them; otherwise I might now easily have found some of these Islands. But my hope was, that if I stood along this Coast till I came to that Part where the *English* Traded, I should find some of their Vessels upon their usual Design of Trade, that would relieve and take us in.

By the best of my Calculation, that Place where I now was, must be that Country, which lying between the Emperor of *Morocco*'s Dominions and the *Negro*'s, lies wast[1] and uninhabited, except by wild Beasts; the *Negroes* having abandon'd it and gone farther South for fear of the *Moors*; and the *Moors* not thinking it worth inhabiting, by reason of its Barrenness; and indeed both forsaking it because of the prodigious Numbers of Tygers, Lyons, Leopards and other furious Creatures which harbour there; so that the *Moors* use it for their Hunting only, where they go like an Army, two or three thousand Men at a time; and indeed for near an hundred Miles together upon this Coast, we saw nothing but a wast uninhabited Country, by Day; and heard nothing but Howlings and Roaring of wild Beasts, by Night.

Once or twice in the Day time, I thought I saw the *Pico* of *Teneriffe*,

1. Changed to "waste" in the fifth edition.

being the high top of the Mountain *Teneriffe* in the *Canaries*; and had
a great mind to venture out in hopes of reaching thither; but having
tried twice I was forced in again by contrary Winds, the Sea also going
too high for my little Vessel, so I resolved to pursue my first Design and
keep along the Shoar.

Several times I was obliged to land for fresh Water, after we had left
this Place; and once in particular, being early in the Morning, we came
to an Anchor under a little Point of Land which was pretty high, and
the Tide beginning to flow, we lay still to go farther in; *Xury*, whose
Eyes were more about him than it seems mine were, calls softly to me,
and tells me that we had best go farther off the Shoar, for, says he, look
yonder lies a dreadful Monster on the side of that Hillock fast asleep: I
look'd where he pointed, and saw a dreadful Monster indeed, for it was
a terrible great Lyon that lay on the Side of the Shoar, under the Shade
of a Piece of the Hill that hung as it were a little over him. *Xury*, says
I, you shall go on Shoar and kill him; *Xury* look'd frighted, and said,
Me kill! he eat me at one Mouth; one Mouthful he meant; however, I
said no more to the Boy, but bad him lye still, and I took our biggest
Gun, which was almost Musquetbore, and loaded it with a good Charge
of Powder, and with two Slugs, and laid it down; then I loaded another
Gun with two Bullets, and the third, for we had three Pieces, I loaded
with five smaller Bullets. I took the best aim I could with the first Piece
to have shot him into the Head, but he lay so with his Leg rais'd a little
above his Nose, that the Slugs hit his Leg about the Knee, and broke
the Bone. He started up growling at first, but finding his Leg broke fell
down again, and then got up upon three Legs and gave the most hideous
Roar that ever I heard; I was a little surpriz'd that I had not hit him on
the Head; however I took up the second Piece immediately, and tho'd
he began to move off fir'd again, and shot him into the Head, and had
the Pleasure to see him drop, and make but little Noise, but lay struggling
for Life. Then *Xury* took Heart, and would have me let him go on
Shoar: Well, go said I; so the Boy jump'd into the Water, and taking a
little Gun in one Hand swam to Shoar with the other Hand, and coming
close to the Creature, put the Muzzle of the Piece to his Ear, and shot
him into the Head again which dispatch'd him quite.

This was Game indeed to us, but this was no Food, and I was very
sorry to lose three Charges of Powder and Shot upon a Creature that
was good for nothing to us. However *Xury* said he would have some of
him; so he comes on board, and ask'd me to give him the Hatchet; for
what, *Xury*, said I? *Me cut off his Head*, said he. However *Xury* could
not cut off his Head, but he cut off a Foot and brought it with him,
and it was a monstrous great one.

I bethought my self however, that perhaps the Skin of him might one
way or other be of some Value to us; and I resolved to take off his Skin
if I could. So *Xury* and I went to work with him; but *Xury* was much

the better Workman at it, for I knew very ill how to do it. Indeed it took us up both the whole Day, but at last we got off the Hide of him, and spreading it on the top of our Cabbin, the Sun effectually dried it in two Days time, and it afterwards serv'd me to lye upon.

After this Stop we made on to the Southward continually for ten or twelve Days, living very sparing on our Provisions, which began to abate very much, and going no oftner into the Shoar than we were oblig'd to for fresh Water; my Design in this was to make the River *Gambia* or *Senegall*, that is to say, any where about the *Cape de Verd*, where I was in hopes to meet with some *European* Ship, and if I did not, I knew not what Course I had to take, but to seek out for the *Islands*, or perish there among the *Negroes*. I knew that all the Ships from *Europe*, which sail'd either to the Coast of *Guiney*, or to *Brasil*, or to the *East-Indies*, made this *Cape* or those *Islands*; and in a word, I put the whole of my Fortune upon this single Point, either that I must meet with some Ship, or must perish.

When I had pursued this Resolution about ten Days longer, as I have said, I began to see that the Land was inhabited, and in two or three Places as we sailed by, we saw People stand upon the Shoar to look at us, we could also perceive they were quite Black and Stark-naked. I was once inclin'd to ha' gone on Shoar to them; but *Xury* was my better Councellor, and said to me, *no go, no go*; however I hal'd in nearer the Shoar that I might talk to them, and I found they run along the Shoar by me a good way; I observ'd they had no Weapons in their Hands, except one who had a long slender Stick, which *Xury* said was a Lance, and that they would throw them a great way with good aim; so I kept at a distance, but talk'd with them by Signs as well as I could; and particularly made Signs for some thing to Eat, they beckon'd to me to stop my Boat, and that they would fetch me some Meat; upon this I lower'd the top of my Sail, and lay by, and two of them run up into the Country, and in less than half an Hour came back and brought with them two Pieces of dry Flesh and some Corn, such as is the Produce of their Country, but we neither knew what the one or the other was; however we were willing to accept it, but how to come at it was our next Dispute, for I was not for venturing on Shore to them, and they were as much afraid of us; but they took a safe way for us all, for they brought it to the Shore and laid it down, and went and stood a great way off till we fetch'd it on Board, and then came close to us again.

We made Signs of Thanks to them, for we had nothing to make them amends; but an Opportunity offer'd that very Instant to oblige them wonderfully, for while we were lying by the Shore, came two mighty Creatures one pursuing the other, (as we took it) with great Fury, from the Mountains towards the Sea; whether it was the Male pursuing the Female, or whether they were in Sport or in Rage, we could not tell, any more than we could tell whether it was usual or strange, but I believe it was the latter; because in the first Place, those ravenous Creatures seldom appear but in the Night; and in the second Place, we found the People terribly frighted, especially the Women. The Man that had the Lance or Dart did not fly from them, but the rest did; however as the two Creatures ran directly into the Water, they did not seem to offer to fall upon any of the Negroes, but plung'd themselves into the Sea and swam about as if they had come for their Diversion; at last one of them began to come nearerr our Boat than at first I expected, but I lay ready for him, for I had loaded my Gun with all possible Expedition, and bad Xury load both the other; as soon as he came fairly within my reach, I fir'd and shot him directly into the Head; immediately he sunk down into the Water, but rose instantly and plung'd up and down as if he was struggling for Life; and so indeed he was, he immediately made to the Shore, but between the Wound which was his mortal Hurt, and the strangling of the Water, he dyed just before he reach'd the Shore.

It is impossible to express the Astonishment of these poor Creatures at the Noise and the Fire of my Gun; some of them were even ready to dye for Fear, and fell down as Dead with the very Terror. But when they saw the Creature dead and sunk in the Water, and that I made Signs to them to come to the Shore; they took Heart and came to the Shore and began to search for the Creature, I found him by his Blood staining the Water, and by the help of a Rope which I slung round him and gave the Negroes to hawl, they drag'd him on Shore, and found that it was a most curious Leopard, spotted and fine to an admirable Degree, and the Negroes held up their Hands with Admiration to think what it was I had kill'd him with.

The other Creature frighted with the flash of Fire and the Noise of the Gun swam on Shore, and ran up directly to the Mountains from whence they came, nor could I at that Distance know what it was. I found quickly the Negroes were for eating the Flesh of this Creature, so I was willing to have them take it as a Favour from me, which when I made Signs to them that they might take him, they were very thankful for, immediately they fell to work with him, and tho' they had no Knife, yet with a sharpen'd Piece of Wood they took off his Skin as readily and much more readily than we cou'd have done with a Knife; they offer'd me some of the Flesh, which I declined, making as if I would give it them, but made Signs for the Skin, which they gave me very freely, and brought me a great deal more of their Provision, which tho' I did not understand, yet I accepted; then I made Signs to them for some Water, and held out one of my Jarrs to them, turning it bottom upward, to shew that it was empty, and that I wanted to have it filled. They call'd immediately to some of their Friends, and there came two Women and brought a great Vessel made of Earth, and burnt as I suppose in the Sun; this they set down for me, as before, and I sent Xury on Shore with my Jarrs, and filled them all three: The Women were as stark Naked as the Men.

I was now furnished with Roots and Corn, such as it was, and Water, and leaving my friendly Negroes, I made forward for about eleven Days more without offering to go near the Shoar, till I saw the Land run out a great Length into the Sea, at about the Distance of four or five Leagues before me, and the Sea being very calm I kept a large offing[2] to make this Point; at length, doubling the Point at about two Leagues from the Land, I saw plainly Land on the other Side to Seaward; then I concluded, as it was most certain indeed, that this was the *Cape de Verd*, and those the *Islands*, call'd from thence *Cape de Verd Islands*. However they were at a great Distance, and I could not well tell what I had best to do, for if I should be taken with a Fresh of Wind I might neither reach one or other.

In this Dilemna, as I was very pensive, I stept into the Cabbin and sat me down, *Xury* having the Helm, when on a suddain the Boy cry'd out, *Master, Master, a Ship with a Sail*, and the foolish Boy was frighted out of his Wits, thinking it must needs be some of his Master's Ships sent to pursue us, when, I knew we were gotten far enough out of their reach. I jump'd out of the Cabbin, and immediately saw not only the Ship, but what she was, (*viz.*) that is was a *Portuguese* Ship, and as I thought was bound to the Coast of *Guinea* for *Negroes*. But when I observ'd the Course she steer'd, I was soon convinc'd they were bound some other way, and did not design to come any nearer to the Shoar; upon which I stretch'd out to Sea as much as I could, resolving to speak with them if possible.

With all the Sail I could make, I found I should not be able to come in their Way, but that they would be gone by, before I could make any Signal to them; but after I had crowded to the utmost,[3] and began to despair, they it seems saw me by the help of their Perspective-Glasses,[4] and that it was some *European* Boat, which as they supposed must belong to some Ship that was lost, so they shortned Sail to let me come up. I was encouraged with this, and as I had my Patron's Antient on Board, I made a Waft of it to them for a Signal of Distress, and fir'd a Gun, both which they saw, for they told me they saw the Smoke, tho' they did not hear the Gun; upon these Signals they very kindly brought too, and lay by for me, and in about three Hours time I came up with them.

They ask'd me what I was, in *Portuguese*, and in *Spanish*, and in *French*, but I understood none of them; but as last a *Scots* Sailor who was on board, call'd to me, and I answer'd him, and told him I was an *Englishman*, that I had made my escape out of Slavery from the *Moors* at *Sallee*; then they bad me come on board, and very kindly took me in, and all my Goods.

It was an inexpressible Joy to me, that any one will believe, that I was thus deliver'd, as I esteem'd it, from such a miserable and almost

2. Kept well away from shore.
3. Spread all the sail possible.
4. Telescopes.

hopeless Condition as I was in, and I immediately offered all I had to the Captain of the Ship, as a Return for my Deliverance; but he generously told me, he would take nothing from me, but that all I had should be deliver'd safe to me when I came to the *Brasils*, for says he, *I have sav'd your Life on no other Terms than I would be glad to be saved my self, and it may one time or other be my Lot to be taken up in the same Condition; besides,* said he, *when I carry you to the* Brasils, *so great a way from your own Country, if I should take from you what you have, you will be starved there, and then I only take away that Life I have given.* No, no, Seignor Inglese, says he, Mr. Englishman, *I will carry you thither in Charity, and those things will help you to buy your Subsistance there and your Passage home again.*

As he was Charitable in his Proposal, so he was Just in the Performance to a tittle, for he ordered the Seamen that none should offer to touch any thing I had; then he took every thing into his own Possession, and gave me back an exact Inventory of them, that I might have them, even so much as my three Earthen Jarrs.

As to my Boat it was a very good one, and that he saw, and told me he would buy it of me for the Ship's use, and ask'd me what I would have for it? I told him he had been so generous to me in every thing, that I could not offer to make any Price of the Boat, but left it entirely to him, upon which he told me he would give me a Note of his Hand to pay me 80 Pieces of Eight[5] for it at *Brasil,* and when it came there, if any one offer'd to give more he would make it up; he offer'd me also 60 Pieces of Eight more for my Boy *Xury,* which I was loath to take, not that I was not willing to let the Captain have him, but I was very loath to sell the poor Boy's Liberty, who had assisted me so faithfully in procuring my own. However when I let him know my Reason, he own'd it to be just, and offer'd me this Medium,[6] that he would give the Boy an Obligation[7] to set him free in ten Years, if he turn'd Christian; upon this, and *Xury* saying he was willing to go to him, I let the Captain have him.

We had a very good Voyage to the *Brasils,* and arriv'd in the *Bay de Todos los Santos,* or *All-Saints Bay,*[8] in about Twenty-two Days after. And now I was once more deliver'd from the most miserable of all Conditions of Life, and what to do next with my self I was now to consider.

The generous Treatment the Captain gave me, I can never enough remember; he would take nothing of me for my Passage, gave me twenty Ducats[9] for the Leopard's Skin, and forty for the Lyon's Skin which I had in my Boat, and caused every thing I had in the Ship to be punctually

5. Spanish silver dollars marked with the figure eight.
6. Compromise.
7. Contractual agreement.
8. Harbor in northern Brazil where San Salvador, then the capital, was located.
9. Gold coins.

deliver'd me, and what I was willing to see he bought, such as the Case of Bottles, two of my Guns, and a Piece of the Lump of Bees-wax, for I had made Candles of the rest; in a word, I made about 220 Pieces of Eight of all my Cargo, and with this Stock I went on Shoar in the *Brasils*.

I had not been long here, but being recommended to the House of a good honest Man like himself, who had an *Ingenio* as they call it; that is, a Plantation and a Sugar-House. I lived with him some time, and acquainted my self by that means with the Manner of their planting and making of Sugar; and seeing how well the Planters liv'd, and how they grew rich suddenly, I resolv'd, if I could get Licence to settle there, I would turn Planter among them, resolving in the mean time to find out some Way to get my Money which I had left in *London* remitted to me. To this Purpose getting a kind of a Letter of Naturalization, I purchased as much Land that was Uncur'd, as my Money would reach, and form'd a plan for my Plantation and Settlement, and such a one as might be suitable to the Stock which I proposed to myself to receive from *England*.

I had a Neighbour, a *Portugueze* of *Lisbon*, but born of *English* Parents, whose Name was *Wells*, and in much such Circumstances as I was. I call him my Neighbour, because his Plantation lay next to mine, and we went on very sociably together. My Stock was but low as well as his; and we rather planted for Food than any thing else, for about two Years. However, we began to increase, and our Land began to come into Order; so that the third Year we planted some Tobacco, and made each of us a large Piece of Ground ready for planting Canes in the Year to come; but we both wanted Help, and now I found more than before, I had done wrong in parting with with my Boy *Xury*.

But alas! for me to do wrong that never did right, was no great Wonder: I had no Remedy but to go on; I was gotten into an Employment quite remote to my Genius, and directly contrary to the Life I delighted in, and for which I forsook my Father's House, and broke thro' all his good Advice; nay, I was coming into the very Middle Station, or upper Degree of low Life, which my Father advised me to before; and which if I resolved to go on with, I might as well ha' staid at Home, and never have fatigu'd my self in the World as I had done; and I used often to say to my self, I could ha' done this as well in *England* among my Friends, as ha' gone 5000 Miles off to do it among Strangers and Savages in a Wilderness, and at such a Distance, as never to hear from any Part of the World that had the least Knowledge of me.

In this manner I used to look upon my Condition with the utmost Regret. I had no body to converse with but now and then this Neighbour; no Work to be done, but by the Labour of my Hands; and I used to say, I liv'd just like a Man cast away upon some desolate Island, that had no body there but himself. But how just has it been, and how should all Men reflect, that when they compare their present Conditions with others that are worse, Heaven may oblige them to make the Exchange, and be convinc'd of their former Felicity by their Experience: I say, how just has it been, that the truly solitary Life I reflected on in an Island of meer Desolation should be my Lot, who had so often unjustly compar'd it with the Life which I then led, in which had I continued, I had in all Probability been exceeding prosperous and rich.

I was in some Degree settled in my Measures for carrying on the Plantation, before my kind Friend the Captain of the Ship that took me up at Sea, went back; for the Ship remained there in providing his Loading, and preparing for his Voyage, near three Months, when telling him what little Stock I had left behind me in *London*, he gave me this friendly and sincere Advice, *Seignior Inglese, says he;* for so he always called me, if you will give me Letters, and a Procuration here in Form to me, with Orders to the Person who has your Money in *London*, to send your Effects to *Lisbon*, to such Persons as I shall direct, and in such Goods as are proper for this Country, I will bring you the Produce of them, God willing, at my Return; but since human Affairs are all subject to Changes and Disasters, I would have you give Orders but for One Hundred Pounds *Sterl.* which you say is Half your Stock, and let the Hazard be run for the first; so that if it come safe, you may order the rest the same Way; and if it miscarry, you may have the other Half to have Recourse to for your Supply.

This was so wholesom Advice, and look'd so friendly, that I could not but be convinc'd it was the best Course I could take; so I accordingly prepared Letters to the Gentlewoman with whom I had left my Money, and a Procuration to the *Portuguese* Captain, as he desired.

I wrote the *English* Captain's Widow a full Account of all my Adventures, my Slavery, Escape, and how I had met with the *Portugal* Captain at Sea, the Humanity of his Behaviour, and in what Condition I was now in, with all other necessary Directions for my Supply; and when this honest Captain came to *Lisbon*, he found means by some of the *English* Merchants there, to send over not the Order only, but a full Account of my Story to a Merchant at *London*, who represented it effectually to her; whereupon, she not only delivered the Money, but out of her own Pocket sent the *Portugal* Captain a very handsom Present for his Humanity and Charity to me.

The Merchant in *London* vesting[1] this Hundred Pounds in *English* Goods, such as the Captain had writ for, sent them directly to him at *Lisbon*, and he brought them all safe to me to the *Brasils*, among which, without my Direction (for I was too young in my Business to think of them) he had taken Care to have all Sorts of Tools, Iron-Work, and Utensils necessary for my Plantation, and which were of great Use to me.

When this Cargo arrived, I thought my Fortunes made, for I was

1. Investing.

surprised with the Joy of it; and my good Steward the Captain had laid out the Five Pounds which my Friend had sent him for a Present for himself, to purchase, and bring me over a Servant under Bond for six Years Service, and would not accept of any Consideration, except a little Tobacco, which I would have him accept, being of my own Produce.

Neither was this all; but my Goods being all *English* Manufactures, such as Cloath, Stuffs, Bays,[2] and things particularly valuable and desirable in the Country, I found means to sell them to a very great Advantage; so that I might say, I had more than four times the Value of my first Cargo, and was now infinitely beyond my poor Neighbour, I mean in the Advancement of my Plantation; for the first thing I did, I bought me a Negro Slave, and an *European* Servant also; I mean another besides that which the Captain brought me from *Lisbon*.

But as abus'd Prosperity is oftentimes made the very Means of our greatest Adversity, so was it with me. I went on the next Year with great Success in my Plantation: I raised fifty great Rolls of Tobacco on my own Ground, more than I had disposed of for Necessaries among my Neighbours; and these fifty Rolls being each of above a 100 W*t*. were well cur'd and laid by against the Return of the Fleet from *Lisbon*: and now increasing in Business and in Wealth, my Head began to be full of Projects and Undertakings beyond my Reach; such as are indeed often the Ruine of the best Heads in Business.

Had I continued in the Station I was now in, I had room for all the happy things to have yet befallen me, for which my Father so earnestly recommended a quiet retired Life, and of which he had so sensibly describ'd the middle Station of Life to be full of; but other things attended me, and I was still to be the wilful Agent of all my own Miseries; and particularly to encrease my Fault and double the Reflections upon my self, which in my future Sorrows I should have leisure to make; all these Miscarriages were procured by my apparent obstinate adhering to my foolish inclination of wandring abroad and pursuing that Inclination, in contradiction to the clearest Views of doing my self good in a fair and plain pursuit of those Prospects and those measures of Life, which Nature and Providence concurred to present me with, and to make my Duty.

As I had once done thus in my breaking away from my Parents, so I could not be content now, but I must go and leave the happy View I had of being a rich and thriving Man in my new Plantation, only to pursue a rash and immoderate Desire of rising faster than the Nature of the Thing admitted; and thus I cast my self down again into the deepest Gulph of human Misery that ever Man fell into, or perhaps could be consistent with Life and a State of Health in the World.

To come then by the just Degrees, to the Particulars of this Part of

2. Baize.

my Story; you may suppose, that having now lived almost four Years in the *Brasils*, and beginning to thrive and prosper very well upon my Plantation; I had not only learn'd the language, but had contracted Acquaintances and Friendship among my Fellow-Planters, as well as among the Merchants at St. *Salvadore*, which was our Port; and that in my Discourses among them, I had frequently given them an Account of my two Voyages to the Coast of *Guinea*, the manner of Trading with the *Negroes* there, and how easy it was to purchase upon the Coast, for Trifles, such as Beads, Toys, Knives, Scissars, Hatchets, bits of Glass, and the like; not only Gold Dust, *Guinea* Grains,[3] Elephants Teeth, &c. but *Negroes*, for the Service of the *Brasils*, in great Numbers.

They listened always very attentively to my Discourses on these Heads, but especially to that Part which related to the buying *Negroes*, which was a Trade at that time not only not far entred into, but as far as it was, had been carried on by the Assiento's,[4] or Permission of the Kings of *Spain* and *Portugal*, and engross'd in the Publick, so that few *Negroes* were brought, and those excessive dear.

It happen'd, being in Company with some Merchants and Planters of my Acquaintance, and talking of those things very earnestly, three of them came to me the next Morning, and told me they had been musing very much upon what I had discoursed with them of, the last Night, and they came to make a secret Proposal to me; and after enjoining me Secrecy, they told me, that they had a mind to fit out a Ship to go to *Guinea*, that they had all Plantations as well as I, and were straiten'd[5] for nothing so much as Servants; that as it was a Trade that could not be carried on, because they could not publickly sell the *Negroes* when they came home, so they desired to make but one Voyage, to bring the *Negroes* on Shoar privately, and divide them among their own Plantations; and in a Word, the Question was, whether I would go their Super-Cargo in the Ship to manage the Trading Part upon the Coast of *Guinea?* And they offer'd me that I should have my equal Share of the *Negroes* without providing any Part of the Stock.

This was a fair Proposal it must be confess'd, had it been made to any one that had not had a Settlement and Plantation of his own to look after, which was in a fair way of coming to be very Considerable, and with a good Stock upon it. But for me that was thus entered and established, and had nothing to do but go on as I had begun for three or four Years more, and to have sent for the other hundred Pound from *England*, and who in that time, and with that little Addition, could scarce ha' fail'd of being worth three or four thousand Pounds Sterling, and that encreasing too; for me to think of such a Voyage, was the most

3. Seeds of African plants valued as spices.
4. Contracts for furnishing the colonies of Spain and Portugal with African slaves on very profitable terms.
5. Constrained.

preposterous Thing that ever Man in such Circumstances could be guilty of.

But I that was born to be my own Destroyer, could no more resist the Offer than I could restrain my first rambling Designs, when my Father's good Counsel was lost upon me. In a word, I told them I would go with all my Heart, if they would undertake to look after my Plantation in my Absence, and would dispose of it to such as I should direct if I miscarry'd. This they all engag'd to do, and entred into Writings or Covenants to do so; and I made a formal Will, disposing of my Plantation and Effects, in Case of my Death, making the Captain of the Ship that had sav'd my Life, as before, my universal Heir, but obliging him to dispose of my Effects as I had directed in my Will, one half of the Produce being to himself, and the other to be ship'd to *England*.

In short, I took all possible Caution to preserve my Effects, and keep up my Plantation; had I used half as much Prudence to have look'd into my own Intrest, and have made a Judgment of what I ought to have done, and not to have done, I had certainly never gone away from so prosperous an Undertaking, leaving all the probable Views of a thriving Circumstance, and gone upon a Voyage to Sea, attended with all its common Hazards; to say nothing of the Reasons I had to expect particular Misfortunes to my self.

But I was hurried on, and obey'd blindly the Dictates of my Fancy rather than my Reason; and accordingly the Ship being fitted out, and the Cargo furnished, and all things done as by Agreement, by my Partners in the Voyage, I went on Board in an evil Hour, the [first] of [*September*], [*1659*],[6] being the same Day eight Year that I went from my Father and Mother at *Hull*, in order to act the Rebel to their Authority, and the Fool to my own Interest.

Our Ship was about 120 Tun Burthen,[7] carried 6 Guns, and 14 Men, besides the Master, his Boy, and my self; we had on board no large Cargo of Goods, except of such Toys as were fit for our Trade with the *Negroes*, such as Beads, bits of Glass, Shells, and odd Trifles, especially little Looking-Glasses, Knives, Scissars, Hatchets, and the like.

The same Day I went on board we set sail, standing away to the Northward upon our own Coast, with Design to stretch over for the *Affrican* Coast, when they came about 10 or 12 Degrees of Northern Latitude, which it seems was the manner of their Course in those Days. We had very good Weather, only excessive hot, all the way upon our own Coast, till we came the Height of *Cape St. Augustino*, from whence keeping farther off at Sea we lost Sight of Land, and steer'd as if we was bound for the Isle *Fernand de Noronba* holding our Course N.E. by N. and leaving those Isles on the East; in this Course we past the Line

---

6. Spaces were left for the day, month, and year in the first three editions of the text, and the inserted dates appeared in the fourth and subsequent editions.
7. Cargo capacity of about 120 tons.

in about 12 Days time, and were by our last Observation in 7 Degrees 22 Min. Northern Latitude, when a violent Tournado or Hurricane took us quite out of our Knowledge; it began from the South-East, came about to the North-West, and then settled into the North-East, from whence it blew in such a terrible manner, that for twelve Days together we could do nothing but drive, and scudding away before it, let it carry us whither ever Fate and the Fury of the Winds directed; and during these twelve days, I need not say, that I expected every Day to be swallowed up, nor indeed did any in the Ship expect to save their Lives.

In this Distress, we had besides the Terror of the Storm, one of our Men dyed of the Calenture, and one Man and the Boy wash'd over board; about the 12th Day the Weather abating a little, the Master made an Observation as well as he could, and found that he was in about 11 Degrees North Latitude, but that he was 22 Degrees of Longitude difference West from *Cape* St. *Augustino*; so that he found he was gotten upon the Coast of *Guinea*,[8] or the North Part of *Brasil*, beyond the River *Amozones*, toward that of the River *Oronoque*, commonly call'd the *Great River*, and began to consult with me what Course he should take, for the Ship was leaky and very much disabled, and he was going directly back to the Coast of *Brasil*.

I was positively against that, and looking over the Charts of the Sea-Coast of *America* with him, we concluded there was no inhabited Country for us to have recourse to, till we came within the Circle of the *Carribee-Islands*, and therefore resolved to stand away for *Barbadoes*, which by keeping off at Sea, to avoid the Indraft of the Bay or Gulph of *Mexico*, we might easily perform, as we hoped, in about fifteen Days Sail; whereas we could not possibly make our Voyage to the Coast of *Affrica* without some Assistance, both to our Ship and to our selves.

With this Design we chang'd our Course and steer'd away N.W. by W. in order to reach some of our *English* Islands, where I hoped for Relief; but our Voyage was otherwise determined, for being in the Latitude of 12 Deg. 18 Min. a second Storm came upon us, which carry'd us away with the same Impetuosity Westward, and drove us so out of the very Way of all humane Commerce, that had all our Lives been saved, as to the Sea, we were rather in Danger of being devoured by Savages than ever returning to our own Country.

In this Distress, the Wind still blowing very hard, one of our Men early in the Morning, cry'd out, *Land*; and we had no sooner run out of the Cabbin to look out in hopes of seeing where abouts in the World we were; but the Ship struck upon a Sand, and in a moment her Motion being so stopp'd, the Sea broke over her in such a manner, that we expected we should all have perish'd immediately, and we were immediately driven into our close Quarters to shelter us from the very Foam and Sprye[9] of the Sea.

8. Corrected to "*Guiana*" in the fourth and subsequent editions.
9. Variant spelling for *Spray* in the text.

It is not easy for any one, who has not been in the like Condition, to describe or conceive the Consternation of Men in such Circumstances; we knew nothing where we were, or upon what Land it was we were driven, whether an Island or the Main, whether inhabited or not inhabited; and as the Rage of the Wind was still great, tho' rather less than at first, we could not so much as hope to have the Ship hold many Minutes without breaking in Pieces, unless the Winds by a kind of Miracle should turn immediately about. In a word, we sat looking upon one another, and expecting Death every Moment, and every Man acting accordingly, as preparing for another World, for there was little or nothing more for us to do in this; that which was our present Comfort, and all the Comfort we had, was, that contrary to our Expectation the Ship did not break yet, and that the Master said the Wind began to abate.

Now tho' we thought that the Wind did a little abate, yet the Ship having thus struck upon the Sand, and sticking too fast for us to expect her getting off, we were in a dreadful Condition indeed, and had nothing to do but to think of saving our Lives as well as we could; we had a Boat at our Stern just before the Storm, but she was first stav'd by dashing against the Ship's Rudder, and in the next Place she broke away, and either sunk or was driven off to Sea, so there was no hope from her; we had another Boat on board, but how to get her off into the Sea, was a doubtful thing; however there was no room to debate, for we fancy'd the Ship would break in Pieces every Minute, and some told us she was actually broken already.

In this Distress the Mate of our Vessel lays hold of the Boat, and with the help of the rest of the Men, they got her slung over the Ship's-side, and getting all into her, let go, and committed our selves being Eleven in Number, to God's Mercy, and the wild Sea; for tho' the Storm was abated considerably, yet the Sea went dreadful high upon the Shore, and might well be call'd, *Den wild Zee*,[1] as the *Dutch* call the Sea in a Storm.

And now our Case was very dismal indeed; for we all saw plainly, that the Sea went so high, that the Boat could not live, and that we should be inevitably drowned. As to making Sail, we had none, nor, if we had, could we ha' done any thing with it; so we work'd at the Oar towards the Land, tho' with heavy Hearts, like Men going to Execution; for all we knew, that when the Boat came nearer the Shore, she would be dash'd in a Thousand Pieces by the Breach[2] of the Sea. However, we committed our Souls to God in the most earnest Manner, and the Wind driving us towards the Shore, we hasten'd our Destruction with our own Hands, pulling as well as we could towards Land.

What the Shore was, whether Rock or Sand, whether Steep or Shoal, we knew not; the only Hope that could rationally give us the least Shadow of Expectation, was, if we might happen into some Bay or Gulph, or

1. Literally "the wild sea."
2. Breaking waves.

the Mouth of some River, where by great Chance we might have run our Boat in, or got under the Lee of the Land, and perhaps made smooth Water. But there was nothing of this appeared; but as we made nearer and nearer the Shore, the Land look'd more frightful than the Sea.

After we had row'd, or rather driven about a League and a Half, as we reckon'd it, a raging Wave, Mountain-like, came rowling a-stern of us, and plainly bad us expect the *Coup de Grace*.[3] In a word, it took us with such a Fury, that it overset the Boat at once; and separating us as well from the Boat, as from one another, gave us not time hardly to say, O God! for we were all swallowed up in a Moment.

Nothing can describe the Confusion of Thought which I felt when I sunk into the Water; for tho' I swam very well, yet I could not deliver my self from the Waves so as to draw Breath, till that Wave having driven me, or rather carried me a vast Way on towards the Shore, and having spent it self, went back, and left me upon the Land almost dry, but half-dead with the Water I took in. I had so much Presence of Mind as well as Breath left, that seeing my self nearer the main Land than I expected, I got upon my Feet, and endeavoured to make on towards the Land as fast as I could, before another Wave should return, and take me up again. But I soon found it was impossible to avoid it; for I saw the Sea come after me as high as a great Hill, and as furious as an Enemy which I had no Means or Strength to contend with; my Business was to hold my Breath, and raise my self upon the Water, if I could; and so by swimming to preserve my Breathing, and Pilot my self towards the Shore, if possible; my greatest Concern now being, that the Sea, as it would carry me a great Way towards the Shore when it came on, might not carry me back again with it when it gave back towards the Sea.

The Wave that came upon me again, buried me at once 20 or 30 Foot deep in its own Body; and I could feel my self carried with a mighty Force and Swiftness towards the Shore a very great Way: but I held my Breath, and assisted my self to swim still forward with all my Might. I was ready to burst with holding my Breath, when, as I felt my self rising up, so to my immediate Relief, I found my Head and Hands shoot out above the Surface of the Water; and tho' it was not two Seconds of Time that I could keep my self so, yet it reliev'd me greatly, gave me Breath and new Courage. I was covered again with Water a good while, but not so long but I held it out; and finding the Water had spent it self, and began to return, I strook[4] forward against the Return of the Waves, and felt Ground again with my Feet. I stood still a few Moments to recover Breath, and till the Water went from me, and then took to my Heels, and run with what Strength I had farther towards the Shore. But neither would this deliver me from the Fury of the Sea, which came

3. The final fatal blow.
4. Changed to "struck" in the fifth and sixth editions.

pouring in after me again, and twice more I was lifted up by the Waves, and carried forwards as before, the Shore being very flat.

The last Time of these two had well near been fatal to me; for the Sea having hurried me along as before, landed me, or rather dash'd me against a Piece of a Rock, and that with such Force, as it left me senseless, and indeed helpless, as to my own Deliverance; for the Blow taking my Side and Breast, beat the Breath as it were quite out of my Body; and had it returned again immediately, I must have been strangled in the Water; but I recover'd a little before the return of the Waves, and seeing I should be cover'd again with the Water, I resolv'd to hold fast by a Piece of the Rock, and so to hold my Breath, if possible, till the Wave went back; now as the Waves were not so high as at first, being nearer Land, I held my Hold till the Wave abated, and then fetch'd another Run, which brought me so near the Shore, that the next Wave, tho' it went over me, yet did not so swallow me up as to carry me away, and the next run I took, I got to the main Land, where, to my great Comfort, I clamber'd up the Clifts of the Shore, and sat me down upon the Grass, free from Danger, and quite out of the Reach of the Water.

I was now landed, and safe on Shore, and began to look up and thank God that my Life was sav'd in a Case wherein there was some Minutes before scarce any room to hope. I believe it is impossible to express to the Life what the Extasies and Transports of the Soul are, when it is so sav'd, as I may say, out of the very Grave; and I do not wonder now at that Custom, *viz.* That when a Malefactor who has the Halter about his Neck, is tyed up, and just going to be turn'd off,[5] and has a Reprieve brought to him: I say, I do not wonder that they bring a Surgeon with it, to let him Blood that very Moment they tell him of it, that the Surprise may not drive the Animal Spirits from the Heart, and overwhelm him:

For sudden Joys, like Griefs, confound at first.[6]

I walk'd about on the Shore, lifting up my Hands, and my whole Being, as I may say, wrapt up in the Contemplation of my Deliverance, making a Thousand Gestures and Motions which I cannot describe, reflecting upon all my Comrades that were drown'd, and that there should not be one Soul sav'd but my self; for, as for them, I never saw them afterwards, or any Sign of them, except three of their Hats, one Cap, and two Shoes that were not Fellows.

I cast my Eyes to the stranded Vessel, when the Breach and Froth of the Sea being so big, I could hardly see it, it lay so far off, and considered, Lord! how was it possible I could get on Shore?

After I had solac'd my Mind with the comfortable Part of my Condition, I began to look round me to see what kind of Place I was in,

5. Slang for *killed*.
6. Source of quotation is not known.

and what was next to be done, and I soon found my Comforts abate, and that in a word I had a dreadful Deliverance: For I was wet, had no Clothes to shift me, nor any thing either to eat or drink to comfort me, neither did I see any Prospect before me, but that of perishing with Hunger, or being devour'd by wild Beasts; and that which was particularly afflicting to me, was, that I had no Weapon either to hunt and kill any Creature for my Sustenance, or to defend my self against any other Creature that might desire to kill me for theirs: In a Word, I had nothing about me but a Knife, a Tobacco-pipe, and a little Tobacco in a Box, this was all my Provision, and this threw me into terrible Agonies of Mind, that for a while I run about like a Mad-man; Night coming upon me, I began with a heavy Heart to consider what would be my Lot if there were any ravenous Beasts in that Country, seeing at Night they always come abroad for their Prey.

All the Remedy that offer'd to my Thoughts at that Time, was, to get up into a thick bushy Tree like a Firr, but thorny, which grew near me, and where I resolv'd to sit all Night, and consider the next Day what Death I should dye, for as yet I saw no Prospect of Life; I walk'd about a Furlong from the Shore, to see if I could find any fresh Water to drink, which I did, to my great Joy; and having drank and put a little Tobacco in my Mouth to prevent Hunger, I went to the Tree, and getting up into it, endeavour'd to place my self so, as that if I should sleep I might not fall; and having cut me a short Stick, like a Truncheon, for my Defence, I took up my Lodging, and having been excessively fatigu'd, I fell fast asleep, and slept as comfortably as, I believe, few could have done in my Condition, and found my self the most refresh'd with it, that I think I ever was on such an Occasion.

When I wak'd it was broad Day, the Weather clear, and the Storm abated, so that the Sea did not rage and swell as before: But that which surpris'd me most, was, that the Ship was lifted off in the Night from the Sand where she lay, by the Swelling of the Tyde, and was driven up almost as far as the Rock which I first mention'd, where I had been so bruis'd by the dashing me against it; this being within about a Mile from the Shore where I was, and the Ship seeming to stand upright still, I wish'd my self on board, that, at least, I might save some necessary things for my use.

When I came down from my Appartment in the Tree, I look'd about me again, and the first thing I found was the Boat, which lay as the Wind and the Sea had toss'd her up upon the Land, about two Miles on my right Hand. I walk'd as far as I could upon the Shore to have got to her, but found a Neck or Inlet of Water between me and the Boat, which was about half a Mile broad, so I came back for the present, being more intent upon getting at the Ship, where I hop'd to find something for my present Subsistence.

A little after Noon I found the Sea very calm, and the Tyde ebb'd so far out, that I could come within a Quarter of a Mile of the Ship; and here I found a fresh renewing of my Grief, for I saw evidently, that if we had kept on board, we had been all safe, that is to say, we had all got safe on Shore, and I had not been so miserable as to be left entirely destitute of all Comfort and Company, as I now was; this forc'd Tears from my Eyes again, but as there was little Relief in that, I resolv'd, if possible, to get to the Ship, so I pull'd off my Clothes, for the Weather was hot to Extremity, and took the Water, but when I came to the Ship, my Difficulty was still greater to know how to get on board, for as she lay a ground, and high out of the Water, there was nothing within my Reach to lay hold of, I swam round her twice, and the second Time I spy'd a small Piece of a Rope, which I wonder'd I did not see at first, hang down by the Fore-Chains so low, as that with great Difficulty I got hold of it, and by the help of that Rope, got up into the Forecastle of the Ship, here I found that the Ship was bulg'd,[7] and had a great deal of Water in her Hold, but that she lay so on the Side of a Bank of hard Sand, or rather Earth, that her Stern lay lifted up upon the Bank, and her Head low almost to the Water; by this Means all her Quarter was free, and all that was in that Part was dry; for you may be sure my first Work was to search and to see what was spoil'd and what was free; and first I found that all the Ship's Provisions were dry and untouch'd by the Water, and being very well dispos'd to eat, I went to the Bread-room and fill'd my Pockets with Bisket, and eat it as I went about other things, for I had no time to lose; I also found some Rum in the great Cabbin, of which I took a large Drain, and which I had indeed need enough of to spirit me for what was before me: Now I wanted nothing but a Boat to furnish my self with many things which I foresaw would be very necessary to me.

It was in vain to sit still and wish for what was not to be had, and this Extremity rouz'd my Application; we had several spare Yards, and two or three large sparrs of Wood, and a spare Top-mast or two in the Ship; I resolv'd to fall to work with these, and I flung as many of them over board as I could manage for their Weight, tying every one with a Rope that they might not drive away; when this was done I went down the Ship's Side, and pulling them to me, I ty'd four of them fast together at both Ends as well as I could, in the Form of a Raft, and laying two or three short Pieces of Plank upon them crossways, I found I could walk upon it very well, but that it was not able to bear any great Weight, the Pieces being too light; so I went to work, and with the Carpenter's Saw I cut a spare Top-mast into three Lengths, and added them to my Raft, with a great deal of Labour and Pains, but hope of furnishing my self with Necessaries, encourag'd me to go beyond what I should have been able to have done upon another Occasion.

7. Bilged.

My Raft was now strong enough to bear any reasonable Weight; my next Care was what to load it with, and how to preserve what I laid upon it from the Surf of the Sea; But I was not long considering this, I first laid all the Planks or Boards upon it that I could get, and having consider'd well what I most wanted, I first got three of the Seamens Chests, which I had broken open and empty'd, and lower'd them down upon my Raft; the first of these I fill'd with Provision, *viz.* Bread, Rice, three Dutch Cheeses, five Pieces of dry'd Goat's Flesh, which we liv'd much upon, and a little Remainder of *European* Corn which had been laid by for some Fowls which we brought to Sea with us, but the Fowls were kill'd, there had been some Barly and Wheat together, but, to my great Disappointment, I found afterwards that the Rats had eaten or spoil'd it all; as for Liquors, I found several Cases of Bottles belonging to our Skipper, in which were some Cordial Waters, and in all about five or six Gallons of Rack,[8] these I stow'd by themselves, there being no need to put them into the Chest, nor no room for them. While I was doing this, I found the Tyde began to flow, tho' very calm, and I had the Mortification to see my Coat, Shirt, and Wast-coat which I had left on Shore upon the Sand, swim away; as for my Breeches which were only Linnen and open knee'd, I swam on board in them and my Stockings: However this put me upon rummaging for Clothes, of which I found enough, but took no more than I wanted for present use, for I had other things which my Eye was more upon, as first Tools to work with on Shore, and it was after long searching that I found out the Carpenter's Chest, which was indeed a very useful Prize to me, and much more valuable than a Ship Loading of Gold would have been at that time; I got it down to my Raft, even whole as it was, without losing time to look into it, for I knew in general what it contain'd.

My next Care was for some Ammunition and Arms; there were two very good Fowling-pieces in the great Cabbin, and two Pistols, these I secur'd first, with some Powder-horns, and a small Bag of Shot, and two old rusty Swords; I knew there were three Barrels of Powder in the Ship, but knew not where our Gunner had stow'd them, but with much search I found them, two of them dry and good, the third had taken Water, those two I got to my Raft, with the Arms, and now I thought my self pretty well freighted, and began to think how I should get to Shore with them, having neither Sail, Oar, or Rudder, and the least Cap full of Wind would have overset all my Navigation.

I had three Encouragements, 1. A smooth calm Sea, 2. The Tide rising and setting in to the Shore, 3. What little Wind there was blew me towards the Land; and thus, having found two or three broken Oars belonging to the Boat, and besides the Tools which were in the Chest, I found two Saws, an Axe, and a Hammer, and with this Cargo I put

8. Arrack, an intoxicating liquor made by natives, often from palm sap or coconuts.

to Sea: For a Mile, or thereabouts, my Raft went very well, only that I found it drive a little distant from the Place where I had landed before, by which I perceiv'd that there was some Indraft of the Water, and consequently I hop'd to find some Creek or River there, which I might make use of as a Port to get to Land with my Cargo.

As I imagin'd, so it was, there appear'd before me a little opening of the Land, and I found a strong Current of the Tide set into it, so I guided my Raft as well as I could to keep in the Middle of the Stream: But here I had like to have suffer'd a second Shipwreck, which, if I had, I think verily would have broke my Heart, for knowing nothing of the Coast, my Raft run a-ground at one End of it upon a Shoal, and not being a-ground at the other End, it wanted but a little that all my Cargo had slip'd off towards that End that was a-float, and so fall'n into the Water: I did my utmost by setting my Back against the Chests, to keep them in their Places, but could not thrust off the Raft with all my Strength, neither durst I stir from the Posture I was in, but holding up the Chests with all my Might, stood in that Manner near half an Hour, in which time the rising of the Water brought me a little more upon a Level, and a little after, the Water still rising, my Raft floated again, and I thrust her off with the Oar I had, into the Channel, and then driving up higher, I at length found my self in the Mouth of a little River, with Land on both Sides, and a strong Current or Tide running up, I look'd on both Sides for a proper Place to get to Shore, for I was not willing to be driven too high up the River, hoping in time to see some Ship at Sea, and therefore resolv'd to place my self as near the Coast as I could.

At length I spy'd a little Cove on the right Shore of the Creek, to which with great Pain and Difficulty I guided my Raft, and at last got so near, as that, reaching Ground with my Oar, I could thrust her directly in, but here I had like to have dipt all my Cargo in the Sea again; for that Shore lying pretty steep, that is to say sloping, there was no Place to land, but where one End of my Float, if it run on Shore, would lie so high, and the other sink lower as before, that it would endanger my Cargo again: All that I could do, was to wait 'till the Tide was at the highest, keeping the Raft with my Oar like an Anchor to hold the Side of it fast to the Shore, near a flat Piece of Ground, which I expected the Water would flow over; and so it did: As soon as I found Water enough, for my Raft drew about a Foot of Water, I thrust her on upon that flat Piece of Ground, and there fasten'd or mor'd her by sticking my two broken Oars into the Ground; one on one Side near one End, and one on the other Side near the other End; and then I lay 'till the Water ebb'd away, and left my Raft and all my Cargoe safe on Shore.

My next Work was to view the Country, and seek a proper Place for my Habitation, and where to stow my Goods to secure them from whatever might happen; where I was, I yet knew not, whether on the Continent or on an Island, whether inhabited or not inhabited, whether in Danger of wild Beasts or not: There was a Hill not above a Mile from me, which rose up very steep and high, and which seem'd to over-top some other Hills, which lay as in a Ridge from it northward; I took out one of the fowling Pieces, and one of the Pistols, and an Horn of Powder, and thus arm'd I travell'd for Discovery up to the Top of that Hill, where after I had with great Labour and Difficulty got to the Top, I saw my Fate to my great Affliction, (viz.) that I was in an Island environ'd every Way with the Sea, no Land to be seen, except some Rocks which lay a great Way off, and two small Islands less than this, which lay about three Leagues to the West.

I found also that the Island I was in was barren, and, as I saw good Reason to believe, un-inhabited, except by wild Beasts, of whom however I saw none, yet I saw Abundance of Fowls, but knew not their Kinds, neither when I kill'd them could I tell what was fit for Food, and what not; at my coming back, I shot at a great Bird which I saw sitting upon a Tree on the Side of a great Wood, I believe it was the first Gun that had been fir'd there since the Creation of the World; I had no sooner fir'd, but from all the Parts of the Wood there arose an innumerable Number of Fowls of many Sorts, making a confus'd Screaming, and crying every one according to his usual Note; but not one of them of any Kind that I knew: As for the Creature I kill'd, I took it to be a Kind of a Hawk, its Colour and Beak resembling it, but had no Talons or Claws more than common, its Flesh was Carrion and fit for nothing.

Contented with this Discovery, I came back to my Raft, and fell to Work to bring my Cargoe on Shore, which took me up the rest of that Day, and what to do with my self at Night I knew not, nor indeed where to rest; for I was afraid to lie down on the Ground, not knowing but some wild Beast might devour me, tho', as I afterwards found, there was really no Need for those Fears.

However, as well as I could, I barricado'd my self round with the Chests and Boards that I had brought on Shore, and made a Kind of a Hut for that Night's Lodging; as for Food, I yet saw not which Way to supply my self, except that I had seen two or three Creatures like Hares run out of the Wood where I shot the Fowl.

I now began to consider, that I might yet get a great many Things out of the Ship, which would be useful to me, and particularly some of the Rigging, and Sails, and such other Things as might come to Land, and I resolv'd to make another Voyage on Board the Vessel, if possible; and as I knew that the first Storm that blew must necessarily break her all in Pieces, I resolv'd to set all other Things apart, 'till I got every Thing out of the Ship that I could get; then I call'd a Council, that is to say, in my Thoughts, whether I should take back the Raft, but this appear'd impracticable; so I resolv'd to go as before, when the Tide was down, and I did so, only that I stripp'd before I went from my Hut, having nothing on but a Chequer'd Shirt, and a Pair of Linnen Drawers, and a Pair of Pumps[9] on my Feet.

I got on Board the Ship, as before, and prepar'd a second Raft, and having had Experience of the first, I neither made this so unweildy, or loaded it so hard, but yet I brought away several Things very useful to me; as first, in the Carpenter's Stores I found two or three Bags full of Nails and Spikes, a great Skrew-Jack,[1] a Dozen or two of Hatchets, and above all, that most useful Thing call'd a Grindstone; all these I secur'd together, with several Things belonging to the Gunner, particularly two or three Iron Crows,[2] and two Barrels of Musquet Bullets, seven Musquets, and another fowling Piece, with some small Quantity of Powder more; a large Bag full of small Shot, and a great Roll of Sheet Lead: But this last was so heavy, I could not hoise[3] it up to get it over the Ship's Side.

Besides these Things, I took all the Mens Cloaths that I could find, and a spare Fore-top-sail, a Hammock, and some Bedding; and with this I loaded my second Raft, and brought them all safe on Shore to my very great Comfort.

I was under some Apprehensions during my Absence from the Land, that at least my Provisions might be devour'd on Shore; but when I came back, I found no Sign of any Visitor, only there sat a Creature like a wild Cat upon one of the Chests, which when I came towards it, ran away a little Distance, and then stood still; she sat very compos'd, and unconcern'd, and look'd full in my Face, as if she had a Mind to be acquainted with me, I presented my Gun at her, but as she did not understand it, she was perfectly unconcern'd at it, nor did she offer to stir away; upon which I toss'd her a Bit of Bisket, tho' by the Way I was not very free of it, for my Store was not great: However, I spar'd her a Bit, I say, and she went to it, smell'd of it, and ate it, and look'd (as pleas'd) for more, but I thanked her, and could spare no more; so she march'd off.

Having got my second Cargoe on Shore, tho'd I was fain[4] to open the Barrels of Powder, and bring them by Parcels, for they were too heavy, being large Casks, I went to work to make me a little Tent with the Sail and some Poles which I cut for that Purpose, and into this Tent I brought every Thing that I knew would spoil, either with Rain or Sun, and I piled all the empty Chests and Casks up in a Circle round the Tent, to fortify it from any sudden Attempt, either from Man or Beast.

When I had done this I block'd up the Door of the Tent with some Boards within, and an empty Chest set up on End without, and spreading

9. Low shoes.
1. A tool for lifting heavy objects.
2. Crowbars.
3. Changed to "hoist" in the sixth edition.
4. Obliged.

one of the Beds upon the Ground, laying my two Pistols just at my Head, and my Gun at Length by me, I went to Bed for the first Time, and slept very quietly all Night, for I was very weary and heavy, for the Night before I had slept little, and had labour'd very hard all Day, as well to fetch all those Things from the Ship, as to get them on Shore.

I had the biggest Maggazin[5] of all Kinds now that ever were laid up, I believe, for one Man, but I was not satisfy'd still; for while the Ship sat upright in that Posture, I thought I ought to get every Thing out of her that I could; so every Day at low Water I went on Board, and brought away some Thing or other: But particularly the third Time I went, I brought away as much of the Rigging as I could, as also all the small Ropes and Rope-twine I could get, with a Piece of spare Canvaass, which was to mend the Sails upon Occasion, the Barrel of wet Gunpowder: In a Word, I brought away all the Sails first and last, only that I was fain to cut them in Pieces, and bring as much at a Time as I could; for they were no more useful to be Sails, but as meer Canvass only.

But that which comforted me more still was, that at last of all, after I had made five or six such Voyages as these, and thought I had nothing more to expect from the Ship that was worth my meddling with, I say, after all this, I found a great Hogshead[6] of Bread and three large Runlets[7] of Rum or Spirits, and a Box of Sugar, and a Barrel of fine Flower; this was surprizing to me, because I had given over expecting any more Provisions, except what was spoil'd by the Water: I soon empty'd the Hogshead of that Bread, and wrapt it up Parcel by Parcel in Pieces of the Sails, which I cut out; and in a Word, I got all this safe on Shore also.

The next Day I made another Voyage; and now having plunder'd the Ship of what was portable and fit to hand out, I began with the Cables; and cutting the great Cable into Pieces, such as I could move, I got two Cables and a Hawser on Shore, with all the Iron Work I could get; and having cut down the Sprit-sail-yard, and the Missen-yard, and every Thing I could to make a large Raft, I loaded it with all those heavy Goods, and came away: But my good Luck began now to leave me; for this Raft was so unweildy, and so overloaden, that after I was enter'd the little Cove, where I had landed the rest of my Goods, not being able to guide it so handily as I did the other, it overset, and threw me and all my Cargoe into the Water; as for myself it was no great Harm, for I was near the Shore; but as to my Cargoe, it was great Part of it lost, especially the Iron, which I expected would have been of great Use to me: However, when the Tide was out, I got most of the Pieces of Cable ashore, and some of the Iron, tho' with infinite Labour; for I was fain

---

5. Corrected to "Magazine" in the second and subsequent editions.
6. A large barrel.
7. A cask of varying capacity, usually holding about eighteen gallons.

to dip for it into the Water, a Work which fatigu'd me very much: After this I went every Day on Board, and brought away what I could get.

I had been now thirteen Days on Shore, and had been eleven Times on Board the Ship; in which Time I had brought away all that one Pair of Hands could well be suppos'd capable to bring, tho' I believe verily, had the calm Weather held, I should have brought away the whole Ship Piece by Piece: But preparing the 12th Time to go on Board, I found the Wind begin to rise; however at low Water I went on Board, and tho' I thought I had rumag'd the Cabbin so effectually, as that nothing more could be found, yet I discover'd a Locker with Drawers in it, in one of which I found two or three Razors, and one Pair of large Sizzers, with some ten or a Dozen of good Knives and Forks; in another I found about Thirty six Pounds value in Money, some *European* Coin, some *Brasil*, some Pieces of Eight, some Gold, some Silver.

I smil'd to my self at the Sight of this Money. O Drug! said I aloud, what art thou good for? Thou art not worth to me, no not the taking off of the Ground; one of those Knives is worth all this Heap; I have no Manner of use for thee, e'en remain where thou art, and go to the Bottom as a Creature whose Life is not worth saving. However, upon Second Thoughts, I took it away, and wrapping all this in a Piece of Canvas, I began to think of making another Raft; but while I was preparing this, I found the Sky overcast, and the Wind began to rise, and in a Quarter of an Hour it blew a fresh Gale from the Shore; it presently occur'd to me, that it was in vain to pretend to make a Raft with the Wind off Shore, and that it was my Business to be gone before the Tide of Flood began, otherwise I might not be able to reach the Shore at all: Accordingly I let my self down into the Water, and swam cross the Channel, which lay between the Ship and the Sands, and even that with Difficulty enough, partly with the Weight of the Things I had about me, and partly the Roughness of the Water, for the Wind rose very hastily, and before it was quite high Water, it blew a Storm.

But I was gotten home to my little Tent, where I lay with all my Wealth about me very secure. It blew very hard all that Night, and in the Morning when I look'd out, behold no more Ship was to be seen; I was a little surpriz'd, but recover'd my self with this satisfactory Reflection, *viz.* That I had lost no time, nor abated no Dilligence to get every thing out of her that could be useful to me, and that indeed there was little left in her that I was able to bring away if I had had more time.

I now gave over any more Thoughts of the Ship, or of any thing out of her, except what might drive on Shore from her Wreck, as indeed divers Pieces of her afterwards did; but those things were of small use to me.

My Thoughts were now wholly employ'd about securing my self against either Savages, if any should appear, or wild Beasts, if any were in the Island; and I had many Thoughts of the Method how to do this, and what kind of Dwelling to make, whether I should make me a Cave in the Earth, or a Tent upon the Earth: And, in short, I resolv'd upon both, the Manner and Discription of which, it may not be improper to give an Account of.

I soon found the Place I was in was not for my Settlement, particularly because it was upon a low moorish Ground near the Sea, and I believ'd would not be wholesome, and more particularly because there was no fresh Water near it, so I resolv'd to find a more healthy and more convenient Spot of Ground.

I consulted several Things in my Situation which I found would be proper for me, 1st. Health, and fresh Water I just now mention'd, 2dly. Shelter from the Heat of the Sun, 3dly. Security from ravenous Creatures, whether Men or Beasts, 4thly. a View to the Sea, that if God sent any Ship in Sight, I might not lose any Advantage for my Deliverance, of which I was not willing to banish all my Expectation yet.

In search of a Place proper for this, I found a little Plain on the Side of a rising Hill, whose Front towards this little Plain, was steep as a House-side, so that nothing could come down upon me from the Top; on the Side of this Rock there was a hollow Place worn a little way in like the Entrance or Door of a Cave, but there was not really any Cave or Way into the Rock at all.

On the Flat of the Green, just before this hollow Place, I resolv'd to pitch my Tent: This Plain was not above an Hundred Yards broad, and about twice as long, and lay like a Green before my Door, and at the End of it descended irregularly every Way down into the Low-grounds by the Sea side. It was on the N.N.W. Side of the Hill, so that I was shelter'd from the Heat every Day, till it came to a W. and by S. Sun, or thereabouts, which in those Countries is near the Setting.

Before I set up my Tent, I drew a half Circle before the hollow Place, which took in about Ten Yards in its Semi-diameter from the Rock, and Twenty Yards in its Diameter, from its Beginning and Ending.

In this half Circle I pitch'd two Rows of strong Stakes, driving them into the Ground till they stood very firm like Piles, the biggest End being out of the Ground about Five Foot and a Half, and sharpen'd on the Top: The two Rows did not stand above Six Inches from one another.

Then I took the Pieces of Cable which I had cut in the Ship, and I laid them in Rows one upon another, within the Circle, between these two Rows of Stakes up to the Top, placing other Stakes in the In-side, leaning against them, about two Foot and a half high, like a Spurr to a Post, and this Fence was so strong, that neither Man or Beast could get into it or over it: This cost me a great deal of Time and Labour, especially to cut the Piles in the Woods, bring them to the place, and drive them into the Earth.

The Entrance into this Place I made to be not by a Door, but by a short Ladder to go over the Top, which Ladder, when I was in, I lifted over after me, and so I was compleatly fenc'd in, and fortify'd, as I thought, from all the World, and consequently slept secure in the Night, which otherwise I could not have done, tho', as it appear'd afterward, there was no need of all this Caution from the Enemies that I apprehended Danger from.

Into this Fence or Fortress, with infinite Labour, I carry'd all my Riches, all my Provisions, Ammunition and Stores, of which you have the Account above, and I made me a large Tent, which, to preserve me from the Rains that in one Part of the Year are very violent there, I made double, *viz.* One smaller Tent within, and one larger Tent above it, and cover'd the uppermost with a large Tarpaulin which I had sav'd among the Sails.

And now I lay no more for a while in the Bed which I had brought on Shore, but in a Hammock, which was indeed a very good one, and belong'd to the Mate of the Ship.

Into this Tent I brought all my Provisions, and every thing that would spoil by the Wet, and having thus enclos'd all my Goods, I made up the Entrance, which till now I had left open, and so pass'd and re-pass'd, as I said by a short Ladder.

When I had done this, I began to work my Way into the Rock, and bringing all the Earth and Stones that I dug down out thro' my Tent, I laid 'em up within my Fence in the Nature of a Terras,[8] that so it rais'd the Ground within about a Foot and a Half; and thus I made me a Cave just behind my Tent, which serv'd me like a Cellar to my House.

It cost me much Labour, and many Days, before all these Things were brought to Perfection, and therefore I must go back to some other Things which took up some of my Thoughts. At the same time it happen'd after I had laid my Scheme for the setting up my Tent and making the Cave, that a Storm of Rain falling from a thick dark Cloud, a sudden Flash of Lightning happen'd, and after that a great Clap of Thunder, as is naturally the Effect of it; I was not so much surpris'd with the Lightning as I was with a Thought which darted into my Mind as swift as the Lightning it self: O my Powder! My very Heart sunk within me, when I thought, that at one Blast all my Powder might be destroy'd, on which, not my Defence only, but the providing me Food, as I thought, entirely depended; I was nothing near so anxious about my own Danger, tho' had the Powder took fire, I had never known who had hurt me.

Such Impression did this make upon me, that after the Storm was over, I laid aside all my Works, my Building, and Fortifying, and apply'd my self to make Bags and Boxes to separate the Powder, and keep it a little and a little in a Parcel, in hope, that whatever might come, it

8. Corrected to "Terrace" in the sixth edition.

might not all take Fire at once, and to keep it so apart that it should
not be possible to make one part fire another: I finish'd this Work in
about a Fortnight, and I think my Powder, which in all was about
240 l. weight was divided in not less than a Hundred Parcels; as to the
Barrel that had been wet, I did not apprehend any Danger from that,
so I plac'd it in my new Cave, which in my Fancy I call'd my Kitchin,
and the rest I hid up and down in Holes among the Rocks, so that no
wet might come to it, marking very carefully where I laid it.

In the Interval of time while this was doing I went out once at least
every Day with my Gun, as well to divert my self, as to see if I could
kill any thing fit for Food, and as near as I could to acquaint my self
with what the Island produc'd. The first time I went out I presently
discover'd that there were Goats in the Island, which was a great Satisfaction to me; but then it was attended with this Misfortune to me,
viz. That they were so shy, so subtile, and so swift of Foot, that it was
the difficultest thing in the World to come at them: But I was not
discourag'd at this, not doubting but I might now and then shoot one,
as it soon happen'd, for after I had found their Haunts a little, I laid
wait in this Manner for them: I observ'd if they saw me in the Valleys,
tho' they were upon the Rocks, they would run away as in a terrible
Fright; but if they were feeding in the Valleys, and I was upon the Rocks,
they took no Notice of me, from whence I concluded, that by the Position
of their Opticks,[9] their Sight was so directed downward, that they did
not readily see Objects that were above them; so afterward I took this
Method, I always clim'd the Rocks first to get above them, and then
had frequently a fair Mark. The first shot I made among these Creatures,
I kill'd a She-Goat which had a little Kid by her when she gave Suck
to, which griev'd me heartily; but when the Old one fell, the Kid stood
stock still by her till I came and took her up, and not only so, but when
I carry'd the Old one with me upon my Shoulders, the Kid follow'd me
quite to my Enclosure, upon which I laid down the Dam, and took the
Kid in my Arms, and carry'd it over my Pale, in hopes to have bred it
up tame, but it would not eat, so I was forc'd to kill it and eat it myself;
these two supply'd me with Flesh a great while, for I eat sparingly; and
sav'd my Provisions (my Bread especially) as much as possibly I could.

Having now fix'd my Habitation, I found it absolutely necessary to
provide a Place to make a Fire in, and Fewel to burn; and what I did
for that, as also how I enlarg'd my Cave, and what Conveniences I
made, I shall give a full Account of in its Place: But I must first give
some little Account of my self, and of my Thoughts about Living, which
it may well be suppos'd were not a few.

I had a dismal Prospect of my Condition, for as I was not cast away
upon that Island without being driven, as is said, by a violent Storm
quite out of the Course of our intended Voyage, and a great Way, *viz,*

9. Eyes.

some Hundreds of Leagues out of the ordinary Course of the Trade of Mankind, I had great Reason to consider it as a Determination of Heaven, that in this desolate Place, and in this desolate Manner I should end my Life; the Tears would run plentifully down my Face when I made these Reflections, and sometimes I would expostulate with my self, Why Providence should thus compleatly ruine its Creatures, and render them so absolutely miserable, so without Help abandon'd, so entirely depress'd, that it could hardly be rational to be thankful for such a Life.

But something always return'd swift upon me to check these Thoughts, and to reprove me; and particularly one Day walking with my Gun in my Hand by the Sea-side, I was very pensive upon the Subject of my present Condition, when Reason as it were expostulated with me t'other Way, thus: Well, you are in a desolate Condition 'tis true, but pray remember, Where are the rest of you? Did not you come Eleven of you into the Boat, where are the Ten? Why were not they sav'd and you lost? Why were you singled out? Is it better to be here or there, and then I pointed to the Sea? All Evils are to be consider'd with the Good that is in them, and with what worse attends them.

Then it occurr'd to me again, how well I was furnish'd for my Subsistence, and what would have been my Case if it had not happen'd. *Which was an Hundred Thousand to one*, that the Ship floated from the Place where she first struck and was driven so near to the Shore that I had time to get all these Things out of her? What would have been my Case, if I had been to have liv'd in the Condition in which I at first came on Shore, without Necessaries of Life, or Necessaries to supply and procure them? Particularly said I aloud, (tho' to my self) what should I ha' done without a Gun, without Ammunition, without any Tools to make any thing, or to work with, without Clothes, Bedding, a Tent, or any manner of Covering, and that now I had all these to a Sufficient Quantity, and was in a fair way to provide my self in such a manner, as to live without my Gun when my Ammunition was spent; so that I had a tollerable View of subsisting without any Want as long as I liv'd; for I consider'd from the beginning how I would provide for the Accidents that might happen, and for the time that was to come, even not only after my Ammunition should be spent, but even after my Health or Strength should decay.

I confess I had not entertain'd any Notion of my Ammunition being destroy'd at one Blast, I mean my Powder being blown up by Lightning, and this made the Thoughts of it so surprising to me when it lighten'd and thunder'd, as I observ'd just now.

And now being to enter into a melancholy Relation of a Scene of silent Life, such perhaps as was never heard of in the World before, I shall take it from its Beginning, and continue it in its Order. It was, by my Account, the 30th. of *Sept.* when, in the Manner as above said, I first set Foot upon this horrid Island, when the Sun being, to us, in its

Autumnal Equinox, was almost just over my Head, for I reckon'd my self, by Observation, to be in the Latitude of 9 Degrees 22 Minutes North of the Line.

After I had been there about Ten or Twelve Days, it came into my Thoughts, that I should lose my Reckoning of Time for want of Books and Pen and Ink, and should even forget the Sabbath Days from the working Days; but to prevent this I cut it with my Knife upon a large Post, in Capital Letters, and making it into a great Cross I set it up on the Shore where I first landed, *viz. I come on Shore here on the 30th of Sept.* 1659. Upon the Sides of this square Post I cut every Day a Notch with my Knife, and every seventh Notch was as long again as the rest, and every first Day of the Month as long again as that long one, and thus I kept my Kalander, or weekly, monthly, and yearly reckoning of Time.

In the next place we are to observe, that among the many things which I brought out of the Ship in the several Voyages, which, as above mention'd, I made to it, I got several things of less Value, but not at all less useful to me, which I omitted setting down before; as in particular, Pens, Ink, and Paper, several Parcels in the Captain's, Mate's, Gunner's, and Carpenter's keeping, three or four Compasses, some Mathematical Instruments, Dials, Perspectives,[1] Charts, and Books of Navigation, all which I huddled together, whether I might want them or no; also I found three very good Bibles which came to me in my Cargo from *England*, and which I had pack'd up among my things: some *Portugueze* Books also, and among them two or three Popish Prayer-Books, and several other Books, all which I carefully secur'd. And I must not forget, that we had in the Ship a Dog and two Cats, of whose eminent History I may have occasion to say something in its place; for I carry'd both the Cats with me, and as for the Dog, he jump'd out of the Ship of himself, and swam on Shore to me the Day after I went on Shore with my first Cargo, and was a trusty Servant to me many Years; I wanted[2] nothing that he could fetch me, nor any Company that he could make up to me, I only wanted to have him talk to me, but that would not do: As I observ'd before, I found Pen, Ink and Paper, and I husbanded them to the utmost, and I shall shew, that while my Ink lasted, I kept things very exact, but after that was gone I could not, for I could not make any Ink by any Means that I could devise.

And this put me in mind that I wanted many things, notwithstanding all that I had amass'd together, and of these, this of Ink was one, as also Spade, Pick-Axe, and Shovel to dig or remove the Earth, Needles, Pins, and Thread; as for Linnen, I soon learn'd to want[3] that without much Difficulty.

1. Spyglasses or telescopes.
2. Lacked.
3. Do without.

This want of Tools made every Work I did go on heavily, and it was near a whole Year before I had entirely finish'd my little Pale or surrounded Habitation: The Piles or Stakes, which were as heavy as I could well lift, were a long time in cutting and preparing in the Woods, and more by far in bringing home, so that I spent some times two Days in cutting and bringing home one of those Posts, and a third Day in driving it into the Ground; for which Purpose I got a heavy Piece of Wood at first, but at last bethought my self of one of the Iron Crows, which however tho' I found it, yet it made driving those Posts or Piles very laborious and tedious Work.

But what need I ha' been concern'd at the Tediousness of any thing I had to do, seeing I had time enough to do it in, nor had I any other Employment if that had been over, at least, that I could foresee, except the ranging the Island to seek for Food, which I did more or less every Day.

I now began to consider seriously my Condition, and the Circumstance I was reduc'd to, and I drew up the State of my Affairs in Writing, not so much to leave them to any that were to come after me, for I was like to have but few Heirs, as to deliver my Thoughts from daily poring upon them, and afflicting my Mind; and as my Reason began now to master my Despondency, I began to comfort my self as well as I could, and to set the good against the Evil, that I might have something to distinguish my Case from worse, and I stated it very impartially, like Debtor and Creditor, the Comforts I enjoy'd, against the Miseries I suffer'd, Thus,

EVIL.	GOOD.
I am cast upon a horrible desolate Island, void of all Hope of Recovery.	But I am alive, and not drown'd as all my Ship's Company was.
I am singl'd out and separated, as it were, from all the World to be miserable.	But I am singl'd out too from all the Ship's Crew to be spar'd from Death; and he that miraculously sav'd me from Death, can deliver me from this Condition.
I am divided from Mankind, a Solitaire, one banish'd from humane Society.	But I am not starv'd and perishing on a barren Place, affording no Sustenance.
I have not Clothes to cover me.	But I am in a hot Climate, where if I had Clothes I could hardly wear them.
I am without any Defence or Means to resist any Violence of Man or Beast.	But I am cast on an Island, where I see no wild Beasts to hurt me, as I saw on the Coast of Africa: And what if I had been Shipwreck'd there?

I have no Soul to speak to, or relieve me.	But God wonderfully sent the Ship in near enough to the Shore, that I have gotten out so many necessary things as will either supply my Wants, or enable me to supply my self even as long as I live.

Upon the whole, here was an undoubted Testimony, that there was scarce any Condition in the World so miserable, but there was something *Negative* or something *Positive* to be thankful for in it; and let this stand as a Direction from the Experience of the most miserable of all conditions in this World, that we may always find in it something to comfort our selves from, and to set in the description of Good and Evil, on the Credit Side of the Accompt.[4]

Having now brought my Mind a little to relish my Condition, and given over looking out to Sea to see if I could spy a Ship, I say, giving over these things, I began to apply my self to accommodate my way of Living, and to make things as easy to me as I could.

I have already describ'd my Habitation, which was a Tent under the Side of a Rock, surrounded with a strong Pale of Posts and Cables, but I might now rather call it a Wall, for I rais'd a kind of Wall up against it of Turfs, about two Foot thick on the Outside, and after some time, I think it was a Year and a Half, I rais'd Rafters from it leaning to the Rock, and thatch'd or cover'd it with Bows of Trees, and such things as I could get to keep out the Rain, which I found at some times of the Year very violent.

I have already observ'd how I brought all my Goods into this Pale, and into the Cave which I had made behind me: But I must observe too, that at first this was a confus'd Heap of Goods, which as they lay in no Order, so they took up all my Place, I had no room to turn my self; so I set my self to enlarge my Cave and Works farther into the Earth, for it was a loose sandy Rock, which yielded easily to the Labour I bestow'd on it; and so when I found I was pretty safe as to Beasts of Prey, I work'd side-ways to the Right Hand into the Rock, and then turning to the Right again, work'd quite out and made me a Door to come out, on the Out-side of my Pale or Fortification.

This gave me not only Egress and Regress, as it were a back Way to my Tent and to my Storehouse, but gave me room to stow my Goods.

And now I began to apply my self to make such necessary things as I found I most wanted, as particularly a Chair and a Table, for without these I was not able to enjoy the few Comforts I had in the World, I could not write, or eat, or do several things with so much Pleasure without a Table.

So I went to work; and here I must needs observe, that as Reason is

4. Corrected to "Account" in the second and subsequent editions.

the Substance and Original of the Mathematicks, so by stating and squaring every thing by Reason, and by making the most rational Judgment of things, every Man may be in time Master of every mechanick Art. I had never handled a Tool in my Life, and yet in time by Labour, Application, and Contrivance, I found at last that I wanted nothing but I could have made it, especially if I had had Tools; however I made abundance of things, even without Tools, and some with no more Tools than an Adze and a Hatchet, which perhaps were never made that way before, and that with infinite Labour: For Example, If I wanted a Board, I had no other Way but to cut down a Tree, set it on an Edge before me, and hew it flat on either Side with my Axe, till I had brought it to be thin as a Plank, and then dubb it smooth with my Adze. It is true, by this Method I could make but one Board out of a whole Tree, but this I had no Remedy for but Patience, any more than I had for the prodigious deal of Time and Labour which it took me up to make a Plank or Board: But my Time or Labour was little worth, and so it was as well employ'd one way as another.

However, I made me a Table and a Chair, as I observ'd above, in the first Place, and this I did out of the short Pieces of Boards that I brought on my Raft from the Ship: But when I had wrought out some Boards, as above I made large Shelves of the Breadth of a Foot and a Half one over another, all along one Side of my Cave, to lay all my Tools, Nails, and Iron-work, and in a Word, to separate every thing at large in their Places, that I must come easily at them; I knock'd Pieces into the Wall of the Rock to hang my Guns and all things that would hang up.

So that had my Cave been to be seen, it look'd like a general Magazine of all Necessary things, and I had every thing so ready at my Hand, that it was a great Pleasure to me to see all my Goods in such Order, and especially to find my Stock of all Necessaries so great.

And now it was when I began to keep a Journal of every Day's Employment, for indeed at first I was in too much Hurry, and not only Hurry as to Labour, but in too much Discomposure of Mind, and my Journal would ha' been full of many dull things: For Example, I must have said thus. *Sept.* the 30th. After I got to Shore and had escap'd drowning, instead of being thankful to God for my Deliverance, having first vomited with the great Quantity of salt Water which has gotten into my Stomach, and recovering my self a little, I ran about the Shore, wringing my Hands and beating my Head and Face, exclaiming at my Misery, and crying out, I was undone, undone, till tyr'd and faint I was forc'd to lye down on the Ground to repose, but durst not sleep for fear of being devour'd.

Some Days after this, and after I had been on board the Ship, and got all that I could out of her, yet I could not forbear getting up to the Top of a little Mountain and looking out to Sea in hopes of seeing a

Ship, then fancy at a vast Distance I spy'd a Sail, please my self with the Hopes of it, and then after looking steadily till I was almost blind, lose it quite, and sit down and weep like a Child, and thus encrease my Misery by my Folly.

But having gotten over these things in some Measure, and having settled my household Stuff and Habitation, made me a Table and a Chair, and all as handsome about me as I could, I began to keep my Journal, of which I shall here give you the Copy (tho' in it will be told all these Particulars over again) as long as it lasted, for having no more Ink I was forc'd to leave it off.

THE JOURNAL

September 30, 1659. I poor miserable *Robinson Crusoe*, being ship-wreck'd, during a dreadful Storm, in the offing,[5] came on Shore on this dismal unfortunate Island, which I call'd *the Island of Despair*, all the rest of the Ship's Company being drown'd, and my self almost dead.

All the rest of that Day I spent in afflicting my self at the dismal Circumstances I was brought to, *viz.* I had neither Food, House, Clothes, Weapon, or Place to fly to, and in Despair of any Relief, saw nothing but Death before me, either that I should be devour'd by wild Beasts, murther'd by Savages, or starv'd to Death for Want of Food. At the Approach of Night, I slept in a Tree for fear of wild Creatures, but slept soundly tho' it rain'd all Night.

October 1. In the Morning I saw to my great Surprise the Ship had floated with the high Tide, and was driven on Shore again much nearer the Island, which as it was some Comfort on one hand, for seeing her sit upright, and not broken to Pieces, I hop'd, if the Wind abated, I might get on board, and get some Food and Necessaries out of her for my Relief; so on the other hand, it renew'd my Grief at the Loss of my Comrades, who I imagin'd if we had all staid on board might have sav'd the Ship, or at least that they would not have been all drown'd as they were; and that had the Men been sav'd, we might perhaps have built us a Boat out of the Ruins of the Ship, to have carried us to some other Part of the World. I spent great Part of this Day in perplexing my self on these things; but at length seeing the Ship almost dry, I went upon the Sand as near as I could, and then swam on board; this Day also it continu'd raining, tho' with no Wind at all.

From the 1st of *October*, to the 24th. All these Days entirely spent in many several Voyages to get all I could out of the Ship, which I brought on Shore, every Tide of Flood, upon Rafts. Much Rain also in these Days, tho' with some Intervals of fair Weather: But, it seems, this was the rainy Season.

Oct. 20. I overset my Raft, and all the Goods I had got upon it, but

5. Faraway from shore.

being in shoal[6] Water, and the things being chiefly heavy, I recover'd many of them when the Tide was out.

Oct. 25. It rain'd all Night and all Day, with some Gusts of Wind, during which time the Ship broke in Pieces, the Wind blowing a little harder than before, and was no more to be seen, except the Wreck of her, and that only at low Water. I spent this Day in covering and securing the Goods which I had sav'd, that the Rain might not spoil them.

Oct. 26. I walk'd about the Shore almost all Day to find out a place to fix my Habitation, greatly concern'd to secure my self from an Attack in the Night, either from wild Beasts or Men. Towards Night I fix'd upon a proper Place under a Rock, and mark'd out a Semi-Circle for my Encampment, which I resolv'd to strengthen with a Work, Wall, or Fortification made of double Piles, lin'd within with Cables, and without with Turf.

From the 26th. to the 30th. I work'd very hard in carrying all my Goods to my new Habitation, tho' some Part of the time it rain'd exceeding hard.

The 31st. in the Morning I went out into the Island with my Gun to see for some Food, and discover the Country, when I kill'd a She-Goat, and her Kid follow'd me home, which I afterwards kill'd also because it would not feed.

November 1. I set up my Tent under a Rock, and lay there for the first Night, making it as large as I could with Stakes driven in to swing my Hammock upon.

Nov. 2. I set up all my Chests and Boards, and the Piecs of Timber which made my Rafts, and with them form'd a Fence round me, a little within the Place I had mark'd out for my Fortification.

Nov. 3. I went out with my Gun and kill'd two Fowls like Ducks, which were very good Food. In the Afternoon went to work to make me a Table.

Nov. 4. This Morning I began to order my times of Work, of going out with my Gun, time of Sleep, and time of Diversion, *viz.* Every Morning I walk'd out with my Gun for two or three Hours if it did not rain, then employ'd my self to work till about Eleven a-Clock, then eat what I had to live on, and from Twelve to Two I lay down to sleep, the Weather being excessive hot, and then in the Evening to work again: The working Part of this Day and of the next were wholly employ'd in making my Table, for I was yet but a very sorry Workman, tho' Time and Necessity made me a compleat natural Mechanick soon after, as I believe it would do any one else.

Nov. 5. This Day went abroad with my Gun and my Dog, and kill'd a wild Cat, her Skin pretty soft, but her Flesh good for nothing: Every Creature I kill'd I took off the Skins and preserv'd them: Coming back

6. Shallow.

by the Sea Shore, I saw many Sorts of Sea Fowls which I did not understand, but was surpris'd and almost frighted with two or three Seals, which, while I was gazing at, not well knowing what they were, got into the Sea and escap'd me for that time.

Nov. 6. After my Morning Walk I went to work with my Table again, and finish'd it, tho' not to my liking; nor was it long before I learn'd to mend it.

Nov. 7. Now it begain to be settled fair Weather. The 7th, 8th, 9th, 10th, and Part of the 12th. (for the 11th. was Sunday) I took wholly up to make me a Chair, and with much ado brought it to a tolerable Shape, but never to please me, and even in the making I pull'd it in Pieces several times. *Note,* I soon neglected my keeping Sundays, for omitting my Mark for them on my Post, I forgot which was which.

Nov. 13. This Day it rain'd, which refresh'd me exceedingly, and cool'd the Earth, but it was accompany'd with terrible Thunder and Lightning, which frighted me dreadfully for fear of my Powder; as soon as it was over, I resolv'd to separate my Stock of Powder into as many little Parcels as possible, that it might not be in Danger.

Nov. 14, 15, 16. These three Days I spent in making little square Chests or Boxes, which might hold a Pound or two Pound, at most, of Powder, and so putting the Powder in, I stow'd it in Places as secure and remote from one another as possible. On one of these three Days I kill'd a large Bird that was good to eat, but I know not what to call it.

Nov. 17. This Day I began to dig behind my Tent in to the Rock to make room for my farther Conveniency: *Note,* Two Things I wanted exceedingly for this Work *viz.* A Pick-axe, a Shovel, and a Wheel-barrow or Basket, so I desisted from my Work, and began to consider how to supply that Want and make me some Tools; as for a Pick-axe, I made use of the Iron Crows, which were proper enough, tho' heavy; but the next thing was a Shovel or Spade, this was so absolutely necessary, that indeed I could do nothing effectually without it, but what kind of one to make I knew not.

Nov. 18. The next Day in searching the Woods I found a Tree of that Wood, or like it, which, in the *Brasils* they call the *Iron Tree,* for its exceeding Hardness, of this, with great Labour and almost spoiling my Axe, I cut a Piece, and brought it home too with Difficulty enough, for it was exceeding heavy.

The excessive Hardness of the Wood, and having no Other Way, made me a long while upon this Machine, for I work'd it effectually by little and little into the Form of a Shovel or Spade, the Handle exactly shap'd like ours in *England,* only that the broad Part having no Iron shod upon it at Bottom, it would not last me so long, however it serv'd well enough for the uses which I had occasion to put it to; but never was a Shovel, I believe, made after that Fashion, or so long a making.

I was still deficient, for I wanted a Basket or a Wheel-barrow, a Basket

I could not make by any Means, having no such things as Twigs that would bend to make Wicker Ware, at least none yet found out; and as to a Wheel-barrow, I fancy'd I could make all but the Wheel, but that I had no Notion of, neither did I know how to go about it; besides I had no possible Way to make the Iron Gudgeons for the Spindle or Axis of the Wheel to run in, so I gave it over, and so for carrying away the Earth which I dug out of the Cave, I made me a Thing like a Hodd, which the Labourers carry Morter in, when they serve the Bricklayers.

This was not so difficult to me as the making the Shovel; and yet this, and the Shovel, and the Attempt which I made in vain, to make a Wheel-Barrow, took me up no less than four Days, I mean always, excepting my Morning Walk with my Gun, which I seldom fail'd, and very seldom fail'd also bringing Home something fit to eat.

Nov. 23. My other Work having now stood still, because of my making these Tools; when they were finish'd, I went on, and working every Day, as my Strength and Time allow'd, I spent eighteen Days entirely in widening and deepening my Cave, that it might hold my Goods commodiously.

Note, During all this Time, I work'd to make this Room or Cave spacious enough to accommodate me as a Warehouse or Magazin, a Kitchen, a Dining-room, and a Cellar; as for my Lodging, I kept to the Tent, except that some Times in the wet Season of the Year, it rain'd so hard, that I could not keep my self dry, which caused me afterwards to cover all my Place within my Pale with long Poles in the Form of Rafters leaning against the Rock, and load them with Flaggs[7] and large Leaves of Trees like a Thatch.

December 10th, I began now to think my Cave or Vault finished, when on a Sudden, (it seems I had made it too large) a great Quantity of Earth fell down from the Top and one Side, so much, that in short it frighted me, and not without Reason too; for if I had been under it I had never wanted a Grave-Digger: Upon this Disaster I had a great deal of Work to do over again; for I had the loose Earth to carry out; and which was of more Importance, I had the Seiling to prop up, so that I might be sure no more would come down.

Dec. 11. This Day I went to Work with it accordingly, and got two Shores or Posts pitch'd upright to the Top, with two Pieces of Boards a-cross over each Post, this I finish'd the next Day; and setting more Posts up with Boards, in about a week more I had the Roof secur'd and the Posts standing in Rows, serv'd me for Partitions to part of my House.

Dec. 17. From this Day to the Twentieth I plac'd Shelves, and knock'd up Nails on the Posts to hang every Thing up that could be hung up, and now I began to be in some Order within Doors.

Dec. 20. Now I carry'd every Thing into the Cave, and began to

---

7. Plants with long ensiform leaves used in thatching or tying.

furnish my House, and set up some Pieces of Boards, like a Dresser, to order my Victuals upon, but Boards began to be very scarce with me; also I made me another Table.

Dec. 24. Much Rain all Night and all Day, no stirring out.

Dec. 26. Rain all Day.

Dec. 26. No Rain, and the Earth much cooler than before, and pleasanter.

Dec. 27. Kill'd a young Goat, and lam'd another so as that I catch'd it, and led it Home in a String; when I had it Home, I bound and splinter'd up its Leg which was broke, *N.B.* I took such Care of it, that it liv'd, and the Leg grew well, and as strong as ever; but by my nursing it so long it grew tame, and fed upon the little Green at my Door, and would not go away: This was the first Time that I entertain'd a Thought of breeding up some tame creatures, that I might have Food when my Powder and Shot was all spent.

Dec. 28, 29, 30. Great Heats and no Breeze; so that there was no Stirring abroad, except in the Evening for Food; this Time I spent in putting all my Things in Order within Doors.

January 1. Very hot still, but I went abroad early and late with my Gun, and lay still in the Middle of the Day; this Evening going farther into the Valleys which lay towards the Center of the Island, I found there was plenty of Goats, tho' exceeding shy and hard to come at, however I resolv'd to try if I could not bring my Dog to hunt them down.

Jan. 2. Accordingly, the next Day, I went out with my Dog, and set him upon the Goats; but I was mistaken, for they all fac'd about upon the Dog, and he knew his Danger too well, for he would not come near them.

Jan. 3. I began my Fence or Wall; which being still jealous[8] of my being attack'd by some Body, I resolv'd to make very thick and strong.

> *N.B.* This Wall being describ'd before, I purposely omit what was said in the Journal; it is sufficient to observe, that I was no less Time than from the 3d of *January* to the 14th of *April*, working, finishing, and perfecting this Wall, tho' it was no more than about 24 Yards in Length, being a half Circle from one Place in the Rock to another Place about eight Yards from it, the Door of the Cave being in the Center behind it.

All this Time I work'd very hard, the Rains hindering me many Days, nay sometimes Weeks together; but I thought I should never be perfectly secure 'till this Wall was finish'd; and it is scarce credible what inexpressible Labour every Thing was done with, especially the bringing Piles out of the Woods, and driving them into the Ground, for I made them much bigger than I need to have done.

8. Apprehensive.

When this Wall was finished, and the Out-side double fenc'd with a Turf-Wall rais'd up close to it, I perswaded my self, that if any People were to come on Shore there, they would not perceive any Thing like a Habitation; and it was very well I did so, as may be observ'd hereafter upon a very remarkable Occasion.

During this Time, I made my Rounds in the Woods for Game every Day when the Rain admitted me, and made frequent Discoveries in these Walks of something or other to my Advantage; particularly I found a Kind of wild Pidgeons, who built not as Wood Pidgeons in a Tree, but rather as House Pidgeons, in the Holes of the Rocks; and taking some young ones, I endeavoured to breed them up tame, and did so; but when they grew older they flew all away, which perhaps was at first for Want of feeding them, for I had nothing to give them; however I frequently found their nests, and got their young ones, which were very good Meat.

And now, in the managing my household Affairs, I found my self wanting in many Things, which I thought at first it was impossible for me to make, as indeed as to some of them it was; for *Instance*, I could never make a Cask to be hooped, I had a small Runlet or two, *as I observed before*, but I cou'd never arrive to the Capacity of making one of them, tho' I spent many Weeks about it; I could neither put in the Heads, or joint the Staves so true to one another, as to make them hold Water, so I gave that also over.

In the next Place, I was at a great Loss for Candle; so that as soon as ever it was dark, which was generally by Seven-a-Clock, I was oblig'd to go to Bed: But I remembered the Lamp of Bees-wax with which I made Candles in my *African* Adventure, but I had none of that now; the only Remedy I had was, that when I had kill'd a Goat, I sav'd the Tallow, and with a little Dish made of Clay, which I bak'd in the Sun, to which I added a Wick of some Oakum,[9] I made me a Lamp; and this gave me Light, tho' not a clear steady Light like a Candle; in the Middle of all my Labours it happen'd, that rummaging in my Things, I found a little Bag, which, as I hinted before, had been fill'd with Corn for the feeding of Poultry, not for this Voyage, but before, as I suppose, when the Ship came from *Lisbon*, what little Remainder of Corn had been in the Bag, was all devour'd with the Rats, and I saw nothing in the Bag but Husks and Dust; and being willing to have the Bag for some other Use, I think it was to put Powder in, when I divided it for Fear of the Lightning, or some such Use, I shook the Husks of Corn out of it on one Side of my Fortification under the Rock.

It was a little before the great Rains, just now mention'd, that I threw this Stuff away, taking no Notice of any Thing, and not so much as remembering that I had thrown any Thing there; when about a Month

9. Fiber obtained by untwisting old hemp rope.

after, or thereabout, I saw some few Stalks of something green, shooting out of the Ground, which I fancy'd might be some Plant I had not seen, but I was surpriz'd and perfectly astonish'd, when, after a little longer Time, I saw about ten or twelve Ears come out, which were perfect green Barley of the same Kind as our *European*, nay, as our *English* Barley.

It is impossible to express the Astonishment and Confusion of my Thoughts on this Occasion; I had hitherto acted upon no religious Foundation at all, indeed I had very few Notions of Religion in my Head, or had entertain'd any Sense of any Thing that had befallen me, otherwise than as a Chance, or, as we lightly say, what pleases God; without so much as enquiring into the End of Providence in these Things, or his Order in governing Events in the World: But after I saw Barley grow there, in a Climate which I know was not proper for Corn, and especially that I knew not how it came there, it startl'd me strangely, and I began to suggest, that God had miraculously caus'd this Grain to grow without any Help of Seed sown, and that it was directed purely for my Sustenance, on that wild miserable Place.

This touch'd my Heart a little, and brought Tears out of my Eyes, and I began to bless my self, that such a Prodigy of Nature should happen upon my Account; and this was the more strange to me, because I saw near it still all along by the Side of the Rock, some other straggling Stalks, which prov'd to be Stalks of Ryce,[1] and which I knew, because I had seen it grow in *Africa* when I was ashore there.

I not only thought these the pure Productions of Providence for my Support, but not doubting, but that there was more in the Place, I went all over that Part of the Island, where I had been before, peering in every Corner, and under every Rock, to see for more of it, but I could not find any; at last it occur'd to my Thoughts, that I had shook a Bag of Chickens Meat[2] out in that Place, and then the Wonder began to cease; and I must confess, my religious Thankfulness to God's Providence began to abate too upon the Discovering that all this was nothing but what was common; tho' I ought to have been as thankful for so strange and unforseen Providence, as if it had been miraculous; for it was really the Work of Providence as to me, that should order or appoint, that 10 or 12 Grains of Corn should remain unspoil'd, (when the Rats had destroy'd all the rest,) as if it had been dropt from Heaven; as also, that I should throw it out in that particular Place, where it being in the Shade of a high Rock, it sprang up immediately; whereas, if I had thrown it anywhere else, at that Time, it had been burnt up, and destroy'd.

I carefully sav'd the Ears of this Corn you may be sure in their Season, which was about the End of *June*, and laying up every Corn, I resolv'd to sow them all again, hoping in Time to have some Quantity sufficient

1. Corrected to "Rice" in the second and subsequent editions.
2. Chicken feed, grain.

to supply me with Bread; But it was not till the 4th Year that I could allow my self the least Grain of this Corn to eat, and even then but sparingly, as I shall say afterwards in its Order; for I lost all that I sow'd the first Season, by not observing the proper Time; for I sow'd it just before the dry Season, so that it never came up at all, at least, not as it would ha' done: Of which in its Place.

Besides this Barley, there was, as above, 20 or 30 Stalks of Ryce, which I preserv'd with the same Care, and whose Use was of the same Kind or to the same Purpose, (*viz.*) to make me Bread, or rather Food; for I found Ways to cook it up without baking, tho' I did that also after some Time. But to return to my Journal.

I work'd excessive hard these three or four Months to get my Wall done; and the 14th of *April* I closed it up, contriving to go into it, not by a Door, but over the Wall by a Ladder, that there might be no Sign in the Out-side of my Habitation.

April 16. I finish'd the Ladder, so I went up with the Ladder to the Top, and then pull'd it up after me, and let it down in the In-side: This was a compleat Enclosure to me; for within I had Room enough, and nothing could come at me from without, unless it could first mount my Wall.

The very next Day after this Wall was finish'd, I had almost had all my Labour overthrown at once, and my self kill'd, the Case was thus, As I was busy in the Inside of it, behind my Tent, just in the Entrance into my Cave, I was terribly frighted with a most dreadful surprising Thing indeed; for all on a sudden I found the Earth come crumbling down from the Roof of my Cave, and from the Edge of the Hill over my Head, and two of the Posts I had set up in the Cave crack'd in a frightful Manner; I was heartily scar'd, but thought nothing of what was really the Cause, only thinking that the Top of my Cave was falling in, as some of it had done before; and for Fear I shou'd be bury'd in it, I ran foreward to my Ladder, and not thinking my self safe there neither, I got over my Wall for Fear of the Pieces of the Hill which I expected might roll down upon me: I was no sooner stepp'd down upon the firm Ground, but I plainly saw it was a terrible Earthquake, for the Ground I stood on shook three Times at about eight Minutes Distance, with three such Shocks as would have overturn'd the strongest Building that could be suppos'd to have stood on the Earth, and a great Piece of the Top of a Rock, which stood about half a Mile from me next the Sea, fell down with such a terrible Noise as I never heard in all my Life: I perceiv'd also, the very Sea was put into violent Motion by it; and I believe the Shocks were stronger under the Water than on the Island.

I was so amaz'd with the Thing it self, having never felt the like, or discours'd with any one that had, that I was like one dead or stupify'd; and the Motion of the Earth made my Stomach sick like one that was toss'd at Sea, but the Noise of the falling of the Rock awak'd me as it were, and rousing me from the stupify'd Condition I was in, fill'd me with Horror, and I thought of nothing then but the Hill falling upon my Tent and all my houshold Goods, and burying all at once; and this sunk my very Soul within me a second Time.

After the third Shock was over, and I felt no more for some Time, I began to take Courage, and yet I had not Heart enough to go over my Wall again, for Fear of being buried alive, but sat still upon the Ground, greatly cast down and disconsolate, not knowing what to do: All this while I had not the least serious religious Thought, nothing but the common, *Lord ha' Mercy upon me*; and when it was over, that went away too.

While I sat thus, I found the Air over-cast, and grow cloudy, as if it would Rain; soon after that the Wind rose by little and little, so that, in less than half an Hour, it blew a most dreadful Hurricane: The Sea was all on a Sudden cover'd over with Foam and Froth, the Shore was cover'd with the Breach of the Water, the Trees were torn up by the Roots, and a terrible Storm it was; and this held about three Hours, and then began to abate, and in two Hours more it was stark calm, and began to rain very hard.

All this while I sat upon the Ground very much terrify'd and dejected, when on a sudden it came into my thoughts, that these Winds and Rain being the Consequences of the Earthquake, the Earthquake it self was spent and over, and I might venture into my Cave again: With this Thought my Spirits began to revive, and the Rain also helping to perswade me, I went in and sat down in my Tent, but the Rain was so violent, that my Tent was ready to be beaten down with it, and I was forc'd to go into my Cave, tho' very much afraid and uneasy for fear it should fall on my Head.

This violent Rain forc'd me to a new Work, *viz.* To cut a Hole thro' my new Fortification like a Sink to let the Water go out, which would else have drown'd my Cave. After I had been in my Cave some time, and found still no more Shocks of the Earthquake follow, I began to be more compos'd; and now to support my Spirits, which indeed wanted it very much, I went to my little Store and took a small Sup of Rum, which however I did then and always very sparingly, knowing I could have no more when that was gone.

It continu'd raining all that Night, and great Part of the next Day, so that I could not stir abroad, but my Mind being more compos'd, I began to think of what I had best do, concluding that if the Island was subject to these Earthquakes, there would be no living for me in a Cave, but I must consider of building me some little Hut in an open Place which I might surround with a Wall as I had done here, and so make my self secure from wild Beasts or Men; but concluded, if I staid where I was, I should certainly, one time or other, be bury'd alive.

With these Thoughts I resolv'd to remove my Tent from the Place where it stood, which was just under the hanging Precipice of the Hill, and which, if it should be shaken again, would certainly fall upon my Tent: And I spent the two next Days, being the 19th and 20th of *April*, in contriving where and how to remove my Habitation.

The fear of being swallow'd up alive, made me that[3] I never slept in quiet, and yet the Apprehensions of lying abroad without any Fence was almost equal to it; but still when I look'd about and saw how every thing was put in order, how pleasantly conceal'd I was, and how safe from Danger it made me very loath to remove.

In the mean time it occur'd to me that it would require a vast deal of time for me to do this, and that I must be contented to run the Venture where I was, till I had form'd a Camp for my self, and had secur'd it so as to remove to it: So with this Resolution I compos'd my self for a time, and resolv'd that I would go to work with all Speed to build me a Wall with Piles and Cables, &c. in a Circle as before, and set my Tent up in it when it was finish'd, but that I would venture to stay where I was till it was finish'd and fit to remove to. This was the 21st.

April 22. The next Morning I began to consider of Means to put this Resolve in Execution, but I was at a great loss about my Tools; I had three large Axes and abundance of Hatchets, (for we carried the Hatchets for Traffick with the *Indians*)[4] but with much chopping and cutting knotty hard Wood, they were all full of Notches and dull, and tho' I had a Grindstone, I could not turn it and grind my Tools too, this cost me as much Thought as a Statesman would have bestow'd upon a grand Point of Politicks, or a Judge upon the Life and Death of a Man. At length I contriv'd a Wheel with a String, to turn it with my Foot, that I might have both my Hands at Liberty: *Note*, I had never seen any such thing in *England*, or at least not to take Notice how it was done, tho' since I have observ'd it is very common there; besides that, my Grindstone was very large and heavy. This Machine cost me a full Weeks Work to bring it to Perfection.

April 28, 29. These two whole Days I took up in grinding my Tools, my Machine for turning my Grindstone performing very well.

April 30. Having perceiv'd my Bread had been low a great while, now I took a Survey of it, and reduc'd my self to one Bisket-cake a Day, which made my Heart very heavy.

May 1. In the Morning looking towards the Sea-side, the Tide being low, I saw something lye on the Shore bigger than ordinary, and it look'd like a Cask, when I came to it, I found a small Barrel, and two or three Pieces of the Wreck of the Ship, which were driven on Shore by the late Hurricane, and looking towards the Wreck itself I thought it seem'd to lye higher out of the Water than it us'd to do; I examin'd the Barrel

3. So that.
4. African natives.

which was driven on Shore, and soon found it was a Barrel of Gun-
powder, but it had taken Water, and the Powder was cak'd as hard as a
Stone, however I roll'd it farther on Shore for the present, and went on
upon the Sands as near as I could to the Wreck of the Ship to look for
more.

When I came down to the Ship I found it strangely remov'd, The
Fore-castle which lay before bury'd in Sand, was heav'd up at least Six
Foot, and the Stem which was broke to Pieces and parted from the rest
by the Force of the Sea soon after I had left rummaging her, was toss'd,
as it were, up, and cast on one Side, and the Sand was thrown so high
on that Side next her Stern, that whereas there was a great Place of
Water before, so that I could not come within a Quarter of a Mile of
the Wreck without swimming, I could now walk quite up to her when
the Tide was out; I was surpris'd with this at first, but soon concluded
it must be done by the Earthquake, and as by this Violence the Ship
was more broken open than formerly, so many Things came daily on
Shore, which the Sea had loosen'd, and which the Winds and Water
rolled by Degrees to the Land.

This wholly diverted my Thoughts from the Design of removing my
Habitation; and I busied my self mightily that Day especially, in searching whether I could make any Way into the Ship, but I found nothing
was to be expected of that Kind, for that all the In-side of the Ship was
choak'd up with Sand: However, as I had learn'd not to despair of any
Thing, I resolv'd to pull every Thing to Pieces that I could of the Ship,
concluding, that every Thing I could get from her would be of some
Use or other to me.

May 3. I began with my Saw, and cut a Piece of a Beam thro', which
I thought held some of the upper Part or Quarter-Deck together, and
when I had cut it thro', I clear'd away the Sand as well as I could from
the Side which lay highest; but the Tide coming in, I was oblig'd to
give over for that Time.

May 4. I went a fishing, but caught not one Fish that I durst eat of,
till I was weary of my Sport, when just going to leave off, I caught a
young Dolphin. I had made me a long Line of some Rope Yarn, but I
had no Hooks, yet I frequently caught Fish enough, as much as I car'd
to eat; all which I dry'd in the Sun, and eat them dry.

May 5. Work'd on the Wreck, cut another Beam asunder, and brought
three great Fir Planks off from the Decks, which I ty'd together, and
made swim on Shore when the Tide of Flood came on.

May 6. Work'd on the Wreck, got several Iron Bolts out of her, and
other Pieces of Iron Work, work'd very hard, and came Home very
much tyr'd, and had Thoughts of giving it over.

May 7. Went to the Wreck again, but with an Intent not to work,
but found the Weight of the Wreck had broke itself down, the Beams
being cut, that several Pieces of the Ship seem'd to lie loose, and the

In-side of the Hold lay so open, that I could see into it, but almost full of Water and Sand.

May 8. Went to the Wreck, and carry'd an Iron Crow to wrench up the Deck, which lay now quite clear of the Water or Sand; I wrench'd open two Planks, and brought them on Shore also with the Tide; I left the Iron Crow in the Wreck for next Day.

May 9. Went to the Wreck, and with the Crow made Way into the Body of the Wreck, and felt several Casks, and loosen'd them with the Crow, but could not break them up; I felt also the Roll of *English* Lead, and could stir it, but it was too heavy to remove.

May 10, 11, 12, 13, 14. Went every Day to the Wreck, and got a great deal of Pieces of Timber, and Boards, or Plank, and 2 or 300 Weight of Iron.

May 15. I carry'd two Hatchets to try if I could not cut a Piece off of the Roll of Lead, by placing the Edge of one Hatchet, and driving it with the other; but as it lay about a Foot and a half in the Water, I could not make any Blow to drive the Hatchet.

May 16. It had blow'd hard in the Night, and the Wreck appear'd more broken by the Force of the Water but I stay'd so long in the Woods to get Pidgeons for Food, that the Tide prevented me going to the Wreck that Day.

May 17. I saw some Pieces of the Wreck blown on Shore, at a great Distance, near two Miles off me, but resolv'd to see what they were, and found it was a Piece of the Head, but too heavy for me to bring away.

May 24. Every Day to this Day I work'd on the Wreck and with hard Labour I loosen'd some Things so much with the Crow, that the first blowing Tide several Casks floated out, and two of the Seamen's Chests; but the Wind blowing from the Shore, nothing came to Land that Day, but Pieces of Timber, and a Hogshead which had some *Brazil* Pork in it, but the Salt-water and the Sand had spoil'd it.

I continu'd this Work every Day to the 15th of *June*, except the Time necessary to get Food, which I always appointed, during this Part of my Employment, to be when the Tide was up, that I might be ready when it was ebb'd out, and by this Time I had gotten Timber, and Plank, and Iron-Work enough, to have builded a good Boat, if I had known how; and also, I got at several Times and in several Pieces, near 100 Weight of the Sheat-Lead.[5]

June 16. Going down to the Sea-side, I found a large Tortoise or Turtle; this was the first I had seen, which it seems was only my Misfortune, not any Defect of the Place, or Scarcity; for had I happen'd to be on the other Side of the Island, I might have had Hundreds of them

5. Corrected to "Sheet-Lead" in the second and subsequent editions. Pieces of lead in sheets each about one quarter of an inch thick.

every Day, as I found afterwards; but perhaps had paid dear enough for them.

June 17. I spent in cooking the Turtle; I found in her three-score Eggs; and her Flesh was to me at that Time the most savoury and pleasant that ever I tasted in my Life, having had no Flesh, but of Goats and Fowls, since I landed in this horrid Place.

June 18. Rain'd all Day, and I stay'd within. I thought at this Time the Rain felt Cold, and I was something chilly, which I knew was not usual in that Latitude.

June 19. Very ill, and shivering, as if the Weather had been cold.

June 20. No rest all Night, violent Pains in my Head, and feverish.

June 21. Very ill, frighted almost to Death with the Apprehensions of my sad Condition, to be sick, and no Help: pray'd to G O D for the first Time since the Storm off of *Hull*, but scarce knew what I said, or why; my Thoughts being all confused.

June 22. A little better, but under dreadful Apprehensions of Sickness.

June 23. Very bad again, cold shivering, and then a violent Head-ach.

June 24. Much better.

June 25. An Ague[6] very violent; the Fit held me seven Hours, cold Fit and hot, with faint Sweats after it.

June 26. Better; and having no Victuals to eat, took my Gun, but found my self very weak; however I kill'd a She-Goat, and with much Difficulty got it Home, and broil'd some of it, and eat; I wou'd fain have stew'd it, and made some Broath, but had no Pot.

June 27. The Ague again so violent, that I lay a-Bed all Day, and neither eat or drank. I was ready to perish for Thirst, but so weak, I had not Strength to stand up, or to get my self any Water to drink: Pray'd to God again, but was light-headed, and when I was not, I was so ignorant, that I knew not what to say; only I lay and cry'd, *Lord look upon me, Lord pity me, Lord have Mercy upon me:* I suppose I did nothing else for two or three Hours, till the Fit wearing off, I fell asleep, and did not wake till far in the Night; when I wak'd, I found my self much refresh'd, but weak, and exceeding thirsty: However, as I had no Water in my whole Habitation, I was forc'd to lie till Morning, and went to sleep again: In this second Sleep, I had this terrible Dream.

I thought, that I was sitting on the Ground on the Outside of my Wall, where I sat when the Storm blew after the Earthquake, and that I saw a Man descend from a great black Cloud, in a bright Flame of Fire, and light upon the Ground: He was all over as bright as a Flame, so that I could but just bear to look towards him; his Countenance was most inexpressibly dreadful, impossible for Words to describe; when he stepp'd upon the Ground with his Feet, I thought the Earth trembl'd,

6. A malarial illness characterized by chills, fever, and sweating.

just as it had done before in the Earthquake, and all the Air look'd, to my Apprehension, as if it had been fill'd with Flashes of Fire.

He was no sooner landed upon the Earth, but he moved forward towards me, with a long Spear or Weapon in his Hand, to kill me; and when he came to a rising Ground, at some Distance, he spoke to me, or I heard a Voice so terrible, that it is impossible to express the Terror of it; all that I can say I understood, was this, *Seeing all these Things have not brought thee to Repentance, now thou shalt die*: At which Words, I thought he lifted up the Spear that was in his Hand, to kill me.

No one, that shall ever read this Account, will expect that I should be able to describe the Horrors of my Soul at this terrible Vision, I mean, that even while it was a Dream, I even dreamed of those Horrors; nor is it any more possible to describe the Impression that remain'd upon my Mind when I awak'd and found it was but a Dream.

I had alas! no divine Knowledge; what I had received by the good Instruction of my Father was then worn out by an uninterrupted Series, for 8 Years, of Seafaring Wickedness, and a constant Conversation with nothing but such as were like my self, wicked and prophane to the last Degree: I do not remember that I had in all that Time one Thought that so much as tended either to looking upwards toward God, or inwards towards a Reflection upon my own Ways; But a certain Stupidity of Soul, without Desire of Good, or Conscience of Evil, had entirely overwhelm'd me, and I was all that the most hardned, unthinking, wicked Creature among our common Sailors, can be supposed to be, not having the least Sense, either of the Fear of God in Danger, or of Thankfulness to God in Deliverances.

In the relating what is already past of my Story, this will be the more easily believ'd, when I shall add, that thro' all the Variety of Miseries that had to this Day befallen me, I have never had so much as one Thought of it being the Hand of God, or that it was a just Punishment for my Sin; my rebellious Behaviour against my Father, or my present Sins which were great; or so much as a Punishment for the general Course of my wicked Life. When I was on the desperate Expedition on the desert[7] Shores of *Africa*, I never had so much as one Thought of what would become of me; or one Wish to God to direct me whither I should go, or to keep me from the Danger which apparently surrounded me, as well from voracious Creatures as cruel Savages: But I was meerly[8] thoughtless of a God, or a Providence; acted like a meer Brute from the Principles of Nature, and by the Dictates of common Sense only, and indeed hardly that.

When I was deliver'd and taken up at Sea by the *Portugal* Captain, well us'd, and dealt justly and honourably with, as well as charitably, I

---

7. Corrected to "desert" in the second and fourth editions.
8. Completely.

had not the least Thankfulness on my Thoughts: When again I was shipwreck'd, ruin'd, and in Danger of drowning on this Island, I was as far from Remorse, or looking on it as a Judgment; I only said to my self often, that I was *an unfortunate Dog*, and born to be always miserable.

It is true, when I got on Shore first here, and found all my Ship's Crew drown'd, and my self spar'd, I was surpriz'd with a Kind of Extasie, and some Transports of Soul, which, had the Grace of God assisted, might have come up to true Thankfulness; but it ended where it begun, in a meer common Flight of Joy, or as I may say, *being glad I was alive*, without the least Reflection upon the distinguishing Goodness of the Hand which had preserv'd me, and had singled me out to be preserv'd, when all the rest were destroy'd; or an Enquiry why Providence had been thus merciful to me; even just the same common Sort of Joy which Seamen generally have after they are got safe ashore from a Shipwreck, which they drown all in the next Bowl of Punch, and forget almost as soon as it is over, and all the rest of my Life was like it.

Even when I was afterwards, on due Consideration, made sensible of my Condition, how I was cast on this dreadful Place, out of the Reach of humane Kind, out of all Hope of Relief, or Prospect of Redemption, as soon as I saw but a Prospect of living, and that I should not starve and perish for Hunger, all the Sense of my Affliction wore off, and I begun to be very easy, apply'd my self to the Works proper for my Preservation and Supply, and was far enough from being afflicted at my Condition, as a Judgment from Heaven, or as the Hand of God against me; these were Thoughts which very seldom enter'd into my Head.

The growing up of the Corn, as is hinted in my Journal, had at first some little Influence upon me, and began to affect me with Seriousness, as long as I thought it had something miraculous in it; but as soon as ever that Part of the Thought was remov'd, all the Impression which was rais'd from it, wore off also, as I have noted already.

Even the Earthquake, tho' nothing could be more terrible in its Nature, or more immediately directing to the Invisible Power which alone directs such Things, yet no sooner was the first Fright over, but the Impression it had made went off also. I had no more Sense of God or his Judgments, much less of the present Affliction of my Circumstances being from his Hand, than if I had been in the most prosperous Condition of Life.

But now when I began to be sick, and a leisurely View of the Miseries of Death came to place itself before me; when my Spirits began to sink under the Burthen of a strong Distemper, and Nature was exhausted with the Violence of the Fever; Conscience that had slept so long, begun to awake, and I began to reproach my self with my past Life, in which I had so evidently, by uncommon Wickedness, provok'd the Justice of God to lay me under uncommon Strokes, and to deal with me in so vindictive a Manner.

These Reflections oppress'd me for the second or third Day of my Distemper, and in the Violence, as well of the Fever; as of the dreadful Reproaches of my Conscience, extorted some Words from me, like praying to God, tho' I cannot say they were either a Prayer attended with Desires or with Hopes; it was rather the Voice of meer Fright and Distress; my Thoughts were confus'd, the Convictions great upon my Mind, and the Horror of dying in such a miserable Condition rais'd Vapours into my Head with the meer Apprehensions; and in these Hurries of my Soul, I know not what my Tongue might express: but it was rather Exclamation, such as Lord! what a miserable Creature am I? If I should be sick, I shall certainly die for Want of Help, and what will become of me! Then the Tears burst out of my Eyes, and I could say no more for a good while.

In this Interval, the good Advice of my Father came to my Mind, and presently his Prediction which I mention'd at the Beginning of this Story, *viz. That if I did take this foolish Step, God would not bless me, and I would have Leisure hereafter to reflect upon having neglected his Counsel, when there might be none to assist in my Recovery.* Now, said I aloud, My dear Father's Words are come to pass: God's Justice has overtaken me, and I have none to help or hear me: I rejected the Voice of Providence, which had mercifully put me in a Posture or Station of Life, wherein I might have been happy and easy; but I would neither see it my self, or learn to know the Blessing of it from my Parents; I left them to mourn over my Folly, and now I am left to mourn under the Consequences of it; I refus'd their Help and Assistance who wou'd have lifted me into the World, and wou'd have made every Thing easy for me, and now I have Difficulties to struggle with, too great even for Nature itself to support, and no Assistance, no Help, no Comfort, no Advice; then I cry'd out, *Lord be my Help, for I am in great Distress.*

This was the first Prayer, if I may call it so, that I had made for many Years: But I return to my Journal.

June 28. Having been somewhat refresh'd with the Sleep I had had, and the Fit being entirely off, I got up; and tho' the Fright and Terror of my Dream was very great, yet I consider'd, that the Fit of the Ague wou'd return again the next Day, and now was my Time to get something to refresh and support my self when I should be ill; and the first thing I did, I fill'd a large square Case Bottle with Water, and set it upon my Table, in Reach of my Bed; and to take off the chill or aguish Disposition of the Water, I put about a Quarter of a Pint of Rum into it, and mix'd them together; then I got me a Piece of the Goat's Flesh, and broil'd it on the Coals, but could eat very little; I walk'd about, but was very weak, and withal very sad and heavy-hearted in the Sense of my miserable Condition; dreading the Return of my Distemper the next Day; at Night I made my Supper of three of the Turtle's Eggs, which I roasted in the Ashes, and eat, as we call it, in the Shell; and this was the first Bit of

Meat I had ever ask'd God's Blessing to, even as I cou'd remember, in my whole Life.

After I had eaten, I try'd to walk, but found my self so weak, that I cou'd hardly carry the Gun, (for I never went out without that) so I went but a little Way, and sat down upon the Ground, looking out upon the Sea, which was just before me, and very calm and smooth: As I sat here, some such Thoughts as these occurred to me.

What is this Earth and Sea of which I have seen so much, whence is it produc'd, and what am I, and all the other Creatures, wild and tame, humane and brutal, whence are we?

Such we are all made by some secret Power, who form'd the Earth and Sea, the Air and Sky; and who is that?

Then it follow'd most naturally, It is God that has made it all: Well, but then it came on strangely, if God has made all these Things, He guides and governs them all, and all Things that concern them; for the Power that could make all Things, must certainly have Power to guide and direct them.

If so, nothing can happen in the great Circuit of his Works, either without his Knowledge or Appointment.

And if nothing happens without his Knowledge, he knows that I am here, and am in this dreadful Condition; and if nothing happens without his Appointment, he has appointed all this to befal me.

Nothing occurr'd to my Thought to contradict any of these Conclusions; and therefore it rested upon me with the greater Force, that it must needs be, that God had appointed all this to befal me; that I was brought to this miserable Circumstance by his Direction, he having the sole Power, not of me only, but of every Thing that happen'd in the World. Immediately it follow'd,

Why has God done this to me? What have I done to be thus us'd?

My Conscience presently check'd me in that Enquiry, as if I had blasphem'd, and methought it spoke to me like a Voice; *W R E T C H ! dost thou ask what thou hast done!* Look back upon a dreadful mis-spent Life, and ask thy self *what thou hast not done? Ask,* Why is it *that thou wert not long ago destroy'd?* Why *wert thou not drown'd in* Yarmouth Roads? *Kill'd in the Fight when the Ship was taken by* the Sallee man of War? *Devour'd by the wild Beasts on the* Coast of Africa? Or, *Drown'd H E R E, when all the Crew perish'd but thy self?* Dost thou ask, *What have I done?*

I was struck dumb with these Reflections, as one astonish'd, and had not a Word to say, no not to answer to my self, but rose up pensive and sad, walk'd back to my Retreat, and went up over my Wall, as if I had been going to Bed, but my Thoughts were sadly disturb'd, and I had no Inclination to Sleep; so I sat down in my Chair, and lighted my Lamp, for it began to be dark: Now as the Apprehension of the Return of my Distemper terrify'd me very much, it occurr'd to my Thought, that the *Brasilians* take no Physick but their Tobacco, for almost all Distempers; and I had a Piece of a Roll of Tobacco in one of the Chests which was quite cur'd, and some also that was green and not quite cur'd.

I went, directed by Heaven no doubt; for in this Chest I found a Cure, both for Soul and Body, I open'd the Chest, and found what I look'd for, *viz.* the Tobacco; and as the few Books, I had sav'd, lay there too, I took out one of the Bibles which I mention'd before, and which to this Time I had not found Leisure, or so much as Inclination to look into; I say, I took it out, and brought both that and the Tobacco with me to the Table.

What Use to make of the Tobacco, I knew not, as to my Distemper, or whether it was good for it or no; but I try'd several Experiments with it, as if I was resolv'd it should hit one Way or other: I first took a Piece of a Leaf, and chew'd it in my Mouth, which indeed at first almost stupify'd my Brain, the Tobacco being green and strong, and that I had not been much us'd to it: then I took some and steeped it an Hour or two in some Rum, and resolv'd to take a Dose of it when I lay down; and lastly, I burnt some upon a Pan of Coals, and held my Nose close over the Smoke of it as long as I could bear it, as well for the Heat as almost for Suffocation.

In the Interval of this Operation, I took up the Bible and began to read, but my Head was too much disturb'd with the Tobacco to bear reading, at least that Time; only having opened the Book casually, the first Words that occurr'd to me were these, *Call on me in the Day of Trouble, and I will deliver, and thou shalt glorify me.*[9]

The Words were very apt to my Case, and made some Impression upon my Thoughts at the Time of reading them, tho' not so much as they did afterwards; for as for being deliver'd, the Word had no Sound, *as I may say,* to me; the Thing was so remote, so impossible in my Apprehension of Things, that I began to say as the Children of *Israel* did, when they were promis'd Flesh to eat, *Can God spread a Table in the Wilderness?*[1] So I began to say, Can God himself deliver me from this Place? and as it was not for many Years that any Hope appear'd, this prevail'd very often upon my Thoughts: But however, the Words made a great Impression upon me, and I mused upon them very often. It grew now late, and the Tobacco had, as I said, doz'd my Head so much, that I inclin'd to sleep; so I left my Lamp burning in the Cave, least I should want any Thing in the Night, and went to Bed; but before I lay down, I did what I never had done in all my Life, I kneel'd down and pray'd to God to fulfil the Promise to me, that if I call'd upon him in the Day of Trouble, he would deliver me; after my broken and imperfect Prayer was over, I drunk the Rum in which I had steep'd the Tobacco, which was so strong and rank of the Tobacco, that indeed I

9. Psalms 50.15.
1. Psalms 78.19.

could scarce get it down; immediately upon this I went to Bed, I found presently it flew up in my Head violently, but I fell into a sound Sleep, and wak'd no more 'till by the Sun it must necessarily be near Three a-Clock in the Afternoon the next Day; nay, to this Hour, I'm partly of the Opinion, that I slept all the next Day and Night, and 'till almost Three that Day after; for otherwise I knew not how I should lose a Day out of my Reckoning in the Days of the Week, as it appear'd some Years after I had done: for if I had lost it by crossing and re-crossing the Line,[2] I should have lost more than one Day: But certainly I lost a Day in my Accompt, and never knew which Way.

Be that however one Way or th' other, when I awak'd I found my self exceedingly refresh'd, and my Spirits lively and chearful; when I got up, I was stronger than I was the Day before, and my Stomach better, for I was hungry; and in short, I had no Fit the next Day, but continu'd much alter'd for the better; this was the 29th.

The 30th was my well Day of Course, and I went abroad with my Gun, but did not care to travel too far, I kill'd a Sea Fowl or two, something like a brand Goose, and brought them Home, but was not very forward to eat them; so I ate some more of the Turtle's Eggs, which were very good: This Evening I renew'd the Medicine which I had suppos'd did me good the Day before, *viz.* the Tobacco steep'd in Rum, only I did not take so much as before, nor did I chew any of the Leaf, or hold my Head over the Smoke; however I was not so well the next Day, which was the first of *July*, as I hop'd I shou'd have been; for I had a little Spice of the cold Fit, but it was not much.

July 2. I renew'd the Medicine all the three Ways, and doz'd my self with it as at first; and doubled the Quantity which I drank.

3. I miss'd the Fit for good and all, tho' I did not recover my full Strength for some Weeks after; while I was thus gathering Strength, my Thoughts run exceedingly upon this Scripture, *I will deliver thee*, and the Impossibility of my Deliverance lay much upon my Mind in Barr of my ever expecting it: But as I was discouraging my self with such Thoughts, it occurr'd to my Mind, that I pored so much upon my Deliverance from the main Affliction, that I disregarded the Deliverance I had receiv'd; and I was, as it were, made to ask my self such Questions as these, *viz.* Have I not been deliver'd, and wonderfully too, from Sickness? from the most distress'd Condition that could be, and that was so frightful to me, and what Notice I had taken of it: Had I done my Part, *God had deliver'd me, but I had not glorify'd him*; that is to say, I had not own'd and been thankful for that as a Deliverance, and how cou'd I expect greater Deliverance?

This touch'd my Heart very much, and immediately I kneel'd down and gave God Thanks aloud, for my Recovery from my Sickness.

2. Equator. However, days are not lost by crossing the equator, so Crusoe may have in mind the international date line.

July 4. In the Morning I took the Bible, and beginning at the New Testament, I began seriously to read it, and impos'd upon my self to read a while every Morning and every Night, not tying my self to the Number of Chapters, but as long as my Thoughts shou'd engage me: It was not long after I set seriously to this Work, but I found my Heart more deeply and sincerely affected with the Wickedness of my past Life: The Impression of my Dream reviv'd, and the Words, *All these Things have not brought thee to Repentance*, ran seriously in my Thought: I was earnestly begging of God to give me Repentance, when it happen'd providentially the very Day that reading the Scripture, I came to these Words, *He is exalted a Prince and a Saviour, to give Repentance, and to give Remission:*[3] I threw down the Book, and with my Heart as well as my Hands lifted up to Heaven, in a Kind of Extasy of Joy, I cry'd out aloud, *Jesus, thou Son of* David, *Jesus, thou exalted Prince and Saviour, give me Repentance!*

This was the first time that I could say, in the true Sense of the Words, that I pray'd in all my Life; for now I pray'd with a Sense of my Condition, and with a true Scripture View of Hope founded on the Encouragement of the Word of God; and from this Time, I may say, I began to have Hope that God would hear me.

Now I began to construe the Words mentioned above, *Call on me, and I will deliver you*, in a different Sense from what I had ever done before; for then I had no Notion of any thing being call'd Deliverance, but my being deliver'd from the Captivity I was in; for tho' I was indeed at large in the Place, yet the Island was certainly a Prison to me, and that in the worst Sense in the World; but now I learn'd to take it in another Sense: Now I look'd back upon my past Life with such Horrour, and my Sins appear'd so dreadful, that my Soul sought nothing of God, but Deliverance from the Load of Guilt that bore down all my Comfort: As for my solitary Life it was nothing; I did not so much as pray to be deliver'd from it, or think of it; It was all of no Consideration in Comparison to this: And I add this Part here, to hint to whoever shall read it, that whenever they come to a true Sense of things, they will find Deliverance from Sin a much greater Blessing than Deliverance from Affliction.

But leaving this Part, I return to my Journal.

My Condition began now to be, tho' not less miserable as to my Way of living, yet much easier to my Mind; and my Thoughts being directed, by a constant reading the Scripture, and praying to God, to things of a higher Nature: I had a great deal of Comfort within, which till now I knew nothing of; also, as my Health and Strength returned, I bestirr'd my self to furnish my self with every thing that I wanted, and make my Way of living as regular as I could.

3. Acts 5.31.

From the 4th of *July* to the 14th, I was chiefly employ'd in walking about with my Gun in my Hand, a little and a little, at a Time, as a Man that was gathering up his Strength after a Fit of Sickness: For it is hardly to be imagin'd, how low I was, and to what Weakness I was reduc'd. The Application which I made Use of was perfectly new, and perhaps what had never cur'd an Ague before, neither can I recommend it to any one to practise, by this Experiment; and tho' it did carry off the Fit, yet it rather contributed to weakening me; for I had frequent Convulsions in my Nerves and Limbs for some Time.

I learn'd from it also this in particular, that being abroad in the rainy Season was the most pernicious thing to my Health that could be, especially in those Rains which came attended wtih Storms and Hurricanes of Wind; for as the Rain which came in the dry Season was always most accompany'd with such Storms, so I found that Rain was much more dangerous than the Rain which fell in *September* and *October*.

I had been now in this unhappy Island above 10 Months, all Possibility of Deliverance from this Condition, seem'd to be entirely taken from me; and I firmly believed, that no humane Shape had ever set Foot upon that Place. Having now secur'd my Habitation, as I thought, fully to my Mind, I had a great Desire to make a more perfect Discovery of the Island, and to see what other Productions I might find, which I yet knew nothing of.

It was the 15th of *July* that I began to take a more particular Survey of the Island it self: I went up the Creek first, where, as I hinted, I brought my Rafts on Shore; I found after I came about two Miles up, that the Tide did not flow any higher, and that it was no more than a little Brook of running Water, and very fresh and good; but this being the dry Season, there was hardly any Water in some Parts of it, at least, not enough to run in any Stream so as it could be perceiv'd.

On the Bank of this Brook I found many pleasant *Savana's*, or Meadows; plain, smooth, and cover'd with Grass; and on the rising Parts of them next to the higher Grounds, where the Water, as it might be supposed, never overflow'd, I found a great deal of Tobacco, green, and growing to a great and very strong Stalk; there were divers other Plants which I had no Notion of, or Understanding about, and might perhaps have Vertues of their own, which I could not find out.

I searched for the *Cassava* Root,[4] which the *Indians* in all that Climate make their Bread of, but I could find none. I saw large Plants of Alloes,[5] but did not then understand them. I saw several Sugar Canes, but wild, and for want of Cultivation, imperfect. I contented my self with these Discoveries for this Time, and came back musing with my self what Course I might take to know the Vertue and Goodness of any of the

4. Tropical plant with a fleshy rootstock that yields a nutritious starch.
5. Aloes, a purgative or tonic drug from the dried juice of aloe leaves.

Fruits or Plants which I should discover; but could bring it to no Conclusion; for in short, I had made so little Observation while I was in the
Brasils, that I knew little of the Plants in the Field, at least very little
that might serve me to any Purpose now in my Distress.

The next Day, the 16th, I went up the same Way again, and after
going something farther than I had gone the Day before, I found the
Brook, and the *Savana's* began to cease, and the Country became more
woody than before; in this Part I found different Fruits, and particularly
I found Mellons upon the Ground in great Abundance, and Grapes
upon the Trees; the Vines had spread indeed over the Trees, and the
Clusters of Grapes were just now in their Prime, very ripe and rich: This
was a surprising Discovery, and I was exceeding glad of them; but I was
warn'd by my Experience to eat sparingly of them, remembering, that
when I was ashore in *Barbary*, the eating of Grapes kill'd several of our
English Men who were Slaves there, by throwing them into Fluxes[6] and
Fevers: But I found an excellent Use for these Grapes, and that was to
cure or dry them in the Sun, and keep them as dry'd Grapes or Raisins
are kept, which I thought would be, as indeed they were, as wholesom,
as agreeable to eat, when no Grapes might be to be had.

I spent all that Evening there, and went not back to my Habitation,
which, by the Way was the first Night as I might say, I had lain from
Home. In the Night I took my first Contrivance, and got up into a Tree,
where I slept well, and the next Morning proceeded upon my Discovery,
travelling near four Miles, as I might judge by the Length of the Valley,
keeping still due North, with a Ridge of Hills on the South and North-
side of me.

At the End of this March I came to an Opening, where the Country
seem'd to descend to the West, and a little Spring of fresh Water which
issued out of the Side of the Hill by me, run the other Way, that is due
East; and the Country appear'd so fresh, so green, so flourishing, every
thing being in a constant Verdure, or Flourish of *Spring*, that it looked
like a planted Garden.

I descended a little on the Side of that delicious Vale, surveying it
with a secret Kind of Pleasure, (tho' mixt with my other afflicting
Thoughts) to think that this was all my own, that I was King and Lord
of all this Country indefeasibly, and had a Right of Possession; and if I
could convey it, I might have it in Inheritance, as compleatly as any
Lord of a Mannor in *England*. I saw here Abundance of Cocoa Trees,
Orange, and Lemon, and Citron Trees; but all wild, and very few bearing
any Fruit, at least not then: However, the green Limes that I gathered,
were not only pleasant to eat, but very wholesome; and I mix'd their
Juice afterwards with Water, which made it very wholesome, and very
cool, and refreshing.

6. Dysentery.

I found now I had Business enough to gather and carry Home; and I resolv'd to lay up a Store, as well of Grapes, as Limes and Lemons, to furnish my self for the wet Season, which I knew was approaching.

In Order to this, I gather'd a great Heap of Grapes in one Place, and a lesser Heap in another Place, and a great Parcel of Limes and Lemons in another Place; and taking a few of each with me, I travell'd homeward, and resolv'd to come again, and bring a Bag or Sack, or what I could make to carry the rest Home.

Accordingly, having spent three Days in this Journey, I came Home; so I must now call my Tent and my Cave: But, before I got thither, the Grapes were spoil'd, the Richness of the Fruits, and the Weight of the Juice having broken them, and bruis'd them, they were good for little or nothing; as to the Limes, they were good, but I could bring but a few.

The next Day, being the 19th, I went back, having made me two small Bags to bring Home my Harvest: But I was surpriz'd, when coming to my Heap of Grapes, which were so rich and fine when I gather'd them, I found them all spread about, trod to Pieces; and dragg'd about some here, some there, and Abundance eaten and devour'd: By this I concluded, there were some wild Creatures therabouts, which had done this; but what they were, I knew not.

However, as I found that there was no laying them up on Heaps, and no carrying them away in a Sack, but that one Way they would be destroy'd, and the other Way they would be crush'd with their own Weight, I took another Course; for I gather'd a large Quantity of the Grapes, and hung them up upon the out Branches of the Trees, that they might cure and dry in the Sun; and as for the Limes and Lemons, I carry'd as many back as I could well stand under.

When I came Home from this Journey, I contemplated with great Pleasure the Fruitfulness of that Valley, and the Pleasantness of the Situation, the Security from Storms on that Side the Water, and the Wood, and concluded, that I had pitch'd upon a Place to fix my Abode, which was by far the worst Part of the Country. Upon the Whole I began to consider of removing my Habitation; and to look out for a Place equally safe, as where I now was situate, if possible, in that pleasant fruitful Part of the Island.

This Thought run long in my Head, and I was exceeding fond of it for some Time, the Pleasantness of the Place tempting me; but when I came to a nearer View of it, and to consider that I was now by the Sea-Side, where it was at least possible that something might happen to my Advantage, and by the same ill Fate that brought me hither, might bring some other unhappy Wretches to the same Place; and tho' it was scarce probable that any such Thing should ever happen, yet to enclose my self among the Hills and Woods, in the Center of the Island, was to anticipate my Bondage, and to render such an Affair not only Improb-

able, but Impossible; and that therefore I ought not by any Means to
remove.

However, I was so Enamour'd of this Place, that I spent much of my
Time there, for the whole remaining Part of the Month of *July*; and
tho' upon second Thoughts I resolv'd as above, not to remove, yet I
built me a little kind of a Bower, and surrounded it at a Distance with
a strong Fence, being a double Hedge, as high as I could reach, well
stak'd, and fill'd between with *Brushwood*; and here I lay very secure,
sometimes two or three Nights, together, always going over it with a
Ladder, as before; so that I fancy'd now I had my Country-House, and
my Sea-Coast-House: And this Work took me up to the Beginning of
August.

I had but newly finish'd my Fence, and began to enjoy my Labour,
but the Rains came on, and made me stick close to my first Habitation;
for tho' I had made me a Tent like the other, with a Piece of a Sail,
and spread it very well; yet I had not the Shelter of a Hill to keep me
from Storms, nor a Cave behind me to retreat into, when the Rains
were extraordinary.

About the Beginning of *August, as I said*, I had finish'd my Bower,
and began to enjoy my self. The third of *August*, I found the Grapes I
had hung up were perfectly dry'd, and indeed, were excellent good
Raisins of the Sun; so I began to take them down from the Trees, and
it was very happy that I did so; for the Rains which follow'd would have
spoil'd them, and I had lost the best Part of my Winter Food; for I had
above two hundred large Bunches of them. No sooner had I taken them
all down, and carry'd most of them Home to my Cave, but it began to
rain, and from hence, which was the fourteenth of *August*, it rain'd
more or less, every Day, till the Middle of *October*; and sometimes so
violently, that I could not stir out of my Cave for several Days.

In this Season I was much surpriz'd with the Increase of my Family;
I had been concern'd for the Loss of one of my Cats, who run away
from me, or as I thought had been dead, and I heard no more Tale or
Tidings of her, till to my Astonishment she came Home about the End
of *August*, with three *Kittens*; this was the more strange to me, because
tho' I had kill'd a wild Cat, as I call'd it, with my Gun; yet I thought
it was a quite differing Kind from our *European* Cats; yet the young
Cats were the same Kind of House breed like the old one; and both my
Cats being Females, I thought it very strange: But from these three Cats,
I afterwards came to be so pester'd with Cats, that I was forc'd to kill
them like Vermine, or wild Beasts, and to drive them from my House
as much as possible.

From the fourteenth of *August* to the twenty sixth, incessant Rain,
so that I could not stir, and was now very careful not to be much wet.
In this Confinement I began to be straitned for Food, but venturing out
twice, I one Day kill'd a Goat, and the last Day, which was the twenty

sixth, found a very large Tortoise, which was a Treat to me, and my Food was regulated thus; I eat a Bunch of Raisins for my Breakfast, a Piece of the Goat's Flesh, or of the Turtle for my Dinner broil'd; for to my great Misfortune, I had no Vessel to boil or stew any Thing; and two or three of the Turtle's Eggs for my Supper.

During this Confinement in my Cover, by the Rain, I work'd daily two or three Hours at enlarging my Cave, and by Degrees work'd it on towards one Side, till I came to the Out-Side of the Hill, and made a Door or Way out, which came beyond my Fence or Wall, and so I came in and out this Way; but I was not perfectly easy at lying so open; for as I had manag'd my self before, I was in a perfect Enclosure, whereas now I thought I lay expos'd, and open for any Thing to come in upon me; and yet I could not perceive that there was any living Thing to fear, the biggest Creature that I had yet seen upon the Island being a Goat.

September the thirtieth, I was now come to the unhappy Anniversary of my Landing. I cast up the Notches on my Post, and found I had been on Shore three hundred and sixty five Days. I kept this Day as a Solemn Fast, setting it apart to Religious Exercise, prostrating my self on the Ground with the most serious Humiliation, confessing my Sins to God, acknowledging his Righteous Judgments upon me, and praying to him to have Mercy on me, through Jesus Christ; and having not tasted the least Refreshment for twelve Hours, even till the going down of the Sun, I then eat a Bisket Cake, and a Bunch of Grapes, and went to Bed, finishing the Day as I began it.

I had all this Time observ'd no Sabbath-Day; for as at first I had no Sense of Religion upon my Mind, I had after some Time omitted to distinguish the Weeks, by making a longer Notch than ordinary for the Sabbath-Day, and so did not really know what any of the Days were; but now having cast up the Days, as above, I found I had been there a Year; so I divided it into Weeks, and set apart every seventh Day for a Sabbath; though I found at the End of my Account I had lost a Day or two in my Reckoning.

A little after this my Ink began to fail me, and so I contented my self to use it more sparingly, and to write down only the most remarkable Events of my Life, without continuing a daily *Memorandum* of other Things.

The rainy Season, and the dry Season, began now to appear regular to me, and I learn'd to divide them so, as to provide for them accordingly. But I bought all my Experience before I had it; and this I am going to relate, was one of the most discouraging Experiments that I made at all: I have mention'd that I had sav'd the few Ears of Barley and Rice, which I had so surprizingly found spring up, as I thought, of themselves, and believe there was about thirty Stalks of Rice, and about twenty of Barley; and now I thought it a proper Time to sow it after the Rains, the Sun being in its *Southern* Position going from me.

Accordingly I dug up a Piece of Ground as well as I could with my wooden Spade, and dividing it into two Parts, I sow'd my Grain; but as I was sowing, it casually occur'd to my Thoughts, that I would not sow it all at first, because I did not know when was the proper Time for it; so I sow'd about two Thirds of the Seed, leaving about a Handful of each.

It was a great Comfort to me afterwards, that I did so, for not one Grain of that I sow'd this Time came to any Thing; for the dry Months following, the Earth having had no Rain after the Seed was sown, it had no Moisture to assist its Growth, and never came up at all, till the wet Season had come again, and then it grew as if it had been but newly sown.

Finding my first Seed did not grow, which I easily imagin'd was by the Drought, I sought for a moister Piece of Ground to make another Trial in, and I dug up a Piece of Ground near my new Bower, and sow'd the rest of my Seed in *February*, a little before the *Vernal Equinox*; and this having the rainy Months of *March* and *April* to water it, sprung up very pleasantly, and yielded a very good Crop; but having Part of the Seed left only, and not daring to sow all that I had, I had but a small Quantity at last, my whole Crop not amounting to above half a Peck of each kind.

But by this Experiment I was made Master of my Business, and knew exactly when the proper Season was to sow; and that I might expect two Seed Times, and two Harvests every Year.

While this Corn was growing, I made a little Discovery which was of use to me afterwards: As soon as the Rains were over, and the Weather began to settle, which was about the Month of *November*, I made a Visit up the Country to my Bower, where though I had not been some Months, yet I found all Things just as I left them. The Circle or double Hedge that I had made, was not only firm and entire; but the Stakes which I had cut out of some Trees that grew thereabouts, were all shot out and grown with long Branches, as much as a Willow-Tree usually shoots the first Year after lopping its Head. I could not tell what Tree to call it, that these Stakes were cut from. I was surpriz'd, and yet very well pleas'd, to see the young Trees grow; and I prun'd them, and led them up to grow as much alike as I could; and it is scarce credible how beautiful a Figure they grew into in three Years; so that though the Hedge made a Circle of about twenty five Yards in Diameter, yet the Trees, for such I might now call them, soon cover'd it; and it was a compleat Shade, sufficient to lodge under all the dry season.

This made me resolve to cut some more Stakes, and make me a Hedge like this in a Semicircle round my Wall; I mean that of my first Dwelling, which I did; and placing the Trees or Stakes in a double Row, at about eight Yards distance from my first Fence, they grew presently, and were at first a fine Cover to my Habitation, and afterward serv'd for a Defence also, as I shall observe in its Order.

I found now, That the Seasons of the Year might generally be divided, not into *Summer* and *Winter*, as in *Europe*; but into the Rainy Seasons, and the Dry Seasons, which were generally thus,

Half *February*,
      March,   Rainy, the *Sun* being then on, or near the *Equinox*.
Half *April*,

Half *April*,
      May,
      June,   Dry, the *Sun* being then to the *North* of the Line.
      July,
Half *August*,

Half *August*,
      September,   Rainy, the *Sun* being then come back.
Half *October*,

Half *October*,
      November,
      December,   Dry , the *Sun* being then to the *South* of the Line.
      January,
Half *February*,

The Rainy Season sometimes held longer or shorter, as the Winds happen'd to blow; but this was the general Observation I made: After I had found by Experience, the ill Consequence of being abroad in the Rain, I took Care to furnish my self with Provisions before hand, that I might not be oblig'd to go out; and I sat within Doors as much as possible during the wet Months.

This Time I found much Employment, (and very suitable also to the Time) for I found great Occasion of many Things which I had no way to furnish my self with, but by hard Labour and constant Application; particularly, I try'd many Ways to make my self a Basket, but all the Twigs I could get for the Purpose prov'd so brittle, that they would do nothing. It prov'd of excellent Advantage to me now, That when I was a Boy, I used to take great Delight in standing at a *Basket-makers*, in the Town where my Father liv'd, to see them make their *Wicker-ware*; and being as Boys usually are, very officious to help, and a great Observer of the Manner how they work'd those Things, and sometimes lending a Hand, I had by this Means full Knowledge of the Methods of it, that I wanted nothing but the Materials; when it came into my Mind, That the Twigs of that Tree from whence I cut my Stakes that grew, might possibly be as tough as the *Sallows*, and *Willows*, and *Ossiers* in *England*, and I resolv'd to try.

Accordingly the next Day, I went to my Country-House, as I call'd it, and cutting some of the smaller Twigs, I found them to my Purpose

as much as I could desire; whereupon I came the next Time prepar'd
with a Hatchet to cut down a Quantity, which I soon found, for there
was great Plenty of them; these I set up to dry within my Circle or Hedge,
and when they were fit for Use, I carry'd them to my Cave, and here
during the next Season, I employ'd my self in making, *as well as I could*,
a great many Baskets, both to carry Earth, or to carry or lay up any
Thing as I had occasion; and tho' I did not finish them very handsomly,
yet I made them sufficiently serviceable for my Purpose; and thus afterwards I took Care never to be without them; and as my *Wicker-ware*
decay'd, I made more, especially, I made strong deep Baskets to place
my Corn in, instead of Sacks, when I should come to have any Quantity
of it.

Having master'd this Difficulty, and employ'd a World of Time about
it, I bestirr'd my self to see if possible how to supply two Wants: I had
no Vessels to hold any Thing that was Liquid, except two Runlets which
were almost full of Rum, and some Glass-Bottles, some of the common
Size, and others which were Case-Bottles square, for the holding of
Waters, Spirits, &c. I had not so much as a Pot to boil any Thing,
except a great Kettle, which I sav'd out of the Ship, and which was too
big for such Use as I desired it, *viz.* To make Broth, and stew a Bit of
Meat by it self. The Second Thing I would fain have had, was a Tobacco-
Pipe; but it was impossible to me to make one, however, I found a
Contrivance for that too at last.

I employ'd my self in Planting my Second Rows of Stakes or Piles
and in this *Wicker* working all the Summer, or dry Season, when another
Business took me up more Time than it could be imagin'd I could spare.

I mention'd before, That I had a great Mind to see the whole Island,
and that I had travell'd up the Brook, and so on to where I built my
Bower, and where I had an Opening quite to the Sea on the other Side
of the Island; I now resolv'd to travel quite Cross to the Sea-Shore on
that Side; so taking my Gun, a Hatchet, and my Dog, and a larger
Quantity of Powder and Shot than usual, with two Bisket Cakes, and a
great Bunch of Raisins in my Pouch for my Store, I began my Journey;
when I had pass'd the Vale where my Bower stood as above, I came
within View of the Sea, to the *West*, and it being a very clear Day, I
fairly descry'd Land, whether an Island or a Continent, I could not tell;
but it lay very high, extending from the *West*, to the W. S. W. at a very
great Distance; by my Guess it could not be less than Fifteen or Twenty
Leagues off.

I could not tell what Part of the World this might be, otherwise than
that I know it must be Part of *America*, and as I concluded by all my
Observations, must be near the *Spanish* Dominions, and perhaps was
all Inhabited by Savages, where if I should have landed, I had been in
a worse Condition than I was now; and therefore I acquiesced in the
Dispositions of Providence, which I began now to own, and to believe,

order'd every Thing for the best; I say, I quieted my Mind with this, and left afflicting my self with Fruitless Wishes of being there.

Besides, after some Pause upon this Affair, I consider'd, that if this Land was the *Spanish* Coast, I should certainly, one Time or other, see some Vessel pass or repass one Way or other; but if not, then it was the *Savage* Coast between the *Spanish* Country and *Brasils*, which are indeed the worst of *Savages*; for they are Cannibals, or Men-eaters, and fail not to murther[7] and devour all the humane Bodies that fall into their Hands.

With these Considerations I walk'd very leisurely forward, I found that Side of the Island where I now was, much pleasanter than mine, the open or *Savanna* Fields sweet, adorn'd with Flowers and Grass, and full of very fine Woods. I saw Abundance of Parrots, and fain I would have caught one, if possible to have kept it to be tame, and taught it to speak to me. I did, after some Pains taking, catch a young Parrot, for I knock'd it down with a Stick, and having recover'd it, I brought it home; but it was some Years before I could make him speak: However, at last I taught him to call me by my Name very familiarly: But the Accident that follow'd, tho' it be a Trifle, will be very diverting in its Place.

I was exceedingly diverted with this Journey: I found in the low Grounds Hares, as I thought them to be, and Foxes, but they differ'd greatly from all the other Kinds I had met with; nor could I satisfy my self to eat them, tho' I kill'd several: But I had no Need to be venturous; for I had no Want of Food, and of that which was very good too; especially these three Sorts, *viz.* Goats, Pidgeons, and Turtle or Tortoise; which, added to my Grapes, *Leaden-hall* Market[8] could not have furnish'd a Table better than I, in Proportion to the Company; and tho' my Case was deplorable enough, yet I had great Cause for Thankfulness, that I was not driven to any Extremities for Food; but rather Plenty, even to Dainties.[9]

I never travell'd in this Journey above two Miles outright in a Day, or thereabouts; but I took so many Turns and Returns, to see what Discoveries I could make, that I came weary enough to the Place where I resolv'd to sit down for all Night; and then I either repos'd my self in a Tree, or surrounded my self with a Row of Stakes set upright in the Ground, either from one Tree to another, or so as no wild Creature could come at me, without waking me.

As soon as I came to the Sea Shore, I was surpriz'd to see that I had taken up my Lot on the worst Side of the Island; for here indeed the Shore was cover'd with innumerable Turtles, whereas on the other Side I had found but three in a Year and half. Here was also an infinite Number of Fowls, of many Kinds, some which I had seen and some

---

7. Spelling for *murder* throughout the text, corrected in the fifth edition.
8. Named for its leaden roof, this was one of the major London markets for food in Defoe's time.
9. Delicacies.

which I had not seen of before, and many of them very good Meat; but such as I knew not the Names of, except those call'd *Penguins*.

I could have shot as many as I pleas'd, but was very sparing of my Powder and Shot; and therefore had more Mind to kill a she Goat, if I could, which I could better feed on; and though there were many Goats here more than on my Side the Island, yet it was with much more Difficulty that I could come near them, the Country being flat and even, and they saw me much sooner than when I was on the Hill.

I confess this Side of the Country was much pleasanter than mine, but yet I had not the least Inclination to remove; for as I was fix'd in my Habitation, it became natural to me, and I seem'd all the while I was here, to be as it were upon a Journey, and from Home: However, I travell'd along the Shore of the Sea, towards the *East*, I suppose about twelve Miles; and then setting up a great Pole upon the Shore for a Mark, I concluded I would go Home again; and that the next Journey I took should be on the other Side of the Island, *East* from my Dwelling, and so round till I came to my Post again: Of which in its Place.

I took another Way to come back than that I went, thinking I could easily keep all the Island so much in my View, that I could not miss finding my first Dwelling by viewing the Country; but I found my self mistaken; for being come about two or three Miles, I found my self descended into a very large Valley; but so surrounded with Hills, and those Hills cover'd with Wood, that I could not see which was my Way by any Direction but that of the Sun, nor even then, unless I knew very well the Position of the Sun at that Time of the Day.

It happen'd to my farther Misfortune, That the Weather prov'd hazey for three or four Days, while I was in this Valley; and not being able to see the Sun, I wander'd about very uncomfortably, and at last was oblig'd to find out the Sea Side, look for my Post, and come back the same Way I went; and then by easy Journies I turn'd Homeward, the Weather being exceeding hot, and my Gun, Ammunition, Hatchet, and other Things very heavy.

In this Journey my Dog surpriz'd a young Kid, and seiz'd upon it, and I running in to take hold of it, caught it, and sav'd it alive from the Dog: I had a great Mind to bring it Home if I could; for I had often been musing, Whether it might not be possible to get a Kid or two, and so raise a Breed of tame Goats, which might supply me when my Powder and Shot should be all spent.

I made a Collar to this little Creature, and with a String which I made of some Rope-Yarn, which I always carry'd about me, I led him along, tho' with some Difficulty, till I came to my Bower, and there I enclos'd him, and left him; for I was very impatient to be at Home, from whence I had been absent above a Month.

I cannot express what a Satisfaction it was to me, to come into my old Hutch, and lye down in my Hamock-Bed: This little wandring

Journey, without settled Place of Abode, had been so unpleasant to me, that my own House, as I call'd it to my self, was a perfect Settlement to me, compar'd to that; and it rendred every Thing about me so comfortable, that I resolv'd I would never go a great Way from it again, while it should be my Lot to stay on the Island.

I respos'd my self here a Week, to rest and regale my self after my long Journey; during which, most of the Time was taken up in the weighty Affair of making a Cage for my Poll, who began now to be a meer Domestick,[1] and to be mighty well acquainted with me. Then I began to think of the poor Kid, which I had penn'd in within my little Circle, and resolv'd to go and fetch it Home, or give it some Food; accordingly I went, and found it where I left it; for indeed it could not get out, but almost starv'd for want of Food: I went and cut Bows of Trees, and Branches of such Shrubs as I could find, and threw it over, and having fed it, I ty'd it as I did before, to lead it away; but it was so tame with being hungry, that I had no need to have ty'd it; for it follow'd me like a Dog; and as I continually fed it, the Creature became so loving, so gentle, and so fond, that it became from that Time one of my Domesticks also, and would never leave me afterwards.

The rainy Season of the *Autumnal Equinox* was now come, and I kept the 30th. of *Sept.* in the same solemn Manner as before, being the Anniversary of my Landing on the Island, having now been there two Years, and no more Prospect of being deliver'd, than the first Day I came there. I spent the whole Day in humble and thankful Acknowledgments of the many wonderful Mercies which my Solitary Condition was attended with, and without which it might have been infinitely more miserable. I gave humble and hearty Thanks[2] that God had been pleas'd to discover to me, even that it was possible I might be more happy in this Solitary Condition, than I should have been in a Liberty of Society, and in all the Pleasures of the World. That he could fully make up to me, the Deficiencies of my Solitary State, and the want of Humane Society by his Presence, and the Communications of his Grace to my Soul, supporting, comforting, and encouraging me to depend upon his Providence here, and hope for his Eternal Presence hereafter.

It was now that I began sensibly to feel how much more happy this Life I now led was, with all its miserable Circumstances, than the wicked, cursed, abominable Life I led all the past Part of my Days; and now I chang'd both my Sorrows and my Joys; my very Desires alter'd, my Affections chang'd their Gusts, and my Delights were perfectly new, from what they were at my first Coming, or indeed for the two Years past.

Before, as I walk'd about, either on my Hunting, or for viewing the Country; the Anguish of my Soul at my Condition, would break out

1. Completely domesticated.
2. Here, as elsewhere, Defoe echoes the Book of Common Prayer and the Bible.

upon me on a sudden, and my very Heart would die within me, to think of the Woods, the Mountains, the Desarts I was in; and how I was a Prisoner, lock'd up with the Eternal Bars and Bolts of the Ocean, in an uninhabited Wilderness, without Redemption: In the midst of the greatest Composures of my Mind, this would break out upon me like a Storm, and make me wring my Hands, and weep like a Child: Sometimes it would take me in the middle of my Work, and I would immediately sit down and sigh, and look upon the Ground for an Hour or two together; and this was still worse to me; for if I could burst out into Tears, or vent my self by Words, it would go off, and the Grief having exhausted it self would abate.

But now I began to exercise my self with new Thoughts; I daily read the Word of God, and apply'd all the Comforts of it to my present State: One Morning being very sad, I open'd the Bible upon those Words, *I will never, never leave thee, nor forsake thee*;[3] immediately it occurr'd, That these Words were to me, Why else should they be directed in such a Manner, just at the Moment when I was mourning over my Condition, as one forsaken of God and Man? Well then, said I, if God does not forsake me, of what ill Consequence can it be, or what matters it, though the World should all forsake me, seeing on the other Hand, if I had all the World, and should lose the Favour and Blessing of God, there wou'd be no Comparison in the Loss.

From this Moment I began to conclude in my Mind, That it was possible for me to be more happy in this forsaken Solitary Condition, than it was probable I should ever have been in any other Particular State in the World; and with this Thought I was going to give Thanks to God for bringing me to this Place.

I know not what it was, but something shock'd my Mind at that Thought, and I durst not speak the Words: How canst thou be such a Hypocrite, (said I, even audibly) to pretend to be thankful for a Condition, which however thou may'st endeavour to be contented with, thou would'st rather pray heartily to be deliver'd from; so I stopp'd there: But though I could not say, I thank'd God for being there; yet I sincerely gave Thanks to God for opening my Eyes, by whatever afflicting Providences, to see the former Condition of My Life, and to mourn for my Wickedness, and repent. I never open'd the Bible, or shut it, but my very Soul within me, bless'd God for directing my Friend in *England*, without any Order of mine, to pack it up among my Goods; and for assisting me afterwards to save it out of the Wreck of the Ship.

Thus, and in this Disposition of Mind, I began my third Year; and tho' I have not given the Reader the Trouble of so particular Account of My Works this Year as the first; yet in General it may be observ'd, That I was very seldom idle; but having regularly divided my Time,

3. Joshua 1.5.

according to the several daily Employments that were before me, such as, *First*, My Duty to God, and the Reading the Scriptures, which I constantly set apart some Time for thrice every Day. *Secondly*, The going Abroad with my Gun for Food, which generally took me up three Hours in every Morning, when it did not Rain. *Thirdly*, The ordering, curing, preserving, and cooking what I had kill'd or catch'd for my Supply; these took up great Part of the Day; also it is to be considered that the middle of the Day when the Sun was in the *Zenith*, the Violence of the Heat was too great to stir out; so that about four Hours in the Evening was all the Time I could be suppos'd to work in; with this Exception, That sometimes I chang'd my Hours of Hunting and Working, and went to work in the Morning, and Abroad with my Gun in the Afternoon.

To this short Time allow'd for Labour, I desire may be added the exceeding Laboriousness of my Work, the many Hours which for want of Tools, want of Help, and want of Skill; every Thing I did, took up out of my Time: For Example, I was full two and forty Days making me a Board for a long Shelf, which I wanted in my Cave; whereas two Sawyers with their Tools, and a Saw-Pit, would have cut six of them out of the same Tree in half a Day.

My Case was this, It was to be a large Tree, which was to be cut down, because my Board was to be a broad one. This Tree I was three Days a cutting down, and two more cutting off the Bows, and reducing it to a Log, or Piece of Timber. With inexpressible hacking and hewing I reduc'd both Sides of it into Chips, till it begun to be light enough to move; than I turn'd it, and made one Side of it smooth, and flat, as a Board from End to End; then turning that Side downward, cut the other Side, till I brought the Plank to be about three Inches thick, and smooth on both Sides. Any one may judge the Labour of my Hands in such a Piece of Work; but Labour and Patience carry'd me through that and many other Things: I only observe this in Particular, to shew The Reason why so much of my Time went away with so little Work, *viz*. That what might be a little to be done with Help and Tools, was a vast Labour, and requir'd a prodigious Time to do alone, and by hand.

But notwithstanding this, with Patience and Labour I went through many Things; and indeed every Thing that my Circumstances made necessary to me to do, as will appear by what follows.

I was now, in the Months of *November* and *December*, expecting my Crop of Barley and Rice. The Ground I had manur'd or dug up for them was not great; for as I observ'd, my Seed of each was not above the Quantity of half a Peck; for I had lost one whole Crop by sowing in the dry Season; but now my Crop promis'd very well, when on a sudden I found I was in Danger of losing it all again by Enemies of several Sorts, which it was scarce possible to keep from it; as First, The Goats, and wild Creatures which I call'd Hares, who tasting the Sweetness of the Blade, lay in it Night and Day, as soon as it came up, and eat it so close, that it could get no Time to shoot up into Stalk.

This I saw no Remedy for, but by making an Enclosure, about it with a Hedge, which I did with a great deal of Toil; and the more, because it requir'd Speed. However, as my Arable Land was but small, suited to my Crop, I got it totally well fenc'd, in about three Weeks Time; and shooting some of the Creatures in the Day Time, I set my Dog to guard it in the Night, tying him up to a Stake at the Gate, where he would stand and bark all Night long; so in a little Time the Enemies forsook the Place, and the Corn grew very strong, and well, and began to ripen apace.

But as the Beasts ruined me before, while my Corn was in the Blade; so the Birds were as likely to ruin me now, when it was in the Ear; for going along by the Place to see how it throve, I saw my little Crop surrounded with Fowls of I know not how many sorts, who stood as it were watching till I should be gone: I immediately let fly among them (for I always had my Gun with me) I had no sooner shot but there rose up a little Cloud of Fowls, which I had not seen at all, from among the Corn it self.

This touch'd me sensibly, for I foresaw, that in a few Days they would devour all my Hopes, that I should be starv'd, and never be able to raise a Crop at all, and what to do I could not tell: However I resolv'd not to loose my Corn, if possible, tho' I should watch it Night and Day. In the first Place, I went among it to see what Damage was already done, and found they had spoil'd a good deal of it, but that as it was yet too Green for them, the Loss was not so great, but that the Remainder was like to be a good Crop if it could be sav'd.

I staid by it to load my Gun, and then coming away I could easily see the Thieves sitting upon all the Trees about me, as if they only waited till I was gone away, and the Event proved it to be so; for as I walk'd off as if I was gone, I was no sooner out of their sight, but they dropt down one by one into the Corn again. I was so provok'd that I could not have Patience to stay till more came on, knowing that every Grain that they eat now, was, *as it might be said,* a Peck-load to me in the Consequence; but coming up to the Hedge I fir'd again, and kill'd three of them. This was what I wish'd for; so I took them up, and serv'd them, as we serve notorious Thieves in *England*, (*viz.*) Hang'd them in Chains for a Terror to others; it is impossible to imagine almost, that this should have such an Effect, as it had; for the Fowls wou'd not only not come at the Corn, but in short they forsook all that Part of the Island, and I could never see a Bird near the Place as long as my Scare-Crows hung there.

This I was very glad of, you may be sure, and about the latter end of *December*, which was our second Harvest of the Year, I reap'd my Crop.

I was sadly put to it for a Scythe or a Sickle to cut it down, and all

I could do was to make one as well as I could out of one of the Broad
Swords or Cutlasses, which I sav'd among the Arms out of the Ship.
However, as my first Crop was but small I had no great Difficulty to
cut it down; in short, I reap'd it my Way, for I cut nothing off but the
Ears, and carry'd it away in a great Basket which I had made, and so
rubb'd it out with my Hands; and at the End of all my Harvesting, I
found that out of my half Peck of Seed, I had near two Bushels of Rice,
and above two Bushels and half of Barley, *that is to say*, by my Guess,
for I had no Measure at that time.

However, this was a great Encouragement to me, and I forsaw that
in time, it wou'd please God to supply me with Bread: And yet here I
was perplex'd again, for I neither knew how to grind or make Meal of
my Corn, or indeed how to clean it and part it; nor if made into Meal,
how to make Bread of it, and if how to make it, yet I knew not how to
bake it; these things being added to my Desire of having a good Quantity
for Store, and to secure a constant Supply, I resolv'd not to taste any of
this Crop but to preserve it all for Seed against the next Season, and in
the mean time to employ all my Study and Hours of Working to accomplish this great Work of Providing my self with Corn and Bread.

It might be truly said, that now I work'd for my Bread; 'tis a little
wonderful, and what I believe few People have thought much upon,
(*viz.*) the strange multitude of little Things necessary in the Providing,
Producing, Curing, Dressing, Making and Finishing this one Article of
Bread.

I that was reduced to a meer[4] State of Nature, found this to my daily
Discouragement, and was made more and more sensible of it every
Hour, even after I had got the first Handful of Seed-Corn, which, as I
have said, came up unexpectedly, and indeed to a surprize.

First, I had no Plow to turn up the Earth, no Spade or Shovel to dig
it. Well, this I conquer'd, by making a wooden Spade, as I observ'd
before; but this did my Work in but a wooden manner, and tho' it cost
me a great many Days to make it, yet for want of Iron it not only wore
out the sooner, but made my Work the harder, and made it be perform'd
much worse.

However this I bore with, and was content to work it out with Patience,
and bear with the badness of the Performance. When the corn was
sow'd, I had no Harrow, but was forced to go over it my self and drag
a great heavy Bough of a Tree over it, to Scratch it, as it may be call'd,
rather than Rake or Harrow it.

When it was growing and grown, I have obser'd already, how many
things I wanted, to Fence it, Secure it, Mow or Reap it, Cure and Carry
it Home, Thrash, Part it from the Chaff, and Save it. Then I wanted
a Mill to Grind it, Sieves to Dress it, Yeast and Salt to make it into

---

4. Complete, absolute.

Bread, and an Oven to bake it, and yet all these things I did without, as shall be observ'd; and yet the Corn was an inestimable Comfort and Advantage to me too. All this, as I said, made every thing laborious and tedious to me, but that there was no help for; neither was my time so much Loss to me, because as I had divided it, a certain Part of it was every Day appointed to these Works; and as I resolv'd to use none of the Corn for Bread till I had a greater Quantity by me, I had the next six Months to apply my self wholly by Labour and Invention to furnish my self with Utensils proper for the performing all the Operations necessary for the making the Corn (when I had it) fit for my use.

But first, I was to prepare more Land, for I had now Seed enough to sow above an Acre of Ground. Before I did this, I had a Week's-work at least to make me a Spade, which when it was done was but a sorry one indeed, and very heavy, and requir'd double Labour to work with it; however I went thro' that, and sow'd my Seed in two large flat Pieces of Ground, as near my House as I could find them to my Mind, and fenc'd them in with a good Hedge, the Stakes of which were all cut of that Wood which I had set before, and knew it would grow, so that in one Year's time I knew I should have a Quick or Living-Hedge, that would want but little Repair. This Work was not so little as to take me up less than three Months, because great Part of that time was of the wet Season, when I could not go abroad.

Within Doors, *that is*, when it rained, and I could not go out, I found Employment on the following Occasions; always observing, that all the while I was at work I diverted my self with talking to my Parrot, and teaching him to Speak, and I quickly learn'd him to know his own Name, and at last to speak it out pretty loud P O L L, which was the first Word I ever heard spoken in the Island by any Mouth but my own. This therefore, was not my Work, but an assistant to my Work, for now, as I said, I had a great Employment upon my Hands, as follows, (*viz.*) I had long study'd by some Means or other, to make my self some Earthen Vessels, which indeed I wanted sorely, but knew not where to come at them: However, considering the Heat of the Climate, I did not doubt but if I could find out any such Clay, I might botch up[5] some such Pot, as might, being dry'd in the Sun, be hard enough, and strong enough to bear handling, and to hold any Thing that was dry, and requir'd to be kept so; and as this was necessary in the preparing Corn, Meal, &c. which was the Thing I was upon, I resolv'd to make some as large as I could, and fit only to stand like Jarrs to hold what should be put into them.

It would make the Reader pity me, or rather laugh at me, to tell how many awkward ways I took to raise this Paste, what odd mishapen ugly things I made, how many of them fell in, and how many fell out, the

5. Construct crudely.

Clay not being stiff enough to bear its own Weight; how many crack'd by the over violent Heat of the Sun, being set out too hastily; and how many fell in pieces with only removing, as well before as after they were dry'd; and in a word, how after having labour'd hard to find the Clay, to dig it, to temper it, to bring it home and work it; I could not make above two large earthen ugly things, I cannot call them Jarrs, in about two Months Labour.

However, as the Sun bak'd these Two, very dry and hard, I lifted them very gently up, and set them down again in two great Wicker-Baskets which I had made on purpose for them, that they might not break, and as between the Pot and the Basket there was a little room to spare, I stuff'd it full of the Rice and Barley Straw, and these two Pots being to stand always dry, I thought would hold my dry Corn, and perhaps the Meal, when the Corn was bruised.

Tho' I miscarried so much in my Design for large Pots, yet I made several smaller things with better Success, such as little round Pots, flat Dishes, Pitchers, and Pipkins,[6] and any things my Hand turn'd to, and the Heat of the Sun bak'd them strangely hard.

But all this would not answer my End, which was to get an earthen Pot to hold what was Liquid, and bear the Fire, which none of these could do. It happen'd after some time, making a pretty large Fire for cooking my Meat, when I went to put it out after I had done with it, I found a broken Piece of one of my Earthen-ware Vessels in the Fire, burnt as hard as a Stone, and red as a Tile. I was agreeably surpris'd to see it, and said to my self, that certainly they might be made to burn whole if they would burn broken.

This set me to studying how to order my Fire, so as to make it burn me some Pots. I had no Notion of Kiln, such as the Potters burn in, or of glazing them with Lead, tho' I had some Lead to do it with; but I plac'd three large Pipkins, and two or three Pots in a Pile one upon another, and plac'd my Fire-wood all round it with a great Heap of Embers under them; I ply'd the Fire with fresh Fuel round the out-side, and upon the top, till I saw the Pots in the inside red hot quite thro', and observ'd that they did not crack at all; when I saw them clear red, I let them stand in that Heat about 5 or 6 Hours, till I found one of them, tho'd it did not crack, did melt or run, for the Sand which was mixed with the Clay melted by the violence of the Heat, and would have run into Glass if I had gone on; so I slack'd my Fire gradually till the Pots began to abate of the red Colour, and watching them all Night, that I might not let the Fire abate too fast, in the Morning I had three very good, I will not say handsome Pipkins; and two other Earthen Pots, as hard burnt as cou'd be desir'd; and one of them perfectly glaz'd with the Running of the Sand.

6. Small earthen pots.

After this Experiment, I need not say that I wanted no sort of Earthen Ware for my Use; but I must needs say, as to the Shapes of them, they were very indifferent, as any one may suppose, when I had no way of making them; but as the Children make Dirt-Pies, or as a Woman would make Pies, that never learn'd to raise Past.

No Joy at a Thing of so mean a Nature was ever equal to mine, when I found I had made an Earthen Pot that would bear the Fire; and I had hardly Patience to stay till they were cold, before I set one upon the Fire again, with some Water in it, to boil me some Meat, which it did admirably well; and with a Piece of a Kid, I made some very good Broth, though I wanted Oatmeal, and several other Ingredients, requisite to make it so good as I would have had it been.

My next Concern was, to get me a Stone Mortar, to stamp or beat some Corn in; for as to the Mill, there was no thought at arriving to that Perfection of Art, with one Pair of Hands. To supply this Want I was at a great Loss; for of all Trades in the World I was as perfectly unqualify'd for a Stone-cutter, as for any whatever; neither had I any Tools to go about it with. I spent many a Day to find out a great Stone big enough to cut hollow, and make fit for a Mortar, and could find none at all; except what was in the solid Rock, and which I had no way to dig or cut out; nor indeed were the Rocks in the Island of Hardness sufficient, but were all of a sandy crumbling Stone, which neither would bear the Weight of a heavy Pestle, or would break the Corn without filling it with Sand; so after a great deal of Time lost in searching for a Stone, I gave it over, and resolv'd to look out for a great Block of hard Wood, which I found indeed much easier, and getting one as big as I had Strength to stir, I rounded it, and form'd it in the Out-side with my Axe and Hatchet, and then with the Help of Fire, and infinite Labour, made a hollow Place in it, as the *Indians* in *Brasil* make their *Canoes*. After this, I made a great heavy Pestle or Beater, of the Wood call'd the Iron-wood, and this I prepar'd and laid by against I had my next Crop of Corn, when I propos'd to my self, to grind, or rather pound my Corn into Meal to make my Bread.

My next Difficulty was to make a Sieve, or Search, to dress my Meal, and to part it from the Bran, and the Husk, without which I did not see it possible I could have any Bread. This was a most difficult Thing, so much as but to think on; for to be sure I had nothing like the necessary Thing to make it; I mean fine thin Canvas, or Stuff, to search the Meal through. And here I was at a full Stop for many Months; nor did I really know what to do; Linnen I had none left, but what was meer Rags; I had Goats Hair, but neither knew I how to weave it, or spin it; and had I known how, here was no Tools to work it with; all the Remedy that I found for this, was, That at last I did remember I had among the Seamens Cloaths which were sav'd out of the Ship, some Neckcloths of Callicoe, or Muslin; and with some Pieces of these, I made three

small Sieves, but proper enough for the Work; and thus I made shift
for some Years; how I did afterwards, I shall shew in its Place.

The baking part was the next Thing to be consider'd, and how I should
make Bread when I came to have Corn; for first I had no Yeast; as to
that Part, as there was no supplying the Want, so I did not concern my
self much about it; But for an Oven, I was indeed in great Pain, at
length I found out an Experiment for that also, which was this; I made
some Earthen Vessels very broad, but not deep; that is to say, about two
Foot Diameter, and not above nine Inches deep; these I burnt in the
Fire, as I had done the other, and laid them by; and when I wanted to
bake, I made a great Fire upon my Hearth, which I had pav'd with
some square Tiles of my own making, and burning also; but I should
not call them square.

When the Fire-wood was burnt pretty much into Embers, or live
Coals, I drew them forward upon this Hearth so as to cover it all over,
and there I let them lye, till the Hearth was very hot, then sweeping
away all the Embers, I set down my Loaf, or Loaves, and whelming
down the Earthen Pot upon them, drew the Embers all round the Out-
side of the Pot, to keep in, and add to the Heat; and thus, as well as in
the best Oven in the World, I bak'd my Barley Loaves, and became in
little Time a meer Pastry-Cook into the Bargain; for I made my self
several Cakes of the Rice, and Puddings; indeed I made no Pies, neither
had I any Thing to put into them, supposing I had, except the Flesh
either of Fowls or Goats.

It need not be wondred at, if all these Things took me up most Part
of the third Year of my Abode here; for it is to be observ'd, That in the
Intervals of these Things, I had my new Harvest and Husbandry to
manage; for I reap'd my Corn in its Season, and carry'd it Home as well
as I could, and laid it up in the Ear, in my large Baskets, till I had Time
to rub it out; for I had no Floor to thrash it on, or Instrument to thrash
it with.

And now indeed my Stock of Corn increasing, I really wanted to
build my Barns bigger. I wanted a Place to lay it up in; for the Increase
of the Corn now yielded me so much that I had of the Barley about
twenty Bushels, and of the Rice as much, or more; insomuch, that now
I resolv'd to begin to use it freely; for my Bread had been quite gone a
great while; Also I resolv'd to see what Quantity would be sufficient for
me a whole Year, and to sow but once a Year.

Upon the whole, I found that the forty Bushels of Barley and Rice,
was much more than I could consume in a Year; so I resolv'd to sow
just the same Quantity every Year, that I sow'd the last, in Hopes that
such a Quantity would fully provide me with Bread, &c.

All the while these Things were doing, you may be sure my Thoughts
run many times upon the Prospect of Land which I had seen from the
other Side of the Island, and I was not without secret Wishes that I were

on Shore there, fancying the seeing the main Land, and in an inhabited Country, I might find some Way or other to convey myself farther, and perhaps at last find some Means of Escape.

But all this while I made no Allowance for the Dangers of such a Condition, and how I might fall into the Hands of Savages, and perhaps such as I might have Reason to think far worse than the Lions and Tigers of Africa. That if I once came into their Power, I should run a Hazard more than a thousand to one of being kill'd, and perhaps of being eaten; for I had heard that the People of the *Carribean* Coast were Canibals, or Man-eaters; and I knew by the Latitude that I could not be far from that Shore. That suppose they were not Canibals, yet that they might kill me, as many *Europeans* who had fallen into their Hands had been serv'd, even when they had been ten or twenty together; much more I that was but one, and could make little or no Defence: All these Things, I say, which I ought to have consider'd well of, and did cast up in my Thoughts afterwards, yet took up none of my Apprehensions at first; but my Head run mightily upon the Thought of getting over to the Shore.

Now I wish'd for my Boy *Xury*, and the long Boat, with the Shoulder of Mutton Sail, with which I sail'd above a thousand Miles on the Coast of *Africk*; but this was in vain. Then I thought I would go and look at our Ship's Boat, which, as I have said, was blown up upon the Shore, a great Way in the Storm, when we were first cast away. She lay almost where she did at first, but not quite; and was turn'd by the Force of the Waves and the Winds almost Bottom upward, against a high Ridge of Beachy[7] rough Sand; but no Water about her as before.

If I had had Hands to have refitted her, and to have launch'd her into the Water, the Boat would have done well enough, and I might have gone back into the *Brasils* with her easily enough; but I might have forseen, That I could no more turn her, and set her upright upon her Bottom, than I could remove the Island: However, I went to the Woods, and cut Levers and Rollers, and brought them to the Boat, resolv'd to try what I could do, suggesting to my self, That if I could but turn her down, I might easily repair the Damage she had receiv'd, and she would be a very good Boat, and I might go to Sea in her very easily.

I spar'd no Pains indeed, in this Piece of fruitless Toil, and spent, I think, three or four Weeks about it; at last finding it impossible to heave it up with my little Strength, I fell to digging away the Sand, to undermine it, and so to make it fall down, setting Pieces of Wood to thrust and guide it right in the Fall.

But when I had done this, I was unable to stir it up again, or to get under it, much less to move it forward, towards the Water; so I was forc'd to give it over; and yet, though I gave over the Hopes of the Boat,

7. Gravelly.

my desire to venture over for the Main increased, rather than decreased, as the Means for it seem'd impossible.

This at length put me upon thinking, Whether it was not possible to make my self a *Canoe*, or *Periagua*, such as the Natives of those Climates make, even without Tools, or, as I might say, without Hands, *viz.* of the Trunk of a great Tree. This I not only thought possible, but easy, and pleas'd my self extreamly with the Thoughts of making it, and with my having much more Convenience for it than any of the *Negroes* or *Indians*; but not at all considering the particular Inconveniences which I lay under, more than the *Indians* did, *viz.* Want of Hands to move it, when it was made, into the Water, a Difficulty much harder for me to surmount, than all the Consequences of Want of Tools could be to them; for what was it to me, That when I had chosen a vast Tree in the Woods, I might with much Trouble cut it down, if after I might be able with my Tools to hew and dub the Outside into the proper Shape of a Boat, and burn or cut out the In-side to make it hollow, so to make a Boat of it: If after all this, I must leave it just there where I found it, and was not able to launch it into the Water.

One would have thought, I could not have had the least Reflection upon my Mind of my Circumstance, while I was making this Boat; but I should have immediately thought how I should get it into the Sea; but my Thoughts were so intent upon my Voyage over the Sea in it, that I never once consider'd how I should get it off of the Land; and it was really in its own Nature more easy for me to guide it over forty five Miles of Sea, than about forty five Fathom of Land, where it lay, to set it a float in the Water.

I went to work upon this Boat, the most like a Fool, that ever Man did, who had any of his Senses awake. I pleas'd my self with the Design, without determining whether I was ever able to undertake it; not but that the Difficulty of launching my Boat came often into my Head; but I put a stop to my own Enquiries into it, by this foolish Answer which I gave my self, *Let's first make it, I'll warrant I'll find some Way or other to get it along, when 'tis done.*

This was a most preposterous Method; but the Eagerness of my Fancy prevail'd, and to work I went. I fell'd a Cedar Tree: I question much whether *Solomon*[8] ever had such a One for the Building of the Temple at *Jerusalem*. It was five Foot ten Inches Diameter at the lower Part next the Stump, and four Foot eleven Inches Diameter at the End of twenty two Foot, after which it lessen'd for a while, and then parted into Branches: It was not without infinite Labour that I fell'd this Tree: I was twenty Days hacking and hewing at it at the Bottom. I was fourteen more getting the Branches and Limbs, and the vast spreading Head of it cut off, which I hack'd and hew'd through with Axe and Hatchet,

8. 1 Kings 5.6ff.

and inexpressible Labour: After this, it cost me a Month to shape it, and dub it to a Proportion, and to something like the Bottom of a Boat, that it might swim upright as it ought to do. It cost me near three Months more to clear the In-side, and work it out so, as to make an exact Boat of it: This I did indeed without Fire, by meer Malett and Chissel, and by the dint of hard Labour, till I had brought it to be a very handsome *Periagua*, and big enough to have carry'd six and twenty Men, and consequently big enough to have carry'd me and all my Cargo.

When I had gone through this Work, I was extremely delighted with it. The Boat was really much bigger than I ever saw a *Canoe*, or *Periagua*, that was made of one Tree, in my Life. Many a weary Stroke it had cost, you may be sure; and there remain'd nothing but to get it into the Water; and had I gotten it into the Water, I make no quesion but I should have began the maddest Voyage, and the most unlikely to be perform'd, that ever was undertaken.

But all my Devices to get it into the Water fail'd me; tho' they cost me infinite Labour too. It lay about one hundred Yards from the Water, and not more: But the first Inconvenience was, it was up Hill towards the Creek; well, to take away this Discouragement, I resolv'd to dig into the Surface of the Earth, and so make a Declivity: This I begun, and it cost me a prodigious deal of Pains; but who grutches[9] Pains, that have their Deliverance in View: But when this was work'd through, and this Difficulty manag'd, it was still much at one; for I could no more stir the *Canoe*, than I could the other Boat.

Then I measur'd the Distance of Ground, and resolv'd to cut a Dock, or Canal, to bring the Water up to the *Canoe*, seeing I could not bring the *Canoe* down to the Water: Well, I began this Work, and when I began to enter into it, and calculate how deep it was to be dug, how broad, how the Stuff to be thrown out, I found, That by the Number of Hands I had, being none but my own, it must have been ten or twelve Years before I should have gone through with it; for the Shore lay high, so that at the upper End, it must have been at least twenty Foot Deep; so at length, tho' with great Reluctancy, I gave this Attempt over also.

This griev'd me heartily, and now I saw, tho' too late, the Folly of beginning a Work before we count the Cost; and before we judge rightly of our own Strength to go through with it.

In the middle of this Work, I finish'd my fourth Year in this Place, and kept my Anniversary with the same Devotion, and with as much Comfort as ever before; for by a constant Study, and serious Application of the Word of God, and by the Assistance of his Grace, I gain'd a different Knowledge from what I had before. I entertain'd different Notions of Things. I look'd now upon the World as a Thing remote,

9. Changed to "grudges" in the second, third, and sixth editions.

which I had nothing to do with, no Expectation from, and indeed no
Desires about: In a Word, I had nothing indeed to do with it, nor was
ever like to have; so I thought it look'd as we may perhaps look upon it
hereafter, *viz.* as a Place I had liv'd in, but was come out of it; and well
might I say, as Father *Abraham* to *Dives, Between me and thee is a
great Gulph fix'd.*[1]

In the first Place, I was remov'd from all the Wickedness of the World
here. I had neither the *Lust of the Flesh, the Lust of the Eye, or the
Pride of Life.*[2] I had nothing to covet; for I had all that I was now capable
of enjoying: I was Lord of the whole Manor; or if I pleas'd, I might call
my self King, or Emperor over the whole Country which I had Possession
of. There were no Rivals. I had not Competitor, none to dispute Sovereignty or Command with me. I might have rais'd Ship Loadings of
Corn; but I had no use for it; so I let as little grow as I thought enough
for my Occasion. I had Tortoise or Turtles enough; but now and then
one, was as much as I could put to any use. I had Timber enough to
have built a Fleet of Ships. I had Grapes enough to have made Wine,
or to have cur'd into Raisins, to have loaded that Fleet, when they had
been built.

But all I could make use of was, All that was valuable. I had enough
to eat, and to supply my Wants, and, what was all the rest to me? If I
kill'd more Flesh than I could eat, the Dog must eat it, or the Vermin.
If I sow'd more Corn than I could eat, it must be spoil'd. The Trees
that I cut down, were lying to rot on the Ground. I could make no more
use of them than for Fewel;[3] and that I had no Occasion for, but to
dress my Food.

In a Word, The Nature and Experience of Things dictated to me
upon just Reflection, That all the good Things of this World, are no
farther good to us, than they are for our Use; and that whatever we may
heap up indeed to give others, we enjoy just as much as we can use,
and no more. The most covetous griping Miser in the World would
have been cur'd of the Vice of Covetousness, if he had been in my Case;
for I possess'd infinitely more than I knew what to do with. I had no
room for Desire, except it was of Things which I had not, and they were
but Trifles, though indeed of great Use to me. I had, as I hinted before,
a Parcel of Money, as well Gold as Silver, about thirty six Pounds
Sterling: Alas! There the nasty sorry useless Stuff lay; I had no manner
of Business for it; and I often thought with my self, That I would have
given a Handful of it for a Gross of Tobacco-Pipes, or for a Hand-Mill
to grind my Corn; nay, I would have given it all for Sixpenny-worth of
Turnip and *Carrot* Seed out of *England,* or for a Handful of *Pease* and
Beans, and a Bottle of Ink: *As it was,* I had not the least Advantage by

1. Luke 16.26.
2. John 2.16.
3. Fuel.

it, or Benefit from it; but there it lay in a Drawer, and grew mouldy
with the Damp of the Cave, in the wet Season; and if I had had the
Drawer full of Diamonds, it had been the same Case; and they had
been of no manner of Value to me, because of no Use.

I had now brought my State of Life to be much easier in itself than
it was at first, and much easier to my Mind, as well as to my Body. I
frequently sat down to my Meat with Thankfulness, and admir'd the
Hand of God's Providence, which had thus spread my Table in the
Wilderness. I learn'd to look more upon the bright Side of my Condition,
and less upon the dark Side; and to consider what I enjoy'd, rather than
what I wanted; and this gave me sometimes such secret Comforts, that
I cannot express them; and which I take Notice of here, to put those
discontented People in Mind of it, who cannot enjoy comfortably what
God has given them; because they see, and covet something that he has
not given them: All our Discontents about what we want, appear'd to
me, to spring from the Want of Thankfulness for what we have.

Another Reflection was of great Use to me, and doubtless would be
so to any one that should fall into such Distress as mine was; and this
was, To compare my present Condition, with what I at first expected it
should be; nay, with what it would certainly have been, if the good
Providence of God had not wonderfully order'd the Ship to be cast up
nearer to the Shore, where I not only could come at her, but could
bring what I got out of her to the Shore, for my Relief and Comfort;
without which I had wanted for Tools to work, Weapons for Defence,
or Gun-Powder and Shot for getting my Food.

I spent whole Hours, I may say whole Days, in representing to my
self in the most lively Colours, how I must have acted, if I had got
nothing out of the Ship. How I could not have so much as got any
Food, except Fish and Turtles; and that as it was long before I found
any of them, I must have perish'd first. That I should have liv'd, if I
had not perish'd, like a meer Savage. That if I had kill'd a Goat, or a
Fowl, by any Contrivance, I had no way to flea[4] or open them, or part
the Flesh from the Skin, and the Bowels, or to cut it up; but must gnaw
it with my Teeth, and pull it with my Claws like a Beast.

These Reflections made me very sensible of the Goodness of Providence to me, and very thankful for my present Condition, with all its
Hardships and Misfortunes: And this Part also I cannot but recommend
to the Reflection of those, who are apt in their Misery to say, *Is any
Affliction like mine!* Let them consider, How much worse the Cases of
some People are, and their Case might have been, if Providence had
thought fit.

I had another Reflection which assisted me also to comfort my Mind
with Hopes; and this was, comparing my present Condition with what

4. Flay.

I had deserv'd, and had therefore Reason to expect from the Hand of Providence. I had liv'd a dreadful Life, perfectly destitute of the Knowledge and Fear of God. I had been well instructed by Father and Mother; neither had they been wanting to me, in their early Endeavours, to infuse a religious Awe of God into my Mind, a Sense of my Duty, and of what the Nature and End of my Being requir'd of me. But alas! falling early into the Seafaring Life, which of all the Lives is the most destitute of the Fear of God, though his Terrors are always before them; I say, falling early into the Seafaring Life, and into Seafaring Company, all that little Sense of Religion which I had entertain'd, was laugh'd out of me by my Mess-Mates, by a harden'd despising of Dangers; and the Views of Death, which grew habitual to me; by my long Absence from all Manner of Opportunities to converse with any thing but what was like my self, or to hear any thing that was good, or tended towards it.

So void was I of every Thing that was good, or of the least Sense of what I was, or was to be, that in the greatest Deliverances I enjoy'd, such as my Escape from *Sallee*; my being taken up by the *Portuguese* Master of the Ship; my being planted so well in the *Brasils*; my receiving the Cargo from *England*, and the like; I never had once the Word *Thank God*, so much as on my Mind, or in my Mouth; nor in the greatest Distress, had I so much as a Thought to pray to him, or so much as to say, *Lord have Mercy upon me*; no nor to mention the Name of God, unless it was to swear by, and blaspheme it.

I had terrible Reflections upon my Mind for many Months, as I have already observ'd, on the Account of my wicked and hardned Life past; and when I look'd about me and considered what particular Providences had attended me since my coming into this Place, and how God had dealt bountifully with me; had not only punished me less than my Iniquity had deserv'd, but had so plentifully provided for me; this gave me great hopes that my Repentance was accepted, and that God hath yet Mercy in store for me.

With these Reflections I work'd my Mind up, not only to Resignation to the Will of God in the present Disposition of my Circumstances; but even to a sincere Thankfulness for my Condition, and that I who was yet a living Man, ought not to complain, seeing I had not the due Punishment of my Sins; that I enjoy'd so many Mercies which I had no reason to have expected in that Place; that I ought never more to repine at my Condition but to rejoyce, and to give daily Thanks for that daily Bread, which nothing but a Croud of Wonders could have brought. That I ought to consider I had been fed even by Miracle, even as great as that of feeding *Elijah*[5] by Ravens; nay, by a long Series of Miracles, and that I could hardly have nam'd a Place in the unhabitable Part of the World where I could have been cast more to my Advantage: A Place,

5. 1 Kings 17.4–6.

where as I had no Society, which was my Affliction on one Hand, so I found no ravenous Beast, no furious Wolves or Tygers to threaten my Life, no venomous Creatures or poisonous, which I might feed on to my Hurt, no Savages to murther and devour me.

In a word, as my Life was a Life of Sorrow, one way, so it was a Life of Mercy, another; and I wanted nothing to make it a Life of Comfort, but to be able to make my Sence of God's Goodness to me, and Care over me in this Condition, be my daily Consolation; and after I did make a just Improvement of these things, I went away and was no more sad.

I had now been here so long, that many Things which I brought on Shore for my Help, were either quite gone, or very much wasted and near-spent.

My Ink, as I observed, had been gone some time, all but a very little, which I eek'd out with Water a little and a little, till it was so pale it scarce left any Appearance of black upon the Paper: As long as it lasted, I made use of it to minute down the Days of the Month on which any remarkable Thing happen'd to me, and first by casting up Times past: I remember that there was a strange Concurrence of Days, in the various Providences which befel me; and which, if I had been superstitiously inclin'd to observe Days as Fatal or Fortunate, I might have had Reason to have look'd upon with a great deal of Curiosity.

First, I had observed, that the same Day that I broke away from my Father and my Friends, and run away to *Hull*, in order to go to Sea; the same Day afterwards I was taken by the *Sallee* Man of War, and made a Slave.

The same Day of the Year that I escaped out of the Wreck of that Ship in *Yarmouth* Roads, that same Day-Year afterwards I made my escape from *Sallee* in the Boat.

The same Day of the Year I was born on (*viz.*)the 30*th* of *September*, that same Day, I had my Life so miraculously saved 26 Year after,[6] when I was cast on Shore in this Island, so that my wicked Life, and my solitary Life begun both on a Day.

The next Thing to my Ink's being wasted,[7] was that of my Bread, I mean the Bisket which I brought out of the Ship; This I had husbanded to the last Degree, allowing my self but one Cake of Bread a Day for above a Year, and yet I was quite without Bread for near a Year before I got any Corn of my own, and great Reason I had to be thankful that I had any at all, the getting it being, as has been already observed, next to miraculous.

My Cloaths began to decay too mightily: As to Linnen, I had had none a good while, except some chequer'd Shirts which I found in the

6. Crusoe's arithmetic is flawed, for he was born in 1632 and shipwrecked in 1659, hence twenty-seven years after.
7. Used up.

Chests of the other Seamen, and which I carefully preserved, because
many times I could bear no other Cloaths on but a Shirt; and it was a
very great help to me that I had among all the Men's Cloaths of the
Ship almost three dozen of Shirts. There were also several thick Watch-
Coats of the Seamens, which were left indeed, but they were too hot
to wear; and tho' it is true, that the Weather was so violent hot, that
there was no need of Cloaths, yet I could not go quite naked; no, tho'
I had been inclin'd to it, which I was not, nor could not abide the
thoughts of it, tho' I was all alone.

The Reason why I could not go quite naked, was, I could not bear
the heat of the Sun so well when quite naked, as with some Cloaths
on; nay, the very Heat frequently blistered my Skin; whereas with a Shirt
on, the Air itself made some Motion and, whistling under that Shirt
w s twofold cooler than without it: no more could I ever bring my self
to go out in the heat of Sun, without a Cap or a Hat; the heat of the
Sun beating with such Violence as it does in that Place, would give me
the Headache presently, by darting so directly on my Head, without a
Cap or Hat on, so that I could not bear it, whereas, if I put on my Hat,
it would presently go away.

Upon those Views I began to consider about putting the few Rags I
had, which I call'd Cloaths, into some Order; I had worn out all the
Wastcoats I had, and my Business was now to try if I could not make
Jackets out of the great Watch-Coats which I had by me, and with such
other Materials as I had, so I set to Work a Tayloring, or rather indeed
a Botching, for I made most piteous Work of it. However, I made shift
to make two or three new Wastcoats, which I hoped wou'd serve me a
great while; as for Breeches or Drawers, I made but a very sorry shift
indeed, till afterward.

I have mentioned that I saved the Skins of all the Creatures that I
kill'd, I mean four-footed ones, and I had hung them up stretch'd out
with Sticks in the Sun, by which means some of them were so dry and
hard that they were fit for little, but others it seems were very useful.
The first thing I made of these was a great Cap for my Head, with the
Hair on the out Side to shoor[8] off the Rain; and this I perform'd so well,
that after this I made me a Suit of Cloaths wholly of these Skins, that
is to say, a Wastcoat, and Breeches open at Knees, and both loose, for
they were rather wanting to keep me cool than to keep me warm. I must
not omit to acknowledge that they were wretchedly made; for if I was a
bad *Carpenter*, I was a worse *Taylor*. However, they were such as I
made very good shift with; and when I was abroad, if it happen'd to
rain, the Hair of my Wastcoat and Cap being outermost, I was kept very
dry.

After this I spent a great deal of Time and Pains to make me an

---

8. Possibly a misprint for "shoot."

Umbrella; I was indeed in great want of one, and had a great Mind to make one; I had seen them made in the *Brasils*, where they are very useful in the great Heats which are there. And I felt the Heats every jo' as great here, and greater too, being nearer the Equinox; besides, as I was oblig'd to be much abroad, it was a most useful thing to me, as well for the Rains as the Heats. I took a world of Pains at it, and was a great while before I could make anything likely to hold; nay, after I thought I had hit the Way, I spoil'd 2 or 3 before I made one to my Mind; but at last I made one that answer'd indifferently well: The main Difficulty I found was to make it to let down. I could make it to spread, but if it did not let down too, and draw in, it was not portable for me any Way but just over my Head, which wou'd not do. However, at last, as I said, I made one to answer, and covered it with Skins, the Hair upwards, so that it cast off the Rains like a Penthouse, and kept off the Sun so effectually, that I could walk out in the hottest of the Weather with greater Advantage than I could before in the coolest, and when I had no need of it, cou'd close it and carry it under my Arm.

Thus I liv'd mighty comfortably, my Mind being entirely composed by resigning to the Will of God, and throwing my self wholly upon the Disposal of his Providence. This made my Life better than sociable, for when I began to regret the want of Conversation, I would ask my self whether thus conversing mutually with my own Thoughts, and, as I hope I may say, with even God himself by Ejaculations, was not better than the utmost Enjoyment of humane Society in the World.

I cannot say that after this, for five Years, any extraordinary thing happened to me, but I liv'd on in the same Course, in the same Posture and Place, just as before; the chief things I was employ'd in, besides my yearly Labour of planting my Barley and Rice, and curing my Raisins, of both which I always kept up just enough to have sufficient Stock of one Year's Provisions beforehand. I say, besides this yearly Labour, and my daily Labour of going out with my Gun, I had one Labour to make me a Canoe, which at last I finished. So that by digging a Canal to it of six Foot wide, and four Foot deep, I brought it into the Creek, almost half a Mile. As for the first, which was so vastly big, as I made it without considering beforehand, as I ought to do, how I should be able to launch it; so never being able to bring it to the Water, or bring the Water to it, I was oblig'd to let it lye where it was, as a *Memorandum* to teach me to be wiser next Time: Indeed, the next Time, tho' I could not get a Tree proper for it, and in a Place where I could not get the Water to it, at any less Distance, than as I have said, near half a Mile; yet as I saw it was practicable at last, I never gave it over; and though I was near two Years about it, yet I never grutch'd[9] my Labour, in Hopes of having a Boat to go off to Sea at last.

9. Changed to "grudg'd" in the third, fourth, and sixth editions.

However, though my little *Periagua* was finish'd, yet the Size of it was not at all answerable to the Design which I had in View, when I made the first; I mean, Of venturing over to the *Terra Firma*, where it was above forty Miles broad; accordingly, the Smallness of my Boat assisted to put an End to that Design, and now I thought no more of it: But as I had a Boat, my next Design was to make a Tour round the Island; for as I had been on the other Side, in one Place, crossing as I have already describ'd it, over the Land; so the Discoveries I made in that little Journey, made me very eager to see other Parts of the Coast; and now I had a Boat, I thought of nothing but sailing round the Island.

For this Purpose, that I might do every Thing with Discretion and Consideration, I fitted up a little Mast to my Boat, and made a Sail to it, out of some of the Pieces of the Ship's Sail, which lay in store; and of which I had a great Stock by me.

Having fitted my Mast and Sail, and try'd the Boat, I found she would sail very well: Then I made little Lockers, or Boxes, at either End of my Boat, to put Provisions, Necessaries and Ammunition, &c. into, to be kept dry, either from Rain, or the Sprye[1] of the Sea; and a little long hollow Place I cut in the In-side of the Boat, where I could lay my Gun, making a Flap to hang down over it to keep it dry.

I fix'd my Umbrella also in a Step[2] at the Stern, like a Mast, to stand over my Head, and keep the Heat of the Sun off of me like an Auning; and thus I every now and then took a little Voyage upon the Sea, but never went far out, nor far from the little Creek; but at last being eager to view the Circumference of my little Kingdom, I resolv'd upon my Tour, and accordingly I victuall'd my Ship for the Voyage, putting in two Dozen of my Loaves (Cakes I should rather call them) of Barley Bread, an Earthen Pot full of parch'd Rice, a Food I eat a great deal of, a little Bottle of Rum, half a Goat, and Powder and Shot for killing more, and two large Watch-coats, of those which, as I mention'd before, I had sav'd out of the Seamen's Chests; these I took, one to lye upon, and the other to cover me in the Night.

It was the sixth of *November*, in the sixth Year of my Reign, or my Captivity, which you please, That I set out on this Voyage, and I found it much longer than I expected; for though the Island it self was not very large, yet when I came to the *East* Side of it, I found a great Ledge of Rocks lye out above two Leagues into the Sea, some above Water, some under it; and beyond that, a Shoal of Sand, lying dry half a League more; so that I was oblig'd to go a great Way out to Sea to double the Point.

When first I discover'd them, I was going to give over my Enterprise, and come back again, not knowing how far it might oblige me to go out to Sea; and above all, doubting how I should get back again; so I

1. Spray.
2. Platform supporting the heel of the mast.

came to an Anchor; for I had made me a kind of an Anchor with a Piece of a broken Graplin,[3] which I got out of the Ship.

Having secur'd my Boat, I took my Gun, and went on Shore, climbing up upon a Hill, which seem'd to overlook that Point, where I saw the full Extent of it, and resolv'd to venture.

In my viewing the Sea from that Hill where I stood, I perceiv'd a strong, and indeed, a most furious Current, which run to the *East*, and even came close to the Point; and I took the more Notice of it, because I saw there might be some Danger; that when I came into it, I might be carry'd out to Sea by the Strength of it, and not be able to make the Island again; and indeed, had I not gotten first up upon this Hill, I believe it would have been so; for there was the same Current on the other Side the Island, only that it set off at a farther Distance; and I saw there was a strong Eddy under the Shore; so I had nothing to do but to get in out of the first Current, and I should presently be in an Eddy.

I lay here, however, two Days; because the Wind blowing pretty fresh at *E. S. E.* and that being just contrary to the said Current, made a great Breach of the Sea upon the Point; so that it was not safe for me to keep too close to the Shore for the Breach,[4] nor to go too far off because of the Stream.

The Third Day in the Morning, the Wind having abated over Night, the Sea was calm, and I ventur'd; but I am a warning Piece again, to all rash and ignorant Pilots; for no sooner was I come to the Point, when even I was not my Boat's Length from the Shore, but I found my self in a great Depth of Water, and a Current like the Sluice of a Mill: It carry'd my Boat a long with it with such Violence, That all I could do, could not keep her so much as on the Edge of it; but I found it hurry'd me farther and farther out from the Eddy, which was on my left Hand. There was no Wind stirring to help me, and all I could do with my Paddlers signify'd nothing, and now I began to give my self over for lost; for as the Current was on both Sides the Island, I knew in a few Leagues Distance they must joyn again, and then I was irrecoverably gone; nor did I see any Possibility of avoiding it; so that I had no Prospect before me but of Perishing; not by the Sea, for that was calm enough, but of starving for Hunger. I had indeed found a Tortoise on the Shore, as big almost as I could lift, and had toss'd it into the Boat; and I had a great Jar of fresh Water, that is to say, one of my Earthen Pots; but what was all this to being driven into the vast Ocean, where to be sure, there was no Shore, no main Land, or Island, for a thousand Leagues at least.

And now I saw how easy it was for the Providence of God to make the most miserable Condition Mankind could be in *worse*. Now I look'd back upon my desolate solitary Island, as the most pleasant Place in the World, and all the Happiness my Heart could wish for, was to be but

3. Grappling iron.
4. Because of the breakers.

there again. I stretch'd out my Hands to it with eager Wishes. O happy Desart, said I, I shall never see thee more. O miserable Creature, said I, whether[5] am I going: Then I reproach'd my self with my unthankful Temper, and how I had repin'd at my solitary Condition; and now what would I give to be on Shore there again. Thus we never see the true State of our Condition, till it is illustrated to us by its Contraries; nor know how to value what we enjoy, but by the want of it. It is scarce possible to imagine the Consternation I was now in, being driven from my beloved Island (for so it appear'd to me now to be) into the wide Ocean, almost two Leagues, and in the utmost Despair of ever recovering it again. However, I work'd hard, till indeed my Strength was almost exhausted, and kept my Boat as much to the *Northward*, that is, towards the Side of the Current which the Eddy lay on, as possibly I could; when about Noon, as the Sun pass'd the Meridian, I thought I felt a little Breeze of Wind in my Face, springing up from the *S. S. E.* This chear'd my Heart a little, and especially when in about half an Hour more, it blew a pretty small gentle Gale. By this Time I was gotten at a frightful Distance from the Island, and had the least Cloud or haizy Weather interven'd, I had been undone another Way too; for I had no Compass on Board, and should never have known how to have steer'd towards the Island, if I had but once lost Sight of it; but the Weather continuing clear, I apply'd my self to get up my Mast again, spread my Sail, standing away to the *North*, as much as possible, to get out of the Current.

Just as I had set my Mast and Sail, and the Boat began to stretch away, I saw even by the Clearness of the Water, some Alteration of the Current was near; for where the Current was so strong, the Water was foul; but perceiving the Water clear, I found the Current abate, and presently I found to the *East*, at about half a Mile, a Breach of the Sea upon some Rocks; these Rocks I found caus'd the Current to part again, and as the main Stress of it ran away more *Southerly*, leaving the Rocks to the *North-East*; so the other return'd by the Repulse of the Rocks, and made a strong Eddy, which run back again to the *North-West*, with a very sharp Stream.

They who know what it is to have a Reprieve brought to them upon the Ladder, or to be rescued from Thieves just a going to murther them, or, who have been in such like Extremities, may guess what my present Suprise of Joy was, and how gladly I put my Boat into the Stream of this Eddy, and the Wind also freshning, how gladly I spread my Sail to it, running chearfully before the Wind, and with a strong Tide or Eddy under Foot.

This Eddy carryed me about a League in my Way back again directly towards the Island, but about two Leagues more to the Northward than the Current which carried me away at first; so that when I came near

5. Whither.

the Island, I found my self open to the Northern Shore of it, that is to say, the other End of the Island opposite to that which I went out from.

When I had made something more than a League of Way by the help of this Current or Eddy, I found it was spent and serv'd me no farther. However, I found that being between the two great Currents, (*viz.*) that on the South Side which had hurried me away, and that on the North which lay about a League on the other Side: I say between these two, in the wake of the Island, I found the Water at least still and running no Way, and having still a Breeze of Wind fair for me, I kept on steering directly for the Island, tho' not making such fresh Way as I did before.

About four a-Clock in the Evening, being then within about a League of the Island, I found the Point of the Rocks which occasioned this Disaster, stretching out as is describ'd before to the South-ward, and casting off the Current more Southwardly, had of Course made another Eddy to the North, and this I found very strong, but not directly setting the Way my Course lay which was due West, but almost full North. However having a fresh Gale, I stretch'd a-cross this Eddy slanting North-west, and in about an Hour came within about a Mile of the Shore, where it being smooth Water, I soon got to Land.

When I was on Shore I fell on my Knees and gave God Thanks for my Deliverance, resolving to lay aside all Thoughts of my Deliverance by my Boat, and refreshing my self with such Things as I had, I brought my Boat close to the Shore in a little Cove that I had spy'd under some Trees, and lay'd me down to sleep, being quite spent with the Labour and Fatigue of the Voyage.

I was now at a great Loss which Way to get Home with my Boat, I had run so much Hazard, and knew too much the Case to think of attempting it by the Way I went out, and what might be at the other Side (I mean the West Side) I knew not, nor had I any Mind to run any more Ventures; so I only resolved in the Morning to make my Way Westward along the Shore and to see if there was no Creek where I might lay up my Frigate in Safety, so as to have her again if I wanted her; in about three Mile or there-about coasting the Shore, I came to a very good Inlet or Bay about a Mile over, which narrowed till it came to a very little Rivulet or Brook, where I found a very convenient Harbour for my Boat and where she lay as if she had been in a little Dock made on Purpose for her. Here I put in, and having stow'd my Boat very safe, I went on Shore to look about me and see where I was.

I soon found I had but a little past by the Place where I had been before, when I travell'd on Foot to that Shore, so taking nothing out of my Boat, but my Gun and my Umbrella, for it was exceeding hot, I began my March: The Way was comfortable enough after such a Voyage as I had been upon, and I reach'd my old Bower in the Evening, where I found every thing standing as I left it; for I always kept it in good Order, being, as I said before, my Country House.

I got over the Fence, and laid me down in the Shade to rest my

Limbs; for I was very weary, and fell asleep: But judge you, if you can, that read my Story, what a Surprize I must be in, when I was wak'd out of my Sleep by a Voice calling me by my Name several times, *Robin, Robin, Robin Crusoe,* poor *Robin Crusoe,* where are you *Robin Crusoe?* Where are you? Where have you been?

I was so dead asleep at first, being fatigu'd with Rowing, or Paddling, as it is call'd, the first Part of the Day, and with walking the latter Part, that I did not wake thoroughly, but dozing between sleeping and waking, thought I dream'd that some Body spoke to me: But as the Voice continu'd to repeat *Robin Crusoe, Robin Crusoe,* at last I began to wake more perfectly, and was at first dreadfully frighted, and started up in the utmost Consternation: But no sooner were my Eyes open, than I saw my *Poll* sitting on the Top of the Hedge; and immediately knew that it was he that spoke to me; for just in such bemoaning Language I had used to talk to him, and teach him; and he had learn'd it so perfectly, that he would sit upon my Finger, and lay his Bill close to my Face, and cry, *Poor* Robin Crusoe, *Where are you? Where have you been? How come you here?* And such things as I had taught him.

However, even though I knew it was the Parrot, and that indeed it could be no Body else, it was a good while before I could compose my self: First, I was amazed how the Creature got thither, and then, how he should just keep about the Place, and no where else: But as I was well satisfied it could be no Body but honest *Poll,* I got it over; and holding out my Hand, and calling him by his Name *Poll,* the sociable Creature came to me, and sat upon my Thumb, as he used to do, and continu'd talking to me, *Poor* Robin Crusoe, and *how did I come here?* and *where had I been?* just as if he had been overjoy'd to see me again; and so I carry'd him Home along with me.

I had now had enough of rambling to Sea for some time, and had enough to do for many Days to sit still, and reflect upon the Danger I had been in: I would have been very glad to have had my Boat again on my Side of the Island; but I knew not how it was practicable to get it about. As to the East Side of the Island, which I had gone round; I knew well enough there was no venturing that Way; my very heart would shrink, and my very Blood run chill but to think of it: And as to the other Side of the Island, I did not know how it might be there; but supposing the Current ran with the same Force against the Shore at the East as it pass'd by it on the other, I might run the same Risk of being driven down the Stream, and carry'd by the Island, as I had been before, of being carry'd away from it; so with these Thoughts I contented my self to be without any Boat, though it had been the Product of so many Months Labour to make it, and of so many more to get it unto the Sea.

In this Government of my Temper, I remain'd near a Year, liv'd a very sedate retir'd Life, as you may well suppose; and my Thoughts being very much composed as to my Condition, and fully comforted in resigning my self to the Dispositions of Providence, I thought I liv'd really very happily in all things, except that of Society.

I improv'd my self in this time in all the mechanick Exercises which my Necessities put me upon applying my self to, and I believe cou'd, upon Occasion, make a very good *Carpenter*, especially considering how few Tools I had.

Besides this, I arriv'd at an unexpected Perfection in my Earthen Ware, and contriv'd well enough to make them with a Wheel, which I found infinitely easyer and better; because I made things round and shapable, which before were filthy things indeed to look on. But I think I was never more vain of my own Performance, or more joyful for any thing I found out, than for my being able to make a Tobacco-Pipe. And tho' it was a very ugly clumsy thing, when it was done, and only burnt red like other Earthen Ware, yet as it was hard and firm, and would draw the Smoke, I was exceedingly comforted with it, for I had been always used to smoke, and there were Pipes in the Ship, but I forgot them at first, not knowing that there was Tobacco in the Island; and afterwards, when I search'd the Ship again, I could not come at any Pipes at all.

In my Wicker Ware also I improved much, and made abundance of necessary Baskets, as well as my Invention shew'd me, tho' not very handsome, yet they were such as were very handy and convenient for my laying things up in, or fetching things home in. For Example, if I kill'd a Goat abroad, I could hang it up in a Tree, flea it, and dress it, and cut it in Pieces, and bring it home in a Basket, and the like by a Turtle, I could cut it up, take out the Eggs, and a Piece or two of the Flesh, which was enough for me, and bring them home in a Basket, and leave the rest behind me. Also large deep Baskets were my Receivers for my Corn, which I always rubb'd out as soon as it was dry, and cured, and kept it in great Baskets.

I began now to perceive my Powder abated considerably, and this was a Want which it was impossible for me to supply, and I began seriously to consider what I must do when I should have no more Powder; that is to say, how I should do to kill any Goat. I had, as is observ'd in the third Year of my being here, kept a young Kid, and bred her up tame, and I was in hope of getting a He-Goat, but I could not by any Means bring it to pass, 'till my Kid grew an old Goat; and I could never find it my Heart to kill her, till she dy'd at last of meer Age.

But being now in the eleventh Year of my Residence and, as I have said, my Ammunition growing low, I set my self to study some Art to trap and snare the Goats, to see whether I could not catch some of them alive, and particularly I wanted a She-Goat great with young.

To this Purpose I made Snares to hamper them, and I do believe they were more than once taken in them, but my Tackle was not good, for I had no Wire, and I always found them broken, and my Bait devoured.

At length I resolv'd to try a Pit-Fall, so I dug several large Pits in the Earth, in Places where I had observ'd the Goats used to feed, and over these Pits I plac'd Hurdles of my own making too, with a great Weight upon them: and several times I put Ears of Barley, and dry Rice, without setting the Trap, and I could easily perceive that the Goats had gone in and eaten up the Corn, for I could see the Mark of their Feet. At length I set three Traps in one Night, and going the next Morning I found them all standing, and yet the Bait eaten and gone: This was very discouraging. However, I alter'd my Trap, and, not to trouble you with Particulars, going one Morning to see my Trap, I found in one of them a large old He-Goat, and in one of the other, three Kids, a Male and two Females.

As to the old one, I knew not what to do with him, he was so fierce I durst not go into the Pit to him; that is to say, to go about to bring him away alive, which was what I wanted. I could have kill'd him, but that was not my Business, nor would it answer my End. So I e'en let him out, and he ran away as if he had been frighted out of his Wits: but I had forgot then what I learn'd afterwards, that Hunger will tame a Lyon. If I had let him stay there three of four Days without Food, and then have carry'd him some Water to drink, and then a little Corn, he would have been as tame as one of the Kids, for they are mighty sagacious tractable Creatures where they are well used.

However, for the present I let him go, knowing no better at that time; then I went to the Three Kids, and taking them one by one, I tyed them with Strings together, and with some Difficulty brought them all home.

It was a good while before they wou'd feed, but throwing them some sweet Corn, it tempted them and they began to be tame; and now I found that if I expected to supply my self with Goat-Flesh when I had no Powder or Shot left, breeding some up tame was my only way, when perhaps I might have them about my House like a Flock of Sheep.

But then it presently occurr'd to me, that I must keep the tame from the wild, or else they would always run wild when they grew up, and the only Way for this was to have some enclosed Piece of Ground, well fenc'd either with Hedge or Pale, to keep them in so effectually, that those within might not break out, or those without break in.

This was a great Undertaking for one Pair of Hands, yet as I saw there was an absolute Necessity of doing it, my first Piece of Work was to find out a proper Piece of Ground, *viz.* where there was likely to be Herbage for them to eat, Water for them to drink, and Cover to keep them from the Sun.

Those who understand such Enclosures will think I had very little Contrivance, when I pitch'd upon a Place very proper for all these, being a plain open Piece of Meadow-Land, or *Savanna*, (as our People call it in the Western Collonies,) which had two or three little Drills[6] of

6. Rills or small streams.

fresh Water in it, and at one end was very woody. I say they will smile at my Forecast, when I shall tell them I began my enclosing of this Piece of Ground in such a manner, that my Hedge or Pale must have been at least two Mile about. Nor was the Madness of it so great as to the Compass, for if it was ten Mile about I was like to have time enough to do it in. But I did not consider that my Goats would be as wild in so much Compass as if they had had the whole Island, and I should have so much Room to chace them in, that I should never catch them.

My Hedge was begun and carry'd on, I believe, about fifty Yards, when this Thought occurr'd to me, so I presently stopt short, and for the first beginning I resolv'd to enclose a Piece of about 150 Yards in length, and 100 Yards in breadth, which as it would maintain as many as I should have in any reasonable time, so as my Flock encreased, I could add more Ground to my Enclosure.

This was acting with some Prudence, and I went to work with Courage. I was about three Months hedging in the first Piece, and till I had done it I tether'd the three Kids in the best part of of it, and us'd them to feed as near me as possible to make them familiar; and very often I would go and carry them some Ears of Barley, or a handful of Rice, and feed them out of my Hand; so that after my Enclosure was finished, and I let them loose, they would follow me up and down, bleating after me for a handful of Corn.

This answer'd my End, and in about a Year and half I had a Flock of about twelve Goats, Kids and all; and in two Years more I had three and forty, besides several that I took and kill'd for my Food. And after that I enclosed five several Pieces of Ground to feed them in, with little Pens to drive them into, to take them as I wanted, and Gates out of one Piece of Ground into another.

But this was not all, for now I not only had Goats Flesh to feed on when I pleas'd, but Milk too, a thing which indeed in my beginning I did not so much as think of, and which, when it came into my Thoughts, was really an agreeable Surprize. For now I set up my Dairy, and had sometimes a Gallon or two of Milk in a Day. And as Nature, who gives Supplies of Food to every Creature, dictates even naturally how to make use of it; so I that had never milk'd a Cow, much less a Goat, or seen Butter or Cheese made, very readily and handily, tho' after a great many Essays and Miscarriages, made me both Butter and Cheese at last, and never wanted it afterwards.

How mercifully can our great Creator treat his Creatures, even in those Conditions in which they seem'd to be overwhelm'd in Destruction. How can he sweeten the bitterest Providences, and give us Cause to praise him for Dungeons and Prisons. What a Table was here spread for me in a Wilderness,[7] where I saw nothing at first but to perish for Hunger.

7. Psalms 78.19.

It would have made a Stoick smile to have seen, me and my little Family sit down to Dinner; there was my Majesty the Prince and Lord of the whole Island; I had the Lives of all my Subjects at my absolute Command. I could hang, draw, give Liberty, and take it away, and no Rebels among all my Subjects.

Then to see how like a King I din'd too all alone, attended by my Servants; *Poll*, as if he had been my Favourite, was the only Person permitted to talk to me. My Dog who was now grown very old and crazy, and had found no Species to multiply his Kind upon, sat always at my Right Hand, and two Cats, one on one Side the Table, and one on the other, expecting now and then a Bit from my Hand, as a Mark of special Favour.

But these were not the two Cats which I brought on Shore at first, for they were both of them dead, and had been interr'd near my Hab-itation by my own Hand; but one of them having multiply'd by I know not what Kind of Creature, these were two which I had preserv'd tame, whereas the rest run wild in the Woods, and became indeed troublesom to me at last; for they would often come into my House, and plunder me too, till at last I was obliged to shoot them, and did kill a great many; at length they left me: With this Attendance, and in this plentiful Manner I lived; neither could I be said to want anything but Society, and of that in some time after this, I was like to have too much.

I was something impatient, as I have observ'd, to have the Use of my Boat; though very loath to run any more Hazards; and therefore some-times I sat contriving Ways to get her about the Island, and at other Times I sat my self down contented enough without her. But I had a strange Uneasiness in my Mind to go down to the Point of the Island, where, as I have said, in my last Ramble, I went up the Hill to see how the Shore lay, and how the Current set, that I might see what I had to do: This Inclination encreas'd upon me every Day, and at length I resolv'd to travel thither by Land, following the Edge of the Shore. I did so: But had any one in *England* been to meet such a Man as I was, it must either have frighted them, or rais'd a great deal of Laughter; and as I frequently stood still to look at my self, I could not but smile at the Notion of my travelling through *Yorkshire* with such an Equipage, and in such a Dress: Be pleas'd to take a Sketch of my Figure as follows.

I had a great high shapeless Cap, made of a Goat's Skin, with a Flap hanging down behind, as well to keep the Sun from me, as to shoot the Rain off from running into my Neck; nothing being so hurtful in these Climates, as the Rain upon the Flesh under the Cloaths.

I had a short Jacket of Goat-Skin, the Skirts coming down to about the middle of my Thighs; and a Pair of open-knee'd Breeches of the same, the Breeches were made of the Skin of an old *He-goat*, whose Hair hung down such a Length on either Side, that like *Pantaloons* it reach'd to the middle of my Legs; Stockings and Shoes I had none, but had made me a Pair of somethings, I scarce know what to call them, like Buskins[8] to flap over my Legs, and lace on either Side like Spatter-dashes;[9] but of a most barbarous Shape, as indeed were all the rest of my Cloaths.

I had on a broad Belt of Goat's-Skin dry'd, which I drew together with two Thongs of the same, instead of Buckles, and in a kind of a Frog[1] on either Side of this. Instead of a Sword and a Dagger, hung a little Saw and a Hatchet, one on one Side, one on the other. I had another Belt not so broad, and fasten'd in the same Manner, which hung over my Shoulder; and at the End of it, under my left Arm, hung two Pouches, both made of Goat's-Skin too; in one of which hung my Powder, in the other my Shot: At my Back I carry'd my Basket, on my Shoulder my Gun, and over my Head a great clumsy ugly Goat-Skin Umbrella, but which, after all, was the most necessary Thing I had about me, next to my Gun: As for my Face, the Colour of it was really not so *Moletta*[2] *like as one might expect from a Man not at all careful of it, and living within nine or ten*[3] *Degrees of the Equinox.* My Beard I had once suffer'd to grow till it was about a Quarter of a Yard long; but as I had both Scissars and Razors sufficient, I had cut it pretty short, except what grew on my upper Lip, which I had trimm'd into a large Pair of *Mahometan* Whiskers, such as I had seen worn by some*Turks*, who I saw at *Sallee*; for the *Moors* did not wear such, tho' the *Turks* did; of these Muschatoes[4] or Whiskers, I will not say they were long enough to hang my Hat upon them; but they were of a Length and Shape monstrous enough, and such as in *England* would have pass'd for frightful.

But all this is by the by; for as to my Figure, I had so few to observe me, that it was of no manner of Consequence; so I say no more to that Part. In this kind of Figure I went my new Journey, and was out five or six Days. I travell'd first along the Sea Shore, directly to the Place where I first brought my Boat to an Anchor, to get up upon the Rocks; and having no Boat now to take care of, I went over the Land a nearer Way to the same Height that I was upon before, when looking forward to the Point of the Rocks which lay out, and which I was oblig'd to double with my Boat, as is said above: I was surpriz'd to see the Sea all smooth and quiet, no Ripling, no Motion, no Current, any more there than in other Places.

I was at a strange Loss to understand this, and resolv'd to spend some Time in the observing it, to see if nothing from the Sets of the Tide

8. Half boots.
9. Leggings. Cf. "spats."
1. Belt loop for a scabbard.
2. Mulatto.
3. The early editions read "nineteen," but the fourth edition corrects it to "nine or ten," which is in line with Crusoe's reckoning of his position earlier.
4. Corrected to "Mustachios" in the fourth and subsequent editions.

had occasion'd it; but I was presently convinc'd how it was, *viz.* That the Tide of Ebb setting from the *West*, and joyning with the Current of Waters from some great river on the Shore, must be the Occasion of this Current; and that according as the Wind blew more forcibly from the *West*, or from the *North*, this Current came nearer, or went farther from the Shore; for waiting thereabouts till Evening, I went up to the Rock again, and then the Tide of Ebb being made, I plainly saw the Current again as before, only, that it run farther off, being near half a League from the Shore; whereas in my Case, it set close upon the Shore, and hurry'd me and my *Canoe* along with it, which at another Time it would not have done.

This Observation convinc'd me, That I had nothing to do but to observe the Ebbing and the Flowing of the Tide, and I might very easily bring my Boat about the Island again: But when I began to think of putting it in Practice, I had such a Terror upon my Spirits at the Remembrance of the Danger I had been in, that I could not think of it again with any Patience; but on the contrary, I took up another Resolution which was more safe, though more laborious; and this was, That I would build, or rather make me another *Periagua* or *Canoe*; and so have one for one Side of the Island, and one for the other.

You are to understand, that now I had, as I may call it, two Plantations in the Island; one my little Fortification or Tent, with the Wall about it under the Rock, with the Cave behind me, which by this Time I had enlarg'd into several Apartments, or Caves, one within another. One of these, which was the dryest, and largest, and had a Door out beyond my Wall or Fortification; that is to say, beyond where my Wall joyn'd to the Rock, was all fill'd up with the large Earthen Pots, of which I have given an Account, and with fourteen or fifteen great Baskets, which would hold five or six Bushels each, where I laid up my Stores of Provision, expecially my Corn, some in the Ear cut off short from the Straw, and the other rubb'd out with my Hand.

As for my Wall made, *as before*, with long Stakes or Piles, those Piles grew all like Trees, and were by this Time grown so big, and spread so very much, that there was not the least Appearance to any one's View of any Habitation behind them.

Near this Dwelling of mine, but a little farther within the Land, and upon lower Ground, lay my two Pieces of Corn-Ground, which I kept duly cultivated and sow'd, and which duly yielded me their Harvest in its Season; and whenever I had occasion for more Corn, I had more Land adjoyning as fit as that.

Besides this, I had my Country Seat, and I had now a tollerable Plantation there also; for first, I had my little Bower, as I call'd it, which I kept in Repair; *that is to say*, I kept the Hedge which circled it in, constantly fitted up to its usual Height, the Ladder standing always in the Inside; I kept the Trees which at first were no more than my Stakes, but were now grown very firm and tall; I kept them always so cut, that they might spread and grow thick and wild, and make the more agreeable Shade, which they did effectually to my Mind. In the Middle of this I had my Tent always standing, being a piece of a Sail spread over Poles set up for that Purpose, and which never wanted any Repair or Renewing; and under this I had made me a Squab or Couch, with the Skins of the Creatures, I had kill'd, and with other soft Things, and a Blanket laid on them, such as belong'd to our Sea-Bedding, which I had saved, and a great Watch-Coat to cover me; and here, whenever I had Occasion to be absent from my chief Seat, I took up my Country Habitation.

Adjoyning to this I had my Enclosures for my Cattle, that is to say, my Goats: And as I had taken an inconceivable deal of Pains to fence and enclose this Ground, so I was so uneasy to see it kept entire, lest the Goats should break thro', that I never left off till with infinite Labour I had stuck the Out-side of the Hedge so full of small Stakes, and so near to one another, that it was rather a Pale than a Hedge, and there was scarce Room to put a Hand thro' between them, which afterwards when those Stakes grew, as they all did in the next rainy Season, made the Enclosure strong like a Wall, indeed stronger than any Wall.

This will testify for me that I was not idle, and that I spared no Pains to bring to pass whatever appear'd necessary for my comfortable Support; for I consider'd the keeping up a Breed of tame Creatures thus at my Hand, would be a living Magazine of Flesh, Milk, Butter and Cheese, for me as long as I liv'd in the Place, if it were to be forty Years; and that keeping them in my Reach, depended entirely upon my perfecting my Enclosures to such a Degree, that I might be sure of keeping them together; which by this Method indeed I so effectually secur'd that, when these little Stakes began to grow, I had planted them so very thick, I was forced to pull some of them up again.

In this Place also I had my Grapes growing, which I principally depended on for my Winter Store of Raisins; and which I never fail'd to preserve very carefully, as the best and most agreeable Dainty of my whole Diet; and indeed they were not agreeable only, but physical,[5] wholesome, nourishing, and refreshing to the last Degree.

As this was also about half Way between my other Habitation, and the Place where I had laid up my Boat, I generally stay'd, and lay here in my Way thither; for I used frequently to visit my Boat, and I kept all Things about or belongings to her in very good Order; sometimes I went out in her to divert my self, but no more hazardous Voyages would I go, nor scarce ever above a Stone's Cast or two from the Shore, I was so apprehensive of being hurry'd out of my Knowledge again by the Currents, or Winds, or any other Accident. But now I come to a new Scene of my Life.

5. Curative, medicinal.

It happen'd one Day about Noon going towards my Boat, I was exceedingly surpriz'd with the Print of a Man's naked Foot on the Shore, which was very plain to be seen in the Sand: I stood like one Thunderstruck, or as if I had seen an Apparition; I listen'd, I look'd round me, I could hear nothing, nor see any Thing; I went up to a rising Ground to look farther; I went up the Shore and down the Shore, but it was all one, I could see no other Impression but that one, I went to it again to see if there were any more, and to observe if it might not be my Fancy; but there was no Room for that, for there was exactly the very Print of a Foot, Toes, Heel, and every Part of a Foot; how it came thither, I knew not, nor could in the least imagine. But after innumerable fluttering Thoughts, like a Man perfectly confus'd and out of my self, I came Home to my Fortification, not feeling, as we say, the Ground I went on, but terrify'd to the last Degree, looking behind me at every two or three Steps, mistaking every Bush and Tree, and fancying every Stump at a Distance to be a Man; nor is it possible to describe how many various Shapes affrighted Imagination represented Things to me in, how many wild Ideas were found every Moment in my Fancy, and what strange unaccountable Whimsies came into my Thoughts by the Way.

When I came to my Castle, for so I think I call'd it ever after this, I fled into it like one pursued; whether I went over by the Ladder as first contriv'd, or went in at the Hole in the Rock, which I call'd a Door, I cannot remember; no, nor could I remember the next Morning, for never frighted Hare fled to Cover, or Fox to Earth, with more Terror of Mind than I to this Retreat.

I slept none that Night; the farther I was from the Occasion of my Fright, the greater my Apprehensions were, which is something contrary to the Nature of such Things, and especially to the usual Practice of all Creatures in Fear: But I was so embarrass'd with my own frightful Ideas of the Thing, that I form'd nothing but dismal Imaginations to my self, even tho' I was now a great way off of it. Sometimes I fancy'd it must be the Devil; and Reason joyn'd in with me upon this Supposition: For how should any other Thing in human Shape come into the Place? Where was the Vessel that brought them? What Marks was there of any other Footsteps! And how was it possible a Man should come there? But then to think that *Satan* should take human Shape upon him in such a Place where there could be no manner of Occasion for it, but to leave the Print of his Foot behind him, and that even for no Purpose too, for he could not be sure I should see it; this was an Amusement[6] the other Way; I consider'd that the Devil might have found out abundance of other Ways to have terrify'd me than this of the single Print of a Foot. That as I liv'd quite on the other Side of the Island, he would

6. Source of bewilderment.

never have been so simple to leave a Mark in a Place where 'twas Ten Thousand to one whether I should ever see it or not, and in the Sand too, which the first Surge of the Sea upon a high Wind would have defac'd entirely: All this seem'd inconsistent with the Thing it self, and with all the Notions we usually entertain of the Subtilty of the Devil.

Abundance of such Things as these assisted to argue me out of all Apprehensions of its being the Devil: And I presently concluded then, that it must be some more dangerous Creature. *(viz.)* That it must be some of the Savages of the main Land over-against me, who had wander'd out to Sea in their *Canoes*; and either driven by the Currents, or by contrary Winds had made the Island; and had been on Shore, but were gone away again to Sea, being as loth, perhaps, to have stay'd in this desolate Island, as I would have been to have had them.

While these Reflections were rowling[7] upon my Mind, I was very thankful in my Thoughts, that I was so happy as not to be thereabouts at that Time, or that they did not see my Boat, by which they would have concluded that some Inhabitants had been in the Place, and perhaps have search'd farther for me: Then terrible Thoughts rack'd my Imagination about their having found my Boat, and that there were People here; and that if so, I should certainly have them come again in greater Numbers, and devour me: that if it should happen so that they should not find me, yet they would find my Enclosure, destroy all my Corn, carry away all my Flock of tame Goats, and I should perish at last for meer Want.

Thus my Fear banish'd all my religious Hope; all that former Confidence in God which was founded upon such wonderful Experience as I had had of his Goodness, now vanished, as if he that had fed me by Miracle hitherto, could not preserve by his Power the Provision which he had made for me by his Goodness: I reproach'd my self with my Easiness, that would not sow any more Corn one Year than would just serve me till the next Season as if no Accident could intervene to prevent my enjoying the Crop that was upon the Ground; and this I thought so just a Reproof, that I resolv'd for the future to have two or three Years Corn beforehand, so that whatever might come, I might not perish for want of Bread.

How strange a Chequer-Work of Providence is the Life of Man! and by what secret differing Springs are the Affections hurry'd about as differing Circumstances present! To Day we love what to Morrow we hate; to Day we seek what to Morrow we shun; to Day we desire what to Morrow we fear; nay even tremble at the Apprehensions of; this was exemplify'd in me at this Time in the most lively Manner imaginable; for I whose only Affliction was, that I seem'd banished from human Society, that I was alone, circumscrib'd by the boundless Ocean, cut

7. Changed to "rolling" in the third and sixth editions.

off from Mankind, and condemn'd to what I call'd silent Life; that I was as one who Heaven thought not worthy to be number'd among the Living, or to appear among the rest of his Creatures; that to have seen one of my own Species, would have seem'd to me a Raising me from Death to Life, and the greatest Blessing that Heaven it self, next to the supreme Blessing of Salvation, could bestow; I say, that I should now tremble at the very Apprehensions of seeing a Man, and was ready to sink into the Ground at but the Shadow or silent Appearance of a Man's having set his Foot in the Island.

Such is the uneven State of human Life: And it afforded me a great many curious Speculations afterwards, when I had a little recover'd my first Surprize; I consider'd that this was the Station of Life the infinitely wise and good Providence of God had determin'd for me, that as I could not foresee what the Ends of Divine Wisdom might be in all this, so I was not to dispute his Sovereignty, who, as I was his Creature, had an undoubted Right by Creation to govern and dispose of me absolutely as he thought fit; and who, as I was a Creature who had offended him, had likewise a judicial Right to condemn me to what Punishment he thought fit: and that it was my Part to submit to bear his Indignation, because I had sinn'd against him.

I then reflected that God, who was not only Righteous but Omnipotent, as he had thought fit thus to punish and afflict me, so he was able to deliver me; that if he did not think fit to do it, 'twas my unquestion'd Duty to resign my self absolutely and entirely to his Will: and on the other Hand, it was my Duty also to hope in him, pray to him, and quitely to attend the Dictates and Directions of his daily Providence.

These Thoughts took me up many Hours, Days; nay, I may say, Weeks and Months; and one particular Effect of my Cogitations on this Occasion, I cannot omit, viz. One Morning early, lying in my Bed, and fill'd with Thought about my Danger from the Appearance of Savages, I found it discompos'd me very much, upon which those Words of the Scripture came into my Thoughts, *Call upon me in the Day of Trouble, and I will deliver, and thou shalt glorify me*[8]

Upon this, rising chearfully out of my Bed, my Heart was not only comforted, but I was guided and encourag'd to pray earnestly to God for Deliverance: When I had done praying, I took up my Bible, and opening it to read, the first Words that presented to me, were *Wait on the Lord, and be of good Cheer, and he shall strengthen thy Heart; wait, I say, on the Lord:*[9] It is impossible to express the Comfort this gave me. In Answer, I thankfully laid down the Book, and was no more sad, at least, not on that Occasion.

In the middle of these Cogitations, Apprehensions and Reflections,

8. Psalms 50.15.
9. Psalms 27.14.

it came into my Thought one Day, that all this might be a meer Chimera of my own; and that this Foot might be the Print of my own Foot, when I came on Shore from my Boat: This chear'd me up a little too, and I began to perswade my self it was all a Delusion; that it was nothing else but my own Foot, and why might not I come that way from the Boat, as well as I was going that way to the Boat; again, I consider'd also that I could by no Means tell for certain where I had trod, and where I had not; and that if at last this was only the Print of my own Foot, I had play'd the Part of those Fools, who strive to make stories of Spectres, and Apparitions; and then are frighted at them more than any body.

Now I began to take Courage, and to peep abroad again; for I had not stirr'd out of my Castle for three Days and Nights; so that I began to starve for Provision; for I had little or nothing within Doors, but some Barley Cakes and Water. Then I knew that my Goats wanted to be milk'd too, which usually was my Evening Diversion; and the poor Creatures were in great Pain and Inconvenience for want of it; and indeed, it almost spoil'd some of them, and almost dry'd up their Milk.

Heartning my self therefore with the Belief that this was nothing but the Print of one of my own Feet, and so I might be truly said to start at my own Shadow, I began to go abroad again, and went to my Country House, to milk my Flock; but to see with what Fear I went forward, how often I look'd behind me, how I was ready every now and then to lay down my Basket, and run for my Life, it would have made any one have thought I was haunted with an evil Conscience, or that I had been lately most terribly frighted, and so indeed I had.

However, as I went down thus two or three Days, and having seen nothing, I began to be a little bolder; and to think there was really nothing in it, but my own Imagination: But I cou'd not perswade my self fully of this, till I should go down to the Shore again, and see this Print of a Foot, and measure it by my own, and see if there was any Similitude or Fitness, that I might be assur'd it was my own Foot: But when I came to the Place, *First*, It appear'd evidently to me, that when I laid up my Boat, I could not possibly be on Shore any where there about. *Secondly*, When I came to measure the Mark with my own Foot, I found my Foot not so large by a great deal; both these Things fill'd my Head with new Imaginations, and gave me the Vapours[1] again, to the highest Degree; so that I shook with cold, like one in an Ague: And I went Home again, fill'd with the Belief that some Man or Men had been on Shore there; or in short, that the Island was inhabited, and I might be surpriz'd before I was aware; and what course to take for my Security I knew not.

O what ridiculous Resolution Men take, when possess'd with Fear! It deprives them of the Use of those Means which Reason offers for

1. Hypochondria or melancholy.

their Relief. The first Thing I propos'd to my self, was, to throw down my Enclosures, and turn all my tame Cattle wild into the Woods, that the Enemy might not find them; and then frequent the Island in Prospect of the same, or the like Booty: Then to the simple Thing of Digging up my two Corn Fields, that they might not find such a Grain there, and still be prompted to frequent the Island; then to demolish my Bower, and Tent, that they might not find such a Grain there, and still be prompted to look farther, in order to find out the Persons inhabiting.

These were the Subject of the first Night's Cogitation, after I was come Home again, while the Apprehensions which had so over-run my Mind were fresh upon me, and my Head was full of Vapours, as above: Thus Fear of Danger is ten thousand Times more terrifying than Danger it self, when apparent to the Eyes; and we find the Burthen of Anxiety greater by much, than the Evil which we are anxious about; and which was worse than all this, I had not that Relief in this Trouble from the Resignation I used to practise, that I hop'd to have. I look'd, I thought, like *Saul*,[2] who complain'd not only that the *Philistines* were upon him; but that God had forsaken him; for I did not now take due Ways to compose my Mind, by crying to God in my Distress, and resting upon his Providence, as I had done before, for my Defence and Deliverance; which if I had done, I had, at least, been more cheerfully supported under this new Surprise, and perhaps carry'd through it with more Resolution.

This Confusion of my Thoughts kept me waking all Night; but in the Morning I fell asleep, and having by the Amusement[3] of my Mind, been, as it were, tyr'd, and my Spirits exhausted; I slept very soundly, and wak'd much better compos'd than I had ever been before; and now I began to think sedately; and upon the utmost Debate with my self, I concluded, That this Island, which was so exceeding pleasant, fruitful, and no farther from the main Land than as I had seen, was not so entirely abandon'd as I might imagine: That altho' there were no stated Inhabitants who liv'd on the Spot; yet that there might sometimes come Boats off from the Shore, who either with Design, or perhaps never, but when they were driven by cross Winds, might come to this Place.

That I had liv'd here fifteen Years now; and had not met with the least Shadow or Figure of any People yet; and that if at any Time they should be driven here, it was probable they went away again as soon as ever they could, seeing they had never thought fit to fix there upon any Occasion, to this Time.

That the most I cou'd suggest any Danger from, was, from any such casual accidental Landing of straggling People from the Main, who, as it was likely if they were driven hither, were here against their Wills; so they made no stay here, but went off again with all possible Speed,

2. 1 Samuel 28.15.
3. Bewilderment.

seldom staying one Night on Shore, least they should not have the Help of the Tides, and Day-light back again; and that therefore I had nothing to do but to consider of some safe Retreat, in Case I should see any Savages land upon the Spot.

Now I began sorely to repent, that I had dug my Cave so large, as to bring a Door through again, which Door, as I said, came out beyond where my Fortification joyn'd to the Rock; upon maturely considering this therefore, I resolv'd to draw me a second Fortification, in the same Manner of a Semicircle, at a Distance from my Wall just where I had planted a double Row of Trees, about twelve Years before, of which I made mention: These Trees having been planted so thick before, they wanted but a few Piles to be driven between them, that they should be thicker, and stronger, and my Wall would be soon finish'd.

So that I had now a double Wall, and my outer Wall was thickned with Pieces of Timber, old Cables, and every Thing I could think of, to make it strong; having in it seven little Holes, about as big as I might put my Arm out at: In the In-side of this, I thickned my Wall to above ten Foot thick, with continual bringing Earth out of my Cave, and laying it at the Foot of the Wall, and walking upon it; and through the seven Holes, I contriv'd to plant the Musquets,[4] of which I took Notice, that I got seven on Shore out of the Ship; these I say, I planted like my Cannon, and fitted them into Frames that held them like a Carriage, that so I could fire all the seven Guns in two Minutes Time: This Wall I was many a weary Month a finishing, and yet never thought my self safe till it was done.

When this was done, I stuck all the Ground without my Wall, for a great way every way, as full with Stakes or Sticks of the *Osier* like Wood, which I found so apt to grow, as they could well stand; insomuch, that I believe I might set in near twenty thousand of them, leaving a pretty large Space between them and my Wall, that I might have room to see an Enemy, and they might have no shelter from the young Trees, if they attempted to approach my outer Wall.

Thus in two Years Time I had a thick Grove and in five or six Years Time I had a Wood before my Dwelling, growing so monstrous thick and strong, that it was indeed perfectly impassable; and no Men of what kind soever, would ever imagine that there was any Thing beyond it, much less a Habitation: As for the Way which I propos'd to my self to go in and out, for I left no Avenue, it was by setting two Ladders, one to a Part of the Rock which was low, and then broke in, and left room to place another Ladder upon that; so when the two Ladders were taken down, no Man living could come down to me without mischieving himself; and if they had come down they were still on the Out-side of my outer Wall.

4. Subsequently spelled "Musket" in text.

Thus I took all the Measures humane Prudence could suggest for my own Preservation; and it will be seen at length, that they were not altogether without just Reason; though I foresaw nothing at that Time, more than my meer Fear suggested to me.

While this was doing, I was not altogether Careless of my other Affairs; for I had a great Concern upon me, for my little Herd of Goats; they were not only a present Supply to me upon every Occasion, and began to be sufficient to me, without the Expence of Powder and Shot; but also without the Fatigue of Hunting after the wild Ones, and I was loth to lose the Advantage of them, and to have them all to nurse up over again.

To this Purpose, after long Consideration, I could think of but two Ways to preserve them; one was to find another convenient Place to dig a Cave Under-ground, and to drive them into it every Night; and the other was to enclose two or three little Bits of Land, remote from one another and as much conceal'd as I could, where I might keep about half a Dozen young Goats in each Place: So that if any Disaster happen'd to the Flock in general, I might be able to raise them again with little Trouble and Time: And this, tho' it would require a great deal of Time and Labour, I thought was the most rational Design.

Accordingly I spent some Time to find out the most retir'd Parts of the Island; and I pitch'd upon one which was as private indeed as my Heart could wish for; it was a little damp Piece of Ground in the Middle of the hollow and thick Woods, where, as is observ'd, I almost lost my self once before, endeavouring to come back that Way from the Eastern Part of the Island: Here I found a clear Piece of Land near three Acres, so surrounded with Woods, that it was almost an Enclosure by Nature, at least it did not want near so much Labour to make it so, as the other Pieces of Ground I had work'd so hard at.

I immediatly went to Work with this Piece of Ground, and in less than a Month's Time, I had so fenc'd it round, that my Flock or Herd, call it which you please, who were not so wild now as at first they might be supposed to be, were well enough secur'd in it. So, without any farther Delay, I removed ten young She-Goats and two He-Goats to this Piece; and when they were there, I continued to perfect the Fence till I had made it as secure as the other, which, however, I did at more Leisure, and it took me up more Time by a great deal.

All this Labour I was at the Expence of, purely from my Apprehensions on the Account of the Print of a Man's Foot which I had seen; for as yet I never saw any human Creature come near the Island, and I had now liv'd two Years under these Uneasinesses, which indeed made my life much less comfortable than it was before; as may well be imagin'd by any who know what it is to live in the constant Snare of *the Fear of Man*; and this I must observe with Grief too, that the Discomposure of my Mind had too great impressions also upon the religious Part of my

Thoughts, for the Dread and Terror of falling into the Hands of Savages and Canibals, lay so upon my Spirits, that I seldom found my self in a due Temper for application to my Maker, at least not with the sedate Calmness and Resignation of Soul which I was wont to do; I rather pray'd to God as under great Affliction and Pressure of Mind, surrounded with Danger, and in Expectation every Night of being murther'd and devour'd before Morning; and I must testify from my Experience, that a Temper of Peace, Thankfulness, Love and Affection, is much more the proper Frame for Prayer than that of Terror and Discomposure; and that under the Dread of Mischief impending, a Man is no more fit for a comforting Performance of the Duty of praying to God, than he is for Repentance on a sick Bed: For these Discomposures affect the Mind as the others do the Body; and the Discomposure of the Mind must necessarily be as great a Disability as that of the Body, and much greater, Praying to God being properly an Act of the Mind, not of the Body.

But to go on; After I had thus secur'd one Part of my little living Stock, I went about the whole Island, searching for another private Place, to make such another Deposit; when wandring more to the *West* Point of the Island, than I had ever gone yet, and looking out to Sea, I thought I saw a Boat upon the Sea, at a great Distance; I had found a Prospective Glass[5] or two, in one of the Seamen's Chests, which I sav'd out of our Ship; but I had it not about me, and this was so remote, that I could not tell what to make of it; though I look'd at it till my eyes were not able to hold to look any longer; whether it was a Boat, or not, I do not know; but as I descended from the Hill, I could see no more of it, so I gave it over; only I resolv'd to go no more out without a Prospective Glass in my Pocket.

When I was come down the Hill, to the End of the Island, where indeed, I had never been before, I was presently convinc'd, that the seeing the Print of a Man's Foot, was not such a strange Thing in the Island as I imagin'd; and but that it was a special Providence that I was cast upon the Side of the Island, where the Savages never came: I should easily have known, that nothing was more frequent than for the *Canoes* from the Main, when they happen'd to be a little too far out at Sea, to shoot over to that Side of the Island for Harbour; likewise as they often met, and fought in their *Canoes*, the Victors having taken any Prisoners, would bring them over to this Shore, where according to their dreadful Customs, being all *Canibals*, they would kill and eat them; of which hereafter.

When I was come down the Hill, to the Shore, as I said above, being the S. W. Point of the Island, I was perfectly confounded and amaz'd; nor is it possible for me to express the Horror of my Mind, at seeing the Shore spread with Skulls, Hands, Feet, and other Bones of humane

5. Perspective glass or telescope.

Bodies; and particularly I observ'd a Place where there had been a Fire made, and a Circle dug in the Earth, like a Cockpit, where it is suppos'd the Savage Wretches had sat down to their inhumane Feastings upon the Bodies of their Fellow-Creatures.

I was so astonish'd with the Sight of these Things, that I entertain'd no Notions of any Danger to my self from it for a long while; All my Apprehensions were bury'd in the Thoughts of such a Pitch of inhuman, hellish Brutality, and the Horror of the Degeneracy of Humane Nature; which though I had heard of often, yet I never had so near a View of before; in short, I turn'd away my Face from the horrid Spectacle; my Stomach grew sick, and I was just at the Point of Fainting, when Nature discharg'd the Disorder from my Stomach, and having vomited with an uncommon Violence, I was a little reliev'd; but cou'd not bear to stay in the Place a Moment; so I got me up the Hill again, with all the Speed I cou'd, and walk'd on towards my own Habitation.

When I came a little out of that Part of the Island, I stood still a while as amaz'd; and then recovering my self, I looked up with the utmost Affection of my Soul, and with a Flood of Tears in my Eyes, gave God Thanks that had cast my first Lot in a Part of the World, where I was distinguish'd from such dreadful Creatures as these; and that though I had esteem'd my present Condition very miserable, had yet given me so many Comforts in it, that I had still more to give Thanks for than to complain of; and this above all, that I had even in this miserable Condition been comforted with the Knowledge of himself, and the Hope of his Blessing, which as a Felicity more than sufficiently equivalent to all the Misery which I had suffer'd, or could suffer.

In this Frame of Thankfulness, I went Home to my Castle, and began to be much easier now, as to the Safety of my Circumstances, than ever I was before; for I observ'd, that these Wretches never came to this Island in search of what they could get; perhaps not seeking, not wanting, or not expecting any Thing here; and having often, no doubt, been up in the cover'd woody Part of it, without finding any Thing to their Purpose. I knew I had been here now almost eighteen Years, and never saw the least Foot-steps of Humane Creature there before; and I might be here eighteen more, as entirely conceal'd as I was now, if I did not discover my self to them, which I had no manner of Occasion to do, it being my only Business to keep my self entirely conceal'd where I was, unless I found a better sort of Creatures than *Canibals* to make my self known to.

Yet I entertain'd such an Abhorrence of the Savage Wretches, that I have been speaking of, and of the wretched inhuman Custom of their devouring and eating one another up, that I continu'd pensive, and sad, and kept close within my own Circle for almost two Years after this: When I say my own Circle, I mean by it, my three Plantations, *viz.* my Castle, my Country Seat, which I call'd my Bower, and my Enclosure in the Woods; nor did I look after this for any other Use than as an Enclosure for my Goats; for the Aversion which Nature gave me to these hellish Wretches, was such, that I was fearful of seeing them, as of seeing the Devil himself; nor did I so much as go to look after my Boat, in all this Time; but began rather to think of making me another; for I cou'd not think of ever making any more Attempts, to bring the other Boat round the island to me, least I should meet with some of these Creatures at Sea, in which, if I had happen'd to have fallen into their Hands, I knew what would have been my Lot.

Time however, and the Satisfaction I had, that I was in no Danger of being discover'd by these People, began to wear off my Uneasiness about them; and I began to live just in the same compos'd Manner as before; only with this Difference, that I used more Caution, and kept my Eyes more about me than I did before, least I should happen to be seen by any of them; and particularly, I was more cautious of firing my Gun, least any of them being on the Island, should happen to hear of it: and it was therefore a very good Providence to me, that I had furnish'd my self with a tame Breed of Goats, and I needed not hunt any more about the Woods, or shoot at them; and if I did catch any of them after this, it was by Traps, and Snares, as I had done before; so that for two years after this, I believe I never fir'd my Gun once off, though I never went out without it; and which was more, as I had sav'd three Pistols out of the Ship, I always carry'd them out with me, or at least two of them, sticking them in my Goat-skin Belt; also I furbish'd up one of the great Cutlashes, that I had out of the Ship, and made me a Belt to put it on also; so that I was now a most formidable Fellow to look at, when I went abroad, if you add to the former Description of my self, the Particular of two Pistols, and a great broad Sword hanging at my Side in a Belt, but without a Scabbard.

Things going on thus, as I have said, for some Time; I seem'd, excepting these Cautions, to be reduc'd to my former calm, sedate Way of Living, all these Things tended to shewing me more and more how far my Condition was from being miserable, compar'd to some others; nay, to many other Particulars of Life, which it might have pleased God to have made my Lot. It put me upon reflecting, How little repining there would be among Mankind, at any Condition of Life, if People would rather compare their Condition with those that are worse, in order to be thankful, than be always comparing them with those which are better, to assist their Murmurings and Complainings.

As in my present Condition there were not really many Things which I wanted; so indeed I thought that the Frights I had been in about these Savage Wretches, and the Concern I had been in for my own Preservation, had taken off the Edge of my Invention for my own Conveniences; and I had dropp'd a good Design, which I had once bent my Thoughts too much upon; and that was, to try if I could not make some

of my Barley into Malt, and then try to brew my self some Beer: This
was really a whimsical Thought, and I reprov'd my self often for the
Simplicity[6] of it; for I presently saw there would be the want of several
Things necessary to the making my Beer, that it would be impossible
for me to supply; as First, Casks to preserve it in, which was a Thing,
that as I have observ'd already, I cou'd never compass; no, though I
spent not many Days, but Weeks, nay, Months, in attempting it, but
to no purpose. In the next Place, I had no Hops to make it keep, no
Yeast to make it work, no Copper or Kettle to make it boil; and yet all
these Things, notwithstanding, I verily believe, had not these Things
interven'd, I mean the Frights and Terrors I was in about the Savages,
I had undertaken it, and perhaps brought it to pass too; for I seldom
gave any Thing over without accomplishing it, when I once had it in
my Head enough to begin it.

But my Invention now run quite another Way; for Night and Day, I
could think of nothing but how I might destroy some of these Monsters
in their cruel bloody Entertainment, and if possible, save the Victim
they should bring hither to destroy. It would take up a larger Volume
than this whole Work is intended to be, to set down all the Contrivances
I hatch'd, or rather brooded upon in my Thought, for the destroying
these Creatures, or at least frightening them, so as to prevent their coming
hither any more; but all was abortive, nothing could be possible to take
effect, unless I was to be there to do it my self; and what could one
Man do among them, when perhaps there might be twenty or thirty of
them together, with their Darts, or their Bows and Arrows, with which
they could shoot as true to a Mark, as I could with my Gun?

Sometimes I contriv'd to dig a Hole under the Place where they made
their Fire, and put in five or six Pound of Gun-Powder, which when
they kindled their Fire, would consequently take Fire, and blow up all
that was near it: but as in the first place I should be very loth to wast
so much Powder upon them, my Store being now within the Quantity
of one Barrel; so neither could I be sure of its going off, at any certain
Time; when it might surprise them, and at best, that it would do little
more than just blow the Fire about their Ears and fright them, but not
sufficient to make them forsake the Place; so I laid it aside, and then
propos'd, that I would place my self in Ambush, in some convenient
Place, with my three Guns, all double loaded; and in the middle of
their bloody Ceremony, let fly at them, when I should be sure to kill
or wound perhaps two or three at ever shoot; and then falling in upon
them with my three Pistols, and my Sword, I made no doubt, but that
if there was twenty I should kill them all: This Fancy pleas'd my Thoughts
for some Weeks, and I was so full of it, that I often dream'd of it; and
sometimes that I was just going to let fly at them in my Sleep.

6. Naïveté.

I went so far with it in my Imagination, that I employ'd my self several Days to find out proper Places to put my self in Ambuscade, as I said, to watch for them; and I went frequently to the Place it self, which was now grown more familiar to me; and especially while my Mind was thus fill'd with Thoughts of Revenge, and of a bloody putting twenty or thirty of them to the Sword, as I may call it; the Horror I had at the Place, and at the Signals[7] of the barbarous Wretches devouring one another, abated[8] my Malice.

Well, at length I found a Place in the Side of the Hill, where I was satisfy'd I might securely wait, till I saw any of their Boats coming, and might then, even before they would be ready to come on Shore, convey my self unseen into Thickets of Trees, in one of which there was a Hollow large enough to conceal me entirely; and where I might sit and observe all their bloody Doings, and take my full aim at their Heads, when they were so close together, as that it would be next to impossible that I should miss my Shoot, or that I could fail wounding three or four of them at the first Shoot.

In this Place then I resolv'd to fix my Design, and accordingly I prepar'd two Muskets, and my ordinary Fowling Piece. The two Muskets I loaded with a Brace of Slugs each, and four or five smaller Bullets, about the Size of Pistol Bullets; and the Fowling Piece I loaded with near a Handful of Swan-shot, of the largest Size; I also loaded my Pistols with about four Bullets each, and in this Posture, well provided with Ammunition for a second and third Charge, I prepar'd my self for my Expedition.

After I had thus laid the Scheme of my Design, and in my Imagination put it in Practice, I continually made my Tour every Morning up to the Top of the Hill, which was from my Castle, as I call'd it, about three Miles, or more, to see if I cou'd observe any Boats upon the Sea, coming near the Island, or standing over towards it; but I began to tire of this hard Duty; after I had for two or three Months constantly kept my Watch; but came always back without any Discovery, there having not in all that Time been the least Appearance, not only on, or near the Shore; but not on the whole Ocean, so far as my Eyes or Glasses could reach every Way.

As long as I kept up my daily Tour to the Hill, to look out; so long also I kept up the Vigour of my Design, and my Spirits seem'd to be all the while in a suitable Form, for so outragious an Execution as the killing twenty or thirty naked Savages, for an Offence which I had not at all entred into a Discussion of in my Thoughts, any farther than my Passions were at first fir'd by the Horror I conceiv'd at the unnatural Custom of that People of the Country, who it seems had been suffer'd by Providence in his wise Disposition of the World, to have no other

7. Signs.
8. Abetted.

Guide than that of their own abominable and vitiated Passions; and consequently were left, and perhaps had been so for some Ages, to act such horrid Things, and receive such dreadful Customs, as nothing but Nature entirely abandon'd of Heaven, and acted[9] by some hellish Degeneracy, could have run them into: But now, when as I have said, I began to be weary of the fruitless Excursion, which I had made so long, and so far, every Morning in vain, so my Opinion of the Action it self began to alter, and I began with cooler and calmer Thoughts to consider what it was I was going to engage in. What Authority, or Call I had, to pretend to be Judge and Executioner upon these Men as Criminals, whom Heaven had thought fit for so many Ages to suffer unpunish'd, to go on, and to be as it were, the Executioners of his Judgments one upon another. How far these People were Offenders against me, and what Right I had to engage in the Quarrel of that Blood, which they shed promiscuously one upon another, I debated this very often with my self thus; How do I know what God himself judges in this particular Case; it is certain these People either do not commit this as a Crime; it is not against their own Consciences reproving, or their Light reproaching them. They do not know it be an Offence, and then commit it in Defiance of Divine Justice, as we do in almost all the Sins we commit, They think it no more a Crime to kill a Captive taken in War, than we do to kill an Ox; nor to eat humane Flesh, than we do to eat Mutton.

When I had consider'd this a little, it follow'd necessarily, that I was certainly in the Wrong in it, that these People were not Murtherers, in the Sense that I had before condemn'd them, in my Thoughts; any more than those Christians were Murtherers, who often put to Death the Prisoners taken in Battle; or more frequently, upon many Occasions, put whole Troops of Men to the Sword, without giving Quarter, though they threw down their Arms and submitted.

In the next Place it occurr'd to me, that albeit the Usage they thus gave one another, was thus brutish and inhumane; yet it was really nothing to me: These People had done me no Injury. That if they attempted me, or I saw it necessary for my immediate Preservation to fall upon them, something might be said for it; but that as I was yet out of their Power, and they had really no Knowledge of me, and consequently no Design upon me; and therefore it could not be just for me to fall upon them. That this would justify the Conduct of the *Spaniards* in all their Barbarities practis'd in *America*, where they destroy'd Millions of these People, who however they were Idolaters and Barbarians, and had several bloody and barbarous Rites in their Customs, such as sacrificing human Bodies to their Idols, were yet, as to the *Spaniards*, very innocent People; and that the rooting them out of the Country, is spoken of with the utmost Abhorrence and Detestation, by even the *Spaniards*

---

9. Actuated, moved to action.

themselves, at this Time; and by all other Christian Nations of *Europe*, as a meer Butchery, a bloody and unnatural Piece of Cruelty, unjustifiable either to God or Man; and such, as for which the very Name of a *Spaniard* is reckon'd to be frightful and terrible to all People of Humanity, or of Christian Compassion: As if the Kingdom of *Spain* were particularly Eminent for the Product of a Race of Men, who were without Principles of Tenderness, or the common Bowels of Pity to the Miserable, which is reckon'd to be a Mark of generous Temper in the Mind.

These Considerations really put me to a Pause, and to a kind of a Full-stop; and I began by little and little to be off of my Design, and to conclude, I had taken wrong Measures in my Resolutions to attack the Savages; that it was not my Business to meddle with them, unless they first attack'd me, and this it was my Business if possible to prevent; but that if I were discover'd, and attack'd, then I knew my Duty.

On the other hand, I argu'd with my self, That this really was the way not to deliver my self, but entirely to ruin and destroy my self; for unless I was sure to kill every one that not only should be on Shore at that Time, but that should ever come on Shore afterwards, if but one of them escap'd, to tell their Country People what had happen'd, they would come over again by Thousands to revenge the Death of their Fellows, and I should only bring upon my self a certain Destruction, which at present I had no manner of occasion for.

Upon the whole I concluded, That neither in Principle or[1] in Policy, I ought one way or other to concern my self in this Affair. That my Business was by all possible Means to conceal my self from them, and not to leave the least Signal to them to guess by, that there were any living Creatures upon the Island; I mean of humane Shape.

Religion joyn'd in with this Prudential,[2] and I was convinc'd now many Ways, that I was perfectly out of my Duty, when I was laying all my bloody Schemes for the Destruction of innocent Creatures, I mean innocent as to me: As to the Crimes they were guilty of towards one another, I had nothing to do with them; they were National, and I ought to leave them to the Justice of God, who is the Governor of Nations, and knows how by National Punishments to make a just Retribution for National Offences; and to bring publick Judgments upon those who offend in a publick Manner, by such Ways as best pleases him.

This appear'd so clear to me now, that nothing was a greater Satisfaction to me, than that I had not been suffer'd to do a Thing which I now saw so much Reason to believe would have been no less a Sin, than that of wilful Murther, if I had committed it; and I gave most humble Thanks on my Knees to God, that had thus deliver'd me from Blood-Guiltiness; beseeching him to grant me the Protection of his

1. Corrected to "nor" in the second and subsequent editions.
2. Worldly wisdom.

Providence, that I might not fall into the Hands of the Barbarians; or that I might not lay my Hands upon them, unless I had a more clear Call from Heaven to do it, in Defence of my own Life.

In this Disposition I continu'd, for near a Year after this; and so far was I from desiring an Occasion for falling upon these Wretches, that in all that Time, I never once went up the Hill to see whether there were any of them in Sight, or to know whether any of them had been on Shore there, or not, that I might not be tempted to renew any of my Contrivances against them, or be provok'd by any Advantage which might present it self, to fall upon them; only this I did, I went and remov'd my Boat, which I had on the other Side of the Island, and carry'd it down to the *East* End of the whole Island, where I ran it into a little Cove which I found under some high Rocks, and where I knew, by Reason of the Currents, the Savages durst not, at least would not come with their Boats, upon any Account whatsoever.

With my Boat I carry'd away every Thing that I had left there belonging to her, though not necessary for the bare going thither, *viz.* A Mast and Sail which I had made for her, and a Thing like an Anchor, but indeed which could not be call'd either Anchor or Grapling; however, it was the best I could make of its kind: All these I remov'd, that there might not be the least Shadow of any Discovery, or any Appearance of any Boat, or of any human Habitation upon the Island.

Besides this, I kept my self, as I said, more retir'd than ever, and seldom went from my Cell, other than upon my constant Employment, *viz.* To milk my She-goats, and manage my little Flock, in the Wood; which as it was quite on the other Part of the Island, was quite out of Danger; for certain it is, that these Savage People who sometimes haunted this Island, never came with any Thoughts of finding any Thing here; and consequently never wandred off from the Coast; and I doubt not, but they might have been several Times on Shore, after my Apprehensions of them had made me cautious as well as before; and indeed, I look'd back with some Horror upon the Thoughts of what my Condition would have been, if I had chop'd upon[3] them, and been discover'd before that, when naked[4] and unarm'd, except with one Gun, and that loaden often only with small Shot, I walk'd every where peeping, and peeping about the Island, to see what I could get; what a Surprise should I have been in, if when I discover'd the Print of a Man's Foot, I had instead of that, seen fifteen or twenty Savages, and found them pursuing me, and by the Swiftness of their Running, no Possibility of my escaping them.

The Thoughts of this sometimes sunk my very Soul within me, and distress'd my Mind so much, that I could not soon recover it, to think what I should have done, and how I not only should not have been

3. Chanced upon.
4. Defenseless.

able to resist them, but even should not have had Presence of Mind enough to do what I might have done; much less, what now after so much Consideration and Preparation I might be able to do: Indeed, after serious thinking of these Things, I should be very Melancholy; and sometimes it would last a great while; but I resolv'd it at last all into Thankfulness to that Providence, which had deliver'd me from so many unseen Dangers, and had kept me from those Mischiefs which I could no way have been the Agent in delivering my self from; because I had not the least Notion of any such Thing depending,[5] or the least Supposition of it being possible.

This renew'd a Contemplation, which often had come to my Thoughts in former Time, when first I began to see the merciful Dispositions of Heaven, in the Dangers we run through in this Life. How wonderfully we are deliver'd, when we know nothing of it. How when we are in (a *Quandary*, as we call it) a Doubt or Hesitation, whether to go this Way, or that Way, a secret Hint shall direct us this Way, when we intended to go that Way; nay, when Sense, our own Inclination, and perhaps Business has call'd to go the other Way, yet a strange Impression upon the Mind, from we know not what Springs, and by we know not what Power, shall over-rule us to go this Way; and it shall afterwards appear, that had we gone that Way which we should have gone, and even to our Imagination ought to have gone, we should have been ruin'd and lost: Upon these, and many like Reflections, I afterwards made it a certain Rule with me, That whenever I found those secret Hints, or pressings of my Mind, to doing, or not doing any Thing that presented; or to going this Way, or that Way, I never fail'd to obey the secret Dictate; though I knew no other Reason for it, than that such a Pressure, or such a Hint hung upon my Mind: I could give many Examples of the Success of this Conduct in the Course of my Life; but more especially in the latter Part of my inhabiting this unhappy Island; besides many Occasions which it is very likely I might have taken Notice of, if I had seen with the same Eyes then, that I saw with now: But 'tis never too late to be wise; and I cannot but advise all considering Men, whose Lives are attended with such extraordinary Incidents as mine, or even though not so extraordinary, not to slight such secret Intimations of Providence, let them come from what invisible Intelligence they will, that[6] I shall not discuss, and perhaps cannot account for; but certainly they are a Proof of the Converse of Spirits, and the secret Communication between those embody'd, and those unembody'd; and such a Proof as can never be withstood: Of which I shall have Occasion to give some very remarkable Instances, in the Remainder of my solitary Residence in this dismal Place.

5. Impending.
6. Defoe's confusing syntax requires the reader to either regard "that" as a relative pronoun equivalent to *which* or to start a new sentence using "that" as a demonstrative pronoun.

I believe the Reader of this will not think strange, if I confess that these Anxieties, these constant Dangers I liv'd in, and the Concern that was now upon me, put an End to all Invention, and to all the Contrivances that I had laid for my future Accommodations and Conveniencies. I had the Care of my Safety more now than upon my Hands, than that of my Food. I car'd not to drive a Nail, or chop a Stick of Wood now, for fear the Noise I should make should be heard; much less would I fire a Gun, for the same Reason; and above all, I was intollerably uneasy at making any Fire, least the Smoke which is visible at a great Distance in the Day should betray me; and for this Reason I remov'd that Part of my Business which requir'd Fire; such as burning of Pots, and Pipes, *etc.* into my new Apartment in the Woods, where after I had been some time, I found to my unspeakable Consolation, a meer natural Cave in the Earth, which went in a vast way, and where, I dare say, no Savage, had he been at the Mouth of it, would be so hardy as to venture in, nor indeed, would any Man else; but one who like me, wanted nothing so much as a safe Retreat.

The Mouth of this Hollow, was at the Bottom of a great Rock, where by meer accident, (I would say, if I did not see abundant Reason to ascribe all such Things now to Providence) I was cutting down some thick Branches of Trees, to make Charcoal; and before I go on, I must observe the Reason of my making this Charcoal; which was thus:

I was afraid of making a Smoke about my Habitation, as I said before; and yet I could not live there without baking my Bread, cooking my Meat, *etc.* so I contriv'd to burn some Wood here, as I had seen done in *England*, under the Turf, till it became Chark, or dry Coal; and then putting the Fire out, I preserv'd the Coal to carrry Home; and perform the other Services which Fire was wanting for at Home without Danger of Smoke.

But this is by the by: While I was cutting down some Wood here, I perceiv'd that behind a very thick Branch of low Brushwood, or Underwood, there was a kind of hollow Place; I was curious to look into it, and getting with Difficulty into the Mouth of it, I found it was pretty large; that is to say, sufficient for me to stand upright in it, and perhaps another with me; but I must confess to you, I made more hast out than I did in, when looking farther into the Place, and which was perfectly dark, I saw two broad shining Eyes of some Creature, whether Devil or Man I knew not, which twinkl'd like two Stars, the dim Light from the Cave's Mouth shining directly in and making the Reflection.

However, after some Pause, I recover'd my self, and began to call my self a thousand Fools, and tell my self, that he that was afraid to see the Devil, was not fit to live twenty Years in an Island all alone; and that I durst to believe there was nothing in this Cave that was more frightful than my self; upon this, plucking up my Courage, I took up a great Firebrand, and in I rush'd again, with the Stick flaming in my

Hand; I had not gone three Steps in, but I was almost as much frighted as I was before; for I heard a very loud Sigh, like that of a Man in some Pain, and it was follow'd by a broken Noise, *as if* of Words half express'd, and then a deep Sigh again: I stepp'd back, and was indeed struck with such a Surprize, that it put me into a cold Sweat; and if I had had a Hat on my Head, I will not answer for it, that my Hair might not have lifted it off. But still plucking up my Spirits as well as I could, and encouraging my self a little with considering that the Power and Presence of God was every where, and was able to protect me; upon this I stepp'd forward again, and by the Light of the Firebrand, holding it up a little over my Head, I saw lying on the Ground a most monstrous frightful old He-goat, just making his Will, as we say, and gasping for Life, and dying indeed of meer old Age.

I stirr'd him a little to see if I could get him out, and he essay'd to get up, but was not able to raise himself; and I thought with my self, he might even lie there; for if he had frighted me so, he would certainly fright any of the Savages, if any of them should be so hardy as to come in there, while he had any Life in him.

I was not recover'd from my Surprise, and began to look round me, when I found the Cave as but very small, that is to say, it might be about twelve Foot over, but in no manner of Shape, either round or square, no Hands having ever been employ'd in making it, but those of meer Nature: I observ'd also, that there was a Place at the farther Side of it, that went in farther, but was so low, that it requir'd me to creep upon my Hands and Knees to go into it, and whither I went I knew not; so having no Candle, I gave it over for some Time; but resolv'd to come again the next Day, provided with Candles, and a Tinder-box, which I had made of the Lock of one of the Muskets, with some wild-fire[7] in the Pan.

Accordingly the next Day, I came provided with six large Candles of my own making; for I made very good Candles now of Goat's Tallow; and going into this low Place, I was oblig'd to creep upon all Fours, *as I have said*, almost ten Yards; which by the way, I thought was a Venture bold enough, considering that I knew not how far it might go, nor what was beyond it. When I was got through the Strait, I found the Roof rose higher up, I believe near twenty Foot; but never was such a glorious Sight seen in the Island, I dare say, as it was, to look around the Sides and Roof of this Vault, or Cave; the Walls reflected 100 thousand Lights to me from my two Candles; what it was in the Rock, whether Diamonds, or any other precious Stones, or Gold, which I rather suppos'd it to be, I knew not.

The Place I was in, was a most delightful Cavity, or Grotto, of its kind, as could be expected, though perfectly dark; the Floor was dry and

7. A highly combustible substance containing gunpowder.

level, and had a sort of small loose Gravel upon it, so that there was
no nauseous or venomous Creature to be seen, neither was there any
damp, or wet, on the Sides or Roof: The only Difficulty in it was the
Entrance, which however as it was a Place of Security, and such a
Retreat as I wanted, I thought that was a Convenience; so that I was
really rejoyc'd at the Discovery, and resolv'd without any Delay, to bring
some of those Things which I was most anxious about, to this Place;
particularly, I resolv'd to bring hither my Magazine of Powder, and all
my spare Arms, *viz.* Two Fowling-Pieces, for I had three in all; and
three Muskets, for of them I had eight in all; so I kept at my Castle only
five, which stood ready mounted like Pieces of Cannon, on my out-
most Fence; and were ready also to take out upon any Expedition.

Upon this Occasion of removing my Ammunition, I took occasion
to open the Barrel of Powder which I took up out of the Sea, and which
had been wet; and I found that the Water had penetrated about three
or four Inches into the Powder, on every Side, which caking and growing
hard, had preserv'd the inside like a Kernel in a Shell; so that I had near
sixty Pound of very good Powder in the Center of the Cask, and this
was an agreeable Discovery to me at that Time; so I carry'd all away
thither, never keeping above two or three Pound of Powder with me in
my Castle, for fear of a Surprize of any kind: I also carried thither all
the Lead I had left for Bullets.

I fancy'd my self now like one of the ancient Giants, which are said
to live in Caves, and Holes, in the Rocks, where none could come at
them; for I perswaded my self while I was here, if five hundred Savages
were to hunt me, they could never find me out; or if they did, they
would not venture to attack me here.

The old Goat who I found expiring, dy'd in the Mouth of the Cave,
the next Day after I made this Discovery; and I found it much easier to
dig a great Hole there, and throw him in, and cover him with Earth,
than to drag him out; so I interr'd him there, to prevent the Offence to
my Nose.

I was now in my twenty third Year of Residence in this Island, and
was so naturaliz'd to the Place, and to the Manner of Living, that could
I have but enjoy'd the Certainty that no Savages would come to the
Place to disturb me, I could have been content to have capitulated for
spending the rest of my Time there, even to the last Moment, till I had
laid me down and dy'd, like the old Goat in the Cave. I had also arriv'd
to some little Diversions and Amusements, which made the Time pass
more pleasantly with me a great deal, than it did before; as First, I had
taught my Poll, as I noted before, to speak; and he did it so familiarly,
and talk'd so articulately and plain, that it was very pleasant to me; and
he liv'd with me no less than six and twenty Years: How long he might
live afterwards, I know not; though I know they have a Notion in the
Brasils, that they live a hundred Years; perhaps poor Poll may be alive

there still, calling after *Poor Robin Crusoe* to this Day, I wish no *English* Man the ill Luck to come there and hear him; but if he did, he would certainly believe it was the Devil. My Dog was a very pleasant and loving Companion to me, for no less than sixteen Years of my Time, and then dy'd, of meer old Age; as for my Cats, they multiply'd as I have observ'd to that Degree, that I was oblig'd to shoot several of them at first, to keep them from devouring me, and all I had; but at length, when the two old Ones I had brought with me were gone, and after some time continually driving them from me, and letting them have no Provision with me, they all ran wild into the Woods, except two or three Favourites, which I kept tame; and whose Young when they had any, I always drown'd; and these were part of my Family: Besides these, I always kept two or three household Kids about me, who I taught to feed out of my Hand; and I had two more Parrots which talk'd pretty well, and would all call *Robin Crusoe*; but none like my first; nor indeed did I take the Pains with any of them that I had done with him. I had also several tame Sea-Fowls, whose Names I know not, who I caught upon the Shore, and cut their Wings; and the little Stakes which I had planted before my Castle Wall being now grown up to a good thick Grove, these Fowls all liv'd among these low Trees, and bred there, which was very agreeable to me; so that as I said above, I began to be very well contented with the Life I led, if it might but have been secur'd from the dread of the Savages.

But it was otherwise directed; and it may not be amiss for all People who shall meet with my Story, to make this just Observation from it, *viz.* How frequently in the Course of our Lives, the Evil which in it self we seek most to shun, and which when we are fallen into it, is the most dreadful to us, is oftentimes the very Means or Door of our Deliverance, by which alone we can be rais'd again from the Affliction we are fallen into. I cou'd give many Examples of this in the Course of my unaccountable Life; but in nothing was it more particularly remarkable, than in the Circumstances of my last Years of solitary Residence in this Island.

It was now the Month of *December*, as I said above, in my twenty third Year; and this being the *Southern* Solstice, for Winter I cannot call it, was the Particular Time of my Harvest, and requir'd my being pretty much abroad in the Fields, when going out pretty early in the Morning, even before it was thorow Daylight, I was surpriz'd with seeing a Light of some Fire upon the Shore, at a Distance from me, of about two Mile towards the End of the Island, where I had observ'd some Savages had been as before; but not on the other Side; but to my great Affliction, it was on my Side of the Island.

I was indeed terribly surpriz'd at the Sight, and stepp'd[8] short within

---

8. A probable printer's error for *stopp'd*, although all the 1719 editions read "stepp'd" or "step'd."

my Grove, not daring to go out, least I might be surpriz'd; and yet I had no more Peace within, from the Apprehensions I had, that if these Savages in rambling over the Island, should find my Corn standing, or cut, or any of my Works and Improvements, they would immediately conclude, that there were People in the Place, and would then never give over till they had found me out: In this Extremity I went back directly to my Castle, pull'd up the Ladder after me, and made all Things without look as wild and natural as I could.

Then I prepar'd my self within, putting my self in a Posture of Defence; I loaded all my Cannon, as I call'd them; that is to say, my Muskets, which were mounted upon my new Fortification, and all my Pistols, and resolv'd to defend my self to the last Gasp, not forgetting seriously to commend my self to the Divine Protection, and earnestly to pray to God to deliver me out of the Hands of the Barbarians; and in this Posture I continu'd about two Hours; but began to be mighty impatient for Intelligence abroad, for I had no Spies to send out.

After sitting a while longer, and musing what I should do in this Case, I was not able to bear sitting in Ignorance any longer; so setting up my Ladder to the Side of the Hill, where there was a flat Place, as I observ'd before, and then pulling the Ladder up after me, I set it up again, and mounted to the Top of the Hill; and pulling out my Perspective Glass, which I had taken on Purpose, I laid me down flat on my Belly, on the Ground, and began to look for the Place; I presently found there was no less than nine naked Savages, sitting round a small Fire, they had made, not to warm them; for they had no need of that, the Weather being extreme hot; but as I suppos'd, to dress some of their barbarous Diet, of humane Flesh, which they had brought with them, whether alive or dead I could not know.

They had two *Canoes* with them, which they had haled up upon the Shore; and as it was then Tide of Ebb, they seem'd to me to wait for the Return of the Flood, to go away again; it is not easy to imagine what Confusion this Sight put me into, especially seeing them come on my Side the Island, and so near me too; but when I observ'd their coming must always be with the Current of the Ebb, I began afterwards to be more sedate in my Mind, being satisfy'd that I might go abroad with Safety all the Time of the Tide of Flood, if they were not on Shore before: And having made this Observation, I went abroad about my Harvest Work with the more Composure.

As I expected, so it proved; for as soon as the Tide made to the *Westward*, I saw them all take Boat, and row (or paddle as we call it) all away: I should have observ'd, that for an Hour and more before they went off, they went to dancing, and I could easily discern their Postures, and Gestures, by my Glasses: I could not perceive by my nicest Observation, but that they were stark naked, and had not the least covering upon them; but whether they were Men or Women, that I could not distinguish.

As soon as I saw them shipp'd, and gone, I took two Guns upon my Shoulders, and two Pistols at my Girdle, and my great Sword by my Side, without a Scabbard, and with all the Speed I was able to make, I went away to the Hill, where I had discover'd the first Appearance of all; and as soon as I gat thither, which was not less than two Hours (for I could not go apace, being so loaden with Arms as I was) I perceiv'd there had been three *Canoes* more of Savages on that Place; and looking out farther, I saw they were all at Sea together, making over for the Main.

This was a dreadful Sight to me, especially when going down to the Shore, I could see the marks of Horror, which the dismal Work they had been about had left behind it, *viz.* The Blood, the Bones, and part of the Flesh of humane Bodies, eaten and devour'd by those Wretches, with Merriment and Sport; I was so fill'd with Indignation at the Sight, that I began now to premeditate the Destruction of the next that I saw there, let them be who, or how many soever.

It seem'd evident to me, that the Visits which they thus make to this Island, are not very frequent; for it was above fifteen Months before any more of them came on Shore there again; that is to say, I neither saw them, or any Footsteps, or Signals of them, in all that Time; for as to the rainy Seasons, then they are sure not to come abroad, at least not so far; yet all this while I liv'd uncomfortably, by reason of the constant Apprehensions I was in of their coming upon me by Surprize; from whence I observe, that the Expectation of Evil is more bitter than the Suffering, especially, if there is no room to shake off that Expectation, or those Apprehensions.

During all this Time, I was in the murthering Humour; and took up most of my Hours, which should have been better employ'd, in contriving how to circumvent, and fall upon them, the very next Time I should see them; especially if they should be divided, as they were the last Time, into two Parties; nor did I consider at all, that if I kill'd one Party, suppose Ten, or a Dozen, I was still the next Day, or Week, or Month, to kill another, and so another, even *ad infinitum*, till I should be at length no less a Murtherer than they were in being Man-eaters; and perhaps much more so.

I spent my Days now in great Perplexity, and Anxiety of Mind, expecting that I should one Day or other fall into the Hands of these merciless Creatures; and if I did at any Time venture abroad, it was not without looking round me with the greatest Care and Caution imaginable; and now I found to my great Comfort, how happy it was that I provided for a tame Flock or Herd of Goats; for I durst not upon any account fire my Gun, especially near that Side of the Island where they usually came, least I should alarm the Savages; and if they had fled from me now, I was sure to have them come back again, with perhaps two or three hundred *Canoes* with them, in a few Days, and then I knew what to expect.

However, I wore out a Year and three Months more, before I ever saw any more of the Savages, and then I found them again, as I shall soon observe. It is true, they might have been there once, or twice; but either they made no stay, or at least I did not hear them; but in the Month of *May*, as near as I could calculate, and in my four and twentieth Year, I had a very strange Encounter with them, of which in its Place.

The Perturbation of my Mind, during this fifteen or sixteen Months Interval, was very great; I slept unquiet, dream'd always frightful Dreams, and often started out of my Sleep in the Night: In the Day great Troubles overwhelm'd my Mind, and in the Night I dream'd often of killing the Savages, and of the Reasons why I might justify the doing of it: but to wave all this for a while; it was in the middle of *May*, on the sixteenth Day I think, as well as my poor wooden Calendar would reckon; for I markt all upon the Post still; I say, it was the sixteenth of *May*, that it blew a very great Storm of Wind, all Day, with a great deal of Lightning, and Thunder, and a very foul Night it was after it; I know not what was the particular Occasion of it; but as I was reading in the Bible, and taken up with very serious Thoughts about my present Condition, I was sur-priz'd with a Noise of a Gun as I thought fir'd at Sea.

This was to be sure a Surprize of a quite different Nature from any I had met with before; for the Notions this put into my Thoughts, were quite of another kind. I started up in the greatest haste imaginable, and in a trice clapt my Ladder to the middle Place of the Rock, and pull'd it after me, and mounting it the second Time, got to the Top of the Hill, the very Moment, that a Flash of Fire bid me listen for a second Gun, which accordingly, in about half a Minute I heard; and by the sound, knew that it was from that Part of the Sea where I was driven down the Current in my Boat.

I immediately consider'd that this must be some Ship in Distress, and that they had some Comrade, or some other Ship in Company, and fir'd these Guns for Signals of Distress, and to obtain Help: I had this Presence of Mind at that Minute, as to think that though I could not help them, it may be they might help me; so I brought together all the dry Wood I could get at hand, and making a good handsome Pile, I set it on Fire upon the Hill; the Wood was dry, and blaz'd freely; and though the Wind blew very hard, yet it burnt fairly out; that I was certain, if there was any such Thing as a Ship, they must needs see it, and no doubt they did; for as soon as ever my Fire blaz'd up, I heard another Gun, and after that several others, all from the same Quarter; I ply'd my Fire all Night long, till Day broke; and when it was broad Day, and the Air clear'd up, I saw something at a great Distance at Sea, full *East* of the Island, whether a Sail, or a Hull, I could not distinguish, no not with my Glasses, the Distance was so great, and the Weather still some-thing haizy also; at least it was so out at Sea.

I look'd frequently at it all that Day, and soon perceiv'd that it did not move; so I presently concluded, that it was a Ship at an Anchor, and being eager, you may be sure, to be satisfy'd, I took my Gun in my Hand, and run toward the *South* Side of the Island, to the Rocks where I had formerly been carry'd away with the Current, and getting up there, the Weather by this Time being perfectly clear, I could plainly see to my great Sorrow, the Wreck of a Ship cast away in the Night, upon those concealed Rocks which I found, when I was out in my Boat; and which Rocks, as they check'd the Violence of the Stream, and made a kind of Counter-stream, or Eddy, were the Occasion of my recovering from the most desperate hopeless Condition that ever I had been in, in all my Life.

Thus what is one Man's Safety, is another Man's Destruction; for it seems these Men, whoever they were, being out of their Knowledge, and the Rocks being wholly under Water, had been driven upon them in the Night, the Wind blowing hard at *E.* and *E.N.E.*: Had they seen the Island, as I must necessarily suppose they did not, they must, as I thought have endeavour'd to have sav'd themselves on Shore by the Help of their Boat; but their firing of Guns for Help, especially when they saw, as I imagin'd, my Fire, fill'd me with many Thoughts: First, I imagin'd that upon seeing my Light, they might have put themselves into their Boat, and have endeavour'd to make the Shore; but that the Sea going very high, they might have been cast away; other Times I imagin'd, that they might have lost their Boat before, as might be the Case many Ways; as particularly by the Breaking of the Sea upon their Ship, which many Times obliges Men to stave, or take in Pieces their Boat; and sometimes to throw it over-board with their own Hands: Other Times I imagin'd, they had some other Ship, or Ships in Company, who upon the Signals of Distress they had made, had taken them up, and carry'd them off: Other whiles I fancy'd, they were all gone off to Sea in their Boat, and being hurry'd away by the Current that I had been formerly in, were carry'd out into the great Ocean, where there was nothing but Misery and Perishing; and that perhaps they might by this Time think of starving, and of being in a Condition to eat one another.

As all these were but Conjectures at best; so in the Condition I was in, I could do no more than look upon the Misery of the poor Men, and pity them, which had still this good Effect on my Side that it gave me more and more Cause to give Thanks to God who had so happily and comfortably provided for me in my desolate Condition; and that of two Ships Companies who were now cast away upon this part of the World, not one Life should be spar'd but mine: I learn'd here again to observe, that it is very rare that the Providence of God casts us into any Condition of Life so low, or any Misery so great, but we may see something or other to be thankful for; and may see others in worse Circumstances than our own.

Such certainly was the Case of these Men, of whom I could not so much as see room to suppose any of them were sav'd; nothing could make it rational, so much as to wish, or expect that they did not all perish there; except the Possibility only of their being taken up by another Ship in Company, and this was but meer Possibility indeed; for I saw not the least Signal or Appearance of any such Thing.

I cannot explain by any possible Energy of Words what a strange longing or hankering of Desires I felt in my Soul upon this Sight; breaking out sometimes thus; O that there had been but one or two; nay, or but one Soul sav'd out of this Ship, to have escap'd to me, that I might but have had one Companion, one Fellow-Creature to have spoken to me, and to have convers'd with! In all the Time of my solitary Life, I never felt so earnest, so strong a Desire after the Society of my Fellow-Creatures, or so deep a Regret at the want of it.

There are some secret moving Springs in the Affections,[9] which when they are set a going by some Object in view; or be it some Object, though not in view, yet rendered present to the Mind by the Power of Imagination, that Motion[1] carries out the Soul by its Impetuosity to such violent eager embracings of the Object, that the Absence of it is insupportable.

Such were these earnest Wishings, That but one Man had been sav'd! *O that it had been but One!* I believe I repeated the Words, *O that it had been but One!* a thousand Times; and the Desires were so mov'd by it, that when I spoke the Words, my Hands would clinch together, and my Fingers press the Palms of my Hands, that if I had had any soft Thing in my Hand, it would have crusht it involuntarily; and my Teeth in my Head wou'd strike together, and set against one another so strong, that for some time I cou'd not part them again.

Let the Naturalists[2] explain these Things, and the Reason and Manner of them; all I can say to them, is, to describe the Fact, which was even surprising to me when I found it; though I knew not from what it should proceed; it was doubtless the effect of ardent Wishes, and of strong Ideas form'd in my Mind, realizing the Comfort, which the Conversation of one of my Fellow-Christians would have been to me.

But it was not to be; either their Fate or mine, or both, forbid it; for till the last Year of my being on this Island, I never knew whether any were saved out of that Ship or no; and had only the Affliction some Days after, to see the Corps of a drownded[3] boy come on Shore, at the End of the Island which was next the Shipwreck: He had on no Cloaths, but a Seamen's Wastcoat, a pair of open knee'd Linnen Drawers, and a blew[4] Linnen Shirt; but nothing to direct me so much as to guess what

9. Emotions or feelings.
1. Emotional longing or craving.
2. Believers in the doctrine that all phenomena have natural causes and explanations, not supernatural or spiritual ones.
3. Changed to "drown'd" in the second and subsequent editions.
4. Changed to "blue" in the third and fifth editions.

Nation he was of: He had nothing in his Pocket, but two Pieces of Eight, and a Tobacco-Pipe; the last was to me of ten times more value than the first.

It was now calm, and I had a great mind to venture out in my Boat, to this Wreck; not doubting but I might find something on board, that might be useful to me; but that did not altogether press me so much, as the Possibility that there might be yet some living Creature on board, whose Life I might not only save, but might by saving that Life, comfort my own to the last Degree; and this Thought clung so to my Heart, that I could not be quiet, Night or Day, but I must venture out in my Boat on board this Wreck; and committing the rest to God's Providence, I thought the Impression was so strong upon my Mind, that it could not be resisted, that it must come from some invisible Direction, and that I should be wanting to my self if I did not go.

Under the Power of this Impression, I hasten'd back to my Castle, prepar'd every Thing for my Voyage, took a Quantity of Bread, a great Pot for fresh Water, a Compass to steer by, a Bottle of Rum; for I had still a great deal of that left; a Basket full of Raisins: And thus loading my self with every Thing necessary; I went down to my Boat, got the Water out of her, and got her afloat, loaded all my Cargo in her, and then went Home again for more; my second Cargo was a great Bag full of Rice, the Umbrella to set up over my Head for Shade; another large Pot full of fresh Water, and about two Dozen of my small Loaves, or Barley Cakes, more than before, with a Bottle of Goat's-Milk, and a Cheese; all which, with great Labour and Sweat, I brought to my Boat; and praying to God to direct my Voyage, I put out, and Rowing or Padling the Canoe along the Shore, I came at last to the utmost Point of the Island on that Side, (*viz.*) N.E. And now I was to launch out into the Ocean, and either to venture, or not to venture. I look'd on the rapid Currents which ran constantly on both Sides of the Island, at a Distance, and which were very terrible to me, from the Remembrance of the Hazard I had been in before, and my Heart began to fail me; for I foresaw that if I was driven into either of those Currents, I should be carry'd a vast Way out to Sea, and perhaps out of my Reach, or Sight of the Island again; and that then, as my Boat was but small, if any little Gale of Wind should rise, I should be inevitably lost.

These Thoughts so oppress'd my Mind, that I began to give over my Enterprize, and having haled my Boat into a little Creek on the Shore, I stept out, and sat me down upon a little rising bit of Ground, very pensive and anxious, between Fear and Desire about my Voyage; when as I was musing, I could perceive that the Tide was turn'd, and the Flood come on, upon which my going was for so many Hours impracticable; upon this presently it occur'd to me, that I should go up to the highest Piece of Ground I could find, and observe, if I could, how the Sets of the Tide, or Currents lay, when the Flood came in, that I might judge whether if I was driven one way out, I might not expect to be driven another way home, with the same Rapidness of the Currents: This Thought was no sooner in my Head, but I cast my Eye upon a little Hill, which sufficiently over-look'd the Sea both ways, and from whence I had a clear view of the Currents, or Sets of the Tide, and which way I was to guide my self in my Return; here I found, that as the Current of the Ebb set out close by the South Point of the Island; so the Current of the Flood set in close by the Shore of the North Side, and that I had nothing to do but to keep to the North of the Island in my Return, and I should do well enough.

Encourag'd with this Observation, I resolv'd the Next Morning to set out with the first of the Tide; and reposing my self for the Night in the Canoe, under the great Watch-coat, I mention'd, I launched out: I made first a little out to Sea full North, till I began to feel the Benefit of the Current, which set Eastward, and which carry'd me at a great rate, and yet did not so hurry me as the Southern Side Current had done before, and so as to take from me all Government of the Boat; but having a strong Steerage with my Paddle, I went at a great rate, directly for the Wreck, and in less than two Hours I came up to it.

It was a dismal Sight to look at: The Ship, which by its building was *Spanish*, stuck fast, jaum'd in between two Rocks; all the Stern and Quarter of her was beaten to Pieces with the Sea; and as her Forecastle, which stuck in the Rocks, had run on with great Violence, her Mainmast and Foremast were brought by the Board; that is to say, broken short off; but her Boltsprit[5] was sound and the Head and Bow appear'd firm; when I came close to her, a Dog appear'd upon her, who seeing me coming, yelp'd, and cry'd; and as soon as I call'd him, jump'd into the sea, to come to me, and I took him into the Boat; but found him almost dead for Hunger and Thirst: I gave him a Cake of my Bread, and he eat it like a ravenous Wolf, that had been starving a Fortnight in the Snow: I then gave the poor Creature some fresh Water, with which, if I would have let him he would have burst himself.

After this I went on board; but the first Sight I met with, was two Men drown'd, in the Cook-room, or Forecastle of the Ship, with their Arms fast about one another: I concluded, as is indeed probable, that when the Ship struck, it being in a Storm, the Sea broke so high, and so continually over her, that the Men were not able to bear it, and were strangled with the constant rushing in of the Water, as much as if they had been under Water. Besides the Dog, there was nothing left in the Ship that had life; nor any Goods that I could see, but what were spoil'd by the Water. There were some Casks of Liquor, whether Wine or Brandy, I knew not, which lay lower in the Hold; and which, the Water being ebb'd out, I could see; but they were too big to meddle with: I saw several Chests, which I believ'd belong'd to some of the Seamen;

5. Bowsprit.

and I got two of them into the Boat, without examining what was in them.

Had the Stern of the Ship been fix'd, and the Forepart broken off, I am perswaded I might have made a good Voyage; for by what I found in these two Chests, I had room to suppose, the Ship had a great deal of Wealth on board; and if I may guess by the course she steer'd, she must have been bound from the *Buenos Ayres*, or the *Rio de la Plata*, in the South Part of *America*, beyond the *Brasils*, to the *Havana*, in the Gulph of *Mexico*, and so perhaps to *Spain*: She had no doubt a great Treasure in her; but of no Use at that Time to any Body; and what became of the rest of her People, I then knew not.

I found besides these Chests, a little Cask full of Liquor, of about twenty Gallons, which I got into my Boat, with much Difficulty; there were several Muskets in a Cabin, and a great Powderhorn, with about 4 Pounds of Powder in it; as for the Muskets I had no occasion for them; so I left them, but took the Powderhorn: I took a Fire Shovel and Tongs, which I wanted extremely; as also two little Brass Kettles, a Copper Pot to make Chocolate, and a Gridiron; and with this Cargo, and the Dog, I came away, the Tide beginning to make home again; and the same Evening, about an Hour within Night, I reach'd the Island again, weary and fatigue'd to the last Degree.

I repos'd that Night in the Boat, and in the Morning I resolved to harbour what I had gotten in my new Cave, not to carry it home to my Castle. After refreshing my self, I got all my Cargo on Shore, and began to examine the Particulars: The Cask of Liquor I found to be a kind of Rum, but not such as we had at the *Brasils*; and in a Word, not at all good; but when I came to open the Chests, I found several Things, of great Use to me: For Example, I found in one, a fine Case of Bottles, of an extraordinary kind, and fill'd with Cordial Waters, fine, and very good; the Bottles held about three Pints each, and were tipp'd with Silver: I found two Pots of very good Succades,[6] or Sweetmeats, so fastned also on top, that the Salt Water had not hurt them; and two more of the same, which the Water had spoil'd: I found some very good Shirts, which were very welcome to me; and about a dozen and half of Linnen white Handkerchiefs, and colour'd Neckcloths; the former were also very welcome, being exceeding refreshing to wipe my Face in a hot Day; besides this, when I came to the Till in the Chest, I found there three great Bags of Pieces of Eight, which held about eleven hundred Pieces in all; and in one of them, wrapt up in a Paper, six Doubloons[7] of Gold, and some small Bars or Wedges of Gold; I suppose they might all weigh near a Pound.

The other Chest I found had some Cloaths in it, but of little Value; but by the Circumstances it must have belong'd to the Gunner's Mate;

6. Candied fruit.
7. Spanish gold coins.

though there was no Powder in it; but about two Pound of fine glaz'd Powder, in three small Flasks, kept, I suppose, for charging their Fowling-Pieces on occasion: Upon the whole, I got very little by this Voyage, that was of any use to me; for as to the Money, I had no manner of occasion for it: 'Twas to me as the Dirt under my Feet; and I would have given it all for three or four pair of *English* Shoes and Stockings, which were Things I greatly wanted, but had not had on my Feet now for many Years: I had indeed gotten two pair of Shoes now, which I took off of the Feet of the two drown'd Men, who I saw in the Wreck; and I found two pair more in one of the Chests, which were very welcome to me; but they were not like our *English* Shoes, either for Ease, or Service; being rather what we call Pumps, than Shoes: I found in this Seaman's Chest, about fifty Pieces of Eight in Royals,[8] but no Gold; I suppose this belong'd to a poorer Man than the other, which seem'd to belong to some Officer.

Well, however, I lugg'd this Money home to my Cave, and laid it up, as I had done that before which I brought from our own Ship; but it was great Pity as I said, that the other Part of this Ship had not come to my Share; for I am satisfy'd I might have loaded my *Canoe* several Times over with Money, which if I had ever escap'd to *England*, would have lain here safe enough, till I might have come again and fetch'd it.

Having now brought all my Things on Shore, and secur'd them, I went back to my Boat, and row'd, or paddled her along the Shore, to her old Harbour, where I laid her up, and made the best of my way to my old Habitation, where I found everything safe and quiet; so I began to repose my self, live after my old Fashion, and take care of my Family Affairs; and for a while, I liv'd easy enough; only that I was more vigilant than I us'd to be, look'd out oftner, and did not go abroad so much; and if at any time I did stir with any Freedom, it was always to the *East* Part of the Island, where I was pretty well satisfy'd the Savages never came, and where I could go without so many Precautions, and such a Load of Arms and Ammunition, as I always carry'd with me, if I went the other way.

I liv'd in this Condition near two Years more; but my unlucky Head, that was always to let me know it was born to make my Body miserable, was all this two Years fill'd with Projects and Designs, how, if it were possible, I might get away from this Island; for sometimes I was for making another Voyage to the Wreck, though my Reason told me that there was nothing left there, worth the Hazard of my Voyage; Sometimes for a Ramble one way, sometimes another; and I believe verily, if I had had the Boat that I went from *Sallee* in, I should have ventur'd to Sea, bound any where, I knew not whither.

I have been in all my Circumstances a *Memento*[9] to those who are

8. Spanish silver coins. (Misspelled "Ryals" in the first edition.)
9. An emblematic reminder and warning.

touched with the general Plague of Mankind, whence, for ought I know, one half of their Miseries flow; I mean, that of not being satisfy'd with the Station wherein God and Nature has plac'd them; for not to look back upon my primitive[1] Condition, and the excellent Advice of my Father, the Opposition to which, was, *as I may call it*, my ORIGINAL SIN; my subsequent Mistakes of the same Kind had been the Means of my coming into this miserable Condition; for had that Providence, which so happily had seated me at the *Brasils*, as a Planter, bless'd me with confin'd Desires, and I could have been contented to have gone on gradually, I might have been by this Time; *I mean, in the Time of my being in this Island*, one of the most considerable Planters in the *Brasils*, nay, I am perswaded, that by the Improvements I had made, in that little Time I liv'd there, and the Encrease I should probably have made, if I had stay'd, I might have been worth an hundred thousand *Moydors*;[2] and what Business had I to leave a settled Fortune, a well stock'd Plantation, improving and encreasing, to turn *Supra-Cargo* to *Guinea*, to fetch Negroes; when Patience and Time would have so encreas'd our Stock at Home, that we could have bought them at our own Door, from those whose Business it was to fetch them; and though it had cost us something more, yet the Difference of that Price was by no Means worth saving, at so great a Hazard.

But as this is ordinarily the Fate of young Heads, so Reflection upon the Folly of it, is as ordinarily the Exercise of more Years, or of the dear bought Experience of Time; and so it was with me now; and yet so deep had the Mistake taken root in my Temper, that I could not satisfy my self in my Station, but was continually poring upon the Means, and Possibility of my Escape from this Place; and that I may with the greater Pleasure to the Reader, bring on the remaining Part of my Story, it may not be improper, to give some Account of my first Conceptions on the Subject of this foolish Scheme for my Escape; and how, and upon what Foundation I acted.

I am now to be suppos'd retir'd into my Castle, after my late Voyage to the Wreck, my Frigate laid up, and secur'd under Water, as usual, and my Condition restor'd to what it was before: I had more Wealth indeed than I had before, but was not at all the richer; for I had no more use for it, than the *Indians of Peru* had, before the *Spaniards* came there.

It was one of the Nights in the rainy Season in *March*, the four and twentieth Year of my first setting Foot in this Island of Solitariness; I was lying in my bed, or Hammock, awake, very well in Health, had no Pain, no Distemper, no Uneasiness of Body; no, nor any Uneasiness of Mind, more than ordinary; but could by no means close my Eyes; that

1. Earlier, original.
2. *Moidores* were gold coins of Portugal and Brazil in circulation in the seventeenth and eighteenth centuries.

is, so as to sleep; no, not a Wink all Night long, otherwise than as follows:

It is as impossible, as needless, to set down the innumerable Crowd of Thoughts that whirl'd through that great thorow-fare of the Brain, the Memory, in this Night's Time: I ran over the whole History of My Life in Miniature, or by Abridgement, *as I may call it*, to my coming to this Island, and also of the Part of my Life, since I came to this Island. In my Reflections upon the State of my Case, since I came on Shore on this Island, I was comparing the happy Posture of my Affairs, in the first Years of my Habitation here, compar'd to the Life of Anxiety, Fear and Care, which I had liv'd ever since I had seen the Print of a Foot in the Sand; not that I did not believe the Savages had frequented the Island even all the while, and might have been several Hundreds of them at Times on Shore there; but I had never known it, and was incapable of any Apprehensions about it; my Satisfaction was perfect, though my Danger was the same; and I was as happy in not knowing my Danger, as if I had never really been expos'd to it: This furnish'd my Thoughts with many very profitable Reflections, and particularly this one, How infinitely Good that Providence is, which has provided in its Government of Mankind, such narrow bounds to his Sight and Knowledge of Things, and though he walks in the midst of so many thousand Dangers, the Sight of which, if discover'd to him, would distract his Mind, and sink his Spirits; he is kept serene, and calm, by having the Events of Things hid from his Eyes, and knowing nothing of the Dangers which surround him.

After these Thoughts had for some Time entertain'd[3] me, I came to reflect seriously upon the real Danger I had been in, for so many Years, in this very Island; and how I had walk'd about in the greatest Security, and with all possible Tranquillity; even when perhaps nothing but a Brow of a Hill, a great Tree, or the casual Approach of Night, had been between me and the worst kind of Destruction, *viz.* That of falling into the Hands of Cannibals, and Savages, who would have seiz'd on me with the same View, as I did of a Goat, or a Turtle; and have thought it no more a Crime to kill and devour me, than I did of a Pidgeon, or a Curlieu: I would unjustly slander my self, if I should say I was not sincerely thankful to my great Preserver, to whose singular Protection I acknowledg'd, with great Humility, that all these unknown Deliverances were due; and without which, I must inevitably have fallen into their merciless Hands.

When these Thoughts were over, my Head was for some time taken up in considering the Nature of these wretched Creatures; I mean, the Savages; and how it came to pass in the World, that the wise Governour of all Things should give up any of his Creatures to such Inhumanity;

3. Preoccupied.

nay, to something so much below, even Brutality itself, as to devour its own Kind; but as this ended in some (at that Time fruitless) Speculations, it occurr'd to me to enquire, what Part of the World these Wretches liv'd in; how far off the Coast was from whence they came; what they ventur'd over so far from home for; what kind of Boats they had; and why I might not order my self, and my Business so, that I might be as able to go over thither, as they were to come to me.

I never so much as troubl'd my self, to consider what I should do with my self, when I came thither; what would become of me, if I fell into the Hands of the Savages; or how I should escape from them, if they attempted[4] me; no, nor so much as how it was possible for me to reach the Coast, and not be attempted by some or other of them, without any Possibility of delivering my self; and if I should not fall into their Hands, what I should do for Provision, or whither I should bend my Course; none of these Thoughts, I say, so much as came in my way; but my mind was wholly bent upon the Notion of my passing over in my Boat, to the Main Land: I look'd back upon my present Condition, as the most miserable that could possibly be, that I was not able to throw my self into any thing but Death, that could be call'd worse; that if I reached the Shore of the Main,[5] I might perhaps meet with Relief, or I might coast along, as I did on the Shore of *Africk*, till I came to some inhabited Country, and where I might find some Relief; and after all perhaps, I might fall in with some Christian Ship, that might take me in; and if the worse came to the worst, I could but die, which would put an end to all these Miseries at once. Pray note, all this was the fruit of a disturb'd Mind, an impatient Temper, made as it were desperate by the long Continuance of my Troubles and the Disappointments I had met in the Wreck, I had been on board of; and where I had been so near the obtaining what I so earnestly long'd for, *viz.* Some-Body to speak to, and to learn some Knowledge from of the Place where I was, and of the probable Means of my Deliverance; I say, I was agitated wholly by these Thoughts: All my Calm of Mind in my Resignation to Providence, and waiting the Issue of the Dispositions of Heaven, seem'd to be suspended; and I had, as it were, no Power to turn my Thoughts to any thing, but to the Project of a Voyage to the Main, which came upon me with such Force, and such an Impetuosity of Desire, that it was not to be resisted.

When this had agitated my Thoughts for two Hours, or more, with such Violence, that it set my very Blood into a Ferment, and my Pulse beat as high as if I had been in a Feaver, meerly with the extraordinary Fervour of my Mind about it; Nature, as if I had been fatigued and exhausted with the very Thought of it, threw me into a sound Sleep; one would have thought, I should have dream'd of it: But I did not,

4. Tried to capture or kill.
5. Mainland.

nor of any Thing relating to it; but I dream'd, that as I was going out in the Morning as usual from my Castle, I saw upon the Shore, two *Canoes*, and eleven Savages coming to Land, and that they brought with them another Savage, who they were going to kill, in Order to eat him; when on a sudden, the Savage that they were going to kill, jumpt away, and ran for his Life; and I thought in my Sleep, that he came runing into my little thick Grove, before my Fortification, to hide himself; and that I seeing him alone, and not perceiving that the other sought him that Way, show'd my self to him, and smiling upon him, encourag'd him; that he kneel'd down to me, seeming to pray me to assist him; upon which I shew'd my Ladder, made him go up, and carry'd him into my Cave, and he became my Servant; and that as soon as I had gotten this Man, I said to my self, now I may certainly venture to the main Land; for this Fellow will serve me as a Pilot, and will tell me what to do, and whether[6] to go for Provisions; and whether not to go for fear of being devoured, what Places to venture into, and what to escape: I wak'd with this Thought, and was under such inexpressible Impressions of Joy, at the Prospect of my Escape in my Dream, that the Disappointments which I felt upon coming to my self, and finding it was no more than a Dream, were equally extravagant the other Way, and threw me into a very great Dejection of Spirit.

Upon this, however, I made this Conclusion, that my only Way to go about an Attempt for an Escape, was, if possible, to get a Savage into my Possession; and if possible, it should be one of their Prisoners, who they had condemn'd to be eaten, and should bring thither to kill; but these Thoughts still were attended with this Difficulty, that it was impossible to effect this, without attacking a whole Caravan of them, and killing them all; and this was not only a very desperate Attempt, and might miscarry; but on the other Hand, I had greatly scrupled the Lawfulness of it to me; and my Heart trembled at the thoughts of shedding so much Blood, tho' it was for my Deliverance. I need not repeat the Arguments which occurr'd to me against this, they being the same mention'd before; but tho' I had other Reasons to offer now (*viz.*) that those Men were Enemies to my Life, and would devour me, if they could; that it was Self-preservation in the highest Degree, to deliver my self from this Death of a Life, and was acting in my own Defence, as much as if they were actually assaulting me, and the like. I say, tho' these Things argued for it, yet the Thoughts of shedding Humane Blood for my Deliverance, were very Terrible to me, and such as I could by no Means reconcile my self to, a great while.

However, at last, after many secret Disputes with my self, and after great Perplexities about it, for all these Arguments one Way and another struggl'd in my Head a long Time, the eager prevailing Desire of Deliverance at length master'd all the rest; and I resolved, if possible, to

6. Whither.

get one of those Savages into my Hands, cost what it would. My next Thing then was to contrive how to do it, and this indeed was very difficult to resolve on: But as I could pitch upon no probable Means for it, so I resolv'd to put my self upon the Watch, to see them when they came on Shore, and leave the rest to the Event, taking such Measures as the Opportunity should present, let be what would be.

With these Resolutions in my Thoughts, I set my self upon the Scout, as often as possible, and indeed so often till I was heartily tir'd of it, for it was above a Year and a Half that I waited, and for great part of that Time went out to the *West* End, and to the *South West* Corner of the Island, almost every Day, to see for Canoes, but none appear'd. This was very discouraging, and began to trouble me much, tho' I cannot say that it did in this Case, as it had done some time before that, (*viz.*) wear off the Edge of my Desire to the Thing. But the longer it seem'd to be delay'd, the more eager I was for it; in a Word, I was not at first so careful to shun the sight of these Savages, and avoid being seen by them, as I was now eager to be upon them.

Besides, I fancied my self able to manage One, nay, Two or Three Savages, if I had them, so as to make them entirely Slaves to me, to do whatever I should direct them, and to prevent their being able at any time to do me any Hurt. It was a great while, that I pleas'd my self with this Affair, but nothing still presented; all my Fancies and Schemes came to nothing, for no Savages came near me for a great while.

About a Year and half after I had entertain'd these Notions, and by long musing, had as it were resolved them all into nothing, for want of an Occasion to put them in Execution, I was surpriz'd one Morning early, with seeing no less than five *Canoes* all on Shore together on my side the Island, and the People who belong'd to them all landed, and out of my sight: The Number of them broke all my Measures, for seeing so many, and knowing that they always came four or six, or sometimes more in a Boat, I could not tell what to think of it, or how to take my Measures, to attack Twenty or Thirty Men single handed; so I lay still in my Castle, preplex'd and discomforted: However I put my self into all the same Postures for an Attack that I had formerly provided, and was just ready for Action, if any Thing had presented. Having waited a good while, listening to hear if they made any Noise; at length being very impatient, I set my Guns at the Foot of my Ladder, and clamber'd up to the Top of the Hill, by my two Stages as usual; standing so however that my Head did not appear above the Hill, so that they could not perceive me by any Means: Here I observ'd by the help of my Perspective Glass, that they were no less than Thirty in Number, that they had a Fire kindled, that they had had Meat dress'd. How they had cook'd it, that I knew not, or what it was; but they were all Dancing in I know not how many barbarous Gestures and Figures, their own Way, round the Fire.

While I was thus looking on them, I perceived by my Perspective, two miserable Wretches dragg'd from the Boats, where it seems they were laid by, and were now brought out for the Slaughter. I perceived one of them immediately fell, being knock'd down, I suppose with a Club or Wooden Sword, for that was their way, and two or three others were at work immediately cutting him open for their Cookery, while the other Victim was left standing by himself, till they should be ready for him. In that very Moment this poor Wretch seeing himself a little at Liberty, Nature inspir'd him with Hopes of Life, and he started away from them, and ran with incredible Swiftness along the Sands directly towards me, I mean towards that part of the Coast, where my Habitation was.

I was dreadfully frighted, (that I must acknowledge) when I perceived him to run my Way; and especially, when as I thought I saw him pursued by the whole Body, and now I expected that part of my Dream was coming to pass, and that he would certainly take shelter in my Grove; but I could not depend by any means upon my Dream for the rest of it, (viz.) that the other Savages would not pursue him thither, and find him there. However, I kept my Station, and my Spirits began to recover, when I found that there was not above three Men that follow'd him, and still more was I encourag'd, when I found that he outstrip'd them exceedingly in running, and gain'd Ground of them, so that if he could but hold it for half an Hour, I saw easily he would fairly get away from them all.

There was between them and my Castle, the Creek which I mention'd often at the first part of my Story, when I landed my Cargoes out of the Ship; and this I saw plainly, he must necessarily swim over, or the poor Wretch would be taken there: But when the Savage escaping came thither, he made nothing of it, tho' the Tide was then up, but plunging in, swam thro' in about Thirty Strokes or thereabouts, landed and ran on with exceeding Strength and Swiftness; when the Three Persons came to the Creek, I found that Two of them could Swim, but the Third cou'd not, and that standing on the other Side, he look'd at the other, but went no further; and soon after went softly[7] back again, which as it happen'd, was very well for him in the main.

I observ'd, that the two who swam, were yet more than twice as long swimming over the Creek, as the Fellow was, that fled from them: It came now very warmly[8] upon my Thoughts, and indeed irresistbly, that now was my Time to get me a Servant, and perhaps a Companion, or Assistant; and that I was call'd plainly by Providence to save this poor Creature's Life; I immediately run down the Ladders with all possible Expedition, fetch'd my two Guns, for they were both but at the Foot of the Ladders, as I observ'd above; and getting up again, with the same haste, to the Top of the Hill, I cross'd toward the Sea; and having a

7. Quietly, slowly.
8. Strongly.

very short Cut, and all down Hill, clapp'd my self in the way, between the Pursuers, and the Pursu'd; hallowing aloud to him that fled, who looking back, was at first perhaps as much frighted at me, as at them; but I beckon'd with my Hand to him, to come back; and in the mean time, I slowly advanc'd towards the two that follow'd; then rushing at once upon the foremost, I knock'd him down with the Stock of my Piece; I was loath to fire, because I would not have the rest hear; though at that distance, it would not have been easily heard, and being out of Sight of the Smoke too, they woul'd not have easily known what to make of it: Having knock'd this Fellow down, the other who pursu'd with him stopp'd, as if he had been frighted; and I advanc'd a-pace towards him; but as I came nearer, I perceiv'd presently, he had a Bow and Arrow, and was fitting it to shoot at me; so I was then necessitated to shoot at him first, which I did, and kill'd him at the first Shoot; the poor Savage who fled, but had stopp'd; though he saw both his Enemies fallen, and kill'd, as he thought; yet was so frighted with the Fire, and Noise of my Piece; that he stood Stock still, and neither came forward or went backward, tho' he seem'd rather enclin'd to fly still, than to come on; I hollow'd again to him, and made Signs to come forward, which he easily understood, and came a little way, then stopp'd again, and then a little further, and stopp'd again, and I cou'd then perceive that he stood trembling, as if he had been taken Prisoner, and had just been to be[9] kill'd, as his two Enemies were. I beckon'd him again to come to me, and gave him all the Signs of Encouragement that I could think of, and he came nearer and nearer, kneeling down every Ten or Twelve steps in token of acknowledgement for my saving his Life: I smil'd at him, and look'd pleasantly, and beckon'd to him to come still nearer; at length he came close to me, and then he kneel'd down again, kiss'd the Ground, and laid his Head upon the Ground, and taking me by the Foot, set my Foot upon his Head; this it seems was in token of swearing to be my Slave for ever; I took him up, and made much of him, and encourag'd him all I could. But there was more work to do yet, for I perceived the Savage who I knock'd down, was not kill'd, but stunn'd with the blow, and began to come to himself; so I pointed to him, and showing him the Savage, that he was not dead; upon this he spoke some Words to me, and though I could not understand them, yet I thought they were pleasant to hear, for they were the first sound of a Man's Voice, that I had heard, *my own excepted*, for above Twenty Five Years. But there was no time for such Reflections now, the Savage who was knock'd down recover'd himself so far, as to sit up upon the Ground, and I perceived that my Savage began to be afraid; but when I saw that, I presented my other Piece at the Man, as if I would shoot him, upon this my Savage, *for so I call him now*, made a Motion to me to lend

9. Been about to be.

him my Sword, which hung naked in a Belt by my side; so I did: he no sooner had it, but he runs to his Enemy, and at one blow cut off his Head as cleaverly,[1] no Executioner in *Germany* could have done it sooner or better; which I thought very strange, for one who I had Reason to believe never saw a Sword in his Life before, except their own Wooden Swords; however, it seems, as I learn'd afterwards, they make their Wooden Swords so sharp, so heavy, and the Wood is so hard, that they will cut off Heads even with them, ay and Arms and that at one blow too; when he had done this, he comes laughing to me in Sign of Triumph, and brought me the Sword again, and with Abundance of Gestures which I did not understand, laid it down with the Head of the Savage, that he had kill'd just before me.

But that which astonish'd him most, was to know how I had kill'd the other Indian so far off, so pointing to him, he made Signs to me to let him go to him, so I bad him go, as well as I could; when he came to him, he stood like one amaz'd, looking at him, turn'd him first on one side, then on t'other, look'd at the Wound the Bullet had made, which it seems was just in his Breast, where it had made a Hole, and no great Quantity of Blood had follow'd, but he had bled inwardly, for he was quite dead: He took up his Bow, and Arrows, and came back, so I turn'd to go away, and beckon'd to him to follow me, making Signs to him, that more might come after them.

Upon this he sign'd to me, that he should bury them with Sand, that they might not be seen by the rest if they follow'd; and so I made Signs again to him to do so; he fell to Work, and in an instant he had scrap'd a Hole in the Sand, with his Hands, big enough to bury the first in, and then dragg'd him into it, and cover'd him, and did so also by the other; I believe he had bury'd them both in a Quarter of an Hour; then calling him away, I carry'd him not to my Castle, but quite away to my Cave, and the farther Part of the Island; so I did not let my Dream come to pass in that Part. *viz.* That he came into my Grove for shelter.

Here I gave him Bread, and a Bunch of Raisins to eat, and a Draught of Water, which I found he was indeed in great Distress for, by his Running; and having refresh'd him, I made Signs for him to go lie down and sleep; pointing to a Place where I had laid a great Parcel of Rice Straw, and a Blanket upon it, which I used to sleep upon my self sometimes; so the poor Creature laid down, and went to sleep.

He was a comely handsome Fellow, perfectly well made; with straight strong Limbs, not too large; tall and well shap'd, and as I reckon, about twenty six Years of Age. He had a very good Countenance, not a fierce and surly Aspect; but seem'd to have something very manly in his Face, and yet he had all the Sweetness and Softness of an *European* in his Countenance too, especially when he smil'd. His Hair was long and

1. Pun? Corrected to "cleverly" in the second and subsequent editions.

black, not curl'd like Wool; his Forehead very high, and large, and a great Vivacity and sparkling Sharpness in his Eyes. The Colour of his Skin was not quite black, but very tawny;[2] and yet not of an ugly yellow nauseous tawny, as the *Brasilians*, and *Virginians*, and other Natives of *America* are; but of a bright kind of a dun[3] olive Colour, that had in it something very agreeable; tho' not very easy to describe. His Face was round, and plump; his Nose small, not flat like the Negroes, a very good Mouth, thin Lips, and his fine Teeth well set, and white as Ivory. After he had slumber'd, rather than slept, about half an Hour, he wak'd again, and comes out of the Cave to me; for I had been milking my Goats, which I had in the Enclosure just by: When he espy'd me, he came running to me, laying himself down again upon the Ground, with all the possible Signs of an humble thankful Disposition, making a many antick[4] Gestures to show it: At last he lays His Head flat upon the Ground, close to my Foot, and sets my other Foot upon his Head, as he had done before; and after this; made all the Signs to me of Subjection, Servitude, and Submission imaginable, to let me know, how he would serve me as long as he liv'd. I understood him in many Things, and let him know, I was very well pleas'd with him; in a little Time I began to speak to him, and teach him to speak to me; and first I made him know his Name should be *Friday*, which was the Day I sav'd his Life; I call'd him so for the Memory of the Time; I likewise taught him to say *Master*, and then let him know, that was to be my Name; I likewise taught him to say, Y E S, and N O, and to know the Meaning of them; I gave him some Milk, in an earthen Pot, and let him see me Drink it before him, and sop my Bread in it; and I gave him a Cake of Bread, to do the like, which he quickly comply'd with, and made Signs that it was very good for him.

I kept there with him all that Night; but as soon as it was Day, I beckon'd to him to come with me, and let him know, I would give him some Cloths, at which he seem'd very glad, for he was stark naked: As we went by the Place where he had bury'd the two Men, he pointed exactly to the Place, and shew'd me the Marks that he had made to find them again, making Signs to me, that we should dig them up again, and eat them; at this I appear'd very angry, express'd my Abhorrence of it, made as if I would vomit at the Thoughts of it, and beckon'd with my Hand to him to come away, which he did immediately, with great Submission. I then led him up to the Top of the Hill, to see if his Enemies were gone; and pulling out my Glass, I look'd, and saw plainly the Place where they had been, but no appearance of them, or of their *Canoes*; so that it was plain they were gone, and had left their two Comrades behind them, without any search after them.

2. Brown.
3. Dark.
4. Grotesque, bizarre.

But I was not content with this Discovery; but having now more Courage, and consequently more Curiosity, I took my Man *Friday* with me, giving him the Sword in his Hand, with the Bow and Arrows at his Back, which I found he could use very dextrously, making him carry one Gun for me, and I two for myself, and away we march'd to the Place, where these Creatures had been; for I had a Mind now to get some fuller Intelligence of them: When I came to the Place, my very Blood ran chill in my Veins, and my Heart sunk within me, at the Horror of the Spectacle: Indeed it was a dreadful Sight, at least it was so to me; though *Friday* made nothing of it: The Place was cover'd with humane Bones, the Ground dy'd with their Blood, great Pieces of Flesh left here and there, half eaten, mangl'd and scorch'd; and in short, all the Tokens of the triumphant Feast they had been making there, after a Victory over their Enemies. I saw three Skulls, five Hands, and the Bones of three or four Legs and Feet, and abundance of other Parts of the Bodies; and *Friday*, by his Signs, made me understand, that they brought over four Prisoners to feast upon; that three of them were eaten up, and that he, pointing to himself, was the fourth: That there had been a great Battle between them, and their next King, whose Subjects it seems he had been one of; and that they had taken a great Number of Prisoners, all which were carry'd to several Places by those that had taken them in the Fight, in order to feast upon them, as was done here by these Wretches upon those they brought hither.

I caus'd *Friday* to gather all the Skulls, Bones, Flesh, and whatever remain'd, and lay them together on a Heap, and make a great Fire upon it, and burn them all to Ashes: I found *Friday* had still a hankering Stomach after some of the Flesh, and was still a Cannibal in his Nature; but I discover'd[5] so much Abhorrence at the very Thoughts of it, and at the least Appearance of it, that he durst not discover it; for I had by some Means let him know, that I would kill him if he offer'd it.

When we had done this, we came back to our Castle, and there I fell to work for my Man *Friday*; and first of all, I gave him a pair of Linnen Drawers, which I had out of the poor Gunner's Chest I mentioned, and which I found in the Wreck; and which with a little Alteration fitted him very well; then I made him a Jerkin[6] of Goat's-skin, as well as my Skill would allow; and I was now grown a tollerable good Taylor; and I gave him a Cap, which I had made of a Hare-skin, very convenient, and fashionable enough; and thus he was cloath'd for the present, tollerably well; and was mighty well pleas'd to see himself almost as well cloath'd as his Master: It is true, he went awkwardly in these Things at first, wearing the Drawers was very awkward to him, and the Sleeves of the Wastcoat gall'd his Shoulders, and the inside of his Arms; but a little easing them where he complain'd they hurt him, and using himself to them, at length he took to them very well.

5. Displayed.
6. A waistcoat.

The next Day after I came home to my Hutch with him, I began to consider where I should lodge him; and that I might do well for him, and yet be perfectly easy my self, I made a little Tent for him in the vacant Place between my two Fortifications, in the inside of the last, and in the outside of the first, and as there was a Door, or Entrance there into my Cave, I made a formal fram'd Door Case, and a Door to it of Boards, and set it up in the Passage, a little within the Entrance; and causing the Door to open on the inside, I barr'd it up in the Night, taking in my Ladders too; so that *Friday* could no way come at me in the inside of my innermost wall, without making so much Noise in getting over, that it must needs waken me; for my first Wall had now a compleat Roof over it of long Poles, covering all my Tent, and leaning up to the side of the Hill, which was again laid cross with smaller Sticks instead of Laths, and then thatch'd over a great Thickness, with the Rice Straw, which was strong like Reeds; and at the Hole or Place which was left to go in or out by the Ladder, I had plac'd a kind of Trap-door, which if it had been attempted on the outside, would not have open'd at all, but would have fallen down, and made a great Noise; and as to Weapons, I took them all in to my Side every Night.

But I needed none of all this Precaution; for never Man had a more faithful, loving, sincere Servant, than *Friday* was to me; without Passions, Sullenness or Designs, perfectly oblig'd and engag'd; his very Affections were ty'd to me, like those of a Child to a Father; and I dare say, he would have sacrific'd his Life for the saving mine upon any occasion whatsoever; the many Testimonies he gave me of this, put it out of doubt, and soon convinc'd me, that I needed to use no Precautions as to my Safety on his Account.

This frequently gave me occasion to observe, and that with wonder, that however it had pleas'd God, in his Providence, and in the Government of the Works of his Hands, to take from so great a Part of the World of his Creatures, the best Uses to which their Faculties, and the Powers of their Souls are adapted; yet that he has bestow'd upon them the same Powers, the same Reason, the same Affections, the same Sentiments of Kindness and Obligation, the same Passions and Resentments of Wrongs; the same Sense of Gratitude, Sincerity, Fidelity, and all the Capacities of doing Good, and receiving Good, that he has given to us; and that when he pleases to offer to them Occasions of exerting these, they are as ready, nay, more ready to apply them to the right Uses for which they were bestow'd, than we are: and this made me very melancholly sometimes, in reflecting as the several Occasions presented, how mean a Use we make of all these, even though we have these Powers enlighten'd by the great Lamp of Instruction, the Spirit of God, and by the Knowledge of his Word, added to our Understanding; and why it has pleas'd God to hide the like saving Knowledge from so many Millions of Souls, who if I might judge by this poor Savage, would make a much better use of it than we did.

From hence, I sometimes was led too far to invade the Soverainty of *Providence*, and as it were arraign the Justice of so arbitrary a Disposition of Things, that should hide that Light from some, and reveal it to others, and yet expect a like Duty from both: But I shut it up, and check'd my Thoughts with this Conclusion, (1st.) That we did not know by what Light and Law these should be Condemn'd; but that as God was necessarily, and by the Nature of his Being, infinitely Holy and Just, so it could not be, but that if these Creatures were all sentenc'd to Absence from himself, it was on account of sinning against that Light which, as the Scripture says, was a Law to themselves,[7] and by such Rules as their Consciences would acknowledge to be just tho' the Foundation was not discover'd to us: And (2d.) that still as we are all the Clay in the Hand of the Potter,[8] no Vessel could say to him, Why hast thou form'd me thus?

But to return to my New Companion; I was greatly delighted with him, and made it my Business to teach him every Thing, that was proper to make him useful, handy, and helpful; but especially to make him speak, and understand me when I spake, and he was the aptest Schollar that ever was, and particularly was so merry, so constantly diligent, and so pleas'd, when he cou'd but understand me, or make me understand him, that it was very pleasant to me to talk to him; and now my Life began to be so easy, that I began to my self, that could I but have been safe from more Savages, I cared not, if I was never to remove from the place while I lived.

After I had been two or three Days return'd to my Castle, I thought that, in order to bring *Friday* off from his horrid way of feeding, and from the Relish of a Cannibal's Stomach, I ought to let him taste other Flesh; so I took him out with me one Morning to the Woods: I went indeed intending to kill a Kid out of my own Flock, and bring him home and dress it. But as I was going, I saw a She Goat lying down in the Shade, and two young Kids sitting by her. I catch'd hold of *Friday*, Hold, says I, stand still; and made Signs to him not to stir, immediately I presented my Piece, shot and kill'd one of the Kids. The poor Creature who had at a Distance indeed seen me kill the Savage his Enemy, but did not know, or could imagine how it was done, was sensibly surpriz'd, trembled, and shook, and look'd so amaz'd, that I thought he would have sunk down. He did not see the Kid I shot at, or perceive I had kill'd it, but ripp'd up his Wastcoat to feel if he was not wounded, and as I found, presently thought I was resolv'd to kill him; for he came and kneel'd down to me, and embracing my Knees, said a great many Things I did not understand; but I could easily see that the meaning was to pray me not to kill him.

I soon found a way to convince him that I would do him no harm,

7. Romans 2.14.
8. Jeremiah 18.6; Isaiah 45.9.

and taking him up by the Hand laugh'd at him, and pointed to the Kid which I had kill'd, beckoned to him to run and fetch it, which he did; and while he was wondering and looking to see how the Creature was kill'd, I loaded my Gun again, and by and by I saw a great Fowl like a Hawk sit upon a Tree within Shot; so to let *Friday* understand a little what I would do, I call'd him to me again, pointed at the Fowl which was indeed a Parrot, tho' I thought it had been a Hawk, I say pointing to the Parrot, and to my Gun, and to the Ground under the Parrot, to let him see I would make it fall, I made him understand that I would shoot and kill that Bird; according I fir'd and bad him look, and immediately he saw the Parrot fall, he stood like one frighted again, notwithstanding all I had said to him; and I found he was the more amaz'd because he did not see me put any Thing into the Gun; but thought that there must be some wonderful Fund of Death and Destruction in that Thing, able to kill Man, Beast, Bird, or any Thing near, or far off, and the Astonishment this created in him was such, as could not wear off for a long Time; and I believe, if I would have let him, he would have worshipp'd me and my Gun: As for the Gun it self, he would not so much as touch it for several Days after; but would speak to it, and talk to it, as if it had answer'd him, when he was by himself; which, as I afterwards learn'd of him, was to desire it not to kill him.

Well, after his Astonishment was a little over at this, I pointed to him to run and fetch the Bird I had shot, which he did, but stay'd some Time; for the Parrot not being quite dead, was flutter'd away a good way off from the Place where she fell; however, he found her, took her up, and brought her to me; and as I had perceiv'd his Ignorance about the Gun before, I took this Advantage to charge the Gun again, and not let him see me do it, that I might be ready for any other Mark that might present; but nothing more offer'd at that Time; so I brought home the Kid, and the same Evening I took the Skin off, and cut it out as well as I could; and having a Pot for that purpose, I boil'd, or stew'd some of the Flesh, and made some very good Broth; and after I had begun to eat some, I gave some to my Man, who seem'd very glad of it, and lik'd it very well; but that which was strangest to him, was, to see me eat Salt with it; he made a sign to me, that the Salt was not good to eat, and putting a little into his own Mouth, he seem'd to nauseate it, and would spit and sputter at it, washing his Mouth with fresh Water after it; on the other hand, I took some Meat in my Mouth without Salt, and I pretended to spit and sputter for want of Salt, as fast as he had done at the Salt; but it would not do, he would never care for Salt with his Meat, or in his Broth; at least not a great while, and then but a very little.

Having thus fed him with boil'd Meat and Broth, I was resolv'd to feast him the next Day with roasting a Piece of the Kid; this I did by hanging it before the Fire, in a string, as I had seen many People do in *England*, setting two Poles up, one on each side the Fire, and one cross on the Top, and tying the String to the Cross-stick, letting the Meat turn continually: This *Friday* admir'd very much; but when he came to taste the Flesh, he took so many ways to tell me how well he lik'd it, that I could not but understand him; and at last he told me he would never eat Man's flesh any more, which I was very glad to hear.

The next Day I set him to work to beating some Corn out, and sifting it in the manner I us'd to do, as I observ'd before, and he soon understood how to do it as well as I, especially after he had seen what the Meaning of it was, and that it was to make my Bread, and bake it too, and in a little Time *Friday* was able to do all the Work for me, as well as I could do it my self.

I begun now to consider, that having two Mouths to feed, instead of one, I must provide more Ground for my Harvest, and plant a larger Quantity of Corn, than I us'd to do; so I mark'd out a larger Piece of Land, and began the Fence in the same Manner as before, in which *Friday* not only work'd very willingly, and very hard; but did it very chearfully; and I told him what it was for; that it was for Corn to make more Bread, because he was now with me, and that I might have enough for him, and my self too: He appear'd very sensible of that Part, and let me know, that he thought I had much more Labour upon me on his Account, than I had for my self; and that he would work the harder for me, if I would tell him what to do.

This was the pleasantest Year of all the Life I led in this Place; *Friday* began to talk pretty well, and understand the Names of almost every Thing I had occasion to call for, and of every Place I had to send him to, and talk'd a great deal to me; so that in short I began now to have some Use for my Tongue again, which indeed I had very little occasion for before; that is to say, *about Speech*; besides the Pleasures of talking to him, I had a singular Satisfaction in the Fellow himself; his simple unfeign'd Honesty, appear'd to me more and more every Day, and I began really to love the Creature; and on his Side, I believe he lov'd me more than it was possible for him ever to love any Thing before.

I had a Mind once to try if he had any hankering Inclination to his own Country again, and having learn'd him *English* so well that he could answer me almost any Questions, I ask'd him whether the Nation that he belong'd to never conquer'd in Battle, at which he smil'd; and said; yes, yes, we always fight the better; that is, he meant always get the better in Fight; and so we began the following Discourse: You always fight the better, said I, How came you to be taken Prisoner then, *Friday*?

Friday, My Nation beat much, for all that.

Master, How beat; if your Nation beat them, how came you to be taken?

Friday, They more many than my Nation in the Place where me was; they take one, two, three, and me; my Nation over-beat them in the yonder Place, where me no was; there my Nation take one, two, great Thousand.

Master, But why did not your Side recover you from the Hands of your Enemies then?

Friday, They run one, two, three, and me, and make go in the *Canoe*; my Nation have no *Canoe* that time.

Master, Well *Friday,* and What does your Nation do with the Men they take, do they carry them away, and eat them, as these did?

Friday, Yes, my Nation eat Mans too, eat all up.

Master, Where do they carry them?

Friday, Go to other Place where they think.

Master, Do they come hither?

Friday, Yes, yes, they come hither; come other else Place.

Master, Have you been here with them?

Friday, Yes, I been here; [*points to the N.W. Side of the Island, which it seems was their Side.*]

By this I understood, that my Man *Friday* had formerly been among the Savages, who us'd to come on Shore on the farther Part of the Island, on the same Man eating Occasions that he was now brought for; and sometime after, when I took the Courage to carry him to that Side, being the same I formerly mention'd, he presently knew the Place, and told me, he was there once when they eat up twenty Men, two Women, and one Child; he could not tell[9] Twenty in *English*; but he numbered them by laying so many Stones on a Row, and pointing to me to tell them over.

I have told this Passage, because it introduces what follows; that after I had had this Discourse with him, I ask'd him how far it was from our Island to the Shore, and whether the *Canoes* were not often lost; he told me, there was no Danger, no *Canoes* ever lost; but that after a little way out to the Sea, there was a Current, and Wind, always one way in the Morning, the other in the Afternoon.

This I understood to be no more than the Sets of the Tide, as going out, or coming in; but I afterwards understood, it was occasion'd by the great Draft and Reflex of the mighty River *Oroonooko*; in the Mouth, or the Gulph of which River, as I found afterwards, our Island lay; and this Land which I perceiv'd to the W. and N.W. was the great Island *Trinidad*, on the *North* Point of the Mouth of the River: I ask'd *Friday* a thousand Questions about the Country, the Inhabitants, the Sea, the Coast, and what Nations were near; he told me all he knew with the greatest Openness imaginable; I ask'd him the Name of the several Nations of his Sort of People; but could get no other Name than *Caribs*; from whence I easily understood, that these were the *Caribbees*, which our Maps place on the Part of *America*, which reaches from the Mouth

9. Count.

of the River *Oroonooko* to *Guiana*, and onwards to *St. Martha*:[1] He
told me that up a great way beyond the Moon, that was, beyond the
Setting of the Moon, which must be W. from their Country, there dwelt
white bearded Men, like me; and pointed to my great Whiskers, which
I mention'd before; and that they had kill'd *much Mans*, that was his
Word; by all which I undersood, he meant the *Spaniards*, whose Cruelties in *America* had been spread over the whole Countries, and was
remember'd by all the Nations from Father to Son.

I enquir'd if he could tell me how I might come from this Island,
and get among those white Men; he told me, yes, yes, I might go *in
two Canoe*; I could not understand what he meant, or make him describe
to me what he meant by *two Canoe* till at last with great Difficulty, I
found he meant it must be in a large great Boat, as big as *two Canoes*.

This Part of *Friday*'s Discourse began to relish with me very well,
and from this Time I entertain'd some Hopes, that one Time or other,
I might find an Opportunity to make my Escape from this Place; and
that this poor Savage might be a Means to help me to do it.

During the long Time that *Friday* has now been with me, and that
he began to speak to me, and understand me, I was not wanting to lay
a Foundation of Religious Knowledge in his Mind; particularly I ask'd
him one Time who made him? The poor Creature did not understand
me at all, but thought I had ask'd him who was his Father; but I took
it by another handle, and ask'd him who made the Sea, the Ground we
walk'd on, and the Hills, and Woods; he told me it was one old *Benamuckee*, that liv'd beyond all: He could describe nothing of this great
Person, but that he was very old; much older he said than the Sea, or
the Land, than the Moon, or the Stars: I ask'd him then, if this old
Person had made all Things, why did not all Things worship him; he
look'd very grave and with a perfect Look of Innocence, said, *All Things
do say O to him*: I ask'd him if the People who die in his Country went
away any where? He said, Yes, they all went to *Benamuckee*: Then I
ask'd him, Whether these they eat up went thither too? He said, Yes.

From these Things, I began to instruct him in the Knowledge of the
true God: I told him that the great Maker of all Things liv'd up there,
pointing up towards Heaven: That he governs the World by the same
Power and Providence by which he had made it: That he was omnipotent, could do every Thing for us, give every Thing to us, take every
Thing from us; and thus by Degrees I open'd his Eyes. He listned with
great Attention, and receiv'd with Pleasure the Notion of *Jesus Christ*
being sent to redeem us, and of the Manner of making our Prayers to
God, and his being able to hear us, even into Heaven. He told me one
Day, that if our God could hear us up beyond the Sun, he must needs
be a greater God than their *Benamuckee*, who liv'd but a little way off,

1. In Colombia.

and yet could not hear, till they went up to the great Mountains where he dwelt, to speak to him: I ask'd him if ever he went thither, to speak to him? He said, No, they never went that were young Men; none went thither but the old Men, who he call'd their *Oowocakee*, that is, as I made him explain it to me, their Religious, or Clergy, and that they went to say O, (so he call'd saying Prayers) and then came back, and told them what *Benamuckee* said. By this I observ'd, That there is *Priest-craft*, even amongst the most blinded ignorant Pagans in the World; and the Policy of making a secret Religion, in order to preserve the Veneration of the People to the Clergy, is not only to be found in the *Roman*, but perhaps among all Religions in the World, even among the most brutish and barbarous Savages.

I endeavour'd to clear up this Fraud, to my Man *Friday*, and told him, that the Pretence of their old Men going up the Mountains, to say O to their God *Benamuckee*, was a Cheat, and their bringing Word from thence what he said, was much more so; that if they met with any Answer, or spoke with any one there, it must be with an evil Spirit: And then I entred into a long Discourse with him about the Devil, the Original of him, his Rebellion against God, his Enmity to Man, the Reason of it, his setting himself up in the dark Parts of the World to be Worship'd instead of God, and as God; and the many Stratagems he made use of to delude Mankind to his Ruine; how he had a secret access to our Passions, and to our affections, to adapt his Snares so to our Inclinations, as to cause us even to be our own Tempters, and to run upon our Destruction by our own Choice.

I found it was not so easie to imprint right Notions in his Mind about the Devil, as it was about the Being of a God. Nature assisted all my Arguments to Evidence to him, even the Necessity of a great first Cause and overruling governing Power; a secret directing Providence, and of the Equity, and Justice, of paying Homage to him that made us, and the like. But there appeared nothing of all this in the Notion of an Evil Spirit; of his Original, his Being, his Nature, and above all of his Inclination to do Evil, and to draw us in to do so too; and the poor Creature puzzl'd me once in such a manner, by a Question meerly natural and innocent, that I scarce knew what to say to him. I had been talking a great deal to him of the Power of God, his Omnipotence, his dreadful Nature to Sin, his being a consuming Fire[2] to the Workers of Iniquity; how, as he had made us all, he could destroy us and all the World in a Moment; and he listen'd with great Seriousness to me all the while.

After this, I had been telling him how the Devil was God's Enemy in the Hearts of Men, and used all his Malice and Skill to defeat the good Designs of Providence, and to ruine the Kingdom of Christ in the World; and the like. Well, says *Friday*; but you say, God is so strong,

2. Crusoe echoes the Bible: Deuteronomy 4.24

so great, is he not much strong, much might as the Devil? Yes, yes, says I, *Friday*, God is stronger than the Devil, God is above the Devil, and therefore we pray to God to tread him down under our Feet, and enable us to resist his Temptations and quench his fiery Darts.[3] *But*, says he again, *if God much strong, much might as the Devil, why God no kill the Devil, so make him no more do wicked?*

I was strangely surpriz'd at his Question, and after all, tho' I was now an old Man, yet I was but a young Doctor,[4] and ill enough quallified for a Casuist,[5] or a Solver of Difficulties: And at first I could not tell what to say, so I pretended not to hear him, and ask'd him what he said? But he was too earnest for an Answer to forget his Question; so that he repeated it in the very same broken Words, as above. By this time I had recovered my self a little, and I said, *God will at last punish him severely; he is reserv'd for the Judgment, and is to be cast into the Bottomless-Pit, to dwell with everlasting Fire:*[6] This did not satisfie *Friday*, but he returns upon me, repeating my Words, R E S E R V E , A T L A S T , *me no understand; but, Why not kill the Devil now, not kill great ago?* You may as well ask me *said I*, Why God does not kill you and I, when we do wicked Things here that offend him? We are preserv'd to repent and be pardon'd: He muses a while at this; *Well, well*, says he, mighty affectionately, *that well; so you, I, Devil, all wicked, all preserve, repent, God pardon all.* Here I was run down again by him to the last Degree, and it was a Testimony to me, how the meer Notions of Nature, though they will guide reasonable Creatures to the Knowledge of a God, and of a Worship or Homage due to the supreme Being, of a God as the Consequence of our Nature; yet nothing but divine Revelation can form the Knowledge of *Jesus Christ*, and of a Redemption purchas'd for us, of a Mediator of the new Covenant, and of an Intercessor, at the Foot-stool of God's Throne; I say, nothing but a Revelation from Heaven, can form these in the Soul, and that therefore the Gospel of our Lord and Saviour *Jesus Christ*; I mean, the Word of God, and the Spirit of God promis'd for the Guide and Sanctifier of his People, are the absolutely necessary Instructors of the Souls of Men, in the saving Knowledge of God, and the Means of Salvation.

I therefore diverted the present Discourse between me and my Man, rising up hastily, as upon some sudden Occasion of going out; then sending him for something a good way off, I seriously pray'd to God that he would enable me to instruct savingly this poor Savage, assisting by his Spirit the Heart of the poor ignorant Creature, to receive the Light of the Knowledge of God in *Christ*, reconciling him to himself, and would guide me to speak so to him from the Word of God, as his

3. Romans 16.20; Ephesians 6.16.
4. Teacher.
5. One skilled in dealing with cases of conscience.
6. More biblical echoes: 2 Peter 2.4; Revelation 20.1ff.

Conscience might be convinc'd, his Eyes open'd, and his Soul sav'd. When he came again to me, I entred into a long Discourse with him upon the Subject of the Redemption of Man by the Saviour of the World, and of the Doctrine of the Gospel preach'd from Heaven, *viz.* of Repentance towards God, and Faith in our Blessed Lord *Jesus.* I then explain'd to him, as well as I could, why our Blessed Redeemer took not on him the Nature of Angels, but the Seed of *Abraham,* and how for that Reason the fallen angels had no Share in the Redemption; that he came only to the lost Sheep of the House of *Israel,* and the like.

I had, *God knows,* more Sincerity than Knowledge, in all the Methods I took for this poor Creature's Instruction, and must acknowledge what I believe all that act upon the same Principle will find, That in laying Things open to him, I really inform'd and instructed myself in many Things, that either I did not know, or had not fully consider'd before; but which occurr'd naturally to my Mind, upon my searching into them, for the Information of this poor Savage; and I had more Affection[7] in my Enquiry after Things upon this Occasion, than ever I felt before; so that whether this poor wild Wretch was the better for me, or no, I had great Reason to be thankful that ever he came to me: My Grief set lighter upon me, my Habitation grew comfortable to me beyond Measure; and when I reflected that in this solitary Life which I had been confin'd to, I had not only been moved my self to look up to Heaven, and to seek to the Hand that had brought me there; but was now to be made an Instrument under Providence to save the Life; and *for ought I knew,* the Soul of a poor Savage, and bring him to the true Knowledge of Religion, and of the Christian Doctrine, that he might know Christ Jesus, *to know whom is Life eternal.* I say, when I reflected upon all these Things, a secret Joy run through every Part of my Soul, and I frequently rejoyc'd that ever I was brought to this Place, which I had so often thought the most dreadful of all Afflictions that could possibly have befallen me.

In this thankful Frame I continu'd all the Remainder of my Time, and the Conversation which employ'd the Hours between *Friday* and I, was such, as made the three Years which we liv'd there together perfectly and compleatly happy, *if any such Thing as compleat Happiness can be form'd in a sublunary*[8] *State.* The Savage was now a good Christian, a much better than I; though I have reason to hope, and bless God for it, that we were equally penitent, and comforted restor'd Penitents; we had here the Word of God to read, and no farther off from his Spirit to instruct, than if we had been in *England.*

I always apply'd my self in Reading the Scripture, to let him know, as well as I could, the Meaning of what I read; and he again, by his serious Enquiries, and Questionings, made me, *as I said before,* a much better Scholar in the Scripture Knowledge, than I should ever have been

7. Zeal.
8. Earthly.

by my own private meer Reading. Another thing I cannot refrain from observing here also from Experience, in this retir'd Part of my Life, *viz.* How infinite, and inexpressible a Blessing it is, that the Knowledge of God, and of the Doctrine of Salvation by *Christ Jesus*, is so plainly laid down in the Word of God; so easy to be receiv'd and understood: That as the bare reading the Scripture made me capable of understanding enough of my Duty, to carry me directly on to the great Work of sincere Repentance for my Sins, and laying hold of a Saviour for Life and Salvation, to a stated Reformation in Practice, and Obedience to all God's Commands, and this without any Teacher or Instructer (I mean, humane) so the same plain Instruction sufficiently serv'd to the enlightening this Savage Creature, and bringing him to be such a Christian, as I have known few equal to him in my Life.

As to all the Disputes, Wranglings, Strife and Contention, which has happen'd in the World about Religion, whether Niceties in Doctrines, or Schemes of Church Government, they were all perfectly useless to us; as for ought I can yet see, they have been to all the rest of the World: We had the *sure Guide* to Heaven, *viz.* The Word of God; and we had, *blessed be God*, comfortable Views of the Spirit of God teaching and instructing us by his Word, *leading us into all Truth*, and making us both willing and obedient to the Instruction of his Word, and I cannot see the least Use that the greatest Knowledge of the disputed Points in Religion which have made such Confusions in the World would have been to us, if we could have obtain'd it; but I must go on with the Historical Part of Things, and take every Part in its order.

After *Friday* and I became more intimately acquainted, and that he could understand almost all I said to him, and speak fluently, though in broken *English* to me; I acquainted him with my own Story, or at least so much of it as related to my coming into the Place, how I had liv'd there, and how long. I let him into the Mystery, for such it was to him, of Gunpowder, and Bullet, and taught him how to shoot: I gave him a Knife, which he was wonderfully delighted with, and I made him a Belt, with a Frog hanging to it, such as in *England* we wear Hangers[9] in; and in the Frog,[1] instead of Hanger, I gave him a Hatchet, which was not only as good a Weapon in some Cases, but much more useful upon other Occasions.

I describ'd to him the Country of *Europe*, and particularly *England*, which I came from; how we liv'd, how we worshipp'd God, how we behav'd to one another; and how we traded in Ships to all Parts of the World: I gave him an Account of the Wreck which I had been on board of, and shew'd him as near as I could, the Place where she lay; but she was all beaten in Pieces before, and gone.

I shew'd him the Ruins of our Boat, which we lost when we escap'd,

9. Short sword.
1. Belt loop for a scabbard.

and which I could not stir with my whole Strength then; but was now fallen almost to Pieces: Upon seeing this Boat, *Friday* stood musing a great while, and said nothing; I ask'd him what it was he study'd upon, at last says he, *me see such Boat like come to Place at my Nation.*

I did not understand him a good while; but at last, when I had examin'd farther into it, I understood by him, that a Boat, such as that had been, came on Shore upon the Country where he liv'd; that is, as he explain'd it, was driven thither by Stress of Weather: I presently imagin'd, that some *European* Ship must have been cast away upon their Coast, and the Boat might get loose, and drive a-Shore; but was so dull, that I never once thought of Men making escape from a Wreck thither, much less whence they might come; so I only enquir'd after a Description of the Boat.

Friday describ'd the Boat to me well enough; but brought me better to understand him, when he added with some Warmth, *we save the White Mans from drown:* Then I presently ask'd him, if there was any *white Mans*, as he call'd them, in the Boat; *yes*, he said, *the Boat full white Mans:* I ask'd him how many; he told upon his Fingers seventeen: I ask'd him then what become of them; he told me, *they live, they dwell at my Nation.*

This put new Thoughts into my Head; for I presently imagin'd, that these might be the Men belonging to the Ship, that was cast away in Sight of *my Island*, as I now call it; and who after the Ship was struck on the Rock, and they saw her inevitably lost, had sav'd themselves in their Boat, and were landed upon that wild Shore among the Savages.

Upon this, I enquir'd of him more critically, What was become of them? He assur'd me they lived still there; that they had been there about four Years; that the Savages let them alone, and gave them Victuals to live. I ask'd him, How it came to pass they did not kill them and eat them? He said, *No, they make Brother with them*; that is, as I understood him, a Truce: And then he added, *They no eat Mans but when makes the War fight*; that is to say, they never eat any Men but such as come to fight with them, and are taken in Battle.

It was after this some considerable Time, that being upon the Top of the Hill, at the *East* Side of the Island, from whence as I have said, I had in a clear Day discover'd the Main, or Continent of *America*; *Friday*, the Weather being very serene, looks very earnestly towards the Main Land, and in a kind of Surprise, falls a jumping and dancing, and calls out to me, for I was at some Distance from him: I ask'd him, What was the Matter? *O joy!* Says he, *O glad! There see my Country, there my Nation!*

I observ'd an extraordinary Sense of Pleasure appear'd in his Face, and his Eyes sparkled, and his Countenance discover'd a strange Ea-gerness, as if he had a Mind to be in his own Country again; and this Observation of mine, put a great many Thoughts into me, which made me at first not so easy about my new Man *Friday* as I was before; and I made no doubt, but that if *Friday* could get back to his own Nation again, he would not only forget all his Religion, but all his Obligation to me; and would be forward enough to give his Countrymen an Account of me, and come back perhaps with a hundred or two of them, and make a Feast upon me, at which he might be as merry as he us'd to be with those of his Enemies, when they were taken in War.

But I wrong'd the poor honest Creature very much, for which I was very sorry afterwards. However, as my Jealousy[2] encreased, and held me some Weeks, I was a little more circumspect, and not so familiar and kind to him as before; in which I was certainly in the Wrong too, the honest grateful Creature having no thought about it, but what consisted with the best Principles, both as a religious Christian, and as a grateful Friend, as appeared afterwards to my full Satisfaction.

While my Jealousy of him lasted, you may be sure I was every Day pumping him to see if he would discover any of the new Thoughts, which I suspected were in him; but I found every thing he said was so Honest, and so Innocent, that I could find nothing to nourish my Suspicion; and in spight of all my Uneasiness he made me at last entirely his own again, nor did he in the least perceive that I was Uneasie, and therefore I could not suspect him of Deceit.

One Day walking up the same Hill, but the Weather being haizy at Sea, so that we could not see the Continent, I call'd to him, and said, *Friday*, do not you wish your self in your own Country, your own Nation? Yes, he said, *he be much O glad to be at his own Nation.* What would you do there, said I, would you turn Wild again, eat Mens Flesh again, and be a Savage as you were before? He lookt full of Concern, and shaking his Head said, *No no,* Friday *tell them to live Good,* tell them *to pray God,* tell them *to eat Corn bread, Cattle-flesh, Milk, no eat Man again:* Why then, said I to him, *They will kill you.* He look'd grave at that, and then said, *No, they no kill me, they willing love learn:* He meant by this, they would be willing to learn. He added, they learn'd much of the Bearded-Mans that come in the Boat. Then I ask'd him if he would go back to them? He smil'd at that, and told me he could not swim so far. I told him I would make a *Canoe* for him. He told me, *he would go, if I would go with him.* I go! says I, why they will Eat me if I come there? No, no, says he, *me make they no Eat you; me make they much Love you:* He meant he would tell them how I had kill'd his Enemies, and sav'd his Life, and so he would make them love me; then he told me as well as he could, how kind they were to seventeen White-men, or Bearded-men, as he call'd them, who came on Shore there in Distress.

From this time I confess I had a Mind to venture over, and see if I

2. Suspicion.

could possibly joyn with these Bearded-men, who I made no doubt were *Spaniards* or *Portuguese*; not doubting but if I could we might find some Method to Escape from thence, being upon the Continent, and a good Company together; better than I could from an Island 40 Miles off the Shore, and alone without Help. So after some Days I took *Friday* to work again, by way of Discourse, and told him I would give him a Boat to go back to his own Nation; and accordingly I carry'd him to my Frigate which lay on the other Side of the Island, and having clear'd it of Water, for I always kept it sunk in the Water; I brought it out, shewed it him, and we both went into it.

I found he was a most dextrous Fellow at managing it, would make it go almost as swift and fast again as I could; so when he was in, I said to him, Well now, *Friday*, shall we go to your Nation? He look'd very dull at my saying so, which it seems was, because he thought the Boat too small to go so far. I told him then I had a bigger; so the next Day I went Day I went to the Place where the first Boat lay which I had made, but which I could not get into Water: He said that was big enough; but then as I had taken no Care of it, and it had lain two or three and twenty Years there, the Sun had split and dry'd it, that it was in a manner rotten. *Friday* told me such a Boat would do very well, and would carry *much enough* V*ittle*,[3] *Drink, Bread,* that was his Way of Talking.

Upon the whole, I was by this Time so fix'd upon my Design of going over with him to the Continent, that I told him we would go and make one as big as that, and he should go home in it. He answer'd not one Word, but look'd very grave and sad: I ask'd him what was the matter with him? He ask'd me again thus; *Why, you angry mad with* Friday, *what me done?* I ask'd him what he meant; I told him I was not angry with him at all. *No angry! No angry!* says he, repeating the Words several Times, *Why send* Friday *home away to my Nation?* Why, (says I) *Friday,* did you not say you wish'd you were there? *Yes, yes,* says he, *wish be both there, no wish* Friday *there, no Master there.* In a Word, he would not think of going there without me; *I go there!* Friday, (says I) *what shall I do there?* He turn'd very quick upon me at this: *You do great deal much good,* says he, *you teach wild Mans be good sober tame Mans; you tell them know God, pray God, and live new Life. Alas!* Friday, (says I) *thou knowest not what thou sayest, I am but an ignorant Man my self. Yes, yes,* says he, *you teachee me Good, you teachee them Good. No, no,* Friday, (says I) *you shall go without me, leave me here to live by my self, as I did before.* He look'd confus'd again at that Word, and running to one of the Hatchets which he used to wear, he takes it up hastily, comes and gives it me, *What must I do with this?* says I to him. *You take, kill* Friday; (says he.) *What must I kill you for?* said I again. He returns very quick, *What you send* Friday *away for? take, kill*

3. Victual.

Friday, *no send* Friday *away*. This he spoke so earnestly, that I saw
Tears stand in his Eyes: In a Word, I so plainly discover'd the utmost
Affection in him to me, and a firm Resolution in him, that I told then,
and often after, that I would never send him away from me, if he was
willing to stay with me.

Upon the whole, as I found by all his Discourse a settled Affection
to me, and that nothing should part him from me, so I found all the
Foundation of his Desire to go to his own Country, was laid in his
ardent Affection to the People, and his Hopes of my doing them good;
a Thing which as I had no Notion of my self, so I had not the least
Thought or Intention, or Desire of undertaking it. But still I found a
strong Inclination to my attempting an Escape as above, founded on
the Supposition gather'd from the Discourse, (*viz.*) That there were
seventeen bearded Men there; and therefore, without any more Delay,
I went to Work with *Friday* to find out a great Tree proper to fell, and
make a large Periagua or Canoe to undertake the Voyage. There were
Trees enough in the Island to have built a little Fleet, not of Periagua's
and Canoes, but even of good large Vessels. But the main Thing I look'd
at, was to get one so near the Water that we might launch it when it
was made, to avoid the Mistake I committed at first.

At last, *Friday* pitch'd upon a Tree, for I found he knew much better
than I what kind of Wood was fittest for it, nor can I tell to this Day
what Wood to call the Tree we cut down, except that it was very like
the Tree we call *Fustic*,[4] or between that and the *Nicaragua* Wood,[5]
for it was much of the same Colour and Smell. *Friday* was for burning
the Hollow or Cavity of this Tree out to make it for a Boat. But I shew'd
him how rather to cut it out with Tools, which, after I had shew'd him
how to use, he did very handily, and in about a Month's hard Labour,
we finished it, and made it very handsome, especially when with our
Axes, which I shew'd him how to handle, we cut and hew'd the out-
side into the true Shape of a Boat; after this, however, it cost us near a
Fortnight's Time to get her along as it were Inch by Inch upon great
Rowlers into the Water. But when she was in, she would have carry'd
twenty Men with great Ease.

When she was in the Water, and tho' she was so big, it amazed me
to see with what Dexterity and how swift my Man *Friday* would manage
her, turn her, and paddle her along; so I ask'd him if he would, and if
we might venture over in her; *Yes*, he said, *he venture over in her very
well, tho' great blow Wind*. However, I had a farther Design that he
knew nothing of, and that was to make a Mast and Sail and to fit her
with an Anchor and Cable: As to a Mast, that was easy enough to get;
so I pitch'd upon a strait young Cedar-Tree, which I found near the
Place, and which there was great Plenty of in the Island, and I set *Friday*

4. A common tropical American tree that yields a light yellow dye.
5. A species of South American redwood, also called Brazil wood.

to Work to cut it down, and gave him Directions how to shape and order it. But as to the Sail, that was my particular Care; I knew I had old Sails, or rather Pieces of old Sails enough; but as I had had them now six and twenty Years by me, and had not been very careful to preserve them, not imagining that I should ever have this kind of Use for them, I did not doubt but they were all rotten, and indeed most of them were so; however, I found two Pieces which appear'd pretty good, and with these I went to Work, and with a great deal of Pains, and awkward tedious stitching (you may be sure) for Want of Needles, I at length made a three Corner'd ugly Thing, like what we call in *England*, a Shoulder of Mutton Sail, to go with a Boom at bottom, and a little short Sprit at the Top, such as usually our Ship's Long-Boats sail with, and such as I best knew how to manage; because it was such a one as I had to the Boat, in which I made my Escape from *Barbary*, as related in the first Part of my Story.

I was near two Months performing this last Work, *viz.* rigging and fitting my Mast and Sails; for I finish'd them very compleat, making a small Stay, and a Sail, or Foresail to it, to assist, if we should turn to Windward; and which was more than all, I fix'd a Rudder to the Stern of her, to steer with; and though I was but a bungling Shipwright, yet as I knew the Usefulness, and even Necessity of such a Thing, I apply'd my self with so much Pains to do it, that at last I brought it to pass; though considering the many dull Contrivances I had for it that fail'd, I think it cost me almost as much Labour as making the Boat.

After all this was done too, I had my Man *Friday* to teach as to what belong'd to the Navigation of my Boat; for though he knew very well how to paddle a *Canoe*, he knew nothing what belong'd to a Sail, and a Rudder; and was the most amaz'd, when he saw me work the Boat too and again in the Sea by the Rudder, and how the Sail gy'b,[6] and fill'd this way, or that way, as the Course we sail'd chang'd; I say, when he saw this, he stood like one, astonish'd, and amaz'd: However, with a little Use, I made all these Things familiar to him; and he became an expert Sailor, except that as to the Compass, I could make him understand very little of that. On the other hand, as there was very little cloudy Weather, and seldom or never any Fogs in those Parts, there was the less occasion for a Compass, seeing the Stars were always to be seen by Night, and the Shore by Day, except in the rainy Seasons, and then no body car'd to stir abroad, either by Land or Sea.

I was now entred on the seven and twentieth Year of my Captivity in this Place; though the three last Years that I had this Creature with me, ought rather to be left out of the Account, my Habitation being quite of another kind than in all the rest of the Time. I kept the Anniversary of my landing here with the same Thankfulness to God for

6. Jibbed, swung round or shifted.

his Mercies, as at first; and if I had such Cause of Acknowledgment at first, I had much more so now, having such additional Testimonies of the Care of Providence over me, and the great Hopes I had of being effectually, and speedily deliver'd; for I had an invincible Impression upon my Thoughts, that my Deliverance was at hand, and that I should not be another Year in this Place: However, I went on with my Husbandry, digging, planting, fencing, as usual; I gather'd and cur'd my Grapes, and did every necessary Thing as before.

The rainy Season was in the mean Time upon me, when I kept more within Doors than at other Times; so I had stow'd our new Vessel as secure as we could, bringing her up into the Creek, where as I said, in the Beginning I landed my Rafts from the Ship, and haling her up to the Shore, at high Water mark, I made my Man *Friday* dig a little Dock, just big enough to hold her, and just deep enough to give her Water enough to float in; and then when the Tide was out, we made a strong Dam cross the End of it, to keep the Water out; and so she lay dry, as to the Tide from the Sea; and to keep the Rain off, we laid a great many Boughs of Trees, so thick, that she was as well thatch'd as a House; and thus we waited for the Month of *November* and *December*, in which I design'd to make my Adventure.

When the settled Season began to come in, as the thought of my Design return'd with the fair Weather, I was preparing daily for the Voyage; and the first Thing I did, was to lay by a certain Quantity of Provisions, being the Stores for our Voyage; and intended in a Week or a Fortnight's Time, to open the Dock, and launch out our Boat. I was busy one Morning upon some Thing of this kind, when I call'd to *Friday*, and bid him go to the Sea Shore, and see if he could find a Turtle, or Tortoise, a Thing which we generally got once a Week, for the Sake of the Eggs, as well as the Flesh: *Friday* had not been long gone, when he came running back, and flew over my outer Wall, or Fence, like one that felt not the Ground, or the Steps he set his Feet on; and before I had time to speak to him, he cries out to me, *O Master! O Master! O Sorrow! O bad!* What's the Matter, *Friday*, says I; *O yonder, there*, says he, *one, two, three Canoe! one, two, three!* By his way of speaking, I concluded there were six; but on enquiry, I found it was but three: Well, *Friday*, says I, do not be frighted; so I heartned him up as well as I could: However, I saw the poor Fellow was most terribly scar'd; for nothing ran in his Head but that they were come to look for him, and would cut him in Pieces, and eat him; and the poor Fellow trembled so, that I scarce knew what to do with him: I comforted him so well as I could, and told him I was in as much Danger as he, and that they would eat me as well as him; *but*, says I, *Friday, we must resolve to fight them: Can you fight*, Friday? *Me shoot*, says he, *but there come many great Number.* No matter for that, said I again, our Guns will fright them that we do not kill; so I ask'd him, Whether if I resolv'd to defend him, he would defend me, and stand by me, and do just as I bid him? He said, *Me die, when you bid die, Master*; so I went and fetch'd a good Dram of Rum, and gave him; for I had been so good a Husband of my Rum, that I had a great deal left: When he had drank it, I made him take the two Fowling-Pieces, which we always carry'd, and load them with large Swan-Shot, as big as small Pistol Bullets; then I took four Muskets, and loaded them with two Slugs, and five small Bullets each; and my two Pistols I loaded with a Brace of Bullets each; I hung my great Sword as usual, naked by my Side, and gave *Friday* his Hatchet.

When I had thus prepar'd my self, I took my Perspective-Glass, and went up to the Side of the Hill, to see what I could discover; and I found quickly, by my Glass, that there were one and twenty Savages, three Prisoners, and three *Canoes*; and that their whole Business seem'd to be the triumphant Banquet upon these three humane Bodies, (a barbarous Feast indeed) but nothing more than as I had observ'd was usual with them.

I observ'd also, that they were landed not where they had done, when *Friday* make his Escape; but nearer to my Creek, where the Shore was low, and where a thick Wood came close almost down to the Sea: This, with the Abhorrence of the inhumane Errand these Wretches came about, fill'd me with such Indignation, that I came down again to *Friday*, and told him, I was resolv'd to go down to them, and kill them all; and ask'd him, If he would stand by me? He was now gotten over his Fright, and his Spirits being a little rais'd, with the Dram I had given him, he was very chearful, and told me, as before, *he would die, when I bid die.*

In this Fit of Fury, I took first and divided the Arms which I had charg'd, as before, between us; I gave *Friday* one Pistol to stick in his Girdle, and three Guns upon his Shoulder; and I took one Pistol, and the other three my self; and in this Posture we march'd out: I took a small Bottle of Rum in my Pocket, and gave *Friday* a large Bag, with more Powder and Bullet; and as to Orders, I charg'd him to keep close behind me, and not to stir, or shoot, or do any Thing, till I bid him; and in the mean Time, not to speak a Word: In this Posture I fetch'd a Compass[7] to my Right-Hand, of near a Mile, as well to get over the Creek, as to get into the Wood; so that I might come within shoot[8] of them, before I should be discover'd, which I had seen by my Glass, it was easy to do.

While I was making this March, my former Thoughts returning, I began to abate my Resolution; I do not mean, that I entertain'd any Fear of their Number; for as they were naked, unarm'd Wretches, 'tis certain I was superior to them; nay, though I had been alone; but it occurr'd to my Thoughts, What Call? What Occasion? much less, What

7. Circled.
8. Corrected to "Shot" in the third and subsequent editions.

Necessity I was in to go and dip my Hands in Blood, to attack People, who had neither done, or intended me any Wrong? Who as to me were innocent, and whose barbarous Customs were their own Disaster, being in them a Token indeed of God's having left them, with the other Nations of that Part of the World, to such Stupidity, and to such inhumane Courses; but did not call me to take upon me to be a Judge of their Actions, much less an Executioner of his Justice; that whenever he thought fit, he would take the Cause into his own Hands, and by national Vengeance punish them as a People, for national Crimes; but that in the mean time, it was none of my Business; that it was true, *Friday* might justify it, because he was a declar'd Enemy, and in a State of War with those very particular People; and it was lawful for him to attack them; but I could not say the same with respect to me: These Things were so warmly press'd upon my Thoughts, all the way as I went, that I resolv'd I would only go and place my self near them, that I might observe their barbarous Feast, and that I would act then as God should direct; but that unless something offer'd that was more a Call to me than yet I knew of, I would not meddle with them.

With this Resolution I enter'd the Wood, and with all possible Waryness and Silence, *Friday* following close at my Hells, I march'd till I came to the Skirt of the Wood, on the Side which was next to them; only that one Corner of the Wood lay between me and them; here I call'd softly to *Friday*, and shewing him a great Tree, which was just at the Corner of the Wood, I bad him go to the Tree, and bring me Word if he could see there plainly what they were doing; he did so, and came immediately back to me, and told me they might be plainly view'd there; that they were all about their Fire, eating the Flesh of one of their Prisoners; and that another lay bound upon the Sand, a little from them, which he said they would kill next, and which fir'd all the very Soul within me; he told me it was not one of their Nation; but one of the bearded Men, who he had told me of, that came to their Country in the Boat: I was fill'd with Horror at the very naming the white-bearded Man, and going to the Tree, I saw plainly by my Glass, a white Man who lay upon the Beach of the Sea, with his Hands and his Feet ty'd, with Flags, or Things like Rushes; and that he was an *European*, and had Cloaths on.

There was another Tree, and a little Thicket beyond it, about fifty Yards nearer to them than the Place where I was, which by going a little way about, I saw I might come at undiscover'd, and that then I should be within half Shot of them; so I with-held my Passion, though I was indeed enrag'd to the highest Degree, and going back about twenty Paces, I got behind some Bushes, which held all the way, till I came to the other Tree; and then I came to a little rising Ground, which gave me a full View of them, at the Distance of about eighty Yards.

I had now not a Moment to loose;[9] for nineteen of the dreadful Wretches sat upon the Ground, all close huddled together, and had just sent the other two to butcher the poor *Christian*, and bring him perhaps Limb by Limb to their Fire, and they were stoop'd down to untie the Bands, at his Feet; I turn'd to *Friday*, now *Friday*, said I, do as I bid thee; *Friday* said he would; then *Friday*, says I, do exactly as you see me do, fail in nothing; so I set down one of the Muskets, and the Fowling-Piece, upon the Ground, and *Friday* did the like by his; and with the other Musket, I took my aim at the Savages, bidding him do the like; then asking him, If he was ready? He said, yes, then fire at them, said I; and the same Moment I fir'd also.

Friday took his Aim so much better than I, that on the Side that he shot, he kill'd two of them, and wounded three more; and on my Side, I kill'd one, and wounded two: They were, you may be sure, in a dreadful Consternation; and all of them, who were not hurt, jump'd up upon their Feet, but did not immediately know which way to run, or which way to look: for they knew not from whence their Destruction came: *Friday* kept his Eyes close upon me, that as I had bid him, he might observe what I did; so as soon as the first Shot was made, I threw down the Piece, and took up the Fowling-Piece, and *Friday* did the like; he see me cock, and present, he did the same again; Are you ready? *Friday*, said I; yes, says he; let fly then, says I, in the Name of God, and with that I fir'd again among the amaz'd Wretches, and so did *Friday*; and as our Pieces were now loaden with what I call'd Swan-Shot, or small Pistol Bullets, we found only two drop; but so many were wounded, that they run about yelling, and skreaming, like mad Creatures, all bloody, and miserably wounded, most of them; whereof three more fell quickly after, though not quite dead.

Now *Friday*, says I, laying down the discharg'd Pieces, and taking up the Musket, which was yet loaden; follow me, says I; which he did, with a great deal of Courage; upon which I rush'd out of the Wood, and shew'd my self, and *Friday* close at my Foot; as soon as I perceiv'd they saw me, I shouted as loud as I could, and bad *Friday* do so too; and running as fast I could, *which by the way, was not very fast, being loaden with Arms as I was*, I made directly towards the poor Victim, who was, as I said, lying upon the Beach, or Shore, between the Place where they sat, and the Sea; the two Butchers who were just going to work with him, had left him, at the Suprize of our first Fire, and fled in a terrible Fright, to the Sea Side, and had jump'd into a *Canoe*, and three more of the rest made the same way; I turn'd to *Friday*, and bid him step forwards, and fire at them; he understood me immediately, and running about forty Yards, to be near them, he shot at them, and I thought he had kill'd them all; for I see them all fall of a heap into the Boat; though

9. Corrected to "lose" in the third and subsequent editions.

I saw two of them up again quickly: However, he kill'd two of them, and wounded the third; so that he lay down in the Bottom of the Boat, as if he had been dead.

While my Man *Friday* fir'd at them, I pull'd out my Knife, and cut the Flags that bound the poor Victim, and loosing his Hands, and Feet, I lifted him up, and ask'd him in the *Portuguese* Tongue, What he was? He answer'd in Latin, *Christianus*; but was so weak, and faint, that he could scarce stand, or speak; I took my Bottle out of my Pocket, and gave it to him, making Signs that he should drink, which he did; and I gave him a Piece of Bread, which he eat; then I ask'd him, What Countryman he was? And he said, *Espagniole*; and being a little recover'd, let me know by all the Signs he could possibly make, how much he was in my Debt for his Deliverance; *Seignior*, said I, with as much *Spanish* as I could make up, we will talk afterwards; but we must fight now, if you have any Strength left, take this Pistol, and Sword, and lay about you; he took them very thankfully, and no sooner had he the Arms in his Hands, but as if they had put new Vigour into him, he flew upon his Murtherers, like a Fury, and had cut two of them in Pieces, in an instant; for the Truth is, as the whole was a Surprize to them; so the poor Creatures were so much frighted with the Noise of our Pieces, that they fell down for meer Amazement, and Fear; and had no more Power to attempt their own Escape, than their Flesh had to resist our Shot; and that was the Case of those Five that *Friday* shot at in the Boat; for as three of them fell with the Hurt they receiv'd; so the other two fell with the Fright.

I kept my Piece in my Hand still, without firing, being willing to keep my Charge ready; because I had given the *Spaniard* my Pistol, and Sword; so I call'd to *Friday*, and bad him run up to the Tree, from whence we first fir'd, and fetch the Arms which lay there, that had been discharg'd, which he did with great Swiftness; and then giving him my Musket, I sat down my self to load all the rest again, and bad them come to me when they wanted: While I was loading these Pieces, there happen'd a fierce Engagement between the *Spaniard*, and one of the Savages, who made at him with one of their great wooden Swords, the same Weapon that was to have kill'd him before, if I had not prevented it: The *Spaniard*, who was as bold, and as brave as could be imagin'd, though weak, had fought this *Indian* a good while, and had cut him two great Wounds on his Head; but the Savage being a stout lusty Fellow, closing in with him, had thrown him down (being faint) and was wringing my Sword out of his Hand, when the *Spaniard*, tho' undermost, wisely quitting the Sword, drew the Pistol from his Girdle, shot the Savage through the Body, and kill'd him upon the Spot; before I, who was running to help him, could come near him.

Friday being now left to his Liberty, pursu'd the flying Wretches with no Weapon in his Hand, but his Hatchet; and with that he dispatch'd those three, who, as I said before, were wounded at first and fallen, and all the rest he could come up with, and the *Spaniard* coming to me for a Gun, I gave him one of the Fowling-Pieces, with which he pursu'd two of the Savages, and wounded them both; but as he was not able to run, they both got from him into the Wood, where *Friday* pursu'd them, and kill'd one of them; but the other was too nimble for him, and though he was wounded, yet had plunged himself into the Sea, and swam with all his might off to those two who were left in the *Canoe*, which three in the *Canoe*, with one wounded, who we know not whether he dy'd or no, were all that escap'd our Hands of one and twenty: The Account of the Rest is as follows;

3 Kill'd at our first Shot from the Tree.
2 Kill'd at the next Shot.
2 Kill'd by *Friday* in the Boat.
2 Kill'd by *Ditto*, of those at first wounded.
1 Kill'd by *Ditto*, in the Wood.
3 Kill'd by the *Spaniard*.
4 Kill'd, being found dropp'd here and there of their Wounds, or kill'd by *Friday* in his Chase of them.
4 Escap'd in the Boat, whereof one wounded if not dead.

--

21 In all.

--

Those that were in the *Canoe*, work'd hard to get out of Gun-Shot; and though *Friday* made two or three Shot at them, I did not find that he hit any of them: *Friday* would fain have had me took[1] one of their *Canoes*, and pursu'd them; and indeed I was very anxious about their Escape, least carrying the News home to their People, they should come back perhaps with two or three hundred of their *Canoes*, and devour us by meer Multitude; so I consented to pursue them by Sea, and running to one of their *Canoes*, I jump'd in, and bad *Friday* follow me; but when I was in the *Canoe*, I was surpriz'd to find another poor Creature lye there alive, bound Hand and Foot, as the *Spaniard* was, for the Slaughter, and almost dead with Fear, not knowing what the Matter was; for he had not been able to look up over the Side of the Boat, he was ty'd so hard, Neck and Heels, and had been ty'd so long, that he had really but little Life in him.

I immediately cut the twisted Flags, or Rushes, which they had bound him with, and would have helped him up; but he could not stand, or speak, but groan'd most piteously, believing it seems still that he was only unbound in order to be kill'd.

When *Friday* came to him, I bad him speak to him, and tell him of

1. Take.

his Deliverance, and pulling out my Bottle, made him give the poor
Wretch a Dram, which, with the News of his being deliver'd, reviv'd
him, and he sat up in the Boat; but when *Friday* came to hear him
speak, and look in his Face, it would have mov'd any one to Tears, to
have seen how *Friday* kiss'd him, embrac'd him, hugg'd him, cry'd,
laugh'd, hollow'd, jump'd about, danc'd, sung, then cry'd again, wrung
his Hands, beat his own Face, and Head, and then sung, and jump'd
about again, like a distracted Creature: It was a good while before I
could make him speak to me, or tell me what was the Matter; but when
he came a little to himself, he told me, that it was his Father.

It is not easy for me to express how it mov'd me to see what Extasy
and filial Affection had work'd in this poor *Savage*, at the Sight of his
Father, and of his being deliver'd from Death; nor indeed can I describe
half the Extravagancies of his Affection after this; for he went into the
Boat and out of the Boat a great many times: When he went in to him,
he would sit down by him, open his Breast, and hold his Father's Head
close to his Bosom, half an Hour together, to nourish it: then he took
his Arms and Ankles, which were numb'd and stiff with the Binding,
and chaffed and rubbed them with his Hands; and I perceiving what
the Case was, gave him some Rum out of my Bottle, to rub them with,
which did them a great deal of Good.

This Action put an End to our Pursuit of the Canoe, with the other
Savages, who were now gotten almost out of Sight; and it was happy
for us that we did not; for it blew so hard within two Hours after, and
before they could be gotten a Quarter of their Way, and continued
blowing so hard all Night, and that from the *North-west*, which was
against them, that I could not suppose their Boat could live, or that they
ever reach'd to their own Coast.

But to return to *Friday*, he was so busy about his Father, that I could
not find in my Heart to take him off for some time: But after I thought
he could leave him a little, I call'd him to me, and he came jumping
and laughing, and pleas'd to the highest Extream; then I ask'd him, If
he had given his Father any Bread? He shook his Head, and said, *None*:
Ugly Dog eat all up self; so I gave him a Cake of Bread out of a little
Pouch I carry'd on Purpose; I also gave him a Dram for himself, but
he would not taste it, but carry'd it to his Father: I had in my Pocket
also two or three Bunches of my Raisins, so I gave him a Handful of
them for his Father. He had no sooner given his Father these Raisins,
but I saw him come out of the Boat, and run away, as if he had been
bewitch'd, he run at such a Rate; for he was the swiftest Fellow of his
Foot that ever I saw; I say, he run[2] at such a Rate, that he was out of
Sight, as it were, in an instant; and though I call'd, and hollow'd too,
after him, it was all one, away he went, and in a Quarter of an Hour,

2. Ran.

I saw him come back again, though not so fast as he went; and as he came nearer, I found his Pace was slacker, because he had something in his Hand.

When he came up to me, I found he had been quite Home for an Earthen Jugg or Pot to bring his Father some fresh Water, and that he had got two more Cakes, or Loaves of Bread: The Bread he gave me, but the Water he carry'd to his Father: However, as I was very thirsty too, I took a little Sup of it. This Water reviv'd his Father more than all the Rum or Spirits I had given him; for he was just fainting with Thirst.

When his Father had drank, I call'd to him to know if there was any Water left; he said, yes; and I bad him give it to the poor *Spaniard*, who was in as much Want of it as his Father; and I sent one of the Cakes, that *Friday* brought, to the *Spaniard* too, who was indeed very weak, and was reposing himself upon a green Place under the Shade of a Tree; and whose Limbs were also very stiff, and very much swell'd with the rude Bandage he had been ty'd with. When I saw that upon *Friday*'s coming to him with the Water, he sat up and drank, and took the Bread, and began to eat, I went to him, and gave him a Handful of Raisins: he look'd up in my Face with all the Tokens of Gratitude and Thankfulness, that could appear in any Countenance; but was so weak, notwithstanding he had so exerted himself in the Fight, that he could not stand up upon his Feet; he try'd to do it two or three times, but was really not able, his Ankles were so swell'd and so painful to him; so I bad him sit still, and caused *Friday* to rub his Ankles, and bathe them with Rum, as he had done his Father's.

I observ'd the poor affectionate Creature every two Minutes, or perhaps less, all the while he was here, turn'd his Head about, to see if his Father was in the same Place, and Posture, as he left him sitting; and at last he found he was not to be seen; at which he started up, and without speaking a Word, flew with that Swiftness to him, that one could scarce perceive his Feet to touch the Ground, as he went: But when he came, he only found he had laid himself down to ease his Limbs; so *Friday* came back to me presently, and I then spoke to the *Spaniard* to let *Friday* help him up if he could, and lead him to the Boat, and then he should carry him to our Dwelling, where I would take Care of him: But *Friday*, a lusty strong Fellow, took the *Spaniard* quite up upon his Back, and carry'd him away to the Boat, and set him down softly upon the Side or Gunnel of the Canoe, with his Feet in the inside of it, and then lifted him quite in, and set him close to his Father, and presently stepping out again, launched the Boat off, and paddled it along the Shore faster than I could walk, tho' the Wind blew pretty hard too; so he brought them both safe into our Creek; and leaving them in the Boat, runs away to fetch the other Canoe. As he pass'd me, I spoke to him, and ask'd him, whither he went, he told me, *Go fetch more Boat*; so away he went like the Wind; for sure never Man or Horse run like him, and he had the other Canoe in the Creek, almost as soon as I got to it by Land; so he wafted me over, and then to help our new Guests out of the Boat, which he did; but they were neither of them able to walk; so that poor *Friday* knew not what to do.

To remedy this, I went to Work in my Thought, and calling to *Friday* to bid them sit down on the Bank while he came to me, I soon made a Kind of Hand-Barrow to lay them on, and *Friday* and I carry'd them up both together upon it between us: But when we got them to the outside of our Wall or Fortification, we were at a worse Loss than before; for it was impossible to get them over; and I was resolv'd not to break it down: So I set to Work again; and *Friday* and I, in about 2 Hours time, made a very handsom Tent, cover'd with old Sails, and above that with Boughs of Trees, being in the Space without our outward Fence, and between that and the Grove of young Wood which I had planted: And here we made them two Beds of such things as I had (*viz.*) of good Rice-Straw, with Blankets laid upon it to lye on, and another to cover them on each Bed.

My island was now peopled, and I thought my self very rich in Subjects; and it was a merry Reflection which I frequently made, How like a King I look'd. First of all, the whole Country was my own meer Property; so that I had an undoubted Right of Dominion. 2*dly*, My People were perfectly subjected: I was absolute Lord and Lawgiver; they all owed their Lives to me, and were ready to lay down their Lives, *if there had been Occasion of it*, for me. It was remarkable too, we had but three Subjects, and they were of three different Religions. My Man *Friday* was a Protestant, his Father was a *Pagan* and a *Cannibal*, and the *Spaniard* was a Papist: However, I allow'd Liberty of Conscience throughout my Dominions: But this is by the Way.

As soon as I had secur'd my two weak rescued Prisoners, and given them Shelter, and a Place to rest them upon, I began to think of making some Provision for them: And the first thing I did, I order'd *Friday* to take a yearling Goat, betwixt a Kid and a Goat out of my particular Flock, to be kill'd: When I cut off the hinder Quarter, and chopping it into small Pieces, I set *Friday* to Work to boiling and stewing, and made them a very good Dish, I assure you, of Flesh and Broth, having put some Barley and Rice also into the Broth; and as I cook'd it without Doors, for I made no Fire within my inner Wall, so I carry'd it all into the new Tent; and having set a Table there for them, I sat down and eat my own Dinner also with them, and, as well as I could, chear'd them and encourag'd them; *Friday* being my Interpreter, especially to his Father, and indeed to the *Spaniard* too; for the *Spaniard* spoke the Language of the *Savages* pretty well.

After we had dined, or rather supped, I order'd *Friday* to take one of the Canoes, and go and fetch our Muskets and other Fire-Arms, which

for Want of time we had left upon the Place of Battle, and the next Day
I order'd him to go and bury the dead Bodies of the Savages, which lay
open to the Sun, and would presently be offensive; and I also ordered
him to bury the horrid Remains of their barbarous Feast, which I knew
were pretty much, and which I could not think of doing my self; nay,
I could not bear to see them, if I went that Way: All which he punctually
performed, and defaced[3] the very Appearance of the *Savages* being there;
so that when I went again, I could scarce know where it was, otherwise
than by the Corner of the Wood pointing to the Place.

I then began to enter into a little Conversation with my two new
Subjects; and first I set *Friday* to enquire of his Father, what he thought
of the Escape of the *Savages* in that Canoe, and whether we might
expect a Return of them with a Power too great for us to resist: His first
Opinion was, that the Savages in the Boat never could live out the Storm
which blew that Night they went off, but must of Necessity be drowned
or driven *South* to those other Shores, where they were as sure to be
devoured as they were to be drowned if they were cast away; but as to
what they would do if they came safe on Shore, he said he knew not;
but it was his Opinion that they were so dreadfully frighted with the
Manner of their being attack'd, the Noise and the Fire, that he believed
they would tell their People, they were all kill'd by Thunder, and Lightning, not by the Hand of Man, and that the two which appear'd, (*viz.*)
Friday and me, were two Heavenly Spirits or Furies, come down to
destroy them, and not Men with Weapons: This he said he knew, because
he heard them all cry out so in their Language to one another, for it
was impossible to them to conceive that a Man could dart Fire, and
speak Thunder, and kill at a Distance without lifting up the Hand, as
was done now: And this old Savage was in the right; for, as I understood
since by other Hands, the Savages never attempted to go over to the
Island afterwards; they were so terrified with the Accounts given by those
four Men, (for it seems they did escape the Sea) that they believ'd whoever
went to that enchanged Island would be destroy'd with Fire from the
Gods.

This however I knew not, and therefore was under continual Apprehensions for a good while, and kept always upon my Guard, me and
all my Army; for as we were now four of us, I would have ventur'd upon
a hundred of a them fairly in the open Field at any Time.

In a little Time, however, no more Canoes appearing, the Fear of
their Coming wore off, and I began to take my former Thoughts of a
Voyage to the Main into Consideration, being likewise assur'd by *Friday's*
Father, that I might depend upon good Usage from their Nation on his
Account, if I would go.

But my Thoughts were a little suspended, when I had a serious Dis-

3. Effaced.

course with the *Spaniard*, and when I understood that there were sixteen
more of his Countrymen and *Portuguese*, who having been cast away,
and made their Escape to that Side, liv'd there at Peace indeed with the
Savages, but were very sore put to it for Necessaries, and indeed for Life:
I ask'd him all the Particulars of their Voyage, and found they were a
Spanish Ship bound from the *Rio de la Plata* to the *Havana*, being
directed to leave their Loading there which was chiefly Hides and Silver,
and to bring back what *European* Goods they could meet with there;
that they had five *Portuguese* Seamen on Board, who they took out of
another Wreck; that five of their own Men were drowned when the first
ship was lost, and that these escaped thro' infinite Dangers and Hazards,
and arriv'd almost starv'd on the *Cannibal* Coast, where they expected
to have been devour'd every Moment.

He told me, they had some Arms with them, but they were perfectly
useless, for that they had neither Powder or Ball, the Washing of the
Sea having spoil'd all their Powder but a little, which they used at their
first Landing to provide themselves some Food.

I ask'd him what he thought would become of them there, and if they
had form'd no Design of making any Escape? He said, They had many
Consultations about it, but that having neither Vessel, or Tools to build
one, or Provisions of any kind, their Councils always ended in Tears
and Despair.

I ask'd him how he thought they would receive a Proposal from me,
which might tend towards an Escape? And whether, if they were all
here, it might not be done? I told him with Freedom, I fear'd mostly
their Treachery and ill Usage of me, if I put my Life in their Hands;
for that Gratitude was no inherent Virtue in the Nature of Man; nor
did Men always square their Dealings by the Obligations they had receiv'd, so much as they did by the Advantages they expected. I told him
it would be very hard, that I should be the Instrument of their Deliverance, and that they should afterwards make me their Prisoner in *New
Spain*,[4] where an *English* Man was certain to be made a Sacrifice, what
Necessity, or what Accident soever, brought him thither: And that I had
rather be deliver'd up to the *Savages*, and be devour'd alive, than fall
into the merciless Claws of the Priests, and be carry'd into the *Inquisition*.
I added, That otherwise I was perswaded, if they were all here, we might,
with so many Hands, build a Bark large enough to carry us all away,
either to the *Brasils* South-ward, or to the Islands, or *Spanish* Coast
North-ward: But that if in Requital they should, when I had put Weapons
into their Hands, carry me by Force among their own People, I might
be ill used for my Kindness to them, and make my Case worse than it
was before.

He answer'd with a great deal of Candor and Ingenuity, That their

4. Spanish colonies in the New World.

Condition was so miserable, and they were so sensible of it, that he believed they would abhor the thought of using any Man unkindly that should contribute to their Deliverance; and that, if I pleased, he would go to them with the old Man, and discourse with them about it, and return again, and bring me their Answer: That he would make Conditions with them upon their solemn Oath, That they should be absolutely under my Leading, as their Commander and Captain; and that they should swear upon the Holy Sacraments and the Gospel, to be true to me, and to go to such Christian Country, as that I should agree to, and no other; and to be directed wholly and absolutely by my Orders, 'till they were landed safely in such Country, as I intended; and that he would bring a Contract from them under their Hands for that Purpose.

Then he told me, he would first swear to me himself, That he would never stir from me as long as he liv'd, 'till I gave him Orders; and that he would take my Side to the last Drop of his Blood, if there should happen the least Breach of Faith among his Country-men.

He told me, they were all of them very civil honest Men, and they were under the greatest Distress imaginable, having neither Weapons or Cloaths, nor any Food, but at the Mercy and Discretion of the *Savages*; out of all Hopes of ever returning to their own Country; and that he was sure, if I would undertake their Relief, they would live and die by me.

Upon these Assurances, I resolv'd to venture to relieve them, if possible, and to send the old *Savage* and this *Spaniard* over to them to treat: But when we had gotten all things in a Readiness to go, the *Spaniard* himself started an Objection, which had so much Prudence in it on one hand, and so much Sincerity on the other hand, that I could not but be very well satisfy'd in it; and by his Advice, put off the Deliverance of his Comrades, for at least half a Year. The Case was thus:

He had been with us now about a Month; during which time, I had let him see in what Manner I had provided, with the Assistance of Providence, for my support; and he saw evidently what Stock of Corn and Rice I had laid up; which as it was more than sufficient for myself, so it was not sufficient, at least without good Husbandry, for my Family; now it was encreas'd to Number four: But much less would it be sufficient, if his Country-men, who were, as he said, fourteen still alive, should come over. And least of all should it be sufficient to victual our Vessel, if we should build one, for a Voyage to any of the Christian Colonies of *America*. So he told me, he thought it would be more advisable, to let him and the two other, dig and cultivate some more Land, as much as I could spare Seed to sow; and that we should wait another Harvest, that we might have a Supply of Corn for his Country-men when they should come; for Want might be a Temptation to them to disagree, or not to think themselves delivered, otherwise than out of one Difficulty into another. You know, says he, the Children of *Israel*,[5] though they rejoyc'd at first for their being deliver'd out of *Egypt*, yet rebell'd even against God himself that deliver'd them, when they came to want Bread in the Wilderness.

His Caution was so seasonable, and his Advice so good, that I could not but be very well pleased with his Proposal, as well as I was satisfy'd with his Fidelity. So we fell to digging all four of us, as well as the Wooden Tools we were furnish'd with permitted; and in about a Month's time, by the End of which it was Seed time, we had gotten as much Land cur'd[6] and trim'd up, as we sowed 22 Bushels of Barley on, and 16 Jarrs of Rice, which was in short all the Seed we had to spare; nor indeed did we leave our selves Barley sufficient for our own Food, for the six Months that we had to expect[7] our Crop, that is to say, reckoning from the time we set our Seed aside for sowing; for it is not to be supposed it is six Months in the Ground in the Country.

Having now Society enough, and our Number being sufficient to put us out of Fear of the *Savages*, if they had come, unless their Number had been very great, we went freely all over the Island, where-ever we found Occasion; and as here we had our Escape or Deliverance upon our Thoughts, it was impossible, *at least for me*, to have the Means of it out of mine; to this Purpose, I mark'd out several Trees which I thought fit for our Work, and I set *Friday* and his Father to cutting them down; and then I caused the *Spaniard*, to whom I imparted my Thought on that Affair, to oversee and direct their Work. I shewed them with what indefatigable Pains I had hewed a large Tree into single Planks, and I caused them to do the like, till they had made about a Dozen large Planks of good Oak, near 2 Foot broad, 35 Foot long, and from 2 Inches to 4 Inches thick: What prodigious Labour it took up, any one may imagine.

At the same time I contrived to encrease my little Flock of tame Goats as much as I could; and to this Purpose, I made *Friday* and the *Spaniard* go out one Day, and my self with *Friday* the next Day; for we took our Turns: And by this Means we got above 20 young Kids to breed up with the rest; for when-ever we shot the Dam, we saved the Kids, and added them to our Flock: But above all, the Season for curing the Grapes coming on, I caused such a prodigious Quantity to be hung up in the Sun, that I believe, had we been at *Alicant*,[8] where the Raisins of the Sun are cur'd, we could have fill'd 60 to 80 Barrels; and these with our Bread was a great Part of our Food, and very good living too, I assure you; for it is an exceeding nourishing Food.

It was now Harvest, and our Crop in good Order; it was not the most

5. Exodus 16.1ff.
6. Cleared.
7. Wait for.
8. Port in southern Spain.

plentiful Encrease I had seen in the Island, but however it was enough to answer our End; for from our 22 Bushels of Barley, we brought in and thrashed out above 220 Bushels; and the like in Proportion of the Rice, which was Store enough for our Food to the next Harvest, tho' all the 16 *Spaniards* had been on Shore with me; or if we had been ready for a Voyage, it would very plentifully have victualled our Ship, to have carry'd us to any Part of the World, that is to say, of *America*.

When we had thus hous'd and secur'd our Magazine of Corn, we fell to Work to make more Wicker Work, (*viz.*) great Baskets in which we kept it; and the *Spaniard* was very handy and dexterous at this Part, and often blam'd me that I did not make some things, for Defence, of this Kind of Work; but I saw no Need of it.

And now having a full Supply of Food for all the Guests I expected, I gave the *Spaniard* Leave to go over to the *Main*, to see what he could do with those he had left behind him there. I gave him a strict Charge in Writing, Not to bring any Man with him, who would not first swear in the Presence of himself and of the old *Savage*, That he would no way injure, fight with, or attack the Person he should find in the Island, who was so kind to send for them in order to their Deliverance; but that they would stand by and defend him against all such Attempts, and where-ever they went, would be entirely under and subjected to his Commands; and that this should be put in Writing, and signed with their Hands: How we were to have this done, when I knew they had neither Pen or Ink; that indeed was a Question which we never asked.

Under these Instructions, the *Spaniard*, and the old *Savage* the Father of *Friday*, went away in one of the Canoes, which they might be said to come in, or rather were brought in, when they came as Prisoners to be devour'd by the *Savages*.

I gave each of them a Musket with a Firelock on it, and about eight Charges of Powder and Ball, charging them to be very good Husbands of both, and not to use either of them but upon urgent Occasion.

This was a chearful Work, being the first Measures used by me in view of my Deliverance for now 27 Years and some Days. I gave them Provisions of Bread, and of dry'd Grapes, sufficient for themselves for many Days, and sufficient for all their Country-men for about eight Days time; and wishing them a good Voyage, I see them go, agreeing with them about a Signal they should hang out at their Return, by which I should know them again, when they came back, at a Distance, before they came on Shore.

They went away with a fair Gale on the Day that the Moon was at Full by my Account, in the Month of *October*: But as for an exact Reckoning of Days, after I had once lost it, I could never recover it again; nor had I kept even the Number of Years so punctually, as to be sure that I was right, tho' as it prov'd, when I afterwards examin'd my Account, I found I had kept a true Reckoning of Years.

It was no less than eight Days I had waited for them, when a strange and unforeseen Accident interven'd, of which the like has not perhaps been heard of in History: I was fast asleep in my Hutch one Morning, when my Man *Friday* came running in to me, and call'd aloud, Master, Master, they are come, they are come.

I jump'd up, and regardless of Danger, I went out, as soon as I could get my Cloaths on, thro' my little Grove, which by the Way was by this time grown to be a very thick Wood; I say, regardless of Danger, I went without my Arms, which was not my Custom to do: But I was surpriz'd, when turning my Eyes to the Sea, I presently saw a Boat at about a league and half's Distance, standing in for the Shore, with a *Shoulder of Mutton Sail*, as they call it; and the Wind blowing pretty fair to bring them in; also I observ'd presently, that they did not come from that Side which the Shore lay on, but from the Southermost End of the Island: Upon this I call'd *Friday* in, and bid him lie close, for these were not the People we look'd for, and that we might not know yet whether they were Friends or Enemies.

In the next Place, I went in to fetch my Perspective Glass, to see what I could make of them; and having taken the Ladder out, I climb'd up to the Top of the Hill, as I used to do when I was apprehensive of any thing, and to take my View the plainer without being discover'd.

I had scarce set my Foot on the Hill, when my Eye plainly discover'd a Ship lying at an Anchor, at about two Leagues and an half's Distance from me South-south-east, but not above a League and an half from the Shore. By my Observation it appear'd plainly to be an English Ship, and the Boat appear'd to be an *English* Long-Boat.

I cannot express the Confusion I was in, tho' the Joy of seeing a Ship, and one who I had Reason to believe was Mann'd by my own Country-men, and consequently Friends, was such as I cannot describe; but yet I had some secret Doubts hung about me, I cannot tell from whence they came, bidding me keep upon my Guard. In the first Place, it occurr'd to me to consider what Business an *English* Ship could have in that part of the World, since it was not the Way to or from any Part of the World, where the *English* had any Traffick; and I knew there had been no Storms to drive them in there, as in Distress; and that if they were *English* really, it was most probable that they were here upon no good Design; and that I had better continue as I was, than fall into the Hands of Thieves and Murtherers.

Let no Man despise the secret Hints and Notices of Danger, which sometimes are given him, when he may think there is no Possibility of its being real. That such Hints and Notices are given us, I believe few that have made any Observations of things, can deny; that they are certain Discoveries[9] of an invisible World, and a Converse[1] of Spirits,

9. Revelations.
1. Communications.

we cannot doubt; and if the Tendency of them seems to be to warn us to Danger, why should we not suppose they are from some friendly Agent, whether supreme, or inferior, and subordinate, is not the Question; and that they are given for our Good?

The present Question abundantly confirms me in the Justice of this Reasoning; for had I not been made cautious by this secret Admonition, come it from whence it will, I had been undone inevitably, and in a far worse Condition than before, as you will see presently.

I had not kept my self long in this Posture, but I saw the Boat draw near the Shore, as if they look'd for a Creek to thrust in at for the Convenience of Landing; however, as they did not come quite far enough, they did not see the little Inlet where I formerly landed my Rafts; but run their Boat on Shore upon the Beach, at about half a Mile from me, which was very happy for me; for otherwise they would have landed just, as I may say, at my Door, and would soon have beaten me out of my Castle, and perhaps have plunder'd me of all I had.

When they were on Shore, I was fully satisfy'd that they were *English* Men; at least, most of them; one or two I thought were *Dutch*; but it did not prove so: There were in all eleven Men, whereof three of them I found were unarm'd, and as I thought, bound; and when the first four or five of them were jump'd on Shore, they took those three out of the Boat as Prisoners: One of the three I could perceive using the most passionate Gestures of Entreaty, Affliction and Despair, even to a kind of Extravagance; the other two I could perceive lifted up their Hands sometimes, and appear'd concern'd indeed, but not to such a Degree as the first.

I was perfectly confounded at the Sight, and knew not what the meaning of it should be. *Friday* call'd out to me in *English*, as well as he could, O Master! *You see* English *Mans eat Prisoner as well as Savage Mans.* Why, says I, *Friday, Do you think they are a going to eat them then! Yes*, says Friday. *They will eat them*: No, *no*, says I, Friday, *I am afraid they will murther them indeed, but you may be sure they will not eat them.*

All this while I had no thought of what the Matter really was; but stood trembling with the Horror of the Sight, expecting every Moment when the three Prisoners should be kill'd; nay, once I saw one of the Villains lift up his Arm with a great Cutlash,[2] as the Seamen call it, or Sword, to strike one of the poor Men; and I expected to see him fall every Moment, at which all the Blood in my Body seem'd to run chill in my Veins.

I wish'd heartily now for my *Spaniard*, and the *Savage* that was gone with him; or that I had any way to have come undiscover'd within shot of them, that I might have rescu'd the three Men; for I saw no Fire

2. Cutlass.

Arms they had among them; but it fell out to my Mind another way.

After I had observ'd the outrageous Usage of the three Men, by the insolent Seamen, I observ'd the Fellows run scattering about the Land, as if they wanted to see the Country: I observ'd that the three other Men had Liberty to go also where they pleas'd; but they sat down all three upon the Ground, very pensive, and look'd like Men in Despair.

This put me in Mind of the first Time when I came on Shore, and began to look about me; How I gave my self over for lost; How wildly I look'd round me: What dreadful Apprehensions I had: And how I lodg'd in the Tree all Night for fear of being devour'd by wild Beasts.

As I knew nothing that night of the Supply I was to receive by the providential Driving of the Ship nearer the Land, by the Storms and Tide, by which I have since been so long nourish'd and supported; so these three poor desolate Men knew nothing how certain of Deliverance and Supply they were, how near it was to them, and how effectually and really they were in a Condition of Safety, at the same Time that they thought themselves lost, and their Case desperate.

So little do we see before us in the World, and so much reason have we to depend chearfully upon the great Maker of the World, that he does not leave his Creatures so absolutely destitute, but that in the worst Circumstances they have always something to be thankful for, and sometimes are nearer their Deliverance than they imagine; nay, are even brought to their Deliverance by the Means by which they seem to be brought to their Destruction.

It was just at the Top of High-Water when these People came on Shore, and while partly they stood parlying with the prisoners they brought, and partly while they rambled about to see what kind of a Place they were in; they had carelessly staid till the Tide was spent, and the Water was ebb'd considerably away, leaving their Boat a-ground.

They had left two Men in the Boat, who as I found afterwards, having drank a little too much Brandy, fell asleep; however, one of them waking sooner than the other, and finding the Boat too fast a-ground for him to stir it, hollow'd for the rest who were straggling about, upon which they all soon came to the Boat; but it was past all their Strength to launch her, the Boat being very heavy, and the Shore on that Side being a soft ousy Sand, almost like a Quick-Sand.

In this Condition, like true Seamen who are perhaps the least of all Mankind given to fore-thought, they gave it over, and away they stroll'd about the Country again; and I heard one of them say aloud to another, calling them off from the Boat, *Why let her alone*, Jack, *can't ye, she will float next Tide*; by which I was fully confirm'd in the main Enquiry, of what Countrymen they were.

All this while I kept myself very close, not once daring to stir out of my Castle, any farther than to my Place of Observation, near the Top of the Hill; and very glad I was, to think how well it was fortify'd: I knew it was no less than ten Hours before the Boat could be on float again, and by that Time it would be dark, and I might be at more Liberty to see their Motions, and to hear their Discourse, if they had any.

In the mean Time, I fitted my self up for a Battle, as before; though with more Caution, knowing I had to do with another kind of Enemy than I had at first: I order'd *Friday* also, who I had made an excellent Marks-Man with his Gun, to load himself with Arms: I took my self two Fowling-Pieces, and I gave him three Muskets; my Figure indeed was very fierce; I had my formidable Goat-Skin Coat on, with the great Cap I have mention'd, a naked Sword by my Side, two Pistols in my Belt, and a Gun upon each Shoulder.

It was my Design, as I said above, not to have made any Attempt till it was Dark: But about Two a Clock, being the Heat of the Day, I found that in short they were all gone straggling into the Woods, and as I thought were laid down to Sleep. The three poor distressed Men, too Anxious for their Condition to get any Sleep, were however set down under the Shelter of a great Tree, at about a quarter of a Mile from me, and as I thought out of sight of any of the rest.

Upon this I resolv'd to discover my self to them, and learn something of their Condition: Immediately I march'd in the Figure as above, my Man *Friday* at a good Distance behind me, as formidable for his Arms as I, but not making quite so staring a *Spectre-like* Figure as I did.

I came as near them undiscover'd as I could, and then before any of them saw me, I call'd aloud to them in *Spanish, What are ye Gentlemen?*

They started up at the Noise, but were ten times more confounded when they saw me, and the uncouth Figure that I made. They made no Answer at all, but I thought I perceiv'd them just going to fly from me, when I spoke to them in *English*: Gentlemen, said I, do not be surpriz'd at me; perhaps you may have a Friend near you when you did not expect it. He must be sent directly from Heaven then, *said one of them very gravely to me, and pulling off his Hat at the same time to me,* for our Condition is past the Help of Man. All Help is from Heaven, Sir, *said I.* But can you put a Stranger in the way how to help you, for you seem to be in some great Distress? I saw you when you landed, and when you seem'd to make Applications to the Brutes that came with you, I saw one of them lift up his Sword to kill you.

The poor Man with Tears running down his Face, and trembling, looking like one astonish'd, return'd, *Am I talking to God, or Man! Is it a real Man, or an Angel!* Be in no fear about that, Sir, *said I,* if God had sent an Angel to relieve you, he would have come better Cloath'd, and Arm'd after another manner than you see me in; pray lay aside your Fears, I am a Man, an *Englishman*, and dispos'd to assist you, you see; I have one Servant only; we have Arms and Ammunition; tell us freely, Can we serve you?—What is your Case?

Our Case, said he, Sir, is too long to tell you, while our Murtherers are so near; but in short, Sir, I was Commander of that Ship, my Men have Mutinied against me; they have been hardly prevail'd on not to Murther me, and at last have set me on Shore in this desolate Place, with these two Men with me; one my Mate, the other a Passenger, where we expected to Perish, believing the Place to be uninhabited, and know not yet what to think of it.

Where are those Brutes, your Enemies, said I, do you know where they are gone? *There they lye*, Sir, said he, pointing to a Thicket of Trees; *my Heart trembles, for fear they have seen us, and heard you speak; if they have, they will certainly Murther us all.*

Have they any Fire-Arms, *said I*, He answered they had only two Pieces, and one which they left in the Boat. Well then, said I, leave the rest to me; I see they are all asleep, it is an easie thing to kill them all; but shall we rather take them Prisoners? He told me there were two desperate Villains among them, that it was scarce safe to shew any Mercy to; but if they were secur'd, he believ'd all the rest would return to their Duty. I ask'd him, which they were? He told me he could not at that distance describe them; but he would obey my Orders in any thing I would direct. Well, says I, let us retreat out of their View or Hearing, least they awake, and we will resolve further; so they willingly went back with me, till the Woods cover'd us from them.

Look you, Sir, said I, if I venture upon your Deliverance, are you willing to make two Conditions with me; he anticipated my Proposals, by telling me, that both he and the Ship, if recover'd, should be wholly Directed and Commanded by me in every thing; and if the Ship was not recover'd, he would live and dye with me in what Part of the World soever I would send him; and the two other Men said the same.

Well, says I, *my Conditions are but two*. 1. That while you stay on this Island with me, you will not pretend to any Authority here; and if I put Arms into your Hands, you will upon all Occasions give them up to me, and do no Prejudice to me or mine, upon this Island, and in the mean time be govern'd by my Orders.

2. That if the Ship is, or may be recover'd, you will carry me and my Man to *England* Passage free.

He gave me all the Assurances that the Invention[3] and Faith of Man could devise, that he would comply with these most reasonable Demands, and besides would owe his Life to me, and acknowledge it upon all Occasions as long as he liv'd.

Well then, *said I*, here are three Muskets for you, with Powder and Ball; tell me next what you think is proper to be done. He shew'd all the Testimony of his Gratitude that he was able; but offer'd to be wholly guided by me. I told him I thought it was hard venturing any thing; but the best Method I could think of was to fire upon them at once, as they

---

3. Act of finding out or discovering.

lay; and if any was not kill'd at the first Volley, and offer'd to submit,
we might save them, and so put it wholly upon God's Providence to
direct the Shot.

He said very modestly, that he was loath to kill them, if he could
help it, but that those two were incorrigible Villains, and had been the
Authors of all the Mutiny in the Ship, and if they escaped, we should
be undone still; for they would go on Board, and bring the whole Ship's
Company, and destroy us all. *Well then*, says I, *Necessity* legitimates
my Advice; for it is the only Way to save our Lives. However, seeing
him still cautious of shedding Blood, I told him they should go themselves, and manage as they found convenient.

In the Middle of this Discourse, we heard some of them awake, and
soon after, we saw two of them on their Feet. I ask'd him, if either of
them were of the Men who he had said were the Heads of the Mutiny?
He said *No*: Well then, said I, you may let them escape, and Providence
seems to have wakned them on Purpose to save themselves. Now, says
I, if the rest escape you, *it is your Fault*.

Animated with this, he took the Musket, I had given him, in his
Hand, and a Pistol in his Belt, and his two Comrades with him, with
each Man a Piece in his Hand. The two Men who were with him, going
first, made some Noise, at which one of the Seamen who was awake,
turn'd about, and seeing them coming, cry'd out to the rest; but it was
too late then; for the Moment he cry'd out, they fir'd; *I mean the two
Men*, the Captain wisely reserving his own Piece: They had so well aim'd
their Shot at the Men they knew, that one of them was kill'd on the
Spot, and the other very much wounded; but not being dead, he started
up upon his Feet, and call'd eagerly for help to the other; but the Captain
stepping to him, told him, 'twas too late to cry for help, he should call
upon God to forgive his Villany, and with that Word knock'd him down
with the Stock of his Musket, so that he never spoke more: There were
three more in the Company, and one of them was also slightly wounded:
By this Time I was come, and when they saw their Danger, and that it
was in vain to resist, they begg'd for Mercy: The Captain told them, he
would spare their Lives, if they would give him any Assurance of their
Abhorrence of the Treachery they had been guilty of, and would swear
to be faithful to him in recovering the Ship, and afterwards in carrying
her back to *Jamaica*, from whence they came: They gave him all the
Protestations of their Sincerity that could be desir'd, and he was willing
to believe them, and spare their Lives, which I was not against, only
that I oblig'd him to keep them bound Hand and Foot while they were
upon the Island.

While this was doing, I sent *Friday* with the Captain's Mate to the
Boat, with orders to secure her, and bring away the Oars, and Sail,
which they did; and by and by, three straggling Men that were (happily
for them) parted from the rest, came back upon hearing the Guns fir'd,

and seeing their Captain, who before was their Prisoner, now their Conqueror, they submitted to be bound also; and so our Victory was compleat.

It now remain'd, that the Captain and I should enquire into one another's Circumstances: I began first, and told him my whole History, which he heard with an Attention even to Amazement; and particularly, at the wonderful Manner of my being furnish'd with Provisions and Ammunition; and indeed, as my Story is a whole Collection of Wonders, it affected him deeply; but when he reflected from thence upon himself, and how I seem'd to have been preserv'd there, on purpose to save his Life, the Tears ran down his Face, and he could not speak a Word more.

After this Communication was at an End, I carry'd him and his two Men into my Apartment, leading them in, just where I came out, *viz.* At the Top of the House, where I refresh'd them with such Provisions as I had, and shew'd them all the Contrivances I had made, during my long, long, inhabiting that Place.

All I shew'd them, all I said to them, was perfectly amazing; but above all, the Captain admir'd my Fortification, and how perfectly I had conceal'd my Retreat with a Grove of Trees, which having been now planted near twenty Years, and the Trees growing much faster than in *England*, was become a little Wood, and so thick, that it was unpassable in any Part of it, but at the one Side, where I had reserv'd my little winding Passage into it: I told him, this was my Castle, and my Residence; but that I had a Seat in the Country, as most Princes have, whither I could retreat upon Occasion, and I would shew him that too another Time; but at present, our Business was to consider how to recover the Ship: He agreed with me as to that; but told me, he was perfectly at a Loss what Measures to take; for that there were still six and twenty Hands on board, who having entred into a cursed Conspiracy, by which they had all forfeited their Lives to the Law, would be harden'd in it now by Desperation; and would carry it on, knowing that if they were reduc'd, they should be brought to the Gallows, as soon as they came to *England*, or to any of the *English* Colonies; and that therefore there would be no attacking them, with so small a Number as we were.

I mus'd for some Time upon what he had said, and found it was a very rational Conclusion; and that therefore something was to be resolv'd on very speedily, as well to draw the Men on board into some Snare for their Surprize, as to prevent their Landing upon us, and destroying us; upon this it presently occurr'd to me, that in a little while the Ship's Crew wondring what was become of their Comrades, and of the Boat, would certainly come on Shore in their other Boat, to see for them, and that then perhaps they might come arm'd, and be too strong for us; this he allow'd was rational.

Upon this, I told him the first Thing we had to do, was to stave the Boat, which lay upon the Beach, so that they might not carry her off;

and taking every Thing out of her, leave her so far useless as not to be fit to swim; accordingly we went on board, took the Arms which were left on board, out of her, and whatever else we found there, which was a Bottle of Brandy, and another of Rum, a few Bisket Cakes, a Horn of Powder, and a great Lump of Sugar, in a Piece of Canvas; the Sugar was five or six Pounds, all which was very welcome to me, especially the Brandy, and Sugar, of which I had had none left for many Years.

When we had carry'd all these Things on Shore (the Oars, Mast, Sail, and Rudder of the Boat, were carry'd away before, as above) we knock'd a great Hole in her Bottom, that if they had come strong enough to master us, yet they could not carry off the Boat.

Indeed, it was not much in my Thoughts, that we could be able to recover the Ship; but my View was that if they went away without the Boat, I did not much question to make her fit again, to carry us away to the *Leeward* Islands, and call upon our Friends, the *Spaniards*, in my Way, for I had them still in my Thoughts.

While we were thus preparing our Designs, and had first, by main Strength heav'd the Boat up upon the Beach, so high that the Tide would not fleet[4] her off at High-Water-Mark; and besides, had broke a Hole in her Bottom, too big to be quickly stopp'd, and were sat down musing what we should do; we heard the Ship fire a Gun, and saw her make a Waft with her Antient,[5] as a Signal for the Boat to come on board; but no Boat stirr'd; and they fir'd several Times, making other Signals for the Boat.

At last, when all their Signals and Firing prov'd fruitless, and they found the Boat did not stir, we saw them by the Help of my Glasses, hoist another Boat out, and row towards the Shore; and we found as they approach'd that there was no less than ten Men in her, and that they had Fire-Arms with them.

As the Ship lay almost two Leagues from the Shore, we had a full View of them as they came, and a plain Sight of the Men even of their Faces, because the Tide having set them a little to the *East* of the other Boat, they row'd up under Shore, to come to the same Place, where the other had landed, and where the Boat lay.

By this Means, I say, we had a full View of them, and the Captain knew the Persons and Characters of all the Men in the Boat, of whom he said, that there were three very honest Fellows, who he was sure were led into this Conspiracy by the rest, being overpower'd and frighted.

But that as for the Boatswain, who it seems was the chief Officer among them, and all the rest, they were as outragious as any of the Ship's Crew, and were no doubt made desperate in their new Enterprize, and terribly apprehensive he was, that they would be too powerful for us.

I smil'd at him, and told him, that Men in our Circumstances were

4. Float.
5. Ancient or ship's flag.

past the Operation of Fear: That seeing almost every Condition that could be, was better than that which we were suppos'd to be in, we ought to expect that the Consequence, whether Death or Life, would be sure to be a Deliverance: I ask'd him, What he thought of the Circumstances of my Life? And, Whether a Deliverance were not worth venturing for? And where, Sir, said I, is your Belief of my being preserv'd here on purpose to save your Life, which elevated you a little while ago? For my Part, said I, there seems to be but one Thing amiss in all the Prospect of it; *What's that?* Says he; why, said I, 'Tis, that as you say, there are three or four honest Fellows among them, which should be spar'd; had they been all of the wicked Part of the Crew, I should have thought God's Providence had singled them out to deliver them into your Hands; for depend upon it, every Man of them that comes a-shore are our own, and shall die, or live, as they behave to us.

As I spoke this with a rais'd Voice and chearful Countenance, I found it greatly encourag'd him; so we set vigorously to our Business: We had upon the first Appearance of the Boat's coming from the Ship, consider'd of separating our Prisoners, and had indeed secur'd them effectually.

Two of them, of whom the Captain was less assur'd than ordinary, I sent with *Friday*, and one of the three (deliver'd Men) to my Cave, where they were remote enough, and out of Danger of being heard or discover'd, or of finding their way out of the Woods, if they could have deliver'd themselves: Here they left them bound, but gave them Provisions, and promis'd them if they continu'd there quietly, to give them their Liberty in a Day or two; but that if they attempted their Escape, they should be put to Death without Mercy: They promis'd faithfully to bear their Confinement with Patience, and were very thankful that they had such good Usage, as to have Provisions, and a Light left them; for *Friday* gave them Candles (such as we made our selves) for their Comfort; and they did not know but that he stood Sentinel over them at the Entrance.

The other Prisoners had better Usage; two of them were kept pinion'd indeed, because the Captain was not free to trust them; but the other two were taken into my Service upon their Captain's Recommendation, and upon their solemnly engaging to live and die with us; so with them and the three honest Men, we were seven Men, well arm'd; and I made no doubt we shou'd be able to deal well enough with the Ten that were coming, considering that the Captain had said, there were three or four honest Men among them also.

As soon as they got to the Place where their other Boat lay, they run their Boat in to the Beach, and came all on Shore, haling the Boat up after them, which I was glad to see; for I was afraid they would rather have left the Boat at an Anchor, some Distance from the Shore, with some Hands in her, to guard her; and so we should not be able to seize the Boat.

Being on Shore, the first Thing they did, they ran all to their other Boat, and it was easy to see that they were under a great Surprize, to find her stripp'd as above, of all that was in her, and a great hole in her Bottom.

After they had mus'd a while upon this, they set up two or three great Shouts, hollowing with all their might, to try if they could make their Companions hear; but all was to no purpose: Then they came all close in a Ring, and fir'd a Volley of their small Arms, which indeed we heard, and the Ecchos made the Woods ring; but it was all one, those in the Cave we were sure could not hear, and those in our keeping, though they heard it well enough, yet durst give no Answer to them.

They were so astonish'd at the Surprize of this, that as they told us afterwards, they resolv'd to go all on board again to their Ship, and let them know, that the Men were all murther'd, and the Long-Boat stav'd; accordingly they immediately launch'd their Boat again, and got all of them on board.

The Captain was terribly amaz'd, and even confounded at this, believing they would go on board the Ship again, and set Sail, giving their Comrades for lost, and so he should still lose the Ship, which he was in Hopes we should have recover'd; but he was quickly as much frighted the other way.

They had not been long put off with the Boat, but we perceiv'd them all coming on Shore again; but with this new Measure in their Conduct, which it seems they consulted together upon, *viz.* To leave three Men in the Boat, and the rest to go on Shore, and go up into the Country to look for their Fellows.

This was a great Disappointment to us; for now we were at a Loss what to do; for our seizing those seven men on Shore would be no Advantage to us, if we let the Boat escape; because they would then row away to the Ship, and then the rest of them would be sure to weigh and set Sail, and so our recovering the Ship would be lost.

However, we had no Remedy, but to wait and see what the Issue of Things might present; the seven Men came on Shore, and the three who remain'd in the Boat, put her off to a good Distance from the Shore, and came to an Anchor to wait for them; so that it was impossible for us to come at them in the Boat.

Those that came on Shore, kept close together, marching towards the Top of the little Hill, under which my Habitation lay; and we could see them plainly, though they could not perceive us: We could have been very glad they would have come nearer to us, so that we might have fir'd at them, or that they would have gone farther off, that we might have come abroad.

But when they were come to the Brow of the Hill, where they could see a great way into the Valleys and Woods, which lay towards the *North-East* Part, and where the Island lay lowest, they shouted, and hollow'd, till they were weary; and not caring it seems to venture far from the Shore, nor far from one another, they sat down together under a Tree, to consider of it: Had they thought fit to have gone to sleep there, as the other Party of them had done, they had done the Jobb for us; but they were too full of Apprehensions of Danger, to venture to go to sleep, though they could not tell what the Danger was they had to fear neither.

The Captain made a very just Proposal to me, upon this Consultation of theirs, *viz*. That perhaps they would all fire a Volley again, to endeavour to make their Fellows hear and that we should all Sally[6] upon them, just at the Juncture when their Pieces were all discharg'd, and they would certainly yield, and we should have them without Bloodshed: I lik'd the Proposal, provided it was done while we were near enough to come up to them, before they could load their Pieces again.

But this Event did not happen, and we lay still a long Time, very irresolute what Course to take; at length I told them, there would be nothing to be done in my Opinion till Night, and then if they did not return to the Boat, perhaps we might find a way to get between them, and the Shore, and so might use some Stratagem with them in the Boat, to get them on Shore.

We waited a great while, though very impatient for their removing; and were very uneasy, when after long Consultations, we saw them start all up, and march down toward the Sea: It seems they had such dreadful Apprehensions upon them, of the Danger of the Place, that they resolv'd to go on board the Ship again, give their Companions over for lost, and so go on with their intended Voyage with the Ship.

As soon as I perceiv'd them go towards the Shore, I imagin'd it to be as it really was, That they had given over their Search, and were for going back again; and the Captain, as soon as I told him my Thoughts, was ready to sink at the Apprehensions of it, but I presently thought of a Stratagem to fetch them back again, and which answer'd my End to at Tittle.

I order'd *Friday*, and the Captain's Mate, to go over the little Creek *Westward*, towards the Place were the *Savages* came on Shore, when *Friday* was rescu'd; and as soon as they came to a little rising Ground, at about half a Mile Distance, I bad them hollow[7] as loud as they could, and wait till they found the Seamen heard them; that as soon as ever they heard the Seamen answer them, they should return it again, and then keeping out of Sight, take a round,[8] always answering when the other hollow'd, to draw them as far into the Island, and among the Woods, as possible, and then wheel about again to me, by such ways as I directed them.

6. Burst forth.
7. Holler.
8. Circle round.

They were just going into the Boat, when *Friday* and the Mate hollow'd, and they presently heard them, and answering, run along the
Shore *Westward*, towards the Voice they heard, where they were presently stopp'd by the Creek, where the Water being up, they could not
get over, and call'd for the Boat to come up, and set them over, as
indeed I expected.

When they had set themselves over, I observ'd, that the Boat being
gone up a good way into the Creek, and as it were, in a Harbour within
the Land, they took one of the three Men out of her to go along with
them, and left only two in the Boat, having fastned her to the Stump
of a little Tree on the Shore.

This was what I wish'd for, and immediately leaving *Friday* and the
Captain's Mate to their Business, I took the rest with me, and crossing
the Creek out of their Sight, we surpriz'd the two Men before they were
aware; one of them lying on Shore, and the other being in the Boat;
the Fellow on Shore, was between sleeping and waking, and going to
start up, the Captain who was foremost, ran in upon him, and knock'd
him down, and then call'd out to him in the Boat, to yield, or he was
a dead Man.

There needed very few Arguments to perswade a single Man to yield,
when he saw five Men upon him, and his Comrade knock'd down;
besides, this was it seems one of the three who were not so hearty in
the Mutiny as the rest of the Crew, and therefore was easily perswaded,
not only to yield, but afterwards to joyn very sincerely with us.

In the mean time, *Friday* and the Captain's Mate so well manag'd
their Business with the rest, that they drew them by hollowing and
answering, from one Hill to another, and from one Wood to another,
till they not only heartily tyr'd them, but left them, where they were
very sure they could not reach back to the Boat, before it was dark; and
indeed they were heartily tyr'd themselves also by the Time they came
back to us.

We had nothing now to do, but to watch for them, in the Dark, and
to fall upon them, so as to make sure work with them.

It was several Hours after *Friday* came back to me, before they came
back to their Boat; and we could hear the foremost of them long before
they came quite up, calling to those behind to come along, and could
also hear them answer and complain, how lame and tyr'd they were,
and not able to come any faster, which was very welcome News to us.

At length they came up to the Boat; but 'tis impossible to express their
Confusion, when they found the Boat fast a-Ground in the Creek, the
Tide ebb'd out, and their two Men gone: We could hear them call to
one another in a most lamentable Manner, telling one another, they
were gotten into an inchanted Island; that either there were Inhabitants
in it, and they should all be murther'd, or else there were Devils and
Spirits in it, and they should be all carry'd away, and devour'd.

They hallow'd[9] again, and call'd their two Comerades by their Names,
a great many times, but no Answer. After some time, we could see
them, by the little Light there was, run about wringing their Hands like
Men in Despair; and that sometimes they would go and sit down in the
Boat to rest themselves, then come ashore again, and walk about again,
and so over the same thing again.

My Men would fain have me give them Leave to fall upon them at
once in the Dark; but I was willing to take them at some Advantage, so
to spare them, and kill as few of them as I could; and especially I was
unwilling to hazard the killing any of our own Men, knowing the other
were very well armed. I resolved to wait to see if they did not separate;
and therefore to make sure of them, I drew my Ambuscade nearer, and
order'd *Friday* and the Captain, to creep upon their Hands and Feet as
close to the Ground as they could, that they might not be discover'd,
and get as near them as they could possibly, before they offered to fire.

They had not been long in that Posture, but that the Boat-swain, who
was the principal Ringleader of the Mutiny, and had now shewn himself
the most dejected and dispirited of all the rest, came walking towards
them with two more of their Crew; the Captain was so eager, as having
this principal Rogue so much in his Power, that he could hardly have
Patience to let him come so near, as to be sure of him; for they only
heard his Tongue before: But when they came nearer, the Captain and
Friday starting up on their Feet, let fly at them.

The Boatswain was kill'd upon the Spot, the next Man was shot into
the Body, and fell just by him, tho' he did not die 'till an Hour or Two
after; and the third run for it.

At the Noise of the Fire, I immediately advanc'd with my whole
Army, which was now 8 men, *viz.* my self *Generalissimo*,[1] *Friday* my
Lieutenant-General, the Captain and his two Men, and the three Pris-
oners of War, who we had trusted with Arms.

We came upon them indeed in the Dark, so that they could not see
our Number; and I made the Man we had left in the Boat, who was
now one of us, call to them by Name, to try if I could bring them to a
Parley, and so might perhaps reduce them to Terms, which fell out just
as we desir'd: for indeed it was easy to think, as their Condition then
was, they would be very willing to capitulate; so he calls out as loud as
he could, to one of them, *Tom Smith, Tom Smith; Tom Smith* answered
immediately, *Who's that*, Robinson? for it seems he knew his Voice:
T'other answered, Ay, *ay; for God's Sake*, Tom Smith, *throw down your
Arms, and yield*, or, *you are all dead Men this Moment.*

Who must we yield to? where are they? (says *Smith* again;) *Here they
are*, says he, here's our Captain, and fifty Men with him, have been
hunting you this two Hours; the Boatswain is kill'd, *Will Frye* is

9. Hollered ("hollow'd" in the third and later editions).
1. Italian superlative for *generale*—hence highest ranking general.

wounded, and I am a Prisoner; and if you do not yield, you are all lost.

Will they give us Quarter then, (says *Tom Smith*) and we will yield? *I'll go and ask, if you promise to yield*, says *Robinson*; so he ask'd the Captain, and the Captain then calls himself out, You *Smith*, you know my Voice, if you lay down your Arms immediately, and submit, you shall have your Lives, all but *Will. Atkins.*

Upon this, *Will Atkins* cry'd out, *For God's sake, Captain, give me Quarter, what have I done? They have been all as bad as I*; which by the Way was not true neither; for it seems this *Will. Atkins* was the first Man that laid hold of the Captain, when they first mutiny'd, and used him barbarously, in tying his Hands, and giving him injurious Language. However, the Captain told him he must lay down his Arms at Discretion, and trust to the Governour's Mercy, by which he meant me; for they all call'd me Governour.

In a Word, they all laid down their Arms, and begg'd their Lives; and I sent the Man that had parley'd with them, and two more, who bound them all; and then my great Army of 50 Men, which particularly with those three, were all but eight, came up and seiz'd upon them all, and upon their Boat, only that I kept my self and one more out of Sight, for Reasons of State.

Our next Work was to repair the Boat, and think of seizing the Ship; and as for the Captain, now he had Leisure to parley with them: He expostulated with them upon the Villany of their Practices with him, and at length upon the farther Wickedness of their Design, and how certainly it must bring them to Misery and Distress in the End, and perhaps to the Gallows.

They all appear'd very penitent, and begg'd hard for their Lives; as for that, he told them, they were none of his Prisoners, but the Commander's of the Island; that they thought they had set him on Shore in a barren uninhabited Island, but it had pleased God so to direct them, that the Island was inhabited, and that the Governour was an *English* Man; that he might hang them all there, if he pleased; but as he had given them all Quarter, he supposed he would send them to *England* to be dealt with there, as Justice requir'd, except *Atkins*, who he was commanded by the Governour to advise to prepare for Death; for that he would be hang'd in the Morning.

Though this was all a Fiction of his own, yet it had its desired Effect; *Atkins* fell upon his Knees to beg the Captain to interceed with the Governour for his Life; and all the rest beg'd of him for God's sake, that they might not be sent to *England.*

It now occurr'd to me, that the time of our Deliverance was come, and that it would be a most easy thing to bring these Fellows in, to be hearty in getting Possession of the Ship; so I retir'd in the Dark from them, that they might not see what Kind of a Governour they had, and call'd the Captain to me; when I call'd, as at a good Distance, one of

the Men was order'd to speak again, and say to the Captain, *Captain,
the Commander calls for you*; and presently the Captain reply'd, *Tell his
Excellency, I am just a coming:* This more perfectly amused[2] them; and
they all believed that the Commander was just by with his fifty Men.

Upon the Captain's coming to me, I told him my Project for seizing
the Ship, which he lik'd of wonderfully well, and resolv'd to put it in
Execution the next Morning.

But in Order to execute it with more Art, and secure of Success, I
told him, we must divide the Prisoners, and that he should go and take
Atkins and two more of the worst of them, and send them pinion'd to
the Cave where the others lay: This was committed to *Friday* and the
two Men who came on Shore with the Captain.

They convey'd them to the Cave, as to a Prison; and it was indeed a
dismal Place, especially to Men in their Condition.

The other I order'd to my *Bower*, as I call'd it, of which I have given
a full Description; and as it was fenc'd in, and they pinion'd, the Place
was secure enough, considering they were upon their Behaviour.

To these in the Morning I sent the Captain, who was to enter into a
Parley with them, in a Word, to try them, and tell me, whether he
thought they might be trusted or no, to go on Board and surprize the
Ship. He talk'd to them of the Injury done him; of the Condition they
were brought to; and that though the Governour had given them Quarter
for their Lives, as to the present Action, yet that if they were sent to
England, they would all be hang'd in Chains, to be sure; but that if
they would join in so just an Attempt, as to recover the Ship, he would
have the Governour's engagement for their Pardon.

Any one may guess how readily such a Proposal would be accepted
by Men in their Condition; they fell down on their Knees to the Captain,
and promised with the deepest Imprecations, that they would be faithful
to him to the last Drop, and that they should owe their Lives to him,
and would go with him all over the World, that they would own him
for a Father to them as long as they liv'd.

Well, says the Captain, I must go and tell the Governour what you
say, and see what I can do to bring him to consent to it: So he brought
me an Account of the Temper he found them in; and that he verily
believ'd they would be faithful.

However, that we might be very secure, I told him he should go back
again, and choose out those five and tell them, they might see that he
did not want Men, that he would take out those five to be his Assistants,
and that the Governour would keep the other two, and the three that
were sent Prisoners to the Castle, (*my Cave*) as Hostages, for the Fidelity
of those five; and that if they prov'd unfaithful in the Execution, the
five Hostages should be hang'd in Chains alive upon the Shore.

2. Tricked.

This look'd severe, and convinc'd them that the Governour was in Earnest; however, they had no Way left them, but to accept it; and it was now the Business of the Prisoners, as much as of the Captain, to perswade the other five to do their Duty.

Our Strength was now thus ordered for the Expedition: 1. The Captain, his Mate, and Passenger. 2. Then the two Prisoners of the first Gang, to whom having their Characters from the Captain, I had given their Liberty, and trusted them with Arms. 3. The other two who I had kept till now, in my Bower, pinion'd; but upon the Captain's Motion, had now releas'd. 4. These five releas'd at last: So that they were twelve in all, besides five we kept Prisoners in the Cave, for Hostages.

I ask'd the Captain, if he was willing to venture with these Hands on Board the Ship; for as for me and my Man *Friday*, I did not think it was proper for us to stir, having seven Men left behind; and it was Employment enough for us to keep them assunder, and supply them with Victuals.

As to the five in the Cave, I resolv'd to keep them fast, but *Friday* went in twice a Day to them, to supply them with Necessaries; and I made the other two carry Provisions to a certain Distance, where *Friday* was to take it.

When I shew'd my self to the two Hostages, it was with the Captain, who told them, I was the Person the Governour had order'd to look after them, and that it was the Governour's Pleasure they should not stir any where, but by my Direction; that if they did, they should be fetch'd into the Castle, and be lay'd in Irons; so that as we never suffered them to see me as Governour, so I now appear'd as another Person, and spoke of the Governour, the Garrison, the Castle, and the like, upon all Occasions.

The Captain now had no Difficulty before him, but to furnish his two Boats, stop the Breach of one, and Man them. He made his Passenger Captain of one, with four other Men; and himself, and his Mate, and five more, went in the other: And they contriv'd their Business very well; for they came up to the Ship about Midnight: As soon as they came within Call of the Ship, he made *Robinson* hale them, and tell them they had brought off the Men and the Boat, but that it was a long time before they had found them, and the like; holding them in a Chat 'till they came to the Ship's Side; when the Captain and the Mate entring first with their Arms, immediately knock'd down the second Mate and Carpenter, with the But-end of their Muskets, being very faithfully seconded by their Men; they secur'd all the rest that were upon the Main and Quarter Decks, and began to fasten the Hatches to keep them down who were below, when the other Boat and their Men entring at the Fore-Chains, secur'd the Fore-Castle of the Ship, and the Scuttle[3] which

3. Hatchway.

went down into the Cook-Room, making three Men they found there Prisoners.

When this was done, and all safe upon Deck, the Captain order'd the Mate with three Men to break into the Round-House[4] where the new Rebel Captain lay, and having taken the Alarm, was gotten up, and with two Men and a Boy had gotten Fire Arms in their Hands; and when the Mate with a Crow split open the Door, the new Captain and his Men fir'd boldly among them, and wounded the Mate with a Musket Ball, which broke his Arm, and wounded two more of the Men but kill'd no Body.

The Mate calling for Help, rush'd however into the Round-House, wounded as he was, and with his Pistol shot the new Captain thro' the Head, the Bullet entring at his Mouth, and came out again behind one of his Ears; so that he never spoke a Word; upon which the rest yielded, and the Ship was taken effectually, without any more Lives lost.

As soon as the Ship was thus secur'd, the Captain order'd seven Guns to be fir'd, which was the Signal agreed upon with me, to give me Notice of his Success, which you may be sure I was very glad to hear, having sat watching upon the Shore for it till near two of the Clock in the Morning.

Having thus heard the Signal plainly, I laid me down; and it having been a Day of great Fatigue to me, I slept very sound, 'till I was something surpriz'd with the Noise of a Gun; and presently starting up, I heard a Man call me by the Name of Governour, Governour, and presently I knew the Captain's Voice, when climbing up to the Top of the Hill, there he stood, and pointing to the Ship, he embrac'd me in his Arms, *My dear Friend and Deliverer,* says he, *there's your Ship, for she is all yours, and so are we and all that belong to her.* I cast my Eyes to the Ship, and there she rode within little more than a half a Mile of the Shore; for they had weighed her Anchor as soon as they were Masters of her; and the Weather being fair, had brought her to an Anchor just against the Mouth of the little Creek; and the Tide being up, the Captain had brought the Pinnace[5] in near the Place where I at first landed my Rafts, and so landed just at my Door.

I was at first ready to sink down with the Surprize. For I saw my Deliverance indeed visibly put into my Hands, all things easy, and a large Ship just ready to carry me away whither I pleased to go. At first, for some time, I was not able to answer him one Word; but as he had taken me in his Arms, I held fast by him, or I should have fallen to the Ground.

He perceived the Surprize, and immediately pulls a Bottle out of his Pocket, and gave me a Dram of Cordial, which he had brought on Purpose for me; after I had drank it, I sat down upon the Ground; and

4. Cabin in the rear of the ship, directly below the poop deck.
5. Ship's tender.

though it brought me to my self, yet it was a good while before I could speak a Word to him.

All this while the poor Man was in as great an Extasy as I, only not under any Surprize, as I was; and he said a thousand kind tender things to me, to compose me and bring me to my self; but such was the Flood of Joy in my Breast, that it put all my Spirits into Confusion; at last it broke out into Tears, and in a little after, I recovered my Speech.

Then I took my Turn, and embrac'd him as my Deliverer; and we rejoyc'd together. I told him, I look'd upon him as a Man sent from Heaven to deliver me, and that the whole Transaction seemed to be a Chain of Wonders; that such things as these were the Testimonies we had of a secret Hand of Providence governing the World, and an Evidence, that the Eyes of an infinte Power could search into the remotest Corner of the World, and send Help to the Miserable whenever he pleased.

I forgot not to lift up my Heart in Thankfulness to Heaven; and what Heart could forbear to bless him, who had not only in a miraculous Manner provided for one in such a Wilderness, and in such a desolate Condition, but from whom every Deliverance must always be acknowledged to proceed.

When we had talk'd a while, the Captain told me, he had brought me some little Refreshment, such as the Ship afforded, and such as the Wretches that had been so long his Master had not plunder'd him of: Upon this he call'd aloud to the Boat, and bid his Men bring the things ashore that were for the Governour; and indeed it was a Present, as if I had been one not that was to be carry'd away along with them, but as if I had been to dwell upon the Island still, and they were to go without me.

First he had brought me a Case of Bottles full of excellent Cordial Waters, six large Bottles of *Madera* Wine; the Bottles held two Quarts a-piece; two Pound of excellent good Tobacco, twelve good Pieces of the Ship's Beef, and six Pieces of Pork, with a Bag of Pease, and about a hundred Weight of Bisket.

He brought me also a Box of Sugar, a Box of Flower,[6] a Bag full of Lemons, and two Bottles of Lime-Juice, and Abundance of other things: But besides these, and what was a thousand times more useful to me, he brought me six clean new Shirts, six very good Neckcloaths, two Pair of Gloves, one Pair of Shoes, a Hat, and one Pair of Stockings, and a very good Suit of Cloaths of his own, which had been worn but very little: In a Word, he cloathed me from Head to Foot.

It was a very kind and agreeable Present, as any one may imagine to one in my Circumstances: But never was any thing in the World of that

6. Flour.

Kind so unpleasant, awkward, and uneasy, as it was to me to wear such Cloaths at their first putting on.

After these Ceremonies past, and after all his good things were brought into my little Apartment, we began to consult what was to be done with the Prisoners we had; for it was worth considering, whether we might venture to take them away with us or no, especially two of them, who we knew to be incorrigible and refractory to the last Degree; and the Captain said, he knew they were such Rogues, that there was no obliging them, and if he did carry them away, it must be in Irons, as Malefactors to be delivered over to Justice at the first *English* Colony he could come at; and I found that the Captain himself was very anxious about it.

Upon this, I told him, that if he desir'd it, I durst undertake to bring the two Men he spoke of, to make it their own Request that he should leave them upon the Island: *I should be very glad of that*, says the Captain, *with all my Heart*.

Well, says I, I will send for them up, and talk with them for you; so I caused *Friday* and the two Hostages, for they were now discharg'd, their Comrades having perform'd their Promise; I say, I caused them to go to the Cave, and bring up the five Men pinion'd, as they were, to the Bower, and keep them there 'till I came.

After some time, I came thither dress'd in my new Habit, and now I was call'd Governour again; being all met, and the Captain with me, I caused the Men to be brought before me, and I told them, I had had a full Account of their villanous Behaviour to the Captain, and how they had run away with the Ship, and were preparing to commit farther Robberies, but that Providence had ensnar'd them in their own Ways, and that they were fallen into the Pit which they had digged for others.

I let them know, that by my Direction the Ship had been seiz'd, that she lay now in the Road; and they might see by and by, that their new Captain had receiv'd the Reward of his Villany; for that they might see him hanging at the Yard-Arm.

That as to them, I wanted to know what they had to say, why I should not execute them as Pirates taken in the Fact, as by my Commission they could not doubt I had Authority to do.

One of them answer'd in the Name of the rest, That they had nothing to say but this, That when they were taken, the Captain promis'd them their Lives, and they humbly implor'd my Mercy; But I told them, I knew not what Mercy to shew them; for as for my self, I had resolv'd to quit the Island with all my Men, and had taken Passage with the Captain to go for *England*: And as for the Captain, he could not carry them to *England*, other than as Prisoners in Irons to be try'd for Mutiny, and running away with the Ship; the Consequence of which, they must needs know, would be the Gallows; so that I could not tell which was best for them, unless they had a Mind to take their Fate in the Island; if they desir'd that, I did not care, as I had Liberty to leave it, I had some Inclination to give them their Lives, if they thought they could shift on Shore.

They seem'd very thankful for it, said they would much rather venture to stay there, than to be carry'd to *England* to be hang'd; so I left it on that Issue.

However, the Captain seem'd to make some Difficulty of it, as if he durst not leave them there: Upon this I seem'd a little angry with the Captain, and told him, That they were my Prisoners, not his; and that seeing I had offered them so much Favour, I would be as good as my Word; and that if he did not think fit to consent to it, I would set them at Liberty, as I found them; and if he did not like it, he might take them again if he could catch them.

Upon this they appear'd very thankful, and I accordingly set them at Liberty, and bad them retire into the Woods to the Place whence they came, and I would leave them some Fire Arms, some Ammunition, and some Directions how they should live very well, if they thought fit.

Upon this I prepar'd to go on Board the Ship, but told the Captain, that I would stay that Night to prepare my things, and desir'd him to go on Board in the mean time, and keep all right in the Ship, and send the Boat on Shore the next Day for me; ordering him in the mean time to cause the new Captain who was kill'd, to be hang'd at the Yard-Arm that these Men might see him.

When the Captain was gone, I sent for the Men up to me to my Apartment, and entred seriously into Discourse with them of their Circumstances; I told them, I thought they had made a right Choice; that if the Captain carry'd them away, they would certainly be hang'd. I shewed them the new Captain, hanging at the Yard-Arm of the Ship, and told them they had nothing less to expect.

When they had all declar'd their Willingness to stay, I then told them, I would let them into the Story of my living there, and put them into the Way of making it easy to them: Accordingly I gave them the whole History of the Place, and of my coming to it; shew'd them my Fortifications, the Way I made my Bread, planted my Corn, cured my Grapes; and in a Word, all that was necessary to make them easy: I told them the Story also of the sixteen *Spaniards* that were to be expected; for whom I left a Letter, and made them promise to treat them in common with themselves.

I left them my Fire Arms, *viz.* Five Muskets, three Fowling Pieces, and three Swords. I had above a Barrel and half of Powder left; for after the first Year or two, I used but little, and wasted none. I gave them a Description of the Way I manag'd the Goats, and Directions to milk and fatten them, and to make both Butter and Cheese.

In a Word, I gave them every Part of my own Story; and I told them, I would prevail with the Captain to leave them two Barrels of Gun-Powder more, and some Garden-Seeds, which I told them I would have been very glad of; also I gave them the Bag of Pease which the Captain had brought me to eat, and bad them be sure to sow and encrease them.

Having done all this, I left them the next Day, and went on Board the Ship: We prepared immediately to sail, but did not weigh that Night: The next Morning early, two of the five Men came swimming to the Ship's Side, and making a most lamentable Complaint of the other three, begged to be taken into the Ship, for God's Sake, for they should be murthered, and begg'd the Captain to take them on Board, tho' he hang'd them immediately.

Upon this the Captain pretended to have no Power without me; But after some Difficulty, and after their solemn Promises of Amendment, they were taken on Board, and were some time after soundly whipp'd and pickl'd;[7] after which, they prov'd very honest and quiet Fellows.

Some time after this, the Boat was order'd on Shore, the Tide being up, with the things promised to the Men, to which the Captain at my Intercession caused their Chests and Cloaths to be added, which they took, and were very thankful for; I also encourag'd them, by telling them, that if it lay in my Way to send any Vessel to take them in, I would not forget them.

When I took leave of this Island, I carry'd on board for Reliques, the great Goat's-Skin-Cap I had made, my Umbrella, and my Parrot; also I forgot not to take the Money I formerly mention'd, which had lain by me so long useless, that it was grown rusty, or tarnish'd, and could hardly pass for Silver, till it had been a little rubb'd, and handled; as also the Money I found in the Wreck of the *Spanish* Ship.

And thus I left the Island, the Nineteenth of *December* as I found by the Ship's Account, in the Year 1686, after I had been upon it eight and twenty Years, two Months, and 19 Days;[8] being deliver'd from this second Captivity, the same Day of the Month, that I first made my Escape in the *Barco-Longo*,[9] from among the *Moors* of *Sallee*.

In this Vessel, after a long Voyage, I arriv'd in *England*, the Eleventh of *June*, in the Year 1687, having been thirty and five Years absent.

When I came to *England*, I was as perfect a Stranger to all the World, as if I had never been known there. My Benefactor and faithful Steward, who I had left in Trust with my Money, was alive; but had had great Misfortunes in the World; was become a Widow the second Time, and very low in the World; I made her easy as to what she ow'd me, assuring her, I would give her no Trouble; but on the contrary, in Gratitude to her former Care and Faithfulness to me, I reliev'd her as my little Stock would afford, which at that Time would indeed allow me to do but little for her; but I assur'd her, I would never forget her former Kindness to

---

7. Rubbing salt and vinegar on back wounds after whipping, both to heighten the punishment and to prevent infection.
8. Crusoe's arithmetic, here as elsewhere, is inaccurate.
9. *Longboat* in Spanish.

me; nor did I forget her, when I had sufficient to help her, as shall be observ'd in its Place.

I went down afterwards into *Yorkshire*; but my Father was dead, and my Mother, and all the Family extinct, excpet that I found two Sisters, and two of the Children of one of my Brothers; and as I had been long ago given over for dead, there had been no Provision made for me; so that in a Word, I found nothing to relieve, or assist me; and that little Money I had, would not do much for me, as to settling in the World.

I met with one Piece of Gratitude indeed, which I did not expect; and this was, That the Master of the Ship, who I had so happily deliver'd, and by the same Means sav'd the Ship and Cargo, having given a very handsome Account to the Owners, of the Manner how I had sav'd the Lives of the Men, and the Ship, they invited me to meet them, and some other Merchants concern'd, and altogether made me a very handsome Compliment upon the Subject, and a Present of almost two hundred Pounds Sterling.

But after making several Reflections upon the Circumstances of my Life, and how little way this would go towards settling me in the World, I resolv'd to go to *Lisbon*, and see if I might not come by some Information of the State of my Plantation in the *Brasils*, and of what was become of my Partner, who I had reason to suppose had some Years now given me over for dead.

With this View I took Shipping for *Lisbon*, where I arriv'd in *April* following; my Man *Friday* accompanying me very honestly in all these Ramblings, and proving a most faithful Servant upon all Occasions.

When I came to *Lisbon*, I found out by Enquiry, and to my particular Satisfaction, my old Friend the Captain of the Ship, who first took me up at Sea, off of the Shore of *Africk*: He was now grown old, and had left off the Sea, having put his Son, who was far from a young Man, into his Ship; and who still used the *Brasil* Trade. The old Man did not know me, and indeed, I hardly knew him; but I soon brought him to my Remembrance, and as soon brought my self to his Remembrance, when I told him who I was.

After some passionate Expressions of the old Acquaintance, I enquir'd, you may be sure, after my Plantation and my Partner: The old Man told me he had not been in the *Brasils* for about nine Years; but that he could assure me, that when he came away, my Partner was living, but the Trustees, who I had join'd with him to take Cognizance of my Part, were both dead; that however, he believ'd that I would have a very good Account of the Improvement of the Plantation; for that upon the general Belief of my being cast away, and drown'd, my Trustees had given in the Account of the Produce of my Part of the Plantation, to the Procurator Fiscal, who had appropriated it, in Case I never came to claim it; one Third to the King, and two Thirds to the Monastery of St. *Augustine*, to be expended for the Benefit of the Poor, and for the

Conversion of the *Indians* to the Catholick Faith; but that if I appear'd, or any one for me, to claim the Inheritance, it should be restor'd; only that the Improvement, or Annual Production, being distributed to charitable Uses, could not be restor'd; but he assur'd me, that the Steward of the King's Revenue (from Lands) and the Proviedore, or Steward of the Monastery, had taken great Care all along, that the Incumbent, that is to say my Partner, gave every Year a faithful Account of the Produce, of which they receiv'd duly my Moiety.

I ask'd him if he knew to what height of Improvement he had brought the Plantation? And, Whether he thought it might be worth looking after? Or, Whether on my going thither, I should meet with no Obstruction to my Possessing my just Right in the Moiety?

He told me, he could not tell exactly, to what Degree the Plantation was improv'd; but this he knew, that my Partner was grown exceeding Rich upon the enjoying but one half of it; and that to the best of his Remembrance, he had heard, that the King's Third of my Part, which was it seems granted away to some other Monastery, or Religious House, amounted to above two hundred Moidores a Year; that as to my being restor'd to a quiet Possession of it, there was no question to be made of that, my Partner being alive to witness my Title, and my Name being also enrolled in the Register of the Country; also he told me, That the Survivors of my two Trustees, were very fair honest People, and very Wealthy; and he believ'd I would not only have their Assistance for putting me in Possession, but would find a very considerable Sum of Money in their Hands, for my Account; being the Produce of the Farm while their Fathers held the Trust, and before it was given up as above, which as he remember'd, was for about twelve Years.

I shew'd my self a little concern'd, and uneasy at this Account, and enquir'd of the old Captain, How it came to pass, that the Trustees should thus dispose my Effects, when he knew that I had made my Will, and had made him, the *Portuguese* Captain, my universal Heir, &c.

He told me, that was true; but that as there was no Proof of my being dead, he could not act as Executor, until some certain Account should come of my Death, and that besides, he was not willing to intermeddle with a thing so remote; that it was true he had registered my Will, and put in his Claim; and could he have given any Account of my being dead or alive, he would have acted by Procuration, and taken Possession of the *Ingenio*, so they call'd the Sugar-House, and had given his Son, who was now at the *Brasils*, Order to do it.

But, says the Old Man, I have one Piece of News to tell you, which perhaps may not be so acceptable to you as the rest, and that is, That believing you were lost, and all the World believing so also, your Partner and Trustees did offer to accompt to me in your Name, for six or eight of the first Years of Profits, which I receiv'd; but there being at that time,

says he, great Disbursements for encreasing the Works, building an
Ingenio, and buying Slaves, it did not amount to near so much as
afterwards it produced: However, says the old Man, I shall give you a
true Account of what I have received in all, and how I have disposed
of it.

After a few Days farther Conference with this ancient Friend, he
brought me an Account of the six first Years Income of my Plantation,
sign'd by my Partner and the Merchants Trustees, being always deliver'd
in Goods, *viz.* Tobacco in Roll, and Sugar in Chests, besides Rum,
Molossus,[1] &c. which is the Consequence[2] of a Sugar Work; and I found
by this Account, that every Year the Income considerably encreased;
but as above, the Disbursement being large, the Sum at first was small:
However, the old Man let me see, that he was Debtor to me 470
Moidores of Gold, besides 60 Chests of Sugar, and 15 double Rolls of
Tobacco which were lost in his Ship; he having been Ship-wreck'd
coming Home to *Lisbon* about 11 Years after my leaving the Place.

The good Man then began to complain of his Misfortunes, and how
he had been obliged to make Use of my Money to recover his Losses,
and buy him a Share in a new Ship: However, my old Friend, says he,
you shall not want a Supply in your Necessity; and as soon as my Son
returns, you shall be fully satisfy'd.

Upon this, he pulls out an old Pouch, and gives me 160 *Portugal*
Moidores in Gold; and giving me the Writing of his Title to the Ship,
which his Son was gone to the *Brasils* in, of which he was a Quarter
Part Owner, and his Son another, he puts them both into my Hands
for Security of the rest.

I was too much mov'd with the Honesty and Kindness of the poor
Man, to be able to bear this; and remembering what he had done for
me, how he had taken me up at Sea, and how generously he had used
me on the Occasions, and particularly, how sincere a Friend he was
now to me, I could hardly refrain Weeping at what he said to me:
Therefore, first I asked him, if his Circumstances admitted him to spare
so much Money at that time, and if it would not straiten him? He told
me, he could not say but it might straiten him a little; but however it
was my Money, and I might want it more than he.

Every thing the good Man said was full of Affection, and I could
hardly refrain from Tears while he spoke: In short, I took 100 of the
Moidores, and call'd for a Pen and Ink to give him a Receipt for them;
then I returned him the rest, and told him, If ever I had Possession of
the Plantation, I would return the other to him also, as indeed I afterwards did; and that as to the Bill of Sale of his Part in his Son's Ship,
I would not take it by any Means; but that if I wanted the Money, I
found he was honest enough to pay me; and if I did not, but came to

1. Molasses.
2. By-product.

receive what he gave me reason to expect, I would never have a Penny
more from him.

When this was pass'd, the old Man began to ask me, If he should
put me into a Method to make my Claim to my Plantation? I told him,
I thought to go over to it my self: He said, I might do so if I pleas'd;
but that if I did not, there were Ways enough to secure my Right, and
immediately to appropriate the Profits to my Use; and as there were
Ships in the River of *Lisbon*,[3] just ready to go away to *Brasil*, he made
me enter my Name in a Publick Register, with his Affidavit, affirming
upon Oath that I was alive, and that I was the same Person who took
up the Land for the Planting the said Plantation at first.

This being regularly attested by a Notary, and a Procuration affix'd,
he directed me to send it with a Letter of his Writing, to a Merchant
of his Acquaintance at the Place, and then propos'd my staying with
him till an Account came of the Return.

Never any Thing was more honourable, than the Proceedings upon
this Procuration; for in less than seven Months, I receiv'd a large Packet
from the Survivors of my Trustees the Merchants, for whose Account
I went to Sea, in which were the following particular Letters and Papers
enclos'd.

First, There was the Account Current of the Produce of my Farm,
or Plantation, from the Year when their Fathers had balanc'd with my
old *Portugal* Captain, being for six Years; the Ballance appear'd to be
1174 Moidores in my Favour.

Secondly, There was the Account of four Years more while they kept
the Effects in their Hands, before the Government claim'd the Administration, as being the Effects of a Person not to be found, which they
call'd *Civil Death*; and the Ballance of this, the Value of the Plantation encreasing, amounted to [38,892] Cruisadoes,[4] which made 3241
Moidores.

Thirdly, There was the Prior of the *Augustin*'s Account, who had
receiv'd the Profits for above fourteen Years; but not being to account
for what was dispos'd to the Hospital, very honestly declar'd he had 872
Moidores not distributed, which he acknowledged to my Account; as to
the King's Part, that refunded nothing.

There was a Letter of my Partner's, congratulating me very affectionately upon my being alive, giving me an Account how the Estate was
improv'd, and what it produced a Year, with a Particular of the Number
of Squares or Acres that it contained; how planted, how many Slaves
there were upon it; and making two and twenty Crosses for Blessings,
told me he had said so many *Ave Marias* to thank the Blessed Virgin

3. Tagus River.
4. Defoe apparently failed to calculate the precise amount, for the 1719 editions all leave a blank
   space. The amount has been estimated as above (W. P. Trent). "Cruisadoes" (*crusadoes*) are
   Portuguese silver coins bearing a cross.

that I was alive; inviting me very passionately to come over and take Possession of my own; and in the mean time to give him Orders to whom he should deliver my Effects, if I did not come my self; concluding with a hearty Tender of his Friendship, and that of his Family, and sent me, as a Present, seven fine Leopard's Skins, which he had it seems received from *Africa*, by some other Ship which he had sent thither, and who it seems had made a better Voyage than I: He sent me also five Chests of excellent Sweet-meats, and an hundred Pieces of Gold uncoin'd, not quite so large as Moidores.

By the same Fleet, my two Merchant Trustees shipp'd me 1200 Chests of Sugar, 800 Rolls of Tobacco, and the rest of the whole Accompt in Gold.

I might well say, now indeed, That the latter End of *Job*[5] was better than the Beginning. It is impossible to express here the Flutterings of my very Heart, when I look'd over these Letters, and especially when I found all my Wealth about me; for as the *Brasil* Ships come all in Fleets, the same Ships which brought my Letters, brought my Goods; and the Effects were safe in the River before the Letters came to my Hand. In a Word, I turned pale, and grew sick; and had not the old Man run and fetch'd me a Cordial, I believe the sudden Surprize of Joy had overset Nature, and I had dy'd upon the Spot.

Nay after that, I continu'd very ill, and was so some Hours, 'till a Physician being sent for, and something of the real Cause of my Illness being known, he order'd me to be let Blood; after which, I had Relief, and grew well: But I verily believe, if it had not been eas'd by a Vent given in that Manner, to the Spirits, I should have dy'd.

I was now Master, all on a Sudden, of above 5000. *l. Sterling* in Money, and had an Estate, as I might well call it, in the *Brasils*, of above a thousand Pounds a Year, as sure as an Estate of Lands in *England*:[6] And in a Word, I was in a Condition which I scarce knew how to understand, or how to compose my self, for the Enjoyment of it.

The first thing I did, was to recompense my original Benefactor, my good old Captain, who had been first charitable to me in my Distress, kind to me in my Beginning, and honest to me at the End: I shew'd him all that was sent me, I told him, that next to the Providence of Heaven, which disposes all things, it was owing to him; and that it now lay on me to reward him, which I would do a hundred fold: So I first return'd to him the hundred Moidores I had receiv'd of him, then I sent for a Notary, and caused him to draw up a general Release or Discharge for the 470 Moidores, which he had acknowledg'd he ow'd me in the fullest and firmest Manner possible; after which, I caused a

5. Job 42.12.
6. Crusoe's "Estate" in cash and lands is comparable to that of the lesser landed gentry of England in the early eighteenth century.

Procuration to be drawn, impowering him to be my Receiver of the
annual Profits of my Plantation, and appointing my Partner to accompt
to him, and make the Returns by the usual Fleets to him in my Name;
and a Clause in the End, being a Grant of 100 Moidores a Year to him,
during his Life, out of the Effects, and 50 Moidores a Year to his Son
after him, for his Life: And thus I requited my old Man.

I was now to consider which Way to steer my Course next, and what
to do with the Estate that Providence had thus put into my Hands; and
indeed I had more Care upon my Head now, than I had in my silent
State of Life in the Island, where I wanted nothing but what I had, and
had nothing but what I wanted: Whereas I had now a great Charge upon
me, and my Business was how to secure it. I had ne'er a Cave now to
hide my Money in, or a Place where it might lye without Lock or Key,
'till it grew mouldy and tarnish'd before any Body would meddle with
it: On the contrary, I knew not where to put it, or who to trust with it.
My old Patron, the Captain, indeed was honest, and that was the only
Refuge I had.

In the next Place, my Interest in the *Brasils* seem'd to summon me
thither; but now I could not tell, how to think of going thither, 'till I
had settled my Affairs, and left my Effects in some safe Hands behind
me. At first I thought of my old Friend the Widow, who I knew was
honest, and would be just to me; but then she was in Years, and but
poor, and for ought I knew, might be in Debt; so that in a Word, I had
no Way but to go back to *England* my self, and take my Effects with
me.

It was some Months however before I resolved upon this; and therefore, as I had rewarded the old Captain fully, and to his Satisfaction,
who had been my former Benefactor, so I began to think of my poor
Widow, whose Husband had been my first Benefactor, and she, while
it was in her Power, my faithful Steward and Instructor. So the first
thing I did, I got a Merchant in *Lisbon* to write to his Correspondent
in *London*, not only to pay a Bill, but to go find her out, and carry her
in Money, an hundred Pounds from me, and to talk with her, and
comfort her in her Poverty, by telling her she should, if I liv'd, have a
further Supply: At the same time I sent my two Sisters in the Country,
each of them an Hundred Pounds, they being, though not in Want,
yet not in very good Circumstances; one having been marry'd, and left
a Widow; and the other having a Husband not so kind to her as he
should be.

But among all my Relations, or Acquaintances, I could not yet pitch
upon one, to whom I durst commit the Gross of my Stock, that I might
go away to the *Brasils*, and leave things safe behind me; and this greatly
perplex'd me.

I had once a Mind to have gone to the *Brasils*, and have settled my
self there; for I was, as it were, naturaliz'd to the Place; but I had some

little Scruple in my Mind about Religion, which insensibly drew me back, of which I shall say more presently. However, it was not Religion that kept me from going there for the present; and as I had made no Scruple of being openly of the Religion of the Country, all the while I was among there, so neither did I yet; only that now and then having of late thought more of it, (than formerly) when I began to think of living and dying among them, I began to regret my having profess'd my self a Papist, and thought it might not be the best Religion to die with.

But, as I have said, this was not the main thing that kept me from going to the *Brasils*, but that really I did not know with whom to leave my Effects behind me; so I resolv'd at last to go to *England* with it, where, if I arrived, I concluded I should make some Acquaintance, or find some Relations that would be faithful to me; and according I prepar'd to go for *England* with all my Wealth.

In order to prepare things for my going Home, I first, the *Brasil* Fleet being just going away, resolved to give Answers suitable to the just and faithful Account of things I had from thence; and first to the Prior of St. *Augustine* I wrote a Letter full of Thanks for their just Dealings, and the Offer of the 872 Moidores, which was indisposed of, which I desir'd might be given 500 to the Monastery, and 372 to the Poor, as the Prior should direct, desiring the good *Padres* Prayers for me, and the like.

I wrote next a Letter of Thanks to my two Trustees, with all the Acknowledgment that so much Justice and Honesty call'd for; as for sending them any Present, they were far above having any Occasion of it.

Lastly, I wrote to my Partner, acknowledging his Industry in the Improving the Plantation, and his Integrity in encreasing the Stock of the Works, giving him Instructions for his future Government of my Part, according to the Powers I had left with my old Patron, to whom I desir'd him to send whatever became due to me, 'till he should hear from me more particularly; assuring him that it was my Intention, not only to come to him, but to settle my self there for the Remainder of my Life: To this I added a very handsom Present of some *Italian* Silks for his Wife, and two Daughters, for such the Captain's Son inform'd me he had; with two Pieces of fine *English* broad Cloath, the best I could get in *Lisbon*, five Pieces of black Bays, and some *Flanders* Lace of a good Value.

Having thus settled my Affairs, sold my Cargoe, and turn'd all my Effects into good Bills of Exchange, my next Difficulty was, which Way to go to *England*: I had been accustomed enough to the Sea, and yet I had a strange Aversion to going to *England* by Sea at that time; and though I could give no Reason for it, yet the Difficulty encreas'd upon me so much, that though I had once shipp'd my Baggage, in order to go, yet I alter'd my Mind, and that not once, but two or three times.

It is true, I had been very unfortunate by Sea, and this might be some

of the Reason: But let no Man slight the strong Impulses of his own
Thoughts in Cases of such Moment: Two of the Ships which I had
singl'd out to go in, I mean, more particularly singl'd out than any other,
that is to say, so as in one of them to put my things on Board, and in
the other to have agreed with the Captain; I say, two of these Ships
miscarry'd, *viz*. One was taken by the *Algerines*,[7] and the other was cast
away on the *Start*[8] near *Torbay*, and all the People drown'd except three;
so that in either of those Vessels I had been made miserable; and in
which most, it was hard to say.

Having been thus harass'd in my Thoughts, my old Pilot, to whom
I communicated every thing, press'd me earnestly not to go by Sea, but
either to go by Land to the *Groyne*,[9] and cross over the Bay of *Biscay*
to *Rochell*, from whence it was but an easy and safe Journey by Land
to *Paris*, and so to *Calais* and *Dover*; or to go up to *Madrid*, and so all
the Way by Land thro' *France*.

In a Word, I was so prepossess'd against my going by Sea at all, except
from *Calais* to *Dover*, that I resolv'd to travel all the Way by Land;
which as I was not in Haste, and did not value the Charge, was by much
the pleasanter Way; and to make it more so, my old Captain brought
an *English* Gentleman, the Son of a Merchant in *Lisbon*, who was
willing to travel with me: After which, we pick'd up two more *English*
Merchants also, and two young *Portuguese* Gentlemen, the last going
to *Paris* only; so that we were in all six of us, and five Servants; the two
Merchants and the two *Portuguese*, contenting themselves with one
Servant, between two, to save the Charge; and as for me, I got an *English*
Sailor to travel with me as a Servant, besides my Man *Friday*, who was
too much a Stranger to be capable of supplying the Place of a Servant
on the Road.

In this Manner I set out from *Lisbon*; and our Company being all
very well mounted and armed, we made a little Troop, whereof they
did me the Honour to call me Captain, as well because I was the oldest
Man, as because I had two Servants, and indeed was the Original of
the whole Journey.

As I have troubled you with none of my Sea-Journals, so I shall
trouble you now with none of my Land-Journal: But some Adventures
that happen'd to us in this tedious and difficult Journey, I must not
omit.

When we came to *Madrid*, we being all of us Strangers to *Spain*,
were willing to stay some time to see the Court of *Spain*, and to see
what was worth observing; but it being the latter Part of the Summer,
we hasten'd away, and set out from *Madrid* about the Middle of *October*:
But when we came to the Edge of *Navarre*, we were alarm'd at several

7. Generic term for pirates.
8. Start Point, Devonshire, on the English Channel.
9. Corrupt form of Corunna, a port in northwestern Spain.

Towns on the Way, with an Account, that so much Snow was fallen on the *French* Side of the Mountains, that several Travellers were obliged to come back to *Pampeluna*,[1] after having attempted, at an extream Hazard, to pass on.

When we came to *Pampeluna* it self, we found it so indeed; and to me that had been always used to a hot Climate, and indeed to Countries where we could scarce bear any Cloaths on, the Cold was insufferable; nor indeed was it more painful than it was surprising, to come but ten Days before out of the *Old Castile*[2] where the Weather was not only warm but very hot, and immediately to feel a Wind from the *Pyrenean* Mountains, so very keen, so severely cold, as to be intollerable, and to endanger benumbing and perishing of our Fingers and Toes.

Poor *Friday* was really frighted when he saw the Mountains all cover'd with Snow, and felt cold Weather, which he had never seen or felt before in his Life.

To mend the Matter, when we came to *Pampeluna*, it continued snowing with so much Violence, and so long, that the People said, Winter was come before its time, and the Roads which were difficult before, were now quite impassable: For in a Word, the Snow lay in some Places too thick for us to travel; and being not hard frozen, as is the Case of Northern Countries: There was no going without being in Danger of being bury'd alive every Step. We stay'd no less than twenty Days at *Pampeluna*; when (seeing the Winter coming on, and no Likelihood of its being better; for it was the severest Winter all over *Europe* that had been known in the Memory of Man) I propos'd that we should all go away to *Fonterabia*,[3] and there take Shipping for *Bourdeaux*, which was a very little Voyage.

But while we were considering this, there came in four *French* Gentlemen, who having been stopp'd on the *French* Side of the Passes, as we were on the *Spanish*, had found out a Guide, who traversing the Country near the Head of *Languedoc*,[4] had brought them over the Mountains by such Ways, that they were not much incommoded with the Snow; and where they met with Snow in any Quantity, they said it was frozen hard enough to bear them and their Horses.

We sent for this Guide, who told us, he would undertake to carry us the same Way with no Hazard from the Snow, provided we were armed sufficiently to protect our selves from wild Beasts; for he said, upon these great Snows, it was frequent for some Wolves to show themselves at the Foot of the Mountains, being made ravenous for Want of Food, the Ground being covered with Snow: We told him, we were well enough prepar'd for such Creatures as they were, if he would ensure us from a

1. Pamplona, capital city of the Spanish province of Navarre.
2. Province of Spain (misprinted "old Castile" in the first edition, but corrected after that).
3. Spanish port on the Bay of Biscay.
4. Province in southern France.

Kind of two-legged Wolves, which we were told, we were in most Danger from, especially on the *French* Side of the Mountains.

He satisfy'd us there was no Danger of that kind in the Way that we were to go; so we readily agreed to follow him, as did also twelve other Gentlemen, with their Servants, some *French*, some *Spanish*; who, as I said, had attempted to go, and were oblig'd to come back again.

Accordingly, we all set out from *Pampeluna*, with our Guide, on the fifteenth of *November*; and indeed, I was surpriz'd, when instead of going forward, he came directly back with us, on the same Road that we came from *Madrid*, about twenty Miles; when being pass'd two Rivers, and come into the plain Country, we found our selves in a warm Climate again, where the Country was pleasant, and no Snow to be seen; but on a sudden, turning to his left, he approach'd the Mountains another Way; and though it is true, the Hills and Precipices look'd dreadful, yet he made so many Tours, such Meanders, and led us by such winding Ways, that we were insensibly pass'd the Height of the Mountains, without being much incumber'd with the Snow; and all on a sudden, he shew'd us the pleasant fruitful Provinces of *Languedoc* and *Gascoign*, all green and flourishing; tho' indeed it was at a great Distance, and we had some rough Way to pass yet.

We were a little uneasy however, when we found it snow'd one whole Day, and a Night, so fast, that we could not travel; but he bid us be easy, we should soon be past it all: We found indeed, that we began to descend every Day, and to come more *North* than before; and so depending upon our Guide, we went on.

It was about two Hours before Night, when our Guide being something before us, and not just in Sight, out rushed three monstrous Wolves, and after them a Bear, out of a hollow Way, adjoyning to a thick Wood; two of the Wolves flew upon the Guide, and had he been half a Mile before us, he had been devour'd indeed, before we could have help'd him: One of them fastned upon his Horse, amd the other attack'd the Man with that Violence, that he had not Time, or not Presence of Mind enough to draw his Pistol, but hollow'd and cry'd out to us most lustily; my Man *Friday* being next me, I bid him ride up, and see what was the Matter; as soon as *Friday* came in Sight of the Man, he hollow'd as loud as t'other, O *Master!* O *Master!* But like a bold Fellow, rode directly up to the poor Man, and with his Pistol shot the Wolf that attack'd him into the Head.

It was happy for the poor Man, that it was my Man *Friday*; for he having been us'd to that kind of Creature in his Country, had no Fear upon him; but went close up to him, and shot him as above; whereas any of us, would have fir'd at a farther Distance, and have perhaps either miss'd the Wolf, or endanger'd shooting the Man.

But it was enough to have terrify'd a bolder Man than I, and indeed it alarm'd all our Company, when with the Noise of *Friday*'s Pistol, we heard on both Sides the dismallest Howling of Wolves, and the Noise redoubled by the Eccho of the Mountains, that it was to us as if there had been a prodigious Multitude of them; and perhaps indeed there was not such a Few, as that we had no cause of Apprehensions.

However, as *Friday* had kill'd this Wolf, the other that had fastned upon the Horse, left him immediately, and fled; having happily fastned upon his Head, where the Bosses of the Bridle had stuck in his Teeth; so that he had not done him much Hurt: The Man indeed was most Hurt; for the raging Creature had bit him twice, once on the Arm, and the other Time a little above his Knee; and he was just as it were tumbling down by the Disorder of his Horse, when *Friday* came up and shot the Wolf.

It is easy to suppose, that at the Noise of *Friday*'s Pistol, we all mended our Pace, and rid up as fast as the Way (which was very difficult) would give us leave, to see what was the Matter; as soon as we came clear of the Trees, which blinded us before, we saw clearly what had been the Case, and how *Friday* had disengag'd the poor Guide; though we did not presently discern what kind of Creature it was he had kill'd.

But never was a Fight manag'd so hardily, and in such a surprizing Manner, as that which follow'd between *Friday* and the Bear, which gave us all (though at first we were surpriz'd and afraid for him) the greatest Diversion imaginable. As the Bear is a heavy, clumsey Creature, and does not gallop as the Wolf does, who is swift, and light; so he has two particular Qualities, which generally are the Rule of his Actions; First, As to Men, who are not his proper Prey; I say, not his proper Prey; because tho" I cannot say what excessive Hunger might do, which was now their Case, the Ground being all cover'd with Snow; but as to Men, he does not usually attempt them, unless they first attack him: On the contrary, if you meet him in the Woods, if you don't meddle with him, he won't meddle with you; but then you must take Care to be very Civil to him, and give him the Road; for he is a very nice[5] Gentleman, he won't go a Step out of his Way for a Prince; nay, if you are really afraid, your best way is to look another Way, and keep going on; for sometimes if you stop, and stand still, and look steadily at him, he takes it for an Affront; but if you throw or toss any Thing at him, and it hits him, though it were but a bit of a Stick, as big as your Finger, he takes it for an Affront, and sets all his other Business aside to pursue his Revenge; for he will have Satisfaction in Point of Honour; that is his first Quality: The next is, That if he be once affronted, he will never leave you, Night or Day, till he has his Revenge; but follows at a good round rate, till he overtakes you.

My Man *Friday* had deliver'd our Guide, and when we came up to him, he was helping him off from his Horse; for the Man was both hurt

5. Particular, punctilious.

and frighted, and indeed, the last more than the first; when on the sudden, we spy'd the Bear out of the Wood, and a vast monstrous One it was, the biggest by far that ever I saw: We were all a little surpriz'd, when we saw him; but when *Friday* saw him, it was easy to see Joy and Courage in the Fellow's Countenance; *O! O! O!* Says *Friday*, three Times, pointing to him; O Master! *You give me te Leave! Me shakee te Hand with him: Me make you good laugh.*

I was surpriz'd to see the Fellow so pleas'd; *You Fool you*, says I, *he will eat you up: Eatee me up! Eatee me up!* Says *Friday*, twice over again; *Me eatee him up: Me make you good laugh: You all stay here, me show you good laugh*; so down he sits, and get his Boots off in a Moment, and put on a Pair of Pumps (as we call the flat Shoes they wear) and which he had in his Pocket, gives my other Servant his Horse, and with his Gun away he flew swift like the Wind.

The Bear was walking softly on, and offer'd to meddle with no Body, till *Friday* coming pretty near, calls to him, as if the Bear could understand him; *Hark ye, hark ye*, says *Friday*, *me speakee wit you*: We follow'd at a Distance; for now being come down on the *Gascoign* side of the Mountains, we were entred a vast great Forest, where the Country was plain, and pretty open, though many Trees in it scatter'd here and there.

Friday, who had as we say, the Heels of the Bear, came up with him quickly, and takes up a great Stone, and throws at him, and hit him just on the Head; but did him no more harm, than if he had thrown it against a Wall; but it answer'd *Friday*'s End; for the Rogue was so void of Fear, that he did it purely to make the Bear follow him, and show us some Laugh as he call'd it.

As soon as the Bear felt the Stone, and saw him, he turns about, and comes after him, taking Devilish long Strides, and shuffling along at a strange Rate, so as would have put a Horse to a middling Gallop; away runs *Friday*, and takes his Course, as if he run towards us for Help; so we all resolv'd to fire at once upon the Bear, and deliver my Man; though I was angry at him heartily, for bringing the Bear back upon us, when he was going about his own Business another Way; and especially I was angry that he had turn'd the Bear upon us, and then run away; and I call'd out, *You Dog*, said I, *is this your making us laugh? Come away, and take your Horse, that we may shoot the Creature*; he hears me, and crys out, *No shoot, no shoot, stand still, you get much Laugh*. And as the nimble Creature run two Foot for the Beast's one, he turn'd on a sudden, on one side of us, and seeing a great Oak-Tree, fit for his Purpose, he beckone'd to us to follow, and doubling his Pace, he gets nimbly up the Tree, laying his Gun down upon the Ground, at about five or six Yards from the Bottom of the Tree.

The Bear soon came to the Tree, and we follow'd at a Distance; the first Thing he did, he stopp'd at the Gun, smelt to it, but let it lye, and

up he scrambles into the Tree, climbing like a Cat, though so mon-
strously heavy: I was amaz'd at the Folly, as I thought it, of my Man,
and could not for my Life see any Thing to Laugh at yet, till seeing the
Bear get up the Tree, we all rode nearer to him.

When we came to the Tree, there was *Friday* got out to the small
End of a large Limb of the Tree, and the Bear got about half way to
him; as soon as the Bear got out to that part where the Limb of the Tree
was weaker, *Ha*, says he to us, *now you see me teachee the Bear dance*;
so he falls a jumping and shaking the Bough, at which the Bear began
to totter, but stood still, and begun to look behind him, to see how he
should get back; then indeed we did laugh heartily: But *Friday* had not
done with him by a great deal; when he sees him stand still, he calls
out to him again, as if he had suppos'd the Bear could speak *English*;
What you no come farther, pray you come farther; so he left jumping
and shaking the Bough; and the Bear, just as if he had understood what
he said, did come a little further, then he fell a jumping again, and the
Bear stopp'd again.

We thought now was a good time to knock him on the Head, and I
call'd to *Friday* to stand still, and we would shoot the Bear; but he cry'd
out earnestly, *O pray! O pray! No shoot, me shoot, by and then*; he
would have said, *By and by*: However, to shorten the Story, *Friday*
danc'd so much, and the Bear stood so ticklish, that we had laughing
enough indeed, but still could not imagine what the Fellow would do;
for first we thought he depended upon shaking the Bear off; and we
found the Bear was too cunning for that too; for he would not go out
far enough to be thrown down, but clings fast with his great broad Claws
and Feet, so that we could not imagine what would be the End of it,
and where the Jest would be at last.

But *Friday* put us out of doubt quickly; for seeing the Bear cling fast
to the Bough, and that he would not be perswaded to come any farther;
Well, well, says *Friday*, *you no come farther, me go, me go; you no come
to me, me go come to you*; and upon this, he goes out to the smallest
End of the Bough, where it would bend with his Weight, and gently
lets himself down by it, sliding down the Bough, till he came near
enough to jump down on his Feet, and away he run to his Gun, takes
it up, and stands still.

Well, said I to him *Friday*, What will you do now? Why don't you
shoot him? *No shoots*, says *Friday*, *no yet, me shoot now, me no kill;
me stay, give you one more laugh*; and indeed so he did, as you will see
presently; for when the Bear sees his Enemy gone, he comes back from
the Bough where he stood; but did it mighty leisurely, looking behind
him every Step, and coming backward till he got into the Body of the
Tree; then with the same hinder End foremost, he came down the Tree,
grasping it with his Claws, and moving one Foot at a Time, very leisurely;
at this Juncture, and just before he could set his hind Feet upon the

Ground, *Friday* stept up close to him, clapt the Muzzle of his Piece into his Ear, and shot him dead as a Stone.

Then the Rogue turn'd about, to see if we did not laugh, and when he saw we were pleas'd by our Looks, he falls a laughing himself very loud; *so we kill Bear in my Country*, says *Friday*; so you kill them, says I, Why you have no Guns: No, says he, *no Gun, but shoot, great much long Arrow.*

This was indeed a good Diversion to us; but we were still in a wild Place, and our Guide very much hurt, and what to do we hardly knew; the Howling of Wolves run much in my Head; and indeed, except the Noise I once heard on the Shore of *Africa*, of which I have said something already, I never heard any thing that filled me with so much Horrour.

These things, and the Approach of Night, called us off, or else, as *Friday* would have had us, we should certainly have taken the Skin of this montrous Creature off, which was worth saving; but we had three Leagues to go, and our Guide hasten'd us, so we left him, and went forward on our Journey.

The Ground was still cover'd with Snow, tho' not so deep and dangerous as on the Mountains, and the ravenous Creatures, as we heard afterwards, were come down into the Forest and plain Country, press'd by Hunger to seek for Food; and had done a great deal of Mischief in the Villages, where they surpriz'd the Country People, kill'd a great many of their Sheep and Horses, and some People too.

We had one dangerous Place to pass, which our Guide told us, if there were any more Wolves in the Country, we should find them there; and this was in a small Plain, surrounded with Woods on every Side, and a long narrow Defile or Lane, which we were to pass to get through the Wood, and then we should come to the Village where we were to lodge.

It was within half an Hour of Sun-set when we entred the first Wood; and a little after Sun-set, when we came into the Plain. We met with nothing in the first Wood, except, that in a little Plain within the Wood, which was not above two Furlongs over, we saw five great Wolves cross the Road, full Speed one after another, as if they had been in Chase of some Prey, and had it in View, they took no Notice of us, and were gone, and out of our Sight in a few Moments.

Upon this our Guide, who by the Way was a wretched faint-hearted Fellow, bid us keep in a ready Posture; for he believed there were more Wolves a coming.

We kept our Arms ready, and our Eyes about us, but we saw no more Wolves, 'till we came thro' that Wood, which was near half a League, and entred the Plain; as soon as we came into the Plain, we had Occasion enough to look about us: The first Object we met with, was a dead Horse; that is to say, a poor Horse which the Wolves had kill'd, and at least a Dozen of them at Work; we could not say eating of him, but picking of his Bones rather; for they had eaten up all the Flesh before.

We did not think fit to disturb them at their Feast, neither did they take much Notice of us: *Friday* would have let fly at them, but I would not suffer him by any Means; for I found we were like to have more Business upon our Hands than we were aware of. We were not gone half over the Plain, but we began to hear the Wolves howl in the Wood on our Left, in a frightful Manner, and presently after we saw about a hundred coming on directly towards us, all in a Body, and most of them in a Line, as regularly as an Army drawn up by experienc'd Officers. I scarce knew in what Manner to receive them; but found to draw ourselves in a close Line was the only Way: so we form'd in a Moment: But that we might not have too much Interval, I order'd, that only every other Man should fire, and that the others who had not fir'd should stand ready to give them a second Volley immediately, if they continued to advance upon us, and that then those who had fir'd at first, should not pretend to load their Fuses again, but stand ready with every one a Pistol; for we were all arm'd with a Fusee, and a Pair of Pistols each Man; so we were by this Method able to fire six Volleys, half of us at a Time; however, at present we had no Necessity; for upon firing the first Volley, the Enemy made a full Stop, being terrify'd as well with the Noise, as with the Fire; four of them being shot into the Head, dropp'd; several others were wounded, and went bleeding off, as we could see by the Snow: I found they stopp'd, but did not immediately retreat; whereupon remembring that I had been told, that the fiercest Creatures were terrify'd at the Voice of a Man, I caus'd all our Company to hollow as loud as we could; and I found the Notion not altogether mistaken; for upon our Shout, they began to retire, and turn about; then I order'd a second Volley to be fir'd, in their Rear, which put them to the Gallop, and away they went to the Woods.

This gave us leisure to charge our Pieces again, and that we might loose no Time, we kept going; but we had but little more than loaded our Fusees, and put ourselves into a Readiness, when we heard a terrible Noise in the same Wood, on our Left, only that it was farther onward the same Way we were to go.

The Night was coming on, and the Light began to be dusky, which made it worse on our Side; but the Noise encreasing, we could easily perceive that it was the Howling and Yelling of those hellish Creatures; and on a sudden, we perceiv'd 2 or 3 Troops of Wolves, one on our Left, one behind us, and one on our Front; so that we seem'd to be surrounded with 'em; however, as they did not fall upon us, we kept our Way forward, as fast as we could make our Horses go, which the Way being very rough, was only a good large Trot; and in this Manner we came in View of the Entrance of a Wood, through which we were to pass, at the farther side of the Plain; but we were greatly surpriz'd, when coming nearer the Lane, or Pass, we saw a confus'd Number of Wolves standing just at the Entrance.

On a sudden, at another opening of the Wood, we heard the Noise of a Gun; and looking that Way, out rush'd a Horse, with a Saddle, and a Bridle on him, flying like the Wind, and sixteen or seventeen Wolves after him, full Speed; indeed, the Horse had the Heels of them; but as we suppos'd that he could not hold it at that rate, we doubted not but they would get up with him at last, and no question but they did.

But here we had a most horrible Sight; for riding up to the Entrance where the Horse came out, we found the Carcass of another Horse, and of two Men, devour'd by the ravenous Creatures, and one of the Men was no doubt the same who we heard fir'd the Gun; for there lay a Gun just by him, fir'd off; but as to the Man, his Head, and the upper Part of his Body was eaten up.

This fill'd us with Horror, and we knew not what Course to take, but the Creatures resolv'd us soon; for they gather'd about us presently, in hopes of Prey; and I verily believe there were three hundred of them: It happen'd very much to our Advantage, that at the Entrance into the Wood, but a little Way from it, there lay some large Timber Trees, which had been cut down the Summer before, and I suppose lay there for Carriage; I drew my little Troop in among those Trees, and placing our selves in a Line, behind one long Tree, I advis'd them all to light, and keeping that Tree before us, for a Breast Work, to stand in a Triangle, or three Fronts, enclosing our Horses in the Center.

We did so, and it was well we did; for never was a more furious Charge than the Creatures made upon us in the Place; they came on us with a growling kind of a Noise (and mounted the Piece of Timber, which as I said, was our Breast Work) as if they were only rushing upon their Prey; and this Fury of theirs, it seems, was principally occasion'd by their seeing our Horses behind us, which was the Prey they aim'd at: I order'd our Men to fire as before, every other Man; and they took their Aim so sure, that indeed they kill'd several of the Wolves at the first Volley; but there was a Necessity to keep a continual Firing; for they came on like Devils, those behind pushing on those before.

When we had fir'd our second Volley of our Fusees, we thought they stopp'd a little, and I hop'd they would have gone off; but it was but a Moment; for others came forward again; so we fir'd two Volleys of Our Pistols, and I believe in these four Firings, we had kill'd seventeen or eighteen of them, and lam'd twice as many; yet they came on again.

I was loath to spend our last Shot too hastily; so I call'd my Servant, not my Man *Friday*; for he was better employ'd; for with the greatest Dexterity imaginable, he had charg'd my Fusee, and his own, while we were engag'd; but as I said, I call'd my other Man, and giving him a Horn of Powder, I bad him lay a Train, all along the Piece of Timber, and let it be a large Train; he did so, and had but just Time to get away, when the Wolves came up to it, and some were got up upon it; when I snapping an uncharg'd Pistol, close to the Powder, set it on fire; those that were upon the Timber were scorcht with it, and six or seven of them fell, or rather jump'd in among us, with the Force and Fright of the Fire; we dispatch'd these in an Instant, and the rest were so frighted with the Light, which the Night, for it was now very near Dark, made more terrible, that they drew back a little.

Upon which I order'd our last Pistol to be fir'd off in one Volley, and after that we gave a Shout; upon this, the Wolves turn'd Tail, and we sally'd immediately upon near twenty lame Ones, who we found struggling on the Ground, and fell a cutting them with our Swords, which answer'd our Expectation; for the Crying and Howling they made, was better understood by their Fellows, so that they all fled and left us.

We had, first and last, kill'd about three Score of them; and had it been Day-Light, we had kill'd many more: The Field of Battle being thus clear'd, we made forward again; for we had still near a League to go. We heard the ravenous Creatures houl and yell in the Woods as we went, several Times; and sometimes we fancy'd we saw some of them, but the Snow dazling our Eyes, we were not certain; so in about an Hour more, we came to the Town, where we were to lodge, which we found in a terrible Fright, and all in Arms; for it seems, that the Night before, the Wolves and some Bears had broke into the Village in the Night, and put them in a terrible Fright; and they were oblig'd to keep Guard Night and Day, but especially in the Night, to preserve their Cattle, and indeed their People.

The next Morning our Guide was so ill, and his Limbs swell'd with the rankling[6] of his two Wounds, that he could go no farther; so we were oblig'd to take a new Guide there, and go to *Thoulouse*, where we found a warm Climate, a fruitful pleasant Country, and no Snow, no Wolves, or any Thing like them; but when we told our Story at *Thoulouse*, they told us it was nothing but what was ordinary in the great Forest at the Foot of the Mountains, especially when the Snow lay on the Ground: But they enquir'd much what kind of a Guide we had gotten, that would venture to bring us that Way in such a severe Season: and told us, it was very much we were not all devour'd. When we told them how we plac'd our selves, and the Horses in the Middle, they blam'd us exceedingly, and told us it was fifty to one but we had been all destroy'd; for it was the Sight of the Horses which made the Wolves so furious, seeing their Prey; and that at other Times they are really afraid of a Gun; but the being excessive Hungry, and raging on that Account, the Eagerness to come at the Horses had made them sensless of Danger; and that if we had not by the continu'd Fire, and at last by the Stratagem of the Train of Powder, master'd them, it had been great Odds but that we had been torn to Pieces; whereas had we been content to have sat still on Horseback, and fir'd as Horsemen, they would not

6. Festering.

have taken the Horses for so much their own, when Men were on their Backs, as otherwise; and withal they told us, that at last, if we had stood altogether, and left our Horses, they would have been so eager to have devour'd them, that we might have come off safe, especially having our Fire Arms in our Hands, and being so many in Number.

For my Part, I was never so sensible of Danger in my Life; for seeing above three hundred Devils come roaring and open mouth'd to devour us, and having nothing to shelter us, or retreat to, I gave my self over for lost; and as it was, I believe, I shall never care to cross those Mountains again; I think I would much rather go a thousand Leagues by Sea, though I was sure to meet with a Storm once a Week.

I have nothing uncommon to take Notice of, in my Passage through *France*; nothing but what other Travellers have given an Account of, with much more Advantage than I can. I travell'd from *Thoulouse* to *Paris*, and without any considerable Stay, came to *Callais*, and landed safe at *Dover*, the fourteenth of *January*, after having had a severely cold Season to travel in.

I was now come to the Center of my Travels, and had in a little Time all my new discover'd Estate safe about me, the Bills of Exchange which I brought with me having been very currently paid.

My principal Guide, and Privy Councellor,[7] was my good ancient Widow, who in Gratitude for the Money I had sent her, thought no Pains too much, or Care too great, to employ for me; and I trusted her so entirely with every Thing, that I was perfectly easy as to the Security of my Effects; and indeed, I was very happy from my Beginning, and now to the End, in the unspotted Integrity of this good Gentlewoman.

And now I began to think of leaving my Effects with this Woman, and setting out for *Lisbon*, and so to the *Brasils*; but now another Scruple came in my Way, and that was Religion; for as I had entertain'd some Doubts about the *Roman* Religion, even while I was abroad, especially in my State of Solitude; so I knew there was no going to the *Brasils* for me, much less going to settle there, unless I resolv'd to embrace the *Roman* Catholick Religion, without any Reserve; unless on the other hand, I resolv'd to be a Sacrifice to my Principles, be a Martyr for Religion, and die in the Inquisition; so I resolv'd to stay at Home, and if I could find Means for it, to dispose of my Plantation.

To this Purpose I wrote to my old Friend at *Lisbon*, who in Return gave me Notice, that he could easily dispose of it there: But that if I thought fit to give him Leave to offer it in my Name to the two Merchants, the Survivors of my Trustees, who liv'd in the *Brasils*, who must fully understand the Value of it, who liv'd just upon the Spot, and who I knew were very rich; so that he believ'd they would be fond of buying it; he did not doubt, but I should make 4 or 5000 Pieces of Eight, the more of it.

---

7. Corrected to "Counsellor" in the third, fifth, and sixth editions.

Accordingly I agreed, gave him Order to offer it to them, and he did so; and in about 8 Months more, the Ship being then return'd, he sent me Account, that they had accepted the Offer, and had remitted 33000 Pieces of Eight, to a Correspondent of theirs at *Lisbon*, to pay for it.

In Return, I sign'd the Instrument of Sale in the Form which they sent from *Lisbon*, and sent it to my old Man, who sent me Bills of Exchange for 328000[8] Pieces of Eight to me, for the Estate; reserving the Payment of 100 Moidores a Year to him, the old Man, during his Life, and 50 Moidores afterwards to his Son for his Life, which I had promised them, which the Plantation was to make good as a Rent-Charge. And thus I have given the first Part of a Life of Fortune and Adventure, a Life of Providence's Checquer-Work, and of a Variety which the World will seldom be able to show the like of: Beginning foolishly, but closing much more happily than any Part of it ever gave me Leave so much as to hope for.

Any one would think, that in this State of complicated good Fortune, I was past running any more Hazards; and so indeed I had been, if other Circumstances had concurr'd, but I was inur'd to a wandring Life, had no Family, not many Relations, nor, however rich had I contracted much Acquaintance; and though I had sold my Estate in the *Brasils*, yet I could not keep the Country out of my Head, and had a great Mind to be upon the Wing again, especially I could not resist the strong Inclination I had to see my Island, and to know if the poor *Spaniards* were in Being there, and how the Rogues I left there had used them.

My true Friend, the Widow, earnestly diswaded me from it, and so far prevail'd with me, that for almost seven Years she prevented my running Abroad; during which time, I took my two Nephews, the Children of one of my Brothers into my Care: The eldest having something of his own, I bred up as a Gentleman, and gave him a Settlement of some Addition to his Estate, after my Decease; the other I put out to a Captain of a Ship; and after five Years, finding him a sensible bold enterprising young Fellow, I put him into a good Ship, and sent him to Sea: And this young Fellow afterwards drew me in, as old as I was, to farther Adventures my self.

In the mean time, I in Part settled my self here; for first of all I marry'd, and that not either to my Disadvantage or Dissatisfaction, and had three Children, two Sons and one Daughter: But my Wife dying, and my Nephew coming Home with good Success from a Voyage to *Spain*, my Inclination to go Abroad, and his Importunity prevailed and engag'd me to go in his Ship, as a private Trader to the *East Indies*: This was in the Year 1694.

In this Voyage I visited my new Collony in the Island, saw my Successors the *Spaniards*, had the whole Story of their Lives, and of the Villains I left there; how at first they insulted the poor *Spaniards*, how

8. The fourth edition reads "3288000."

they afterwards agreed, disagreed, united, separated, and how at last the *Spaniards* were oblig'd to use Violence with them, how they were subjected to the *Spaniards*, how honestly the *Spaniards* used them; a History, if it were entred into, as full of Variety and wonderful Accidents, as my own Part, particularly also as to their Battles with the *Carribeans*, who landed several times upon the Island, and as to the Improvement they made upon the Island it self, and how five of them made an Attempt upon the main Land, and brought away eleven Men and five Women Prisoners, by which, at my coming, I found about twenty young Children on the Island.

Here I stay'd about 20 Days, left them Supplies of all necessary things, and particularly of Arms, Powder, Shot, Cloaths, Tools, and two Workmen, which I brought from *England* with me, *viz.* a Carpenter and a Smith.

Besides this, I shar'd the Island into Parts with 'em, reserv'd to my self the Property of the whole, but gave them such Parts respectively as they agreed on; and having settled all things with them, and engaged them not to leave the Place, I left them there.

From thence I touch'd at the *Brasils*, from whence I sent a Bark, which I bought there, with more People to the Island, and in it, besides other Supplies, I sent seven Women, being such as I found proper for Service, or for Wives to such as would take them: As to the *English* Men, I promis'd them to send them some Women from *England*, with a good Cargoe of Necessaries, if they would apply themselves to Planting, which I afterwards perform'd. And the Fellows prov'd very honest and diligent after they were master'd, and had their Properties set apart for them. I sent them also from the *Brasils* five Cows, three of them being big with Calf, some Sheep, and some Hogs, which, when I came again, were considerably encreas'd.

But all these things, with an Account how 300 *Caribbees* came and invaded them, and ruin'd their Plantations, and how they fought with that whole Number twice, and were at first defeated, and three of them kill'd; but at last a Storm destroying their Enemies Canoes, they famish'd or destroy'd almost all the rest, and renew'd and recover'd the Possession of their Plantation, and still liv'd upon the Island.

All these things, with some very surprizing Incidents in some new Adventures of my own, for ten Years more, I may perhaps give a farther Account of hereafter.

F I N I S.

A Note on the Text

The immediate success of *The Life and Strange Surprizing Adventures of Robinson Crusoe* can be measured by the number of editions, both authorized and unauthorized, it underwent in 1719. Defoe's novel was first published by William Taylor on April 25, 1719, and before the year was out Taylor issued another five separate printings of Part I for a total of six editions. Although the number of copies in each of these editions was probably about one thousand, the frequency of editions in the four months following publication compares favorably with such instantly popular works as Swift's *Gulliver's Travels*, Richardson's *Pamela*, and Fielding's *Tom Jones.* [1] The widespread appeal of Crusoe's story is further evidenced by the publication of an abridged piracy by T. Cox in early August and by the serialization starting on October 7, thrice weekly, in the *Original London Post.* [2] Defoe's *Farther Adventures of Robinson Crusoe* was published by Taylor on August 20, and yet a third part, entitled *Serious Reflections during the Life and Surprising Adventures of Robinson Crusoe*, appeared on August 6 of the following year.

Since Taylor in 1719 published Part I of *Robinson Crusoe* only four times (April 25, May 9, June 4, and August 7) and officially named only four "editions," with double printings of the third and fourth editions in June and August, bibliographers traditionally have held that the third and fourth editions each had two "issues." [3] More recent bibliographical research, however, has shown that Taylor's third and fourth editions, although so called on the title pages, each constitute two separate editions and exist in different settings of type. [4] For purposes of chronology and identification we can establish that the true third edition has on the last page of text the tailpiece of a lion and the true fourth edition has on the last page of text the tailpiece of a phoenix rising from the flames; both of these editions have "The Third Edition" on their title pages, and bibliographers have named them

1. K. I. D. Maslen, "Edition Quantities for *Robinson Crusoe*, 1719," *The Library* 24 (1969): 145–50.
2. R. M. Wiles, *Serial Publication in England before 1750* (Cambridge, England, 1957) 27.
3. Publication dates are drawn from John Robert Moore, *A Checklist of the Writings of Daniel Defoe* (Bloomington, 1960) 163; but based upon contemporary newspaper advertisements, Keith Maslen comes up with the following publication dates: second edition, May 8; third edition, June 6; and fourth edition, August 6 (see "The Printers of *Robinson Crusoe*," *The Library* 7 [1952]: 126). Standard bibliographical discussions of the 1719 editions of *Robinson Crusoe* by William Taylor are Henry Clinton Hutchins, *Robinson Crusoe and Its Printing, 1719–1731* (New York, 1925) 52–96, and Lucius L. Hubbard, "Text Changes in the Taylor Editions of *Robinson Crusoe* with Remarks on the Cox Edition," *Papers of the Bibliographical Society of America* 20 (1926): 1–76.
4. Maslen, "The Printers of *Robinson Crusoe*" 124–131, and "Edition Quantities for *Robinson Crusoe*, 1719" 145.

the third "lion" and third "phoenix" editions respectively. Similarly we can establish that the true fifth edition is identified by the absence of a comma after "Life" in the title while the true sixth edition has the comma after "Life"; again both of these editions have "The Fourth Edition" on their title pages and bibliographers have designated them as the fourth A or without-comma and the fourth B or with-comma editions respectively.[5] In this Norton Critical Edition I have followed the more recent bibliographical findings and speak of the *six* editions published by William Taylor in 171ᵒ.

In preparing the text for this edition I have used the excellent Shakespeare Head Press reprint of the first-edition copy of *The Life and Strange Surprizing Adventures of Robinson Crusoe* in the British Museum.[6] I have consulted the British Museum copy of the first edition as well as first-edition copies in the Houghton Library of Harvard University and the Boston Public Library. I have also collated the first-edition text with the remaining five editions published in 1719, copies of which are in the superb William P. Trent Collection in the Rare Book Room of the Boston Public Library, to produce a somewhat revised and annotated text that is faithful to Defoe's *editio princeps* yet also is comprehensible to the student. Occasional printer's errors have been silently corrected, but the rhythms and singularities of Defoe's prose—notably his long sentences, irregular punctuation, variant orthography, curious capitalizations, and casually conversational style— have essentially been retained. Notes have been provided to assist the reader with obscure words and idioms, significant variants, Biblical references, and textual problems.

Although very few of Defoe's manuscripts are extant, we know from what little does survive that his habitual manner of composition posed serious problems for his printers. The editor of Defoe's letters has remarked that his style is characterized by frequent contractions for words, symbols for prefixes, signs for double letters, inconsistent capitalization, variant spelling, and punctuation that "is sometimes confusing and often lacking."[7] Similarly the editor of Defoe's autograph manuscript of *The Compleat English Gentleman* has observed:

> The MS. is well preserved, but the close and hurried writing, the indistinct characters, which may very often mean different letters, the great number of emendations, additions, and deleted passages, the extensive use of contractions and of shorthand and other abbreviations, and the uncommon, irregular, and often curious and faulty spelling make it difficult and sometimes perplexing to read.[8]

Little wonder, then, that the compositors of *Robinson Crusoe*, working under pressure and in poor conditions, encountered uncommon difficulties in setting type from Defoe's manuscript copy, if a scholar, working carefully

5. Hutchins 72–80; Hubbard 2–3; Maslen, "The Printers of *Robinson Crusoe*" 125–26.
6. The Shakespeare Head Edition was a limited printing of 750 copies issued by Basil Blackwell, Oxford, in 1927, and the text was "reprinted from the British Museum copy (c. 30.f.6) of the first edition, compared with the third edition, in which certain alterations were included. The 'Errata' given in a list at the end of the first edition have been incorporated in the text" (vi).
7. *The Letters of Daniel Defoe*, ed. George Harris Healey (Oxford, 1955) 7–8.
8. *The Compleat English Gentleman*, ed. Karl D. Bülbring (London, 1890) xvii.

and patiently in the serene setting of the British Museum, found Defoe's
writing almost indecipherable!

The textual problems arising when editing a Defoe work are considerable
and complex. Since the author's handwritten manuscript for *Robinson Crusoe* is lost, we have only the first and subsequent editions available to us.
The "Errata" list provided at the end of the first edition is only a publisher's
gesture, for the text abounds with errors, omissions, inconsistencies, and
irregularities. In the following editions we discern a gradual but limited
process of correction, so that the sixth edition offers a relatively cleaner and
more finished text than the first. But with each setting and resetting of type,
new errors were introduced as old ones were corrected. The textual variants
among the first six editions by Taylor, all appearing in a period of four
months, number in the thousands, most of them being changes in punctuation, capitalization, and spelling.[9]

Punctuation is a considerable problem with Defoe's writings because he
rarely put any breaks in his notoriously long sentences. We can assume,
therefore, that the compositors working from the manuscript had to supply
much of the punctuation for the first-edition text, especially the commas.
Oftentimes the punctuation is irregular, if not capricious, depending on the
compositor. In a few instances where the punctuation renders the prose
almost illiterate, I have followed the somewhat more uniform and correct
punctuation of the sixth edition. The most notable example of this occurs
in the passage where Crusoe finds the money in the wreck of the ship. I
offer both versions so the reader can see why I have chosen the later punctuation for this short but important passage:

FIRST EDITION	SIXTH EDITION
I smil'd to my self at the Sight of this Money, O Drug! Said I aloud, what art thou good for, Thou art not worth to me, no not the taking off of the Ground, one of those Knives is worth all this Heap, I have no Manner of use for thee, e'en remain where thou art, and go to the Bottom as a Creature whose Life is not worth saving. However upon Second Thoughts, I took it away, and wrapping all this in a Piece of Canvas, I began to think of making another Raft, but	I smil'd to my self at the Sight of this Money. O Drug! said I aloud, what art thou good for? Thou art not worth to me, no not the taking off of the Ground; one of those Knives is worth all this Heap; I have no Manner of use for thee, e'en remain where thou art, and go to the Bottom as a Creature whose life is not worth saving. However, upon Second Thoughts, I took it away, and wrapping all this in a Piece of Canvas, I began to think of making another Raft;

9. The William P. Trent Collection of Defoe at the Boston Public Library includes a heavily
annotated copy, in Professor Trent's hand, of the second edition of *Robinson Crusoe* with
marginal notes on textual variants in the early editions. In consulting this volume, I arrived
at the estimate that the variants run in the thousands, but most are of minor significance.
The editor of the Oxford English Novels text of *Robinson Crusoe* (Oxford, 1972), J. Donald
Crowley, who had collated "the first eight authorized editions," noted that "more than 14,000
changes were made," but most appear in the last two editions, after the Taylor copyright was
sold to other publishers (307). Unfortunately Professor Crowley collated only four Taylor
editions of 1719; consequently the number of "authorized" editions cited is misleading.

but while I was preparing this, I while I was preparing this, I found the Sky over-cast, and the Wind began to rise, and in a Quarter of an Hour it blew a fresh Gale from the Shore;

found the Sky over-cast, and the Wind began to rise, and in a Quarter of an Hour it blew a fresh Gale from the Shore;

(Page 66, lines 4–16)

Even though we cannot know what Defore wrote in his manuscript, it seems clear that the compositor or corrector for the sixth-edition copy had a better sense of the punctuation for this passage than the compositor of the first edition.

I have, however, kept such emendations in the text of this Norton Critical Edition to a minimum because I thought it best to preserve the text of the first edition as much as possible and, therefore, limited my improvements only where all the editions indicated an obvious printer's error. Otherwise I have confined my role as editor to the footnotes, and here, again, I have been studious of restricting my notes to the more significant or characteristic features of the text to aid the reader's comprehension. For once the reader gets into the text and becomes familiar with Defoe's style, the power of the story will take over and the reader will share something akin to what the first readers and subsequent generations of readers experienced from this classic work of English fiction.

CONTEXTS

Contemporary Accounts
of Marooned Men

WILLIAM DAMPIER

[Rescue of a "Moskito Indian" Marooned over Three
Years on Juan Fernandez Island]†

* * *

March the 22d, 1684, we came in sight of the Island, and the next
day got in and anchored in a Bay at the South end of the Island, in 25
fathom Water, not two Cables lengths from the shore. We presently got
out our Canoa, and went ashore to see for a *Moskito Indian*, whom we
left here when we were chased hence by 3 *Spanish* Ships in the year
1681, a little before we went to *Africa*; Capt. *Watlin* being then our
Commander, after Capt. *Sharp*, was turn'd out.

This *Indian* lived here alone above 3 years, and altho' he was several
time sought after by the *Spaniards*, who knew he was left on the Island,
yet they could never find him. He was in the Woods, hunting for Goats,
when Capt. *Watlin* drew off his Men, and the Ship was under sail before
he came back to shore. He had with him his Gun and a Knife, with a
small Horn of Powder, and a few Shot; which being spent, he contrived
a way by notching his Knife, to saw the Barrel of his Gun into small
Pieces, wherewith he made Harpoons, Lances, Hooks and a long Knife;
heating the pieces first in the fire, which he struck with his Gunflint,
and a piece of the Barrel of his Gun, which he hardned; having learnt
to do that among the *English*. The hot pieces of Iron he would hammer
out and bend as he pleased with Stones, and saw them with his jagged
Knife, or grind them to an Edge by long labour, and harden them to a

† From *A New Voyage round the World* . . . , 5th ed. (London, 1703) 84–88.
    William Dampier (1652–1715), privateer, naval captain, navigator, and hydrographer, de-
scribed his sailing adventures as a buccaneer from 1679 on in his *New Voyage round the
World*, which was first published in 1697, and in subsequent volumes. In September 1703,
he sailed for the South Seas as commander of a privateering enterprise consisting of the two
ships *St. George* and *Cinque Ports*. It was on this voyage that Alexander Selkirk (1676–1721),
a Scotsman who served as sailing master of the *Cinque Ports*, quarreled with his captain and
was left on the island of Juan Fernandez in 1704. (See following accounts.)

good temper as there was occasion. All this may seem strange to those that are not acquainted with the sagacity of the *Indians*; but it is no more than these *Moskito* Men are accustomed to in their own Country, where they make their own Fishing and striking Instruments, without either Forge or Anvil; tho' they spend a great deal of time about them.

* * * But to return to our *Moskito* Man on the Isle of *J. Fernando.* With such Instruments as he made in that manner, he got such Provision as the Island afforded; either Goats or Fish. He told us that at first he was forced to eat Seal, which is very ordinary Meat, before he had made hooks: but afterwards he never killed any Seals but to make Lines, cutting their Skins into Thongs. He had a little House or Hut half a mile from the Sea, which was lined with Goats Skin; his Couch or Barbecu of Sticks lying along about 2 foot distant from the Ground, was spread with the same, and was all his Bedding. He had no Cloaths left, having worn out those he brought from *Watlin's* Ship, but only a Skin about his Waste. He saw our Ship the day before we came to an Anchor, and did believe we were *English*, and therefore kill'd 3 Goats in the Morning, before we came to an Anchor, and drest them with Cabbage, to treat us when we came ashore. He came then to the Sea side to congratulate our safe arrival. And when we landed, a *Moskito Indian*, named *Robin*, first leap'd ashore, and running to his Brother *Moskito* Man, threw himself flat on his face at his feet, who helping him up, and embracing him, fell flat with his face on the Ground at *Robin's* feet, and was by him taken up also. We stood with pleasure to behold the suprize and tenderness, and solemnity of this interview, which was exceedingly affectionate on both sides; and when their Ceremonies of Civility were over, we also that stood gazing at them drew near, each of us embracing him we had found here, who was overjoyed to see so many of his old Friends come hither as he thought purposely to fetch him. He was named *Will*, as the other was *Robin*. These were names given them by the *English*, for they have no Names among themselves; and they take it as a great favour to be named by any of us; and will complain for want of it, if we do not appoint them some name when they are with us: saying of themselves they are poor Men, and have no Name.

This Island is in lat. 34 d. 15 m. and about 120 leagues from the Main. It is about 12 leagues round, full of high Hills, and small pleasant Valleys, which if manured, would probably produce any thing proper for the Climate. The sides of the Mountains are part Savannahs, part Wood-land. Savannahs' are clear pieces of Land without Woods; not because more barren than the Wood-land, for they are frequently spots of as good Land as any, and often are intermixt with Wood-land. In the Bay of *Campeachy* are very large Savannahs, which I have seen full of Cattle: But about the River of *Plate* are the largest that ever I heard of, 50, 60, or 100 Miles in length; and *Jamaica*, *Cuba* and *Hispaniola*, have many Savannahs intermixt with Woods. Places cleared of Wood by Art and Labour do not go by this Name, but those only which are found so in the uninhabited parts of *America*, such as this Isle of *John Fernando's*; or which were originally clear in other parts.

The Grass in these Savannahs at *John Fernando's* is not a long flaggy Grass, such as is usually in the Savannahs in the *West-Indies*, but a sort of kindly Grass, both thick and flourishing the biggest part of the year. The Woods afford divers sorts of Trees; some large and good Timber for Building, but none fit for Masts. The Cabbage Trees of this Isle are but small and low; yet afford a good head, and the Cabbage very sweet. * * *

The Savannahs are stocked with Goats in great Herds: but those that live on the East end of the Island are not so fat as those on the West end; for though there is much more Grass, and plenty of Water in every Valley, nevertheless they thrive not so well here as on the West-end, where there is less Food; and yet there are found greater Flocks, and those too fatter and sweeter.

That West end of the Island is all high Champion Ground without any Valley, and but one place to land; there is neither Wood nor any fresh Water, and the Grass short and dry.

Goats were first put on the Island by *John Fernando*, who first discovered it in his Voyage from *Lima* to *Baldivia*; (and discovered also another Island about the same bigness, 20 leagues to the Westward of this.) From those Goats these were propagated, and the Island hath taken its Name from this its first Discoverer; who, when he returned to *Lima*, desired a Patent for it, designing to settle here; and it was in his second Voyage hither that he set ashore 3 or 4 Goats, which have since, by their increase, so well stock'd the whole Island. But he could never get a Patent for it, therefore it lies still destitute of Inhabitants, tho' doubtless capable of maintaing 4 or 500 Families, by what may be produced off the Land only. I speak much within compass; for the Savannahs would at present feed 1000 Head of Cattle besides Goats, and the Land being cultivated would probably bear Corn, or Wheat, and good Pease, Yams, or Potatoes; for the Land in their Valleys and sides of the Mountains, is of a good black fruitful Mould. The Sea about it is likewise very productive of its Inhabitants. *Seals* swarm as thick about this Island, as if they had no other place in the World to live in; for there is not a Bay nor Rock that one can get ashoar on, but is full of them. *Sea Lyons* are here in great Companies, and Fish, particularly Snappers and Rock-fish, are so plentiful, that two Men in an hours time will take with Hook and Line, as many as will serve 100 Men.

EDWARD COOKE

[Rescue of Alexander Selkirk from Juan Fernandez Island]†

Tuesday, February 1. In the Morning tack'd and stood to the *Westward;* but the Wind shrinking, and blowing off the Island in Squals, could not get in 'till Eight in the Evening, when having little Wind, we row'd and tow'd into the great Bay, and came to an Anchor in 50 Fathom Water with our best Bower, carrying our Stream-Anchor in with the Shore. All this Day had a clear Ship, hoping to get some Purchase, but saw no Vessel, only one Man ashore, with a white Ensign, which made us conclude, that some Men had been left there by some Ship, because the Island is not inhabited. The *Duke's* Boat went ashore, and found one *Alexander Selkirk*, who had been formerly Master of the *Cinque Ports* Galley, an *English* Privateer in those Parts; and having some Difference with the Captain of the said Ship, and she being leaky, he left the said Capt. *Stradling*, going ashore on this Island, where he continu'd four Years and four Months, living on Goats and Cabbages that grow on Trees, Turnips, Parsnips, &c. He told us a *Spanish* Ship or two which touch'd there, had like to have taken him, and fir'd some Shot at him. He was cloath'd in a Goat's Skin Jacket, Breeches, and Cap, sew'd together with Thongs of the same. He tam'd some wild Goats and Cats, whereof there are great Numbers.

WOODES ROGERS

[Account of Alexander Selkirk's Solitary Life on Juan Fernandez Island for Four Years and Four Months]‡

Jan. 31. * * * At seven this morning we made the Island of *Juan Fernandez* * * *
February 1. About two yesterday in the Afternoon we hoisted our

† From A *Voyage to the South Sea, and around the World* (London, 1712) 36–37.
   Captain Cooke sailed with the privateering expedition led by Captain Woodes Rogers in 1708. He served as second captain of the *Duchess* and, after the return of the expedition in 1711, he published his account of the voyage in 1712. His mention of Selkirk's rescue was the first to appear in print.
‡ From A *Cruising Voyage round the World* (London, 1712) 121–31.
   Captain Woodes Rogers (d. 1732) was a sea captain who, in 1708, accepted command of a privateering expedition by the ships *Duke* and *Duchess* to prey on Spanish shipping in the South Seas. He returned to England after a successful voyage in 1711, and then in 1712 published an account of the trip, A *Cruising Voyage round the World*, which included a detailed firsthand version of Selkirk's rescue from the island of Juan Fernandez in 1709. Rogers was later appointed governor of the Bahama Islands.

Pinnace out; Capt *Dover* with the Boats Crew went in her to go ashore, tho we could not be less than 4 Ls. off. As soon as the Pinnace was gone, I went on board the *Duchess*, who admir'd our Boat attempted going ashore at that distance from Land: 'twas against my Inclination, but to oblige Capt. *Dover* I consented to let her go. As soon as it was dark, we saw a Light ashore; our Boat was then about a League from the Island, and bore away for the Ships as soon as she saw the Lights. We put out Lights abroad for the Boat, tho some were of opinion the Lights we saw were our Boats Lights; but as Night came on, it appear'd too large for that. We fir'd one Quarter-Deck Gun and several Muskets, showing Lights in our Mizen and Fore-Shrouds, that our Boat might find us, whilst we ply'd in the Lee of the Island. About two in the Morning our Boat came on board, having been two hours on board the *Duchess*, that took 'em up a-stern of us: we were glad they got well off, because it begun to blow. We are all convinc'd the Light in on the shore, and design to make our Ships ready to engage, believing them to be *French* Ships at anchor, and we must either fight 'em or want Water, &c.

Febr. 2. We stood on the back side along the South end of the Island, in order to lay in with the first Southerly Wind, which Capt. *Dampier* told us generally blows there all day long. In the Morning, being past the Island, we tack'd to lay it in close aboard the Land; and about ten a clock open'd the South End of the Island, and ran close aboard the Land that begins to make the North-East side. The Flaws[1] came heavy off shore, and we were forc'd to reef our Top-sails when we open'd the middle Bay, where we expected to find our Enemy, but saw all clear, and no Ships in that nor the other Bay next the N W. End. These two Bays are all that Ships ride in which recruit on this Island, but the middle Bay is by much the best. We guess'd there had been Ships there, but that they were gone on sight of us. We sent our Yall ashore about Noon, with Capt. *Dover*, Mr. *Frye*, and six Men, all arm'd; mean while we and the *Duchess* kept turning to get in, and such heavy Flaws came off the Land, that we were forc'd to let fly our Topsail-Sheet, keeping all Hands to stand by our Sails, for fear of the Wind's carrying 'em away: but when the Flaws were gone, we had little or no Wind. These Flaws proceeded from the Land, which is very high in the middle of the Island. Our Boat did not return, so we sent our Pinnace with the Men arm'd, to see what was the occasion of the Yall's stay; for we were afraid that the *Spaniards* had a Garison there, and might have seizd 'em. We put out a Signal for our Boat, and the *Duchess* show'd a *French* Ensign. Immediately our Pinnace return'd from the shore, and brought abundance of Craw-fish, with a Man cloth'd in Goat-Skins, who look'd wilder than the first Owners of them. He had been on the Island four Years and four Months, being left there by Capt. *Stradling* in the *Cinque-*

1. Blasts of wind.

Ports; his Name was *Alexander Selkirk* a *Scotch* Man, who had been Master of the *Cinque-Ports*, a Ship that came here last with Capt. *Dampier*, who told me that this was the best Man in her; so I immediately agreed with him to be a Mate on board our Ship. 'Twas he that made the Fire last night when he saw our Ships, which he judg'd to be *English*. During his stay here, he saw several Ships pass by, but only two came in to anchor. As he went to view them, he found 'em to be *Spaniards*, and retir'd from 'em; upon which they shot at him. Had they been *French*, he would have submitted; but chose to risque his dying alone on the Island, rather than fall into the hands of the *Spaniards* in these parts, because he apprehended they would murder him, or make a Slave of him in the Mines, for he fear'd they would spare no Stranger that might be capable of discovering the *South-Sea*. The *Spaniards* had landed, before he knew what they were, and they came so near him that he had much ado to escape; for they not only shot at him but pursu'd him into the Woods, where he climb'd to the top of a Tree, at the foot of which they made water, and kill'd several Goats just by, but went off again without discovering him. He told us that he was born at *Largo* in the County of *Fife* in *Scotland*, and was bred a Sailor from his Youth. The reason of his being left here was a difference betwixt him and his Captain; which, together with the Ships being leaky, made him willing rather to stay here, than go along with him at first; and when he was at last willing, the Captain would not receive him. He had been in the Island before to wood and water, when two of the Ships Company were left upon it for six Months till the Ship return'd, being chas'd thence by two *French South-Sea* Ships.

He had with him his Clothes and Bedding, with a Firelock, some Powder, Bullets, and Tobacco, a Hatchet, a Knife, a Kettle, a Bible, some practical Pieces, and his Mathematical Instruments and Books. He diverted and provided for himself as well as he could; but for the first eight months had much ado to bear up against Melancholy, and the Terror of being left alone in such a desolate place. He built two Hutts with Piemento Trees, cover'd them with long Grass, and lin'd them with the Skins of Goats, which he kill'd with his Gun as he wanted, so long as his Powder lasted, which was but a pound; and that being near spent, he got fire by rubbing two sticks of Piemento Wood together upon his knee. In the lesser Hutt, at some distance from the other, he dress'd his Victuals, and in the larger he slept, and employ'd himself in reading, singing Psalms, and praying; so that he said he was a better Christian while in this Solitude than ever he was before, or than, he was afraid, he should ever be again. At first he never eat any thing till Hunger constrain'd him, partly for grief and partly for want of Bread and Salt; nor did he go to bed till he could watch no longer: the Piemento Wood, which burnt very clear, serv'd him both for Firing and Candle, and refresh'd him with its fragrant Smell.

He might have had Fish enough, but could not eat 'em for want of Salt, because they occasion'd a Looseness; except Crawfish, which are there as large as our Lobsters, and very good: These he sometimes boil'd, and at other times broil'd, as he did his Goats Flesh, of which he made very good Broth, for they are not so rank as ours: he kept an Account of 500 that he kill'd while there, and caught as many more, which he mark'd on the Ear and let go. When his Powder fail'd, he took them by speed of foot; for his way of living and continual Exercise of walking and running, clear'd him of all gross Humours, so that he ran with wonderful Swiftness thro the Woods and up the Rocks and Hills, as we perceiv'd when we employ'd him to catch Goats for us. We had a Bull-Dog, which we sent with several of our nimblest Runners, to help him in catching Goats; but he distanc'd and tir'd both the Dog and the Men, catch'd the Goats, and brought 'em to us on his back. He told us that his Agility in pursuing a Goat had once like to have cost him his Life; he pursu'd it with so much Eagerness that he catch'd hold of it on the brink of a Precipice, of which he was not aware, the Bushes having hid it from him; so that he fell with the Goat down the said Precipice a great height, and was so stun'd and bruis'd with the Fall, that he narrowly escap'd with his Life, and when he came to his Senses, found the Goat dead under him. He lay there about 24 hours, and was scarce able to crawl to his Hutt, which was about a mile distant, or to stir abroad again in ten days.

   He came at last to relish his Meat well enough without Salt or Bread, and in the Season had plenty of good Turnips, which had been sow'd there by Capt. *Dampier's* Men, and have now overspread some Acres of Ground. He had enough of good Cabbage from the Cabbage-Trees, and season'd his Meat with the Fruit of the Piemento Trees, which is the same as the *Jamaica* Pepper, and smells deliciously. He found there also a black Pepper call'd *Malagita*, which was very good to expel Wind, and against Griping of the Guts. [2]

He soon wore out all his Shoes and Clothes by running thro the Woods; and at last being forc'd to shift without them, his Feet became so hard, that he run every where without Annoyance: and it was some time before he could wear Shoes after we found him; for not being us'd to any so long, his Feet swell'd when he came first to wear 'em again.

After he had conquer'd his Melancholy, he diverted himself some-times by cutting his Name on the Trees, and the Time of his being left and Continuance there. He was at first much pester'd with Cats and Rats, that had bred in great numbers from some of each Species which had got ashore from Ships that put in there to wood and water. The Rats gnaw'd his Feet and Clothes while asleep, which oblig'd him to cherish the Cats with his Goats-flesh; by which many of them became

2. Constipation.

so tame, that they would lie about him in hundreds, and soon deliver'd him from the Rats. He likewise tam'd some Kids, and to divert himself would now and then sing and dance with them and his Cats: so that by the Care of Providence and Vigour of his Youth, being now but about 30 years old, he came at last to conquer all the Inconveniences of his Solitude, and to be very easy. When his Clothes wore out, he made himself a Coat and Cap of Goat-Skins, which he stitch'd together with little Thongs of the same, that he cut with his Knife. He had no other Needle but a Nail; and when his Knife was wore to the back, he made others as well as he could of some Iron Hoops that were left ashore, which he beat thin and ground upon Stones. Having some Linen Cloth by him, he sow'd himself Shirts with a Nail, and stitch'd 'em with the Worsted of his old Stockings, which he pull'd out on purpose. He had his last Shirt on when we found him in the Island.

At his first coming on board us, he had so much forgot his Language for want of Use, that we could scarce understand him, for he seem'd to speak his words by halves. We offer'd him a Dram, but he would not touch it, having drank nothing but Water since his being there, and 'twas some time before he could relish our Victuals.

He could give us an account of no other Product of the Island than what we have mention'd, except small black Plums, which are very good, but hard to come at, the Trees which bear 'em growing on high Mountains and Rocks. Piemento Trees are plenty here, and we saw some of 60 foot high, and about two yards thick; and Cotton Trees higher, and near four fathom round in the Stock.

The Climate is so good, that the Trees and Grass are verdant all the Year. The Winter lasts no longer than June and July, and is not then severe, there being only a small Frost and a little Hail, but sometimes great Rains. The Heat of the Summer is equally moderate, and there's not much Thunder or tempestuous Weather of any sort. He saw no venomous or savage Creature on the Island, nor any other sort of Beast but Goats, &c. as above-mention'd; the first of which had been put ashore here on purpose for a Breed by *Juan Fernando* a *Spaniard*, who settled there with some Families for a time, till the Continent of *Chili* began to submit to the *Spaniards*; which being more profitable, tempted them to quit this Island, which is capable of maintaining a good number of People, and of being made so strong that they could not be easily dislodg'd.

Ringrose[3] in his Account of Capt. *Sharp*'s Voyage and other Buccaneers, mentions one who had escap'd ashore here out of a Ship which was cast away with all the rest of the Company, and says he liv'd five years alone before he had the opportunity of another Ship to carry him

---

3. Basil Ringrose (d. 1686), buccaneer and author, sailed to the West Indies in 1679 and a year later joined the privateering expedition operating off the coast of South America under Captain Bartholomew Sharpe. On his return to England he prepared for the press his journal, which was published in 1685 as a second volume of the *History of the Buccaneers*.

off. Capt. *Dampier* talks of a *Moskito Indian* that belong'd to Capt. *Watlin*,[4] who being a hunting in the Woods when the Captain left the Island, liv'd here three years alone, shifted much in the same manner as Mr. *Selkirk* did, till Capt. *Dampier* came hither in 1684, and carry'd him off. The first that went ashore was one of his Countrymen, and they saluted one another first by prostrating themselves by turns on the ground, and then embracing. But whatever there is in these Stories, this of Mr. *Selkirk* I know to be true; and his Behaviour afterwards gives me reason to believe the Account he gave me how he spent his time, and bore up under such an Affliction, in which nothing but the Divine Providence could have supported any Man. By this one may see that Solitude and Retirement from the World is not such an unsufferable State of Life as most Men imagine, especially when People are fairly call'd or thrown into it unavoidably, as this Man was; who in all probability must otherwise have perish'd in the Seas, the Ship which left him being cast away not long after, and few of the Company escap'd. We may perceive by this Story the Truth of the Maxim, That Necessity is the Mother of Invention, since he found means to supply his Wants in a very natural manner, so as to maintain his Life, tho not so conveniently, yet as effectually as we are able to do with the help of all our Arts and Society. It may likewise instruct us, how much a plain and temperate way of living conduces to the Health of the Body and the Vigour of the Mind, both which we are apt to destroy by Excess and Plenty, especially of strong Liquor, and the Variety as well as the Nature of our Meat and Drink: for this Man, when he came to our ordinary method of Diet and Life, tho he was sober enough, lost much of his Strength and Agility. But I must quit these Reflections, which are more proper for a Philosopher and Divine than a Mariner, and return to my own Subject.

RICHARD STEELE

[On Alexander Selkirk]†

Talia monstrabat relegens errata retrorsum.[1] Virg.

Under the Title of this Paper, I do not think it foreign to my Design, to speak of a Man born in Her Majesty's Dominions, and relate an Adventure in his Life so uncommon, that it's doubtful whether the like

4. John Watlin (d. 1681), a fellow buccaneer serving with Dampier, commanded a ship that was in 1681 forced by Spanish ships to flee from Juan Fernandez. In the hasty departure a Mosquito Indian from the ship's crew was left alone on the island until March of 1684, when Dampier rescued him (see Dampier's account of the rescue). Watlin was killed in action against the Spanish less than a month after quitting Juan Fernandez.

† Richard Steele, *The Englishman*, No. 26, "[Thursday] December 3, [1713]."

1. *Aeneid* 3.690: "Such things . . . he pointed out as he retraced his former wanderings."

has happen'd to any other of human Race. The Person I speak of i:
Alexander Selkirk, whose Name is familiar to Men of Curiosity, from
the Fame of his having lived four years and four Months alone in the
Island of *Juan Fernandez*. I had the pleasure frequently to converse with
the Man soon after his Arrival in *England*, in the Year 1711. It was
matter of great Curiosity to hear him, as he is a Man of good Sense,
give an Account of the different Revolutions in his own Mind in that
long Solitude. When we consider how painful Absence from Company
for the space of but one Evening, is to the generality of Mankind, we
may have a sense how painful this necessary and constant Solitude was
to a Man bred a Sailor, and ever accustomed to enjoy and suffer, eat,
drink, and sleep, and perform all Offices of Life, in Fellowship and
Company. He was put ashore from a leaky Vessel, with the Captain of
which he had had an irreconcileable difference; and he chose rather to
take his Fate in this place, than in a crazy Vessel, under a disagreeable
Commander. His Portion were a Sea-Chest, his wearing Cloaths and
Bedding, a Fire-lock, a Pound of Gun-powder, a large quantity of Bullets, a Flint and Steel, a few Pounds of Tobacco, an Hatchet, a Knife,
a Kettle, a Bible, and other Books of Devotion, together with Pieces
that concerned Navigation, and his Mathematical Instruments. Re-
sentment against his Officer, who had ill used him, made him look
forward on this Change of Life, as the more eligible one, till the Instant
in which he saw the Vessel put off; at which moment, his Heart yearned
within him, and melted at the parting with his Comrades and all Human
Society at once. He had in Provisions for the Sustenance of Life but
the quantity of two Meals, the Island abounding only with wild Goats,
Cats and Rats. He judged it most probable that he should find more
immediate and easy Relief, by finding Shell-fish on the Shore, than
seeking Game with his Gun. He accordingly found great quantities of
Turtles, whose Flesh is extreamly delicious, and of which he frequently
eat very plentifully on his first Arrival, till it grew disagreeable to his
Stomach, except in Jellies. The Necessities of Hunger and Thirst, were
his greatest Diversions from the Reflection on his lonely Condition.
When those Appetites were satisfied, the Desire of Society was as strong
a Call upon him, and he appeared to himself least necessitious when
he wanted every thing; for the Supports of his Body were easily attained,
but the eager Longings for seeing again the Face of Man during the
Interval of craving bodily Appetites, were hardly supportable. He grew
dejected, languid, and melancholy, scarce able to refrain from doing
himself Violence, till by Degrees, by the Force of Reason, and frequent
reading of the Scriptures, and turning his Thoughts upon the Study of
Navigation, after the Space of eighteen Months, he grew thoroughly
reconciled to his Condition. When he had made this Conquest, the
Vigour of his Health, Disengagement from the World, a constant, chearful, serene Sky, and a temperate Air, made his Life one continual Feast,

and his Being much more joyful than it had before been irksome. He now taking Delight in every thing, made the Hutt in which he lay, by Ornaments which he cut down from a spacious Wood, on the side of which it was situated, the most delicious Bower, fann'd with continual Breezes, and gentle Aspirations of Wind, that made his Repose after the Chase equal to the most sensual Pleasures.

I forgot to observe, that during the Time of his Dissatisfaction, Monsters of the Deep, which frequently lay on the Shore, added to the Terrors of his Solitude; the dreadful Howlings and Voices seemed too terrible to be made for human Ears; but upon the Recovery of his Temper, he could with Pleasure not only hear their Voices, but approach the Monsters themselves with great Intrepidity. He speaks of Sea-Lions, whose Jaws and Tails were capable of seizing or breaking the Limbs of a Man, if he approached them: But at that Time his Spirits and Life were so high, and he could act so regularly and unconcerned, that meerly from being unruffled in himself, he killed them with the greatest Ease imaginable: For observing, that though their Jaws and Tails were so terrible, yet the Animals being mighty slow in working themselves round, he had nothing to do but place himself exactly opposite their Middle, and as close to them as possible, and he dispatched them with his Hatchet at Will.

THE Precaution which he took against Want, in case of Sickness, was to lame Kids when very young, so as that they might recover their Health, but never be capable of Speed. These he had in great Numbers about his Hutt; and when he was himself in full Vigour, he could take at full Speed the swiftest Goat running up a Promontory, and never failed of catching them but on a Descent.

HIS Habitation was extremely pester'd with Rats, which gnaw'd his Cloaths and Feet when sleeping. To defend him against them, he fed and tamed Numbers of young Kitlings, who lay about his Bed, and preserved him from the Enemy. When his Cloaths were quite worn out, he dried and tacked together the skins of Goats, with which he cloathed himself, and was enured to pass through Woods, Bushes, and Brambles with as much Carelessness and Precipitance as any other Animal. It happened once to him, that running on the Summit of a Hill, he made a Stretch to seize a Goat, with which under him, he fell down a Precipice, and lay sensless for the Space of three Days, the Length of which Time he Measured by the Moon's Growth since his last Observation. This manner of life grew so exquisitely pleasant, that he never had a Moment heavy upon his Hands; his Nights were untroubled, and his Days joyous, from the Practice of Temperance and Exercise. It was his Manner to use stated Hours and Places for Exercises of Devotion, which he performed aloud, in order to keep up the Faculties of Speech, and to utter himself with greater Energy.

WHEN I first saw him, I thought, if I had not been let into his Character and Story, I could have discerned that he had been much separated from Company, from his Aspect and Gesture; there was a strong but chearful Seriousness in his Look, and a certain Disregard to the ordinary things about him, as if he had been sunk in Thought. When the Ship which brought him off the Island came in, he received them with the greatest Indifference, with relation to the Prospect of going off with them, but with great Satisfaction in an Opportunity to refresh and help them. The Man frequently bewailed his Return to the World, which could not, he said, with all its Enjoyments, restore him to the Tranquility of his Solitude. Though I had frequently conversed with him, after a few Months Absence he met me in the Street, and though he spoke to me, I could not recollect that I had seen him; familiar Converse in this Town had taken off the Loneliness of his Aspect, and quite altered the Air of his Face.

THIS plain Man's Story is a memorable Example, that he is happiest who confines his Wants to natural Necessities; and he that goes further in his Desires, increases his Wants in Proportion to his Acquisitions; or to use his own Expression, *I am now worth 800 Pounds, but shall never be so happy, as when I was not worth a Farthing.*

Autobiography:
Robinson Crusoe
as Allegorical History

DANIEL DEFOE

[Preface to Volume II of *Robinson Crusoe*]†

The Success the former Part of this Work has met with in the World, has yet been no other than is acknowledg'd to be due to the surprising Variety of the Subject, and to the agreeable Manner of the Performance.

All the Endeavours of envious People to reproach it with being a Romance, to search it for Errors in Geography, Inconsistency in the Relation, and Contradictions in the Fact, have proved abortive, and as impotent as malicious.

The just Application of every Incident, the religious and useful Inferences drawn from every Part, are so many Testimonies to the good Design of making it publick, and must legitimate all the Part that may be call'd Invention, or Parable in the Story.

The Second Part, if the Editor's Opinion may pass, is (contrary to the Usage of Second Parts,) every Way as entertaining as the First, contains as strange and surprising Incidents, and as great a Variety of them; nor is the Application less serious, or suitable; and doubtless will, to the sober, as well as ingenious Reader, be every way as profitable and diverting; and this makes the abridging this Work,[1] as scandalous, as it is knavish and ridiculous; seeing, while to shorten the Book, that they may seem to reduce the Value, they strip it of all those Reflections, as well religious as moral, which are not only the greatest Beautys of the Work, but are calculated for the infinite Advantage of the Reader.

By this they leave the Work naked of its brightest Ornaments; and if

---

† From *The Farther Adventures of Robinson Crusoe* (London, 1719) Ar2–Ar4.
1. A pirated abridgment, printed for T. Cox at the Amsterdam Coffee-House, appeared on sale early in August for two shillings, thus competing with the sale of W. Taylor's authorized edition of *Robinson Crusoe*, which sold for five shillings.

they would, at the same Time pretend, that the Author has supply'd the Story out of his Invention, they take from it the Improvement, which alone recommends that Invention to wise and good Men.

The Injury these Men do the Proprietor of this Work, is a Practice all honest Men abhor; and he believes he may challenge them to shew the Difference between that and Robbing on the Highway, or Breaking open a House.

If they can't shew any Difference in the Crime, they will find it hard to shew why there should be any Difference in the Punishment: And he will answer for it, that nothing shall be wanting on his part, to do them Justice.

DANIEL DEFOE

[Preface to Volume III of *Robinson Crusoe*]†

As the Design of every Thing is said to be first in the Intention, and last in the Execution; so I come now to acknowledge to my Reader, That the present Work is not merely the Product of the two first Volumes, but the two first Volumes may rather be called the Product of this: The Fable[1] is always made for the Moral, not the Moral for the Fable.

I have heard, that the envious and ill-disposed Part of the World have rais'd some Objections against the two first Volumes, on Pretence, *for want of a better Reason*; That (*as they say*) the Story is feign'd, that the Names are borrow'd, and that it is all a Romance;[2] that there never were any such Man or Place, or Circumstances in any Mans Life; that it is all form'd and embellish'd by Invention to impose upon the World.

I *Robinson Crusoe* being at this Time in perfect and sound Mind and Memory, Thanks be to God therefore; do hereby declare, their Objection is an Invention scandalous in Design, and false in Fact; and do affirm, that the Story, though Allegorical, is also Historical;[3] and that it is the beautiful Representation of a Life of unexampled Misfortunes, and of a Variety not to be met with in the World, sincerely adapted to, and intended for the common Good of Mankind, and designed at first, *as it is now farther apply'd*, to the most serious Uses possible.

Farther, that there is a Man alive, and well known too, the Actions of whose Life are the just Subject of these Volumes, and to whom all or most Part of the Story most directly alludes, this may be depended upon for Truth, and to this I set my Name.

The famous History of *Don Quixot*, a Work which thousands read

---

† From *Serious Reflections during the Life and Surprising Adventures of Robinson Crusoe* (London, 1720) Ar2–Ar7.
1. Plot or story.
2. Fiction.
3. That is, factual and true.

with Pleasure, to one that knows the Meaning of it, was an emblematic
History of,[4] and a just Satyr[5] upon the Duke *de Medina Sidonia*; a
Person very remarkable at that Time in *Spain*: To those who knew the
Original, the Figures were lively and easily discovered themselves, as
they are also here, and the Images were just; and therefore, when a
malicious, but foolish Writer,[6] in the abundance of his Gall, spoke of
the Quixotism of R. *Crusoe*, as he called it, he shewed evidently, that
he knew nothing of what he said; and perhaps will be a little startled,
when I shall tell him, that what he meant for a Satyr, was the greatest
of Panegyricks.

Without letting the Reader into a nearer Explication of the Matter,
I proceed to let him know, that the happy Deductions I have employ'd
myself to make from all the Circumstances of my Story, will abundantly
make him amends for his not having the Emblem explained by the
Original; and that when in my Observations and Reflexions of any Kind
in this Volume, I mention my Solitudes and Retirements, and allude
to the Circumstances of the former Story, all those Parts of the Story
are real Facts in my History, whatever borrow'd Lights they may be
represented by: Thus the Fright and Fancies which succeeded the Story
of the Print of a Man's Foot, and Surprise of the old Goat, and the
Thing rolling on my Bed, and my jumping out in a Fright, are all
Histories and real Stories; as are likewise the Dream of being taken by
Messengers, being arrested by Officers, the Manner of being driven on
Shore by the Surge of the Sea, the Ship on Fire, the Description of
starving; the Story of my Man *Friday*, and many more most material
Passages observ'd here, and on which any religious Reflections are made,
are all historical and true in Fact: It is most real, that I had a Parrot,
and taught it to call me by my Name, such a Servant a Savage, and
afterwards a Christian, and that his Name was called *Friday*, and that
he was ravish'd from me by Force, and died in the Hands that took
him, which I represent by being killed; this is all litterally true, and
should I enter into Discoveries, many alive can testify them: His other
Conduct and Assistance to me also have just References in all their Parts
to the Helps I had from that faithful Savage, in my real Solitudes and
Disasters.

The Story of the Bear in the Tree, and the Fight with the Wolves in
the Snow, is likewise Matter of real History; and in a Word, the Adventures of *Robinson Crusoe*, are one whole Scheme of a real Life of
eight and twenty Years, spent in the most wandring desolate and afflicting
Circumstances that ever Man went through, and in which I have liv'd
so long in a Life of Wonders in continu'd Storms, fought with the worse
kind of Savages and Maneaters, by unaccountable supprising Incidents;

4. Symbolic yet realistic representation of.
5. Satire.
6. Charles Gildon's pamphlet, entitled "The Life and Strange Surprizing. Adventures of Mr.
D——— De F———," appeared in 1719 and attacked Defoe and the first two volumes of *Robinson
Crusoe*. This preface to volume three is in large part an answer to Gildon's criticisms.

fed by Miracles greater than that of Ravens, suffered all Manner of Violences and Oppressions, injurious Reproaches, contempt of Men, Attacks of Devils, Corrections from Heaven, and Opposi[ti]ons on Earth; have had innumerable Ups and Downs in Matters of Fortune, been in Slavery worse than *Turkish*, escaped by an exquisite Management, as that in the Story of *Xury*, and the Boat at *Sallee*, been taken up at Sea in Distress, rais'd again and depress'd again, and that oftner perhaps in one Man's Life than ever was known before; Shipwreck'd often, tho' more by Land than by Sea: In a Word, there's not a Circumstance in the imaginary Story, but has its just Allusion to a real Story, and chimes Part for Part, and Step for Step with the inimitable Life of *Robinson Crusoe*.

In like Manner, when in these Reflections, I speak of the Times and Circumstances of particular Actions done, or Incidents which happened in my Solitude and Island-Life, an impartial Reader will be so just to take it as it is; *viz.* that it is spoken or intended of that Part of the real Story, which the Island-Life is a just Allusion to; and in this the Story is not only illustrated, but the real Part I think most justly approv'd: *For Example*, in the latter Part of this Work called the Vision, I begin this, *When I was in my Island Kingdom, I had abundance of strange Notions of my seeing Apparitions,* &c. all these Reflections are just History of a State of forc'd Confinement, which in my real History is represented by a confin'd Retreat in an Island; and 'tis as reasonable to represent one kind of Imprisonment by another, as it is to represent any Thing that really exists, by that which exists not.[7] The Story of My Fright with something on my Bed, was Word for Word a History of what happened, and indeed all those Things received very little Alteration, except what necessarily attends removing the Scene from one Place to another.

My Observations upon Solitude are the same, and I think I need say no more, than that the same Remark is to be made upon all the References made here, to the Transactions of the former Volumes, and the Reader is desired to allow for it as he goes on.

Besides all this, here is the just and only good End of all Parable or Allegorick History brought to pass, *viz.* for moral and religious Improvement. Here is invincible Patience recommended under the worst of Misery; indefatigable Application and undaunted Resolution under the greatest and most discouraging Circumstances; I say, these are recommended, as the only Way to work through those Miseries, and their Success appears sufficient to support the most dead-hearted Creature in the World.

Had the common Way of Writing a Mans private History been taken, and I had given you the Conduct or Life of a Man you knew, and whose Misfortunes and Infirmities, perhaps you had sometimes unjustly triumph'd over; all I could have said would have yielded no Diversion,

7. Albert Camus quotes this observation as the epigraph to his novel *The Plague*, 1948.

and perhaps scarce have obtained a Reading, or at best no Attention; the Teacher, *like a greater*, having no Honour in his own Country. Facts that are form'd to touch the Mind, must be done a great Way off, and by somebody never heard of: Even the Miracles of the Blessed Saviour of the World suffered Scorn and Contempt, when it was reflected, that they were done by the Carpenter's Son; one whose Family and Original they had a mean Opinion of, and whose Brothers and Sisters were ordinary People like themselves.

There even yet remains a Question, whether the Instruction of these Things will take place, when you are supposing the Scene, which is placed so far off, had its Original so near Home.

But I am far from being anxious about that, feeling I am well assur'd, that if the Obstinacy of our Age should shut their Ears against the just Reflections made in this Volume, upon the Transactions taken Notice of in the former, there will come an Age, when the Minds of Men shall be more flexible, when the Prejudices of their Fathers shall have no Place, and when the Rules of Vertue and Religion justly recommended, shall be more gratefully accepted than they may be now, that our Children may rise up in Judgment against their fathers, and one Generation be edified by the same Teaching, which another Generation had despised.

ROB. CRUSOE.

DANIEL DEFOE

Serious Observations†

Introduction

I Must have made very little Use of my solitary and wandring Years, if after such a Scene of Wonders, as my Life may be justly call'd, I had nothing to say, and had made no Observations which might be useful and instructing, as well as pleasant and diverting to those that are to come after me.

Chap. I

OF SOLITUDE

How uncapable to make us happy, and
How unqualify'd to a Christian Life.

I have frequently look'd back, you may be sure, and that with different Thoughts, upon the Notions of a long tedious Life of Solitude, which

† From *Serious Reflections during the Life and Surprising Adventures of Robinson Crusoe* (London, 1720) 1–4.

I have represented to the World, and of which you must have formed some Ideas from the Life of a Man in an Island. Sometimes I have wonder'd how it could be supported, especially for the first Years, when the Change was violent and impos'd, and Nature unacquainted with any thing like it. Sometimes I have as much wonder'd, why it should be any Grievance or Affliction; seeing upon the whole View of the Stage of Life which we act upon in this World, it seems to me, that Life in general is, or ought to be, but one universal Act of Solitude: But I find it is natural to judge of Happiness, by its suiting or not suiting our own Inclinations. Every Thing revolves in our Minds by innumerable circular Motions, all centring in our selves. We judge of Prosperity, and of Affliction, Joy and Sorrow, Poverty, Riches, and all the various Scenes of Life: I say, we judge of them by our selves: Thither we bring them Home, as Meats touch the Palat, by which we try them; the gay Part of the World, or the heavy Part; it is all one, they only call it pleasant or unpleasant, as they suit our Taste.

The World, I say, is nothing to us, but as it is more or less to our Relish: All Reflection is carry'd Home, and our Dear-self is, in one Respect, the End of Living. Hence Man may be properly said to be *alone* in the Midst of the Crowds and Hurry of Men and Business: All the Reflections which he makes, are to himself; all that is pleasant, he embraces for himself; all that is irksome and grievous, is tasted but by his own Palat.

What are the Sorrows of other Men to us? And what their Joy? Something we may be touch'd indeed with, by the Power of Sympathy, and a secret Turn of the Affections; but all the solid Reflection is directed to our selves. Our Meditations are all Solitude in Perfection; our Passions are all exercised in Retirement; we love, we hate, we covet, we enjoy, all in Privacy and Solitude: All that we communicate of those Things to any other, is but for their Assistance in the Pursuit of our Desires; the End is at Home; the Enjoyment, the Contemplation, is all Solitude and Retirement; 'tis for our selves we enjoy, and for our selves we suffer.

What then is the Silence of Life? And, How is it afflicting, while a Man has the Voice of his Soul to speak to God, and to himself? That Man can never want Conversation, who is Company for himself; and he that cannot converse profitably with himself, is not fit for any Conversation at all; and yet there are many good Reasons why a Life of Solitude, as Solitude is now understood by the Age, is not at all suited to the Life of a Christian, or of a wise Man. Without enquiring therefore into the Advantages of Solitude, and how it is to be managed, I desire to be heard concerning what Solitude really is; for I must confess, I have different Notions about it, far from those which are generally understood in the World, and far from all those Notions upon which those People in the primitive Times, and since that also, acted, who separated themselves into Desarts and unfrequented Places, or confin'd themselves to Cells, Monasteries, and the like, retir'd, as they call it, from the World; All which, I think, have nothing of the Thing I call Solitude in them, nor do they answer any of the true Ends of Solitude, much less those Ends which are pretended to be sought after, by those who have talk'd most of those Retreats from the World.

As for Confinement in an Island, if the Scene was plac'd there for this very End, it were not at all amiss. I must acknowledge, there was Confinement from the Enjoyments of the World, and Restraint from human Society: *But all that was no Solitude*; indeed no Part of it was so, except that which, as in my Story, I apply'd to the Contemplation of sublime Things, and that was but a very little, as my Readers well know, compar'd to what a Length of Years my forced Retreat lasted.

It is evident then, that as I see nothing but what is far from being retir'd, in the forced Retreat of an Island, the Thoughts being in no Composure suitable to a retired Condition, no not for a great While; so I can affirm, that I enjoy much more Solitude in the Middle of the greatest Collection of Mankind in the World, I mean, at *London*, while I am writing this, than ever I could say I enjoy'd in eight and twenty Years Confinement to a desolate Island.

* * *

The Puritan Emblematic Tradition

J. PAUL HUNTER

[The "Guide" Tradition]†

Defoe himself worked in the guide tradition, but his method differs from that of the typical Puritan moralist. *The Family Instructor* (published, in two volumes, shortly before *Robinson Crusoe*) shares the typical concerns of guide books, but it relies primarily on example rather than exhortation. "The Way I have taken," says Defoe in Volume I (1715), ". . . is *Entirely New*, and at first *perhaps* it may appear something *Odd*. . . ."[1] In Volume I, Defoe presents the spiritual history of an entire family, from the father's first attempt to Christianize it, up to the conversion or apparent damnation of each family member. The work is divided into sections dealing with specific problems, and each section has an introduction and commentary, but the major portion of the work is devoted to the story itself. Defoe emphasizes the essentially dramatic character of the work by having the story unfold through dialogue. "The whole Work being design'd both to divert and instruct," Defoe says, "the Author has endeavored to adapt it as much as possible to both those uses, from whence some have called it a Religious Play. . . ."[2] The story is complete as story (though perhaps not very compelling for the modern reader), but the emphasis is of course placed upon the lesson it teaches, rather like an extended *exemplum*. Volume II, published less than a year before *Robinson Crusoe*, employs a similar method to inculcate similar morals. The appeal of Defoe's "new" method of guiding Christians is attested by *The Family Instructor*'s popularity: Volume I had reached an eighth edition by 1720, and throughout the eighteenth century it was republished almost as often as was *Robinson Crusoe*. Later, Defoe wrote again in the guide tradition, publishing *Religious Court-*

---

† From *The Reluctant Pilgrim*, by J. Paul Hunter, copyright The Johns Hopkins University Press, 1966, pp. 44–50. Reprinted by permission of the publisher and author.
1. I have quoted from the second edition (1715), p. 2.
2. Preface to the second edition, fol. [A4].

ship in 1722 and *The New Family Instructor* in 1727. In *The Complete English Tradesman* (1725), *The Complete English Gentlemen* (published posthumously), and in several tracts his aims were apparently similar.

George A. Aitken has been criticized sharply for saying that the difference between Defoe's moral treatises and his novels is "one of degree rather than kind." "The difference [in the novels]" according to Professor Aitken, "lay chiefly in the prominence now given the story, which took the leading place, hitherto occupied by the moral."[3] While his statement oversimplifies the issue, it at least indicates a relationship which has been, during the last half-century, too often overlooked. *Robinson Crusoe* is, of course, far more than a guide for youth about to embark on life's journey. But it does bear important thematic affinities to treatises whose primary concern is religious and moral, affinities which would have been obvious to a contemporary reader who might well have grouped it (lacking a more precise category) with *The Practice of Piety*. Whatever the qualities that ultimately separate it from Puritan tracts, *Robinson Crusoe* speaks to the same concerns as do guide books, and it shares their theological and moral point of view. The 1715 volume of *The Family Instructor* introduces us to a son who tires of his father's efforts to tether him. "I'll be content to go to the *West-Indies*, or be a *Foot-soldier*, or anything, rather than be made such a Recluse,"[4] he threatens. This rebellious young man might well be an embryonic Crusoe or Crusoe's brother,[5] and he himself may be descended from one or more of the rebellious young *exempla* who people seventeenth-century guide books. But whether or not Defoe proceeded gradually to thematic fiction from didactic treatise—whether or not *The Family Instructor* was his stepping stone to fictional form—the guide tradition provides one vital perspective from which to view fictional theme in *Robinson Crusoe* and from which to ask larger questions about the relationship between didacticism and literary form. More important than the "source" of *Robinson Crusoe* in another book or in several books is the *manner* in which ideas in the guide tradition become embodied in fiction. Rather than having an "original" somewhere in fact or fiction, *Robinson Crusoe* seems not to follow a specific "original," borrowing neither a particular

3. General Introduction, *Romances and Narratives by Daniel Defoe* (16 vols.; London, 1895), I, xxix. Arthur W. Secord (*Studies in the Narrative Method of Defoe* ["University of Illinois Studies in Language and Literature," IX; Urbana, 1924]) finds this position extreme (p. 17). A half century ago, Charlotte E. Morgan noted the significance of Defoe's guide books in relation to the novel of manners; in her *Rise of the Novel of Manners: A Study of English Prose Fiction between 1600 and 1740* (New York, 1911), she briefly discusses *The Family Instructor*, but she does not suggest any relationship between guide books and Defoe's own fiction. For a more recent discussion which elaborates Miss Morgan's suggestion, see Alan D. McKillop, *Early Masters of English Fiction* (Lawrence, Kans., 1956). Few recent critics, however, seem aware of the relation of Defoe's guide books to his fiction.
4. Pp. 135–36.
5. Crusoe's second brother, who might well have provided an emblem for Crusoe, simply disappears after leaving home.

incident nor a specific writer's attitudes, but rather concretizes in dramatic, symbolic particulars the saga of life as seen by the Puritan mind.

Once *Robinson Crusoe's* relation to the guide tradition is noted, the name of its hero takes on added significance. Of the possible "sources" of the name suggested by scholars, the most prominent has been that of Timothy Cruso, though no one has explained why Defoe should have used the name of a former schoolmate.[6] Nothing is known of any personal relationship between Defoe and Cruso after their schooling at Morton's Academy, but Defoe must have known of Cruso's reputation as a preacher and casuist. Cruso was renowned enough to be selected for the famous Merchant's Lectures at Pinner's Hall (he delivered twenty-four lectures), and his bibliography of a dozen extant books includes three youth guides: *The Usefullnesse of Spiritual Wisdom with a Temporal Inheritance* (written specifically for a young man about to embark on his calling), 1689; *The Necessity and Advantage of an Early Victory over Satan*, 1693; and *God the Guide of Youth*, 1695. Cruso's early death (brought on, according to his admirers, by his zeal for his work), ended a writing career begun only eight years earlier, and there is no evidence that his work had a significant vogue later. But even though he was not of the first rank of Dissenting divines, his work was important enough that readers of 1719 might well be expected (especially in view of the rarity of his surname) to remember him and to associate Defoe's hero with his name.

One of Cruso's guides is particularly interesting, for although it is short (about the length of an average sermon) it deals with most of the major problems involved in *Robinson Crusoe*. In *God the Guide*, Cruso argues the necessity of early choice of God as guide so that one's life may be properly ordered. "The proper work of a Guide," he says, "is to *direct* the Ignorant Traveller in a strange Land, and unknown Countrey. Such is our Case during the *time of our Sojourning* here in this World; and it is the work of the *only wise God, to guide our feet; and direct our steps* for us, which he will do if we sincerely resign ourselves

6. Defoe's latest biographer, John Robert Moore, simply says that "Defoe had a classmate at Morton's academy, Timothy Cruso or Crusoe, whose name (perhaps recalled by the island Curaçao [which Defoe spelled Curasoe] in the Caribbean) suggested the most famous name in all fiction" (*Daniel Defoe: Citizen of the Modern World* [Chicago, 1958], p. 225. Professor Moore had earlier (*N & Q*, CLXIV [1933], 26) suggested the possibility of Curaçao. Others have suggested that Defoe derived the name linguistically, through Creutznaer (Crusoe says that was his family name originally), from *kreutzen* (see Secord, *Studies*, pp. 42–43), or from Creutzinsel in Grimmelshausen's *Simplicissimus* (see Erwin Gustav Gudde, "Grimmelshausen's Simplicius Simplicissimus and Defoe's Robinson Crusoe," *PQ*, IV [1925], 110–20). Another argument, which I am unable to follow in detail, is given by Willard H. Bonner, *Captain William Dampier* (Palo Alto, Calif., 1934), p. 86 ff. Professor Bonner thinks that some connection exists between "Crusoe" and "cruise." In the nineteenth century quite a battle raged in *Notes and Queries* about the origin of the name Crusoe, and I should be content to leave it there, except that Timothy Cruso's writings seem to me to illuminate a tradition vital to *Robinson Crusoe* and to suggest new conclusions about Defoe's allusiveness.

to him. That which undoes us, is not God's *unwillingness* to *instruct us*, but our own unteachableness. . . ." Cruso places heavy emphasis upon filial obedience: "It is very *becoming* to take [parents'] Advice in all weighty and eminent Cases; it is *necessary* to receive and perform their Commands in all things lawful. . . ." And he promises dreadful consequences for those who refuse God's promptings: "Tho you be placed in Lawful Callings, and prosecute them with the greatest *diligence*, I must denounce this Sentence against you in the Name of God, That the *fruit of your labour* will have a *blast* upon it . . . ; either your Undertakings, or your very *Blessings* will be *Curst*. . . . If your Voyage be successful, and you come home *richly laden*, yet God not being concern'd in the *steering* of your Course, your Misery will be the greater."[7]

One might argue that such a tract stimulated Defoe to stretch a story over its ideological framework and that, to pay his debt, he named his hero after his source of inspiration. It is possible that Cruso's language and metaphor prodded Defoe at some stage of conception or execution, but such a specific obligation would be hard to prove, especially since Cruso's guide (though more compact and pointed than many others), conveys ideas characteristic of the guide tradition generally. Or one might construct a wildly elaborate schematization of Defoe's psychological process of creation and imagine that he felt guilty for leaving the profession (the ministry) for which Morton's Academy prepared him, that he recalled his schoolmate's later success in discussing such problems, and that somehow he assuaged his guilt and ordered his mind by writing a therapeutic, somewhat "allegorical" account of his own life, with Cruso—now become Crusoe—as hero. Or one might speculate about Cruso's life and imagine that his children, about whom it is known only that they died before their father, were rebellious like Defoe's own son. And so on.

But we are, of course, unlikely ever to find out whether anything remotely like the processes described above occurred in Defoe's mind. What does seem certain is this: as a student with Timothy Cruso at a small academy, Defoe would have known of Cruso's later work and modest renown; as a writer of guide literature, Defoe would have been aware of themes, methods, and metaphors of the tradition; in naming his hero he could scarcely have forgotten Cruso and chosen the name by coincidence. It is more likely that he expected contemporary readers to recognize his allusion and associate the name with thematic aspects of his book, for one of his aims was certainly to deal with the problems which the guide tradition had previously faced. For the modern reader, the name provides a directional signal for a segment of ideological and subliterary background now largely forgotten. *Robinson Crusoe* ulti-

7. Pp. 12–13, 20, 31–32.

mately is much more complex than any of the traditions which nourish it, but the complexity should not obscure the ancestry. Failure to recognize *Robinson Crusoe*'s relation to guide literature is to miss not only an illuminating segment of eighteenth-century background; it is to misinterpret significant developments in the narrative itself and to be misled on the tantalizing question of the relationship between the new prose fiction and the conventional didactic literature which helped form the minds of that fiction's first creators.

J. PAUL HUNTER

[The "Providence" Tradition]†

In surveying the providence literature before 1719, one might easily beguile oneself into errors made by students of sources, for the providence tradition affords many parallels to *Robinson Crusoe*. But ultimately the striking thing is not the similarity of fact and event between *Robinson Crusoe* and its analogues, but the similarity of meaning given to stories of physical and spiritual castaways. Factual accounts in both providence and travel literature reflect events which recur again and again in an age of increasing maritime exploration and colonization, but, unlike the travel tradition, the providence tradition focuses upon the strange and surprising aspects of these events and interprets them within a religious and philosophical framework which invests them with important meaning. And providence literature reflects the pattern of Christian experience central to the Puritan myth and organizes its *exempla* into a dramatic realization of the historical cycle, seen teleologically.

In 1704, Defoe had himself written in the providence tradition and had showed himself familiar with its ideas and conventions. In *The Storm: Or, a Collection of the Most Remarkable Casualties and Disasters Which Happen'd in the Late Dreadful Tempest, Both by Sea and Land*, Defoe interprets a spectacular storm as a judgment upon the sins of England (he uses a similar theme in *Journal of the Plague Year*, also related to the providence tradition) and says that he offers the anthology "to preserve the Remembrance of Divine Vengeance."[1] Defoe's Preface sets forth his aim: "The main Inference I shall pretend to make . . . is, the strong Evidence God has been pleas'd to give in this terrible manner to his own Being, which Mankind began more than ever to affront and despise. . . ."[2] The rendering and pointing of the accounts in *The Storm* suggests that Defoe well knew the matter and manner of his tradition

† From *The Reluctant Pilgrim*, by J. Paul Hunter, copyright The Johns Hopkins University Press, 1966, pp. 73–75. Reprinted by permission of the publisher and author.
1. P. 84.
2. Fols. A5ᵛ–A6.

and that, long before he undertook the art of fiction, he understood how to give anecdotes a thematic unity in the Puritan manner.

Defoe's prefatory statement in *Robinson Crusoe* that he sought to *"justify and honour the Wisdom of Providence in all the Variety of our Circumstances, let them happen how they will"* suggests that *Robinson Crusoe* shares the aims of the providence tradition, but Defoe goes beyond the tradition in contrasting the episodic appearance of events with the real orderliness of all. The dialectic of fall and recovery which is finally submerged by the total life pattern of Crusoe (an imitation, in little, of the process of history according to the Puritan myth) ultimately both subtilizes and expands the providence tradition's way of rendering *exempla*, and for this subtlety and expansion Defoe draws upon other Puritan literary traditions, particularly those of spiritual biography and pilgrim allegory. *Robinson Crusoe* is not, like *God's Protecting Providence*, merely an account of the workings of providence; unlike the stark *exempla* of Turner's *Compleat History* or the undeveloped spiritual history of Alexander Selkirk in *Providence Displayed*, it achieves a meaning that goes beyond a paraphrase of its theme. The polemical anecdotes in providence literature only illustrate a lesson, and the characters who people them (although historical) are both less humanized and less individualized than the fictional Crusoe. *Robinson Crusoe* is not adequately defined as a providence book any more than as a youth guide. But in its way of interpreting events according to a thematic scheme, and in its organizing pattern, *Robinson Crusoe* relies upon providence literature in a manner which Defoe could expect his contemporaries to recognize. When he told them that he was justifying God's ways to man, he may have spoken only part of the truth, but he was not lying. *Robinson Crusoe* rises above the polemics of the providence tradition and, ultimately, above all the Puritan subliterary traditions, but the quality of Defoe's originality should not obscure the nature of his dependence upon those traditions. The imagination which gave birth to *Robinson Crusoe* and which generated a new set of possibilities in prose fiction was steeped in the theological-moral tradition of lay polemics and was trained in the habitual patterns of the Puritan mind.

J. PAUL HUNTER

[Spiritual Biography]†

The dominant characteristics of both the personal diary and the funeral sermon are merged in spiritual biography in a way that writers hoped would be educational, inspiring, and productive of greater piety and

† From *The Reluctant Pilgrim*, by J. Paul Hunter, copyright The John Hopkins University Press, 1966, pp. 88–92. Reprinted by permission of the publisher and author.

higher morality. Usually, information and hortatory sections more or less alternate throughout the work, though the better written biographies attempt to make as much instruction as possible implicit in the narrative sections. The purposeful pattern of the subject's life is superimposed over the chronological record of events, and the commentary and exhortation seem to draw the events to their inevitable conclusion in the ultimate spiritual victory of the subject. Stylistically and artistically the biographies vary widely, from the wild, ranting, shrill harangues of the more emotional sects to the calm, reasoned way of Richard Baxter's *Autobiography* and the later anthologies of Clarke. The rhythm of spiritual success and failure varies with the "altitudos" or "backslides" of each individual and with the particular meanings of event patterns revealed to the hero or to the interpreter writing about the hero. But all spiritual biographies (like private forms concerned with the spiritual regeneration of man) share one pattern: the tracing of a rebellion-punishment-repentance-deliverance sequence described from the earliest moment of Christendom as characteristic of fallen men who are accorded God's grace.[1]

Readers of *The Pilgrim's Progress*, as well as of *Grace Abounding*, will recognize the basic pattern of spiritual biography, for ultimately the pilgrimage of an allegorical figure through life is not far from the typical journey through life of a real person. *Robinson Crusoe* is shaped more directly by the pilgrim allegories which grow out of the spiritual biography tradition, but the line of ancestry is clear. The organizational pattern of *Robinson Crusoe* follows chronological lines, but, as in a typical spiritual biography, a thematic superstructure is the real unifying principle. Events in *Robinson Crusoe*, like those in spiritual biographies, are validated relative to the total pattern of an individual's life, and the events are "improved" appropriately in order to draw the reader himself to a special view of religion and to a personal practice of higher morality.

Arthur W. Secord's statement that "the resemblance . . . of *Robinson Crusoe* to biography is easy to exaggerate" results from a faulty understanding of what biography was for Defoe's audience and from an inaccurate appraisal of Defoe's artistic intention. "In spite of the title," says Secord, "the story is almost wholly limited to an account of Crusoe's adventures at sea and on his island."[2] Secord ignores the fundamental historical fact that Defoe follows the way of *spiritual* biography in depicting adventures which are at once most dramatic and most specifically related to the basic pattern of his subject's life. And Defoe does tell us

1. For excellent discussions of Christian life pattern, and the centricity of conversion, see Roger Sharrock's Introduction to *Grace Abounding* (London, 1962), pp. xxvii–xxx; and G. A. Starr, *Defoe and Spiritual Autobiography* (Princeton, 1965), pp. 39 ff.
2. *Studies in the Narrative Method of Defoe* ("University of Illinois Studies in Language and Literature," IX; Urbana, 1924), p. 16.

of Crusoe's early life insofar as it is related to the pattern which emerges later in his life.[3]

Defoe's awareness of spiritual biography as a tradition is dramatically suggested by his early authorship of two brief items. One, a poem about Defoe's former pastor, Dr. Samuel Annesley, was published in 1703 and contains rather general biographical eulogy. As poetry, it rates little attention, and one could hardly predict Defoe's later interest in biography on the basis of its factual contents. But it does suggest an awareness of typical Puritan didactic application:

> But would you like a Man, or Christian grieve
> When others die, be thankful you're alive;
> Improve the Great Examples you look on,
> And take their Deaths for Warnings of your own.[4]

The second, Memoirs of the Life and Eminent Conduct of That Learned and Reverend Divine, Daniel Williams,[5] is longer and more elaborate and suggests a more intimate acquaintance with the conventions of spiritual biography. Defoe declines to employ most of the conventions, but his decision is calculated. "I shall not," he says at the beginning, "as is usual in Histories of this kind, trouble my self or the Reader of these Sheets with the looking back to his Nativity, Genealogy, or Introduction into the World, or into that Sphere of Action which he was in his Childhood appointed to move in. . . . But proceed to the more weighty Affairs of his Life, and of the Times he liv'd in. . . ." At the end, he again sums up his procedures and notes their departure from "usual" practice.[6]

Defoe's knowledge of the "usual" suggests an awareness of the tradition that corresponds with his awareness of other Puritan subliterary forms. The Family Instructor, with its "Entirely New Way" of constructing a guide, puts some of this awareness to use, but its full potential is not realized until he turns to fiction, building novels upon a structure developed in spiritual biography and upon themes and aims developed in other Puritan traditions.

Spiritual biography, drawing also from these other traditions, is polemical biography, and it selects facts to accord with its thesis. In Robinson Crusoe Defoe is also selective, and it is the particular principle of selectivity involved, rather than the quantity or completeness of information, which is significant. The artistry of Robinson Crusoe cannot be

3. The influence of spiritual biography upon the literary form of biography has not been adequately discussed. It seems to me likely that the use of extraordinary detail and the attempt to isolate a thematic pattern—characteristic of early biography—derive from the same philosophical basis as the emphasis on detail and pattern in early fiction.
4. "The Character of the Late Dr. Samuel Annesley, by Way of Elegy," in A True Collection of the Writings of the Author of The True Born English-man (London, 1703), p. 111.
5. London, 1718.
6. Pp. 1, 84. Italics mine.

fully described in terms of previous biographical traditions, not even in terms of the "fictional" tradition (pilgrim allegory) which descends from spiritual biography. But a look at the biographical traditions that Defoe and his readers knew reveals ancestors of *Robinson Crusoe* which, if they are less developed and polished, still show us a crude form of what is to come and enable us to isolate a family line that finds its finest expression much later in Hawthorne, Melville, and the symbolic novel.

EIGHTEENTH- AND NINETEENTH-CENTURY OPINIONS

CHARLES GILDON

The Life and Strange Surprizing Adventures of Mr. D—— De F——†

The Preface[1]

If ever the story of any private Man's Adventures in the World were worth making publick, and were acceptable when publish'd, the Editor of this Account thinks this will be so.

The Wonders of this Man's Life exceed all that (he thinks) is to be found Extant; the Life of one Man being scarce capable of greater Variety.

The Story is told with greater Modesty than perhaps some Men may think necessary to the Subject, the Hero of our Dialogue not being very conspicuous for that Virtue, a more than common Assurance carrying him thro' all those various Shapes and Changes which he has pass'd without the least Blush. The Fabulous *Proteus* of the Ancient Mythologist was but a very faint Type of our Hero, whose Changes are much more numerous, and he far more difficult to be constrain'd to his own Shape. If his Works should happen to live to the next Age, there would in all probability be a greater Strife among the several Parties, whose he really was, than among the seven *Graecian* Cities, to which of them *Homer* belong'd: The *Dissenters* first would claim him as theirs, the *Whigs* in general as theirs, the *Tories* as theirs, the *Non-jurors* as theirs, the *Papists* as theirs, the *Atheists* as theirs, and so on to what Subdivisions there may be among us; so that it cannot be expected that I should give you in this short Dialogue his Picture at length; no, I only pretend to present you with him in Miniature, in Twenty Fours, and not in Folio. But of all these Things, with some very surprizing Incidents in some new Adventures of his own for the rest of his Life, I may perhaps give a farther Account hereafter.[2]

---

† From *The Life and Strange Surprizing Adventures of Mr. D—— De F——* (London, 1719) iii–iv, 67–80.

    Charles Gildon (1665–1721) was a minor playwright and political pamphleteer who earned his living by his pen and, toward the end of his life, was a blind and embittered man. He and Defoe disliked each other, and the success of *Robinson Crusoe* excited Gildon's envy and prompted him to attack the book and its author. Gildon's pamphlet appeared in late September, after the publication in August of Defoe's *Farther Adventures of Robinson Crusoe.*

1. The preface, like the title page, of Gildon's pamphlet, is designed as a broad parody of Defoe's title page and preface to *Robinson Crusoe.*
2. Compare this last sentence with the final sentence of Defoe's *Robinson Crusoe.*

A
Dialogue
betwixt
D———— F————e,
Robinson Crusoe,
and His Man
Friday

SCENE, *A great field betwixt* Newington-Green *and* Newington *Town*,[3]
at one a Clock in a Moon-light Morning.

Enter D———F———*with two Pocket Pistols.*

D————*l.* A Fine pleasurable Morning, I believe about one a Clock;
and, I suppose, all the Lazy Kidnapping Rogues are by this Time got
drunk with *Geneva*[4] or Malt-Spirits to Bed, and I may pass Home without
any farther Terror. However, I am pretty well arm'd to keep off their
unsanctified Paws from my Shoulder————

Bless my Eye-Sight, what's this I see! I was secure too soon here, the
Philistines are come upon me; this is the Effect of my not obeying the
Secret Hint I had not to come Home this Night. But, however, here
they shall have a couple of Bullets in their Bellies———— ha! two of them,
great tall Gigantick Rogues, with strange High-crown'd Caps, and Flaps
hanging upon their Shoulders, and two Muskets a-piece, one with a
Cutlass, and the other with a Hatchet; e—g–d I'll e'en run back again
to the Green.   [*Turns and runs.*]

Oh, plague upon that swift leg'd Dog, he's got before me; I must now
stand upon my Guard, for he turns upon me and presents his Musket
———— Gentlemen, what would you have? would you murder me? Take
what I have, and save my Life.

Cru. Why, Father D————*n,* dost thou not know thy own Children?
art thou so frighted at Devils of thy own raising? I am thy *Robinson
Crusoe,* and that, my Man *Friday.*

D————*l. poor* Crusoe, *how came you hither? what do you do here?*

Cru. Ho, ho, do you know me now? You are like the Devil in *Milton,*
that could not tell the Offspring of his own Brain, *Sin* and *Death,* till
Madam Sin discover'd to him who they were. Yes, it is *Crusoe* and his
Man *Friday,* who are come to punish thee now, for making us such
Scoundrels in thy Writing: Come *Friday,* make ready, but don't shoot
till I give the Word.

Fri. No shoot, Master, no shoot: me will show you how we use
Scribblers in my Country.

Cru. In your Country *Friday,* why, you have no Scribblers there?

Fri. No Matter that Master, we have as many Scribblers as Bears in

3. The scene is set in the vicinity of where Defoe was educated (Newington Green Academy)
and where he lived when he wrote *Robinson Crusoe* (Stoke Newington).
4. Gin, a cheap liquor imported in large quantities from Holland in the early eighteenth century.

my Country; and me will make Laugh, me will make D——l dance
upon a Tree like *Bruin*. Oh! me will make much Laugh, and then me
will shoot.

D——l. Why, ye airy Fantoms, are you not my Creatures? mayn't I
make of you what I please?

Cru. Why, yes, you may make of us what you please; but when you
raise Beings contradictory to common Sense, and destructive of Religion
and Morality; they will rise up against you in *Foro Conscientiae*;[5] that
Latin I learn'd in my *Free-School* and *House Education*.

D——l. Hum, hum—— well, and what are your Complaints of me?

Cru. Why, that you have made me a strange whimsical, inconsistent
Being, in three Weeks losing all the Religion of a Pious Education; and
when you bring me again to a Sense of the Want of Religion, you make
me quit that upon every Whimsy; you make me extravagantly Zealous,
and as extravagantly Remiss; you make me an Enemy to all *English*
Sailors, and a Panegyrist upon all other Sailors that come in your way:
Thus, all the *English* Seamen laugh'd me out of Religion, but the
Spanish and *Portuguese* Sailors were honest religious Fellows; you make
me a Protestant in *London*, and a Papist in *Brasil*; and then again, a
Protestant in my own Island, and when I get thence, the only Thing
that deters me from returning to *Brasil*, is meerly, because I did not like
to die a Papist; for you say, *that* Popery *may be a good Religion to live
in, but not to die in*; as if that Religion could be good to live in, which
was not good to die in; for, Father *D——l*, whatever you may think,
no Man is sure of living one Minute. But tho' you keep me thus by
Force a Sort of Protestant, yet, you all along make me very fond of
Popish Priests and the Popish Religion; nor can I forgive you the making
me such a Whimsical Dog, to ramble over three Parts of the World
after I was sixty five. Therefore, I say, *Friday*, prepare to shoot.

Fri. No shoot yet Master, me have something to say, he much Injure
me too.

D——l. Injure you too, how the Devil have I injur'd you?

Fri. Have injure me, to make me such Blockhead, so much contradiction, as to be able to speak *English tolerably well* in a Month or two,
and not to speak it better in twelve Years after; to make me go out to
be kill'd by the Savages, only to be a Spokesman to them, tho' I did not
know, whether they understood one Word of my Language; for you
must know, Father *D——*, that almost ev'ry Nation of us *Indians* speak
a different Language. Now Master shall me shoot?

Cru. No *Friday*, not yet, for here will be several more of his Children
with Complaints against him; here will be the *French Priest, Will Atkins*,
the Priest in *China*, his Nephews Ship's Crew, and——[6]

D——l. Hold, hold, dear Son *Crusoe*, hold, let me satisfy you first
before any more come upon me. You are my Hero, I have made you,

5. The forum of conscience.
6. The reference is to *The Farther Adventures of Robinson Crusoe*.

out of nothing, fam'd from *Tuttle-Street* to *Limehousehole*; there is not an old Woman that can go to the Price of it, but buys thy Life and Adventures, and leaves it as a Legacy, with the *Pilgrims Progress*, the *Practice of Piety*, and *God's Revenge against Murther*,[7] to her Posterity.

Cru. Your Hero! Your Mob Hero! your *Pyecorner* Hero! on a foot with *Guy* of *Warwick*, *Bevis of Southampton*, and the *London Prentice*![8] for *M——w——r* has put me in that Rank, and drawn me much better; therefore, Sir, I say——

D——l. Dear Son *Crusoe*, be not in a Passion, hear me out.

Cru. Well, Sir, I will hear you out for once.

D——l. Then know, my dear Child, that you are a greater Favorite to me than you imagine; you are the true Allegorick Image of thy tender Father *D——l*; I drew thee from the consideration of my own Mind; I have been all my Life that Rambling, Inconsistent Creature, which I have made thee. * * *

* * * And now you have my Picture, Son *Crusoe*, as well as my Justification in my Draught of yours; I would not have you therefore complain any more of the Contradiction of your character, since that is of a Piece with the whole Design of my Book. I made you set out as undutiful and disobedient to your Parents; and to make your Example deter all others, I make you Fortunate in all your Adventures, even in the most unlucky, and give you at last a plentiful Fortune and a safe Retreat, Punishments so terrible, that sure the Fear of them must deter all others from Disobedience to Parents, and venturing to Sea: And now, as for you *Friday*, I did not make you speak broken *English*, to represent you as a Blockhead, incapable of learning to speak it better, but meerly for the Variety of Stile, to intermix some broken *English* to make my Lie go down the more glibly with the Vulgar Reader; and in this, I use you no worse than I do the *Bible* itself, which I quote for the very same End only.

Cru. Enough, Enough, Father *D——n*, you have confest enough, and now prepare for your Punishment, for here come all the rest of our Number which we expected; come *Friday*, pull out the Books, you have both Volumes, have you not *Friday*?

Fri. Yes Master, and me will make him swallow his own Vomit.

Cru. Here, Gentlemen, every one hold a Limb of him.

D——l. Oh, Oh, Mercy! Mercy!

Fri. Swallow, swallow, Father *D——n*, your Writings be good for the Heartburn, swallow, Father *D——n* — so me have cram'd down one Volume, must he have the other now Master?

Cru. Yes, yes, Friday, or else the Dose will not be compleat, and so perhaps mayn't work and pass thro' him kindly.

---

7. Three of the most popular devotional books of the seventeenth and early eighteenth centuries.
8. Pye Corner was in a slum section of London. Guy of Warwick, Bevis of Southampton, and the London Prentice were legendary English heroes whose exploits were widely circulated in cheap ballads and chapbooks in the seventeenth and eighteenth centuries.

Fri. Come, Father D——n, t'other Pill, or I think I may call it *Bolus*[9]
for the bigness of it, it is good for your Health; come, if you will make
such large Compositions, you must take them for your Pains.

D——l. Oh, oh, oh, oh.

Cru. Now, gentlemen, each Man take his Part of the Blanket and
toss him immoderately; for you must know, Gentlemen, that this is a
sort of Physick, which never works well without a violent Motion.

> *They toss him lustily, he crying out all
> the while.*

Cru. Hold, Gentlemen, I think our Business is done; for by the
unsavoury Stench which assaults my Nostrils, I find the Dose is past
thro' him, and so good Morrow, Father D——n. *Past three a Clock
and a Moon light Morning.*   *They all vanish.*

> D——l *solus.*

Bless me! what Company have I been in? or rather, what Dream have
I had? for certainly 'tis nothing but a Dream; and yet I find by the Effects
in my Breeches, that I was most damnably frighted with this Dream;
nay, more than ever I was in my Life; even more, than when we had
News that King *William* design'd to take into *Flanders* the *Royal Regiment.* But this is a fresh Proof of my Observation in the second Volume
of my *Crusoe, that there's no greater Evidence of an invisible World,
than that Connexion betwixt second Causes,* (as that in my Trowsers)
and those Ideas we have in our Minds.

> The End of the Dialogue.

ALEXANDER POPE

[On Defoe]†

The first part of Robinson Crusoe is very good.—De Foe wrote a vast
many things; and none bad, though none excellent, except this. There
is something good in all he has written. [1742]

THEOPHILUS CIBBER

[The Success of *Robinson Crusoe*]‡

His imagination was fertile, strong, and lively, as may be collected
from his many works of fancy, particularly his Robinson Crusoe, which

9. A large pill, commonly associated with quack medicine.
† From Joseph Spence, *Observations, Anecdotes, and Characters, of Books and Men,* ed. Samuel
  Weller Singer (London, 1820) 258–59.
‡ From *The Lives of the Poets* (London, 1753) 4.322.

was written in so natural a manner, and with so many probable incidents, that, for some time after its publication, it was judged by most people to be a true story. It was indeed written upon a model entirely new, and the success and esteem it met with, may be ascertained by the many editions it has sold, and the sums of money which have been gained by it.

JEAN-JACQUES ROUSSEAU

[A Treatise on Natural Education]†

I hate books; they only teach people to talk about what they don't understand. * * *

Is there no expedient to be thought of, to collect the various instructions, scattered up and down in so many voluminous tomes? to unite them under one general head, which may be easy to comprehend, interesting to pursue, and which may serve as a *stimulus*, even to children of this age?[1] If one could but conceive a situation, in which all the natural wants of man would be displayed, in a manner adapted to the understanding of a child, and wherein the means of satisfying those wants are gradually discovered with the same ease and simplicity, it would be in a just and lively description of such a state, that we should first exercise his imagination.

* * * Since we must have books, there is already one which, in my opinion, affords a complete treatise on natural education. This book shall be the first Emilius[2] shall read: In this, indeed, will, for a long time, consist his whole library, and it will always hold a distinguished place among others. It will afford us the text, to which all our conversations on the objects of natural science, will serve only as a comment. It will serve as our guide during our progress to a state of reason; and will even afterwards give us constant pleasure unless our taste be totally vitiated. You ask impatiently, what is the title of this wonderful book? Is it Aristotle, Pliny, or Buffon?[3] No. It is Robinson Crusoe.

Robinson Crusoe, cast ashore on a desolate island, destitute of human assistance, and of mechanical implements, providing, nevertheless, for his subsistence, for self-preservation, and even procuring for himself a

† From *Emilius and Sophia: or, A New System of Education* (London, 1762) 2.58–66. This is the first English translation and edition of *Émile* (1762).
1. Children aged twelve to fifteen.
2. Latinized form of Émile, the name of Rousseau's imaginary pupil in this treatise.
3. Aristotle (384–322 B.C.) was a classical Greek philosopher and teacher whose many influential writings include works on politics, ethics, poetics, rhetoric, metaphysics, logic, and natural history. Pliny the Elder (*ca.* A.D. 23–79) was the author of the monumental *Naturalis historia*, a compendium in thirty-seven books on all aspects of learning from art to zoology. George Louis Leclerc, Comte de Buffon (1707–88), was a celebrated French naturalist whose massive *Histoire naturelle, générale et particulière* (1749) was a multivolumed encyclopedia of the sciences.

kind of competency. In these circumstances, I say, there cannot be an object more interesting to persons of every age; and there are a thousand ways to render it agreeable to children. Such a situation, I confess, is very different from that of man in a state of society. Very probably it will never be that of Emilius; but it is from such a state he ought to learn to estimate others. The most certain method for him to raise himself above vulgar prejudices and to form his judgment on the actual relations of things, is to take on himself the character of such a solitary adventurer, and to judge of every thing about him, as a man in such circumstances would, by its real utility. This romance beginning with his shipwreck on the island, and ending with the arrival of the vessel that brought him away, would, if cleared of its rubbish, afford Emilius, during the period we are now treating of, at once both instruction and amusement. I would have him indeed personate the hero of the tale, and be entirely taken up with his castle, his goats and his plantations; he should make himself minutely acquainted, not from books but circumstances, with every thing requisite for a man in such a situation. He should affect even his dress, wear a coat of skins, a great hat, a large hanger, in short, he should be entirely equipt in his grotesque manner, even with his umbrello, though he would have no occasion for it. I would have him when at a loss about the measures necessary to be taken for his provision or security, upon this or the other occasion, examine the conduct of his hero; he should see if he omitted nothing, or if any thing better could be substituted in the room of what was actually done; and, on the discovery of any mistake in Robinson, should amend it in a similar case himself: for I doubt not but he will form a project of going to make a like settlement. * * *

What opportunities of instruction would such an amusement afford an able preceptor, who should project it only with a view to that end! The pupil, eager to furnish a magazine for his island, would be more ready to learn than his tutor to teach him. He would be solicitous to know every thing that is useful, and nothing else: You would in such a case have no more occasion to direct; but only to restrain him. Let us hasten, therefore, to establish him in this imaginary isle, since to this he confines his present happiness; for the time will now soon come, in which, if he is desirous of life, it is not to live alone, and in which even a man *Friday*, the want of whom does not now affect him, would not be long satisfactory.

The practice of simple manual arts, to the exercise of which the abilities of the individual are equal, leads to the invention of the arts of industry, the exercise of which requires the concurrence of many. The former may be practised by hermits, and savages; but the latter can be exercised only in a state of society, and render that state necessary. * * *

Emilius will see things in a very different light, while he is employed in furnishing his island. Robinson Crusoe would have set a greater value on the stock in trade of a petty ironmonger, than on that of the most magnificent and best furnished toy-shop in Europe. The first had appeared to him a respectable personage, while the owner of the latter had been despised as frivolous and contemptible.

SAMUEL JOHNSON

[In Praise of Defoe and *Robinson Crusoe*]†

Alas, Madam! (continued he) how few books are there of which one ever can possibly arrive at the *last* page! Was there ever yet any thing written by mere man that was wished longer by its readers, excepting *Don Quixote, Robinson Crusoe,* and the *Pilgrim's Progress?*

[Samuel Johnson] told us, that he had given Mrs. Montagu a catalogue of all of Daniel Defoe's works of imagination; most, if not all of which, as well as of his other works, he now enumerated, allowing a considerable share of merit to a man, who, bred a tradesman, had written so variously and so well. Indeed, his *Robinson Crusoe* is enough to establish his reputation. [1778]

HUGH BLAIR

[Fictitious History]‡

No fiction, in any language, was ever better supported than the Adventures of Robinson Crusoe. While it is carried on with that appearance of truth and simplicity, which takes a strong hold of the imagination of all Readers, it suggests, at the same time, very useful instruction; by showing how much the native powers of man may be exerted for surmounting the difficulties of any external situation.

† From Hester Lynch Piozzi, *Anecdotes of . . . Samuel Johnson* (London, 1786) 281, and *Boswell's Life of Johnson,* ed. G. B. Hill (Oxford, 1887) 3.267–268.
‡ From *Lectures on Rhetoric and Belles Lettres* (London, 1783) 2.309.

JAMES BEATTIE

[The Morality of *Robinson Crusoe*]†

Some have thought, that a lovetale is necessary to make a romance interesting. But Robinson Crusoe, though there is nothing of love in it, is one of the most interesting narratives that ever was written; at least in all that part which relates to the desert island: being founded on a passion still more prevalent than love, the desire of self-preservation; and therefore likely to engage the curiosity of every class of readers, both old and young, both learned and unlearned.

* * * Robinson Crusoe must be allowed, by the most rigid moralist, to be one of those novels, which one may read, not only with pleasure, but also with profit. It breathes throughout a spirit of piety and benevolence: it sets in a very striking light, as I have elsewhere observed, the importance of the mechanick arts, which they, who know not what it is to be without them, are so apt to undervalue: it fixes in the mind a lively idea of the horrors of solitude, and, consequently, of the sweets of social life, and of the blessings we derive from conversation, and mutual aid: it shows, how, by labouring with one's own hands, one may secure independence, and open for one's self many sources of health and amusement. I agree, therefore, with Rousseau, that this is one of the best books that can be put in the hands of children.—The style is plain, but not elegant, nor perfectly grammatical: and the second part of the story is tiresome.

GEORGE CHALMERS

[The Popularity of *Robinson Crusoe*]‡

But the time at length came, when De Foe was to deliver to the world the most popular of all his performances. In April 1719, he published the well-known *Life and surprising Adventures of Robinson Crusoe*. The reception was immediate and universal. * * * It if be inquired by what charm it is that these *surprising Adventures* should have instantly pleased, and always pleased, it will be found, that few books have ever so naturally mingled amusement with instruction. The attention is fixed, either by the simplicity of the narration, or by the variety of the incidents; the heart is amended by a *vindication of the ways of God to man*: and the

† From *Dissertations Moral and Critical* (London, 1783) 566–67.
‡ From *The Life of Daniel De Foe* (London, 1790) 52–53.

understanding is informed by various examples, how much utility ought
to be preferred to ornament: the young are instructed, while the old are
amused.

[JOHN BALLANTYNE]

[On Defoe]†

Perhaps there exists no work, either of instruction or entertainment,
in the English language, which has been more generally read, and more
universally admired, than the *Life and Adventures of Robinson Crusoe*.
It is difficult to say in what the charm consists, by which persons of all
classes and denominations are thus fascinated; yet the majority of readers
will recollect it is among the first works which awakened and interested
their youthful attention; and feel, even in advanced life, and in the
maturity of their understanding, that there are still associated with Robinson Crusoe, the sentiments peculiar to that period, when all is new,
all glittering in prospect, and when those visions are most bright, which
the experience of afterlife tends only to darken and destroy.

This work was first published in April, 1719; its reception, as may be
supposed, was universal. It is a singular circumstance, that the Author,
* * * after a life spent in political turmoil, danger, and imprisonment,
should have occupied himself, in its decline, in the production of a
work like the present; unless it may be supposed, that his wearied heart
turned with disgust from society and its institutions, and found solace
in picturing the happiness of a state, such as he has assigned to his hero.
Be this as it may, society is for ever indebted to the memory of De Foe
for his production of a work, in which the ways of Providence are simply
and pleasingly vindicated, and a lasting and useful moral is conveyed
through the channel of an interesting and delightful story.

* * *

There scarce exists a work so popular as *Robinson Crusoe*. It is read
eagerly by young people; and there is hardly an elf so devoid of imagination as not to have supposed for himself a solitary island in which
he could act *Robinson Crusoe*, were it but in the corner of the nursery.
To many it has given the decided turn of their lives, by sending them
to sea. For the young mind is much less struck with the hardships of
the anchorite's situation than with the animating exertions which he
makes to overcome them; and *Robinson Crusoe* produces the same

† From *The Prose Works of Sir Walter Scott* (Edinburgh and London, 1834) 4.228–29, 279–
81.

   John Ballantyne (1774–1821), Edinburgh publisher and friend of Sir Walter Scott. This
biographical sketch first appeared in a much shorter and less polished version as an introduction
to *Robinson Crusoe* in *The Novels of Daniel De Foe*, ed. Walter Scott (Edinburgh, 1810).

impression upon an adventurous spirit which the *Book of Martyrs*[1] would do on a young devotee, or the *Newgate Calendar*[2] upon an acolyte of Bridewell;[3] both of which students are less terrified by the horrible manner in which the tale terminates, than animated by sympathy with the saints or depredators who are the heroes of their volume. Neither does a re-perusal of *Robinson Crusoe*, at a more advanced age, diminish our early impressions. The situation is such as every man may make his own, and, being possible in itself, is, by the exquisite art of the narrator, rendered as probable as it is interesting. It has the merit, too, of that species of accurate painting which can be looked at again and again with new pleasure.

Neither has the admiration of the work been confined to England, though Robinson Crusoe himself, with his rough good sense, his prejudices, and his obstinate determination not to sink under evils which can be surpassed by exertion, forms no bad specimen of the True-Born Englishman. The rage for imitating a work so popular seems to have risen to a degree of frenzy; and, by a mistake not peculiar to this particular class of the *servum pecus*,[4] the imitators did not attempt to apply De Foe's manner of managing the narrative to some situation of a different kind, but seized upon and caricatured the principal incidents of the shipwrecked mariner and the solitary island. It is computed that within forty years from the appearance of the original work, no less than forty-one different *Robinsons* appeared, besides fifteen other imitations, in which other titles were used. Finally, though perhaps it is no great recommendation, the anti-social philosopher Rousseau will allow no other book than *Robinson Crusoe* in the hands of Emilius.[5] Upon the whole, the work is as unlikely to lose its celebrity as it is to be equalled in its peculiar character by any other of similar excellence.

SAMUEL TAYLOR COLERIDGE

[Crusoe as a Representative of Humanity]†

The charm of De Foe's works, especially of Robinson Crusoe, is founded on the same principle. It always interests, never agitates. Crusoe

1. First printed in English in 1563, Foxe's monumental study dwells on the sufferings of Christian martyrs. Its homely style and animated dialogues between persecutors and martyrs made it an enormously popular devotional book from the seventeenth century on.
2. The original series, published in 1774, offered graphic accounts of the most notorious crimes of the eighteenth century.
3. A famous prison in London.
4. Horace, *Epistles* 1.19.19: "slavish herd."
5. See the excerpt from Rousseau's *Emilius*.
† From *Coleridge's Miscellaneous Criticism*, ed. Thomas Middleton Raysor (Cambridge, Mass., 1936) 194, 293, 299–300.

himself is merely a representative of humanity in general; neither his intellectual nor his moral qualities set him above the middle degree of mankind; his only prominent characteristic is the spirit of enterprise and wandering, which is, nevertheless, a very common disposition. You will observe that all that is wonderful in this tale is the result of external circumstances—of things which fortune brings to Crusoe's hand. [1818]

* * *

[Note: The following observations are STC's annotations in an 1812 edition of Robinson Crusoe he possessed. They were included in his Literary Remains (1830).]

* * * Compare the contemptuous Swift with the contemned De Foe, and how superior will the latter be found. But by what test? Even by this. The writer who makes me sympathise with his presentations with the *whole* of my being, is more estimable than the writer who calls forth and appeals to but a part of my being—my sense of the ludicrous for instance; and again, he who makes me forget my *specific* class, character, and circumstances, raises me into the universal man. Now this is De Foe's excellence. You become a man while you read.

* * *

One excellence of De Foe among many is his sacrifice of lesser interest to the greater because more universal. Had he (as without any improbability he might have done) given his Robinson Crusoe any of the turn for natural history which forms so striking and delightful a feature in the equally uneducated Dampier—had he made him find out qualities and uses in the before (to him) unknown plants of the island, discover a substitute for hops, for instance, or describe birds, etc.—many delightful pages and incidents might have enriched the book; but then Crusoe would cease to be the universal representative, the person for whom every reader could substitute himself. But now nothing is done, thought, or suffered, or desired, but what every man can imagine himself doing, thinking, feeling, or wishing for.

Even so very easy a problem as that of finding a substitute for ink is with exquisite judgment made to baffle Crusoe's inventive faculties. Even in what he does he arrives at no excellence; he does not make basket work like Will Atkins. The carpentering, tailoring, pottery, are all just what will answer his purpose, and those are confined to needs that all men have, and comforts all men desire. Crusoe rises only where all men may be made to feel that they might and that they ought to rise —in religion, in resignation, in dependence on, and thankful acknowledgement of the divine mercy and goodness.

CHARLES LAMB

[On Defoe's Novels]†

* * * "In the appearances of truth, in all the incidents and conversations that occur in them, they exceed any works of fiction that I am
acquainted with. It is perfect illusion. The author never appears in these
self-narratives (for so they ought to be called, or rather auto-biographies)
but the narrator chains us down to an implicit belief in every thing he
says. There is all the minute detail of a log-book in it. Dates are painfully
pressed upon the memory. Facts are repeated over and over in varying
phrases, till you cannot chuse but believe them. It is like reading evidence
in a court of Justice. So anxious the storyteller seems that the truth
should be clearly comprehended, that when he has told us a matter of
fact, or a motive, in a line or two farther down he repeats it, with his
favourite figure of speech, *I say*, so and so, though he had made it
abundantly plain before. This is in imitation of the common people's
way of speaking, or rather of the way in which they are addressed by a
master or mistress, who wishes to impress something upon their memories, and has a wonderful effect upon matter-of-fact readers. Indeed,
it is to such principally that he writes. His style is every where beautiful,
but plain and homely. *Robinson Crusoe* is delightful to all ranks and
classes; but it is easy to see, that it is written in a phraseology peculiarly
adapted to the lower conditions of readers. Hence, it is an especial
favourite with sea-faring men, poor boys, servant-maids, &c. His novels
are capital kitchen-reading, while they are worthy, from their interest,
to find a shelf in the libraries of the wealthiest and the most learned.
His passion for matter-of-fact narrative, sometimes betrayed him into a
long relation of common incidents, which might happen to any man,
and have no interest beyond the intense appearance of truth in them,
to recommend them." [1822]

---

† Quoted in Walter Wilson, *Memoirs of the Life and Times of Daniel Defoe* (London, 1830)
3.428–29 (letter from Lamb to Wilson *re* Defoe, December 1822).

WILLIAM WORDSWORTH

[Crusoe's Extraordinary Energy and Resource]†

[Wordsworth] thought the charm of *Robinson Crusoe* mistakenly ascribed, as it commonly is done, to its *naturalness*. Attaching a full value to the singular yet easily imagined and most picturesque circumstances of the adventurer's position, to the admirable painting of the scenes, and to the knowledge displayed of the working of human feelings, he yet felt sure that the intense interest created by the story arose chiefly from the extraordinary energy and resource of the hero under his difficult circumstances, from their being so far beyond what was natural to expect, or what would have been exhibited by the average of men; and that similarly the high pleasure derived from his successes and good fortunes arose from the peculiar source of these uncommon merits of his character.

EDGAR ALLAN POE

[Defoe's Faculty of Identification]‡

While Defoe would have been fairly entitled to immortality had he never written "Robinson Crusoe" yet his many other very excellent writings have nearly faded from our attention, in the superior lustre of the "Adventures of the Mariner of York." What better possible species of reputation could the author have desired for that book than the species which it has so long enjoyed? It has become a household thing in nearly every family in Christendom. Yet never was admiration of any work— universal admiration—more indiscriminately or more inappropriately bestowed. Not one person in ten—nay, not one person in five hundred—has, during the perusal of "Robinson Crusoe," the most remote conception that any particle of genius, or even of common talent, has been employed in its creation! Men do not look upon it in the light of a literary performance. Defoe has none of their thoughts—Robinson all. The powers which have wrought the wonder have been thrown into obscurity by the very stupendousness of the wonder they have wrought! We read, and become perfect abstractions in the intensity of our interest;

---

† From "Reminiscences of the Rev. R. P. Graves, M.A." in *The Prose Works of William Wordsworth*, ed. Alexander B. Grosart (London, 1876) 3.468.

‡ Poe's observation on Defoe first appeared in the *Southern Literary Messenger* (January 1836). Collected in *Marginalia*; see *The Works of Edgar Allan Poe*, eds. E. O. Stedman and G. E. Woodberry (New York and Pittsburgh, 1903) 7.300–302.

we close the book, and are quite satisfied that we could have written as well ourselves. All this is effected by the potent magic of verisimilitude. Indeed the author of "Crusoe" must have possessed, above all other faculties, what has been termed the faculty of *identification*—that dominion exercised by volition over imagination, which enables the mind to lose its own in a fictitious individuality. This includes, in a very great degree, the power of abstraction; and with these keys we may partially unlock the mystery of that spell which has so long invested the volume before us. But a complete analysis of our interest in it cannot be thus afforded. Defoe is largely indebted to his subject. The idea of man in a state of perfect isolation, although often entertained, was never before so comprehensively carried out. Indeed the frequency of its occurrence to the thoughts of mankind argued the extent of its influence on their sympathies, while the fact of no attempt having been made to give an embodied form to the conception went to prove the difficulty of the undertaking. But the true narrative of Selkirk in 1711, with the powerful impression it then made upon the public mind, sufficed to inspire Defoe with both the necessary courage for his work, and entire confidence in its success. How wonderful has been the result!

WILLIAM HAZLITT

[The Influence of *Robinson Crusoe*]†

The first, and by far the most celebrated, of those works of imagination, which have conferred immortality upon the name of De Foe, appeared in 1719, under the title of "The Life and Strange Surprising Adventures of Robinson Crusoe, of York, Mariner;" &c. Next to the Holy Scriptures, it may safely be asserted that this delightful romance has ever since it was written excited the first and most powerful influence upon the juvenile mind of England, nor has its popularity been much less among any of the nations of Christendom. At a period when few of the productions of English genius had been transferred into any of the languages of foreigners, this masterpiece of the homely, unaffected, unpretending, but rich and masculine intellect of Daniel De Foe, had already acquired, in every cultivated tongue of Europe, the full privileges of a native work.

† From a "memoir" of "The Life of Daniel De Foe" prefixed to *The Works of Daniel De Foe* (London, 1840) 1.cviii–cix.

THOMAS DE QUINCEY

[The Double Character of Defoe's Works]†

De Foe is the only author known, who has so plausibly circumstantiated his false historical records, as to make them pass for genuine, even with literary men and critics. * * * How did he accomplish so difficult an end? Simply by inventing such little circumstantiations of any character or incident, as seen by their apparent inertness of effect, to verify themselves; for, where the reader is told that such a person was the posthumous son of a tanner; that his mother married afterwards a Presbyterian schoolmaster, who gave him a smattering of Latin; but, the schoolmaster dying of the plague, that he was compelled at sixteen to enlist for bread—in all this, as there is nothing at all amusing, we conclude, that the author could have no reason to detain us with such particulars, but simply because they were true. To invent, when nothing at all is gained by inventing, there seems no imaginable temptation. It never occurs to us, that this very construction of the case, this very inference from such neutral details, was precisely the object which De Foe had in view, and by which he meant to profit. He thus gains the opportunity of impressing upon his tales a double character; he makes them so amusing, that girls read them for novels; and he gives them such an air of verisimilitude, that men read them for histories.

GEORGE BORROW

[Inspiration from *Robinson Crusoe*]‡

Reader, is it necessary to name the book which now stood open in my hand, and whose very prints, feeble expounders of its wondrous lines, had produced within me emotions strange and novel? Scarcely, for it was a book which has exerted over the minds of Englishmen an influence certainly greater than any other of modern times; which has been in most people's hands, and with the contents of which even those who cannot read are to a certain extent acquainted; a book from which the most luxuriant and fertile of our modern prose writers have drunk inspiration; a book, moreover, to which, from the hardy deeds which it narrates, and the spirit of strange and romantic enterprise which it tends

† From "Homer and the Homeridae," *Blackwood's Edinburgh Magazine* 50 (December 1841): 754–55.
‡ From *Lavengro* (London, 1851) 1.38–39.

to awaken, England owes many of her astonishing discoveries both by sea and land, and no inconsiderable part of her naval glory.

Hail to thee, spirit of De Foe! What does not my own poor self owe to thee? England has better bards than either Greece or Rome, yet I could spare them easier than De Foe, "un-abashed De Foe," as the hunchbacked rhymer styled him.[1]

THOMAS BABINGTON MACAULAY

[On Defoe]†

"I can not understand the mania of some people about De Foe. They think him a man of the first order of genius, and a paragon of virtue. He certainly wrote an excellent book—the first part of 'Robinson Crusoe'—one of those feats which can only be performed by the union of luck with ability. That awful solitude of a quarter of a century—the strange union of comfort, plenty, and security with the misery of loneliness—was my delight before I was five years old, and has been the delight of hundreds of thousands of boys. But what has De Foe done great except the first part of 'Robinson Cursoe?' The second part is poor in comparison. The 'History of the Plague' and the 'Memoirs of a Cavalier' are in one sense curious works of art. They are wonderfully like true histories; but, considered as novels, which they are, there is not much in them. He had undoubtedly a knack at making fiction look like truth. But is such a knack much to be admired? Is it not of the same sort with the knack of a painter who takes in the birds with his fruit? I have seen dead game painted in such a way that I thought the partridges and pheasants real; but surely such pictures do not rank high as works of art. Villemain, and before him Lord Chatham, were deceived by the 'Memoirs of a Cavalier;' but when those 'Memoirs' are known to be fictitious, what are they worth? How immeasurably inferior to 'Waverley,' or the 'Legend of Montrose,' or 'Old Mortality!' As to 'Moll Flanders,' 'Roxana,' and 'Captain Jack,' they are utterly wretched and nauseous; in no respect, that I can see, beyond the reach of Afra Behn.[1] As a political writer, De Foe is merely one of the crowd. He seems to have been an unprincipled hack, ready to take any side of any question. Of all writers he was the most unlucky in irony. Twice he was prosecuted for what he meant to be ironical; but he was so unskillful that every

1. Pope had satirized Defoe in his *Dunciad* (1728) 2.139: "Earless on high, stood un-abash'd De Foe."
† From G. O. Trevelyan, *The Life and Letters of Lord Macaulay* (New York, 1877) 2.383–84.
1. Aphra Behn (1640–89), minor writer of poems, plays, and novels, of which her *Oroonoko, or the History of the Royal Slave* (1678) is the most celebrated.

body understood him literally. Some of his tracts are worse than immoral; quite beastly. Altogether I do not like him." [1858]

CHARLES DICKENS

[The Want of Emotion in Defoe]†

You remember my saying to you some time ago how curious I thought it that *Robinson Crusoe* should be the only instance of an universally popular book that could make no one laugh and could make no one cry. I have been reading it again just now, in the course of my numerous refreshings at those English wells, and I will venture to say that there is not in literature a more surprising instance of an utter want of tenderness and sentiment, than the death of Friday. It is as heartless as *Gil Blas*, in a very different and far more serious way. But the second part altogether will not bear enquiry. In the second part of *Don Quixote* are some of the finest things. But the second part of *Robinson Crusoe* is perfectly contemptible, in the glaring defect that it exhibits the man who was 30 years on that desert island with no visible effect made on his character by that experience. De Foe's women too—Robinson Crusoe's wife for instance—are terrible dull commonplace fellows without breeches; and I have no doubt he was a precious dry disagreeable article himself—I mean De Foe: not Robinson.

KARL MARX

[Crusoe and Capitalism]‡

Since Robinson Crusoe's experiences are a favorite theme with political economists,[1] let us take a look at him on his island. Moderate though he be, yet some few wants he has to satisfy, and must therefore do a little useful work of various sorts, such as making tools and furniture, taming goats, fishing and hunting. Of his prayers and the like we take

† From John Forster, *The Life of Charles Dickens* (Philadelphia, 1874) 3.135n.
‡ From Karl Marx, *Capital*, tr. Samuel Moore and Edward Aveling (Chicago: Charles H. Kerr, 1921) 1.88–91.
1. Even Ricardo has his stories à la Robinson. "He makes the primitive hunter and the primitive fisher straightway, as owners of commodities, exchange fish and game in the proportion in which labourtime is incorporated in these exchange values. On this occasion he commits the ananchronism of making these men apply to the calculation, so far as their implements have to be taken into account, the annuity tables in current use on the London Exchange in the year 1847. 'The parallelograms of Mr. Owen' appear to be the only form of society, besides the bourgeois form, with which he was acquainted." (Karl Marx: "Critique," &c., 69–70.)

no account, since they are a source of pleasure to him, and he looks upon them as so much recreation. In spite of the variety of his work, he knows that his labour, whatever its form, is but the activity of one and the same Robinson, and consequently, that it consists of nothing but different modes of human labour. Necessity itself compels him to apportion his time accurately between his different kinds of work. Whether one kind occupies a greater space in his general activity than another, depends on the difficulties, greater or less as the case may be, to be overcome in attaining the useful effect aimed at. This our friend Robinson soon learns by experience, and having rescued a watch, ledger, and pen and ink from the wreck, commences, like a true-born Briton, to keep a set of books. His stock-book contains a list of the objects of utility that belong to him, of the operations necessary for their production; and lastly, of the labour time that definite quantities of those objects have, on an average, cost him. All the relations between Robinson and the objects that form this wealth of his own creation, are here so simple and clear as to be intelligible without exertion, even to Mr. Sedley Taylor.[2] And yet those relations contain all that is essential to the determination of value.

Let us now transport ourselves from Robinson's island bathed in light to the European middle ages shrouded in darkness. Here, instead of the independent man, we find everyone dependent, serfs and lords, vassals and suzerains, laymen and clergy. Personal dependence here characterises the social relations of production just as much as it does the other spheres of life organized on the basis of that production. But for the very reason that personal dependence forms the groundwork of society, there is no necessity for labour and its products to assume a fantastic form different from their reality. They take the shape, in the transactions of society, of services in kind and payments in kind. Here the particular and natural form of labour, and not, as in a society based on production of commodities, its general abstract form is the immediate social form of labour. Compulsory labour is just as properly measured by time, as commodity-producing labour; but every serf knows that what he expends in the service of his lord, is a definite quantity of his own personal labour-power. The tithe to be rendered to the priest is more matter of fact than his blessing. No matter, then, what we may think of the parts played by the different classes of people themselves in this society, the social relations between individuals in the performance of their labour, appear at all events as their own mutual personal relations, and are not disguised under the shape of social relations between the products of labour.

For an example of labour in common or directly associated labour, we have no occasion to go back to that spontaneously developed form

2. Sedley Taylor (1834–1920), Cambridge political economist who advocated profit-sharing [Editor].

which we find on the threshold of the history of all civilized races.[3] We have one close at hand in the patriarchal industries of a peasant family, that produces corn, cattle, yarn, linen, and clothing for home use. These different articles are, as regards the family, so many products of its labour, but as between themselves, they are not commodities. The different kinds of labour, such as tillage, cattle tending, spinning, weaving and making clothes, which result in the various products, are in themselves, and such as they are, direct social functions, because functions of the family, which just as much as a society based on the production of commodities, possesses a spontaneously developed system of division of labour. The distribution of the work within the family, and the regulation of the labour-time of the several members, depend as well upon differences of age and sex as upon natural conditions varying with the seasons. The labour-power of each individual, by its very nature, operates in this case merely as a definite portion of the whole labour-power of the family, and therefore, the measure of the expenditure of individual labour-power by its duration, appears here by its very nature as a social character of their labour.

Let us now picture to ourselves, by way of change, a community of free individuals, carrying on their work with the means of production in common, in which the labour-power of all the different individuals is consciously applied as the combined labour-power of the community. All the characteristics of Robinson's labour are here repeated, but with this difference, that they are social, instead of individual. Everything produced by him was exclusively the result of his own personal labour, and therefore simply an object of use for himself. The total product of our community is a social product. One portion serves as fresh means of production and remains social. But another portion is consumed by the members as means of subsistence. A distribution of this portion amongst them is consequently necessary. The mode of this distribution will vary with the productive organization of the community, and the degree of historical development attained by the producers. We will assume, but merely for the sake of a parallel with the production of commodities, that the share of each individual producer in the means of subsistence is determined by his labour-time. Labour-time would, in that case, play a double part. Its apportionment in accordance with a definite social plan maintains the proper proportion between the different kinds of work to be done and the various wants of the community. On

3. "A ridiculous presumption has latterly got abroad that common property in its primitive form is specifically a Slavonian, or even exclusively Russian form. It is the primitive form that we can prove to have existed amongst Romans, Teutons, and Celts, and even to this day we find numerous examples, ruins though they be, in India. A more exhaustive study of Asiatic, and especially of Indian forms of common property, would show how from the different forms of primitive common property, different forms of its dissolution have been developed. Thus, for instance, the various original types of Roman and Teutonic private property are deducible from different forms of Indian common property." (Karl Marx. "Critique," &c., p. 29, footnote.)

the other hand, it also serves as a measure of the portion of the common labour borne by each individual and of his share in the part of the total product destined for individual consumption. The social relations of the individual producers, with regard both to their labour and to its products, are in this case perfectly simple and intelligible, and that with regard not only to production but also to distribution.

JOHN STUART MILL

[The Preeminence of *Robinson Crusoe* in Childhood]†

Of children's books, any more than of playthings, I had scarcely any, except an occasional gift from a relation or acquaintance: among those I had, Robinson Crusoe was preeminent, and continued to delight me through all my boyhood.

LESLIE STEPHEN

[Defoe's Discovery of a New Art Form]‡

It is time, however, to say enough of 'Robinson Crusoe' to justify its traditional superiority to De Foe's other writings. The charm, as some critics say, is difficult to analyse; and we do not profess to demonstrate mathematically that it must necessarily be, what it is, the most fascinating boy's book even written, and one which older critics may study with delight. * * *

* * * In his first discovery of a new art [De Foe] shows the freshness so often conspicuous in first novels. The scenery was just that which had peculiar charms for his fancy; it was one of those half-true legends of which he had heard strange stories from seafaring men, and possibly from the acquaintances of his hero himself. He brings out the shrewd vigorous character of the Englishman thrown upon his own resources with evident enjoyment of his task. Indeed, De Foe tells us very emphatically that in Robinson Crusoe he saw a kind of allegory of his own fate. He had suffered from solitude of soul. Confinement in his prison is represented in the book by confinement in an island; and even a particular incident, here and there, such as the fright he receives one night from something in his bed, 'was word for word a history of what happened.' In other words, his novel too, like many of the best ever

† From *Autobiography* (London, 1873) 9.
‡ From "De Foe's Novels," in *Hours in a Library* (London, 1874) 51, 54–58.

written, has in it the autobiographical element which makes a man speak from greater depths of feeling than in a purely imaginary story.

It would indeed be easy to show that the story, though in one sense marvellously like truth, is singularly wanting as a psychological study. Friday is no real savage, but a good English servant without plush. He says 'muchee' and 'speakee,' but he becomes at once a civilised being, and in his first conversation puzzles Crusoe terribly by that awkward theological question, why God did not kill the devil—for characteristically enough Crusoe's first lesson includes a little instruction upon the enemy of mankind. He found, however, that it was 'not so easy to imprint right notions in Friday's mind about the devil, as it was about the being of a God.' This is comparatively a trifle; but Crusoe himself is all but impossible. Steele, indeed, gives an account of Selkirk, from which he infers that 'this plain man's story is a memorable example that he is happiest who confines his wants to natural necessities;' but the facts do not warrant this pet doctrine of an old-fashioned school. Selkirk's state of mind may be inferred from two or three facts. He had almost forgotten to talk; he had learnt to catch goats by running on foot; and he had acquired the exceedingly difficult art of making fire by rubbing two sticks. In other words, his whole mind was absorbed in providing a few physical necessities, and he was rapidly becoming a savage—for a man who can't speak and can make fire is very near the Australian. We may infer, what is probable from other cases, that a man living fifteen years by himself, like Crusoe, would either go mad or sink into the semi-savage state. De Foe really describes a man in prison, not in solitary confinement. We should not be so pedantic as to call for accuracy in such matters; but the difference between the fiction and what we believe would have been the reality is significant. De Foe, even in 'Robinson Crusoe,' gives a very inadquate picture of the mental torments to which his hero is exposed. He is frightened by a parrot calling him by name, and by the strangely picturesque incident of the footmark on the sand; but, on the whole, he takes his imprisonment with preternatural stolidity. His stay on the island produces the same state of mind as might be due to a dull Sunday in Scotland. For this reason, the want of power in describing emotion as compared with the amazing power of describing facts, 'Robinson Crusoe' is a book for boys rather than men, and, as Lamb says, for the kitchen rather than for higher circles. It falls short of any high intellectual interest. When we leave the striking situation and get to the second part, with the Spaniards and Will Atkins talking natural theology to his wife, it sinks to the level of the secondary stories. But for people who are not too proud to take a rather low order of amusement 'Robinson Crusoe' will always be one of the most charming of books. We have the romantic and adventurous incidents upon which the most unflinching realism can be set to work without danger of vulgarity. Here is precisely the story suited to De Foe's strength and weakness. He is forced to be artistic in spite of himself. He cannot lose the thread of the narrative and break it into disjointed fragments, for the limits of the island confine him as well as his hero. He cannot tire us with details, for all the details of such a story are interesting; it is made up of petty incidents, as much as the life of a prisoner reduced to taming flies, or making saws out of penknives. The island does as well as the Bastille for making trifles valuable to the sufferer and to us. The facts tell the story of themselves, without any demand for romantic power to press them home to us; and the efforts to give an air of authenticity to the story, which sometimes makes us smile, and sometimes rather bore us, in other novels, are all to the purpose; for there is a real point in putting such a story in the mouth of the sufferer, and in giving us for the time an illusory belief in his reality. It is one of the exceptional cases in which the poetical aspect of a position is brought out best by the most prosaic accuracy of detail; and we imagine that Robinson Crusoe's island, with all his small household torments, will always be more impressive than the more gorgeously coloured island of Enoch Arden.[1] When we add that the whole book shows the freshness of a writer employed on his first novel—though at the mature age of fifty-eight; seeing in it an allegory of his own experience embodied in the scenes which most interested his imagination, we see some reasons why 'Robinson Crusoe' should hold a distinct rank by itself amongst his works. As De Foe was a man of very powerful but very limited imagination—able to see certain aspects of things with extraordinary distinctness, but little able to rise above them—even his greatest book shows his weakness, and scarcely satisfies a grown-up man with a taste for high art. In revenge, it ought, according to Rousseau, to be for a time the whole library of a boy, chiefly, it seems, to teach him that the stock of an iron-monger is better than that of a jeweller. We may agree in the conclusion without caring about the reason; and to have pleased all the boys in Europe for near a hundred and fifty years is, after all, a remarkable feat.

---

1. Titular hero of a poem by Tennyson (1864); he is shipwrecked for more than ten years on an island [*Editor*].

TWENTIETH-CENTURY
CRITICISM

VIRGINIA WOOLF

Robinson Crusoe†

There are many ways of approaching this classical volume; but which shall we choose? Shall we begin by saying that, since Sidney died at Zutphen leaving the *Arcadia* unfinished, great changes had come over English life, and the novel had chosen, or had been forced to choose, its direction? A middle class had come into existence, able to read and anxious to read not only about the loves of princes and princesses, but about themselves and the details of their humdrum lives. Stretched upon a thousand pens, prose had accommodated itself to the demand; it had fitted itself to express the facts of life rather than the poetry. That is certainly one way of approaching *Robinson Crusoe*—through the development of the novel; but another immediately suggests itself— through the life of the author. Here too, in the heavenly pastures of biography, we may spend many more hours than are needed to read the book itself from cover to cover. The date of Defoe's birth, to begin with, is doubtful—was it 1600 or 1661? Then again, did he spell his name in one word or in two? And who were his ancestors? He is said to have been a hosier; but what, after all, was a hosier in the seventeenth century? He became a pamphleteer, and enjoyed the confidence of William the Third; one of his pamphlets caused him to be stood in the pillory and imprisoned at Newgate; he was employed by Harley and later by Godolphin; he was the first of the hireling journalists; he wrote innumerable pamphlets and articles; also *Moll Flanders* and *Robinson Crusoe*; he had a wife and six children; was spare in figure, with a hooked nose, a sharp chin, grey eyes and a large mole near his mouth. Nobody who has any slight acquaintance with English literature needs to be told how many hours can be spent and how many lives have been spent in tracing the development of the novel and in examining the chins of the novelists. Only now and then, as we turn from theory to biography and from biography to theory, a doubt insinuates itself—if we knew the very moment of Defoe's birth and whom he loved and why, if we had by heart the history of the origin, rise, growth, decline, and fall of the English novel from its conception (say) in Egypt to its decease in the wilds (perhaps) of Paraguay, should we suck an ounce of additional pleasure from *Robinson Crusoe* or read it one whit more intelligently?

For the book itself remains. However we may wind and wriggle, loiter and dally in our approach to books, a lonely battle waits us at the end.

† From *The Second Common Reader* by Virginia Woolf, copyright, 1932, by Harcourt & Company and renewed 1960, by Leonard Woolf, pp. 50–58. Reprinted by permission of the publisher.

There is a piece of business to be transacted between writer and reader before any further dealings are possible, and to be reminded in the middle of this private interview that Defoe sold stockings, had brown hair, and was stood in the pillory is a distraction and a worry. Our first task, and it is often formidable enough, is to master his perspective. Until we know how the novelist orders his world, the ornaments of that world, which the critics press upon us, the adventures of the writer, to which biographers draw attention, are superfluous possessions of which we can make no use. All alone we must climb upon the novelist's shoulders and gaze through his eyes until we, too, understand in what order he ranges the large common objects upon which novelists are fated to gaze: man and men; behind them Nature; and above them that power which for convenience and brevity we may call God. And at once confusion, misjudgment, and difficulty begin. Simple as they appear to us, these objects can be made monstrous and indeed unrecognisable by the manner in which the novelist relates them to each other. It would seem to be true that people who live cheek by jowl and breathe the same air vary enormously in their sense of proportion; to one the human being is vast, the tree minute; to the other, trees are huge and human beings insignificant little objects in the background. So, inspite of the text-books, writers may live at the same time and yet see nothing the same size. Here is Scott, for example, with his mountains looming huge and his men therefore drawn to scale; Jane Austen picking out the roses on her tea-cups to match the wit of her dialogues; while Peacock bends over heaven and earth one fantastic distorting mirror in which a tea-cup may be Vesuvius or Vesuvius a tea-cup. Nevertheless Scott, Jane Austen, and Peacock lived through the same years; they saw the same world; they are covered in the text-books by the same stretch of literary history. It is in their perspective that they are different. If, then, it were granted us to grasp this firmly, for ourselves, the battle would end in victory; and we could turn, secure in our intimacy, to enjoy the various delights with which the critics and biographers so generously supply us.

But here many difficulties arise. For we have our own vision of the world; we have made it from our own experience and prejudices, and it is therefore bound up with our own vanities and loves. It is impossible not to feel injured and insulted if tricks are played and our private harmony is upset. Thus when *Jude the Obscure* appears or a new volume of Proust, the newspapers are flooded with protests. Major Gibbs of Cheltenham would put a bullet through his head tomorrow if life were as Hardy paints it; Miss Wiggs of Hampstead must protest that though Proust's art is wonderful, the real world, she thanks God, has nothing in common with the distortions of a perverted Frenchman. Both the gentleman and the lady are trying to control the novelist's perspective so that it shall resemble and reinforce their own. But the great writer —the Hardy or the Proust—goes on his way regardless of the rights of private property; by the sweat of his brow he brings order from chaos; he plants his tree there, and his man here; he makes the figure of his deity remote or present as he wills. In masterpieces—books, that is, where the vision is clear and order has been achieved—he inflicts his own perspective upon us so severely that as often as not we suffer agonies—our vanity is injured because our own order is upset; we are afraid because the old supports are being wrenched from us; and we are bored—for what pleasure or amusement can be plucked from a brand new idea? Yet from anger, fear, and boredom a rare and lasting delight is sometimes born.

Robinson Crusoe, it may be, is a case in point. It is a masterpiece, and it is a masterpiece largely because Defoe has throughout kept consistently to his own sense of perspective. For this reason he thwarts us and flouts us at every turn. Let us look at the theme largely and loosely, comparing it with our preconceptions. It is, we know, the story of a man who is thrown, after many perils and adventures, alone upon a desert island. The mere suggestion—peril and solitude and a desert island—is enough to rouse in us the expectation of some far land on the limits of the world; of the sun rising and the sun setting; of man, isolated from his kind, brooding alone upon the nature of society and the strange ways of men. Before we open the book we have perhaps vaguely sketched out the kind of pleasure we expect it to give us. We read; and we are rudely contradicted on every page. There are no sunsets and no sunrises; there is no solitude and no soul. There is, on the contrary, staring us full in the face nothing but a large earthenware pot. We are told, that is to say, that it was the 1st of September 1651; that the hero's name is Robinson Crusoe; and that his father has the gout. Obviously, then, we must alter our attitude. Reality, fact, substance is going to dominate all that follows. We must hastily alter our proportions throughout; Nature must furl her splendid purples; she is only the giver of drought and water; man must be reduced to a struggling, life-preserving animal; and God shrivel into a magistrate whose seat, substantial and somewhat hard, is only a little way above the horizon. Each sortie of ours in pursuit of information upon these cardinal points of perspective—God, man, Nature—is snubbed back with ruthless commonsense. Robinson Crusoe thinks of God: "sometimes I would expostulate with myself, why providence should thus completely ruin its creatures. . . . But something always return'd swift upon me to check these thoughts." God does not exist. He thinks of Nature, the fields "adorn'd with flowers and grass, and full of very fine woods", but the important thing about a wood is that it harbours an abundance of parrots who may be tamed and taught to speak. Nature does not exist. He considers the dead, whom he has killed himself. It is of the utmost importance that they should be buried at once, for "they lay open to the sun and would presently be offensive". Death does not exist. Nothing exists except an earthenware pot. Finally, that is to say, we are forced to drop our own preconceptions and to accept what Defoe himself wishes to give us.

Let us then go back to the beginning and repeat again, "I was born in the year 1632 in the city of York of a good family". Nothing could be plainer, more matter of fact, than that beginning. We are drawn on soberly to consider all the blessings of orderly, industrious middle-class life. There is no greater good fortune we are assured than to be born of the British middle class. The great are to be pitied and so are the poor; both are exposed to distempers and uneasiness; the middle station between the mean and the great is the best; and its virtues—temperance, moderation, quietness, and health—are the most desirable. It was a sorry thing, then, when by some evil fate a middle-class youth was bitten with the foolish love of adventure. So he proses on, drawing, little by little, his own portrait, so that we never forget it—imprinting upon us indelibly, for he never forgets it either, his shrewdness, his caution, his love of order and comfort and respectability; until by whatever means, we find ourselves at sea, in a storm; and, peering out, everything is seen precisely as it appears to Robinson Crusoe. The waves, the seamen, the sky, the ship—all are seen through those shrewd, middle-class, uni-maginative eyes. There is no escaping him. Everything appears as it would appear to that naturally cautious, apprehensive, conventional, and solidly matter-of-fact intelligence. He is incapable of enthusiasm. He has a natural slight distaste for the sublimities of Nature. He suspects even Providence of exaggeration. He is so busy and has such an eye to the main chance that he notices only a tenth part of what is going on round him. Everything is capable of a rational explanation, he is sure, if only he had time to attend to it. We are much more alarmed by the "vast great creatures" that swim out in the night and surround his boat than he is. He at once takes his gun and fires at them, and off they swim—whether they are lions or not he really cannot say. Thus before we know it we are opening our mouths wider and wider. We are swallowing monsters that we should have jibbed at if they had been offered us by an imaginative and flamboyant traveller. But anything that this sturdy middle-class man notices can be taken for a fact. He is for ever counting his barrels, and making sensible provisions for his water supply; nor do we ever find him tripping even in a matter of detail. Has he forgotten, we wonder, that he has a great lump of beeswax on board? Not at all. But as he had already made candles out of it, it is not nearly as great on page thirty-eight as it was on page twenty-three. When for a wonder he leaves some inconsistency hanging loose—why if the wild cats are so very tame are the goats so very shy?—we are not seriously perturbed, for we are sure that there was a reason, and a very good one, had he time to give it us. But the presence of life when one is fending entirely for oneself alone on a desert island is really no laughing matter.

It is no crying one either. A man must have an eye to everything; it is no time for raptures about Nature when the lightning may explode one's gunpowder—it is imperative to seek a safer lodging for it. And so by means of telling the truth undeviatingly as it appears to him—by being a great artist and forgoing this and daring that in order to give effect to his prime quality, a sense of reality—he comes in the end to make common actions dignified and common objects beautiful. To dig, to bake, to plant, to build—how serious these simple occupations are; hatchets, scissors, logs, axes—how beautiful these simple objects become. Unimpeded by comment, the story marches on with magnificent downright simplicity. Yet how could comment have made it more impressive? It is true that he takes the opposite way from the psychologist's—he describes the effect of emotion on the body, not on the mind. But when he says how, in a moment of anguish, he clinched his hands so that any soft thing would have been crushed; how "my teeth in my head would strike together, as set against one another so strong, that for the time I could not part them again", the effect is as deep as pages of analysis could have made it. His own instinct in the matter is right. "Let the naturalists", he says, "explain these things, and the reason and manner of them; all I can say to them is, to describe the fact. . . ." If you are Defoe, certainly to describe the fact is enough; for the fact is the right fact. By means of this genius for fact Defoe achieves effects that are beyond any but the great masters of descriptive prose. He has only to say a word or two about "the grey of the morning" to paint vividly a windy dawn. A sense of desolation and of the deaths of many men is conveyed by remarking in the most prosaic way in the world, "I never saw them afterwards, or any sign of them except three of their hats, one cap, and two shoes that were not fellows". When at last he exclaims, "Then to see how like a king I din'd too all alone, attended by my servants"—his parrot and his dog and his two cats, we cannot help but feel that all humanity is on a desert island alone—though Defoe at once informs us, for he had a way of snubbing off our enthusiasms, that the cats were not the same cats that had come in the ship. Both of those were dead; these cats were new cats, and as a matter of fact cats became very troublesome before long from their fecundity, whereas dogs, oddly enough, did not breed at all.

Thus Defoe, by reiterating that nothing but a plain earthenware pot stands in the foreground, persuades us to see remote islands and the solitudes of the human soul. By believing fixedly in the solidity of the pot and its earthiness, he has subdued every other element to his design; he has roped the whole universe into harmony. And is there any reason, we ask as we shut the book, why the perspective that a plain earthenware pot exacts should not satisfy us as completely, once we grasp it, as man himself in all his sublimity standing against a background of broken mountains and tumbling oceans with stars flaming in the sky?

IAN WATT

Robinson Crusoe as a Myth†

We do not usually think of *Robinson Crusoe* as a novel. Defoe's first full-length work of fiction seems to fall more naturally into place with *Faust, Don Juan,* and *Don Quixote,* the great myths of our civilization. What these myths are about it is fairly easy to say. Their basic plots, their enduring images, all exhibit a single-minded pursuit by the protagonist of one of the characteristic aspirations of Western man. Each of their heroes embodies an *arete* and a *hubris,* an exceptional prowess and a vitiating excess, in spheres of action that are peculiarly important in our culture. Don Quixote, the impetuous generosity and the limiting blindness of chivalric idealism; Don Juan, pursuing and at the same time tormented by the idea of boundless experience of women; Faustus, the great knower, whose curiosity, always unsatisfied, brings damnation.

Crusoe does not at first seem a likely companion for these other culture heroes. They lose the world for an idea; he, for gain. Their aspirations are conscious and defiant, so that when retribution comes it is half expected and already understood; whereas Robinson Crusoe, disclaiming heroism or even pride, stolidly insists that he is not more than he seems, that you would do the same in the circumstances.

Yet there can be no doubt of his apotheosis. By the end of the nineteenth century, *Crusoe* had appeared in at least seven hundred editions, translations, and imitations, not to mention a popular eighteenth-century pantomime and an opera by Offenbach.[1] There are other more picturesque examples of his fame. In 1848 an enterprising French industrialist started a restaurant up a tree, a particularly fine chestnut in a wood near Paris: he called it "Robinson," and now restaurateurs vie for the title in a village of that name.[2] In France, again, "un robinson" has become a popular term for a large umbrella.

Nor, as Virginia Woolf has pointed out,[3] is Robinson Crusoe usually thought of as a hero of fiction. Instead, partly because of Defoe's verisimilitude and partly for deeper reasons, his author's name has been forgotten, while he himself has acquired a kind of semihistorical status,

---

† Slightly revised by the author from *Essays in Criticism: A Quarterly Journal of Literary Criticism* (April 1951): 95–119. Reprinted by permission of the publisher and author.
1. For a survey of the work done on this subject, with very full references, see Phillip Babcock Gove, *The Imaginary Voyage in Prose Fiction* (New York: 1941). The study of *Robinsonaden* is particularly connected with the name of Hermann Ullrich, author of *Robinson und Robinsonaden* (Weimar: 1898), and *Defoes Robinson Crusoe, Geschichte eines Weltbuches* (Leipzig: 1924). H. C. Hutchins has studied the early editions of *Robinson Crusoe* in his *Robinson Crusoe and Its Printing* (New York: 1925), and William-Edward Mann is responsible for a useful study of *Robinson Crusoë en France* (Paris: 1916).
2. René Pottier, *Histoire d'un Village* (Paris: 1941), pp. 171–74.
3. Daniel Defoe, *The Common Reader,* first series (London: 1925).

like the traditional heroes of myth. When his story appeared it is reported to have been "universally received and credited as a genuine history";[4] and we today can surely apply to it. Malinowski's description of primitive myths: "It is not of the nature of fiction, such as we read today in a novel, but it is a living reality, believed to have once happened in primeval times, and continuing ever since to influence the world and human destinies."[5]

Almost universally known, almost universally thought of as at least half real, Robinson Crusoe cannot be refused the status of myth. But the myth of what?

It is at first difficult to answer, especially if we take into account the later portions of the Crusoe trilogy. For Defoe at once cashed in on the success of the *Strange and Surprising Adventures of Robinson Crusoe* with two other books, the *Farther Adventures* and the *Serious Reflections*. They complicate the answer because, though the character is the same, he is no longer on the island. But perhaps there is no need to consider them in detail. Myth always tends in transmission to be whittled down to a single, significant situation. Hardly anyone knows the later books of the trilogy; the stark facts of the hero's island existence occupy almost all our attention, and the rest is largely forgotten. Even the other portions of the first volume of the trilogy, comprising the early adventures and the eventual return to civilization, are hardly part of the myth, which retains only the island episode. But merely for that one episode, that solitude, many possible meanings suggest themselves.

Defoe himself gives two main explanations for Crusoe's solitude. At times Crusoe feels he is being punished for irreligion;[6] at others for his filial disobedience in leaving home—in the *Farther Adventures* he even accuses himself of having "killed his father."[7] But Crusoe as a man isolated from God, or as a modern Oedipus, is not our subject here. For the myth as it has taken shape in our minds is surely not primarily about religious or psychological alienation, nor even about solitude as such. Crusoe lives in the imagination mainly as a triumph of human achievement and enterprise, and as a favorite example of the elementary processes of political economy. So, in our attempt to understand the causes for Crusoe's apotheosis, we will look first at the relationship of his story to some of the enduring traits of our social and economic history.

We can briefly designate them as "Back to Nature," "The Dignity of Labor," and "Economic Man." Robinson Crusoe seems to have become

4. Max Günther, *Entstehungsgeschichte von Defoes Robinson Crusoe* (Griefswald: 1909), p. 29.
5. Bronislaw Malinowski, *Myth in Primitive Psychology* (London: 1926), pp. 18–19.
6. *The Life and Strange Surprising Adventures of Robinson Crusoe*, George A. Aitken, ed. (London: 1902), pp. 41–43, 95–100, and *passim*. [29–31, 64–67] [NCE page numbers appear in brackets.]
7. *The Farther Adventures of Robinson Crusoe*, G. A. Aitken, ed. (London: 1902), pp. 149–50. Also *Life and Strange Surprising Adventures*, p. 216. [141]

a kind of culture hero representing all three of these related but not wholly congruent ideas. It is true that if we examine what Defoe actually wrote and what he may be thought to have intended, it appears that *Robinson Crusoe* hardly supports some of the symbolic uses to which the pressure of the needs of our society has made it serve. But this, of course, is in keeping with the status of *Robinson Crusoe* as a myth, for we learn as much from the varied shapes that a myth takes in men's minds as from the form in which it first arose. It is not an author but a society that metamorphoses a story into a myth, by retaining only what its unconscious needs dictate and forgetting everything else.

I

The term "Back to Nature" covers the many and varied forms of primitivism, of revulsion from the contemporary complexities of civilization into a simpler and more "natural" order. The movement necessarily features two forms of regress: technological and topographical; a simpler economic structure and its associated rural setting. Both are involved in *Robinson Crusoe*, and it is interesting to see that Rousseau, the great prophet of both these trends, was the first to see in it something which far transcended the status of a mere adventure story. The book played an important role in his imaginative experience, and he frequently referred to it. The most famous reference occurs in *Émile*.[8] There, after announcing that in principle "he hates books" and that he is determined to correct the predominantly bookish tendency of traditional methods of education, Rousseau solemnly proclaims an exception. One book exists which teaches all that books can teach. It is "the first that my Émile will read; it will for a long time be the whole contents of his library; and it will always hold an honoured place there. . . . What then is this marvelous book? Is it Aristotle? Is it Pliny? Is it Buffon? No, it is *Robinson Crusoe*."

The hero, alone on his island, deprived of all assistance from his fellows, and nevertheless able to look after himself, is obviously a figure that will enthral readers of all ages. The book's consequent entertainment value renders palatable the moral and philosophical teachings which are Rousseau's main concern. We cannot here give a full account of them, but two are particularly relevant. One is based on the descriptions of Crusoe's labors: they will fire Émile's imagination with the practical, natural, and manual education to which he is destined. Bacon, Comenius, and Locke had urged this change of emphasis, but Rousseau takes it very much further; Defoe's story, a box of tools, and the philosopher of Geneva, these will suffice Émile: anything more would be superfluous, nay vicious.

But the pattern which Émile must imitate is not only that of the simple life of toil. Crusoe also stands for another of Rousseau's favorite ideas—radical individualism. To attain this way of life, Rousseau be-

8. *Émile, ou De L'Éducation*, F. and P. Richard, eds. (Paris: 1939), pp. 210–14.

lieves that "the surest way to raise oneself above prejudices and to order one's judgment on the real relationship between things, is to put oneself in the place of an isolated man, and to judge of everything as that man would judge them, according to their actual usefulness."[9] Hence, again, the pre-eminent utility of *Robinson Crusoe* as a basic text: for the hero's life is its demonstration.

The book as Defoe wrote it (strictly speaking, the *Life and Strange Surprising Adventures* as Saint Hyacinthe and Van Effen transposed it into the more formal French literary tradition)[1] is not perfect. So Rousseau proposes a version freed of all "fatras";[2] one which was in fact that of the myth. The story was to begin with the shipwreck and to end with the rescue: Émile's book would be less instructive if it ended in the way Defoe's actually does—with a return to civilization.

Defoe, of course, would have been surprised at this canonization of his story. His surprise would have been increased by Rousseau's other references where Crusoe becomes a sort of John the Baptist, who in his solitude made straight the ways of the final incarnation of the extravagancies of romantic individualism. For Crusoe is after all a "*solitaire malgré lui*," as Paul Nourrison points out in his *Jean-Jacques Rousseau et Robinson Crusoë*.[3] He is an involuntary and unappreciative prisoner of the beauties of nature. Rousseau was a botanist but Crusoe is a seed merchant: and the moral of his activities is quite different from that which Rousseau extracts. Indeed, if we, perhaps unwisely, attempt to draw a general conclusion from Crusoe's life on the island, it must surely be that out of humanity's repertoire of conceivable designs for living, rational economic behavior alone is entitled to ontological status. Crusoe "returns to nature" only according to Defoe's characteristic definition of that accommodating word: in his newspaper, the *Review*, Defoe had written that "Nothing follows the course of Nature more than Trade. There Causes and Consequences follow as directly as day and night."[4] So in the island the nature of the universe is most importantly manifested in the rationality of the processes of economic life. There are the "real relationships between things" which Crusoe discovers, relationships whose value and interest come from the way they help man to secure the maximum utility from his environment.

Defoe's "nature" appeals not for adoration but for exploitation: the island solitude is an exceptional occasion not for undisturbed self-communion, but for strenuous efforts at self-help. Inspired with this belief, Crusoe observes nature, not with the eyes of a pantheist primitive,

9. *Ibid.*, p. 211.
1. See Gove, *The Imaginary Voyage*, p. 36; Mann, *Robinson Crusoë en France*, pp. 51–55 and 102; W. J. B. Pienaar, *English Influences in Dutch Literature and Justus Van Effen as Intermediary* (Cambridge: 1929), pp. 248–49.
2. *Émile*, p. 211.
3. (Paris: 1931), p. 30. This hostile and somewhat exaggerated polemic discusses Rousseau's other references to *Robinson Crusoe*.
4. *Review*, II, 26; *cit.*, Walter Wilson, *Memoirs of the Life and Times of Daniel Defoe* (London: 1830), II, p. 319.

but with the calculating gaze of a colonial capitalist; wherever he looks he sees acres that cry out for improvement, and as he settles down to the task he glows, not with noble savagery, but purposive possession.

The interest of Rousseau and Defore in a "state of nature" has only one motive in common: it and it alone will allow them to realize without interference their own thwarted vocations. The island offers exemplary opportunities for total laissez faire: or perhaps we should say, for *laisse-moi-faire*—to put the doctrine in the psychological terms which explain its appeal to Rousseau.

But the vocations are different, and indeed contradictory. The primitive setting of the island which is Rousseau's goal is only a starting point for Crusoe. Rousseau wanted to flee the complication and corruptions of the town, to take refuge in a solitary pastoral retreat: Defoe's solution of the dilemma is much more deeply representative of our culture. If the pace gets too fast at home, go overseas—not to pastoral retreats but to colonies. There the imagination is fired by the splendid prospect of how to resolve the ancient conflict between urban and rural ways of life—the urbanization of the countryside. The new culture hero's task is done only when he has taken possession of his colony and stocked it with an adequate labor force; presumably Rousseau did not read *The Farther Adventures of Robinson Crusoe*, where his favorite hero rejoices that "never was there such a little city in a wood."[5] But this is the ultimate message of Defoe's story. The most desolate island cannot retain its natural order; wherever the white man brings his rational technology there can only be manmade order, and the jungle itself must succumb to the irresistible teleology of capitalism.

II

That is the direction which Defoe gives his story. It is fundamentally antiprimitivist. If many readers have interpreted it as a "back to nature" story, they have done so to satisfy their own needs, and quite contrary to Defoe's general development of his theme. The implications of *Robinson Crusoe* are equally equivocal as regards "the dignity of labor": but the immediate justification for seeing in it a panegyric of work is a good deal stronger.

Rousseau saw Defoe's story as an object lesson in the educational virtues of manual labor; and Crusoe does indeed draw the correct moral from this activity:

> By stating and squaring everything by reason, and by making the most rational judgment of things, every man may be in time master of every mechanic art. I had never handled a tool in my life, and yet in time, by labour, application and contrivance, I found at last that I wanted nothing but I could have made it, especially if I had had tools.[6]

5. P. 118.
6. *Life and Strange Surprising Adventures*, p. 74. [51]

The pleasures of this discovery to Crusoe and his readers are largely the result of the *division of labor*. The term is Adam Smith's, but he was to a large extent anticipated by Defoe's contemporary, Bernard Mandeville.[7] The process to which the term refers, and which, of course began very early in human history, was at that time as far advanced in England as anywhere. This advanced development of the division of labor is an important condition of the creation and immediate success of *Robinson Crusoe*, just as the later accelerated development of the process is a condition of the subsequent triumph of the myth. For the main processes by which man secures food, clothing, and shelter are only likely to become interesting when they have become alien to man's common, everyday experience. To enjoy the description of the elementary productive processes takes a sophisticated taste. Obviously, primitive peoples can never forget for a day what Crusoe announces with the tones of one making a discovery: "It might be truly said that now I began to work for my bread. 'Tis a little wonderful, and what I believe few people have thought much upon, viz., the strange multitude of little things necessary in the providing, producing, curing, dressing, making and finishing this one article of bread."[8] The account continues for seven pages, and each detail is new or at least unfamiliar, and reminds us of the vast ignorance that separated production and consumption in the London of Defoe's day, an ignorance that has enormously increased since then, and that surely explains much of the fascination we find in reading the detailed descriptions of Crusoe's island labors.

Rousseau was very much aware of these factors. In his political and economic writings the development of the arts and sciences past the stage of patriarchal simplicity, and the consequent growth of the division of labor, urbanization, and the political state, are the villains.[9] One deplorable result is to separate manual from mental labor. For Rousseau's purposes, therefore, *Robinson Crusoe* was a valuable corrective to the unnatural intellectualism which society inflicts upon the middle class.

Progressive education and the arts and crafts movement both owe a good deal to Rousseau's pages on *Robinson Crusoe* in *Émile*. Educationalists try to rectify many of the results of the division of labor and urbanization by including in the curriculum many of the practical and manual activities which Crusoe pursued on the island and which Rousseau recommended for his pupil. In the adult sphere, many reformers have attempted to bridge the gap between the allegedly inventive, satisfying, and humanizing processes of primitive methods of production and the dehumanizing effects of most economic activities under capitalism.. The Arts and Crafts movement, for example, and the cult of the rough edge, are two of the most obvious attempts to remedy the

7. *The Fable of the Bees*, F. B. Kaye, ed. (Oxford: 1924), I, cxxxiv–cxxxv; II, 142*n*.
8. *Life and Strange Surprising Adventures*, p. 130. [86]
9. See Arthur Lovejoy, "The Supposed Primitivism of Rousseau's *Discourse on Inequality*," *Essays in the History of Ideas* (Baltimore: 1948).

social and esthetic effects of the division of labor in industrial capitalism with an artificial primitivism in technique and way of life. The same attempted diagnosis and remedy—in which one can often detect a residue of moral and religious overtones—can be traced in many of the modern forms of leisure activity. It seems typical of our civilization to try to palliate the distortions of specialization by reintroducing the basic economic processes in the guise of recreations. In such pursuits as gardening, home weaving, woodwork, the keeping of pets, it is suggested, we can all partake of Crusoe's character-forming satisfactions.

There are other aspects of the glorification of labor which are relevant to the function of *Robinson Crusoe* as a myth. Many political reformers since Rousseau have been occupied with the idea of rectifying the effects of the division of labor upon the whole economic and political system. Both on the right and the left they have tried to realize in practice, by new social arrangements, the ideal of the dignity of labor.

For Marx, man and his universe are the products of work. Marx's political system was designed with the idea that human labor under changed conditions could undo the contemporary estrangement of most men from their labor and recreate a society where all economic activities would increase each individual's moral stature. William Morris and the Guild Socialists in advocating a return to a simpler communal economy suggested a different road: but they were trying to achieve the same moral end, and accepted, in the main, Marx's analysis of the real conditions of human labor in the society of their day. And on the right, Samuel Smiles, for example, was also trying to persuade us that hard work even in the present state of society is the key to all: that *labor omnia vincit*.[1] Much of Carlyle's political theory and moral teaching derives from his idea that the great lesson is "Know what thou canst work at." All these and many others—educationalists, moralists, social and political reformers, publicists, economic theorists—seem to base them-

1. Smiles gives this epigraph to his delightfully entitled *Life and Labour or Characteristics of Men of Industry, Culture and Genius*, attributing it to Virgil. Virgil actually wrote, of the coming of the Age of Iron:

labor omnia vicit
improbus et duris urgens in rebus egestas.
(*Georgics*. I, 145–46)

The time-hallowed misquotation is an interesting example of the forces which have made *Robinson Crusoe* into a myth. That labor does and always will conquer all is a modern view which cannot be derived from Virgil. There seems no reason to consider *vicit* as a gnomic perfect: Conington remarks that "the poet is narrating, not uttering a sentiment," although he approves of the general characterization of the *Georgics* as a "glorification of labour." (P. *Vergili Maronis Opera* . . . (London: 1881), I, 151–55). F. Plessis and P. Lejay comment acidly: "*Le poëte n'éxalte pas le travail pour luimême, ce qui est une affectation toute moderne, une idée d'Encyclopédiste, mais pour ses résultats.*" (*Œuvres* (Paris: 1945), p. 29), L. P. Wilkinson, in a recent article, writes, "The text of Virgil's Gospel of Work was not *laborare et orare*, as some have suggested, but *laborare et vivere*." ("The Intention of Virgil's *Georgics*," *Greece and Rome*, XVIII (1950), 24.) Virgil's interpretation of the end of the Golden Age bears obvious resemblances to the Christian, and especially Protestant, welcome to the loss of Eden; as Adam says in *Paradise Lost*, "Idleness had been worse." See also A. Lovejoy and G. Boas, *Primitivism and Related Ideas in Antiquity* (Baltimore: 1935), p. 370.

selves upon a dogma which finds its supreme narrative realization on Crusoe's island.

The reader's ignorance of the basic processes of production is not the only source of the appeal of Crusoe's island labors. He is also affected by the obscure ethical and religious overtones which pervade Defoe's intense concentration upon each stage of Crusoe's exertions. Eventually, they fasten upon our imaginative life a picture of the human lot as heroic only when productive, and of man as capable of redemption only through untiring labor. As we read we share in an inspiring and yet wholly credible demonstration of the vitality and interest of all the basic economic pursuits. If we draw a moral, it can only be that for all the ailments of man and his society, Defoe confidently prescribes the therapy of work.

The extent both of Defoe's concern with labor, and that of the whole ideology of our culture, is certainly unprecedented. Older cultural traditions would probably have seen *Robinson Crusoe* as a glorification of the purely contingent (if not wholly deplorable) aspects of human experience. Certainly most of their myths, the Golden Fleece, Midas, and the Rheingold are concerned, not with the process by which people ordinarily manage to subsist, but with the sudden magical seizure of wealth: ultimately, they are inspired by the prospect of never having to work again.

Defoe's interest in labor is part of the ideology of a new and vast historical process. The dignity of labor is the central creed of the religion of capitalism. In this religion Marx figures as the arch-schismatic who —like all heretics—became so by taking one part of the creed too seriously and trying to apply it with inconvenient thoroughness.

It is impossible to deal summarily with this creed. But some attention to that part of it which is directly related to the creation of *Robinson Crusoe* seems necessary.

It is no accident that the idea of the dignity of labor sounds typical of the Victorian Age, for it was then that the new ideology was most publicly and variously established. But actually, of course, the "gospel of work" was by no means new even in 1719. In ancient Greece, Cynics and Stoics had opposed the denigration of manual labor which is a necessary part of a slave-owning society's scale of values. In the Christian tradition labor had never been a dishonorable estate. In the sixteenth century, Protestantism, in harmony with the obscure needs of social and economic change, revived and expanded an old belief until it loomed much larger in the total picture of the human lot. The Biblical view that labor was a curse for Adam's disobedience was displaced by the idea that hard work—untiring stewardship of the gifts of God—was a paramount ethical obligation.

The extent of this shift of values can be measured by comparing Defoe's attitude to work with that of Sir Thomas More. In More's *Utopia* hours of work are limited to six, and all surpluses of production are redistributed in the form of extra holidays.[2] Defoe, in *The Complete Tradesman*, proposes very long hours and insists that leisure activities, even an inordinate craving for sermons, must be kept in check.[3] The same tendency can be observed in the practice of Robinson Crusoe, to whom More's ideal would have seemed moral laxness. For Crusoe hard work seems to be a condition of life itself, and we notice that the arrival of Friday is a signal, not for increased leisure, but for expanded production.

One of the reasons for the canonization of *Robinson Crusoe* is certainly its consonance with the modern view that labor is both the most valuable form of human activity in itself, and at the same time the only reliable way of developing one's spiritual biceps. Defoe's version of this attitude is at times overtly religious in tone. Crusoe's successful improvisations, his perfectly controlled economy, foreshadow his ultimate standing in the divine design. From his own Dissenting milieu Defoe has taken an idea, now familiar to us from the writings of Weber, Troeltsch, and Tawney, and given it a fascinating narrative form.

The combination of this aspect of the ideology of Ascetic Protestantism, or Puritanism, with a kind of return to nature, is particularly happy. Defoe thereby embodies in the same story two historically associated aspirations of the bourgeois class with whom he and his hero have been long and justly identified. In his epic of individual enterprise he bequeathed them both a program of further economic action and a figure on whom to project a quasi-religious mystique which retained from the ebbing fervors of Calvinism its essential social and economic teaching. The program of action is Empire: and it includes, as we have seen, temporary submission to primitivism, or at least to the lure of the wide open places. The mystique is one which distracts attention from the enormous and rapidly growing differences between the kinds of work and their economic rewards, by erecting a creed which bestows the same high "dignity" on *all* the forms of activity which can be subsumed under the one word labor.

That the mystique of the dignity of labor helped to ensure the later success of *Robinson Crusoe* as a myth seems certain. It needed a gospel. But much of what Defoe actually wrote had to be overlooked. This may seem surprising, since Defoe, the complacent apologist of nascent industrial capitalism, certainly approved of the new ideology. But as a writer his eye was so keenly on the object, and second thoughts so rarely checked the flow of his pen, that he reported, not his wishes, but the plausible image of the moment, what he knew people would actually

2. *Ideal Commonwealths*, H. Morley, ed. (London: 1899), pp. 97, 101.
3. *The Complete English Tradesman* (Oxford: 1841), I, 32–34. See also, A. E. Levett, "Daniel Defoe," *Social and Political Ideas of Some English Thinkers of the Augustan Age*, F. J. C. Hearnshaw, ed. (London: 1928), p. 180.

do. So it is that he tells us much which, if analyzed, questions not only the simple message of the myth, but even some of his own cherished beliefs. And as these details do not protrude, we must consider them a little more closely.

On the desert island Robinson Crusoe turns his forsaken estate into a triumph. This is a flagrant unreality. Other castaways in the past, including Defoe's main model, Alexander Selkirk, were reduced to an extremely primitive condition, and in the space of a few years.[4] Harrassed by fear, dogged by ecological degradation, they sank more and more to the level of animals: in some authentic cases they forgot the use of speech, went mad, or died of inanition. One book which Defoe has almost certainly read, *The Voyages and Travels of J. Albert de Mandelso*, tells two such cases: of a Frenchman who, after two years of solitude on Mauritius, tore his clothing to pieces in a fit of madness brought on by a diet of raw tortoise;[5] and of a Dutch seaman on St. Helena who disinterred the body of a buried comrade and set out to sea in the coffin.[6]

Defoe's readers, perhaps, from their own ordinary experiences of solitude, may suspect as much, even if in a less dramatic form. But as they read *Robinson Crusoe* they forget that isolation can be painful or boring, that it tends in their own lives toward apathetic animality and mental derangement. Instead, they rejoice to find that isolation can be the beginning of a new realization of the potentialities of the individual. Their inertias are cheered by a vicarious participation in Crusoe's twenty-three years of lonely and triumphant struggle. They imagine themselves to be sharing each representative step in his conquest of the environment and perform with him a heartening recapitulation of humanity's success story.

To all who feel isolated or who get tired of their jobs—and who at times does not?—the story has a deep appeal and sends our critical faculties asleep. Inspired by the theme, and blinded, perhaps, by our wishes and dreams, we avert our attention from the subtle ways by which a consolatory unreality has been made to appear real.

The psychological unreality has its complement in the material one. The normal economic picture—that known to most of Defoe's readers—has been tampered with, unobtrusively but decisively. Defoe's hero—unlike most of us—has been endowed with the basic necessities for the successful exercise of free enterprise. He is not actually a primitive or a proletarian or even a professional man, but a capitalist. He owns, freehold, an estate which is rich, though unimproved. It is not a desert island in the geographical sense—it is merely barren of owners or competitors; and, above all, the very event which brings him there, the shipwreck, which is supposed to be a retributive disaster, is in fact a

4. A. W. Secord, *Studies in the Narrative Method of Defoe* (Urbana, Illinois: 1924), p. 26.
5. *Ibid.*, p. 28.
6. *Ibid.*

miraculous gift of the means of production, and one rendered particularly felicitous by the death of all the other passengers. Crusoe complains that he is "reduced to a state of nature"; in fact he secures from the wreck "the biggest magazine of all kinds . . . that ever was laid out . . . for one man."[7]

The possession of this original stock, which Defoe's imitators usually retain, usually on a more lavish and less utilitarian scale, is the major practical unreality overlooked by many of his admirers of the classic idyll of individual enterprise. Yet it alone is enough to controvert the myth's wishful affirmation of a flagrant economic naïveté—the idea that anyone has ever attained comfort and security entirely by his own efforts.

The myth demanded that the storm be presented as a tragic peripety, although it is really the *deus ex machina* which makes its message plausible. Some such legerdemain was necessary before solitary labor could even appear to be not an alternative to a death sentence, but a solution to the perplexities of economic and social reality.

The dignity of labor is salvaged, then, under the most apparently adverse conditions, mainly because Crusoe has been lucky with capital stock. One wonders whether his "instinct of workmanship"would have been of any avail if he had really begun from scratch. Certainly Johann Heinrich Campe, the head master of the *Philanthropium* at Dessau, felt that there was a logical objection here which should be countered. He acted on Rousseau's suggestion that only the island episode was improving, and produced a *Nouveau Robinson* for the young which superseded Defoe's original version both in France and Germany. In it, the stock of tools was omitted.[8]

This version imposes a severe strain on our credulity, at least on that of anyone who does not live in a *Philanthropium*. But even if we grant the possibility of an isolated man reaching a high technological level unaided, there remain other more drastic difficulties in interpreting *Robinson Crusoe* as a myth of autarchic individual enterprise—difficulties based on the fact that the island is, after all, an island, and that whatever happens there is exceptional and does not seem to happen anywhere else.

On the island there is—with one exception to which we shall return—only real wealth. The perplexities of money and the price mechanism do not exist. There is there, as perhaps nowhere else, a direct relation between production and consumption. That is one obvious reason why we should not argue from it to our society; another follows from the fact that Crusoe did not want to go to the island, and once there, doesn't want to stay. The fact that he is forced to be a model of

7. *Life and Strange Surprising Adventures*, p. 60. [42]
8. See Mann, *Robinson Crusoë en France*, pp. 85–101. It was this version which H. H. Gossen used in deriving economic laws from *Crusoe* (W. Stark, *The Ideal Foundations of Economic Thought* [London: 1948], p. 159): and was probably that of Frédéric Bastiat in his *Harmonies Économiques* (Brussels: 1850), pp. 99f., 214f.

industry does not mean that he likes work. Actually, in the total setting of the trilogy, it becomes clear that Crusoe regards his little profits on the island as only a consolation prize. What he wanted (and later obtained) were unearned increments from the labor of others. In Brazil he had soon tired even of the tasks of a sugar plantation owner, and it was his quest of the more spectacular rewards of the slave trade which took him to the island.[9] To use Max Weber's distinction, he preferred the speculative rewards of "adventurer's capitalism" to the uneventful, though regular, increments which are typical of the modern economic order.[1] And after Crusoe leaves the island, he again succumbs to the lure of foreign trade, which at that time gave the highest and quickest returns on capital.[2] It is only on his island that Crusoe shows the regulated diligence combined with accurate planning and stocktaking which is so important in modern economic organization. Defoe knew this theoretically; he dealt with such matters in his economic manuals. But he himself had not been able to put his economic ideals into practice. They were to be realized only on Crusoe's "island of despair" which is actually a utopia, though of a new and peculiar kind.

Most utopias have been based upon the ideal of a more harmonious relationship among men. Those of Plato and More are wholly social in inspiration. They, and many later utopias, are also characterized by a certain static quality, and by the fact that people seem to do much less work and get much more for it than in the real world. But this new utopia is the answer, not to the easy and expansive yearnings of the heart for individual happiness and social harmony, nor even to Crusoe's acquisitive instincts; it is the answer only to a very rigorous conception of what kind of life Defoe feels is good for other people.

Crusoe, in fact, has been stranded in the utopia of the Protestant Ethic. There temptation, whether economic or moral, is wholly absent. Crusoe's energies cannot be deflected, either by the picnic promises of pastoral utopias, or by the relaxing and uneconomic piety of the hermits and mystics who are the heroes of an earlier form of Christianity, heroes whose faith is measured by their certainty that "God will provide." On Crusoe's island, unremitting toil is obligatory; there, and only there, it is instinct with both moral value and calculable personal reward.

If we look further afield for economic motivation in Defoe, if we leave the island, we find a very different picture. The other adventures of Robinson Crusoe, and the lives of Defoe's other heroes and heroines do not point in the direction of the dignity of labor. Defoe knew very

---

9. *Life and Strange Surprising Adventures*, pp. 40–42. [29–31] See also, *Farther Adventures*, p. 66, where Defoe shows his awareness of the dangers of this type of enterprise by attributing it to idle ne'er-do-wells.
1. Weber, *The Protestant Ethic and the Spirit of Capitalism*, trans. T. Parsons (London: 1930), pp. 21, 74–78; and *The Theory of Economic and Social Organization*, trans. T. Parsons and A. M. Henderson (New York: 1947), pp. 50–52, 279ff.
2. A. L. Merson, "The Revolution and the British Empire," *The Modern Quarterly*, IV (1949), p. 152.

well that the normal social conditions of his time caused very different adjustments to the environment. Moll Flanders, Roxana, and Colonel Jacque satisfy their needs in ways which no one would propose for imitation. Indeed, their exploits demonstrate quite another type of political economy, and point the moral that—to those outside Crusoe's island, and without his heaven-bestowed capital—*La propriété, c'est le vol.*[3]

Defoe, then, is a realist about the individual and his economic environment. He has no illusions about the dignity of the labors of most people in the England of his day. He expressed their lot in a moving passage which William Morris used as epigraph to his lecture on "The Art of the People": "And the men of labour spend their strength in daily strugglings for bread to maintain the vital strength they labour with, so living in a daily circulation of sorrow, living but to work, and working but to live, as if daily bread were the only end of wearisome life, and a wearisome life the only occasion of daily bread."[4]

If we wish to trace in Defoe any universal and overriding idea, it is certainly not that of the dignity of labor as a social fact or even as a moral dogma. The key to the basic motivation of his characters and the hypothesis that best explains their history both apply to Crusoe. For he is only a special case of economic man. Just as the doctrine of the dignity of labor can be understood as the optimistic and deluding myth which hides the realities involved in the division of labor, so the fortitude of Defoe's isolated man withdraws from general attention the true lineaments of that lonely and unlovely archetpye of our civilization, *homo economicus*, who is also mirrored in *Robinson Crusoe*.

III

Homo economicus is, of course, a fiction. There has long been a conflict about the utility of the abstraction. Briefly, the classical political economists found in the idea of Robinson Crusoe, the solitary individual on a desert island, a splendid example for their system building. On the other hand, their critics who, like Marx, were concerned to prove that economics can be a guide to reality only when it is a historical and a social science, have denied the relevance of Robinson Crusoe to any realistic economic thinking.

Marx began his polemic against classical political economy by insisting on the social nature of production. He, therefore, attacked the starting points of Adam Smith and Ricardo—the isolated hunters and fishers, who were, he said, "Robinsonades," and belonged to "the insipid illusions of the Eighteenth Century."[5] Later, in *Capital*, he appropriated

---

3. J. Sutherland points out that on the island, although stealing is impossible, the satisfactory emotions of successful theft are suggested by the looting of the wreck. *Defoe* (London: 1937), p. 232.
4. *Farther Adventures*, pp. 7–8.
5. *A Contribution to the Critique of Political Economy* (1st edition, 1859; New York: 1904), pp. 265–66.

Crusoe to support his own theory of value. For Crusoe, "in spite of the variety of his work . . . knows that his labour whatever its form, is but the activity of one and the same Robinson, and consequently, that it consists of nothing but different modes of human labor. . . . All the relations between Robinson and the objects that form this wealth of his own creation, are here so simple and clear as to be intelligible without exertion."[6] But it is only on the island that the value of any object is directly proportional to the quantity of labor expended upon it. In Western capitalism the rewards of labor and the price of commodities are subject to market considerations which are capricious and unjust, especially to labor.[7] The use of Crusoe as an example therefore distracts attention from the realities of the economic system as it is.

Marx does not make the useful polemic point which Crusoe's fortunate acquisition of capital might have afforded him. Nor does he mention the extent to which his personality embodies the moral evils which he ascribed to capitalism. This is no doubt because he is using Crusoe only as an example of one particular theme, and not for any general purpose. For actually Crusoe exexmplifies another aspect of Marx's thought; the process of alienation by which capitalism tends to convert man's relationships with his fellows, and even with his own self, into commodities to be manipulated.

This view of economic man is not, of course, limited to Marx. Max Weber's idea that the Protestant Ethic involves a thorough systematization of behavior according to rational norms of personal profit is very similar,[8] and so is Tawney's picture of the acquisitive society composed of individuals pursuing their individual interests without any recognition of social or moral solidarity.[9] But these theoretical formulations had long before been anticipated by literary realization. For, as an ironic commentary upon the myth, the book of *Robinson Crusoe* depicts in its casual reports of the hero's behavior and of his occasional parenthetic reflections, the shameless and pervasive impact of the cash nexus upon the character and personal relationships of the archetypal economic man. Defoe has supplied the antidote to the myth of his unwitting creation —not only in the already mentioned incidental unrealities of the plot, but also in the somber touches which are an overt part of his picture of the personality of the protagonist.

Crusoe treats his personal relationships in terms of their commodity value. The Moorish boy, Xury, for example, helps him to escape from slavery, and on another occasion offers to prove his devotion by sacrificing his own life. Crusoe very properly resolves "to love him ever

---

6. Chap. 1, sec. iv.
7. Defoe had experienced this for himself. His bookseller, Taylor, owned the whole share of all three parts of *Robinson Crusoe* and is said to have made his fortune by it. (Hutchins, *Robinson Crusoe and its Printing*, p. 185.) Defoe worked indefatigably for most of his seventy years of life, and though he was at times rich, he died alone, hiding from a creditor. (Sutherland, *Defoe*, pp. 269–74).
8. Weber, *Theory of Economic and Social Organizations*, pp. 191–249 *et passim*.
9. R. H. Tawney, *The Acquisitive Society* (London: 1921), p. 32.

after,"[1] and promises "to make him a great man." But when chance leads them to the Portuguese trader, and its captain offers Crusoe sixty pieces of eight—twice Judas's figure—he cannot resist the bargain and sells Xury into slavery. He has momentary scruples at the betrayal, it is true, but they are soon economically satisfied by securing from the captain a promise "to set him free in ten years if he turn Christian."[2] Remorse later supervenes, but only when the tasks of his island existence renew his need for a slave.[3]

Slaves, of course, were his original objective in the voyage which brought him to the island. And eventually Providence and his own exertions provide him with Man Friday, who answers his prayers by "swearing to be my slave for ever."[4] The unsolicited promise is as prophetic as the development of the relationship is instructive. Crusoe does not ask Friday his name, he gives him one; and there is throughout a remarkable lack of interest in Friday as a person, as someone worth trying to understand or converse with. Even in language—the medium whereby human beings may achieve something more than animal relationships with each other—Crusoe is a strict utilitarian. "I likewise taught him to say yes and no,"[5] he tells, though, as Defoe's contemporary critic Gildon not unjustly remarked,[6] Friday still speaks pidgin English at the end of their long association.

Yet Crusoe regards the relationship as ideal. In the period alone with Friday he was "perfectly and completely happy, if any such thing as complete happiness can be found in a sublunary state."[7] A functional silence, apparently, adds to the charms of the idyll, broken only by an occasional "No, Friday" or an abject "Yes, Master." Man's social nature is wholly satisfied by the righteous bestowal, or grateful receipt, of benevolent but not undemanding patronage.[8]

Only one doubt ruffles Crusoe's proprietary equanimity. He becomes obsessed with the fear that Friday may be harboring an ungrateful wish to return to his father and his tribe. But the fear proves groundless, and they leave the island together. Crusoe later avoids any possible qualms about keeping Friday in servitude by the deferred altruism of a resolution "to do something considerable for him, if he outlived me."[9] Fortunately, no such sacrifice is called for, as Friday dies at sea, faithful to the end, and rewarded only by a brief word of obituary compassion.

Crusoe's attitude to women is also marked by an extreme inhibition

1. *Life and Strange Surprising Adventures*, p. 27. [20]
2. *Ibid.*, p. 36. [26]
3. *Ibid.*, p. 164. [108]
4. *Ibid.*, p. 226. [147]
5. *Ibid.*, p. 229. [149]
6. *Robinson Crusoe Examin'd and Criticis'd*; P. Dottin, ed. (London and Paris: 1923), pp. 70, 78, 118.
7. *Life and Strange Surprising Adventures*, pp. 245–46. [159–60]
8. The Crusoe-Friday relationship is representative in many other ways, not least in showing how the quest for the white man's burden tends to end in the discovery of the perfect porter.
9. *Farther Adventures*, p. 133.

of what we now consider to be normal human feelings. There are, of course, none on the island, and their absence is not deplored. When Crusoe does notice the lack of "society," he prays for company, but it is for that of a male slave. With Friday he is fully satisfied by an idyll without benefit of woman. It is an interesting break from the traditional expectations aroused by desert islands, from the *Odyssey* to the *New Yorker*.

Defoe's view of the individual was too completely dominated by the rational pursuit of material self-interest to allow any scope either for natural instinct or for higher emotional needs. Even when Crusoe returns to civilization, sex is strictly subordinated to business. Only after his financial position has been fully secured by a further voyage does he marry, "and that not either to my disadvantage or dissatisfaction."[1]

Some of Crusoe's colonists have the same attitude. He tells how they draw lots for five women, and he strongly approves of the outcome: "He that drew to choose first . . . took her that was reckoned the homeliest and eldest of the five, which made mirth enough among the rest . . . but the fellow considered better than any of them, that it was application and business that they were to expect assistance in as much as anything else; and she proved the best wife of all the parcel."[2]

The conflict is put very much in Weber's terms.[3] Sex is seen as a dangerously irrational factor in life which interferes with the pursuit of rational self-interest: and economic and moral worth in the male does not guarantee him a profitable matrimonial investment. On his colony "as it often happens in the world (what the wise ends of God's Providence are in such a disposition of things I cannot say), the two honest fellows had the two worst wives; and the three reprobates, that were scarce worth hanging, . . . had three clever, diligent, careful and ingenious wives."[4] It is therefore no accident that love plays a very minor part in Crusoe's own life, and is eliminated from the scene of his greatest triumphs.

IV

One could illustrate the ideology of *homo economicus* at much greater length from *Robinson Crusoe*. Everything is measured from the rational, asocial, and antitraditional standards of individual self-interest, and some of the results are not pleasant. But these results are surely the lamentable, but necessary, corollaries of the social process which the story reflects; and the common tendency to overlook them in the hero must be attributed to the obscure forces that guard the idols of our society and shape its myths.

1. *Life and Strange Surprising Adventures*, p. 341. [219]
2. *Farther Adventures*, p. 77.
3. Max Weber, *Essays in Sociology*, trans. H. H. Gerth and C. Wright Mills (New York: 1946), p. 350.
4. *Farther Adventures*, p. 78.

Malinowski has said that "myth is . . . an indispensable ingredient of all culture."[5] It would indeed appear to be so, but I have no wish to be numbered among those who would prove our common humanity by putting us back on a level with the Trobriand islanders. The aim of this essay is rather to do something they don't do; that is, scrutinize one small item of our cultural repertoire in the hope of clarifying its role in the past and present of our society.

Much has had to be omitted—the appeal of the adventure in itself, for example, and the theological aspect of the story, which modifies the picture considerably. Some of the social and economic matters have been treated somewhat cavalierly. The case of Robinson Crusoe as *homo economicus* has been somewhat oversimplified—Defoe does suggest on at least one occasion (the famous episode when Crusoe comes across a hoard of gold on the island and, after declaiming on its uselessness, "upon second thoughts" takes it away)[6] the irrationality of the goals which shape the character of economic man and which affect his actions more powerfully than his own understanding of his real needs. And, of course, in a wintry sort of way, Crusoe has his pleasures. He does not, as Selkirk had done, dance with the goats, but he does at least occasionally supplement occupational by recreational therapy. Still, it seems true to say that the reality of Defoe's masterpiece, its ultimate referent, is economic man. So that if we seek a general meaning for his solitude it must be the social atomization which *homo economicus* brings in his train. That, surely, is the main historical basis of this metaphor of human solitude which has haunted the Western consciousness. And the need to obscure the negative social and psychological corollaries of the rise of economic individualism must explain much of the very general disinclination to see the darker side of Defoe's hero.

It is certainly curious to observe how all but universal has been the reluctance to challenge Crusoe as a model for imitation and inspiration. In some cases there may be other explanations for this. The myth of national character, for example. Some foreign commentators have had ulterior motives in presenting Robinson Crusoe as the typical Englishman. Marx calls him a "true-born Briton";[7] and Dibelius echoes the impeachment of a nation of shopkeepers with more obvious venom.[8] For France, de Vogüé, in his study of what he calls *"Le livre anglais,"* though more polite, is equally disparaging by implication.[9] What is curious is to find that most English writers, too, have tended to accept Crusoe as the typical Englishman, apparently undeterred by any of his antisocial idiosyncrasies.

There have been occasional dissentients. Dickens, for example, was

5. *Myth in Primitive Psychology*, p. 125.
6. *Life and Strange Surprising Adventures*, p. 62. [43]
7. *Capital*, chap. 1, sec. vi.
8. *Englische Romankunst* (Berlin: 1910), I, p. 36.
9. *Revue des deux Mondes* (October 1, 1895), as is Jean Giraudoux in *Suzanne et le Pacifique* (Paris: 1921), pp. 228–33.

revolted by Crusoe's attitudes toward the death of Friday, and to women generally; and he wrote in a letter that Defoe must have been a "precious dry and disagreeable article himself."[1] Ruskin—another critic of the mentality of industrial capitalism—uses the phrase "a very small, perky, contented, conceited, Cock-Robinson-Crusoe, sort of life."[2] Yet on the whole, Crusoe has been accepted as the typical Englishman by his fellow countrymen, although, as it happens, Defoe made Crusoe's father "a foreigner of Bremen."

In some ways, of course, the character of Robinson Crusoe is a national one. Courage, practical intelligence, not making a fuss, these are not the least of the virtues, and their combination in Crusoe does seem to be according to an English pattern. But these virtues cannot be regarded as exemplary and sufficient. Dickens wrote of *Robinson Crusoe* that it is "the only instance of a universally popular book that could make no one laugh and no one cry."[3] This suggests the major flaw. Defoe's epic of the stiff upper lip does not propose a wholly satisfactory ideal. For Crusoe's merits are combined with a stolid and inhibited self-sufficiency which is disastrous both for the individual and for society. That is Crusoe's *hubris*—a defect not unlike Rousseau's *hypertrophie du moi*.

There is, even on Crusoe's own showing, very little content or peace in this way of life. Pascal said that the misery of man can be traced from a single fact, his inability to stay still in his own room. Crusoe can never stay still. His brisk and businesslike exterior cannot wholly conceal the deadening compulsion of an alienation which is assuaged only by ceaseless economic activity. He is modern economic man putting a poker face on the fate that Pascal found intolerable. "Nothing else offering, and finding that really stirring about and trading, the profit being so great, and, as I may say, certain, had more pleasure in it, and more satisfaction to the mind, than sitting still, which, to me especially, was the unhappiest part of life. . . ." So, in the *Farther Adventures*, he sets out on yet another lucrative Odyssey.

His author, deeply implicated in the character that Walter de la Mare has called Defoe's "Elective Affinity,"[4] appears to approve. But he certainly does not see his work in an optimistic vein: "Nothing else offering . . ." suggests why. Defoe wrestles with the meanings of his creation in the essay "On Solitude," which begins the *Serious Reflections*. The essay is inconclusive, and there are several different strands of thought in it. But the bitterness of isolation as the primordial fact repeatedly moves Defoe to a great fervor of communication. One of the passages seems a particularly moving commentary on the isolation which the pursuit of individual self-interest creates in the human spirit.

1. John Forster, *Life of Charles Dickens*, rev. by J. W. T. Ley (London, 1928), p. 611.
2. Peter Quennell, *John Ruskin* (London: 1949), p. 15.
3. Forster, loc. cit.
4. *Desert Islands and Robinson Crusoe* (London: 1930), p. 7.

What are the sorrows of other men to us, and what their joy? Sometimes we may be touched indeed by the power of sympathy, and a secret turn of the affections; but all the solid reflection is directed to ourselves. Our meditations are all solitude in perfection; our passions are all exercised in retirement; we love, we hate, we covet, we enjoy, all in privacy and solitude. All that we communicate of those things to any other is but for their assistance in the pursuit of our desires; the end is at home; the enjoyment, the contemplation, is all solitude and retirement; it is for ourselves we enjoy, and for ourselves we suffer.[5]

The loneliness of economic man was a tragic fact. Many Stoic or Christian thinkers might have said "We love, we hate . . . all in privacy and solitude." But "we covet, we enjoy" is characteristic of a later ideology. To the solitude of the soul which so many have expressed, Defoe adds "all we communicate of those things to any other is but for their assistance in the pursuit of our desires." A rationally conceived self-interest makes a mockery of speech, and suggests silence.

So, although *Robinson Crusoe* is a mutation of a very ancient theme, its specific cause and nature are wholly modern. And now that it is possible to see fairly clearly the realities of which Crusoe is the menacing symbol, we must surely question his desirability as an ideal prototype. What has happened in the last two hundred years has shown that where Defoe's new culture hero is admitted into the pantheon of myth, he soon crowds out or subjugates the other figures, whether comic or tragic, round whom have gathered those more generous aspirations that occasionally mitigate the bitterness of history.

ERIC BERNE

The Psychological Structure of Space with Some Remarks on *Robinson Crusoe*†

Interest in space is a sublimation useful in many occupations. This interest has three varieties, depending upon the predominant instinctual drive it expresses: the exploration of space, the measurement of space, and the utilization of space. The interest may be intellectual, as in the case of philosophers, geometricians, and planners; or physical, as in the case of explorers, surveyors, and builders. The manifest attitude of the explorer is incorporative (this island will be incorporated into the Empire), or mastering (the conquest of Mount Everest); the surveyor insists

5. *Serious Reflections of Robinson Crusoe,* G. A. Aitken, ed. (London: 1902), pp. 2–3.
† From *The Psychoanalytic Quarterly* 25 (1956): 549–67. Reprinted by permission of *The Psychoanalytic Quarterly* and the executor of the author's estate.

on orderliness and exactitude; and the builder and his colleagues are intrusive (dig here, drill there), or 'erective.' These three interests may be characterized as predominantly oral, anal, and phallic sublimations, respectively. Although exploration is predominantly an oral sublimation, anal and phallic drives also come into play in proper sequence. The original object of exploration is not hard to discover: every child is an explorer.

*   *   *

* * * One of the most detailed accounts in any literature of the psychological process of organizing space into a structure is Daniel Defoe's description of Robinson Crusoe's adventures with insular fear and anxiety. Any psychoanalyst who has not reread this remarkable work since childhood may find its depth and interest far beyond his expectations.

* * * Crusoe's problem was [to be] thrown out of the comfortable bowl of a ship onto a strange island where he was beset with two powerful fears: 'of perishing with hunger, or being devoured by wild beasts'. He thinks only of getting up 'into a thick busy tree' once he has found water to drink. After he has salvaged what he can from the ship, '. . . my next work was to view the country, and seek a proper place for my habitation', where he can enclose himself in a place completely secure 'from ravenous creatures, whether man or beasts'. Later he begins to explore his island, both for diversion and to seek what he can kill for food. But in the midst of all this, he feels an urgent necessity to keep his identity by maintaining his orientation in time and reckoning the days as they go by, as well as ordering his times of work, hunting, sleep, and diversion. He is also careful to determine his position in space, as precisely as he is able, by determining his latitude and longitude.

Only after he has spent ten months securing his habitation is he free 'to take a more particular survey of the island itself'; and it is five years before he begins to think 'of nothing but sailing round the island'. This project almost ends in disaster. He is in danger of perishing 'not by the sea, but of starving for hunger'. By this time, the internal structure of his island is well begun. The most important loci are his plantations. The first of these is a fortification full of food with two pieces of land planted in corn; the second a similarly fortified 'bower' where he keeps cattle to supply him with flesh, milk, butter, and cheese; and near by is his vineyard. He is also familiar with some points of land and some creeks into which he can run his boat safely. At this point comes one of the most dramatic moments in all literature: his discovery of a solitary human footprint on the shore. This means to him only two things: it is either the mark of the devil, or of savages who will return to devour him, or at least destroy his food supply and leave him to perish from want. Shortly afterward, his worst fears seem confirmed by the discovery of dismembered bodies and a roasting pit. For two years after that, he keeps close to his 'three plantations'.

All this makes him 'very melancholy' and the result is that he 'afterward made it a certain rule' never to fail to obey 'secret hints or pressings of mind', that is, his intuition. One night, shortly after he plundered a ship wrecked near by, obtaining some very good cordials and sweetmeats and two pairs of shoes which he took off the feet of some drowned men, he reflects how for many years he has without knowing it been in real danger of 'the worst kind of destruction . . .had walked about with all possible tranquility' when mere chance had preserved him from 'falling into the hands of cannibals who would have seized on me with the same view as I would on a goat or turtle, and have thought it no more a crime to devour me than I did a pigeon or a curlew'. He wants so badly to get away that the thought sends his very blood into a ferment; but instead of dreaming of it or 'of anything relating to it', he dreams that a victim of the cannibals escapes and Crusoe carries him to his cave, thinking that this man will serve as a pilot and tell him 'whither to go for provisions, and whither not to go for fear of being devoured'.

When his dream comes true, one of the first things Crusoe does is make his man Friday burn the remains of the cannibal feast. He finds that Friday 'had still a hankering stomach after some of the flesh'. Crusoe lets him know that he will kill him if he tries it.

It is noteworthy that not only is Crusoe afraid of starving and of being eaten; he is also afraid of being poisoned by 'venomous or poisonous creatures, which I might feed on to my hurt'. He is grateful for being mercifully spared from these three dangers. The blessings he counts before he learns about the cannibals are as follows: 'I was here removed from all the wickedness of the world; I had neither the lust of the flesh, the lust of the eye, nor the pride of life. I had nothing to covet, for I had all that I was now capable of enjoying: I was lord of the whole manor, I might call myself a king or emperor over the whole country which I had possession of; there were no rivals; I had no competitor, none to dispute sovereignty or command with me.' These considerations make him feel that he has made his conquest.

It is not difficult to perceive in Robinson Crusoe the simple fantasy of the author. The main problem is to have now all you want to eat and the indefinite assurance of future nourishment to avert the danger of starving to death. But there are the two other dangers of being poisoned and of being eaten. When you think you are secure, having possession of everything on the body of land and no one to dispute your sovereignty, along comes somebody who wants to eat you, somebody who has been lurking in the background all along and who now must be dealt with face to face. It seems that after Crusoe had incorporated his island as far as he dared through exploration and exploitation, he felt guilty; he thought the devil should surely come after him and sure enough he did. Crusoe's anxieties were based on the principle: 'He who eats shall be eaten'. The whole sequence of events, including his dreams, is an elaboration of this theme with familiar clinical variations. In this case * * *

the anal and phallic elements are minimal, highly obscure, and inde-
cisively expressed.

*   *   *

Two types of psychological structure of geographical space are constructed by the adult. In the first the terrain is arranged beforehand by
obligations which occupy the ego and form the framework for its activity,
so that 'exploration' becomes a subsidiary activity obscured by the more
pressing obligations. In the second, exploration is an end in itself and
external determinants of behavior (structure predetermined by obligations) are minimal. In the latter case, the ego is free to follow, as it
were, the program of the id, and this program is a derivative of archaic
patterns.

In so far, then, as exploration is a productive or a creative activity, it
becomes an art. Like all the arts it is restricted by its medium, but within
those restrictions its creativity is the result of guidance from the id and
represents a sublimation of pregenital strivings. * * * Crusoe, because
of his oral fixation and the accompanying intense anxiety, never did
explore the whole extent of his island effectively.

MAXIMILLIAN E. NOVAK

Robinson Crusoe and the State of Nature†

I

. . . 'tis a little wonderful, and what I believe few People have
thought much upon, (viz.) the strange multitude of little Things
necessary in the Providing, Producing, Curing, Dressing, Making
and Finishing this one Article of Bread.

I that was reduced to a meer State of Nature, found this to my
daily Discouragement. . . .

Defoe, The Life and Surprising Adventures of Robinson Crusoe¹

When Crusoe remarks that he is in a 'State of Nature', Defoe's audience must have recognized both the aptness and the ambiguity of this
statement. By 1719, when Robinson Crusoe was first published, the
problem of defining natural man and the state of nature had been the
subject of considerable speculation. Arthur Lovejoy suggested that there
were three principle meanings for the term 'state of nature' in the eighteenth century. It could be used in an historical or anthropological sense

† From Defoe and the Nature of Man (New York and London, 1963) 22–36. Copyright © 1963
Oxford University Press. Reprinted by permission of the Clarendon Press, Oxford, and the
author.
1. In the Shakespeare Head Edition of the Novels and Selected Writings of Daniel Defoe (1927),
i. 135 [86]. Subsequent references to this edition of Defoe's writings will be cited as Shakespeare
Head ed. [NCE page numbers appear in brackets.]

to refer to the 'primeval condition of man'; in a 'cultural sense' to refer to a stage of society in which the arts and sciences had not yet progressed beyond a few primitive tools; or in a political sense to indicate the relationships between men before the creation of government.[2] Although there are some notable omissions, Lovejoy's triad is a convenient classification for a discussion of *Robinson Crusoe*, for Defoe was not only delineating the condition of man in the state of nature but also the cultural and political evolution which, by transforming the state of nature, created civilization and government.

Lovejoy's scheme omits two important ideas. He makes no mention of the theological implications of man's natural state—the idea that every man has a law of reason written in his heart by God. In this sense, the state of nature refers to any condition which is governed by the laws of nature. This is what Crusoe means when he remarks that before his religious conversion he 'acted like a meer Brute from the Principles of Nature'.[3] Secondly, Lovejoy does not explain that in the seventeenth and eighteenth centuries, discussions of the primitive state of man almost always commenced with the image of an isolated being, abstracted from society and religion. Three opinions on the solitary natural man were current in Defoe's day. Some writers believed that the isolated natural man might, through the use of his reason, achieve the same moral and intellectual condition as the human being raised in society. Others, following certain hints in Lucretius, suggested that he would be savage and brutal and have greater freedom and happiness and fewer vices than civilized man. The majority of writers, however, argued that man was a social animal, that the bestial life of the solitary savage was insecure, and that so far from being happy, the isolated natural man lived in constant fear of death. Although most modern critics have regarded Crusoe as an embodiment of the enterprising, fearless economic man, Crusoe clearly belongs to the third category. He survives his solitude, but he is always afraid, always cautious. Defoe recognized the benefits of the state of nature, but he believed that the freedom and purity of Crusoe's island were minor advantages compared to the comfort and security of civilization.

II

Man is a creature so formed for society, that it may not only be said that it is not good for him to be alone, but 'tis really impossible he should be alone.

Defoe, *Serious Reflections of Robinson Crusoe*[4]

In 1708, the year that Alexander Selkirk was rescued from the island of Juan Fernandez and eleven years before the appearance of *Robinson*

2. Arthur Lovejoy, 'The supposed Primitivism of Rousseau's *Discourses on Inequality*' in *Essays in the History of Ideas* (1948), pp. 14–15.
3. *Robinson Crusoe*, i. 101. [65]
4. P. 12. Defoe is probably echoing John Norris's essay 'Of Solitude'. See *A Collection of Miscellanies*, 3rd ed. (1699), pp. 125–8.

Crusoe, Abu ibn al-Tufail's *The Improvement of Human Reason*, a narrative of another solitary, was translated into English. Robinson Crusoe was to replace both Tufail's hero, Hai Ibn Yokdhan, and Selkirk as the paradigm of the isolated natural man, but for Alexander Pope, writing in 1719, Selkirk and Yokdhan were still the best examples.[5] Yokdhan's story was widely read in an earlier Latin translation, and in 1702 he appeared in a dialogue with the Turkish Spy as a spokesman for natural rights and freedom.[6] He was entirely a child of nature. While yet a baby, Yokdhan was wafted by the waves to a desert island, where he was suckled by a doe and reared as an animal. After the death of his foster-mother, he rejected his brute existence and began to examine his world and its principles. By the use of his reason Yokdhan eventually discovers the secret of life, hell, heaven, and God. A religious hermit who arrives at the island teaches Yokdhan how to speak and discovers to his astonishment that what Yokdhan has learned from nature is the same as the knowledge contained in the *Koran*. After a time, they leave the island to visit the world, where Yokdhan is disappointed to find everyone pursuing worldly pleasures and wealth.

Parallels with the life of Crusoe are remarkable. The hero is completely isolated for more than twenty years, dresses in animal skins, and indulges in religious speculations. He even has a 'Vision of the Angelic World' in the manner of Defoe's hero; so that one is led to speculate as to whether or not Defoe knew the story of Yokdhan. Yet so far from being the 'idea' of *Robinson Crusoe* as one writer has suggested, it is almost the complete reverse.[7]

'He', wrote Aristotle, 'who is unable to live in society, or who has no need because he is sufficient for himself, must be either a beast or a god.'[8] Some critics have decided that Robinson Crusoe is indeed almost godlike, that he is an economic superman, enjoying his exploitation of the resources of the island and regretting his solitude only when he needs a helper in his labours. Such a view probably did not occur to Defoe. Commenting on Crusoe's life through the mask of his narrator, Defoe remarked: 'Here is invincible patience recommended under the worst of misery, indefatigable application and undaunted resolution under the greatest and most discouraging circumstances.'[9] Behind this statement lies Aristotle's view of man as a social animal, for whom loneliness was a terrifying condition. Not very long after Defoe's death, Rousseau eulogized the happiness of the solitary savage. But for Defoe, solitude was 'a rape upon human nature',[1] the worst of all punishments for his erring hero.

Cut off from the world, Crusoe's mind is dominated by fear. 'This

5. Alexander Pope, *Correspondence*, ed. George Sherburn (1956), ii. 13.
6. See *Memoirs for the Curious*, i (1701), 47–50.
7. See A. C. R. Pastor, *The Idea of Robinson Crusoe* (1930), p. 1.
8. *Politics, Works*, trans. Benjamin Jowett (1952), x, 1253[a].
9. *Serious Reflections*, p. xii.
1. Ibid., p. 6.

bold man', Giraudoux observed, 'was constantly trembling with fear and
it was thirteen years before he dared to reconnoitre all his island.'[2] Upon
reaching land, the sole survivor of a terrible shipwreck, Crusoe might
be expected to express some joy at his salvation from the sea; instead his
first reaction is panic:

> I had a dreadful Deliverance: For I was wet, had no Clothes to
> shift me, nor any thing either to eat or drink to comfort me, neither
> did I see any Prospect before me, but that of perishing with Hunger,
> or being devour'd by wild Beasts; and that which was particularly
> afflicting to me was that I had no Weapon either to hunt and kill
> any Creature for my Sustenance, or to defend my self against any
> other Creature that might desire to kill me for theirs: In a Word,
> I had nothing about me but a Knife, a Tobacco-pipe, and a little
> Tobacco in a Box, this was all my Provision, and threw me into
> terrible Agonies of Mind, that for a while I run about like a Mad-
> man; Night coming upon me, I began with a heavy Heart to con-
> sider what would be my Lot if there were any ravenous Beasts in
> that Country, seeing at Night they always come abroad for their
> Prey.[3]

Climbing into a tree for the night, Crusoe contemplates what he regards
as his inevitable fate—destruction by violence or starvation.

Such a reaction may not seem unlikely under the circumstances, but
Crusoe returns to the memory of this scene throughout the work, dwelling on and embellishing the description of his fear. He tells the reader:
'I ran about the Shore, wringing my Hands and beating my Head and
Face, exclaiming at my Misery, and crying out, I was undone.'[4] When
he sees the English captain in despair at being abandoned on the island
by his mutinous crew, Crusoe is reminded of his emotions when he
first arrived: 'How I gave myself over for lost; How wildly I look'd round
me: What dreadful Apprehensions I had: and how I lodg'd in the Tree
all Night for fear of being devour'd by wild Beasts.'[5] In his journal, he
recalls his despair and fear of starvation, recounting how, instead of
searching for food and shelter, he could only think about the necessities
he lacked: 'Food, House, Clothes, Weapon, or Place to fly to.'[6] During
these first hours on the island, Crusoe lacks all the resources of mind
which are usually associated with his adventure.

Fear, Defoe was clearly saying, is the dominant passion of a man in
Crusoe's condition. His isolation identifies him with the state of nature
which precedes society, a condition in which man could live alone not
because he was godlike, but because he was bestial. Probably the best
contemporary description of man in his natural state was provided by

2. Jean Giraudoux, *Suzanne and the Pacific*, trans. Ben Redman (1923), p. 225.
3. *Robinson Crusoe*, i. 52. [36]
4. Ibid., i. 78. [51]
5. Ibid., ii. 43. [182]
6. Ibid., i. 79. [52]

Samuel Pufendorf in his *De Jure Naturae et Gentium* and *De Officio Hominis et Civis*. The 'ingenious Puffendorf', as Defoe called him,[7] pictured the natural state as 'opposed to a life improved by the industry of men'—a life which must have been filled with continual fears and doubts and 'more wretched than that of any wild beast'.[8]

Pufendorf's description of natural man born into a state of isolation loosely parallels Crusoe's condition:

> Now to form in our Minds some Image of this Natural State, as such as it would be if destitute of all Arts and Assistances either invented by Men, or reveal'd by GOD, we must fancy a Man thrown at a venture into the World, and then left entirely to himself without receiving any farther Help or Benefit from others, than his bare Nativity; we must likewise suppose him to be furnish'd with no larger Endowments of Body or Mind, than such as we can now discover in men antecedent to all Culture and Information; and lastly, we must take it for granted, that he is not foster'd under the peculiar Care and Concern of Heaven. The Condition of such a Person could not prove otherwise than extreamly miserable, whether he were thus cast upon the Earth in Infancy, or in Maturity of Stature and of Strength. If an Infant, he could not but have sadly perish'd, unless some Brute Creature had by a kind of Miracle offer'd its Duggs for his Support; and then he must necessarily have imbib'd a fierce and savage Temper, under the Nursery and Education of Beasts. If in Perfection of Limbs and Size, we must however conceive him Naked, able to utter but an inarticulate Sound, . . . amaz'd and startled at the things about him, and even at his own Being.[9]

Although such a passage may, at first, seem more applicable to the life of Hai Ibn Yokdhan than to Defoe's hero, actually it reveals precisely the same attitude toward isolation which appears in the *Serious Reflections*. Certainly Crusoe has an education and considers himself under the special care of heaven, but like Pufendorf's abstraction, he is the ordinary man separated from the rest of humanity and forced to struggle for survival in a natural environment.

Pufendorf described how this natural man would react. First he would feel hunger and thirst; then he would search eagerly for the means to satisfy his needs. After satisfying these instincts, he would fall asleep among the trees. Crusoe does precisely the same thing, quenching his thirst and falling asleep in spite of his fears. But fear does not disappear with sleep. It remains the dominant emotion of natural man:

> What a wretched Creature we should at last behold! A mute and an ignoble Animal, Master of no Powers or Capacities any farther than to pluck up the Herbs and Roots that grow about him; to

---

7. *The Interest of the Several Princes and States of Europe* (1698), p. 13.
8. *De Officio Hominis et Civis*, trans. Frank Moore (1927), ii. 89 (II. i. 4).
9. *Law of Nature*, p. 79 (II. ii. 2).

> gather the Fruits which he did not plant; to quench his Thirst at
> the first River, or Fountain or Ditch, that he finds out in his way;
> to creep into a Cave for Shelter from the Injuries of Weather, or
> to cover over his Body with Moss and Grass and Leaves; Thus
> would he pass a heavy Life in most tedious Idleness; would tremble
> at every Noise, and be scar'd at the approach of any of his Fellow
> Creatures, till at last his miserable days were concluded by the
> Extremity of Hunger or Thirst, or by the Fury of a ravenous Beast. [1]

Like Pufendorf's abstraction, Crusoe eventually finds a cave to hide in
and surrounds his shelter with an impenetrable wall of stakes. He fears
every noise, in spite of his failure to discover the wild beasts which he
imagines are in possession of the island. After one of his few attempts
at exploration, Crusoe mentions how happy he is to return to the security
of his home. When he decides to make another entrance to his cave,
he is seized with a sudden anxiety. 'I was not perfectly easy at lying so
open,' he says, 'for as I had manag'd my self before, I was in a perfect
Enclosure, whereas now I thought I lay expos'd'. [2] He fears the attack
of some enemy although he admits that he has not seen anything on
the island more dangerous than a goat. Such a reaction might be considered normal enough during his first few days on the island, but Crusoe
still lives in fear a year after his arrival.

In the *Serious Reflections* Crusoe remarks than an 'eminent poet tells
us that all courage is fear'. [3] The poet is Rochester, and the passage is
significant, for it deduces all the passions from the ruling passion of fear.
Rochester compared the wisdom of animals, who only fight for love or
hunger to man who fights from fear:

> For fear he armes, and is of Armes afraid,
> By fear, to fear, successively betray'd
> Base fear, the source whence his best passion[s] came,
> His boasted Honor, and his dear bought Fame.
>
> . . . .
> Look to the bottom, of his vast design,
> Wherein *Mans* Wisdom, Pow'r, and Glory joyn;
> The good he acts, the ill he does endure,
> 'Tis all for fear, to make himself secure. [4]

Crusoe quotes a large part of the *Satyr Against Mankind* as well as
sections of Creech's translation of Lucretius. The combination is significant, for Lucretius's discussion of man in the state of nature formed
the basis for Rochester's theories as well as those of Hobbes.

Although Rochester and Hobbes argued that man in his natural state
would be divided by his lust after power and his fears, most philosophers

1. *Law of Nature*, p. 78 (II. i. 8).
2. *Robinson Crusoe*, i. 118. [76]
3. *Serious Reflections*, p. 25.
4. 'Satyr Against Mankind', *Poems*, ed. Vivian de Sola Pinto (1953), p. 122.

contended that fear was the dominant passion. Montesquieu's brief view of natural man in his *Spirit of the Laws* was approximately the same as Pufendorf's:

> Man in a state of nature would have the faculty of knowing, before he had acquired any knowledge. Plain it is that his first ideas would not be of a speculative nature; he would think of the preservation of his being, before he would investigate its origin. Such a man would feel nothing in himself at first but impotency and weakness; his fears and apprehensions would be excessive; as appears from instances (were there any necessity of proving it) of savages found in forests, trembling at the motion of a leaf, and flying from every shadow.[5]

The reference which Montesquieu supplies for what he obviously regards as a self-evident statement is to a 'savage' found in the forests of Hanover and brought over to England in 1726. The arrival of this natural man, Peter the Wild Boy, in England produced a flood of anonymous pamphlets and poems and one long work, *Mere Nature Delineated*, by Defoe. Most of the pamphlets contained some form of satire on Walpole or the court; all of them suggested ideas on primitivism which were more typical of the period after Rousseau than the time of *Gulliver's Travels*. Later in the century, Rousseau's British disciple, Lord Monboddo, used Peter's case to illustrate man's happy animalism in the state of nature, but his exposition, while clearly more serious, offered few ideas which had not been suggested when Peter first arrived in England. In the *Manifesto of Lord Peter* the Wild Boy is seen searching for a wife who is free from the evil influences of a civilized education 'which may have corrupted the Simplicity of Nature';[6] while the narrator of *It Cannot Rain But It Pours* tells of the rumour that

> . . . the new Sect of Herb-eaters intend to follow him into the Fields. . . . And that there are many of them now thinking of turning their Children into Woods to Graze with the Cattle, in hopes to raise a healthy and moral Race, refin'd from the Corruptions of this Luxurious World.[7]

In reply to these pamphlets and their half-joking suggestions that by creating governments and erecting cities man had destroyed the purity of his feral state, Defoe issued his *Mere Nature Delineated*. The title suggests that the work is related to William Wollaston's *Religion of Nature Delineated*, which probably antagonized Defoe by attempting to construct a system of natural morality. But although Defoe unquestionably objected to some of Wollaston's premises, he would have been in complete agreement with Wollaston's attack on those philosophers who

5. Trans. Thomas Nugent (1949), p. 4.
6. (London, 1726), p. 9. See also David Lewis ed., *Miscellaneous Poems* (1726), p. 305.
7. (1726), p. 8.

believed that men could attain virtue by following nature. Like Defoe, Wollaston praised civilization for elevating man's reason above his passions, remarking that if there were another Flood, only the 'natural fools' would return to the woods. He also argued that man was a social creature and that '. . . it is certain that absolute and perpetual solitude has something in it very disagreeable, and hideous.'[8] These, however, are ideas which Defoe had formulated long before Wollaston's book appeared in 1722. It must be concluded that Defoe merely adapted the title of a popular and controversial work to draw attention to his own study of a very different subject: the problems raised by the discovery of man in his natural state.

Defoe's observations on Peter are important because they show his disagreement with the central moral of Hai Ibn Yokdhan's life: that '. . . nature of its meer undirected inclination guided mankind to make the best choice of things, and rejecting the pleasing objects of sence, led him to choose vertue by a meer propensity of will without instruccion or example'.[9] In regard to Peter's condition, Defoe remarked that the Wild Boy was 'passive, weak, foolish, as well as wild', not strong and fearless as Hobbes suggested natural man would be.[1] Defoe speculated on this being in a 'State of Meer Nature' wondering whether he could reason or form ideas without the power of language. The main trouble with Peter, Defoe concluded, was that he lacked any kind of education or civilization. Comparing him to a deaf girl who had learned how to speak at the age of fourteen, Defoe remarked that the natural man was 'a plain coarse Piece of Work', and that without some kind of learning a knowledge of language or religion would be impossible.[2]

Both Crusoe and Peter the Wild Boy were in a natural state because they were solitaries, entirely outside of society. By the end of the eighteenth century, Zimmermann was to write a book praising some kinds of solitude as remedies for many problems of the mind and heart, but even he regarded absolute isolation with distrust. The possibility of a *dementia ex separatione* was clearly perceived by writers of the seventeenth and eighteenth centuries. Stories of men isolated for long periods, such as that of Pedro Serrano in Garcilaso de la Vega's *Royal Commentaries of the Yncas*, parallel Crusoe's adventure in many ways, but after three years on his island Serrano said that 'he would have been glad to end his misery by death'.[3] Serrano was almost reduced to the condition of an animal; so that when a companion finally came to the island, he could not believe Serrano was a human being. Because isolation was regarded with such horror, pirates often assumed that marooning a victim on an uninhabited island would be worse punishment

8. (1722), pp. 67, 107.
9. *Compleat English Gentleman*, p. 111.
1. *Mere Nature Delineated* (1726), p. 8.
2. Ibid., p. 68.
3. Trans. Clements Markham (1869), i. 44.

than death. After only five days alone, Richard Norwood, one of the early settlers of Bermuda, had sunk into despair:

> This five days seemed to me the most tedious and miserable time that I ever underwent in all my life, yea, though I had had experience of sundry difficulties, dangers, and hard conditions before; yet till then I never seemed to understand what misery was; yet I had victuals sufficient, only I seemed banished from human society and knew not how long it might last. Yet at other times I was apt to retire myself much from company, but at this time I thought it was one of the greatest punishments in the world, yea, I thought it was one of the greatest punishments in hell, and the sense and apprehension of it made me to think of hell as of hell indeed, a condition most miserable.[4]

Norwood, like Serrano, thought that he would rather suffer any torture than be deprived of human society, but Serrano and several others endured this loneliness for many years.

Perhaps the best example of this ability to endure loneliness was Alexander Selkirk. Although he experienced some fear, Selkirk 'came at last to conquer all the inconveniences of his solitude, and to be very easy'.[5] Around Selkirk's life two myths have arisen which seem to have little factual basis. The first concerned Steele's statement that Selkirk '. . . frequently bewailed his return to the world, which could not . . . with all its enjoyments, restore him to the tranquility of his solitude'.[6] The second is the idea that Selkirk had slipped back into animalism and lost the use of speech.[7] Steele's version turned Selkirk's experience into something not very different from the life of Hai Ibn Yokdhan; whereas followers of Rousseau, like Monboddo, pointed to Selkirk as proof that when returned to the state of nature, man quickly reverts to his bestial origins.

Defoe adapted neither of these myths. From time to time Crusoe has a certain nostalgia for the primitive conditions of his island, but never does he suggest that he would like to return to his solitary state of nature. In the *Serious Reflections* Defoe repeated the story of Saint Hilarion, who spent his life in the desert only to discover that a simple labourer, living in the midst of a city, had led a more holy life than he:

> There is no need of a wilderness to wander among wild beasts, no necessity of a cell on the top of a mountain, or a desolate island in the sea; if the mind be confirmed, if the soul be truly master of

4. *The Journal of Richard Norwood*, ed. Wesley Craven and Walter Hayward (1945), p. 54. For a modern study of isolation see A. L. Singh and Robert Zingg, *Wolf Children and Feral Man* (1942), pp. 247–9.
5. Woodes Rogers, A *Cruising Voyage Round the World*, in Defoe, *Romances*, Dent ed., iii. 322.
6. Richard Steele, *The Englishman*, in Defoe, *Romances*, Dent ed., iii. 328.
7. See Isaac James, *Providence Displayed* (1800), p. 100; and James Burnet, Lord Monboddo, *Of the Origin and Progress of Language*, 2nd ed. (1774), i. 198.

itself, all is safe; for it is certainly and effectually master of the body, and what signify retreats, especially a forced retreat as mine was?[8]

Defoe probably realized that Crusoe's isolation on his island was almost the same as the isolation of the desert fathers. Living in a cave, dividing his life between work and prayer, seeing visions, Crusoe seems not very different from a religious hermit. But Defoe rejected this idea by pointing to his hero's misery and to his inability to leave the island. Crusoe insists that he could 'enjoy much more solitude in the middle of the greatest collection of mankind in the world' than in twenty-eight years of isolation.[9] Crusoe is not a saint. Charles Kingsley called him a 'Protestant monk', but this is paradoxical.[1] Crusoe's real life was to be lived in the world, following his calling, not on the island where much of his time was spent in hiding from imaginary enemies.

Although Crusoe's manufacturing, farming, and building are given most space in the novel, much of his time is devoted to self-defence:

> The anxiety of my circumstances there, I can assure you, was such for a time as was very unsuitable to heavenly meditations, and even when that was got over, the frequent alarms from the savages put the soul sometimes to such extremities of fear and horror, that all manner of temper was lost, and I was no more fit for religious exercises than a sick man is fit for labour.[2]

Crusoe lives in a 'brutal solitude' and, like Pufendorf's natural man, leads a life of 'perpetual doubt and danger'.[3] Pufendorf described such an existence as being worse than that of a beast. Nothing can be considered secure, and within the soul the passions rule instead of reason. Lacking the aid of his fellow man and forced to meet every enemy alone, the isolated natural man passes his life in continual expectation of destruction.[4] Crusoe is rescued from this condition by his tools, the symbols of learning, the arts, society, and that civilization which is the reverse of man's natural state. But as soon as he discovers the footprint in the sand, Crusoe returns to his original state in which fear rules every aspect of life.

'O what ridiculous Resolution Men take', says Crusoe, 'when posses'd with Fear! It deprives them of the Use of those Means which Reason

8. *Serious Reflections*, p. 6.
9. The comparison between Selkirk's isolation and that of the desert fathers was apparent to Captain Edward Cooke, who urged his readers to peruse the 'Lives of ancient Anchorites, who spent many years in the Deserts of *Thebaida* in *Egypt*' if they wanted to learn about the moral benefits of isolation instead of wasting their time on a 'downright Sailor, whose only Study was how to support himself, during his Confinement, and all his Conversation with Goats'. A *Voyage to the South Sea* (1712), II, xix.
1. Introduction, *The Surprising Adventures of Robinson Crusoe* (1868), p. xxii.
2. *Serious Reflections*, p. 7.
3. Defoe, *An Historical Account of the Voyages and Adventures of Sir Walter Raleigh* (1719), p. 44.
4. *De Officio Hominis et Civis*, ii. 90–93 (II. i. 7–11).

offers for their Relief.'[5] Ruled by his passions, Crusoe thinks of destroying everything which might indicate to the savage who made that single footprint the possibility of some inhabitant on the island. He contemplates letting his goats run loose, digging up his corn fields, and even destroying his beloved cave and enclosure. Searching desperately for some means of defence, Crusoe forgets the consolation which religion offered him. Recalling these emotions from the safety of his study in England, he moralizes on the senselessness of his behaviour:

> Thus Fear of Danger is ten thousand Times more terrifying than Danger it self, when apparent to the Eyes; and we find the Burthen of Anxiety greater by much, than the Evil which we are anxious about. . . .[6]

Crusoe was incapable of such moralizing on the island, for he passed most of his time attempting to ensure his safety. The impassable wood is now made ten feet thick, and after he has completed his fortification, Crusoe hides himself in his cave, afraid to leave, living 'in the constant Snare of the *Fear of Man*'.[7]

Crusoe remarks on the effect which his fear has upon his efforts at improving the conditions of his life: 'the Frights I had been in about these Savage Wretches, and the Concern I had been in for my own Preservation, had taken off the Edge of my Invention for my own Conveniences.'[8] Instead of making beer and providing for his comforts, Crusoe is forced to abandon even his most simple improvements. Defoe's concept is the same as that contained in one of the best-known passages from Hobbes's *Leviathan* describing the state of nature:

> In such condition, there is no place for Industry; because the fruit thereof is uncertain: and consequently no Culture of the Earth; no Navigation, nor use of the commodities that may be imported by Sea; no commodius Building; no Instruments of moving, and removing such things as require much force; no Knowledge of the face of the Earth; no account of Time; no Arts; no Letters; no Society; and which is worst of all, continuall feare, and danger of violent death; And the life of man, solitary, poore, nasty, brutish, and short.[9]

Defoe, like Pufendorf, would have objected that such a picture could only apply to a society of solitary males, but this is precisely Crusoe's condition. Nor is this state of war a matter of a few days or the length of time required to fight a battle; it is rather a continual state of mind. Crusoe is no longer able to perfect his bread or invent a new type of grindstone; all

5. *Robinson Crusoe*, i. 184. [115]
6. Ibid., i. 184. [116]
7. Ibid., i. 189. [118]
8. Ibid., i. 194. [121]
9. p. 84.

his labour is directed to the task of preserving his life. Looking back, Crusoe is amused at the time and energy which he devoted to works of defence 'on the Account of the Print of a Man's Foot which I had seen; for as yet I never saw any human Creature come near the Island'.[1] But this is written from the safety of Crusoe's study in England. While he is on the island, he is unable to achieve this objectivity about his fears.

Crusoe recalls with longing the happiness of the first two years on the island, comparing them to 'the Life of Anxiety, Fear and Care' which have plagued him since his discovery of the cannibals.[2] And he rationalizes that the state of fear which these savages have induced in him is enough to justify his slaughtering them. 'It was Self-preservation in the highest Degree', he remarks, 'to deliver myself from this Death of a Life, and was acting in my own Defence, as much as if they were actually assaulting me.'[3] Only the arrival of Friday relieves him from his care and returns him to the life of peace and industry. With the coming of social life, man gladly abandons his isolation and enters the comparative security of the social state of nature.

FRANK BUDGEN

[On Joyce's Admiration of Defoe]†

Joyce was a great admirer of Defoe. He possessed his complete works, and had read every line of them. Of only three other writers, he said, could he make this claim: Flaubert, Ben Jonson and Ibsen. *Robinson Crusoe* he called the English *Ulysses*.

JAMES JOYCE

Daniel Defoe‡

* * * The first English author to write without imitating or adapting foreign works, to create without literary models and to infuse into the

---

1. *Robinson Crusoe*, i. 188. [118]
2. Ibid., i. 227. [142]
3. Ibid., i. 231. [144]
   † From *James Joyce and the Making of Ulysses* (Bloomington: Indiana University Press, 1960), p. 181. By permission of Indiana University Press and Oxford University Press. Frank Budgen, friend and critic of Joyce, was associated with him in Zurich during World War I.
   ‡ From *Buffalo Studies* 1.1 (1964): 7, 11–13, 22–25. Edited from Italian manuscripts and translated by Joseph Prescott, the introduction, translation, and notes are copyrighted by Joseph Prescott, © 1964 renewed 1992. Reprinted by permission of Joseph Prescott and the State University of New York at Buffalo.

creatures of his pen a truly national spirit, to devise for himself an artistic form which is perhaps without precedent, except for the brief monographs of Sallust and Plutarch, is Daniel Defoe, father of the English novel.

* * * [Defoe] then turned (he was past sixty)[1] to literature properly so called and in the first years of the reign of George I (Defoe's eventful life extends across seven reigns) he wrote and published the first part of *Robinson Crusoe*. This book had been offered by the author to nearly all of the capital's publishing houses, which, with great perspicacity, had rejected it.[2] It saw the light in April, 1719; at the end of August, the fourth edition was already on sale.[3] Eighty thousand copies were sold, a record circulation for those times. The public, far from tiring of the adventures of Defoe's hero, demanded more. And as Conan Doyle, yielding to the insistence of the contemporary public, revived his lean puppet Sherlock Holmes to send him off again in pursuit of rogues and criminals, even so the sixty-year-old Defoe followed the first part of his novel with a second in which the protagonist feels the wanderlust once more and returns to his "island home." This second part was followed by a third, *Serious Reflections of Robinson Crusoe*. Defoe, good soul, perceiving rather tardily that in his matter-of-fact realism he had taken little account of the spiritual side of his hero,[4] made a collection in the third part of serious reflections upon man, human destiny, the Creator—reflections and thoughts which decorate the figure of the rude sailor neither more nor less than the votive talismans which hang about the neck and from the outstretched hands of a miracle-working Madonna. The famous book even had the supreme luck to be parodied by a London wag who also amassed a fortune on the sale of a whimsical satire entitled *The Life and Surprizing Strange Adventures of a Certain Daniel Defoe, Wool Merchant, Who Lived All Alone in the Uninhabited Island of Great Britain.*[5]

In 1912 Joyce delivered a lecture in Italian on Daniel Defoe at the Università Popolare Triestina. Joyce's text of this lecture in manuscript form is in the possession of the State University of New York at Buffalo.

1. Joyce's arithmetic is unreliable since he gives Defoe's birth year as 1661 and the date of *Robinson Crusoe* as 1719.
2. Joyce could hardly have failed to recognize parallels between Defoe's career and his own. Thus, the bitterness which impelled him to throw the manuscript of *Stephen Hero* into the fire would seem to pervade his account of the numerous rejections of Defoe's masterpiece. See John J. Slocum and Herbert Cahoon, A *Bibliography of James Joyce* [1882–1941] (New Haven, 1953), item E3d. For a different view of Defoe's experience, see Hutchins [H. C. Hutchins, *Robinson Crusoe and Its Printing* (New York, 1925)], pp. 44ff., and J. R. Moore, A *Checklist of the Writings of Daniel Defoe* (Bloomington, 1960), item 412.
3. According to Moore, ibid., the fourth edition appeared on August 7.
4. In 1895—according to Kevin Sullivan, *Joyce among the Jesuits* (New York, 1958), p. 238— *Robinson Crusoe*, ed. W. H. Lambert (Ginn, Heath, & Co.), formed part of Joyce's studies at Belvedere College. Joyce differs with Lambert's view that the story contains "lengthy moral reflections" (*Life and Adventures of Robinson Crusoe* [Boston: Ginn, Heath, & Co., 1883], p. iv).
5. The beginning of the correct title, taken from a microfilm of the copy in the British Museum, is *The Life and Strange Surprising Adventures of Mr. D—— De F——, of London, Hosier, Who Has liv'd above fifty Years by himself, in the Kingdoms of North and South Britain.* Joyce

Pedants strained to expose the paltry errors into which the great pre-
cursor of the realist movement had fallen. How could Crusoe stuff his
pockets with biscuits if he had stripped before swimming from the beach
to the stranded vessel? How could he see the goat's eyes in the pitch-
dark cave? How could the Spaniards give Friday's father an agreement
in writing when they had neither ink nor pen? Are there any bears or
not on the West Indian islands?[6] And so on. The pedants are right: the
errors are there; but the broad river of the new realism carries them off
majestically like bushes and reeds uprooted by the flood.

Modern realism is perhaps a reaction. The great French nation, which
venerates the legend of the Maid of Orleans, nevertheless disfigures her
through the mouth of Voltaire, lasciviously defiles her in the hands of
the engravers of the nineteenth century, riddles and shreds her in the
twentieth century with the cutting style of Anatole France. The very
intensity, the very refinement of French realism betray its spiritual
origins. But you will search in vain in the works of Defoe for that wrathful
ardor of corruption which illumines with pestiferous phosphorescence
the sad pages of Huysmans. You will search in vain in the works of a
writer who, two centuries before Gorki or Dostoevski, brought into
European literature the lowest dregs of the population—the foundling,
the pickpocket, the go-between, the prostitute, the witch, the robber,
the castaway—for that studied ardor of indignation and protest which
lacerates and caresses. You will find, if anything, beneath the rude
exterior of his characters an instinct and a prophecy. His women have
the indecency and the continence of beasts; his men are strong and silent
as trees. English feminism and English imperialism already lurk in these
souls which are just emerging from the animal kingdom. The African
proconsul Cecil Rhodes descends in a direct line from Captain Singleton,
and the afore-praised Mrs. Christian Davies is the presumptive great-
great-grandmother of Mrs. Pankhurst.

Defoe's masterpiece, *Robinson Crusoe*, is the full artistic expression
of this instinct and this prophecy. In the life of the pirate and explorer
Captain Singleton and in the story of *Colonel Jack*, suffused by such
generous and sad compassion, Defoe presents studies and sketches for
that great solitary character who later, with the approbation of so many
simple-hearted men and boys, achieved citizenship in the world of let-

may have found his error in Minto [William Minto, *Daniel Defoe* (London, 1879)], who gives
the title as *"The life and strange surprising adventures of Daniel de Foe, of London, Hosier,
who lived all alone in the unihabited island of Great Britain, and so forth."* (pp. 150–51) The
phrase *"who lived . . . all alone in an un-inhabited island"* occurs in the title of *Robinson
Crusoe*.

      For a reprint of the parody and an account of its author, see Paul Dottin, ed., *Robinson
Crusoe Examin'd and Criticis'd, or A New Edition of Charles Gildon's Famous Pamphlet . . .*
(London & Paris, 1923).

6. All four objections occur in the same sequence in Gildon (1st ed., pp. 15–16, 26, 26–27, 28
[cf. p. vii]); but they occur in the same sequence and together in Minto, p. 146, introduced
by the statement "He did not mind the sneers of hostile critics" (Joyce's introductory "Pedants"?). Moreover, Joyce's wording is much closer to Minto's than to Gildon's.

ters.[7] The story of the shipwrecked sailor who lived on the desert island for four years reveals, as perhaps no other book throughout the long history of English literature does, the wary and heroic instinct of the rational animal and the prophecy of the empire.

European criticism has striven for many generations, and with a not entirely friendly insistence, to explain the mystery of the unlimited world conquest accomplished by that mongrel breed which lives a hard life on a small island in the northern sea and was not endowed by nature with the intellect of the Latin, nor with the patience of the Semite, nor with Teutonic zeal, nor with the sensitiveness of the Slav. European caricature has amused itself for many years in contemplating, with a gaiety not unmixed with distress, an exaggerated man with the jaws of an ape, checkered clothes that are too short and too tight, and enormous feet; or the traditional John Bull, the corpulent trader with the fatuous, rubicund moonface and the diminutive top hat. Neither of these lay figures would have conquered a handbreadth of ground in a thousand ages. The true symbol of the British conquest is Robinson Crusoe, who, cast away on a desert island, in his pocket a knife and a pipe, becomes an architect, a carpenter, a knife grinder, an astronomer, a baker, a shipwright, a potter, a saddler, a farmer, a tailor, an umbrella-maker, and a clergyman. He is the true prototype of the British colonist, as Friday (the trusty savage who arrives on an unlucky day) is the symbol of the subject races. The whole Anglo-Saxon spirit is in Crusoe: the manly independence; the unconscious cruelty; the persistence; the slow yet efficient intelligence; the sexual apathy; the practical, well-balanced religiousness; the calculating taciturnity. Whoever rereads this simple, moving book in the light of subsequent history cannot help but fall under its prophetic spell.

Saint John the Evangelist saw on the island of Patmos the apocalyptic ruin of the universe and the building of the walls of the eternal city sparkling with beryl and emerald, with onyx and jasper, with sapphire and ruby. Crusoe saw only one marvel in all the fertile creation around him, the print of a naked foot in the virgin sand. And who knows if the latter is not more significant than the former?

GEORGE A. STARR

Robinson Crusoe and the Myth of Mammon†

What we make of the hero's labor greatly influences our response to *Robinson Crusoe*. Indeed, from Rousseau's day to our own, most dif-

7. Joyce is having difficulty with chronology. *Robinson Crusoe* appeared in 1719, *Captain Singleton* in 1720, and *Colonel Jack* in 1722. See Moore, *Checklist*, items 412, 435, 452.
† From *Defoe and Spiritual Autobiography* (copyright © 1965 by Princeton University Press), pp. 185 through 197. Reprinted by permission of Princeton University Press and the author.

ferences of interpretation are traceable to this single factor, the varying significance attached to Crusoe's work.[1] One recent commentator, for instance, finds implicit in it the creed of the dignity of labor: on his reading, Crusoe's efforts signify that the human lot is heroic only when productive, and that man is capable of redemption only through untiring labor. "If we draw a moral," this critic maintains, "it can only be that for all the ailments of man and his society, Defoe confidently prescribes the therapy of work."[2]

We may question, however, whether such an interpretation does justice either to Defoe's intention or to the facts of the narrative. The ideology here ascribed to Defoe had found expression long before the appearance of *Robinson Crusoe*: Mammon, after all, is traditionally its most eloquent advocate. It is he who counsels his fellows in Pandaemonium not to attempt further insurrections.

> but rather seek
> Our own good from ourselves, and from our own
> Live to ourselves, though in this vast recess,
> Free, and to none accountable, preferring
> Hard liberty before the easie yoke
> Of servil Pomp. Our greatness will appear
> Then most conspicuous, when great things of small,
> Useful of hurtful, prosperous of adverse,
> We can create, and in what place so e're
> Thrive under evil, and work ease out of pain
> Through labour and endurance.[3]

To be sure, Milton makes clear from the outset that Mammon is "the least erected Spirit that fell from Heav'n"; yet some modern criticism would have us see such a figure in Robinson Crusoe.

In my opinion there is a vast difference in spirit between Mammon, that prototypical *homo economicus*, and the regenerate Crusoe. Before examining Defoe's hero, however, we might glance briefly at *The Faerie Queene*, for in the second book Spenser presents not only Mammon but the opposite extreme, in the figure of Phaedria. In fact, Phaedria's song to Cymochles (II. vi. 15–17) leads us back to an important source of the entire problem, the passage in the Sermon on the Mount (Matthew 6:24–34) in which Christ urges that man take no thought for the morrow. "Ye cannot serve God and Mammon," Christ warns, and Phaedria's

1. See Charles Eaton Burch, "British Criticism of Defoe as a Novelist, 1719–1860," *E.S.*, Vol. 67 (1932), pp. 178–98, and "Defoe's British Reputation 1869–1894," *E.S.*, Vol. 68 (1934), pp. 410–23.
2. Ian Watt, "*Robinson Crusoe* as a Myth," pp. 165, 166 and *passim*; *The Rise of the Novel*, pp. 72–74. Cf. Max Weber, *The Protestant Ethic and the Spirit of Capitalism* (N.Y., 1958), pp. 171–72 and *passim*.
3. John Milton, *Paradise Lost*, II, 252–62, in *Poetical Works*, edited by Helen Darbishire, 2 vols. (Oxford, 1952), I, 32–33.

song is in its own way a powerful dissuasive from laying up treasures upon earth.[4]

No critic, it is true, identifies Crusoe's island with Phaedria's. But to establish the fact that he is not cast away in Mammon's cave, either, we should consider some other views on the Mammon-versus-Phaedria dilemma, for there are numerous discussions of it during the seventeenth century. These often take the form of discourses on that portion of the Sermon on the Mount which Phaedria has glossed for us, after her fashion. They sometimes occur in sermons on other texts, such as I Peter 5:7, "Casting all your care upon him, for he careth for you," or Philippians 4:6, "Be careful for nothing"; and they frequently appear in practical works other than sermons, notably in treatises on Providence. Occasionally these discussions will crop out even in the works of self-examination and meditation, and I shall begin by citing one such instance, since it puts very concisely the usual solution of this dilemma. Bishop Hall declares in the 287th of his *Meditations and Vows, Divine and Moral* that "there is an holy carelessness, free from idleness, free frorm distrust. In these earthly things I will so depend on my Maker, that my trust in him may not exclude all my labour; and yet so labour, upon my confidence on him, as my endeavour may be void of perplexity."[5] That idleness was anathema to the seventheenth-century English mind we have been told sufficiently; a point we tend to lose sight of is that distrust was to be just as carefully avoided. If divines of that era seem to have had ringing in their ears God's sentence on the fallen Adam, "In the sweat of thy face shalt thou eat bread, till thou return unto the ground" (Genesis 3:19), they were equally conscious of Christ's words in the Sermon on the Mount.

When they called attention to this paradox, they did so in order to show that the alternatives were not in fact mutually exclusive. Like the relation of faith to works as a basis for salvation, labor and dependence on God came to be regarded as a "both/and," not an "either/or" relationship. Just as true faith, far from obviating works, would be productive of them, so the right kind of dependence on God, far from ruling out human effort, would give it impetus and sanction. The two problems were frequently treated as analogous, and resolved in much the same way: thus Thomas Lye, one of the preachers at Dr. Annesley's Cripplegate Exercises, observes that "As faith shows itself by its works (James 2:18), so trust discovers itself by its obedience, especially in the use of such means as God prescribes for the bringing about his appointed end. . . . God's means are to be used, as well as God's blessing to be ex-

4. Phaedria's argument is defective, of course, in its failure to advise instead that one lay up treasures in heaven. She agrees with Christ in repudiating "fruitlesse toile," but differs greatly in her motive for doing so: namely, her conviction that man should "present pleasures chuse." Moreover, she appeals to the sheer abundance of nature, rather than the fact of divine provision, as grounds for casting off care.

5. *Works*, VII, 515; cf. No. 126, VII, 467.

pected."[6] There is little suggestion here that one claim takes precedence over the other, let alone that the two are antagonistic. Both obligations are binding, but each is qualified by the other: Christ had not countermanded God's bidding, but had amplified it, had ordered man to go about his tasks in a new spirit. Even though God fully determines the outcome of every action, man is expected to cooperate; he is responsible for the performance, if not for the result. As one writer says, "The use of means in matters is Man's work; the Issue or success of means, is God's work"; or as another remarks, "Tho we are sure God has decreed the certain event of such a thing, yet we must not encourage our *idleness*, but our diligence."[7]

When Lye and others spoke of "the use of means," they frequently wanted to stress that God not only compels man to exert himself, but guides and assists him in his exertions. Stephen Charnock, an Emmanuel-trained Presbyterian writing in the 1670's, is typical in asserting that Providence "directs us by means; not to use them is to tempt our Guardian; where it intends any great thing for our good, it *opens* a door, and puts such circumstances into our hands, as we may use without the breach of any Command, or the neglect of our Duty."[8] The splendid thing about Providence, in the eyes of such writers, is not that it simply "provides" for man, but rather that it affords him—if he is attentive and obedient to its dictates—the means of providing for himself. Thus Providence does not excuse man from action, but calls him to it and sustains him in it. Richard Sibbes, whose *Soul's Conflict* (1635) Walton piously bequeathed to his son, insists that "We must not put all carelessly upon a providence, but first consider what is our part; and, so far as God presents us with light, and affords us help and means, we must not be failing in our duty. We should neither outrun nor be wanting to Providence."[9] Nearly a century later, Defoe himself was to assert that "To be utterly careless of ourselves,, and talk of trusting Providence, is a lethargy of the worst nature; for as we are to trust Providence with our estates, but to use, at the same time, all diligence in our callings, so we are to trust Providence with our safety, but with our eyes open to all its necessary cautions, warnings, and instructions."[1]

6. "How are we to live by faith on divine providence?" in *Cripplegate Exercises*, I, 374.
7. T[homas] C[rane], *Isagoge*, p. 475; Stephen Charnock, *Works*, p. 531. See Edward Synge, *A Gentlemen's Religion* (1700), pp. 173–74; Jeremy Collier, *Several Discourses upon Practical Subjects* (1725), pp. 103–04; and John Tillotson, "The Necessity of Supernatural Grace, in order to a Christian Life," in *Works*, VIII, 506.
8. Charnock, *Works*, p. 531; cf. Samuel Scattergood (1646–1696), *Fifty-Two Sermons, Upon Several Occasions*, 2 vols. (Oxford, 1810), I, 173; Benjamin Whichcote, *Works*, I, 359–60; John Tillotson, "The Wisdom of God in his Providence," *Works*, VI, 409.
9. *The Soul's Conflict with Itself, and Victory Over Itself by Faith*, in *Complete Works*, I, 209, Cf. [Richard Allestree], "Of Trust in God," in *The Whole Duty of Man*, Sunday, I, Par. 55. The very phrasing is similar in William Burkitt's *The Poor Man's Help, and Young Man's Guide* (N.Y., 1788; 1st edition, 1693), p. 14.
1. *Serious Reflections*, pp. 190–91; cf. p. 183 and *passim*; *The Compleat English Tradesman*, 2nd edition (1727), II, 183. See also Samuel Slater, *Cripplegate Exercises*, III, 327–28; John Tillotson, "Success not always answerable to the probability of Second Causes," in *Works*, II,

Providence, in short, imposes obligations: it indicates solutions rather than simply performing them, it evokes effective action rather than obviating it, and confers human responsibility rather than precluding it.

All this would tend to refute Phaedria, who makes the bounty of Nature an argument for sloth, but it may seem to guard less effectively against the opposite danger, that of robust Mammonism. We should bear in mind, however, the conviction that just as man must heed and apply strenuously the lessons that Providence teaches, so conversely his efforts will be fruitless if he sets about them without a due regard for Providence. Total self-reliance and unaided human labor are regarded as vain, blind, and perverse, since God is never a mere spectator and since, as the preachers were fond of repeating, the race is not to the swift, nor the battle to the strong, neither yet bread to the wise, nor yet riches to men of understanding, nor yet favor to men of skill. Since God can interrupt or deflect the ordinary sequence of cause and effect to work his will in the world, it is both impious and imprudent to rely on one's own efforts and calculations.

It is this end of the stick that was used to beat the followers of Mammon. We have seen Thomas Lye's warning against sloth, that "God's means are to be used, as well as God's blessing to be expected"; his onslaught against Mammon is even more forceful. The man of faith, he says, "leaves it to the atheist in being *fortunae suae faber*; or, with that dunghill wretch who, being excited to thank God for a rich crop of corn, replies, "Thank God shall I! Nay, rather thank my dung-cart!' "[2] The other divines cited earlier express similar sentiments, though seldom in such earthy terms.[3] Moreover, various Biblical texts were used to support the argument. In a sermon preached before the House of Commons, William Jane urges his listeners "not to boast of the arm of flesh, *to sacrifice to our net, or burn incense to our drag* (Habakkuk 1:16), or say with the Assyrian (Isaiah 10:13), *By the might of my hands I have*

357; and Lancelot Andrewes *Ninety-six Sermons*, 5 vols. (Oxford, 1841–43), IV, 68.

2. *Cripplegate Exercises*, I, 383. This attitude was satirized throughout the period; see Francis Quarles's portrait of "The Wordly Man's Verdour," in *Judgement and Mercy for Afflicted Souls* (1646), in *Works*, edited by A. B. Grosart, 3 vols. (Edinburgh, 1880), I, 87. Cf. the merchant's assertions in "Man's Injustice towards Providence" (1713), in *The Poems of Anne Countess of Winchilsea*, edited by Myra Reynolds (Chicago, 1903), pp. 196–98. Finally, the conclusion of Pope's Epistle to Bathurst lies partly within this tradition in such lines as the following:

> Behold Sir Balaam, now a man of spirit,
> Ascribes his gettings to his parts and
>   merit;
> What late he call'd a Blessing, now was
>   Wit,
> And God's good Providence, a lucky Hit.

(Epistle III, "Of the Use of Riches," ll. 375–78, in *Epistles to Several Persons*, edited by F. W. Bateson [1951], p. 120.)

3. William Gurnal had used the same anecdote some years earlier, however, in *The Christian in Compleat Armour*, p. 313.

done this, and by my wisdome, for I am prudent."[4] What is to be avoided
is the extreme position of those who, in Samuel Clarke's words, "rely
with such confidence on the Effects of their own Wisdom and Industry,
and so presumptuously depend upon the natural and regular Tendencies
of second Causes; as if they thought, either there was no Superior Cause
at all, on which the Fame of Nature depended; or at least, that the
Providence of God did not condescend to direct the Events of Things,
in this lower and uncertain World."[5] Industry, then, has no intrinsic
merit; it becomes valuable only when coupled with an acknowledgment
of God's ultimate power to further or thwart it. Mammon's independence
and self-reliance, far from being redeeming features, are at the very core
of his inquity, since they involve a denial of God's sovereignty.[6]

   This rapid survey would indicate that the seventeenth-century attitude
towards diligence and sloth was somewhat more subtle than generally
recognized. Instead of lauding the one and castigating the other, preachers and poets alike arrived at a sort of compromise: what they wanted
was an alert, active acquiescence, and a humble, resigned striving. It
remains to show that Crusoe, following his conversion, comes to fulfill
this ideal, rather than the one embodied and proposed by Spenser's and
Milton's Mammon. The first thing to consider is Crusoe's behavior
between his shipwreck and his conversion. With as yet no sense that he
is an object either of Providential chastisement or care, Crusoe's initial
reaction to his situation is one of despondence. It is noteworthy that

4. *A Sermon Preached . . . the 26th of November, 1691* (Oxford, 1691), pp. 8–9; on the texts
   from Habakkuk and Isaiah see Edward Waple, *Thirty Sermons*, pp. 139–40, 142; Thomas
   Manton, *Sermons* (1678), pp. 267–68; Jeremy Collier, "Of Discontent," in *Essays upon Several
   Subjects*, Part III, 3rd edition (1720), pp. 86–87. Compare *The Compleat English Tradesman*,
   II, 235; speaking of the way a tradesman should behave when successful, Defoe says that "To
   boast of his own Wisdom in the amassing his Money, and insult the Senses and Understanding
   of every Man that has miscarried, is not only a Token of Immodesty, but . . . 'tis the infallible
   Mark of Irreligion; 'tis sacrificing to his own Net, and to his own Drag, to his own Head, and
   to his own Hands."
5. "The Event of Things not always answerable to Second Causes," in *Sermons*, VI, 187–89.
   The proper relation between diligence and dependence had been summed up memorably by
   Donne a century earlier in the third verse letter "To The Countesse of Bedford" (*Poetical
   Works*, edited by H. J. C. Grierson [Oxford, 1912], p. 173):

> Who prayer-lesse labours, or without this,
>   prayes,
> Doth but one halfe that's none; He which
>   said, Plough
> And looke not back, to looke up doth
>   allow.

   Donne alludes to Luke 9:62; John Flavel was to make a similar point in *The Seaman's
   Companion* (1676), in *Whole Works*, II, 267.
6. Compare Benjamin Whichcote, "The Conversion of a Sinner," in *Works*, I, 218: "It was
   never God's intention when he made man at first, to put him into a state of absolute *inde-
   pendency*, or *self-sufficiency*. And therefore whosoever assumes it to himself, doth assume that
   which never did belong to a creature-state."
      Mammon is guilty of that kind of "thoughtfulness for the morrow" that necessarily proceeds,
   as John Howe expresses it, "from an ungovernable spirit, a heart not enough subdued to the
   ruling power of God in the world." Howe's treatise "Of Thoughtfulness for the Morrow," first
   published in 1681, is one of the most systematic explorations of this whole question: see his
   Works, pp. 328–48, esp. p. 333f.

until his conversion he calls his new setting the "Island of Despair," and always refers to it as "a horrible desolate island," "this horrid island," "this dismal unfortunate island," or "that wild miserable place" (pp. 76, 69, 72, 85) [52,49, etc.]. At the outset, then, he does not see wherever he looks acres that cry out for improvement, nor does he settle down to his task glowing with purposive possession.[7] He does set to work, however, and it is worth examining the nature and results of his labors. Two episodes can be singled out which seem to characterize them all, up to the time of his conversion: the springing up of the barley affords one kind of commentary on his efforts, the partial destruction of his cave by earthquake another.

Near his fortification Crusoe shakes out a grain-bag, in which he sees nothing but husks and dust; after the rainy season he finds barley growing on the spot. Dry husks drove the prodigal back to his father's home, and ten or twelve ears of green English barley nearly have the same effect on Crusoe. At first he takes this for a miracle, and begins to bless himself that such a prodigy of nature should happen on his account; he is ready to acknowledge himself the beneficiary of Providence. But when he recalls shaking out the bag in that place, he confesses that "the wonder began to cease" and "my religious thankfulness began to abate, too, upon the discovering that all this was nothing but what was common." As he goes on to reflect, however, "I ought to have been thankful for so strange and unforeseen providence, as if it had been miraculous, for it really was the work of Providence as to me" (pp. 84–86) [58]. In other words, he relapses quickly into what he himself late condemns as an exclusive attention to second causes; he fails to look beyond them to a first cause. He is still the "dunghill wretch" Thomas Lye spoke of, who attributes a crop to natural causes rather than thanking God for it.[8]

The relation between Crusoe's own efforts and God's doing also emerges clearly from the earthquake episode. With his improvised tools, Crusoe struggles to make his cave "spacious enough to accomodate [him] as a warehouse or magazine, a kitchen, a diningroom, and a cellar." In eight minutes an earthquake threatens to ruin the work of six months.

---

7. Crusoe is thus in no frame of mind to exlaim, with Mammon,

> This Desart soile
> Wants not her hidd'n lustre, Gemms and
>   Gold;
> Nor want we skill or art, from whence to
>   raise
> Magnificence; and what can Heav'n shew
>   more?

(P.L., II, 270–78; but cf. Watt, "Robinson Crusoe as a Myth," p. 162.)

8. On the necessity of distinguishing between "second causes" and a "first cause," see Richard Baxter, The Divine Life (1664), in Practical Works (1830), XIII, 32; Isaac Barrow, "On the Gunpowder Treason," in Theological Works (Oxford, 1859), I, 448–49; Samuel Clarke, Sermons, X, 11–12; Joseph Hall, Works, VIII, 28–29. Defoe himself frequently deplored, as in the Review, I, (IX), 2, that "second Causes have the Blessings or Curses of every Action, without any regard to the great first moving Cause of all Things."

But once again, he fails to see God's hand in the matter. As he later remarks, "though nothing could be more terrible in its nature, or more immediately directing to the invisible Power, which alone directs such things, yet no sooner was the first fright over, but the impression it had made went off also."[9] Thus he repeats his error over the barley. In the former case, Providence negates his most assiduous toils. Each episode minimizes, in a different way, the role of Crusoe's own efforts, and correspondingly magnifies the role of Providence. On both occasions Crusoe frustrates the divine intention, for neither blessing nor alarm brings him to a sense of his dependence on God.

Eventually he does gain this awareness; what happens, in fact, is that the labors of the regenerate Crusoe come to fulfill the wishes of the divines quoted earlier. After conversion he does not slacken his efforts, but goes about them in an altogether different spirit. Recognizing that providence plays a decisive and benign role in all his affairs, he learns thankfulness and resignation. Previously, he reports, "the anguish of my soul at my condition would break out upon me on a sudden, and my very heart would die within me. . . . In the midst of the greatest composures of my mind, this would break out upon me like a storm, and make me wring my hands, and weep like a child" (p. 125) [83]. But now, comforted by the Biblical assurance that "I will never, never leave thee, nor forsake thee," Crusoe attains a serenity that no subsequent crises and alarms can long interrupt. It is not the therapy of work that confers this security, but the realization that he is the object of what one bishop calls "that special providence of God, which is man's only security."[1] He gains a sense of well-being, not through purposive possession, but through understanding that God has furnished him a table in the wilderness.[2] What affords him peace of mind is not his success in the role of *homo economicus*, but the discovery that he can rely on Providence for direction and support. By making himself amenable to expressions of the divine will, by becoming alert and tractable, he can at once avail himself of divine assistance, and free himself of the immoderate care rebuked in the Sermon on the Mount. If, as Mr. Watt rightly observes, Crusoe "turns his forsaken estate into a triumph," it is less through sheer labor than through acquiring a sense of dependence; and it is this sense of God's concern and provision for him that keeps such a triumph from being, as Mr. Watt finds it, "a flagrant unreality."[3]

9. Pp. 79, 83, 87, 81, 99; cf. p. 88, [NCE] [55f., 66; cf. p. 60] where Crusoe says, "All this while I had not the least serious religious thought, nothing but the common 'Lord, have mercy upon me!' and when it was over, that went away too."

1. George Bull, *Works*, I, 470; cf. Crane, *Isagoge*, pp. 16, 160–61, and 523.

2. In three places Crusoe echoes the passage from Psalm 78:19: see pp. 104, 143, 164. Compare also the allusion to Elijah and the Ravens (I Kings 17:4–6) at p. 146. In his Autobiography (1711), Robert Knox meditates on the same text: see *An Historical Relation of Ceylon together With somewhat concerning Serverall Remarkeable passages of my life that hath hapned since my Deliverance out of my Captivity*, edited by James Ryan (Glasgow, 1911), p. 400.

3. "*Robinson Crusoe as a Myth*," p. 167.

For, as Coleridge observed long ago, "The carpentering, tailoring, pottery, are all just what will answer his purpose, and those are confined
to needs that all men have, and comforts all men desire. Crusoe rises
only where all men may be made to feel that they might and that they
ought to rise—in religion, in resignation, in dependence on, and thankful acknowledgment of the divine mercy and goodness."[4]

J. PAUL HUNTER

The "Occasion" of *Robinson Crusoe*†

Interpretive problems in eighteenth-century fiction result not so much
from a lack of historical interest and knowledge as from a disguised
antihistoricism in applying known facts, for it is often tempting to use
history rather than surrender to it. Defoe study has, I think, more often
settled for the illusion of history than for a full, rigorous, and sensitive
examination of the assumed contexts of a particular work. Old generalizations have often seemed more valid than they really are because a
façade of fact has obscured a flawed foundation of logic. Such methodology has determined the greater part of *Robinson Crusoe* scholarship,
and I wish to examine some of the assumptions of this methodology
before arguing another series of contexts which, it seems to me, are
more relevant to *Robinson Crusoe* and to the energence of the novel as
a form.

Knowledge of Defoe's political journalism has opened some important
windows to his art, but misuse of this knowledge has also led to some
serious misconceptions. One such set of misconceptions involves the
"occasion"of *Robinson Crusoe*, for Defoe students (working upon assumptions about Defoe's journalistic methods) have reconstructed on
the basis of conjecture the events which inspired *Robinson Crusoe* and
also those which effected its ultimate form. Alexander Selkirk's four-
year sojourn on the desolate island of Juan Fernandez is thus usually
considered to be the direct inspiration for *Robinson Crusoe*;[1] and travel
books (such as those by Edward Cooke and Woodes Rogers, which give
accounts of Selkirk's story) are regarded as formative influences on Defoe's art. This account of Defoe's procedure dates from a generation ago,
but because neither its conclusions nor assumptions have been seriously

4. *Coleridge's Miscellaneous Criticism*, edited by T. M. Raysor (Cambridge, Mass., 1936), p. 300.

† From *the Reluctant Pilgrim*, by J. Paul Hunter, copyright The Johns Hopkins University Press, 1966, pp. 1–22. Reprinted by permission of the publisher and author.

1. Arthur W. Secord's assumption is typical: "Selkirk undoubtedly furnished Defoe with the central theme of the story,—a fact upon which too much emphasis cannot be laid and which I shall assume as fundamental" (*Studies in the Narrative Method of Defoe* ["University of Illinois Studies in Language and Literature," IX; Urbana, 1924], p. 31).

questioned the received opinion is still that articulated by Ernest A.
Baker in 1929: "The original incentive to write *Robinson Crusoe* and
the central idea of a man left by himself on a desert island . . . came
to Defoe from the actual experiences of Alexander Selkirk." The novel
must "be considered as [a] fictitious narrative of travel."[2] This account
of Defoe's design and procedure is, I think, inadequate and inaccurate;
and it seriously misleads us as to the rich and complex traditions which
nourish *Robinson Crusoe*—and which influence the form of an emerging
genre.

The Selkirk conjecture dates from the middle of the eighteenth century
and probably originated from rumors during Defoe's own lifetime.[3] Selkirk's adventure was, of course, well known to Defoe's contemporaries,[4]
but Selkirk was only the most recent of several persons who had endured
long isolation in remote places. Many other "miraculous preservations"
were recorded during the late seventeen and early eighteenth centuries,
and Defoe probably knew as much about some of them as he did about
Selkirk. For example, two other men before Selkirk had been stranded
at separate times on Juan Fernandez, one of them for five years.[5] Another
castaway, Ephraim How, for nearly a year was supposed dead before he
was found alone upon a "rocky desolate Island," where he and two
companions had been cast in a storm. After his companions died, he
had survived by using materials washed ashore from the shipwreck.[6] A
fourth castaway, stranded near Scotland in 1616, had become so notable
an *exemplum* that eighteenth-century writers still repeated his story.[7] A
fifth spent two years alone on an island near the Isle of Providence after
nine of his companions perished either on the island or in trying to
swim to civilization.[8] A sixth, Anthony Thatcher, stranded with his wife
in 1635 after a shipwreck had killed their fellow voyagers, survived by
using clothing and debris from the wreck, much as Crusoe does.[9] Many

2. *The History of the English Novel* (10 vols.; London, 1929–39), III, 147–48, 150.
3. Late in the eighteenth century, James Beattie relates, as "the account commonly given," an
   ancedote about Defoe's taking advantage of Selkirk after hearing Selkirk tell his story personally
   (*Dissertations Moral and Critical* [London, 1783], p. 565). Another rumor during Defoe's
   lifetime insisted that *Robinson Crusoe* was really written by the Earl of Oxford.
4. Accounts of it were published not only in standard travel books but in a periodical (*The
   Englishman*, December 1–3, 1713) and a separately issued tract (*Providence Displayed* [London,
   1712]). But Baker probably exaggerates in calling the incident "*the* great sensation of 1712–
   1713" (*History*, III, 148; italics mine).
5. See Woodes Rogers, *A Cruising Voyage Round the World* (London, 1712), pp. 129–30.
6. See Increase Mather, *An Essay for the Recording of Illustrious Providences* (Boston, 1684), pp.
   58–64; and William Turner, *A Compleat History of the Most Remarkable Providences, Both
   of Judgment and Mercy, Which Have Hapned in This Present Age* (London, 1697), p. 110.
7. See James Janeway, *Token for Mariners, Containing Many Famous and Wonderful Instances
   of God's Providence in Sea Dangers and Deliverances, in Mercifully Preserving the Lives of
   His. Poor Creatures, When in Humane Probability, at the Point of Perishing by Shipwreck,
   Famine, or Other Accidents* (London, 1708), pp. 31–33. Janeway retells the story from Adam
   Olearius, *The Voyages and Travels of the Ambassadors*, trans. John Davies (London, 1962).
   * * *
8. See Increase Mather, *Essay*, p. 71, and Turner, *Remarkable Providences*, p. 110.
9. See Mather, *Essay*, p. 13.

castaways, in fact, underwent hardships much like Crusoe's, reacted to them much as he does, and recounted their experiences in a similarly detailed way.[1]

Any of these castaways might have provided some inspiration for Defoe, but, laying aside for a moment the issue of Defoe's possible indebtedness for facts or incidents, one may question whether any cast-away event provided the major impulse for the creation of *Robinson Crusoe*. Selkirk's adventure is closer in time to the publication of *Robinson Crusoe* than are the other adventures I have cited, but almost seven years separate the publication of *Robinson Crusoe* from the publication of accounts of Selkirk. Because the Selkirk conjecture rests primarily on the assumption that Defoe usually "capitalized" on current news events, this seven-year delay would seem crucial. Pope and Horace may have thought a seven-year waiting period advisable, but no journalist would agree.[2]

The assumption that Defoe's writings all stem from current happenings ignores an important distinction about artistic aim. An event often stimulated Defoe to produce a political tract, for his function as a news analyst for the Whigs and/or Tories often demanded that he interpret the current scene so as to influence the English public. But in other kinds of writing Defoe may well have worked differently. In *The Family Instructor*, for example, and in his other clearly moralistic works, he seems to begin with an ideological aim and to accumulate events (factual or fictional) as examples to support his ideology. The antithetical procedures of the journalist and moralist are only two of many authorial

1. See, for example, Janeway, *Token for Mariners*, Mather, *Essay*, or Turner, *Remarkable Providences*.

2. John Robert Moore's doubts about the Selkirk conjecture on first glance seem to represent an advance over received opinion, but although his conclusion differs from the received one, his assumptions have the same weakness. Moore does not think that Selkirk's return to England in 1712 weighed heavily on Defoe's mind in 1719, but he does regard as significant the contemporary economic situation in South America. He points out that England's war with Spain had severed trade relations between South America and England's South Sea Company, and he argues that Defoe's interest in stimulating colonization near the Orinoco led him somehow to write *Robinson Crusoe*, though he is not explicit about how *Robinson Crusoe* delivers Defoe's economic message. Moore argues that "if [Defoe] wrote a novel in 1719, it would likely have something to say of the slave trade, of the jealousy between England and Spain, of pirates and mutineers. . . , and of an island near the mouth of the Orinoco River." He adds that "no one could have foreseen how Defoe would develop his hero's solitary life on the island," and concludes that the develoment was a " 'strange surprise' to Defoe himself" (*Daniel Defoe: Citizen of the Modern World* [Chicago, 1958], pp. 223–24). Another recent critic, Francis Watson, has also been troubled by standard explanations of Defoe's delay in writing the novel; his reading of *Robinson Crusoe* is salutary, but he offers no new insights about the Selkirk conjecture ("Robinson Crusoe: Fact and Fiction," *Listener*, LXII [October 15, 1959], 617–19).

Earlier scholars suggested that a new 1718 edition of Rogers (which contained the Selkirk story) somehow prompted Defoe, but this suggestion does not seem very helpful unless it is meant to indicate that somehow Defoe's memory was jogged. Only briefly has it been suggested that the inspiration is tied to thematic concerns, and these suggestions have been related to biographical conjectures. Moore thinks that Defoe may have felt some concern for having left the calling (the ministry) for which he prepared at Morton's Academy, or that he may have been concerned with the rebellion of his own son, who showed little inclination to obey his father's wishes.

procedures in which Defoe may have engaged, for living by his pen cast him in a variety of roles. And to see what sort of role he assumed in writing *Robinson Crusoe*, one needs to determine what kind of book it is, for his procedures are much more likely to have been dictated by his aim in an individual work than by a standard scheme or method applied indiscriminately to his more than five hundred publications.[3]

* * *

The assumptions which, when pursued in one direction, lead to the Selkirk conjecture, when pursued in another, lead to more serious misconceptions about *Robinson Crusoe*. Because it is assumed that Defoe began with factual information (largely from travel literature), wove various facts together, embroidered his by now fictional fabric with a semblance of truth, and, finally, tried to pass off the result as a true account, the conclusion is that Defoe desired to imitate his sources and that he wrote in the tradition of fictionalized travel literature. In "placing" *Robinson Crusoe* on the basis of assumptions about Defoe's method rather than on the basis of the book's text, Defoe students have diverted critical attention from relevant materials in other subliterary traditions and have instead defined a context which does a serious injustice to *Robinson Crusoe*, for while Defoe's novel bears some resemblances to travel literature, it differs from that literature in crucial ways.[4]

Source studies of half a century ago are largely responsible for this definition of context. The search for sources turned rather naturally to travel books, for source hunters were first looking for sources of *information*, and travel books were the atlases and geographical encyclopedias of Defoe's day. But the search never really got beyond travel books, for the searchers never really looked beyond factual information, even though they implied that Defoe's dependence on travel books was almost total and influenced even the structure of books like *Robinson Crusoe*. Then too, they were greatly encouraged in their efforts by a strange and surprising bibliographical discovery of 1895.

3. Maximillan Novak has recently suggested that thematic concerns are primary in several of Defoe's works (see *Economics and the Fiction of Daniel Defoe* [Berkeley and Los Angeles, 1962]). Received opinion about Defoe is indicated by the response which Professor Novak's suggestion received. See, for example, the review by Michael Shugrue (*JEGP*, LXII [1963], 403–5), in which "Novak's conviction that 'Defoe created his fiction from ideas rather than from incidents' " is regarded as "perhaps the only disturbing note in an otherwise excellent discussion of *Robinson Crusoe*" (p. 404).

4. At one time, Defoe students recognized that a wider context of traditions nourished *Robinson Crusoe*; they usually mentioned biography, picaresque romance, and moral treatise. But events of the late nineteenth century obscured this contextual richness. The eclipse of Defoe's moral reputation, based on discoveries about his political duplicity, was accompanied by decreasing attention to his ideas, especially moral and religious ones, and emphasis shifted quickly to the adventure-story aspects of his work. At the same time, a new consciousness of the novel as an art form stimulated the desire to evaluate Defoe's contributions to the history of fiction; this desire, combined with the shift of emphasis from ideas to events in Defoe, focused attention on materials from which Defoe could have obtained factual information.

For early discussions of the relationship of Defoe's fiction to other traditions in which he wrote, see George A. Aitken, General Introduction, *Romances and Narratives by Daniel Defoe* (16 vols.; London, 1895), I, xxix ff.; and W. P. Trent, *Daniel Defoe: How To Know Him* (Indianapolis, Ind., 1916), pp. 128, 135, 175. For the rationale behind Defoe source study, see Secord, *Studies*, p. 19.

Defoe's library had been sold a few months after his death in 1731, and although the *Daily Advertiser* for November 13, 1731, mentioned a sale catalogue, no copy of it had been found before 1895, when George A. Aitken located one in the British Museum.[5] The value of the find was considerably diminished, however, by the fact that Defoe's books were grouped with those of an Anglican clergyman, Philip Farewell, and the catalogue failed to distinguish individual ownership.[6] Announcing his find in the *Athenaeum*, Aitken admitted that because of the catalogue's grouping he was "in some cases . . . unable to say positively that a certain book was Defoe's," but he thought that "we shall not be far wrong if we set on one side certain classes of works as Dr. Farewell's and attribute the remainder to [Defoe]." On this assumption, Aitken proposed a partial list of Defoe's books, setting aside as Dr. Farewell's "the large array of theological and classical literature." He admitted that "in adopting this course we shall, no doubt, pass over not a few works of Defoe's, but this is unavoidable."[7]

Aitken listed more than three dozen travel books and maps as probably belonging to Defoe, and later source students seem to have trusted Aitken's list completely.[8] Although one cannot be certain, it is likely that Defoe did own most of the books on Aitken's list, but his background and interests make it equally probable that he owned many of the theological and devotional books passed over by Aitken. The authority of Aitken's list has never been seriously challenged, however, and its publication lent considerable support to the growing tendency to pass over Defoe's ideas and his intellectual background in favor of a quest for the sources of his facts in travel literature. During the next thirty years source students found enough "parallels" to "establish" the debt that they had anticipated, and since 1924 (when Arthur W. Secord's *Studies in the Narrative Method of Defoe* was published) their conclusions about Defoe's sources, his method of composition, and his aims have been accepted almost without dissent.[9]

The placing of *Robinson Crusoe* itself in the tradition of travel literature is ultimately the most misleading implication of such source stud-

5. William Lee had noted the sale and lamented the apparent loss of the catalogue. See his *Daniel Defoe: His Life and Recently Disovered Writings 1716–1729* (3 vols.; London, 1869), I, 470–71.

6. Besides, some of Defoe's books were apparently not sold through the catalogue. The fact that the Farewell-Defoe sale catalogue contains only a few of Defoe's own writings suggests that part of the library had been dispersed before the catalogue was printed. This possibility casts even further doubt on the reliability of the catalogue as a guide to Defoe's reading habits.

7. "Defoe's Library," *Athenaeum*, I (1895), 706–7.

8. Not all scholars who have used Aitken's list have been careful to note the conjecture involved and Aitken's own reservations about the limitations of his list, and their footnotes often cite Aitken's list, not the catalogue itself. Secord and Baker assume the authority of Aitken's judgment. See, for example, Secord, *Studies*, pp. 25, 93, and 104n.

9. Since the late nineteen fifties there have been signs of a growing dissatisfaction with received opinion about Defoe * * *, and, although the conclusions of students of the sources have not been attacked explicitly, the growing awareness of Defoe's artistic complexity has cast some doubt on the generally accepted account of Defoe's imaginative act. But for a recent example of the continuing prominence of source students' procedures, see Gary J. Scrimgeour, "The Problem of Realism in Defoe's *Captain Singleton*" (*HLQ*, XXVII [1963], 21–37).

ies, but an examination of the premises and procedures of such studies warns us to be wary of accepting even their general conclusions. Secord quotes approvingly the belief of Ernest Bernbaum that "originals will ultimately be found for all of [Defoe's] longer narratives,"[1] and although they do not say so openly, most Defoe source students seem to operate from such a premise. Often a subtle suggestion of Defoe's dishonesty hovers just beneath the surface of their analyses, and they seem anxious to attribute a very different role to Defoe's imagination than to the imagination of most writers. As a result, they often attach far too much importance to parallels which are either coincidental or indicate nothing more than the common knowledge of an age—errors which raise serious questions about generalizations we have come to accept.

Secord emphasizes Defoe's debt to Robert Knox's *An Historical Relation of . . . Ceylon* and William Dampier's *A New Voyage Round the World*; among the sources of *Robinson Crusoe*, he lists these as two of six "certain" ones.[2] Yet his conception of what their contribution was and his method of arguing Defoe's debt to them are most revealing. Knox's *Ceylon*, according to Secord, provided Defoe with a number of details about resourcefulness in the face of loneliness and hardship, for although Selkirk's adventure provided the inspiration for Defoe, it did not provide sufficient detail for a long story; Defoe therefore turned to Knox, for his *Ceylon* was "less known but more detailed, and more satisfactory to Defoe for both reasons."[3] Secord admits that Knox's external circumstances differ from Crusoe's—"It is true that Knox was a captive on a large and populous island, that he had a dozen or more fellow Englishmen with him so that occasionally they might converse, and that part of their time they were allowed to live together"—but he thinks these "external differences" may have "blinded investigators to the significance of Knox as a prototype of Crusoe. Both were on islands, both were lonely, and both had their existence to maintain under similar handicaps." Secord then notes the stylistic similarities of the two works ("It was now about the year 1673" [Knox]; "It was now the month of December" [Crusoe]), and he next illustrates Defoe's "borrowing" of events. He notes that "the island experiences of each, for instance, begin at about the same time": Knox's ship is disabled on November 19, 1659, and Crusoe is shipwrecked on September 30, 1659. Both have the ague, both wear out their clothes and try to replace them, Knox uses cocoanut oil in his acquired lamp while Crusoe makes a lamp and uses goat's tallow. After several pages of similar "parallels," Secord admits that

1. P. 18. Secord says that Bernbaum offers this conjecture to explain Defoe's large number of publications.
2. Knox's book was first published in 1681, Dampier's (in two volumes) in 1697 and 1699.
3. P. 32. Assumptions about Defoe's deviousness seem clear here, as in Secord's statement elsewhere that "Defoe is compelled in the island story to go to . . . [great] lengths to disguise his materials borrowed from published sources so that those borrowings may not appear" (p. 26).

"many of these similarities are not in themselves very convincing," but because he is sure that Defoe had read Knox he believes the similarities "become of more than superficial importance." "These matters," he concludes, "were known to Defoe and *could not fail* to find some place in Crusoe's endeavors to work out the problem of existence on his island."[4] Even if writers are a part of all that they have met, one may doubt the value of such source study when no specific debt can be discovered.

As he begins to consider Dampier's Voyages, Secord indicates his conception of Defoe's imaginative act: "If we think of Selkirk as having suggested to Defoe the idea of writing a story of desert island life, and of Knox as having provided him with a concrete embodiment of that idea, we shall not go far astray. Defoe's next need would be a large storehouse of details of life under unusual circumstances from which he could clothe the skeleton furnished by Selkirk and Knox. Exactly such a storehouse of details is Dampie's 'Voyages' "[5] One may doubt the accuracy of this description of creation, but Secord's suggestions about how Defoe used Dampier are even more startling. He does not distinguish clearly between facts and suggestions for episodes, and (as in the Knox argument) his case rests primarily on a long list of inexact parallels and a statement that Defoe must surely have read the book. Defoe might indeed have gotten information about South American geography, climate, and customs from Dampier, but he might just as well have gotten this information from a number of other sources, for to find such facts in both books hardly proves borrowing. As a political journalist aware of his expanding world, as a man of trade, and as a key figure in the formulation of the South Sea Company, Defoe might well have stored facts like these in his head; if not, the men with whom he conversed daily could have supplied him from memory with the kind of information found in Dampier. If one considers this sort of information as a literary source, there is no end of source study, for the encyclopedia and the dictionary (and how would one decide *which* encyclopedia, *which* dictionary?) would be only the first sources studied in attempts to uncover an author's "materials."[6]

4. Pp. 32–39. Italics mine.
5. Pp. 49–50. Secord seems to assume the primacy of printed materials as "sources," apparently believing that an author only makes use of oral information if there is no published word on the subject. Secord also assumes the primacy of English over non-English books, apparently on a similar theory, even though Defoe was conversant with several languages.
6. The immoderate judgment of source students is suggested by Secord's discussion of two episodes—Crusoe's making of planks and his discovery of a footprint. He finds Crusoe's plank-making to be based either upon Dampier or upon information in the private unpublished journal of Knox, even though both Knox and Dampier describe how two planks are made from a tree and Crusoe is able to make but one. Such a derivation might still be possible if we assume Crusoe's more primitive method to be a part of Defoe's artistic strategy, but to regard these two accounts as the exclusive possibilities seems excessive, especially since the methods are rather obvious and would probably occur to anyone needing a plank.
  Secord notes three narratives which contain footprint episodes and attaches much importance

The rage for parallel passages as evidence of borrowing has blurred
the one real contribution of source students: evidence that Defoe
grounded his story on the geographical and cultural facts and beliefs of
his contemporaries, just as he grounded the psychology and religion of
his characters on contemporary belief.[7] But by overstating Defoe's debt
to contemporary knowledge and by localizing it too exclusively, they
have seriously misled us about Defoe's imagination. Once we are aware
of the amount and variety of information available to Defoe about shipwrecks, castaways, and primitive life, we are more likely to be impressed
by his ability to distinguish the norm in the experiences of island castaways than to be convinced that he wrote with a specific incident in
mind. And by generalizing about Defoe's method on the basis of inexact
circumstantial evidence and specious logic, source hunters have successfully (but not accurately) promulgated an image of Defoe as a com-
piler whose art consists in the crafty fusion of unrelated anecdotes.[8]
Lately Defoe's imagination and accomplishment have sometimes been
viewed differently, but still too typical is the judgment of the Oxford
literary historian of Defoe's time: *Robinson Crusoe*, he says, "is not so
much invented as compiled from a number of reports."[9]

The artistry of *Robinson Crusoe* is most seriously maligned, however,
not by viewing the novel's parts as somehow dependent upon travel
books, but by considering its total form to be patterned on the travel
tradition. Source hunters did not set out specifically to "place" *Robinson
Crusoe* within any literary tradition, but, because they failed to distinguish between what Defoe worked from (sources) and what he worked
toward (artistic aims), their conclusions have had the effect of defining
Robinson Crusoe itself as a fictionalized travel book.[1] Such a definition

---

to one of them (in Dampier's *Voyages*) because the print evokes fear. Here is his description
and interpretation of the incident:

> Dampier and some others, being ashore to kill cattle on the isle of Pines (near Cuba), landed
> on a sandy bay where they saw "much footing of men and boys; the impressions seemed to
> be about 8 or 10 days old." "This troubled us a little," said Dampier, who strongly suspected
> them of being the tracks of Spaniards; "but it being now their Christmas, we concluded that
> they were gone over to Cuba to keep it there, so we went after our game. . . ." The element
> of fear is, of course, mild in comparison to that in "Robinson Crusoe," but it is there.

One might, I think, more profitably consider the symbolic overtones of the footprint in *The
Pilgrim's Progress*, though not as a "source" in Secord's sense.

7. I have discussed this subject in my essay, "Friday as a Convert: Defoe and the Accounts of
Indian Missionaries" (*RES*, n.s., XIV [1963], 243–48).
8. The illustrations I have drawn from Secord are, I am afraid, too typical of the evidence and
logic of Defoe source study; I choose my examples from Secord not because he is most
vulnerable, but because he is the most articulate and detailed of Defoe source students. It
now seems almost incredible that Secord's book has been the most influential study of Defoe
in the twentieth century; my concern is that these conjectural conclusions have remained
unchallenged for so long, have guided a majority of Defoe studies in our time, and have
obscured aspects of Defoe's background which bear important implications for the novel as a
form.
9. Bonamy Dobrée, "The Matter-of-Fact Novelist," *Listener*, XLV (1951), 468.
1. Even Professor Secord fails to make this important distinction, and slips into a "placing" of
Robinson Crusoe based on sources: " 'Robinson Crusoe,' finally, is not so much a fictitious
autobiography . . . as it is a fictitious book of travel . . ." (p. 111).

has serious implications for the structure and meaning of *Robinson Crusoe*, as today's critical commonplaces about the novel clearly demonstrate, for, like the Selkirk conjecture, it suggests that Defoe's art is fact-centered rather than idea-centered. Because questionable assumptions and procedures have led to such a definition, the validity of the conclusion is at least doubtful, but ultimately such a definition has to rest (as Shakespearean studies ought to have taught us) not upon the matter of source materials at all, but upon questions of Defoe's aims and those of the travel writers. Examined on this basis, the categorizing of *Robinson Crusoe* as travel literature is even less valid than other conclusions of Defoe source studies, for (aside from a few surface similarities) *Robinson Crusoe* makes no attempt to follow the conventional pattern of the travel tradition.

Despite their subliterary status, travel books early in the seventeenth century developed a set of distinguishing characteristics almost as rigid as the conventions of a poetic genre: each book tried to answer the same kind of questions and each was organized in much the same way. Travel books depended for their success on the continued interest of a buying public with specific expectations, and even when their stated purpose was to offer other benefits, travel writers usually fulfilled those expectations.[2] "I know 'tis generally expected," writes Woodes Rogers in his introduction to *A Cruising Voyage Round the World*, "that when far distant Voyages are printed, they should contain new and wonderful Discoveries with surprizing Accounts of People and Animals,"[3] and like other voyagers, Rogers condemns this popular taste. But, also like others, he satisfies the very expectations which he rails against.

The expectations satisfied by the travel writers are of various kinds. For the reader interested in adventure and strange occurrence, a story like Selkirk's is often included, and though the story is advertised blatantly, usually on the title page, very sparing and professedly grudging attention is given to it in the book itself.[4] Other general readers, like those referred to by Rogers, sought encyclopedic information about exotic places and peoples. The writers, however, seem (or pretend) to be concerned with readers who expect more technical information, and they usually profess that their only desire is to disseminate knowledge which will benefit country and commerce. In practice, all these expectations are ministered to according to a procedural formula with little variation.

Basically, the formula may be described as chronological in movement from place to place, topical in describing the particulars of each place.

2. Reader expectation was, of course, largely determined by familiarity with Hakluyt, Purchas, and their seventeenth-century successors. For a good recent account of travel literature, see Percy G. Adams, *Travelers and Travel Liars* (Berkeley and Los Angeles, 1962).

3. P. xiv.

4. See the title page of Edward Cooke, *A Voyage to the South Sea, and Round the World* (2 vols.; London, 1712). It is always difficult to tell whether the travel writers are sincere in their protestations or whether they are simply repeating a conventional attitude toward reader expectations.

Much geographical detail is given about the places and about the natives and their customs, but there is relatively little emphasis on event. When an unusual happening (like the finding of Selkirk) is described, the tone retains the same calm, dispassionate quality that characterizes the rest of the book, for "objectivity" of tone and style characterizes the tradition as a whole.[5] An important aspect of this objectivity is the absence of any informing idea of theme: chronology, replaced by topicality when the narrative is interrupted to describe a particular place, is the only organizing force in the books, thematic considerations being inappropriate to the "pose" or conventions of the form.[6]

Secord notes that Defoe has Crusoe "do a series of things well known in the literature of travel; suffer storm and shipwreck, endure slavery . . . , duplicate the experiences of desert island life, and participate in both commerce and travel," but the resemblances, as Secord's comparison would suggest, are broad ones.[7] Crusoe describes events in chronological order (after a rationale for the first voyage is established) until the "narrator" returns home from his longest, most arduous voyage. The style is matter-of-fact, and the book contains some of the same kinds of "fact" as do the travel books. When Crusoe is at sea, he frequently gives his position, speed, and direction; on land, he describes the animals and the weapons, food, and customs of the natives. About his island he gives full information, detailing its geography, climatic patterns, animal and plant life, and the sailing conditions around it.

But these superficial similarities lose their significance when one notes Defoe's very different emphasis and his considerably different use of similar materials. In *Robinson Crusoe* the facts about various places are never presented as information for its own sake; each fact is introduced because of its function in the narrative situation. Lions and leopards are described in Africa because they represent, in one case, danger to Crusoe

5. See, for example, the Hakluyt Society edition of Lionel Wafer's *A New Voyage & Description of the Isthmus of America* (ed. L. E. Elliott Joyce [Oxford, 1934]), in which the contrast between Wafer's "Secret Report" and the published version of his travels suggests the tone and manner expected of a narrator in travel literature.

6. The typical narrative first states the author's credentials (previous sea experience) and explains the nature and purpose of the current voyage. The ship is decribed (size, number and type of sails), and often the more important members of the crew are introduced. The log of days at sea is detailed enough for a curious reader to trace the journey; masses of information are given about daily locations, winds, currents, and factors affecting the speed and direction of the voyage. Unusual events (storms, sighting of other ships, dietary problems, pirate encounters, crew changes) sometimes are given extended treatment, but such anecdotes seldom extend beyond two or three pages. On the other hand, topical descriptions of places and peoples visited are usually lengthy. The amount of detail for each place varies, of course, with the knowledge of the voyager and with the general importance of the particular place, but ordinarily such matters as the kinds of fish inhabiting the coastal waters or native methods of building huts get far more attention than any event. Such information may or may not have sold the books, but travel writers at least pretend to think it did.

7. Secord, *Studies*, p. 109. The superficiality of the similarities suggests that instead of attempting to imitate the style and format of travel books (which the author of *The Shortest Way with the Dissenters* could surely do, if he tried) Defoe used features like the title page simply to attract a particular kind of reader, one who was perhaps unlikely to be reached by *The Family Instructor*.

and Xury, and, in another, their means of reciprocating the kindness of the natives. The description of the island accumulates gradually as the narrative unfolds; there is no tabular itemizing of descriptive facts. And the island is the only land area which receives anything like a full description. About Brazil the reader learns only a few things pertinent to Crusoe; during the voyage from Sallee, he is given only facts necessary to the narrative. Here, the description serves the narrative; in the travel books, the narrative often merely connects the various descriptions, which are avowedly the most important parts.

Failure to define the rationale and mode of the travel books has led to a general lack of discrimination between various kinds of books concerned with discovery.[8] *Robinson Crusoe* clearly is more like contemporary adventure stories than like the travel books; information is subordinated to event, and the movement is dramatic. Chronology, simply a convenience in the travel books, becomes for Defoe (as for adventure stories) a conscious device to dramatize development.[9] But even more important, *Robinson Crusoe* has a larger coherence than that produced by the narrative sequence—a coherence which ultimately separates *Robinson Crusoe* from both travel literature and adventure stories, for books in both the latter traditions lack an informing idea which gives a meaning to individual events or to the sequence as a whole. These books seem to lack ideological content, and no thematic meaning can be abstracted from them. Some critics have insisted that *Robinson Crusoe* resembles them in this respect, that it is episodic and lacks fundamental unity. Secord states as a truism that *Robinson Crusoe* "imitates life in its very shapelessness."[1] This view, however, ignores the thematic structure of the novel, a structure set up by the artistic (and ultimately philosophical) rationale for all of Crusoe's wanderings.

8. Throughout this study, I use the term "travel literature" to refer only to published reports of such explorers as Dampier, Rogers, and Cooke. This kind of literature was the chief type used by source students in their work; Secord, for example, lists ten such books as "certain" or "probable" sources of *Robinson Crusoe* and its two sequels. However, he also includes Defoe's *The Storm* and the anonymous *Providence Displayed* as sources of the same type. * * *
   The term travel literature is sometimes used in a broader, less precise sense; a recent English Institute program on travel literature contained, for example, a paper on science fiction (as voyages of the mind). Under a broad enough definition of the term, *The Pilgrim's Progress*, *The Odyssey*, and almost every eighteenth-century novel could fit the category. But it is important to distinguish between different types of publications dealing with travel, and because source students have usually used the term "travel literature" to refer to reports like Dampier's, I have retained their term here. I use it, however, *only* to describe writings like Dampier's, not those with different aims and methods.

9. Adventure stories often involve travel to far-off places, but travel books seldom involve much adventure. When writers like Dampier or Cooke do describe exciting events, they de-emphasize the action in accordance with their avowal that their only concern is information. Events only explain delays in the voyage or difficulties of exploration: they do not structure a sequential relation. Chronology is less a conscious structure than a convenience. Adventure stories—factual or fictional, episodic or unified—use chronology to suggest movement; they depend upon a world of time, for they are concerned with event, not fact. Even when based on actual happenings, they obviously filter- and formulate experience, organizing it in a more or less dramatic manner; travel books, by contrast, pretend to be almost photographic. The difference is that between a story and a report.

1. P. 232.

Crusoe is never merely an aventurer who goes from place to place, participating in isolated events. Each of his experiences takes on meaning in relation to a pattern set in motion by his "fatal . . . Propension of Nature" (A2)—an irrational inclination to roam. His "rambling Thoughts" (A1) cause him to rebel against parental authority and against his divinely appointed "station"—a rebellion which he interprets as his "Original Sin" (A225). Crusoe views each subsequent tragic event as punishment for his rebellion, and at last concludes that real deliverance from his plight (both physical and spiritual) is only possible when he resigns himself completely to the will of God.

Robinson Crusoe is structured on the basis of a familiar Christian pattern of disobedience-punishment-repentance-deliverance, a pattern set up in the first few pages of the book. Crusoe sees each event of his life in terms of the conflict between man's sinful natural propensity, which leads him into one difficulty after another, and a watchful providence, which ultimately delivers man from himself. Crusoe's continual appraisal of his situation keeps the conflict at the forefront of the action throughout, for his appraisal is not the superficial, unrelated commentary some critics have described, but rather is an integral part of the thematic pattern set up by Crusoe's rebellion and the prophecy of his father that Crusoe "will be the miserablest Wretch that was ever born" (A6). On the first page Crusoe plunges himself, through disobedience by reason of pride, into the universal predicament of fallen man; the remainder of the narrative describes that predicament in detail and dramatizes Crusoe's attempts to confront his world—and his God.

Despite its bias, Charles Gildon's criticism of *Robinson Crusoe* is historically valuable because it suggests how Defoe's contemporaries viewed his aim and accomplishment. Gildon cites several improbabilities and historical inaccuracies, but his main objection is not to Defoe's passing off fiction as fact, but to the book's moral and religious point of view:

> I am far from being an enemy to the Writers of Fables, since I know every well that this Manner of Writing is not only very Ancient, but very useful, I might say sacred, since it has been made use of by the inspired Writers themselves; but then to render my Fable worthy of being received into the Number of those which are truly valuable, it must naturally produce some useful Moral . . . but this of *Robinson Crusoe* . . . is design'd against . . . publick good.[2]

2. *The Life and Strange Surprizing Adventures of Mr. D—— De F—— of London, Hosier . . .* (London, 1719), p. 2; reprinted in *Robinson Crusoe Examin'd and Criticis'd*, ed. Paul Dottin (London and Paris, 1923), p. 82. Gildon does not accuse Defoe of failing to inculcate a moral, but of not pointing a *useful* moral.

A Roman Catholic turned deist turned Anglican, Gildon was eager to defend what he now considered the orthodox faith, and his charges are directed primarily against a theological point of view which seems to him unsound and ultimately dangerous.[3] He attacks Defoe's use of the supernatural, and (because he holds a very different, much less orthodox view of God's role in human affairs) he takes issue with almost every religious attitude in the novel. Gildon's motives may have been those of personal jealousy and party animus, but the charges themselves are still revealing, for they suggest that Gildon viewed the book in religious terms and felt that he must attack it ideologically rather than simply expose its fictional nature.

In his statement about *Robinson Crusoe*'s popularity, Gildon suggests that other contemporary readers also saw the book in religious terms. People who buy the book, says Gildon, leave it "as a legacy with the *Pilgrim's Progress,* the *Practice of Piety* and *God's Revenge against Murther.*"[4] The juxtaposition and implied comparison is a sneer at the level of Defoe's readership and suggests (from Gildon's point of view) condemnation by association, for the books he mentions all share a Puritan view of morality and theology. Each of them was well known to Gildon's contemporaries. By 1719, Lewis Bayly's *Practice of Piety* (1613) had reached its fiftieth edition and was probably the best-known Puritan manual of piety and conduct. John Reynolds' *The Triumphs of God's Revenge against Murther* (1621–24) had gone through fewer editions, but it was well known for assigning to providence a particularly active role in human affairs. Bunyan's book, then as now, seemed to epitomize the Puritan view of life.

Ultimately, *Robinson Crusoe* is much closer to *The Pilgrim's Progress* than to the other two books, but it bears a significant relationship to the traditions in which all three of the books belong. In his Author's Preface, Defoe gives two aims of *Robinson Crusoe*: (1) to present "*a religious Application of Events . . . [for] the Instruction of others by this Example,*" and (2) "*to justify and honour the Wisdom of Providence in all the Variety of our Circumstances . . .*" (Avii). These moral and ideological aims have often been regarded as Defoe's afterthoughts or rationalizations; modern scholars have seemed reluctant to take seriously a man who can "lie like truth." But Defoe's Preface, like Gildon's scornful comparison, suggests the connection with Puritan religious traditions; once examined,

3. For an account of Gildon's life and a discussion of his various religious positions, see Dottin's "Life of Gildon" in *Crusoe Examin'd and Criticis'd.* Dottin says that Gildon was resolved "to reap the utmost benefit from his conversion" (p. 22).

4. P. x; in Dottin, p. 72. Because these words are placed in the mouth of "Defoe" in a dialogue, one might suspect that Gildon was simply being facetious—if he did not later attack the book for its theological position on various matters.

   In *Tom Jones,* Fielding suggests a similar contemporary classification, even though (like Gildon) he holds very different religious and philosophical positions. Note the kind of books Fielding lists alongside *Robinson Crusoe* in Bk. VIII, chap. v.

these traditions illuminate both the theme and structure of *Robinson Crusoe* and, ultimately, the development of the novel as a literary form.

JAMES SUTHERLAND

[On *Robinson Crusoe*]†

As every schoolboy used to know, the prototype of Robinson Crusoe was a stubborn and refractory Scottish sailor, Alexander Selkirk (1676–1721), who while cruising on a privateering voyage under the command of William Dampier, quarreled with the captain of his ship, and had himself put ashore in 1704 on the uninhabited island of Juan Fernandez. After some initial difficulties, Selkirk managed to make a life of it, and when he was rescued in January 1709 from his self-inflicted exile by Captain Woodes Rogers, he was in good health and apparently quite satisfied with his island life. He consented, however, to sail with Woodes Rogers, who appointed him mate of his ship. Later he was given command of another ship, and returned at last to London in October 1711. Accounts of his life on Juan Fernandez were published in 1712 by Woodes Rogers and by Captain Edward Cooke, and on 3 December 1713 Steele devoted a whole paper to him in his periodical *The Englishman*. Defoe must have known some or all of these accounts, and it is odd that with his interest in voyages and pirates he made no reference to Selkirk in the *Review* or elsewhere. Steele claimed to have had frequent conversations with Selkirk when he came back to London in 1711, and although nothing is known of Defoe having ever met the Scottish sailor, it seems unlikely that he would not seek him out and learn his story from his own lips.[1]

At all events, *Robinson Crusoe* shares with most of Defoe's later fiction a firm basis in actuality: while his fiction *is* fiction, it often starts from, and in some cases stays very close to, a fact or series of facts. Selkirk's story gave Defoe the situation of a marooned mariner and a few accom-

---

† From *Daniel Defoe: A Critical Study*, Riverside Edition, pp. 123–139, 242–243. Copyright © 1971 by Houghton Mifflin Company. Used with permission. NCE page numbers appear in brackets.

1. Woodes Rogers, *A Cruising Voyage round the World* (1712); Edward Cooke, *A Voyage to the South Sea, and round the World*, 2 vols. (1712). Professor J. Paul Hunter has argued strongly against "the received opinion" that Selkirk's experiences on Juan Fernandez gave Defoe the situation on which he based *Robinson Crusoe*, and that the novel must be considered as a fictitious narrative of travel. "This account of Defoe's design and procedure is, I think, inadequate and inaccurate; and it seriously misleads us as to the rich and complex traditions which nourish *Robinson Crusoe*" (*The Reluctant Pilgrim* . . . , Baltimore, 1966, pp. 2 *et seq.*). While I can readily agree that *Robinson Crusoe* has the religious significance that Professor Hunter demonstrates so ably in his study of Defoe's "emblematic method and quest for form," I do not think that he has shaken the traditional view that Selkirk was what Henry James liked to call the *donnée* of Defoe's story.

panying circumstances—the goats which he tamed, the goatskin cloth-ing, the cats, etc. In Steele's account it is related of Selkirk that he went through a period of deep depression, "grew dejected, languid and mel-ancholy," until gradually "by the force of reason, and frequent reading of the scriptures, . . . he grew thoroughly reconciled to his condition." Selkirk's progress from dejection to equanimity is paralleled by that of Crusoe; but Defoe was quite capable of imagining Crusoe's state of mind without having recourse to Selkirk's. On the other hand, Crusoe's de-scription of his religious exercises may owe something to Steele's account of how Selkirk had formed the habit of using "stated hours and places for exercises of devotion." On any count, however, Defoe's indebtedness to the Selkirk narratives was small; and indeed it was essential for him as a writer of fiction to conceal it as much as possible, since Selkirk's strange experience was comparatively fresh in the public mind, and had recently (1718) been recalled to memory by the publication of a second edition of Woodes Rogers' *Cruising Voyage round the World*. Defoe's hero was not therefore marooned on his island, but cast ashore by shipwreck; the imaginary island was not off the west coast of South America, but off the east coast. When Selkirk was put ashore on Juan Fernandez he lived for some time on a diet of turtles until he could stomach them no longer, but Crusoe doesn't mention his first turtle until he has been on the island for the best part of a year. Selkirk was provided with some bedding, a musket, a pound of gunpowder, a large quantity of bullets, a flint and steel, a few pounds of tobacco, a hatchet, a knife, a kettle, a Bible and some other books, and his mathematical instruments: Crusoe had at his disposal a more extensive collection of firearms and ammunition, and a much more miscellaneous quantity of tools and other material which he had saved from the wreck. And of course Crusoe lived for eight and twenty years on his desert island, whereas the isolated existence of Selkirk lasted for rather less than four and a half years.[2]

There were various other accounts of shipwrecked seamen, real or fictitious, on which Defoe could have drawn, and he may have taken a few hints from one or other of those, such as *A Relation of the Great Sufferings . . . of Henry Pitman* (1689). What is not in doubt is the frequent use he made of Dampier's *A New Voyage round the World*; and Professor A. W. Secord has drawn particular attention to two other sources, Robert Knox's *Historical Relation of Ceylon* (1681) and Max-imilien Misson's fictitious *Voyage of François Leguat* (1707). Although Knox's twenty-year captivity in Ceylon was very different from Crusoe's prolonged stay on his desert island, there are a number of resemblances in their activities, and (as Secord pointed out) Knox was much closer in character and personality to Crusoe than was Selkirk, and Defoe may

2. Richard Steele, *The Englishman*, ed. Rae Blanchard (Oxford, 1955), pp. 107, 109, 107.

even have known Knox and have used him as the model for Crusoe.[3]

In Defoe's own day readers of all classes—from Alexander Pope to every "old woman that can go to the price of it"—enjoyed *Robinson Crusoe* as a story of "strange, surprizing adventures." Twentieth-century critics have seen it as more than just that; but it is primarily as an adventure story that it still lives, and its continuing vitality is largely due to the skill and narrative confidence with which Defoe told it. In one of his less generous moments Dr. Johnson, who disliked Jonathan Swift, told Boswell that there was nothing especially remarkable about *Gulliver's Travels*. "When once you have thought of big men and little men," he said, "it is very easy to do all the rest." On the same grounds it might presumably be argued that once Defoe had thought of the desert island, his story of the shipwrecked Crusoe practically wrote itself. Defoe, however, showed a quite unusual ability to enter imaginatively into the situation he was developing, and to devise circumstances and events that would enable, and even compel, the reader to realize Crusoe's predicament and share vicariously in his difficulties. If we are to judge him as a novelist we have to admit that he had serious limitations; but he had in abundant measure one of the most essential gifts of the novelist, the ability to put himself in someone else's place, even to the extent of almost losing his own identity in that of a fictitious character—as he had done with such disastrous results to himself when he wrote *The Shortest Way with the Dissenters*. On the other hand, he is usually able to do this with only one character at a time, the hero (or heroine) who is the teller of the tale: the other characters are apt to be seen from the outside, and to have importance only in so far as they are involved in the life of the chief character. How far something of Defoe himself creeps into his heroes and heroines is a question that will be discussed later.[4]

In all his works of fiction Defoe was almost certainly inventing continuously as he went along. In *Robinson Crusoe*, for example, after twelve separate journeys to the wreck, during which Crusoe brings ashore all that he can lay his hands on and is able to move, a storm blows up, and in the morning the ship has disappeared from view. A few pages further on, however, Crusoe enumerates a number of things that he had "omitted setting down before," including pens, ink, and paper, three Bibles, some mathematical instruments, etc. "And I must not forget that we had in the ship a dog and two cats, of whose eminent history I may have occasion to say something in its place." It is of course entirely natural that Crusoe should temporarily forget some of the things he had saved from the wreck, and their mention a little later certainly

3. Secord, [*Studies in the Narrative Method of Defoe* (Urbana, Illinois, 1924)], p. 109 and *passim*.
4. Charles Gildon, *The Life and Strange Surprizing Adventures of Mr. D——— De F——— of London, Hosier* (1719), p. x (quoted in Lee, i. 298); *Boswell's Life of Johnson*, ed. George Birkbeck Hill, rev. L. F. Powell (Oxford, 1934), ii. 319.

does no damage to the credibility of the narrative. But anyone familiar with Defoe's casual mode of composition will be tempted to see this late introduction of the dog and the two cats as an afterthought. At this point in his narrative he may well have said to himself, "This is my last chance of letting Crusoe save anything more from the wreck. What else would be interesting or useful for him to have?" Later on, the pens, ink, and paper, the faithful dog, the two cats (one of which proves highly fertile), and above all the Bibles, all play their part in Crusoe's story.[5]

It is often possible to look over Defoe's shoulder in this way as he writes, and to watch him correcting or modifying some statement that he has just made. Like Shakespeare, he seems never to have blotted a line, and the stream of his writing merely flowed round any obstacle in its way. Near the end of *Robinson Crusoe*, when the Spaniard whom Crusoe has saved from the cannibals along with Friday's father, plans to return to the mainland and rescue his fellow countrymen and bring them to the island, he wisely suggests that before he makes the attempt it would be advisable to grow enough barley and rice to feed them. Accordingly they all set to work,

> and in about a month's time, by the end of which it was seed time, we had gotten as much land cur'd and trim'd up as we sowed 22 bushels of barley on and 16 jarrs of rice, which was, in short, all the seed we had to spare; nor indeed did we leave our selves barely sufficient for our own food for the six months that we had to expect our crop, that is to say, reckoning from the time we set our seed aside for sowing, for it is not to be supposed it is six months in the ground in the country.

As Defoe was writing this passage, it looks as if he may have been thinking of the six months it would take *in England* from the time of sowing to the ripening and harvesting of a crop of barley; and then, or some time later, he remembered that conditions were very different on the island. Instead of canceling the "six months," however, he preferred to offer the rather lame explanation that he was reckoning from "the time we set our seed aside for sowing." If anyone should argue that the "six months" is not a slip at all, and that if it is, it is Crusoe's, and therefore another example of Defoe's verisimilitude, I cannot prove that he is wrong; but I would suggest that on the balance of probability it is Defoe's mistake rather than Crusoe's. But here, of course, the autobiographical form in which he chose to tell his various stories gives him a complete answer to those critical readers who may detect anomalies or contradictions or repetitions or other defects of composition. None of his heroes or heroines is a professional writer, and some of them have had little or no formal education. What more natural, therefore, for a Crusoe or a Singleton to make mistakes when he has a pen in his hand? Their very

5. *Robinson Crusoe*, i. 73 [48].

mistakes and awkwardnesses are a kind of guarantee of their authenticity: Defoe can't lose.[6]

At all events, he almost certainly wrote his various narratives in much the same way as an adult tells a serial bedtime story to a child, making up most of it as he went along. Anyone who has ever told such a story has probably made some slips which are instantly pounced upon by the vigilant young listener, who would be the first to object that Crusoe couldn't possibly have taken his parrot with him on board the ship that rescued him since he had already said that he left it on the island and that "poor Poll may be alive there still, calling after *Poor Robin Crusoe* to this day." Defoe made many such slips. "I must beg my reader's indulgence," he wrote in his old age, "being the most immethodical writer imaginable. It is true I lay down a scheme, but fancy is so fertile I often start fresh hints, and cannot but pursue them." He had undoubtedly laid down a scheme for *Robinson Crusoe*, but it is equally evident that many of his best things came to him on the spur of the moment. All creative writing is a compromise between the foreseen and the fortuitous. If the novelist foresees everything, we may lose the casual and disorderly and spontaneous impression made by real life; if everything is fortuitous, we have nothing but a chronological and unrelated series of events.[7]

That said, it should be added that the first part of *Robinson Crusoe* shows many indications of having been more carefully planned than most of Defoe's fictitious narratives. One small but significant sign of this is the extent to which he anticipates later developments. In the passage about the dog and the two cats already quoted, it will be remembered that Crusoe adds, "of whose eminent history I may have occasion to say something in its place." They duly reappear, but perhaps the "may" indicates that at this stage in the composition of *Robinson Crusoe* Defoe was not sure what he would do about them, and was therefore making no promises. But there are many phrases like "of which in its place" or "as will be observed hereafter" which indicate that Defoe was thinking ahead, and not just drifting along as his fancy took him. It is true that there are numerous repetitions (some perhaps conscious, others unconscious), loose ends, and contradictory statements; but these are in effect trivial, and due, no doubt, to Defoe's writing at odd times or in haste, and failing to revise his manuscript before publication. All this is very unlike Flaubert or Henry James, but it is not very unlike Sir Walter Scott. Some idea of the speed at which Defoe wrote may be seen from the appearance of *The Farther Adventures of Robinson Crusoe* slightly less than four months after the publication of the first part. At the conclusion of *The Life and Strange Surprizing Adventures* Defoe had dangled the prospect of a sequel before his readers, and had even given a brief forecast of its contents; but it is unlikely that he had written

6. *Ibid.*, ii. 36f [178f.].
7. *Ibid.*, i. 209 [130–31]; *Augusta Triumphans*, 1728 (*Works, 1840*, xvii. 27).

any of it before the success of the first part encouraged him to proceed.[8]

A more important indication of the way in which the first part of *Robinson Crusoe* was planned is to be found in Defoe's careful treatment of the first days on the island. It was wise of him to equip his hero with some tools, but it was still wiser not to give him too many. One of the strongest impressions made upon the reader of *Robinson Crusoe* is the sense of difficulty and frustration encountered by Crusoe in his attempts to create order out of disorder and comfort out of privation. What this unfortunate castaway hasn't got therefore becomes as important as what he has. He has, for example, no needles, pins, or thread; to Crusoe, who has a puritanical horror of going naked, and who keeps his breeches and stockings on when swimming out to the wreck, this was to prove a serious deprivation. When his supply of clothing wore out, he "made but a very sorry shift indeed" to construct breeches and drawers; and when at a later stage he ran together a suit of goatskin, it was "wretchedly made." More serious was his lack of either a pick-axe or a shovel. For the first of these some iron levers proved to be a practical substitute, but the shovel had to be painfully constructed from the wood of a tree "which in the Brasils they call the Iron Tree," hacked and trimmed into shape with his axe. With this primitive implement Crusoe was able to till the ground that later produced his crops of barley and rice, harrowing the freshly-dug soil by dragging "a great heavy bough of a tree over it." Nature duly played her part, but more frustration was to follow: when the corn was in the blade, goats and hares broke in and ate it, and Crusoe was forced to tie his dog to a stake, "where he would stand and bark all night long." He managed to drive off the goats, but most of what was saved in the blade was devoured in the ear when clouds of birds descended on it. All through such trials the reader shares in Crusoe's anxieties and rejoices with him in his little triumphs. "This want of tools," he tells us, "made every work I did go heavily." Yet we watch him making do with what he has, solving one problem after another, and constructing his own clumsy equivalents of chairs, tables, baskets, etc. In this way he contrived to make some earthenware pots after a period of trial and error during which many fell in and others fell out. As the ex-proprietor of a brick and tile factory Defoe could have given Crusoe some useful advice, but he is left to think things out for himself, and do the best he can. He is, as Coleridge said,

> the universal representative, the person for whom every reader could substitute himself. . . . And in what he does, he arrives at no excellence; he does not make basket work like Will Atkins; the carpentering, tailoring, pottery, etc. are all just what will answer his purposes, and those are confined to needs that all men have, and comforts that all men desire."[9]

8. *Robinson Crusoe*, ii. 107 [220].
9. *Ibid.*, i. 155, 172, 83, 136, 133, 133f., 74, 137ff. [98, 108, 54, 86, 85f.; 49, 87ff.]; *The Literary Remains of Samuel Taylor Coleridge*, ed. H. N. Coleridge (1836), i. 197.

Crusoe's successes are nicely balanced by his failures. When he is returning on his raft after his first visit to the wreck, he accidently runs it on to a shoal, and has to use all his strength for the next half hour to keep the cargo from sliding into the water (another memorable picture of frustration), until the rising tide floats the raft level again. On a later journey from the wreck he is less fortunate, and loads the raft so heavily that it oversets and tips the whole cargo into the sea. What is needed for this sort of writing is something that Defoe had in full measure, a talent for make-believe. The process is seen in its purest form in the games played by children when they act out an imaginary situation or series of events. How near Defoe often came to reviving the memories of childhood may be seen from the numerous occasions on which Crusoe contemplates his little kingdom with a sort of naive and playful delight:

> It would have made a stoick smile to have seen me and my little family sit down to dinner. There was My Majesty, the Prince and Lord of the whole island; I had the lives of all my subjects at my absolute command. I could hang, draw, give liberty, and take it away, and no rebels among all my subjects.
>
> Then to see how like a king I din'd too all alone, attended by my servants. Poll, as if he had been my favourite, was the only person permitted to talk to me. My dog, who was now grown very old and crazy, and had found no species to multiply his kind upon, sat always at my right hand, and two cats, one on one side of the table, and one on the other, expecting now and then a bit from my hand, as a mark of special favour.

Similarly, in the *Farther Adventures* Crusoe tells us that his island dominion has been divided up in his absence into three colonies, and that his old habitation under the hill was now "the capital city."[1]

Simple make-believe and empathy may account for much of what Defoe has to give us in *Robinson Crusoe*, but occasionally they are accompanied by a psychological insight that may surprise us. When, for example, Crusoe fells with infinite labor a huge cedar tree and sets to work to hack out of it a periagua big enough to have carried twenty-six men, he has no thought of how he is going to get it to the sea. When he does begin to be conscious of this problem, he still refuses to face it: "I put a stop to my own enquiries into it by this foolish answer which I gave myself, *Let's first make it, I'll warrant I'll find some way or other to get it along when 'tis done.*" This looks very unlike the careful and provident Crusoe that we have come to know; but his normal canniness has given way to the excitement of finding a means to leave the island, and with this *idée fixe* controlling his thoughts he can think of nothing else. "This was a most preposterous method," he admits; "but the eagerness of my fancy prevail'd, and to work I went." The ordinary process

---

1. *Robinson Crusoe*, i. 58, 63f., 171 [39, 42f., 108]; *ibid.*, iii, 12.

of make-believe has here been transformed by the perception of a creative writer who is interested, as Wordsworth was, in "the manner in which we associate ideas in a state of excitement."[2]

"I had never handled a tool in my life," Crusoe tells us, "and yet in time by labour, application, and contrivance, I found at last that I wanted nothing but I could have made it. . . ." When Defoe was writing, the division of labor was already well advanced, and skills which were common even in the Elizabethan age had now become specialized, or had been supplanted by the machine. Even the earliest readers of *Robinson Crusoe*, therefore, were able to find pleasure in Crusoe's primitive carpentry, pottery, bread-making, basket-weaving, etc., with which the growing specialization of industry had begun to make them unfamiliar. If this was true of Defoe's contemporaries, it is still more so today. As Professor Ian Watt has said, the extent to which we have been deprived by economic specialization "is suggested by the way our civilisation has reintroduced some of the basic economic processes as therapeutic recreations: in gardening, home-weaving, pottery, camping, woodwork and keeping pets, we can all participate in the character-forming satisfactions which circumstances force on Defoe's hero. . . ."[3]

Ultimately, much of the power of *Robinson Crusoe* lies in its appeal to the permanent feelings and essential interests of the human race. In this story Defoe achieved a drastic simplification of society and social relationships, and by stripping life of its inessentials he got down to the roots of human experience. This return to the essential can hardly have been difficult for him: he was never far from it in his own life. He had none of the artificiality and little of the sophistication of the polite writers of the day; he habitually wrote plain English, called a rogue a rogue, and a whore a whore, and continually reduced moral and religious problems, political issues, and economic policies to the simplest terms. So much is this sharp dichotomy between good and bad, right and wrong, true and false inseparable from his normal way of thinking, that when, for example, Moll Flanders tell us her story she never pretends that the life she is living is anything but wrong, and the title-page informs us that she was "twelve year a whore" and "twelve year a thief." Defoe's black-and-white view of things undoubtedly leads at times to oversimplification (however effectively it enabled him to make his points as a controversialist), but in *Robinson Crusoe* it tends rather to clear the way for an uncomplicated vision of life lived on its simplest and most essential terms.

In some ways Defoe was the most unpoetical soul alive, and in all his stories we are conscious of the background of the countinghouse, of

2. *Ibid.*, i. 145ff. [92ff.]; Wordsworth, Preface to *Lyrical Ballads*, 1800 (*Wordsworth's Literary Criticism*, ed. Nowell C. Smith, 1905, p. 14).
3. *Robinson Crusoe*, i. 77 [51]; Watt, *The Rise of the Novel* (Berkeley and Los Angeles, 1957), p. 72.

profit and loss and periodical stock-taking. Yet in this famous story, in which he has succeeded in transporting us into a closed world of his own imagining, he comes nearer to being a poet than he had ever been before or would ever be again. It was the belief of Wordsworth that the passions and thoughts and feelings of the poet were essentially those of all men. And with what, he asked, are they connected?

> Undoubtedly with our moral sentiments and animal sensations, and with the causes which excite these; with the operations of the elements, and the appearances of the visible universe; with storm and sunshine, with the revolution of the seasons, with cold and heat, with loss of friends and kindred, with injuries and resentments, gratitude and hope, with fear and sorrow. These, and the like, are the sensations and objects which the Poet describes, as they are the sensations of other men, and the objects which interest them.

There is little in this catalogue that we do not find in *Robinson Crusoe*; and as for "loss of friends and kindred, gratitude and hope, fear and sorrow," we find them on every other page. When, for example, Crusoe has suffered a change of heart as a result of his experiences on the island, and has learned to depend upon God's providence, he looks back on the days of despair before the grace of God had entered his soul:

> Before, as I walk'd about, either on my hunting, or for viewing the country, the anguish of my soul at my condition would break out upon me on a sudden, and my very heart would die within me, to think of the woods, the mountains, the desarts I was in, and how I was a prisoner lock'd up with the eternal bars and bolts of the ocean, in an uninhabited wilderness, without redemption. In the midst of the greatest composures of my mind this would break out upon me like a storm, and make me wring my hands, and weep like a child.

This moving passage (it might be described in Wordsworthian terms as one of emotion recollected in tranquillity) has the large simplicity of Bunyan, and may indeed owe something to the author of *The Pilgrim's Progress*. At all events, the general level of emotion is higher in *Robinson Crusoe* than in any other of Defoe's works of fiction; and to meet with any comparable expressions of feeling we must go to his *Appeal to Honour and Justice*, and to his private correspondence with Harley and others in hours of personal crisis and distress, i.e. to his autobiographical writings. In *Serious Reflections . . . of Robinson Crusoe* he hinted that the whole story was really an allegory of his own life; and however we may judge this claim, the impression remains that he is more deeply involved in the story of his shipwrecked mariner than in any other of his works of fiction. The frequent poignancy of feeling in *Robinson Crusoe*, and the intensity with which Defoe realizes the loneliness and anguish of his hero, are compatible with some kind of self-involvement on the part of the author in the vicissitudes and sufferings that he describes.[4]

As a story, *Robinson Crusoe* has the firm and satisfying structure of a man triumphing over difficulties, creating his own little cosmos out of what, if he had been merely idle and despondent, must have remained chaos. In most of Defoe's fiction the situation is that of the hero or heroine alone against the world, surviving by dint of perseverance and ingenuity and sheer native energy; but nowhere is that situation brought home to us more forcibly than in *Robinson Crusoe*. The hero has his moments of self-pity and even despair, but these have the effect of intensifying our awareness of his desperate plight. If all Defoe's heroes and heroines give the impression of being solitaries, even when they are living in crowded cities, the physical isolation of Crusoe is for many years complete, and, for all he can see, likely to be permanent. Some form of companionship is provided by the faithful dog, the cats, the parrot, the goats, and later by the arrival of Friday on the island. But although Friday provides him with a human companion, and is more useful to Crusoe than his now defunct dog was, he remains essentially a more versatile, articulate, and amusing dog, and Crusoe is still left alone to wrestle with his own thoughts and problems. As Professor Watt notes, his relations with Friday are egocentric: he "does not ask his name, but gives him one"—in the same way in which one names a pet animal. It is not until the arrival of the Spaniards that the spell of loneliness is broken and Crusoe can resume his place in human society which has been for so long in abeyance.[5]

This isolation of a human soul would normally provide the conditions usually associated with tragedy. The story of Crusoe's fight for survival certainly arouses both pity and fear, and in his indomitable struggle with dangers and difficulties he comes near at times to heroic stature. But Defoe avoids the tragic implications of Crusoe's position. Crusoe's very virtues perhaps incapacitate him for being a tragic hero. For one thing, his usual response to the vicissitudes of fortune is not some grand gesture or defiant utterance but immediate practical application. There is something almost ant-like in his activity as he goes to and from the wreck during his first two weeks on the island, carrying back hatchets, Dutch cheeses, bottles of cordial waters, bags of nails, fowling-pieces, and the rest. We expect action from a tragic hero, but not this sort of action, at once so detailed, dispersed, and miscellaneous: when the tragic hero strikes back it is normally with one great blow of gathered strength that brings down the pillars of the temple, and characteristically, too, he enables us to realize his tragic situation by the eloquence and imaginative power of speech. Defoe seems to be almost committed to avoiding such moments of revelation. After his twelfth visit to the wreck Crusoe ex-

4. Wordsworth, Preface to *Lyrical Ballads*, 1800 (ed. cit., pp. 29f.); *Robinson Crusoe*, i. 130 [82–83]; *Serious Reflections . . . of Robinson Crusoe* (1720), Preface.
5. Watt, p. 69.

periences some difficulty in reaching the shore again, for a sudden storm
has made the water rough. None the less, carrying several razors, a pair
of large scissors, some ten or a dozen knives and forks, and about £36
of gold and silver coins, all wrapped up in a piece of canvas, he swims
back through the choppy seas:

> . . . I was gotten home to my little tent, where I lay with all my
> wealth about me very secure. It blew very hard all that night, and
> in the morning when I look'd out, behold no more ship was to be
> seen. I was a little surpriz'd, but recover'd my self with this satis-
> factory reflection, *viz.* that I had lost no time, nor abated no dil-
> ligence to get every thing out of her that could be useful to me,
> and that indeed there was little left in her that I was able to bring
> away if I had had more time.

Behold, no more ship! It is just here that nine out of ten great writers
would have chosen to make the reader feel the full impact of Crusoe's
now complete isolation. As long as the wrecked ship was still there it
was a link of sorts with civilization and with Crusoe's past; but now that
it had disappeared, Crusoe had nothing to look upon but a waste of
waters. Yet so far is Defoe from dwelling on the finality of this event
that he seems to go out of his way to belittle it: Crusoe was "a little
surprized." The practical reflection and self-congratulation that follow
are typical of Crusoe, and no doubt of Defoe himself. To deny heroism
to Crusoe, however, is perhaps to take too histrionic a view of the heroic.
Crusoe has the heroism of London's wartime firemen and air-raid war-
dens digging in the rubble for survivors after an "incident," or of the
blitzed shopkeeper "carrying on" as usual the next morning. This is the
heroism of the practical and the imperturbable; it lives in an atmosphere,
not of cloud-capped towers, but of unemotional comment and habitual
understatement.[6]

Is *Robinson Crusoe* a simple story of adventure, or has it a deeper
significance? In recent years critics have tended to concentrate attention
on the character of Crusoe, and to interpret his story in accordance with
his ruling passion. More especially, they have dwelt upon that "original
sin" about which Crusoe himself expatiates at some length:

> I have been in all my circumstances a *memento* to those who are
> touch'd with the general plague of mankind, whence, for ought I
> know, one half of their miseries flow; I mean that of not being
> satisfy'd with the station wherein God and nature has plac'd them;
> for not to look back upon my primitive condition, and the excellent
> advice of my father, the opposition to which was, as I may call it,
> my ORIGINAL SIN, my subsequent mistakes of the same kind
> had been the means of my coming into this misearable condition;
> for had then Providence, which so happly had seated me at the
> Brasils as a planter, bless'd me with confin'd desires, and I could

6. *Robinson Crusoe*, i, 65 [43].

have been contented to have gone on gradually, I might have been by this time (I mean, in the time of my being in this island) one of the most considerable planters in the Brasils.

To Professor Watt, Crusoe is a characteristic embodiment of economic individualism. "Profit," he assures us, "is Crusoe's only vocation," and "only money—fortune in its modern sense—is a proper cause of deep feeling." Watt therefore claims that Crusoe's motive for disobeying the commands of his father and leaving home was to better his economic condition, and that the argument between himself and his parents in the early pages of the book is really a debate "not about filial duty or religion, but about whether going or staying is likely to be the most advantageous course materially: both sides accept the economic motive as primary." We certainly cannot afford to ignore those passages in which Crusoe attributes his misfortunes to an evil influence that hurried him on to "the wild and indigested notion of raising my fortune," and into "projects and undertakings beyond my reach, such as are indeed often the ruine of the best heads in business," and that drove him "to pursue a rash and immoderate desire of rising faster than the nature of the thing permitted." These are among the very errors and temptations that Defoe was to enlarge upon in *The Complete English Tradesman*, and that had proved fatal to him in his early years as a merchant. But surely the emphasis here is not on the economic motive as such, but on the willingness to gamble and seek for quick profits beyond what "the nature of the thing permitted."[7]

Crusoe's father wished him to take up the law as a profession, and if Crusoe had done so and had prospered he might have become a very wealthy man indeed. Professor Novak seems to come nearer to the truth when he attributes Crusoe's failure to accept his father's choice for him to his personal characteristics: "his lack of economic prudence, his inability to follow a steady profession, his indifference to a calm bourgeois life, and his love of travel." On the very first page Crusoe tells us that he could "be satisfied with nothing but going to sea"; his inclination in that direction was so strong that "there seem'd to be something fatal in that propension of nature tending directly to the life of misery which was to befal me." The modern reader may miss the true force of the word "fatal": Defoe almost certainly intended it to suggest that Crusoe's longing to go to sea was decreed by destiny, and therefore beyond his power to resist. Elsewhere Crusoe tells his father that his thoughts were "so entirely bent upon seeing the world" that he could never bring himself to settle down at home; and looking back on his highly favorable prospects as a planter in the Brasils, he reflects that all his miscarriages had come about "by my apparent obstinate adhering to my foolish inclination of wandring abroad and pursuing that inclination," when he might so easily have prospered by a "plain pursuit of those prospects

7. *Ibid.*, i. 225 [140–41]; Watt, pp. 67, 70, 65; *Robinson Crusoe*, i, 16, 42 [13, 29].

and those measures of life which nature and providence concurred to present me with, and to make my duty." Back in England after his adventures, he married and settled down, but the old restlessness returned on the death of his wife: he was "inur'd to a wandring life," and "had a great mind to be upon the wing again." In the *Farther Adventures* he tells us again of his "native propensity to rambling" and of his inability to resist "the strong inclination I had to go abroad again, which hung about me like a chronical distemper." He even states expressly that his motives were *not* economic, "for I had no fortune to make, I had nothing to seek: if I had gain'd ten thousand pound, I had been no richer." His subsequent travels in the *Farther Adventures* were due to nothing but "a deep relapse into the wandring disposition, which, as I may say, being born in my very blood, soon recover'd its hold of me, and like the returns of a violent distemper, came on with an irresistible force upon me."[8]

Unless we are to say—and we have no right to say it—that Crusoe did not know himself, profit hardly seems to have been his "only vocation." Instead, we are presented with a man who was driven (like so many contemporary Englishmen whom Defoe either admired or was fascinated by) by a kind of compulsion (a "strong inclination") and a fever in the blood ("a chronical distemper," "a violent distemper") to wander footloose about the world. As if to leave no doubt about his restless desire to travel, Crusoe contrasts himself with his partner, the very pattern of the economic motive and of what a merchant ought to be, who would have been quite happy to go on trading on the same route, and "to have gone like a carrier's horse, always to the same inn, backward and forward, provided he could, as he call'd it, *find his account in it*." Crusoe, on the other hand, was like a rambling boy who never wanted to see again what he had already seen. "My eye," he tells us, "which like that which Solomon speaks of, *was never satisfied with seeing*, was still more desirous of wand'ring and seeing." Here it seems to be reasonable to detect an autobiographical element in *Robinson Crusoe*: If Defoe had seen a good deal less of the world than Crusoe, he was none the less an inveterate traveler. He may have made several visits to the continent of Europe in his earlier years, and although the extent of his travels is not certainly known, they have been plausibly pieced together by Professor Moore. In his preface to A *Tour thro' the Whole Island of Great Britain* he claimed to have gathered his material in "seventeen very large circuits, or journeys" and "three general tours over almost the whole English part of the island," besides having "travell'd critically" over most of Scotland. Such tourism was quite exceptional in the early eighteenth century; and as for countries which he had been unable to visit in person, he was still an eager mental traveller, poring over atlases and maps and the accounts of voyagers gathered

8. Maximillian E. Novak, *Economics and the Fiction of Daniel Defoe* (Berkeley and Los Angeles, 1962), p. 32; *Robinson Crusoe*, i. 1f., 2, 5, 42, 104 [4, 6, 29, 67]; *ibid.*, ii. 111, 112, 111, 117.

together by Hakluyt and Purchas, or written by such of his contemporaries as Dampier and Woodes Rogers. At all events, no one was better fitted than Defoe to understand Crusoe's wanderlust.[9]

The refusal of Crusoe to follow the "calling" laid down for him by his father has, as Professor Novak has suggested, religious implications. Those implications have been investigated in greater detail by Professor G. A. Starr, who has shown convincingly how the various stages in Crusoe's religious development—from original sin to spirtual hardening (during the eight years of "seafaring wickedness" when he conversed only with sinners like himself, "wicked and profane to the last degree") to a gradual repentance and ultimate conversion—follow closely the established pattern of seventeenth-century spiritual autobiography. Starr points out that the writers of those autobiographies show the same sort of concern as Crusoe with omens and portents, and with the apparently direct intervention of providence in the life of the individual; and that the imagery by which they seek to express their spiritual travails is often paralleled by the actual physical sufferings and vicissitudes of Crusoe. When all such evidence is taken into account (together with that offered by Professor J. Paul Hunter in a similar study), the religious element in Robinson Crusoe is seen as the common property of English Protestantism; and it is clear that otherworldly concerns do a great deal more than merely punctuate the narrative with what Professor Watt calls "comminatory codas." If Crusoe is not the Platonic pattern of a converted sinner, his life history is at least a progress from the careless self-indulgence of the natural man, without forethought or reflection, to a life of reason and introspection and ultimately of faith; and it is in this progress towards repentance and moral stability that Professor Starr finds the structural unity of Robinson Crusoe. Defoe's hero never shows the least signs of becoming a saint—he remains a man like ourselves—but he ceases to be a mere sinner.[1]

JOHN J. RICHETTI

Robinson Crusoe: The Self as Master†

You are not to take it, if you please, as the saying of an ignorant man, when I express my opinion that such a book as Robinson Crusoe never was written, and never will be written again. I have tried that book for years—generally in combination with a pipe of tobacco—and I have found it my friend in

9. Ibid., iii. 111, 110; Moore, [Daniel Defoe, Citizen of the Modern World (Chicago, 1958)], pp. 276ff.; A Tour thro' . . . Great Britain (Everyman ed., n.d.), p. 3.
1. Novak, op. cit., pp. 40ff.; Starr, passim; J. Paul Hunter, op. cit., passim; Watt, p. 81.
† This essay appeared in a longer version as chapter 2 in Defoe's Narratives, Situations and Structures (Oxford: Clarendon Press, 1975), pp. 21–62. The author has abridged his chapter especially for this edition. © Oxford University Press 1975. By permission of Oxford University Press.

need in all the necessities of this mortal life. When my spirits are bad—
Robinson Crusoe. When I want advice—Robinson Crusoe. In past times,
when my wife plagued me; in present times, when I have had a drop too
much—Robinson Crusoe. I have worn out six stout Robinson Crusoes with
hard work in my service. On my lady's last birthday she gave me a seventh.
I took a drop too much on the strength of it; and Robinson Crusoe put me
right again. Price four shillings and sixpence, bound in blue, with a picture
into the bargain.

Wilkie Collins, *The Moonstone*

Near the very end of his *Farther Adventures*, Robinson Crusoe visits
China and allows himself to describe it as a poor, ignorant, and barbarous
nation. That description strikes Crusoe as a departure from his usual
procedure and he apologizes:

As this is the only excursion of this kind which I have made in
all the account I have given of my travels, so I shall make no more
descriptions of countrys and people; 'tis none of my business, or
any part of my design; but giving an account of my own adventures,
through a life of inimitable wandrings, and a long variety of
changes, which perhaps few that come after me will have heard
the like of; I shall therefore say very little of all the mighty places,
desart countrys, and numerous people I have yet to pass thro', more
than relates to my own story, and which my concern among them
will make necessary.[1]

Such limitation is exactly why we now read Defoe. His achievement,
as Ian Watt has rendered it fairly, was to assert the 'primacy of individual
experience' by a 'total subordination of the plot to the pattern of the
autobiographical memoir'.[2] Crusoe sees more of the world in his sequel
than any ordinary eighteenth-century person could even hope to see,
and yet he calmly denies his readers extensive knowledge of that extraordinarily varied world in order to deliver himself. This audacity
accords perfectly with the egocentric preferences of the novel as a genre
which really cares only for personality and its triumph over environment
and circumstances. As Ortega y Gasset once remarked, characters in
novels 'interest us not because of what they are doing; rather the opposite,
what they do interests us because it is they who do it.[3] Such paradox
seems borne out by the dismal fate of Crusoe's continuation. The tre-
mendous variety of scene the sequel features is, perhaps, part of the
reason for its failure. Crusoe himself tends to fade out of sight and the
exotic locales take over to a degree. In the original, Crusoe is himself
the actor and the stage, the whole theatre.

1. *Robinson Crusoe* (Everyman edition, ed. Guy N. Pocock), p. 387. All further page references
in the text are to this edition. [NCE page numbers appear in brackets.]
2. *The Rise of the Novel*, p. 15.
3. 'Notes on the Novel', in *The Dehumanization of Art and Other Writings* (New York, 1956),
pp. 61–2.

*   *   *

As an archetypcal personage of the last two hundred and fifty years of European consciousness, Crusoe seems to have achieved his popularity by virtue of precisely that versatility and adaptability, able as Wilkie Collins's Betteredge says to provide sage advice 'in cases of doubt and emergency'.[4] As the accumulated reports of more serious Crusoe watchers make clear, he seems at various times to be the embodiment of various ideologies. On the one hand, for observers from Marx to Ian Watt, he is a representative of capitalist ideology, driven to acquire, control, and dominate. On the other hand, if we read with patience the actual text of his story and listen to recent commentators such as J. Paul Hunter and G. A. Starr, he is quite convincing as a man intent upon discovering his ultimate limitations by seeking spiritual definition and divine pattern in his life. His goal is from this point of view to abdicate responsibility, to give God the glory and take whatever shame there is upon himself. I think we must concede the accuracy of *both* these descriptions; Crusoe is in my view neither exclusively a masterful economic individual nor a heroically spiritual slave. He inhabits both ideologies in such a way that he manages to be both at once and therefore to reside in neither. What we may call the real Crusoe, the existential Crusoe that the novel aspires instinctively to deliver, is the personal energy that experiences the contradiction implicit in mimetic narrative: control in a context of helplessness and helplessness in a context of control. Crusoe can be called a converter, turning an ideology to the uses of survival and autonomy by using what it gives and neutralizing its possessive effects. He survives physically on the island by means of a resourcefulness and cunning well beyond probability, but the narrative tries to assure us in various ways that his control is a mere response to circumstances. For the sake of what we must call psychological survival, to get away from the destructive effects of isolation, he realizes on the island that he is a part of providential design. He experiences and accepts divine control but that control can only be realized in the free context he has himself created. And that free context, the narrative makes us remember, is itself the result of determining circumstances stretching back to Crusoe's adolescence. In *Robinson Crusoe*, a position is always relative; the freedom and defining autonomy of the narrative self is in the consciousness (or, better, the enactment) of this dynamic relativity.

*   *   *

Crusoe's energy and its capacity for turning the randomly varied world of mimetic narrative into a self-expressive structure emerge in their fullness on the island, where fidelity to mimetic decorum is naturally more prominent than ever. On the island Defoe's exact rendering of things and events is at its clearest and most intense, partly because

4. *The Moonstone* (Modern Library edition), p. 15.

exactness becomes most necessary here as an opposite to the formlessness of the island. In other words, the technique of self-analysis combined with scrupulous external observation that Defoe gives his hero reveals itself here clearly for what it is: a means of blameless self-assertion. That technique is often praised as an end in itself, an achievement that speaks for itself; but I think it is more important and critically relevant to analyse Crusoe's talents as analytic reporter in the context of their function in the narrative considered as a whole. Crusoe isolated so dramatically is in a position to speak about himself and his circumstances in a new way which eventually allows him that maximum of freedom and virtual autonomy as a character that his narrative aspires to achieve for him. I think we can say that in time he becomes on the island a contemplative consciousness who can literally observe himself at work, resembling in that fruitful split the master in Hegel's formulation who interposes the slave between the thing and himself and thereby achieves freedom.[5]

Crusoe's control is partly an aspect of the retrospective narrative position which he shares with Defoe's other autobiographers. They are writing their own stories, and we are conscious of them as masters of their autobiographies, above events in that elementary sense. But Crusoe's relationship to events has a dynamic quality that we have already experienced if we have read this far in his book, but which becomes more regular and even obtrusive when he reaches the island. Consider the shipwreck itself, a rush of meticulously rendered descriptive details but preceded and indeed punctuated by a phrase which is characteristic of Defoe's narratives at moments of stress. The ship in the storm suddenly strikes a sand bar: 'It is not easy for any one, who has not been in the like condition, to describe or conceive the consternation of men in such circumstances' (33) [33]. What is implicit in such a statement is a world of pure compulsion *as experienced*, that is, of the frenzied simultaneity of a reality which admits of no human mediation at all and which taxes the limited linear resources of the novel. Crusoe's next step is to violate the blurred reality of such a sentence by outlining the situation as a set of possibilities: '. . . we knew nothing where we were, or upon what land it was we were driven, whether an island or the main, whether inhabited or not inhabited; and as the rage of the wind was still great, tho' rather less than at first, we could not so much as hope to have the ship hold many minutes without breaking in pieces, unless the winds by a kind of miracle should turn immediately about' (33) [33]. To provide shape and calm sequence in the middle of the disasters of experience is a function of any retrospective narrator, but Crusoe is also aware of the desirability of conveying the emotional immediacy of the situation. His recourse to the initial formula of the impossibility of rendering experience is evidence of that. What he is in fact doing is establishing a narrative

5. *The Phenomenology of the Spirit*, trans. J. B. Baille, in *The Philosophy of Hegel*, ed. C. J. Friedrich (Modern Library edition), p. 405.

point between the world of experience and the world of narrative, that is, between the unruly and actually incommunicable world of reality as experienced and the lucid, controlled world of narrative. Throughout his narrative, Crusoe will continue to allude to that inchoate world of experience and indeed succeed in making us see it to some extent, but only by constantly giving up the attempt to describe it and rendering it in the solid sequences of orderly narrative. What we read is not simply the sequence but the sequence offering itself again and again as a partial description and evocation of the experience itself. The eventual result of that delicate balance is to give us the world of experience as such where the 'slave' exists and to allow us at the same time to occupy the privileged position of the 'master.'

*   *   *

We are conscious here and elsewhere in the book of a world of unruly and therefore fascinating forces—experience, in short. But in the midst of all that welter of observation are the occasional analytic details which establish human understanding and implicit control of that world. That is the discernible shape and disposition of Defoe's narrative prose; a series of descriptive clauses and then the analytic phrase, the clarifying insight which makes the previous clauses cohere. 'I stood still a few moments to recover breath and till the water went from me, and then took to my heels, and run with what strength I had further towards the shore. But neither would this deliver me from the fury of the sea, which came pouring in after me again, and twice more I was lifted up by the waves and carried forwards as before, the shore being very flat.' (35) [34–35]. Crusoe's understanding of the relationship between surf and shore anticipates his shrewd understanding in time of the island. We are conscious in the very arrangements of Defoe's prose of a continuous and dynamic movement between experience exactly observed and the experiencing and narrating self, and that swing in the prose is a metonymic reflection of the substance of the narrative in its most profound sense.

*   *   *

If we look at Crusoe's survival after the initial shocked stupidity of being thrown upon the beach, it is a continuation of his behaviour in the water: clear-eyed co-operation with circumstances. As the Spaniard remarks after hearing of all this in the *Farther Adventures*, this is a remarkable achievement: ' "had we poor Spaniards been in your case, we should never have gotten half those things out of the ship, as you did: nay," says he, "we should never have found means to have gotten a raft to carry them, or to have gotten the raft on shore without boat or sail; and how much less should we have done," said he, "if any of us had been alone!" ' (294.) Crusoe works with unbelievable care, and the secret of his success lies in watching the tides and co-operating with their flow. But even in the middle of heroic ingenuity and improbable steadiness, there are unstable forces at work, a portion of that formless and hysterical self that threatened him when he landed. In the middle of his tide-watching and planning, Crusoe begins to wonder 'why Providence should thus compleatly ruine its creatures, and render them so absolutely miserable, so without help abandon'd, so entirely depress'd, that it could hardly be rational to be thankful for such a life' (47) [47]. But 'something always return'd swift upon me to check these thoughts' (47) [47]. Crusoe casts up an account at this point and ends rumination with a proverb: 'All evils are to be considered with the good that is in them, and with what worse attends them' (48) [47]. By themselves, such ruminations are uninteresting; proverbs like this one are normally excuses for inaction. But in the context of Crusoe's remarkable feat of survival, the division of experience into good and bad, useful and destructive, and the analysis of circumstances implicit in the proverb are heroic acts which are the centre of Crusoe's character. Just as God co-operates with natural process and even employs disasters to further his mysterious ends, Crusoe finds meaning in flux, holds back his own potential hysteria, and converts disaster and accident into fortune and plan.

*　　*　　*

Crusoe's techniques of self-assurance can be derived from the methods of Protestant self-consciousness, but the meaning and ultimate function of these spiritual techniques are inseparable from Crusoe's position in his book and on his island. Although Crusoe has to learn certain specific techniques such as building, pot-making, baking, etc., he is essentially knowledgeable in the over-all technique and internal disposition for physical survival. He seems to know *how to learn*. He tells us that such is not the case when it comes to spiritual survival; he pictures himself as insensible to God's mercy and goodness, occasionally confused by his bad fortune and indifferent the rest of the time to God's role or presence in his life. The casting of accounts is an effective but temporary stay against confusion, that is against the psycho-spiritual uncertainty that Crusoe tells us was a real danger until his 'conversion'. That conversion occurs slowly, surrounded by the continuing details of survival, and, given the efficiency of Crusoe's proceedings, we may wonder why that conversion is necessary at all. We may easily be tempted and forgiven for dismissing all this religious rigmarole as Defoe's cunning or boring insertion of piety. But Crusoe's story is coherent and whole and the religious experience is part of his total survival. The answer to our unease with it lies, I think, in his solitude, an untenable human situation but a necessary one for the needs of this particular narrative. In our context as readers of the narrative, 'conversion' is an informative pun on what really happens. To be that delicately powerful master-slave the narrative requires, Crusoe has to be converted in part into a passive figure who is delivered by God, that is, whose active survival and the identity which that involves have to be guaranteed by some outside force beyond the random flow of circumstance, some force that is on the side of order and pattern and meaning. Crusoe's competence at survival is a sign of his potentiality for virtual autonomy, but he can hardly be the only one who establishes order and pattern and meaning.

*   *   *

His conversion enables Crusoe to leave his paranoid seclusion and to convert his island from a prison into a garden. From this point on, Crusoe turns to the island itself, exploring it, domesticating it, and indeed enjoying it in various ways. The self, liberated from survival by a reciprocal relationship with an 'other', is free to gratify itself. Crusoe experiences power for the first time, 'a secret kind of pleasure (tho' mixt with my other afflicting thoughts) to think that this was all my own, that I was king and lord of all this country indefeasibly, and had a right of possession' (74) [73]. Now the countryside appears 'so fresh, so green, so flourishing, every thing being in a constant verdure or flourish of spring, that it looked like a planted garden' (74) [73]. In all this, the structure emerges only as something which is suspended in the tentative resolutions of the narrative. Crusoe's condition 'began now to be, tho' not less miserable as to my way of living, yet much easier to my mind' (72) [71]. In time (eleven days we are told) and within the qualifications of psychological relativity, he takes a survey of the island and begins to enumerate its positive side. Like Marvell's sojourner in the garden, he finds 'mellons upon the ground in great abundance, and grapes upon the trees; the vines had spread indeed over the trees, and the clusters of grapes were just now in their prime, very ripe and rich' (74) [73]. But quite unlike Marvell's Adam, he notes that this is an equivocal paradise, the grapes are dangerous if eaten as they are. He remembers several Englishmen in Barbary killed by 'fluxes and feavers' from eating such. Crusoe converts them into raisins by drying them, 'wholesom as agreeable to eat' (74) [73].

That detail of Crusoe's Eden can stand as a perfect example of Crusoe's new condition: the recipient of divine deliverance, he understands that God is only partially present in what he gives, and so he converts or refines nature into that which sustains and nourishes. Having himself experienced pure activity and pure passivity, he can now in his lordship of the island set about reconciling or balancing the contradiction to be found everywhere upon it. It is a new step from the cunning observation and defensive building he did when he first arrived, and it is also unlike the passive stasis of his sickness. His new condition is the synthesis which results from the thesis and antithesis of pure action and pure passivity. This part of the book can therefore display Crusoe as the perfect mediator. Having reconciled contradiction in himself, he moves among contradictions, resolving them. He discovers that the island has wet and dry seasons, he builds a 'villa' for pleasure to balance his secure fortress for survival, he tames wild things (a parrot, then goats), he despises the surplus value of his gold and celebrates useful things but keeps his gold anyway, in effect reconciling the two systems of value. He is able to speak jauntily 'of my reign or my captivity, which you please' (101) [100]. Such activities enable us to see a meaning in Crusoe's new condition which makes it more than the simple religious tranquillity he claims it is. Crusoe sings a *contemptus mundi* tune even while we rejoice in his expanding and ever more orderly island world. Crusoe's independence is really his achievement of the Hegelian mastership; he has done with the thing and is not contained in its being as a thing but 'enjoys it without qualification and without reserve. The aspect of its independence he leaves to the servant, who labors upon it.[6] There is a part of Crusoe which 'labors' upon the island in these various and fascinating ways, but the true gratification Crusoe derives from it is a matter of his freedom from the fact of the island, the island as a constellation of forces and things which threaten his being in their natural formlessness, their character as undifferentiated and (as we know) potentially dangerous phenomena. It is his mastership and the authentic gratification it implies that are being asserted when Crusoe describes his spiritual indifference:

> In the middle of this work [he has been building what will be an unusable boat], I finish'd my fourth year in this place, and kept my anniversary with the same devotion, and with as much comfort as ever before; for by a constant study and serious application of the word of God and by the assistance of His grace, I gain'd a different knowledge from what I had before. I entertain'd different notions of things. I look'd now upon the world as a thing remote, which I had nothing to do with, no expectation from, and indeed no desires about: in a word, I had nothing indeed to do with it, nor was ever like to have; so I thought it look'd as we may perhaps look upon it hereafter, viz. as a place I had liv'd in, but was come out of it, and well might I say, as Father Abraham to Dives, *Between me and thee is a great gulph fix'd*. (94–5) [93–94]

Significantly, it is at this point that Crusoe's self-consciousness develops to the extent that he is able to think in coherent autobiographical terms. Previously, he had only been able to look back at flashes of his past, to regret this or that imprudence or to bewail a present deficiency. Now he reviews his life, considers the causes of his wandering and of his relative indifference to God and finds at last that God has forgiven him and is in process of showing him mercy. His new sense of self, his new mastership, provides access to the Puritan world-view, with its emblems, types, allusions, and metaphors, and that scheme provides his autobiography with a shape by giving him a coherent past. But that world-view is in Crusoe's case expression of an inner coherence which can now recapture the past and enjoy the spectacle of the self surviving

6. *The Phenomenology of the Spirit*, p. 405.

into the present. He spends, he tells us, 'whole hours, I may say whole days' thinking what would have become of him without the goods from the ship. The picture that holds Crusoe's attention is his significant anti-type, either dead or worse, a 'meer savage; that if I had kill'd a goat or a fowl, by any contrivance, I had no way to flea or open them, or part the flesh from the skin and the bowels, or to cut it up; but must gnaw it with my teeth and pull it with my claws like a beast' (96) [95]. The graphic insistence of this vision in the context of Crusoe's order and what we know of its establishment tells us that Crusoe's thankfulness is an indirect expression of his triumph and satisfaction over avoiding that hideous alternative. Crusoe can safely invoke Elijah's survival as a type of his own; he intends no irony and considers the relative benignity of his environment as quite the equivalent of the prophet's ravens. Praising the mildness of his God-given environment is a way of neutralizing what Crusoe fears most, what he stands most clearly against and what we have already defined as the turbulent world of experience *per se* that the novel posits and then refines: 'I found no ravenous beast, no furious wolves or tygers to threaten my life, no venemous creatures, or poisonous, which I might feed on to my hurt, no savages to murther and devour me' (98) [97]. What is chiefly of interest, what we as readers experience through Crusoe's thankful autobiographical pause, is the antithesis between Crusoe as atavistic savage or beast and Crusoe as orderly master of himself and his island. That is the opposition that informs this section, and our calm experience of it is the culmination of our experience so far as readers and satisfied onlookers. In fact, what Crusoe really learns to do in every way through his conversions is to experience by means of contradiction, to keep before himself (in his terms) what he might have been if God had indeed abandoned him. To experience anything properly, that is to see through it and understand its meaning, the event must be doubled, seen as part of a system of alternatives. Of course, what that comes to for Crusoe is keeping before himself the image of various anti-Crusoes, the beast and savage at his fiercest, but also the Crusoe who fails to plan (building a boat too large to move to the water) or the 'rash and ignorant' pilot who finds his boat carried out to sea. In this temporarily hopeless state, Crusoe looks back at the island and reproaches himself with his 'unthankful temper, and how I had repin'd at my solitary condition; and now what would I give to be on shore there again! Thus we never see the true state of our condition till it is illustrated to us by its contraries, nor know how to value what we enjoy, but by the want of it' (102–3) [102].

* * *

It is precisely at this point in the narrative, when the island has been totally possessed by Crusoe, when it is fully an extension of himself, that he discovers the footprint on the beach. Crusoe has all along feared others, although his paranoia has diminished with his growing powers.

That he should now find that he has indeed been in danger all along, that his possession and rule of the island are in some sense illusory is a recapitulation of the primal bourgeois scene. The free individual discovers that he is threatened by other individuals whose claim to freedom is as total as his own. Crusoe's fear and ultimate rage are compounded of classic Hobbesian aggression and jealousy. Moreover, those rivals will turn out to be cannibals, that is, nothing less than full-fledged embodiments of the anti-type of himself that haunts Crusoe's imagination and sustains him in his drive for order and towards civilisation. Crusoe has established 'culture' in nature, but nature returns with a vengeance in the person of the cannibals.

It is worth noticing that there is no novelistic preparation for the footprint, no transition is offered, merely an abrupt new topic: 'But now I come to a new scene of my life' (113) [111]. The abruptness is appropriate in several ways, the first and most obvious one of which may be described as psychological. It is accurate and inevitable that Crusoe's serenity should lead to turbulence, that he should face the greatest danger when he is totally secure. But the inevitable irony of desire thus uncovered is really a way of proving the inevitability of bourgeois society: serenity need not be eternally followed by its psychological opposite, but it must always be so in a bourgeois society where the price of freedom, as politicians still say, is eternal vigilance. Psychological patterns are insisted upon when they coincide with social patterns.

On another level, the abruptness reveals the structure I have been talking about. *Robinson Crusoe* deals in extremes; it presents a world where one state is transformed into its opposite and where the secret of survival is a talent for changing violent transpositions into gradual adaptations. Crusoe is here once again literally hurled back on to the world of mere nature, and that thrust from absolute solitude to dangerous society, from pastoral isolation and mock empire to a realistic state of war, is enacted and heightened dramatically by this violent shift in the action. What Crusoe must learn to do in this section is to repeat the stabilizing and possessive operation he has performed first upon himself and then upon his island, and now upon others, that is, upon society.

That situation and the beginnings of the controlling operation are implicit in Crusoe's rendition of his shock upon seeing the footprint:

> But after innumerable fluttering thoughts, like a man perfectly confus'd and out of my self, I came home to my fortification, not feeling, as we say, the ground I went on, but terrify'd to the last degree, looking behind me at every two or three steps, mistaking every bush and tree, and fancying every stump at a distance to be a man; nor is it possible to describe how many various shapes affrighted imagination represented things to me in, how many wild ideas were found every moment in my fancy, and what strange

unaccountable whimsies came into my thoughts by the way. (113)
[112]

Characteristically, Crusoe refuses to reproduce confused emotions and
delivers a careful rendition of the external facts of behaviour; he sketches
a scenario of movements and alludes to internal disorder too vast to
render. Note the apology ('as we say') for the imprecise, colloquially
figurative expression he needs to describe the physical feeling of terror:
'not feeling . . . the ground I went on' (113) [112]. He is out of himself
and surrounded by others; the most intense subjectivity induced by the
fear of others eliminates the balanced, 'objective' subjectivity Crusoe has
painfully acquired, and he experiences himself as a subject pure and
simple, a wildly erratic collection of responses to threatening stimuli.
The re-introduction of 'spontaneous' subjectivity reveals definitively for
us and Crusoe the dangers and the persistence of nature.

The ensuing long debate that occupies Crusoe for many pages until
the last defeat of the cannibals is still another kind of accounting whereby
Crusoe seeks to escape this destructive spontaneity, to exhaust reality by
listing its alternative formulations, hoping to stand at last quite apart
from their world of cause and effect. What Crusoe really seeks, in short,
is to reenact the mastery he has already achieved. The beginning of that
distancing, the theoretical underpinning for his autonomy, is laid out
at the beginnings of the internal debate: 'How strange a chequer work
of providence is the life of man! and by what secret differing springs are
the affections hurry'd about as differing circumstances present! To day
we love what to morrow we hate; to day we seek what to morrow we
shun; to day we desire what to morrow we fear, nay, even tremble at
the apprehensions of; this was exemplify'd in me at this time in the most
lively manner imaginable' (114–15) [113]. On one level, this is mere
sententious verbalizing, Christian stoicism of an uninteresting sort. But
in the imaginative context of Crusoe's problem within the narrative, it
is an anatomy of experience which enables him to stand both in and
out of experience, to be in those contraries and eventually to stand apart
from them in the moment of action which is a magical combination of
both.

For what Crusoe does in the debate is to explore those contradictions
by verbalizing them intensely. After seeing the cannibals, he jumps
rapidly from violent and eloquent moral disgust and elaborate schemes
for destroying them to impeccably enlightened anthropological and his-
toricist tolerance to clear-headed self-preservation. He embraces all these
positions with equal fervour, seems to hold them all with equal if temporary conviction. His final decision is to do nothing, to leave it all to
God, to obey impulse: in his words, to obey 'a secret hint . . . a strange
impression upon the mind, from we know not what springs' (128) [127].
Thus, when the moment for action finally comes, none of the coherent

plans or postures is quite relevant. Crusoe acts, to be sure, but he acts because of the totally unforeseen and purely haphazard circumstances he is by this time so at home in. Action is a reflex which has little to do with consciousness. Action, in fact, is a matter of watching the unpredictable flow of events for an opening, of co-operating with events at the moment when they will serve, that is, of observation and submission such as Crusoe has used in his previous triumphs. Throughout this long period of suspenseful watching and contradictory planning, Crusoe is changed from a planter-colonist into a fearful observer as much of his own shifting desires and fantasies as of the coastline for cannibal enemies. He comes close to disastrous action, almost reverts to his first condition as a man of naïvely aggressive action: 'All my calm of mind in my resignation to providence, and waiting the issue of the dispositions of Heaven, seem'd to be suspended, and I had, as it were, no power to turn my thoughts to any thing, but to the project of a voyage to the main, which came upon me with such force, and such an impetuosity of desire, that it was not to be resisted' (144) [143]. Such direct human assertion is a vulgar surrender to nature; it reduces reality to a simple challenge issued by nature and places the actor in an impossible heroic situation in which he must struggle directly with oppressive circumstances. Survival in Defoe's narratives typically involves a strong temptation towards such action. Indeed the central problem of all the narratives is to find a mode of action which mediates between the impossible heroic and the untenable actual.

Crusoe is saved from the novelistic disaster of simple heroism by a dream, a remarkably prophetic one. He dreams of 'two canoes and eleven savages' who bring another one to kill and eat. The prisoner escapes and Crusoe takes him in: '. . . he came running into my little thick grove before my fortification, to hide himself; and that I seeing him alone, and not perceiving that the others sought him that way, show'd myself to him, and smiling upon him, encourag'd him; that he kneel'd down to me, seeming to pray me to assist him; upon which I shew'd my ladder, made him go up, and carry'd him into my cave, and he became my servant' (145) [144]. In his dream, Crusoe hopes this servant will guide him to the mainland and escape. His dream strengthens him in his resolve to do nothing directly, for it is a curiously unreal dream in which Crusoe does not really participate but simply watches action with a cool detachment totally foreign to normal dream experience. Crusoe's smile in the dream is a sign of the serenity he is about to achieve, a pleased instinctive recognition of the resolution of his dilemma: doing nothing will involve him in the ultimate act of control —escape. The frantic internal debate over a course of action is resolved by the dream; the ultimate danger represented by the cannibals is to be converted into the source of ultimate deliverance. By standing still and watching the most extreme of his circumstances, Crusoe will be liberated from them. Awake, he realizes that planning is useless, circumstances will provide: 'But as I could pitch upon no probable means for it, so I resolv'd to put myself upon the watch, to see them when they came on shore, and leave the rest to the event, taking such measures as the opportunity should present, let be what would be' (146) [145].

Crusoe's resolution is the most explicit statement of the central satisfaction of his book. His strategy for survival is a means of establishing a relationship between the free self and the determined event so that the self can act upon events and in reaction to events without losing its autonomy. Indeed, the deep fantasy that Crusoe and his story serve is the dream of freedom perfectly reconciled with necessity, the self using necessity to promote its freedom. Crusoe builds up at this point to his greatest and most daring exploit in the enactment of the dream of freedom, and the pervasive antithesis between circumstances and freedom is here at its sharpest. What he proposes (fittingly in a dream, proposing without asserting) is the startling exploitation of his own anti-type, for the cannibals are an externalization of an anti-Crusoe, the natural man he has repressed by various means.

For once, Crusoe is eager, and his readiness endures through the year and a half he tells us he had to wait. Time of this sort is meaningless in *Robinson Crusoe*; the 'years' serve as breaks and transitions between crises. As readers, we feel the stress of ordering experience which rushes by Crusoe: a world of moving details and obstacles rather than the lingering static existence he claims he endured. But even Crusoe's record at this point is of impatience: '*But* the longer it seem'd to be delay'd, the more eager I was for it; in a word, I was not at first so careful to shun the sight of these savages, and avoid being seen by them, as I was now eager to be upon them' (146) [145].

The long break in Crusoe's personal time between his resolve and his opportunity does work, however, to make them surprised when the cannibals actually appear. Moreover, opportunity when it comes never matches plans, so Crusoe finds not the eleven of his dream but thirty. These and subsequent events Crusoe perceives through his telescope, and he reports everything he sees by that means in suitably distanced language, full of the tentative and objective features of vision from a distance. He is really in this scene physically apart from events even as he is tremendously concerned in them; his perspective is literally necessary but structurally coherent as well. Crusoe is on his way to enacting literally what he has been doing thus far in various indirect ways. He becomes at the moment of Friday's deliverance exactly like the deity who delivered him: suddenly visible, powerful, and obviously mysterious in that power. He acquires at the moment of action, that moment when he sees the lone savage pursued by two others, a sense of divine purpose, or, better, his impulses are for the first time in his story fully acceptable as divine urges. Crusoe here begins his final transformation into a quasi-divine, autonomous hero whose desires are no longer self-destructive in their determinate independence but fulfilling and self-constructive in their free dependence on reality. Friday swims from his pursuers (two of them), and at that precise moment when the unmanageable three pursuers are reduced to a workable two, Crusoe is struck with the inevitability of his action: 'It came now very warmly upon my thoughts, and indeed irresistibly, that now was my time to get me a servant, and perhaps a companion or assistant; and that I was call'd plainly by Providence to save this poor creature's life' (147) [146]. The universe has been dramatically realigned; the inevitable is now exactly parallel to Crusoe's desires and needs. By mastering the art of observation, by rejecting in effect all assertive and personal action, Crusoe (telescope in hand) achieves a divine perspective and his action coincides perfectly with the bizarre swing of events.

*   *   *

The huge battle with the cannibals and their bloody defeat is only the first in the climactic series of consistently one-sided triumphs which marks this last phase of Crusoe's career.[7] Crusoe admits that his enemies are so surprised and so frightened by the action of the fire-arms that they 'had no more power to attempt their own escape, than their flesh had to resist our shot' (171) [169]. In other words, Crusoe's triumph is not really or at least not completely the result of bravery but of the power and surprise he commands and the technological world over which he alone on his island presides. He moves, once again, like his God, unexpectedly and irresistibly. On the surface, Crusoe's new political power which follows the battle is adventitious; he refers to it in jest: 'My island was now peopled, and I thought my self very rich in subjects; and it was a merry reflection which I frequently made, how like a king I look'd' (175) [174]. His real power is in his confident movements: his absolutely sure sense of what to do and where to station himself in relation to events and phenomena. His power has the technological-natural inevitability of the bullets which pierce the flesh of the terrified cannibals.

When his last great adventure on the island arrives, when a ship suddenly appears in his harbour, Crusoe's caution is thus appropriately a divine instinct: 'I had some secret doubts hung about me, I cannot tell from whence they came, bidding me keep upon my guard' (182) [180]. He argues darkly that such intuitions are proof of a world of supervising spirits. No matter that Crusoe's reasons for caution are ab-

7. Crucial throughout this analysis is the simple fact that things happen in *Robinson Crusoe* in a certain sequence rather than in any other order. The sequence we read yields a coherent progression of transformations, much as a sentence is what linguists call a transformation of raw information into the resolving order of language. Crusoe's book presents a series of experiences—both the events themselves and the narration which delivers those events to us—and that series constitutes a coherent sequence, an extended sentence. The trouble up to now is that critics have used the partial perspectives of religion, economics, psychology, and literary history and missed or blocked out important parts of that sequence.

solutely sound: 'it occurr'd to me to consider what business an English ship could have in that part of the world, since it was not the way to or from any part of the world where the English had any traffick; and I knew there had been no storms to drive them in there, as in distress; and that if they were English really, it was most probable that they were here upon no good design; and that I had better continue as I was, than fall into the hands of thieves and murtherers' (182) [180]. Crusoe is able to jump neatly from the natural cunning explicit in such observation to the ideological coherence which transforms such sagacity into a link between heaven and earth. Crusoe feels his power, feels a kind of current of energy running through him from natural fact and random circumstance to divine ordering. He is the centre, a heroic mediator of a special kind at this point.

That mediation is nowhere clearer than in the subsequent events. Crusoe sees three men put ashore by mutineers, and their condition, he remarks, is exactly like his when he first landed on the island. He is now in a position to rescue them just as he was rescued by providence in various ways; he becomes providence in effect. When he confronts them, the marvellous audacity iimplicit in Crusoe's new part in the drama of deliverance surfaces in the dialogue:

> 'Gentlemen,' said I, 'do not be surpriz'd at me; perhaps you may have a friend near you when you did not expect it.' 'He must be sent directly from heaven then,' said one of them very gravely to me, and pulling off his hat at the same time to me, 'for our condition is past the help of man.' 'All help is from heaven, sir,' said I. (185) [183]

Naturally, Crusoe disavows his powers and expresses only formal confidence in God's wisdom. But the serene efficiency with which he masterminds the fight against the mutiny is an unmistakable token of the power he now embodies. Crusoe invokes desperation as the psychological source of that serenity, but we know that he has long ago in our experience of him passed through desperation, that his entire story is an effort to exclude the kind of frantic movement within circumstances that desperation implies. His very description of desperation changes it into the calm power we as onlookers are given. Crusoe senses that he is part of a larger pattern, that his story has taken its final shape and established its inevitable direction, and that his and God's purposes are inseparable. The captain is apprehensive, but Crusoe smiles. [8]

> I smil'd at him, and told him that men in our circumstances were past the operation of fear: that seeing almost every condition that could be, was better than that which we were suppos'd to be

8. J. R. Moore notes that 'Defoe smiled often and laughed rarely' and attributed that habit to many of his characters. See *Daniel Defoe: Citizen of the Modern World*, p. 73. Crusoe, at least, only smiles at moments of power.

in, we ought to expect that the consequence, whether death or life, would be sure to be a deliverance. I ask'd him what he thought of the circumstances of my life, and whether a deliverance were not worth venturing for. 'And where, sir,' said I, 'is your belief of my being preserv'd here on purpose to save your life, which elevated you a little while ago? For my part,' said I, 'there seems to be but one thing amiss in all the prospect of it.' 'What's that?' says he. 'Why,' said I, ''tis that as you say, there are three or four honest fellows among them, which should be spar'd; had they been all of the wicked part of the crew, I should have thought God's providence had singled them out to deliver them into your hands; for depend upon it, every man of them that comes a-shore are our own, and shall die or live as they behave to us.' (189) [187–88].

We know from following the sequence of Crusoe's career and watching his successive elevation to higher and higher forms of mastery (the self, the environment, animals, natives, and now Europeans) that he is speaking out of more than a desperate need to leave the island. What we enjoy most as readers and what is truest in all this sequence against the mutineers is our sense of Crusoe's serene omnicompetence, his ability to be above circumstances while immersed in them. Crusoe is so much the master in this passage that he can speak of their situation as only superficially dangerous; it looks dangerous only to an ignorant observer: 'almost every condition that could be, was better than that which we were *suppos'd to be in*'. Crusoe knows his power so exactly that he wonders that some of the mutineers on shore are honest fellows who must be spared. The whole lot, in his view, seem clearly meant to be instruments in his plan rather than individuals with their own fates and power to save themselves.

The actual battle with the mutineers repeats the strategies and satisfactions of the two encounters with the cannibals, although here the manœuvres are appropriately more complicated and extensive, given the higher sophistication of his adversaries. In directing this battle, Crusoe is still quite recognizable as a human imitation of providence: distant, inscrutable, and omnipotent. Matters are arranged so that the captain represents Crusoe as the 'governor and commander' of the island; the effectiveness of their counter-attack depends upon Crusoe's exactly engineered fiction of irresistible power, both military and legal: 'In a word, they all laid down their arms, and begg'd their lives; and I sent the man that had parley'd with them, and two more, who bound them all; and then my great army of 50 men, which, particularly with those three, were all but eight, came up and seiz'd upon them all, and upon their boat, only that I kept myself and one more out of sight, for reasons of state' (194–5) [193].

The pretence continues past the victory. We and Crusoe and his allies from the ship are all in on the elaborate masquerade in which Crusoe is not only transformed for immediate strategic purposes from castaway hermit to colonial proprietor but in which he is given the ship as his political right, clothed by the captain in appropriate European garb, and in which he even extends these outward ceremonies to actual judicial power over the mutineers. Crusoe's transformation is utterly complete; he dispenses justice as it was, in a sense, dispensed to him at the beginning of the island episode. He gives the mutineers the penance of island exile: 'I accordingly set them at liberty, and had them retire into the woods to the place whence they came, and I would leave them some fire arms, some ammunition, and some directions how they should live very well, if they thought fit' (200) [199]. Through all this, Crusoe's acting is suspiciously perfect. He shows them (twice) as evidence of his power the captain of the mutiny hanging at the yard-arm of the ship. He pretends to correct the real captain and reminds him that these men are 'my prisoners, not his; and that seeing I had offered them so much favour, I would be as good as my word; and that if he did not think fit to consent to it, I would set them at liberty, as I found them; and if he did not like it, he might take them again if he could catch them' (200) [199]. Crusoe plays at power and never has to take it quite seriously, simply because he has achieved so much of it. One must never admit to one's power and freedom, since that would falsify their essentially dynamic and relational nature. Power and freedom are states of equilibrium between the self and a constantly unruly and threatening environment and/or society. The elaborate games that Crusoe plays as he ends his story are not only strategies for managing the mutineers; they represent an awareness in the narrative of the nature of freedom. They repeat on that trickiest and most difficult level of reality—the social and political—the games that Crusoe has had to master all through his story in order to 'survive', that is, to achieve a special kind of autonomy.

* * *

LEOPOLD DAMROSCH, JR.

Myth and Fiction in *Robinson Crusoe*†

In 1719, at the age of fifty-nine, the businessman, pamphleteer, and sometime secret agent Daniel Defoe unexpectedly wrote the first English novel. The affinities of *Robinson Crusoe* with the Puritan tradition are unmistakable: it draws on the genres of spiritual autobiography and allegory, and Crusoe's religious conversion is presented as the central

† This essay appeared as part of chapter 5 in *God's Plot and Man's Stories* (Chicago: University of Chicago Press, 1985), pp. 187–212. The author has abridged the essay especially for this edition. By permission of the University of Chicago Press.

event. But this primal novel, in the end, stands as a remarkable instance of a work that gets away from its author, and gives expression to attitudes that seem to lie far from his conscious intention. Defoe sets out to dramatize the conversion of the Puritan self, and he ends by celebrating a solitude that exalts autonomy instead of submission. He undertakes to show the dividedness of a sinner, and ends by projecting a hero so massively self-enclosed that almost nothing of his inner life is revealed. He proposes a naturalistic account of real life in a real world, and ends by creating an immortal triumph of wish-fulfillment. To some extent, of course, Defoe must have been aware of these ambiguities, which are summed up when Crusoe calls the island "my reign, or my captivity, which you please."[1] But it is unlikely that he saw how deep the gulf was that divided the two poles of his story, the Augustinian theme of alienation and the romance theme of gratification.

Recommending *Robinson Crusoe* to his readers as a didactic work, Defoe compared it to *The Pilgrim's Progress* and called it "an allusive allegoric history" designed to promote moral ends, in terms which explicitly distinguish this kind of writing from immoral fictions that are no better than lies:

> The selling [sic] or writing a parable, or an allusive allegoric history, is quite a different case [from lying], and is always distinguished from this other jesting with truth, that it is designed and effectually turned for instructive and upright ends, and has its moral justly applied. Such are the historical parables in the Holy Scriptures, such "The Pilgrim's Progress," and such, in a word, the adventures of your fugitive friend, "Robinson Crusoe."[2]

Crusoe's "original sin," like Adam's, is disobedience to his father. After going to sea against express warnings, he is punished by shipwreck and isolation, converted by God (who communicates through a monitory dream during sickness, an earthquake, and the words of the Bible), and rewarded in the end beyond his fondest hopes. More than once Crusoe likens himself to the Prodigal Son, a favorite emblem for fallen man in Puritan homiletics, and a shipwrecked sea captain indignantly calls him a Jonah. In the providential scheme his sojourn on the island is both punishment and deliverance: punishment, because his wandering disposition must be rebuked; deliverance, because he (alone of the crew) is saved from drowning and then converted by grace that overcomes the earlier "hardening" of his heart (pp. 11, 14) [8, 12]. As Ben Gunn summarizes a similar lesson in *Treasure Island*, "It were Providence that put me here. I've thought it all out in this here lonely island, and I'm back on piety."

1. *The Life and Strange Surprizing Adventures of Robinson Crusoe*, ed. J. Donald Crowley (London, 1972), p. 137 [100]. Further references to *Crusoe* are to this edition. [NCE page numbers appear in brackets.]
2. *Serious Reflections during the Life and Surprising Adventures of Robinson Crusoe*, in *Romances and Narratives of Daniel Defoe*, ed. George A. Aitken (London, 1895), III, 101.

Yet Defoe's story curiously fails to sustain the motif of the prodigal. His father is long dead when Crusoe finally returns—there is no tearful reunion, no fatted calf, not even a sad visit to the father's grave—and by then he has come into a fortune so splendid that he exclaims, "I might well say, now indeed, that the latter end of Job was better than the beginning" (p. 284) [205]. Far from punishing the prodigal Crusoe for disobedience, the novel seems to reward him for enduring a mysterious test. Crusoe's father had wanted him to stay at home and, two elder sons having vanished without a trace, to establish his lineage in a strange land (he was "a foreigner of Bremen" named Kreutznaer, p. 3) [4]. But "a secret over-ruling decree" (p. 14) [12] pushes Crusoe on toward his wayfaring fate, and it is hard not to feel that he does well to submit to it, like the third son in the fairy tales whom magical success awaits.

Robinson Crusoe is the first of a series of novels by Defoe that present the first-person reminiscences of social outsiders, adventurers and criminals. Since the Puritans were nothing if not outsiders, the "masterless men" of the seventeenth century can appear (as Walzer observes) either as religious pilgrims or as picaresque wayfarers.[3] Whether as saints or as rogues they illustrate the equivocal status of the individual who no longer perceives himself fixed in society. And by Defoe's time the attempt to create a counter-*nomos* in the Puritan small group—Bunyan's separated church—was increasingly a thing of the past. Puritanism was subsiding into bourgeois Nonconformity, no longer an ideology committed to reshaping the world, but rather a social class seeking religious "toleration" and economic advantage. The old Puritans, glorying in their differentness, would have regarded the Nonconformists as all too eager to conform.

Defoe was both beneficiary and victim of the new ethic, and two facts are particularly relevant to the allegorical implications of *Crusoe:* he was twice disastrously bankrupt during a rocky career as capitalist and speculator, and he regretted an unexplained failure to enter the Presbyterian ministry—"It was my disaster," he says mysteriously in his one reference to the subject, "first to be set apart for, and then to be set apart from, the honour of that sacred employ."[4] John Richetti, in the subtlest interpretation of *Crusoe* that we have, sees Defoe as celebrating a mastery of self and environment which implicitly contradicts his religious premises: "The narrative problem . . . is to allow Crusoe to achieve and enjoy freedom and power without violating the restrictions of a moral and religious ideology which defines the individual as less than autonomous."[5] But the tension was always present in the ideology itself; it grows directly from the implications of a faith like Bunyan's, in which temptations are projected outside the self and determination is a force with

3. Michael Walzer, *The Revolution of the Saints* (New York, 1974), p. 15.
4. *Defoe's Review*, ed. in facsimile by A. W. Secord (New York, 1938), VI, 341 (22 Oct. 1709).
5. *Defoe's Narratives: Situations and Structures* (Oxford, 1975), p. 63.

which one learns to cooperate. What is new is the effective withdrawal of God from a structure which survives without him, though its inhabitants continue in all sincerity to pay him homage.

At the level of conscious intention Defoe undoubtedly wanted *Robinson Crusoe* to convey a conventional doctrinal message. The island probably suggests the debtors' prison in which he was humiliatingly confined, and it certainly allegorizes the solitude of soul needed for repentance and conversion. "I was a prisoner," Crusoe exclaims, "locked up with the eternal bars and bolts of the ocean. . . . This would break out upon me like a storm, and make me wring my hands and weep like a child" (p. 113) [83]. Very much in the Puritan tradition Crusoe learns to recognize the "particular providences" (p. 132) [96] with which God controls his life. When he discovers turtles on the other side of the island he thinks himself unlucky to have come ashore on the barren side, and only afterwards realizes, on finding the ghastly remains of a cannibal feast, "that it was a special providence that I was cast upon the side of the island where the savages never came" (p. 164) [119]. Once aware of the cannibals he must find a cave in which to conceal his fire, and Providence, having permitted him years of conspicuous fires without harm, now provides the very thing he needs. "The mouth of this hollow was at the bottom of a great rock, where by mere accident (I would say, if I did not see abundant reason to ascribe all such things now to providence) I was cutting down some thick branches of trees to make charcoal . . ." (p. 176) [128]. Most notably of all, Crusoe is rescued from hunger when some spilled chicken-feed sprouts apparently by chance; eventually he understands that although it was natural for the seeds to grow, it was miraculous that they did so in a way that was advantageous to him (pp. 78–79) [58].

In a Puritan view the normal course of nature is simply the sum total of an ongoing chain of special providences, for as a modern expositor of Calvin puts it, "Bread is not the natural product of the earth. In order that the earth may provide the wheat from which it is made, God must intervene, ceaselessly and ever anew, in the 'order of nature,' must send the rain and dew, must cause the sun to rise every morning."[6] In the eighteenth century, however, there was an increasing tendency to define providence as the general order of things rather than as a series of specific interventions. Wesley bitterly remarked that "The doctrine of a particular providence is absolutely out of fashion in England—and any but a particular providence is no providence at all."[7] One purpose of *Robinson Crusoe* is to vindicate God's omnipotence by showing the folly of making such a distinction. And Crusoe's isolation (like Ben Gunn's) encourages

6. Richard Stauffer, *Dieu, la Création et la Providence dans la Prédication de Calvin* (Berne, 1978), p. 268.

7. John Wesley, quoted by Keith Thomas, *Religion and the Decline of Magic* (New York, 1971), p. 640; see Thomas's discussion of this point on pp. 639–40.

him to think the matter through. When Moll Flanders, in Defoe's next major novel, is finally arrested and thrown into Newgate, she suddenly perceives her clever career as the condign punishment of "an inevitable and unseen fate." But she admits that she is a poor moralist and unable to retain the lesson for long: "I had no sense of my condition, no thought of heaven or hell at least, that went any farther than a bare flying touch, like the stitch or pain that gives a hint and goes off."[8] Moll sees only at moments of crisis what Crusoe learns to see consistently.

In keeping with this message the narrative contains many scriptural allusions, which are often left tacit for the reader to detect and ponder. The sprouting wheat, for instance, recalls a central doctrine of the Gospels: "Verily, verily I say unto you, Except a corn of wheat fall into the ground and die, it abideth alone; but if it die, it bringeth forth much fruit. He that loveth his life shall lose it, and he that hateth his life in this world shall keep it unto life eternal" (John 12:24–25). Crusoe's life recapitulates that of everyman, a fictional equivalent of what Samuel Clarke recommended in the study of history: "By setting before us what hath been, it premonisheth us of what will be again; sith the self-same fable is acted over again in the world, the persons only are changed that act it."[9] Like other Puritans Crusoe has to grope toward the meaning of the types embodied in his own biography. Defoe often likened himself to persecuted figures in the Bible, but wrote to his political master Harley that his life "has been and yet remains a mystery of providence unexpounded."[1] Translating his experience into the quasi-allegory of *Crusoe* permits him to define typological connections more confidently, from the coincidence of calendar dates to the overarching theme of deliverance (typified in individuals like Jonah, and in the children of Israel released from Egypt).[2] Thus the temporal world, however circumstantially described, can be seen in the Puritan manner as gathered up into eternity. Crusoe's fever is not only a direct warning from God but also, as Alkon shows, a rupture in his careful recording of chronology by which he is "wrenched outside time," an intimation that the various incidents in the story must be subsumed in a single structure.[3] As in other Puritan narratives, separate moments are valued for their significance in revealing God's will, and become elements in an emblematic pattern rather than constituents of a causal sequence.

Nearly all of the essential issues cluster around the crucial theme of solitude. Defoe clearly gives it a positive valuation, and suggests more than once that Crusoe could have lived happily by himself forever if no

8. *Moll Flanders*, ed. G. A. Starr (London, 1976), pp. 274, 279.
9. *A General Martyrologie* (1677), quoted by J. Paul Hunter, *The Reluctant Pilgrim: Defoe's Emblematic Method and Quest for Form in Robinson Crusoe* (Baltimore, 1966), p. 76.
1. *The Letters of Daniel Defoe*, ed. G. H. Healey (Oxford, 1969), p. 17. See Paula R. Backscheider, "Personality and Biblical Allusion in Defoe's Letters," *South Atlantic Review* 47 (1982), 1–20.
2. See Paul J. Korshin, *Typologies in England, 1650–1820* (Princeton, 1982), pp. 218–21.
3. Paul K. Alkon, *Defoe and Fictional Time* (Athens, Ga., 1979), pp. 61, 146.

other human beings had intruded. "I was now in my twenty-third year of residence in this island, and was so naturalized to the place, and to the manner of living, that could I have but enjoyed the certainty that no savages would come to the place to disturb me, I could have been content to have capitulated for spending the rest of my time there, even to the last moment, till I had laid me down and died like the old goat in the cave" (p. 180) [130]. However obliquely Defoe's *Serious Reflections of Robinson Crusoe* (published in the following year) relates to the novel, it must be significant that it begins with an essay "Of Solitude" which moves at once to the claim that we are solitary even in the midst of society:

> Everything revolves in our minds by innumerable circular motions, all centering in ourselves. . . . All reflection is carried home, and our dear self is, in one respect, the end of living. Hence man may be properly said to be alone in the midst of the crowds and hurry of men and business. . . . Our meditations are all solitude in perfection; our passions are all exercised in retirement; we love, we hate, we covet, we enjoy, all in privacy and solitude. All that we communicate of those things to any other is but for their assistance in the pursuit of our desires; the end is at home; the enjoyment, the contemplation, is all solitude and retirement; it is for ourselves we enjoy, and for ourselves we suffer.[4]

Critics have unfairly quoted this disturbing and memorable passage as symptomatic of a peculiar egotism in Defoe. In fact it reflects the logical consequence of Puritan inwardness, also susceptible of course to the change of egotism—the descent into the interior self that impels Bunyan's Christian to reject his family in order to win eternal life. And it is compatible, as Defoe goes on to make clear, with the traditional view that "Man is a creature so formed for society, that it may not only be said that it is not good for him to be alone, but 'tis really impossible he should be alone" (pp. 11–12). The good man or woman ought to associate with others but seek in meditation that solitude which can be attained anywhere, symbolized in *Robinson Crusoe* by "the life of a man in an island" (p. 2).

In effect Defoe literalizes the metaphor that Descartes (for example) uses: "Among the crowds of a large and active people . . . I have been able to live as solitary and retired as in the remotest desert."[5] But to literalize the metaphor creates profound complications, for it is one thing to live *as if* on a desert island and another to do it in earnest. Jonathan Edwards writes that in his meditations on the Song of Songs, "an inward sweetness . . . would carry me away in my contemplations, . . . and sometimes a kind of vision, or fixed ideas and imaginations,

---

4. *Serious Reflections*, pp. 2–3.
5. René Descartes, *Discours de la Méthode*, final sentence of Part III.

of being alone in the mountains, or some solitary wilderness, far from all mankind, sweetly conversing with Christ, and wrapt and swallowed up in God."[6] This rapture of self-abnegation is very far from Crusoe's experience. The difference is partly explained by the bluff common sense of Crusoe, not to mention of Defoe; Dickens comments, "I have no doubt he was a precious dry disagreeable article himself."[7] But beyond that it is due to the way in which Defoe takes a *topos* of allegory and literalizes it in mimetic narrative. Even though he may believe that the result is still allegorical, he has transformed—to borrow a useful pair of terms from German—*Jenseitigkeit* into *Diesseitigkeit*, collapsing the "other side" of religion into the "this side" of familiar experience. In *The Pilgrim's Progress* everyday images serve as visualizable emblems of an interior experience that belongs to another world. In *Robinson Crusoe* there is no other world.

Another way of saying this is that *Crusoe* reflects the progressive de-sacralizing of the world that was implicit in Protestantism, and that ended (in Weber's phrase) by disenchanting it altogether. Defoe's God may work through nature, but he does so by "natural" cause and effect (the seeds that sprout), and nature itself is not viewed as sacramental. Rather it is the workplace where man is expected to labor until it is time to go to a heaven too remote and hypothetical to ask questions about. "I come from the City of Destruction," Bunyan's Christian says, "but am going to Mount Sion."[8] In *Crusoe*, as is confirmed by the feeble sequel *The Farther Adventures of Robinson Crusoe*, there is no goal at all, at least not in this world. But the world of *The Pilgrim's Progress* was *not* this world: after conversion the believer knew himself to be a stranger in a strange land. Defoe keeps the shape of the allegorical scheme but radically revalues its content.

Defoe is no metaphysician, and his dislocation of the religious schema may seem naive, but in practice if not in theory it subtly images the ambiguity of man's relation to his world, at once a "natural" home and a resistant object to be manipulated. Milton's Adam and Eve fall from the world in which they had been at home, and Bunyan's characters march through the fallen world like soldiers passing through enemy territory. Defoe has it both ways, defining man over against nature and at the same time inventing a fantasy of perfect union with it. As technologist and (halting) thinker Crusoe finds himself in opposition to nature, as when he builds a "periagua" so grotesquely huge that he is unable to drag it to the water, or when he does make a successful canoe but is nearly swept out to sea by unexpected currents. And his concepts function to define his human status in contrast with nature, in keeping

6. *Personal Narrative*, in *Jonathan Edwards: Representative Selections*, ed. Clarence H. Faust and Thomas H. Johnson (New York, 1962), p. 60.
7. From Forster's *Life of Charles Dickens*, reprinted in the Norton Critical Edition of *Robinson Crusoe*, ed. Michael Shinagel (New York, 1975), p. 295 [274].
8. *The Pilgrim's Progress*, ed. Roger Sharrock (Harmondsworth, 1965), p. 56.

with the moral tradition that saw man in a "state of nature" as living in
continual fear of death.[9] But as a concord fiction *Robinson Crusoe* still
more strongly suggests that man can indeed return to union with nature,
so long as other men are not present to disturb him. In important respects
the island is an Eden.

This equivocation between punitive doctrine and liberating romance
has remarkable consequences in Defoe's treatment of psychology. In
effect he carries to its logical conclusion the externalizing of unwanted
impulses which we have seen in Bunyan and other Puritan writers. With
God generalized into an abstract Providence, Crusoe's universe is peopled by inferior beings, angelic spirits who guide him with mysterious
hints and diabolical spirits who seek his ruin. Of these the latter are the
more interesting, and Crusoe is scandalized to find that Friday is unaware
of any Satan, merely saying "O" to a pleasant but ineffectual deity called
Benamuckee who seems not to know to punish men. Defoe needs the
Devil—and this must be his never-articulated answer to Friday's trenchant question, "Why God no kill the Devil?" (p. 218) [158]—because
man's unacknowledged impulses have to be explained. Like the older
Puritans Defoe externalizes such impulses by calling them tricks of Satan,
but he altogether lacks the subtle dialectic by which the Puritans acknowledged man's continued complicity with the hated enslaver.

Defoe's late work *The Political History of the Devil* (1726), once one
gets behind its frequent facetiousness, expresses deep anxiety about the
power of a being who "is with us, and sometimes in us, sees when he
is not seen, hears when he is not heard, comes in without leave, and
goes out without noise; is neither to be shut in or shut out" (II.iii, p.
221). Yet in a sense this ominous figure is welcome, for he furnishes a
comforting explanation of feelings which must otherwise be located in
one's self. After discussing the case of virtuous persons whom the Devil
causes to behave lasciviously in their dreams, Defoe tells the haunting
story of a tradesman, "in great distress for money in his business," who
dreamt that he was walking "all alone in a great wood" where he met
a little child with a bag of gold and a diamond necklace, and was
prompted by the Devil to rob and kill the child.

> He need do no more but twist the neck of it a little, or crush it
> with his knee; he told me he stood debating with himself, whether
> he should do so or not; but that in that instant his heart struck him
> with the word Murther, and he entertained an horror of it, refused
> to do it, and immediately waked. He told me that when he waked
> he found himself in so violent a sweat as he had never known the
> like; that his pulse beat with that heat and rage, that it was like a
> palpitation of the heart to him; and that the agitation of his spirits
> was such that he was not fully composed in some hours; though

9. See Maximillian E. Novak, *Defoe and the Nature of Man* (Oxford, 1963), ch. 2

the satisfaction and joy that attended him, when he found it was but a dream, assisted much to return his spirits to their due temperament. (II.x, pp. 361–62)

One may well suspect that this desperate and guilty tradesman was Defoe himself, and perhaps it is not fanciful to think that the famous episode in *Moll Flanders,* in which Moll robs a child of its watch but resists the temptation to kill it, is a kind of revision and expiation of the dream. Guilty impulses like these are doubly repudiated on Crusoe's island: first, because they are projected on to Satan and the cannibals whom Satan prompts, and second, because so long as Crusoe is alone he could not act upon them even if he wanted to. The return of human beings means the return of the possibility of sin, as indeed he realizes when he longs to gun down the cannibals in cold blood.

In *Robinson Crusoe,* therefore, we see the idea of solitude undergoing a drastic revaluation. Instead of representing a descent into the self for the purpose of repentance, it becomes the normal condition of all selves as they confront the world in which they have to survive. Puritans of Bunyan's generation sometimes welcomed imprisonment because it freed them from external pressures and made self-scrutiny easier. Baxter for example says, "If you be banished, imprisoned, or left alone, it is but a relaxation from your greatest labours; which though you may not cast off yourselves, you may lawfully be sensible of your ease, if God take off your burden. It is but a cessation from your sharpest conflicts, and removal from a multitude of great temptations."[1] This liberation from outer attacks, however, was supposed to encourage a deeper attention to inner conflict, as in the widespread custom of keeping diaries. But that is precisely what Crusoe does not do. He keeps his diary *before* conversion, and stops with the flimsy excuse (on the part of the novelist) that he ran out of ink and could not figure out how to make any. At the very moment when the Puritan's continuous self-analysis begins, Crusoe's ends.

The function of Crusoe's diary, it seems, is not to anatomize the self, but rather to keep track of it in the modern fashion that Riesman describes: "The diary-keeping that is so significant a symptom of the new type of character may be viewed as a kind of inner time-and-motion study by which the individual records and judges his output day by day. It is evidence of the separation between the behaving and the scrutinizing self."[2] This new way of presenting psychology goes far toward explaining what critics of every persuasion have recognized, the peculiar opacity and passivity of character in Defoe's fiction. Novak observes that "frequently a passion appears to be grafted on to the characters, an appendage rather than an organic part of them," and Price says that "conflicts are

1. Richard Baxter, *The Divine Life,* III.iii, in *Practical Works* (London, 1838), III, 868.
2. David Riesman, *The Lonely Crowd,* abridged ed. (New Haven, 1961), p. 44.

settled in Crusoe or for him, not by him."[3] And it also helps to explain
why, as Fletcher notices in his survey of allegory, much in Crusoe is
dispersed into externalized daemonic agents."[4] A similar procedure made
Bunyan's Christian seem more complex and human by analyzing his
psyche into complex elements; it makes Crusoe seem, if not less human,
at least less intelligible, because we are encouraged to look outward
rather than inward. So long as we imagine ourselves looking outward
with Crusoe, we see what he sees and feel what he feels, but what we
perceive is always external. Starr shows in a brilliant essay that Defoe's
prose constantly projects feelings on to the other world, and that the
reality thus presented is subjective rather than interior, a defense of the
ego "by animating, humanizing, and Anglicizing the alien thing he
encounters."[5] If we try to look *into* any of Defoe's characters we find
ourselves baffled; when Crusoe, on seeing the footprint, speaks of being
"confused and out of my self" (p. 154) [112], we have no clear idea of
what kind of self he has when he is in it.

In Defoe's behaviorist psychology, as in that of Hobbes, people live
by reacting to external stimuli, and while we may get a strong sense of
individuality, there is little sense of the psyche. His frightened behavior
after seeing the footprint, Crusoe says, "would have made any one have
thought I was haunted with an evil conscience" (p. 158) [115]. If beasts
and savages are allegorical symbols of inner impulses, then of course he
does have an evil conscience; but in the mimetic fiction they are simply
beasts and savages, and conscience becomes irrelevant. Moreover Crusoe
describes how he *would have looked* to an observer if one had been there,
even though the total absence of other people was precisely what made
him comfortable, and the advent of other people is what filled him with
horrible fears. Riesman's point about the split between the behaving and
the observing self is thus confirmed.

In contrast with the self the Puritans believed in, utterly open to God
and potentially open to careful introspection, the self in Defoe participates in the general cultural revaluation epitomized by Locke: "Man,
though he have great variety of thoughts, and such from which others
as well as himself might receive profit and delight; yet they are all within
his own breast, invisible and hidden from others, nor can of themselves
be made to appear." Locke goes on to describe the role of language in
bridging (but not abolishing) this gap by means of conventional signs.
Hume characteristically goes further and argues that the self is invisible
to itself as well as to others: "Ourself, independent of the perception of
every other object, is in reality nothing; for which reason we must turn

3. Novak, *Defoe and the Nature of Man*, p. 133; Martin Price, *To the Palace of Wisdom: Studies in Order and Energy from Dryden to Blake* (New York, 1965), p. 275.
4. Angus Fletcher, *Allegory: The Theory of a Symbolic Mode* (Ithaca, 1964), p. 53.
5. G. A. Starr, "Defoe's Prose Style: 1. The Language of Interpretation," *Modern Philology* 71 (1974), p. 292.

our view to external objects."[6] This psychology is quite directly a rejection of Puritan introspection, which is not surprising since Locke championed toleration against fanaticism—he wrote a book entitled *The Reasonableness of Christianity*—and Hume turned atheist after a Calvinist upbringing. If God can see every hidden corner of the self, the believer is obliged to try to see it too; but if God withdraws or vanishes, then the anguish of self-examination is no longer necessary.

These considerations suggest a way of reconciling two very different interpretations of Crusoe's psychology. One holds that the self is fragmented in a state of turbulent flux,[7] The other that the self precedes and resists alteration: "We always feel as we read that personality is radically primary, that it existed before events and continues to exist in spite of circumstances that seek to change or even to obliterate it."[8] In effect this is the distinction, already noted, between solitude as self-abnegating introspection and solitude as self-assertive independence. Whenever Defoe allows his narrators to try to look within, they do indeed find a chaos of unfocused sensations, but most of the time they simply avoid introspection and assert themselves tenaciously against a series of manageable challenges. The notoriously extraneous ending of *Robinson Crusoe*, in which the hero successfully organizes his traveling party to fight off wolves in the Pyrenees, may symbolize the mastery that Crusoe has attained on the island, but if so it is a mastery of external objects rather than a richer organization of the psyche. No wonder all of Defoe's characters, like their creator, habitually resort to alias and disguise.

This assertion of the autonomy of the self is mirrored in the disappearance of Crusoe's father, with his oracular warning, "That boy might be happy if he would stay at home, but if he goes abroad he will be the miserablest wretch that was ever born" (p. 7) [7]. What the miserable wretch gets is an idyllic, self-sufficient existence that for generations has made *Robinson Crusoe* a special favorite of children. And Crusoe thereby achieves what Milton's Satan so heretically desired, a condition of self-creation. Despite its mimetic surface, *Robinson Crusoe* closely anticipates the Romantic pattern discussed by Bloom: "All quest-romances of the post-Enlightenment, meaning all Romanticisms whatsoever, are quests to re-beget one's own self, to become one's own Great Original."[9]

The Romantic poets and philosophers interpreted the Fall as the birth of consciousness of one's finite self, and Blake explicitly indentified it with the onset of puberty. *Robinson Crusoe* is a resolutely sexless novel, with only the most covert prurience: "I could not perceive by my nicest

6. John Locke, *An Essay Concerning Human Understanding*, III.ii.1; David Hume, *A Treatise of Human Nature*, ed. L. A. Selby-Bigge (Oxford, 1888), II.ii, p. 340.
7. See esp. Homer O. Brown, "The Displaced Self in the Novels of Daniel Defoe," in *Studies in Eighteenth-Century Culture*, vol. IV, ed. Harold E. Pagliaro (Madison, 1975), pp. 69–94; and Everett Zimmerman, *Defoe and the Novel* (Berkeley, 1975), ch. 2.
8. Richetti, *Defoe's Narratives*, p. 22.
9. Harold Bloom, *The Anxiety of Influence* (London, 1973), p. 64.

observation but that they were stark naked, and had not the least covering upon them; but whether they were men or women, that I could not distinguish" (p. 183) [132]. In fact *Crusoe* is a fantasy of retreat into an innocence before puberty, with a vision of solitude among vegetable riches that literalizes the metaphors of Marvell's "Garden":

> Such was that happy garden-state,
> While man there walked without a mate:
> After a place so pure and sweet,
> What other help could yet be meet!
> But 'twas beyond a moral's share
> To wander solitary there:
> Two paradises 'twere in one
> To live in paradise alone.

Milton's sober Puritanism leads him to elaborate the ways in which the original helpmeets drag each other down, while implying the unacceptability of Marvell's playful fantasy of life without a mate. But Marvell was after all a Puritan, and wrote somberly elsewhere that every man must be "his own expositor, his own both minister and people, bishop and diocese, his own council; and his own conscience excusing or condemning him, accordingly he escapes or incurs his own internal anathema."[1] Defoe evades the internal anathema, invents a world without sexuality, and gives a positive valuation to the shelter behind a wall of trees which in *Paradise Lost* was a guilty escape from God's eye:

> O might I here
> In solitude live savage, in some glade
> Obscured, where highest woods impenetrable
> To star or sunlight, spread their umbrage broad. . . .
> (IX.1084–87)

Adam and Eve are expelled from Eden and sent out into the world of history; Crusoe retreats from history into an Eden innocent of sexuality and of guilt. To be sure, Defoe makes him now and then refer to his "load of guilt" (p. 97) [71] or bewail "the wicked, cursed, abominable life I led all the past part of my days" (p. 112) [82], but no details are ever given, and on the island the absence of other people makes guilt irrelevant.

Solitude is power. "There were no rivals. I had no competitor, none to dispute sovereignty or command with me" (p. 128) [94]. And again: "It would have made a Stoic smile to have seen me and my little family sit down to dinner; there was my majesty the prince and lord of the whole island; I had the lives of all my subjects at my absolute command. I could hang, draw, give liberty, and take it away, and no rebels among

1. "On General Councils" (1676), in *The Complete Works of Andrew Marvell*, ed. A. B. Grosart (New York, 1875), I, 125.

all my subjects" (p. 148) [108]. The subjects are a parrot, a dog, and two cats; the cruelties that might tempt a despot among men would be absurd among pets. Christianity always dealt uneasily with Stoicism, which recommended an indifference to the world that seemed appealing, but also a preoccupation with self that seemed un-Christian. Regal in solitude, Crusoe would indeed make a Stoic smile. Absolute power is a function of freedom from social power; only when the cannibals arrive does the Hobbesian state of nature resume, as Defoe describes it in his poem *Jure Divino* (1706):

> Nature has left this tincture in the blood,
> That all men would be tyrants if they could.
> If they forbear their neighbours to devour,
> 'Tis not for want of will, but want of power.[2]

So long as he is by himself Crusoe escapes Hobbes's war of all against all and rejoices in the war of nobody against nobody.

Defoe makes it absolutely explicit that Crusoe's Eden is an escape from guilt. "I was removed from all the wickedness of the world here. I had neither the *lust of the flesh, the lust of the eye, or the pride of life*" (p. 128 [94]; the reference is to a favorite Puritan text, John 2:16). To be alone with God is to be alone with oneself and to find it good:

> Thus I lived mighty comfortably, my mind being entirely composed by resigning to the will of God, and throwing myself wholly upon the disposal of his Providence. This made my life better than sociable, for when I began to regret the want of conversation, I would ask my self whether thus conversing mutually with my own thoughts, and, as I hope I may say, with even God himself by ejaculations, was not better than the utmost enjoyment of human society in the world. (pp. 135–36) [99]

Crusoe has nothing to hide. Whereas Bunyan trembled in the knowledge that God sees "the most secret thoughts of the heart,"[3] Crusoe often applies the word "secret" to emotions of self-satisfaction: "I descended a little on the side of that delicious vale, surveying it with a secret kind of pleasure" (p. 100) [73]. This is not the Puritan use of the term, but an ethical and aesthetic ideal that Defoe may have picked up from Addison: "A man of a polite imagination . . . meets with a secret refreshment in a description, and often feels a greater satisfaction in the prospect of fields and meadows than another does in the possession."[4] The solitary Crusoe has no one to keep secrets from; the word "secret" defines his privacy, individuality, possessiveness, and sole claim to pleasure.

Self-congratulation merges with the frequently mentioned "secret

2. See Novak, *Defoe and the Nature of Man*, pp. 16–18.
3. *Grace Abounding*, ed. Roger Sharrock (Oxford, 1962), p. 76.
4. *Spectator* 411. There are two similar uses of "secret" in no. 412.

hints" of Providence until Crusoe learns to identify Providence with his own desires. When after a time he reflects on his role in saving Friday from paganism, "A secret joy run through every part of my soul" (p. 220) [159]. For the older Puritans determinism was a crucial issue, whether one concluded like Milton that man was free to cooperate with God's will in his own way, or like Bunyan that man must learn to make his will conform to the irresistible force of predestination. In strictly theological terms Defoe seems to have followed Baxter in stressing God's desire to welcome all of his children, rather than his power of predestination.[5] But imaginatively Defoe shares with the Puritans a feeling of unfreedom, of being compelled to act by some power beyond himself. In the imaginary world of fiction he can embrace that power instead of resisting it. In its simplest terms this amounts to asserting that Crusoe is an agent of Providence as well as its beneficiary, as he himself indicates after masterminding the defeat of the mutineers:

> "Gentlemen," said I, "do not be surprised at me; perhaps you may have a friend near you when you did not expect it." "He must be sent directly from heaven, then," said one of them very gravely to me, and pulling off his hat at the same time to me, "for our condition is past the help of man." "All help is from heaven, sir," said I. (p. 254) [183]

But beyond this, Defoe's determinism becomes a defense of his own impulses, whereas for Puritans it would have been a confirmation of their sinfulness. Providence is seen as responsible not only for what happens but also for what does not, for what Crusoe is not as well as what he is. "Had Providence . . . blessed me with confined desires" (p. 194) [141] none of the misfortunes—and none of the rewards—would have come about. But Providence did not. Where then does repsonsibility lie?

The more one ponders this question, the more equivocal the role of Providence becomes, as is vividly apparent when Crusoe reflects on his very first shipwreck.

> Had I now had the sense to have gone back to Hull and have gone home, I had been happy, and my father, an emblem of our blessed Saviour's parable, had even killed the fatted calf for me; for hearing the ship I went away in was cast away in Yarmouth Road, it was a great while before he had any assurance that I was not drowned.
>
> But my ill fate pushed me on now with an obstinacy that nothing could resist; and though I had several times loud calls from my reason and my more composed judgment to go home, yet I had no power to do it. I know not what to call this, nor will I urge that

> it is a secret overruling decree that hurries us on to be the instruments of our own destruction, even though it be before us, and that we rush upon it with our eyes open. Certainly nothing but some such decreed unavoidable misery attending, and which it was impossible for me to escape, could have pushed me forward against the calm reasonings and persuasions of my most retired thoughts, and against two such visible instructions as I had met with in my first attempt. (p. 14) [12]

The passage is filled with interesting negatives: (1) Crusoe would have been like the prodigal if he had gone home, but he did *not*; (2) he will *not* say that his fate was compelled by "a secret overruling decree"; (3) yet *nothing but* such a decree can account for it.

One can try to explain these complications in orthodox Christian fashion, as Coleridge does:

> When once the mind, in despite of the remonstrating conscience, has abandoned its free power to a haunting impulse or idea, then whatever tends to give depth and vividness to this idea or indefinite imagination increases its despotism, and in the same proportion renders the reason and free will ineffectual. . . . This is the moral of Shakespeare's *Macbeth*, and the true solution of this paragraph —not any overruling decree of divine wrath, but the tyranny of the sinner's own evil imagination, which he has voluntarily chosen as his master.[6]

Coleridge adds, "Rebelling against his conscience he becomes the slave of his own furious will" (p. 316). But Crusoe does not go so far as this toward accepting the orthodox solution. He shows that he is aware of it, and hence hesitates to ascribe misfortunes to fate or God, but nevertheless the sense of involuntary behavior is so strong that he can only attribute it to "some such decreed unavoidable misery."

An emphasis on God's "decrees," comforting for the elect and dreadful for the reprobate, was fundamental to Calvinism. But Crusoe uses Calvinist language here to suggest that he cannot be morally responsible for actions in which he is moved about like a chess piece. In many places Defoe discusses the kinds of necessity in ordinary life (finding food, self-defense) that may not extenuate crime but impel it so irresistibly that the criminal is simply not free to behave otherwise.[7] A character in *Colonel Jack* says, "I believe my case was what I find is the case of most of the wicked part of the world, *viz.* that to be reduced to necessity is to be wicked; for necessity is not only the temptation, but is such a temptation as human nature is not empowered to resist. How good then is that God which takes from you, sir, the temptation, by

6. Samuel Taylor Coleridge, *Complete Works* (New York, 1884), IV, 312.
7. See Novak, *Defoe and the Nature of Man*, ch. 3.

taking away the necessity?"[8] Surely the corollary must also hold: the sinner can hardly be blamed if God does *not* remove the temptation by removing the necessity.

Obeying necessity, Crusoe allows himself to ride the current of his secret destiny and is magnificently rewarded. A Puritan reading of *Robinson Crusoe*—such as Defoe himself might have endorsed—would hold that by seeking self-fulfillment and creating a private *nomos*, Crusoe is an abject sinner. But the logic of the story denies this. Starr has shown that Defoe was fascinated with the science of casuistry,[9] which treats necessity as an ethical excuse for behavior instead of—as in Calvinism—a moral condemnation of it. The inverted egotism of Bunyan's "chief of sinners" is turned right-side-up again, as Crusoe's island refuses to remain a metaphor for captivity and quickly develops positive qualities. Since Crusoe is a fictional character and not a real person, what is really involved is Defoe's imaginative conception of the island. And this at bottom is a powerful fantasy of punishment that can be willingly accepted because it ceases to punish. The autonomy of solitude is the happy culmination of those mysterious impulses that first sent Crusoe to sea, and in achieving it he makes his destiny his choice.

The much-discussed economic aspects of *Robinson Crusoe* are suggestive of ambiguities very like the religious ones. On this topic the *locus classicus* is Ian Watt's chapter on *Crusoe* as a myth of capitalism. It is not really relevant to argue, as critics of Watt have done, that Crusoe has little of the rational calculation of the capitalist. For Watt's point is that the book is a myth and not a literal picture, reflecting the dynamic spirit of capitalism rather than its practical application. "Crusoe's 'original sin' is really the dynamic tendency of capitalism itself, whose aim is never merely to maintain the *status quo*, but to transform it incessantly. Leaving home, improving on the lot one was born to, is a vital feature of the individualist pattern of life."[1] The island permits Crusoe (and Defoe) to evade the contradictions in capitalist individualism, and to imagine a Puritan Eden in which work yields gratification instead of vexation and defeat.

The special status of the island makes possible Crusoe's reaction, in a famous passage, when he finds a quantity of coins on board the wrecked ship.

> I smiled to myself at the sight of this money; "O drug!" said I aloud, "What are thou good for? Thou art not worth to me, no not the taking off of the ground, one of those knives is worth all this heap, I have no manner of use for thee, e'en remain where thou art, and go to the bottom as a creature whose life is not worth saving." However, upon second thoughts, I took it away. . . . (p. 57) [43]

8. *Colonel Jack*, ed. Samuel Holt Monk (London, 1965), p. 161.
9. *Defoe and Casuistry* (Princeton, 1971).
1. *The Rise of the Novel: Studies in Defoe, Richardson, and Fielding* (Berkeley, 1957), ch. 3.

Ever since Coleridge, readers have perceived irony in those second thoughts, but the irony is at society's expense rather than Crusoe's. If ever he returns to the world whose lifeblood is money, then this money will be useful if not indispensable. With his usual good sense he therefore saves it. But on the island, as if by enchantment, money is truly valueless, and Crusoe is free of the whole remorseless system whose lubricant it is. His personification of the coins as a "creature" carries its traditional Puritan meaning: all earthly things are "creatures" which the saint is to restrain himself from loving too much. Only on Crusoe's island is it possible to despise money as a useless and indeed harmful drug.

Crusoe is no anchorite. Things retain their value, and in pillaging the ship he never repents the urge to accumulate. "I had the biggest magazine of all kinds now that ever were laid up, I believe, for one man, but I was not satisfied still" (p. 55) [42]. What matters now is use, exactly as Crusoe indicates in the "O drug" passage, and as he confirms in a later reference to the saved-up coins: "If I had had the drawer full of diamonds it had been the same case; and they had been of no manner of value to me, because of no use" (p. 129) [95]. Crusoe notes about his early voyages that since he was a gentleman, a person with money but no skills (p. 16) [14], he was a mere passenger and could do nothing useful. On the island he has to work with his hands, something no gentlemen would do, and recovers the dignity of labor which his father's "middle station" might have insulated him from. Just as money becomes meaningless, labor becomes meaningful. "A man's labour," Hobbes says, "is a commodity exchangeable for benefit, as well as any other thing."[2] Marx was hardly the first to notice the joylessness of work performed solely for what it can buy. On the island Crusoe has no market in which to sell his labor, and bestows it either on making things he really wants or as an end in itself. It may take him forever to make a pot, but Franklin's maxim has no meaning here: time is not money. Defoe was a speculator and middleman; Crusoe literalizes the labor theory of value in a miniature world where speculation is impossible and the middleman does not exist.

Relating *Robinson Crusoe* to the myth of Mammon, Starr surveys writers who tried to reconcile Christ's injunction "Take no thought for the morrow" with the duty of labor by emphasizing that the labor must be performed in cooperation with Providence.[3] On the island Crusoe need no longer attempt this difficult reconciliation, whereas capitalism, being rational, must always take thought for the morrow. Thus in sociological terms Crusoe escapes the prison of alienated labor, just as in religious terms he escapes the prison of guilt. He inhabits a little world where his tools and products fully embody his desires (or would if he could make ink) and where necessity authenticates his desires instead of

2. Thomas Hobbes, *Leviathan*, ed. Michael Oakeshott (Oxford, 1946), II.xxiv, p. 161.
3. G. A. Starr, *Defoe and Spiritual Autobiography* (Princeton, 1965), pp. 185–97.

punishing them. "The liberty of the individual," Freud says, "is no gift of civilization."[4] It is Defoe's gift to Crusoe.

JOHN BENDER

The Novel and the Rise of the Penitentiary: *Robinson Crusoe*[†]

> *There are in London, and the far
> extended Bounds, which I now call so,
> notwithstanding we are a Nation of Liberty,
> more publick and private Prisons,
> and Houses of Confinement,
> than any City in Europe, perhaps as many
> as in all the Capital Cities of
> Europe put together.*
>
> —DANIEL DEFOE
> A *Tour Thro' the Whole Island of Great Britain*

One of the most explicit motifs in seventeenth- and eighteenth-century prison accounts is the identification of the experience of imprisonment with the point of view of the initiate or neophyte in a ritual. The old-style prisoners were subjects who, to use Victor Turner's word, underwent the "liminal" experience characteristic of rites of passage. * * * Such rites enact symbolic demise and take for granted a randomness that, quite unpredictably, can bring about real death. "The essential feature of these symbolizations," according to Turner, "is that the neophytes are neither living nor dead from one aspect, and both living and dead from another. Their condition is one of ambiguity and paradox, a confusion of all the customary categories."[1] Incessant complaints by eighteenth-century reformers that the old prisons were confused in tone—sites at once of misery and hilarity, punishment and immorality, death and generation—serve, in this context, to affirm their liminality. Randomness was one of the rules in the old prisons:

> the squalor, the disease, the possibility of escape, the periodic jail deliveries voted by Parliment; the chance that your creditors might relent, the courts miscarry, the judges commute death to transportation, your patrons gain a reprieve, your friends revive your

---

4. *Civilization and Its Discontents*, tr. James Strachey (New York, 1962), p. 42.
† This essay appeared as chapter 2 in *Imagining the Penitentiary: Fiction and the Architecture of Mind in Eighteenth-Century England* (Chicago: U. of Chicago P, 1987). The author has abridged the essay especially for this edition. By permission of the University of Chicago Press.
1. See Victor Turner's essay, "Betwixt and Between: The Liminal Period in *Rites de Passage*," reprinted in William A. Lessa and Evon Z. Vogt, eds., *Reader in Comparative Religion: An Anthropological Approach*, 3rd ed. (New York: Harper and Row, 1972), pp. 338–47; p. 340.

corpse after hanging. In the old prisons the real, if transient, danger to the liminal passenger depended, as in carnival, upon losing control within a demarcated arena where new patterns of life could be formulated. "Initiation," at the threshold (*limen, liminis*) separating one role in the larger social structure from another, "is to rouse initiative at least as much as to produce conformity to custom."[2]

The old prisons visibly situated the transient structures of liminality in the topography of the early modern city. They were representational no less than the new penitentiaries that would replace them; the difference lay in the principles governing their form. The old prisons were loose structures bounded by authority yet out of its reach, even as their randomness sustained tradition by clarifying its elemental value. Structurally articulate, yet unpenetrated by systematic governance or precisely formulated rules, the old prisons maintained an account of reality that had informed earlier religious, governmental, and narrational practice and that continued to permeate much of eighteenth-century popular culture.[3]

The new penitentiaries banished chance and fortune—the providential order of things—in favor of human planning and certitude imagined in material terms. Our very words make the case: "rebirth" through initiation or baptism implies mysterious re-creation, whereas "reform" assumes rationally ordered causal sequence and conceives human invention as capable of reconstructing reality. In the words of Sir William Blackstone, one of the several men who shaped the Penitentiary Act and guided it through Parliament during the 1770s:

> If the plan be properly executed, there is reason to hope that such a reformation may be effected in the lower classes of mankind, and such a gradual scale of punishment be affixed to all gradations of guilt, as may in time supersede the necessity of punishment, except for very atrocious crimes.

Penitentiaries have regimes, schedules, disciplines; their inmates progress or regress; and they have stories, not to be told upon release or just prior to execution (like the liminal subjects of the old *Newgate Calendar*), but to be lived out in the penitentiary itself. Much of the history of penology subsequent to the establishment of penitentiaries in England during the last quarter of the eighteenth century is properly described as an attempt to order the prison story generically with divergent classifications of plot for each age, sex, and type of convict. This idea stands, then, at the heart of my argument: the form prisons took when they

2. Victor Turner, *Dramas, Fields, and Metaphors: Symbolic Action in Human Society* (Ithaca: Cornell University Press, 1974), p. 256.
3. See E. P. Thompson, "Patrician Society, Plebian Culture," *Journal of Social History* 7 (1974), p. 391, on the decline of the Church in this role.

were remade in correspondence to and collaboration with the period's new systems of political and moral consciousness was narrative form of a distinctively novelistic kind that I associate with early realist fiction.

* * *

Defoe's fictional representation of the old prisons implied the conception of the new kind of imprisonment structured narratively along the lines of the realistic, consciousness-centered novel. * * * Defoe took two crucial steps toward the full novelistic schematization of confinement in the penitentiary: (1) he subjected experience to a detailed narrative articulation and thereby revealed the high degree of control latent in the novel as a representational form; (2) he showed how, in confinement, the internal forces of psychological motivation fuse dynamically with the physical details of perceptual experience. This is the penitentiary imagined as the meeting point of the individual mind and material causes. Defoe's narratives array the old prisons on detailed representational grids of elapsed time, causal sequence, perceptual registration, and associative psychology. Under these conditions, the liminal prototype gives way to an ideal of confinement as the story of isolated self-consciousness shaped over time, within precise material circumstances, under the regime of narrative discipline: the key terms of what I call the "penitentiary idea." The point is not that Defoe proposes penitentiaries but that he delineates the subjective order—the structure of feeling—that they institutionalize and discloses to that order the power latent in the minutely sequential representations of realist narrative.

* * *

Experiences of transformation in marginal places of confinement figure centrally in *Robinson Crusoe*, which presents a materially realistic delineation of consciousness shaped through the narration of confinement. Here is Crusoe's situation liminally considered. Prior to the wreck, Crusoe lays stress on the unceremonious break with his parents and on the immaturity of obeying "blindly the Dictates of my Fancy rather than my Reason."[4] After the wreck, invoking the metaphor of condemnation and reprieve, he hovers at the boundary between life and death:

> I believe it is impossible to express to the Life what the Extasies and Transports of the Soul are, when it is so sav'd, as I may say, out of the very Grave; and I do not wonder now at that Custom, *viz.* That when a Malefactor who has the Halter about his Neck, is tyed up, and just going to be turn'd off, and has a Reprieve brought to him: I say, I do not wonder that they bring a Surgeon with it, to let him Blood that very Moment they tell him of it, that the Surprise may not drive the Animal Spirits from the Heart, and overwhelm him. (p. 46) [35]

4. Daniel Defoe, *Robinson Crusoe*, ed. J. Donald Crowley (London: Oxford University Press, 1972), p. 40 [31] [NCE page numbers appear in brackets.] Further references are to this edition.

Crusoe's thinking here catches the primitive doubleness of marginal symbolism in the notion of bloodletting at the moment of reprieve: the wound that heals. His overarching metaphor assumes the liminal prison because Newgate launched the condemned onto the infamous road terminating at Tyburn gallows and held the fortunate few who returned with reprieves until their transportation abroad. Indeed, we later discover that Crusoe has been simultaneously alive and dead throughout most of the book, for legally he has undergone *"Civil Death"* (pp. 283–84) [204].

During the island confinement he subjects his entire previous standard of life to criticism; his initiative rises to the re-creation, often in parodic forms, of virtually every craft or social comfort known in England. Time becomes conjectural after he loses track during a delirious, nearly fatal, illness, and its value becomes immeasurably small during his ceaseless labors to shape the island into a microcosm of European life. Having undergone his own rite of passage, Crusoe undertakes Friday's instruction and eventually institutes a facsimile of civil society on the basis of truths he has discovered about human nature. Finally, Crusoe himself, as the Governor, reprieves certain mutineers and commutes their sentences to a form of transportation: the colonization of the island. He thus closes the liminal cycle with full acceptance of axiomatic social values, including the use of reprieves as tokens in the system of partician patronage through which the gentry exercised authority.[5] Although Crusoe never settles down to realize them, the social prospects implied by his entry into the class of substantial landholders have been enacted prospectively on the island through his journeys from sea coast fort to inland country seat, as well as by his exercises in governance. In the end, however much greater his fortunes might have been had he remained in Brazil instead of undertaking the fateful voyage, Crusoe does achieve a new economic status well above his father's "middle state."

Yet the liminal account, like Crusoe's metaphor of reprieve, seems artificial—not false, but insufficient or old-fashioned—because Defoe centers the work on Crusoe's obsession with finding an account of his mental life that coheres sequentially, causally, and spiritually. Solitude is the occasion, narrative the medium, and prison the overarching figure:

> Now I began to construe the Words mentioned above, *Call on me, and I will deliver you*, in a different Sense from what I had ever done before; for then I had no Notion of any thing being call'd Deliverance, but my being deliver'd from the Captivity I was in; for tho' I was indeed at large in the Place, yet the Island was certainly a Prison to me, and that in the worst Sense in the World; but now I learn'd to take it in another Sense: Now I look'd back upon my

5. See Douglas Hay, "Property, Authority, and the Criminal Law," in *Albion's Fatal Tree: Crime and Society in Eighteenth-Century England*, ed. Douglas Hay et al. (New York: Pantheon, 1975), pp. 17–63.

past Life with such Horrour, and my Sins appear'd so dreadful, that my Soul sought nothing of God, but Deliverance from the Load of Guilt that bore down all my Comfort: As for my solitary Life it was nothing; I did not so much as pray to be deliver'd from it, or think of it. (pp. 96–97) [71]

Here, as in the wreck, Crusoe's terms are directly religious. But in context the theological referents are subordinate to the machinations of Defoe's narrative as it struggles—repeatedly retelling the early phases of the story—to trace the reformation of Crusoe's conscience. We move from "just history of fact," to straight journal, to journal interrupted and dissolved by reflection. Defoe uses the "real" words of Crusoe's chronicle to certify the truth of reflections that at first break into the texture of the vital pages surrounding the delirium and eventually overtake them entirely. Narrative in its relation to consciousness is the actual subject here: accounts of the self *are* the self, and fuller, more circumstantial accounts placed in a reflective context are more true than mere chronicles or journals. This section of *Robinson Crusoe* stands at a decisive juncture in the history of the novel because of its literal quest through generic types for some material equivalent to the formation of thought. This quest structures Defoe's "realism" as a mode of representation that incorporates and subordinates the others into what Bakhtin calls polyglossia.[6] Before our very eyes, the new, reflective, consciousness-centered form displaces the genres it has subsumed, a state of affairs traced in Defoe's text by Crusoe's progressive dilution of his ink until the journal fades into illegibility a few pages following the passage quoted above.

During Crusoe's "solemn" observance of the second anniversary of his shipwreck, the prison metaphor recurs, again yoked with solitude. Here the two terms fall into clear opposition, signifying states of mind before and after Crusoe's correct understanding of deliverance some two months earlier. To be imprisoned is to be subject to random misery:

I was a Prisoner lock'd up with the Eternal Bars and Bolts of the Ocean, in an uninhabited Wilderness, without Redemption: In the midst of the greatest Composures of my Mind, this would break out upon me like a Storm, and make me wring my Hands, and weep like a Child: Sometimes it would take me in the middle of my Work, and I would immediately sit down and sigh, and look upon the Ground for an Hour or two togther; and this was still worse to me; for if I could burst out into Tears, or vent my self by Words, it would go off, and the Grief having exhausted it self would abate. (p. 113) [83]

6. On "polyglossia" as a form of contradiction and as the essence of the novel—that is, its ability to contain contradictory voices—see Mikhail Bakhtin, "From the Prehistory of Novelistic Discourse" and "Discourse in the Novel," in *The Dialogic Imagination*, ed. and trans. Michael Holquist and Caryl Emerson (Austin: University of Texas Press, 1981), especially pp. 50–60 and 277–84.

But to comprehend solitude is to be spiritually and mentally whole, as well as to function materially:

> I spent the whole Day in humble and thankful Acknowledgments of the many wonderful Mercies which my Solitary Condition was attended with. . . . I gave humble and hearty Thanks that God had been pleas'd to discover to me, even that it was possible I might be more happy in this Solitary Condition, than I should have been in a Liberty of Society, and in all the Pleasures of the World. That he could fully make up to me, the Deficiencies of my Solitary State, and the want of Humane Society by his Presence . . . supporting, comforting, and encouraging me to depend upon his Providence here, and hope for his Eternal Presence hereafter. (p. 112) [82]

Meanings outnumber terms here as the notion of prison slides from the liminal, arbitrary, openly public realm into the private realm of reflective thought.

Several things are happening. First, the liminal experience, while present, is losing its tangibility, and its habitual, external forms are assuming a negative tinge. Second, the outcome of punishment is now being represented as mental reformation. Third, errant personality is reconstituted as self-consciousness by solitary reflection. Finally, the ability to function materially is specifically attributed to the proper inner comprehension of life as a story, each circumstance of which is meaningful. We see the mythology of reform taking shape here. Prison, now equated with solitary reflection, is first viewed as negative, random, punitive, vengeful; but it slides into another thing entirely—something salubrious, beneficent, reformative, and productive of wealth and social integration. Crusoe's illness can be read, in this light, as a prospective allegory of the move from the old, fever-ridden jails to the clean, healthy, contemplative solitude of the penitentiaries.

Crusoe equates having a self with being able to account for his crime, and his story literally enacts a quest for some narrative equivalent to personality. Just as his construction of material surrogates of European civilization is indistinguishable from the narration of his story, so is novelization inseparable from the reformation of his consciousness. Friday's advent enables Crusoe to test the power of narrative to constitute the self. Crusoe must teach him the causes and raise him up into the crafts before Friday is recognizable as human and Crusoe's self-construction is socially validated.

When Crusoe ends his confinement by subjugating the mutineers with the purely fictional personage of the Governor, both the self and the authority it projects are shown as narrative constructs that effect material ends.

> When I shew'd my self to the two Hostages, it was with the Captain, who told them, I was the Person the Governour had order'd to look

> after them, and that it was the Governour's Pleasure they should
> not stir any where, but by my Direction; that if they did, they
> should be fetch'd into the Castle, and be lay'd in Irons; so that as
> we never suffered them to see me as Governour, so I now appear'd
> as another Person, and spoke of the Governour, the Garrison, the
> Castle, and the like, upon all Occasions. (p. 271) [195]

The fiction of the Governor becomes real through its own enactment:
the mutineers are divided, maneuvered into submission, and, where of
sound character, reconverted to the service of established order. The
five incorrigibles, imprisoned in the island's fortified cave during the
recapture of the English captain's ship, benefit ultimately from clemency
at Crusoe's hand in his role as the Governor; they are left to colonize
the island under threat of execution should they return to England.
Viewed one way, they, like Moll Flanders, are reprieved and transported;
but from another perspective they have become convicts in Crusoe's
penitentiary, condemned to reformation according to a narrative of his
making. His story will be their regime:

> I then told them, I would let them into the Story of my living
> there, and put them into the Way of making it easy to them:
> Accordingly I gave them the whole History of the Place, and of
> my coming to it; shew'd them my Fortifications, the Way I made
> my Bread, planted my Corn, cured my Grapes; and in a Word, all
> that was necessary to make them easy: I told them the Story also
> of the sixteen *Spaniards* that were to be expected; for whom I left
> a Letter, and made them promise to treat them in common with
> themselves. (p. 277) [199]

Crusoe has altered from a lord of nature, alone with the savage Friday,
to a lord of men who appears at last, ceremoniously clothed, in *propria
persona* as the Governor. Having defined a consciousness located at the
juncture of the mental and the material, having mapped it first on the
terrain of his island and then on Friday's malleable mentality, Crusoe
now rehearses his authority and renders it tangible through fiction. Once
he has construed himself and discovered the enabling force of narrative,
Crusoe uses the explanatory power of story-telling to exert control over
the mutineers and to police the future civic order he envisions upon
the arrival of the sixteen Spaniards. Upon Crusoe's departure, the island
and its furniture exchange their metaphorical standing as prison for that
of an actual penal colony with his fortress at its civic center and his story
as its master narrative.

Although Defoe's hero is castaway on a deserted island, the formulation of imprisonment that lies at *Robinson Crusoe*'s figurative core
assumes and incorporates the experience of the city as the seat of power.
Defoe's tale is an archaeology of urban geographical, social, psycholog-

ical, and legal forms. Crusoe maps the island according to the polarity between city and country even before he is able to populate it, and the architectural traces of his ingenuity, so minutely fabricated in the telling, become instruments of power once the mutineers arrive. This is especially clear in the case of Crusoe's fortified cave, the evolution of which is synonymous with the narration of his story, because it serves at once as a prison in which he holds the mutineers and the seat of authority personified in the Governor. Built first to shield its resident from harm and then elaborated to provide a base for his farming and hunting, the fortress becomes a walled city that can contain and subjugate as well as defend. Crusoe's building program retraces the ancient etymology of the English word "town" and the French word "ville," earlier forms of which referred first to enclosed places or camps, then to farms or manors, and finally to governed urban habitations.

Crusoe tests and revalidates forms of hegemony characteristic of urban culture, the ordering principles of the governed city. With the convergence of Friday, the Spanish captain, the mutineers, the English captain, and the prospective arrival of sixteen Spanish castaways from the mainland (signifying, like so many tribes, the varying modes of social order), Defoe retrieves that moment in human history described by Lewis Mumford as "the first time the city proper becomes visible": "The first beginning of urban life . . . was marked by a sudden increase in power in every department and by a magnification of the role of power itself in the affairs of men."[7] Of course Defoe's narrative cannot re-create the original city but instead must represent it from the vantage point of modern civilization—thus Crusoe's salvage operations, and his construction of what amounts to a deserted city waiting for its test of viability. The architectural fabric by which Crusoe laboriously masters the island, like the articles reclaimed from the shipwreck, store up power as surely as gunpowder stores propulsive force. They form a stockpile of the urban estate that, no less than Crusoe's hoard of gold, must wait to be expended.

It has become a commonplace of literary history to trace the emergence of the realist novel to the concentration of literate audiences in early modern cities.[8] Collaterally, from the broad perspective of social theory, the origin of written history within the purview of the city situates narrative in "a special form of 'container,' a crucible for the generation of power on a scale unthinkable in non-urban communities."[9] Critics of the novel risk more by making too little of these congruent analyses than by making too much.

7. Lewis Mumford, "University City," in *City Invincible*, ed. Carl H. Kraeling and Robert M. Adams (Chicago: University of Chicago Press, 1960), p. 7.
8. See especially Watt, *The Rise of the Novel*, pp. 45–46 and 177–82. My treatment of the relationship between narrative and cities, in general, and between the realist novel and the urban metropolis, in particular, is at once more literal, more encompassing, and less dependent upon the concept of class than Watt's.
9. Anthony Giddens, *A Contemporary Critique of Historical Materialism* (Berkeley: University of California Press, 1981), p. 96. In the following section I employ various terms from Giddens.

Traditionally the two most distinctive spatial traits of the city were, at its center, the compound containing governmental and religious buildings and, at its periphery, the surrounding walls. These also were the two habitual sites of prisons, which thus lay deep in the syntactic structure articulating the space of the city. Viewed on the large canvas of world time, written narrative rests with prison at the generative axis of the city as the enclosed seat of authority and the site of surveillance. In ancient Sumer, for example, the origins first of written language and then of inscribed narrative have been traced to the requirements of civic administration:

> The keeping of written "accounts"—regularised information about persons, objects and events—generates power that is unavailable in oral cultures. The list is . . . not just an aid to the memory, but a definite means of encoding information. Lists do not represent speech in any sort of direct way, and . . . the early development of writing thus signals a sharper break with speech than might be imagined if we suppose that writing originated as a visual depiction of the spoken word. In Sumer, listing led eventually to the further development of writing as a mode of chronicling events of a "historical" nature. . . . These "event lists" form the first known "written histories," and eventually built up to span a large number of generations.[1]

Considered on this scale, the claim that novels often lay to the narration of historical truth becomes an assertion of the authority latent in written representation.

As Mikhail Bakhtin says, all of the traditional literary genres, "or in any case their defining features, are considerably older than written language and the book, and to the present day they retain their ancient oral and auditory characteristics. Of all the major genres only the novel is younger than writing and the book: it alone is organically receptive to new forms of mute perception, that is, to reading."[2] The novel, the genre of writing par excellence, formally embodies the fabric of urban culture: the very self-consciousness concerning the narration of minute particulars that defines it implies not merely an awareness of being watched but the technical ability to keep track by writing and to retrieve by reading. Compilation, investigation, justification, adjudication, letters, lists, receipts, journals, records, evidentiary detail, testimony—the written traces of merchandise and manners—here is the stuff both of cities and of novels.

Defoe's pervasive listings—his accountings, inventories, census reports, bills of lading, logs, and diaries—fictionally reinscribe the origins

1. Ibid., p. 95.
2. Bakhtin, *The Dialogic Imagination*, p. 3. I am concerned with the extent to which narrative order itself modifies the diversity and antiauthoritarianism ("heteroglossia") that, for Bakhtin, defines the novel. Chapter 7 of *Imagining the Penitentiary* suggests that transparent representation in the realist novel encompasses, contains, and reshapes apparent heterodoxy.

of writing as the medium of power. Among the first products of Crusoe's confinement are the lists contained in his journal, at once prototypes of his ultimate published narrative and integral parts of it. But early in the story we see writing, the means of civic commerce, go faint as Crusoe dilutes and finally exhausts his ink in a trail of scarcely legible script. Defoe underscores the social structure implicit in records when, because of his delirium, Crusoe's marking of the calendar also becomes indefinite. On the island Crusoe's solitary, gestural use of writing calls attention to its usual function as a medium of exchange. For written language, which represents its objects abstractly and renders them transferable across time and space, is to talk and oral fable as money, which gains value only as a medium of exchange, is to labor and its tangible products. Defoe probes and reoriginates the link between money and writing, which, in recent times, has been traced archaeologically to exceedingly ancient trade tokens, impressions of which appear to have formed the earliest inscriptions, a primitive, protocuneiform script. Crusoe is forced back into an existence based only on use value rather than exchange. He must put aside his hoards of money and stash his manuscripts.

In *Robinson Crusoe*, Defoe stages an explanatory myth showing how Crusoe's isolation and enclosure enable him to constitute power through the storage and allocation of resources. Only gradually does Crusoe master the physical potential of the island and store up enough provisions to consider allocating some to another person. At first his sense of control seems childish or illusory, and he suffers horrible fears that his authoritative resources might not be sufficient to protect him from visiting savages. However, his power becomes instrumental when luck and skillful deployment enable him to subdue the two cannibals who separate from their clan to pursue Friday, the object of their feast. His rescue of Friday provides a subject on whom to exercise authority.

As Friday becomes Crusoe's loyal subject (a human resource), he participates in an elementary linguistic, educational, and social structure in which Crusoe accumulates enough power to mount a direct assault, destroying all but four of the twenty-one cannibals who visit the island intent upon making a banquet of Friday's father and the Spanish captain. Defoe's representation of the signal stages of civilization is lucid. Crusoe represses the primitive, devouring power latent, as Elias Canetti suggests, in the sharp, smooth, orderly array of teeth.[3] His island government sublimates cannibalistic dominance into a mimicry of toleration as state policy:

> My Island was now peopled, and I thought my self very rich in Subjects; and it was a merry Reflection which I frequently made, How like a King I look'd. First of all, the whole Country was my

3. Elias Canetti, *Crowds and Power*, trans. Carol Stewart (New York: Viking Press, 1962), pp. 207–11.

own meer Property; so that I had an undoubted Right of Dominion. *2dly*, My People were perfectly subjected: I was absolute Lord and Law-giver; they all owed their Lives to me, and were ready to lay down their Lives, *if there had been Occasion of it*, for me. It was remarkable too, we had but three Subjects, and they were of three different Religions. My Man *Friday* was a Protestant, his Father was a *Pagan* and a *Cannibal*, and the *Spaniard* was a Papist: However, I allow'd Liberty of Conscience throughout my Dominions: But this is by the Way. (p. 241) [174]

When Defoe has the Spanish captain interpose an objection to immediate colonization of the island by shipmates abandoned among savages on the mainland, he goes out of his way to elucidate the relationship between physical resources and power in social formations:

He told me, he thought it would be more advisable, to let him and the two other [*sic*], dig and cultivate some more Land, as much as I could spare Seed to sow; and that we should wait another Harvest, that we might have a Supply of Corn for his Country-men when they should come; for Want might be a Temptation to them to disagree, or not to think themselves delivered, otherwise than out of one Difficulty into another. You know, says he, the Children of *Israel*, though they rejoyc'd at first for their being deliver'd out of *Egypt*, yet rebell'd even against God himself that deliver'd them, when they came to want Bread in the Wilderness. (p. 246) [177–78]

In this same context, though implements are lacking, writing becomes an issue for the first time since the ink was exhausted more than twenty years before. The authoritative language that Crusoe intends to have the force of a written charge assumes the marked stiffness of legislative prose:

And now having a full Supply of Food for all the Guests I expected, I gave the *Spaniard* Leave to go over to the *Main*, to see what he could do with those he had left behind him there. I gave him a strict Charge in Writing, Not to bring any Man with him, who would not first swear in the Presence of himself and of the old *Savage*, That he would no way injure, fight with, or attack the Person he should find in the Island, who was so kind to send for them in order to their Deliverance; but that they would stand by and defend him against all such Attempts, and where-ever they went, would be entirely under and subjected to his Commands; and that this should be put in Writing, and signed with their Hands: How we were to have this done, when I knew they had neither Pen or Ink; that indeed was a Question which we never asked. (p. 248) [179]

Only eight days later Crusoe sights the mutinous vessel, the mastery of which will prove his salvation.

Except for the one invocation of writing in Crusoe's charge to the

Spanish captain, his ambassador to the mainland castaways, his demonstrations of power remain oral and physical until after he has staged the appearance of a settled government so as to overcome and imprison the mutineers. But at the moment of departure, when he tells the technical secrets of life on the island to the prison colony he leaves behind, Crusoe's letter to the expected Spaniards reintroduces writing in order to explain the constitution of his city-state and to govern its future behavior. His letter attempts to store up authority across time just as his treasure has stored up value. And indeed, as if to acknowledge the ancient covalence of writing and money, within a page of text Defoe refurbishes the disused currency:

> When I took leave of this Island, I carry'd on board for Reliques, the great Goat's-Skin-Cap I had made, my Umbrella, and my Parrot; also I forgot not to take the Money I formerly mention'd, which had lain by me so long useless, that it was grown rusty, or tarnish'd, and could hardly pass for Silver, till it had been a little rubb'd, and handled; as also the Money I found in the Wreck of the *Spanish* Ship. (p. 278) [200]

Money, writing, listing, urban enclosure, social authority, forced confinement—all are obsessions of Defoe's, and these elements remain central to our sense of the novel in general.

Reference to large-scale social theory merely works to confirm motive forces embedded in the novel. The novel acts out, it represents iconically, the interplay between the unbounded heterogeneity of population in cities (their polyglot assembly of voices) and the bounded unity of their walls, fortified compounds, governmental structures, and systems of communication (their inscription of "facts," their insistence on point of view, and their assimilation of authority from approved genres through parody, burlesque, irony). "From the beginning," as Lewis Mumford says, "the city exhibited an ambivalent character it has never wholly lost: it combined the maximum amount of protection with the greatest incentives to aggression: it offered the widest possible freedom and diversity, yet imposed a drastic system of compulsion and regimentation."[4] My stance necessarily stresses the subordination of diversity to civic rule and, in the case of the novel, to narrative order. But the novel's generic instability persists because the diversity it encompasses and the authority it projects are reciprocal opposites, each defined by the representation of its antithesis, each always containing the other. Still, while it remains permissive in many respects, the novel oscillates between points of view that imply surveillance and enclosure. On the one hand stand novels in which readers enter the mental world of a single character and thereby fictionally view reality as a network of contingencies dependent upon observation; on the other lie novels in which readers ally themselves

4. Lewis Mumford, *The City in History* (New York: Harcourt, Brace and World, 1961), p. 46.

with the controlling power of an omniscient narrator. In this light, it is of more than incidental significance that Defoe served as a spy and a government agent—the very human medium of surveillance—and that he repeatedly suffered imprisonment.

MICHAEL McKEON

Defoe and the Naturalization of Desire: *Robinson Crusoe*†

In *Robinson Crusoe*, Defoe's principal response to the central question of narrative epistemology—the question of how to tell the truth in narrative—is evidently the claim to historicity and the quantifying assertions of veracity with which it is conventionally associated. However, the naive empiricism of this approach is modified in several ways. Charles Gildon is only the first of many readers who have suspected that Defoe's purportedly objective protagonist is really a subjective projection.[1] Robinson's island journal, so far from confirming the events of the framing narrative itself, differs enough in minute detail to complicate the historicity of both documents. And yet the effect of these factors may be less to throw the historicity of the travels themselves into question than to sensitize us to the personalized veracity of Robinson's experience, which is all the more authentic for having this subjective volatility.

* * *

The peculiar coexistence of historicity and subjectivity in *Robinson Crusoe*, the early dynamic between journal and narrative and the more general one between Character and Narrator—these exemplify the obvious indebtedness of Defoe's work to the formal procedures of spiritual autobiography. The form would of course have been familiar to Defoe, who had been set apart for the nonconformist ministry until his religious crisis at the age of twenty-one. The gap between the sinful young rambler and the repentant convert from whose perspective the story is told is felt very strongly in the first half of *Robinson Crusoe*. "But if I can express at this Distance the Thoughts I had about me at that time," Robinson says at one point, and we are often aware, through retrospective narrative intrusions, of the great divide between this foolish, thoughtless, headstrong, prodigal, sinful youth whose fortunes we attend, and the au-

† This essay appeared as chapter 9 in *The Origins of the English Novel, 1600–1740* (Baltimore: The Johns Hopkins UP, 1987) 315–37. The author has revised the essay especially for this edition. By permission of The Johns Hopkins Press. NCE page numbers appear in brackets.
1. [Charles Gildon], *The Life and Strange Surprizing Adventures of Mr. D—— De F——* . . . (1719).

thoritiative, prophetic, but disembodied consciousness that hastens us on into the fateful future (11) [10].[2]

Once on the island, the gap between the two begins to close. The sprouting seeds, the earthquake, his illness and dream, are natural events that we watch Robinson painfully and imperfectly learn to spiritualize, to read as signs of God's presence (78–79, 80–81, 87–91) [58–60, 64–67]. In order to treat his ague he looks in his seaman's chest for a roll of tobacco, and finds there "a Cure, both for Soul and Body"—not only the roll but a bible as well. Trying "several Experiments" with the tobacco, he listlessly experiments also with bibliomancy for a cure to the spiritual disease of which he is only now, before our eyes, becoming fully conscious (93–94) [69]. "Deliverance" is the scriptural word that holds his attention, and he learns to read it in such a way as to release, for the first time, its spiritual application:

> Nor I began to construe the Words mentioned above, *Call on me, and I will deliver you*, in a different Sense from what I had ever done before; for then I had no Notion of any thing being call'd Deliverance, but my being deliver'd from the Captivity I was in, for tho' I was indeed at large in the Place, yet the Island was certainly a Prison to me, and that in the worst Sense in the World; but now I learn'd to take it in another Sense: . . . [to seek] Deliverance from the Load of Guilt that bore down all my Comfort . . . Deliverance from Sin [is] a much greater Blessing, than Deliverance from Affliction (96–97) [71].

At this point, Robinson's "load," like that of Bunyan's Christian, falls from his shoulders because he has learned, like Edward Coxere, to spiritualize his island prison as the prison of the world herebelow. It is the beginning of the movement of narrative "atonement," when Character and Narrator come together, and this can be seen in the case with which Robinson will shortly distinguish between not aimless past and repentant future but anguished past and contented present: between "Before," when he felt he "was a Prisoner lock'd up with the Eternal Bars and Bolts of the Ocean," and "now," when "I began to exercise my self with new Thoughts" (113) [83]. Henceforth he will by no means be immune from backslidings, but they will be ostentatious lapses—his construction of the enormous canoe, his panic over the footprint, his rage against the cannibals—whose rapid moralization will only emphasize how far the Character has internalized the spiritualizing powers of the Narrator.[3]

2. See e.g., *Robinson Crusoe*, 3, 5–6, 7–8, 9–10, 14–15,, 16, 17, 19, 35–36, 38, 40 [4, 5–9, 12–15, 27–28, 29, 31]. On Defoe's religious upbringing see Michael Shinagel, *Defoe and Middle-Class Gentility* (Cambridge: Harvard University Press, 1968), chap. 1.
3. See *Robinson Crusoe*, 124–28, 153–57, 168–73 [91–93, 112–14, 122–25]. On the conventionality of postconversion lapses in spiritual autobiography, see George A. Starr, *Defoe and Spiritual Autobiography* (Princeton: Princeton University Press, 1965), 160; Hunter, *Reluctant Pilgrim*, 187.

MICHAEL McKEON

Thus *Robinson Crusoe* can be seen to be in rather close proximity to the preoccupations of Protestant soteriology in general and of spiritual autobiography in particular. With the spiritualization of "deliverance" Robinson's early urge to "ramble" (3) [4] does not disappear, but it is permanently transvalued for him, as we will see. Physical mobility is reconceived in spiritual terms, as movement both "upward" and "inward": after his dream of the avenging angel he realizes that since leaving home he has had not "one Thought that so much as tended either to looking upwards toward God, or inwards towards a Reflection upon my own Ways" (88) [65]. Moreover, the impulse toward introspective veracity that Robinson now evinces is a vital channel for the claim to historicity in spiritual autobiography. But of course the generic status of *Robinson Crusoe* is a good deal more uncertain than this argument would suggest. The dynamic relation between Character and Narrator is, after all, a formal feature of the picaresque as well, and even of that originating strain of picaresque in which the "spiritual" constitution of the protagonist is clearly an "autodidactic" and secular act of self-creation rather than a function of divine creativity. By the same token, we are obliged to recall that the interplay between "journal" and "narrative" is as central to secular travel narrative as to spiritual autobiography.

These fairly random attempts to "place'" *Robinson Crusoe* by associating it with one or another established subgenre recapitulate, in different terms, the most important recent controversy concerning its interpretation. The modern tendency to see Defoe's work as essentially an essay in secular materialism is fairly represented by Ian Watt's view that Robinson's religion is the result of a mechanically Puritan "editorial policy." In reaction to this tendency, the traditions of seventeenth-century Puritan allegory and spiritual autobiography have been reviewed by critics, notably George Starr and Paul Hunter, to the end of assimilating *Robinson Crusoe* to something like an ideal type of Protestant narrative religiosity. Both arguments are made with great skill, but both may appear extreme insofar as they seem unnecessarily obliged to imply a mutual exclusion. As the Weber thesis suggests, in the historically transitional territory of early modern Protestantism, spiritual and secular motives are not only "compatible"; they are inseparable, if ultimately contradictory, parts of a complex intellectual and behavior system.[4]

If, shortly after his conversion, Robinson demonstrates (as in the preface) his ability to use the terms "application" and "improvement" in their spiritual sense (128, 132) [94, 96], throughout the narrative

4. See Ian Watt, *The Rise of the Novel: Studies in Defoe, Richardson, and Fielding* (Berkeley and Los Angeles: University of California Press, 1957), 81 (but Watt's position is not as extreme as it has sometimes been taken to be; see 82–83); Starr, *Defoe and Spiritual Autobiography*; and Hunter, *Reluctant Pilgrim*. Among more recent critics, John J. Richetti has gone furthest in arguing against this mutual exclusion: see his thoughtful discussions in *Popular Fiction before Richardson: Narrative Patterns, 1700–1739* (Oxford: Clarendon Press, 1969), 13–18, 92–96; and *Defoe's Narratives: Situations and Structures* (Oxford: Clarendon Press, 1975), 23 and chap. 2 passim.

he is far more inclined to use these words as synonyms for material industry (4, 49, 68, 144, 182, 195, 280) [4, 37, 51, 105, 132, 141, 202] Yet both usages are consistent with the unstable strategies of Protestant casuistry—which in any case is only one sphere of discourse in which the instability of secularization and reform is registered during this period. And if we wish to appreciate fully the status of *Robinson Crusoe* as a "Protestant narrative," we will need to attend to its filiations not only with *Grace Abounding* but also with the literal plot of *The Pilgrim's Progress*. Of course, Bunyan's entire plot of "romance" adventure exists in order to be spiritualized. In Defoe the balance between spiritualization and the claim to historicity has been reversed, and it is as though he has—not without the spiraling misgivings of the *Serious Reflections*[5]— taken that perilous next step and, in the name of a "positive" secularization, explicitly sanctioned our resistance to allegorical translation. The result is a literal narrative filled with the mutabilities of religion (providence) and romance (pirates, shipwreck), which do not so much undergo in themselves a transformative specification to the mechanics of social mobility, as engineer the conditions under which that mobility is wonderfully enabled to transpire.

* * *

What is Defoe's response to "questions of virtue"—to the problem of how virtue is manifested in social behavior and experience? One focus of the critical controversy to which I have just referred is the question of what Robinson means when he speaks of his "ORIGINAL SIN" in opposing his father's advice that he stay at home and keep to the "middle Station," or "the upper Station of *Low Life*," to which he was born (194, 4–5) [141, 5]. Obviously the term ascribes a religious significance to Robinson's physical mobility; but what sort of social significance does it attribute to it? Should we identify Robinson's "original sin" with capitalist industry; or with an anticapitalist impulse to ramble and to evade his capitalist calling; or with an anti-Puritan motive to evade his Puritan calling; or with a general unregenerate waywardness that really has no special social significance at all?[6] In a certain sense, however, this is to begin at the wrong end. For Robinson's mobility gains its religious overtones only with hindsight, through the retrospective viewpoint of the Narrator. In the present tense of narrative action it is primarily a social *rather* than a religious meaning—even the socially charged meaning of Calvinism—that Robinson's mobility possesses

5. Defoe, *Serious Reflections During the Life and Surprising Adventures of Robinson Crusoe . . .* (1720).
6. See Watt, *The Rise of the Novel*, 65; Starr, *Defoe and Spiritual Autobiography*, 74–81; Hunter, *Reluctant Pilgrim* 38–39; Shinagel, *Defoe and Middle-Class Gentility*, 126–27 and 268–69n. 5; Rogers, *Robinson Crusoe*, 76–77; Maximillian E. Novak, *Economics and the Fiction of Daniel Defoe*, University of California English Studies, no. 24 (Berkeley and Los Angeles: University of California Press, 1962), chap. 2; C.N. Manlove, *Literature and Reality, 1600–1800* (New York: St. Martin's, 1978), chap. 7. Cf. Gildon, *The Life and Strange Surprizing Adventures of Mr. D—— De F——*, 5–6.

when he first leaves home. His father speaks in a general way about the virtues of "Application and Industry," but this is not really the language of labor discipline and the calling (3–6) [4–6]. His appeal is at least as plausibly aristocratic ideology: to a very traditionalistic social stratification and to the advisability of maintaining the station of one's birth. How is it, then, that the young Robinson learns to read the social meaning of his wish to ramble through the religious spectacles of Calvinist discipline? And since the Puritan's pursuit of grace might entail either stasis or pilgrimage, either social stability or change, why should his mobility appear so definitively a sign of his sin rather than a token of his election? When does the language of the calling enter Robinson's vocabulary?

On his first sea voyage, Robinson, in mortal fear, bitterly berates himself for "the Breach of my Duty to God and my Father" (7–8) [7]. Before this the narration of his early life has been relatively free of religious injunction. Robinson's father is a merchant who became successful through the sort of travel he now forbids his son. One of the older sons is dead; the other has disappeared. Designed now for the law and a "settled" life, Robinson thinks himself at eighteen too old to be set an attorney's clerk or an apprentice, and he seems momentarily to attribute his wanderlust to the marginality of his status in the family: "Being the third Son of the Family, and not bred to any Trade, my Head began to be fill'd very early with rambling Thoughts" (3) [4]. But whatever the psychological cause of it, Robinson soon finds a more satisfactory explanation for his unsettledness—more satisfactory because empowered with the ascription of sin—in the idea of a "duty" that has been breached. And this idea he seems to hear first from his friend's father, the master of the ship on which he had made his nearly fatal first voyage. Learning that the youth had sailed with him "only for a Trial in order to go farther Abroad," the master tells Robinson "to take this for a plain and visible Token that you are not to be a Seafaring Man." "Why, Sir," says Robinson, "will you go to Sea no more?" "That is another Case," said he, "it is my Calling, and therefore my Duty" (14–15) [12]. This is Robinson's first lesson in casuistry, at least to our knowledge, and it is an important one. Duty is dictated by calling, and to be out of one's calling is certainly to be in sin. But how do you tell your calling if you have no clear intuition of it and have not been definitively bred to one? Parental authority is one guide. Another is the tokens and signs of divine will that can be read in experience, and it does not require a very subtle interpreter to read God's judgment in this particular case.

At this early stage Robinson is quite blind to providential signs. Yet even so, the narrative voice soon lets us know that returning home is not the only way he might at this point have altered his course for the better. For now Robinson begins to ship on a succession of voyages, and because he has "Money in my Pocket, and good Cloaths upon my Back, I would always go on board in the Habit of a Gentleman" rather than that of a common sailor. Like his creator, he is fond of upwardly mobile masquerade, but the result is that he remains idle and forfeits the opportunity to establish his calling at sea: for "as a Sailor . . . I had learn'd the Duty and Office of a Fore-mast Man; and in time might have quallified my self for a Mate or Lieutenant, if not for a Master" (16) [14]. Despite this bad choice, Robinson is lucky enough to be befriended by an honest Guinea captain, who teaches him some of the skills of both sailor and merchant (17) [14]. But before we can begin to ask if this employment has the potential of being a redemptive discipline, Robinson is captured by pirates and metamorphosed "from a Merchant to a miserable Slave . . . Now the Hand of Heaven had overtaken me, and I was undone without Redemption" (19) [15].

Nor do his spiritual prospects improve when he escapes from Sallee and gains material prosperity as a planter in Brazil. The problem is more general than the fact of his readiness to sell Xury to the Portuguese captain by whom they are "deliver'd" (in any case Defoe seems to exercise some care in formulating the case so as to make it conscientiously acceptable).[7] It is not that Robinson is specifically and spectacularly sacrilegious, but that he is comprehensively devoid of moral and spiritual constraints. The Portuguese captain himself is a man of such exemplary fair dealing that he would seem to epitomize how the merchant is to pursue his calling; and he treats Robinson so "honourably" and "charitably" that the latter's coarse desire to "gr[o]w rich suddenly" can only suffer by comparison (33–34, 37, 89) [26–27, 29, 65]. Rather than follow the rule of charity or regulate his life by the satisfaction of necessities, Robinson simply pursues his self-interest in Brazil. When the captain's good advice leads to his receipt of some valuable goods, Robinson is content to exploit the market for all he can get, selling them "to a very great Advantage; so that I might say, I had more than four times the Value of my first Cargo, and was now infinitely beyond my poor Neighbour." In this way Robinson's overextension and excess are palpably registered by his rapid advancement over others. It is not the fact of being a trader, but his "abus'd Prosperity," his unrationalized exploitation of exchange value, that distinguishes him from those who might be said to pursue their callings (37) [29]. The principles of subsistence and consumption are dominated by the unlimited desire to accumulate, a triumph of excess and waste that is also expressed in the irony that now Robinson "was coming into the very Middle Station, or upper Degree of low Life, which my Father advised me to before; and which if I resolved to go on with, I might as well ha' staid at Home" (35) [27].[8]

7. See, e.g., Richard Baxter's handling of the question, *"Is it lawful to buy and use men as Slaves?"* in *The Catechizing of Families* . . . (1683), 311.
8. On the rule of charity and the limiting standard of the satisfaction of necessities, see my *The Origins of the English Novel, 1600–1740* (Baltimore: The Johns Hopkins University Press), chap. 5, n. 39. On the persistence of a secularized conception of "honor" as "credit" and "trust" in business dealings, ibid., chap. 5, nn. 51–53.

By the same token, the voice of the Narrator makes it clear that despite past sins, having wandered into this way of life, Robinson might yet have made a decent calling of it. It is not strictly required, in other words, that one remain in the station of one's birth. What Robinson fails in for a second time is the identification of "those Prospects and those measures of Life, which Nature and Providence concurred to present me with, and to make my Duty." Our duty and calling are not objective entities, but conditions in which we find ourselves and which we are able to intuit and interpret into fulfillment. "As I had once done thus in my breaking away from my Parents, so I could not be content now, but I must go and leave the happy View I had of being a rich and thriving Man in my new Plantation, only to pursue a rash and immoderate Desire of rising faster than the Nature of the Thing admitted" (38) [29]. An incapacity to limit his desires by sensing the natural and providential limits of his situation is what makes Robinson successively a prodigal son, an unethical trader, and now also an imprudent trader: "Now increasing in Business and in Wealth," says the Narrator, "my Head began to be full of Projects and Undertakings beyond my Reach" (37–38) [29] When he is offered the chance to oversee an illegal and highly profitable shipment of African slaves, he is oblivious to the fact that it would have been "a fair Proposal" only if made to one who did not already possess a "Settlement" in need of looking after. For him to accept the offer is to do "the most preposterous Thing that ever Man in such Circumstances could be guilty of," to abandon the clear possibility of a settled calling. Nevertheless Robinson enters into an agreement with his fellow planters and goes "on Board in an evil Hour" (39–40) [30].

So the prelude to shipwreck is a chronic incapacity to rationalize worldly activity by the sanctions of a perceived moral duty. The many years on the island overcome this incapacity by obliging Robinson, devoid of human society, to experience the society of God. This experience has two crucial dimensions. First, in a state of solitude the greatest impediments to ethical behavior—other people—suddenly disappear. But second, what then remains is the otherness of divinity itself, the absolute moral standard now so inescapable that its very voice may be heard and internalized within one's own desires. Robinson's long isolation schools him in the psychological discipline needed to transform his activity into his calling. * * *

3

Robinson's island conversion depends upon a new-found ability to spiritualize his situation, to detect and interpret the signs of God's presence in his life on the island. As he explains it, the pleasures of this presence do not only compensate for the absence of human society.

They also alter his understanding of his own desires, of what it is he really wants:

> Thus I liv'd mighty comfortably, my Mind being entirely composed by resigning to the Will of God, and throwing my self wholly upon the Disposal of his Providence. This made my Life better than sociable, for when I began to regret the want of Conversation, I would ask my self whether thus conversing mutually with my own Thoughts, and, as I hope I may say, with even God himself by Ejaculations, was not better than the utmost Enjoyment of humane Society in the World.
>
> I gave humble and hearty Thanks that God had been pleas'd to discover to me, even that it was possible I might be more happy in this Solitary Condition, than I should have been in a Liberty of Society, and in all the Pleasures of the World. That he could fully make up to me, the Deficiencies of my Solitary State, and the want of Humane Society by his Presence, and the Communications of his Grace to my Soul . . . my very Desires alter'd, my Affections chang'd their Gusts, and my Delights were perfectly new . . .
>
> I look'd now upon the World as a Thing remote, which I had nothing to do with, no Expectation from, and indeed no Desires about: . . . I had neither the *Lust of the Flesh, the lust of the Eye, or the Pride of Life*. I had nothing to covet; for I had all that I was now capable of enjoying. (135–36, 112–13, 128) [99, 82, 93–94]

At such moments of radiant contentment, Robinson speaks as though he has shed not only all acquisitive appetites but all "worldly" ambition whatsoever, so that even the language of duty, labor discipline, and the calling has become an irrelevance. Yet we know this is not true. It is not only that he tells us that now "I was very seldom idle; but [had] regularly divided my Time, according to the several daily Employments that were before me, such as, *First*, My Duty to God, and the Reading of Scriptures" (114) [83–84]. It is precisely the enterprising and furiously energetic performance of some of those other employments that dominates our permanent impression of this most industrious of narratives. Robinson does not give over vocational ambition; on the contrary, he slowly and steadily makes "all Trades in the World"—farmer, baker, potter, stonecutter, carpenter, tailor, basketmaker—his calling (122) [89]. As he remarks, "By making the most rational Judgment of things, every Man may be in time Master of every mechanick Art . . . I improv'd my self in this time in all the mechanick Exercises which my Necessities put me upon applying my self to" (68, 144) [51, 105].

It is therefore not so much that Robinson moderates the immoderate desires that plagued him in his former life, as that their ethical quality has been altered—limited and therefore detoxified—by the alteration in his external circumstance: by the substitution, that is, of the society of God for human society. What this replacement achieves is, first of all, the transformation of exchange value into value in use. After the shipwreck but before his conversion, Robinson still believes that things acquire their value through commodification in the marketplace: although work on the island is discouragingly primitive, "my Time or Labour was little worth, and so it was as well employ'd one way as another" (68) [51]. But as we know from his celebrated, King James–version disdain for the found money—"O Drug! Said I aloud, what art thou good for, Thou art not worth to me"—Robinson is not slow to realize that there is no marketplace to be found on the island (57) [43]. And after a while he is completely captivated by the distinction between use value and exchange value, which he seizes many opportunities to rehearse. In the following passage he pointedly applies it to his former employment, in which exchange value played such a dominant role:

> I might have rais'd Ship Loadings of Corn; but I had no use for it . . . I had Timber enough to have built a Fleet of Ships. I had Grapes enough to have made Wine, or to have cur'd into Raisins, to have loaded that Fleet, when they had been built. But all I could make use of, was, All that was valuable . . . In a Word, The Nature and Experience of Things dictated to me upon just Reflection, That all the good Things of this World, are no farther good to us, than they are for our Use . . . I possess'd infinitely more than I knew what to do with . . . I had, as I hinted before, a Parcel of Money . . . [But] As it was, I had not the least Advantage by it, or Benefit from it. (128–29) [94]

Robinson's tone of cautionary sobriety should not obscure for us the liberation of being able to "possess infinitely," to accumulate limitless possessions that cannot entail the risk of becoming commodities in exchange. "*Leaden-hall* Market could not have furnish'd a Table better than I, in Proportion to the Company"; and the differences that are disclosed by this analogy are fully as important to Robinson as are the similarities (109) [80]. For here he can lay up great stocks of grain, fully indulging his "Desire of having a good Quantity for Store," without challenging the great end of personal consumption. Indeed, in combining capitalist abstinence with the just belief that "now I work'd for my Bread," Robinson implicity tempers the danger of attributing an imaginary value to capitalist activity with a labor theory of value, so that all this industry may be confidently sanctified by the biblical conviction "that in time, it wou'd please God to supply me with Bread" (117–18, 123–24) [86, 90].[9]

9. Ibid. On capitalist abstinence see, e.g., Eric Roll, *A History of Economic Thought*, 4th ed. rev. (London: Faber and Faber, 1973), 344–46. When Robinson attributes the preservation of the shipwrecked commodities to providence, he associates them with the gift of God's grace and achieves a similar sanctification (*Robinson Crusoe*, 130–31) [95]. See also Ian Watt's discussion of the mystique of the dignity of labor in relation to *Robinson Crusoe* in *"Robinson Crusoe as*

If the absence of human society prohibits the exchange of goods and the dangerous creation of imaginary value, it also precludes the human register of potentially sinful social advancement and excess. Unlike his sojourn in Brazil, here "there were no Rivals. I had no Competitor, none to dispute Sovereignty or Command with me" (128) [94]. Again, this does not prevent Robinson from continuing to behave like a capitalist; it effaces the moral consequences of that behavior. We become aware of this in subtle ways. When he tells us how he first "fenc'd in, and fortify'd," and "enclos'd all my Goods," the voice of the Narrator adds that "there was no need of all this Caution from the Enemies that I apprehended Danger from" (59, 60) [44–45]. But later we see that this is not really so. For once Robinson has again become a farmer in earnest, he finds himself in the position not so much of a Brazilian planter as of an English enclosing landlord. In danger of losing his crop to "Enemies of several Sorts"—goats, hares, and especially birds—he describes his emergency capital improvements in language that is disturbingly evocative of seventeenth- and eighteenth-century agrarian conflicts.[1]

> This I saw no Remedy for, but by making an Enclosure about it with a Hedge, which I did with a great deal of Toil; and the more, because it requir'd Speed. However, as my Arable Land was but small, suited to my Crop, I got it totally well fenc'd, in about three Weeks Time; and shooting some of the Creatures in the Day Time, I set my Dog to guard it in the Night . . . I staid by it to load my Gun, and then coming away I could easily see the Thieves sitting upon all the Trees about me, as if they ony waited till I was gone away, and the Event proved it to be so . . . I was so provok'd . . . knowing that every Grain that they eat now, was, *as it might be said*, a Peck-loaf to me in the Consequence; but coming up to the Hedge, I fir'd again, and kill'd three of them. This was what I wish'd for; so I took them up, and serv'd them as we serve notorious Thieves in *England*, (*viz.*) Hang'd them in Chains for a Terror to others. (116–17) [85]

But although Robinson gives vent here to the deep and disquieting emotions of the enclosing landlord, these "enemies," with whom he is indeed in mortal competition, are not expropriated peasants but birds and beasts of the field. The equivocal appetite for elevating oneself over one's neighbors has been slaked even as the categories by which such elevation might be registered—the social "stations" so significant to

---

a Myth," in *Eighteenth-Century English Literature: Modern Essays in Criticism*, ed. James L. Clifford (New York: Oxford University Press, 1959), 163–67. For Robinson's fascination with use and exchange value, see Robinson Crusoe, 50, 64, 189, 193, 195, 278 [38, 48, 137, 139, 141, 200].

1. For useful treatments of several aspects of the subject see Raymond Williams, *The Country and the City* (New York: Oxford University Press, 1973), chap. 10; Douglas Hay, "Poaching and the Game Laws on Cannock Chase," in *Albion's Fatal Tree: Crime and Society in Eighteenth-Century England* (New York: Pantheon, 1975), 189–253. For a discussion that has bearing on mine here, see Richetti, *Popular Fiction Before Richardson*, 95–96.

MICHAEL MCKEON

Robinson's father—have been erased. And the obscure but pervasive sense of status inconsistency that has all along been expressed in Robinson's persistent desire to "ramble" is quashed under conditions that paradoxically exclude all reference groups whatsoever. There are only himself and God; and the only criteria by which to experience relative deprivation and reward are those dictated by divine justice and mercy.[2]

But as we have just seen in the image of the thieving wildlife, this is only literally true. All readers of *Robinson Crusoe* have been struck by the protagonist's propensity to populate and domesticate his island with figures from home. Unlike many authors of imaginary voyages, Defoe is disinclined to celebrate the reign of use value within the relatively exotic environs of a communist utopia. The passage on the thieving wildlife makes it clear that he is far more attracted by the private property of the landed estate, whose utopian character consists in the "magical extraction," in Raymond Williams's words, of its problematic inhabitants. When Robinson takes his first "Survey of the Island" and comes upon the Edenic valley where he will build the "Bower" that will serve as his "Country-House," he imagines "that this was all my own, that I was King and Lord of all this Country indefeasibly, and had a Right of Possession; and if I could convey it, I might have it in Inheritance, as compleatly as any Lord of a Manor in *England*" (98, 100, 101–2) [72–74]. Later he permits the figure to encompass the entire island: "I was Lord of the whole Mannor; or if I pleas'd, I might call my self King, or Emperor over the whole Country which I had Possession of" (128) [94].[3]

If this fantasy of proprietorship appeals primarily to the impulse toward private ownership and capitalist improvement, there is at least an element here also of contemplative pastoralism and the domestic themes of Horatian retirement. Another way of saying this is that Defoe's island utopia is able to incorporate notions of value that are associated not only with capitalist and laboring industry but also with aristocratic ideology and its location of value in land. Of course, this syncretism can be found in the assimilationist posture of progressive ideology itself. Despite his trenchant attacks on the corruptions of lineage and aristocratic honor, Defoe was obsessed with the illusion of his own gentility, and at various stages in his career he proudly rode in the livery of his merchant's company, outrageously inflated his ancestry, and employed the medium of print to become armigerous and to aristocratize his name from Foe to De Foe. Marx was certainly right to argue that the utopianism of

2. Compare the following passages from *Robinson Crusoe*: "All our Discontents about what we want, appear'd to me, to spring from the Want of Thankfulness for what we have" (130) [95]; and "Thus we never see the true State of our Condition, till it is illustrated to us by its Contraries; nor know how to value what we enjoy, but by the want of it" (139) [102].

3. Defoe was fond of comparing a landowner's absolute possession to a monarch's; my *The Origins of the English Novel*, chap. 5, n. 4. Later, on his return to the island, Robinson "reserv'd to [him] self the Property of the whole" (*Robinson Crusoe*, 305) [220]. For Williams's argument see *Country and City*, 32; his subject is the country-house poems of Jonson and Carew.

Robinson Crusoe is not nostalgically conservative but progressive, that it is not "merely a reaction against oversophistication and a return to a misunderstood natural life," but "rather, the anticipation of 'civil society'."[4]

What must be added to Marx's view of the function of Defoe's utopia is the crucial and complementary religious element. And Robinson's labor discipline is as successful as it is in confirming his sense of election because the neutralization of its social volatility has been ensured by his utter solitude. This solitude is challenged, of course, when Robinson discovers the print of a man's foot on the shore. But it is important to recognize the volatility even of Robinson's imaginative figures, which in truth is essential also to the significance of that discovery. As Maximillian Novak has remarked, "If [Robinson's] triumph over the island is mostly an economic conquest, it is an imaginative conquest as well." But as we know, Defoe was deeply ambivalent about "the Power of Imagination" and imaginative creativity. Some of its riskiness can be felt in the self-conscious drollery with which Robinson extends the figure of his island lordship: "It would have made a Stoick smile to have seen, me and my little Family sit down to Dinner; there was my Majesty the Prince and Lord of the whole Island; I had the Lives of all my Subjects at my absolute Command. I could hang, draw, give Liberty, and take it away, and no Rebels among all my Subjects" (148) [108]. No more than a poignant fiction, of course. But shortly Robinson panics at the thought of being joined by other people, and he is moved not only to reaffirm the old language of social stratification that had been suspended by his utopian solitude but also to remind himself of the *real* sources of absolute sovereignty and creativity: "I consider'd that this was the Station of Life the infinitely wise and good Providence of God had determin'd for me, that . . . I was not to dispute his Sovereignty, who, as I was his Creature, had an undoubted Right by Creation to govern and dispose of me absolutely as he thought fit . . . 'Twas my unquestion'd Duty to resign my self absolutely and entirely to his Will" (157) [114].

Robinson's image of his "little family at dinner" is distracting in part because it suggests the speciousness of a submissive resignation achieved by the brute excision of all opportunities for competitive aggression. Defoe was conscious that his fiction of a desert-island conversion entailed this vulnerability. Still in the voice of Robinson Crusoe he later observed: "It is the Soul's being entangled by outward Objects, that interrupts its Contemplation of divine Objects, which is the Excuse for these Solitudes, and makes the removing the Body from those outward Objects

4. Karl Marx, *Grundrisse*, trans. Martin Nicolaus (Harmondsworth: Penguin, 1973), 83. On Defoe's assimilationism see Shinagel, *Defoe and Middle-Class Gentility*, 29–30, 47–48, 73–74, 103–4. On the retirement themes see Pat Rogers, "Crusoe's Home," *Essays in Criticism*, 24 (1974), 375–90.

seemingly necessary; but what is there of Religion in all this? . . . a vicious Inclination remov'd from the Object, is still a vicious Inclination." Robinson's imaginative enclosures are more treacherous than his physical ones because they cannot be held accountable to a standard that is clearly distinct from their own. At least part of his island experience, he speculates, was a function of "the brain-sick Fancy, the vapourish Hypochondriack Imagination . . . it was not meer Imagination, but it was the Imagination rais'd up to Disease." As we have seen, Robinson's conversion depends on his capacity to look both upward and inward. The lesson of the sprouting seeds, as he tells us pointedly, is not that God works miracles but that he works through us: "For it was really the Work of Providence as to me, that should order or appoint, that 10 or 12 Grains of Corn should remain unspoil'd . . . As also, that I should throw it out in that particular Place" (79) [58]. But once the saint has learned to read the presence of God in his own acts and intuitions, he has also become adept at discovering his own intuitions in the world at large. This dialectic is intensified considerably once Robinson finds the human footprint.[5]

4

Remarking on "how many various Shapes affrighted Imagination represented Things to me in," Robinson passes rapidly through several interpretations of the print: that it is his own fancy; the work of the Devil; the mark of a savage from the mainland; even that it "might be a meer Chimera of [his] own; and that this Foot might be the Print of [his] own Foot" (154, 157) [114–15]. This last possibility suggests to him that in his panic he has been like the credulous author of an apparition narrative, that "[he] had play'd the Part of those Fools, who strive to make stories of Spectres, and Apparitions; and then are frighted at them more than any body" (158) [115]. But Robinson's relief "to think that there was really nothing in it, but my own Imagination" is short-lived. He cannot resist subjecting the print to empirical measurement, and the disconfirmation "fill'd my Head with new Imaginations, and gave me the Vapours again to the highest Degree" (158, 159) [115]. His response to this renewed fear of the presence of other people is basically double. On the one hand, as we have seen, he ostentatiously resubmits himself to God's absolute will and sovereignty. On the other hand he apparently forgets this strategy of submission, and, like Saul, thinks "not only that the *Philistines* were upon him; but that God had forsaken him" (159) [116]. That the presence of human society should seem to threaten the absence of God's society is built in, of course, to the utopian mechanism of

---

5. Defoe, *Serious Reflections*, 8; idem, *A Vision of the Angelick World*, 12, 11 (ibid., new pagination); idem. *Meditations* (written 1681), 5, quoted in Shinagel, *Defoe and Middle-Class Gentility*, 16.

Robinson's solitude, and he now hits upon a strategy that, ostensibly directed at the putative savages, is also symbolically aimed at a divine audience and in fact only extends his other strategy, that of humble submission: "The first Thing I propos'd to my self, was, to throw down my Enclosures, and turn all my tame Cattle [i.e., his goats] wild into the Woods, that the Enemy might not find them . . . Then to the simple Thing of Digging up my two Corn Fields . . . [and] then to demolish my Bower, and Tent" (159) [116]. Physical, like metaphorical, enclosures bespeak a vanity whose traces must be destroyed. Robinson soon thinks better of this wholesale act of decreation, but he does plant a thick grove around his principal fortification so as to ensure that "no Men of what kind soever, would ever imagine that there was any Thing beyond it, much less a Habitation"; and he makes "all Things without look as wild and natural as [he can]" (161, 182) [117, 132].

These frantic oscillations and adjustments suggest in Robinson a fundamental confusion—of self and other, of self and "the enemy," of God and the enemy, of God and self—born of his incomplete internalization of divine righteousness and autonomy. In wishing now to destroy the unnatural signs of his own inventiveness with which he has defaced the landscape, Robinson recurs to the terms of his father, by which he saw himself as a young man bent on rebellion against God and "nature" (5, 38, 194) [5, 29, 141]. But the young Robinson was not only unnatural; he was also *too* natural, a "wild" man who "acted like a meer Brute from the Principles of Nature," devoid of revelation, and who had to be ensnared, enclosed, and tamed by God on the island (16, 88) [13, 65]. Robinson has learned to internalize this principle of divine cultivation to some degree, for he has trapped, "penn'd," and domesticated the wild beasts of his island, most notably its goats.[6] Now he wavers in his confidence, fearing that his cultured creativity bespeaks only the old wildness and rebellion. But the very cause of his fear ultimately helps solidify his conviction.

Robinson is repelled by the savages, by their "unnatural Custom" of cannibalism and by "the Degeneracy of Humane Nature" that it represents, and for a while his "Invention" and "Imagination" and "Fancy" are completely absorbed with alternative schemes for their efficient massacre (165, 168, 169, 170) [118f.] But in a satiric movement characteristic of travel narrative, he soon reflects that the culpability of these savages may yet be less than that of corrupted Europeans (his own early prodigality being a case in point), since "they do not know it to be an Offence, and then commit it in Defiance of Divine Justice, as we do in almost all the Sins we commit" (171) [124].[7] Robinson re-

---

6. See e.g., *Robinson Crusoe*, 111–12, 145–46 [81–82, 105–6]. For this point see Richetti, *Defoe's Narratives*, 50.

7. Compare the passage on 251 [181], where Friday suspects the English mutineers are going to eat their prisoners: "*No, no, says I, Friday, I am afraid they will murther them indeed, but you may be sure they will not eat them*" (an irony that takes in Robinson's own, initial murderous desires with respect to the savages).

pudiates his bloody imaginings by intuiting that they do not issue from a divine source. Pondering the case at hand, he asks himself: "What Authority, or Call I had, to pretend to be Judge and Executioner upon these Men as Criminals . . . How do I know what God himself judges in this particular Case? . . . I was perfectly out of my Duty, when I was laying all my bloody Schemes . . . I gave most humble Thanks on my Knees to God, that had thus deliver'd me from Blood-Guiltiness; beseeching him . . . that I might not lay my Hands upon them, unless I had a more clear Call from Heaven to do it, in Defence of my own Life" (170–71, 173) [124–26]. As the language of duty and the calling imply, Robinson shows, in the very censoring of his first impulses, that he has learned to read the signs of God's will in his conscience sufficiently well to know how to act upon them. If the savages "have no other Guide than that of their own abominable and vitiated Passions" (170) [124], Robinson is indeed (as he had vainly thought at first) now "distinguish'd from such dreadful Creatures as these" because he has begun to internalize a divine guide whereby to moderate and limit his own abominable passions. And so it becomes "a certain Rule with me, That whenever I found those secret Hints, or pressings of my Mind . . . I never fail'd to obey the secret Dictate; though I knew no other Reason for it, than that such a Pressure, or such a Hint hung upon my Mind." The very persistence of an impulse, in other words, may argue its affiliation with the "secret Intimations of Providence" (175, 176) [127]. In the remainder of the narrative, Robinson's increasing exposure to elements of external, human society will proceed alongside his increasingly confident internalization of God's society.

The first test of his capacity to read the marks of God on his own mind comes not from the savages but from a Spanish ship that appears one day on the horizon. Robinson's mind is filled with imaginings, fancies, and conjectures that are violently "rendred present to [his] Mind by the Power of Imagination": "In all the Time of my solitary Life, I never felt so earnest, so strong a Desire after the Society of my Fellow-Creatures, or so deep a Regret at the want of it" (188) [136]. Are these "ardent Wishes" the secret hints of providence? It soon appears that the ship has been broken apart by the sea, and the question then becomes whether "there might be yet some living Creature on board, whose Life I might not only save, but might by saving that Life, comfort my own to the last Degree; and . . . I thought the Impression was so strong upon my Mind, that it could not be resisted, that it must come from some invisible Direction" (189) [137]. Nothing comes of the rescue mission, but it provides Robinson with experience both in the identification of his desires as heaven-sent and in the way this internalization of providence entails a reciprocal expansion of his own identity as one not only delivered by God but able to deliver others as well. However, the mechanism is still uncertain, and the experiment is not without its costs.

Robinson is soon beset with guilt for his preoccupation with a physical deliverance from the island, and it is now that he recalls his "ORIGINAL SIN" of leaving home and its recurrence in Brazil, when he could not be content with the "confin'd Desires" with which providence had blessed him. Here he is once more "fill'd with Projects and Designs . . . for a Ramble" (194) [140]. Yet this episode of backsliding does not end, like earlier ones, with a chastening moralization. Or rather it extends that series into new territory.

What happens is that Robinson remains completely oblivious to the "Calm of Mind in my Resignation to Providence" that he had felt earlier, and his obsession with a physical deliverance becomes so palpable that he has "no Power to turn my Thoughts to any thing, but to the Project of a Voyage to the Main[land], which came upon me with such Force, and such an Impetuosity of Desire, that it was not to be resisted" (198) [143]. We recognize here, in the distinctive language of God's secret workings on the mind, the logic of inner conviction Robinson has prescribed for himself. A passion that is initially distinguished explicitly from providential directive succeeds, through the sheer force of its persistence, in redefining itself as nothing other than the irresistible dictate of providence. This transvaluation of desire, extraordinary as it is, is given yet more explicit form in what immediately ensues. Agitated beyond description, Robinson falls asleep and dreams that he delivers a savage from the cannibals, who afterward becomes his servant (198–99) [144]. And as he had said on an earlier and different occasion, "As I imagin'd, so it was" (51) [39]. For a year and a half later the dream materializes before his eyes, and Robinson behaves like nothing so much as the creative author of this drama, dutifully playing his assigned role but sometimes also exercising the playwright's revisionary prerogative when it pleases him to do so.[8]

What of his earlier intuition that the murder of savages is not part of his call or duty? Robinson does indeed recollect now that "I had greatly scrupled the Lawfulness of it to me," and although he knows he might rationalize the breaking of these scruples by arguments of self-preservation and self-defense, the real sanction is simply that "the eager prevailing Desire of Deliverance at length master'd all the rest" (199–200) [144]. So when the savages and their escaping prisoner, far down the beach, begin to run toward him, he tells us, in a suggestive choice of words, "I kept my Station." And when it appears that Friday (for it is of course he) will reach Robinson well before the savages do, "It came now very warmly upon my Thoughts, and indeed irresistibly . . . that I was call'd plainly by Providence to save this poor Creature's Life" (202) [146]. Providence, rebuffed when it counseled resignation, turns out to have been counseling impassioned activity all along. Divine and natural

8. See the following passages: "I could not depend on any means upon my Dream for the rest of it" (202) [146]; and "I did not let my Dream come to pass in that Part" (205) [148].

law, abandoning the posture of a moderating and limiting authority over and against human desire, now boldly join forces with it.[9]

When Robinson "saves" Friday from the cannibals, he becomes his deliverer. As God has communicated with Robinson, so Robinson speaks to Friday by "making Signs to him" (203–5) [147–48]. Friday soon learns enough broken English to say, *"You teach wild Mans be good sober tame Mans"*: as God tamed Robinson, so Robinson now tames this brute, and he has reason to hope that he has been "made an Instrument under Providence to save" not just the life but "the Soul of a poor Savage" (226, 220) [163, 160]. Friday, for his part, makes "all the Signs to me of Subjection, Servitude, and Submission imaginable, to let me know, how he would serve me as long as he liv'd" (206) [149]. Thus is this necessarily metaphorical relationship of creator to creature quickly literalized into one of sociopolitical subordination, and with this pledge Robinson's dominion on the island ceases to be figurative. Now he names Friday and tells him that his own name will be *"Master"*; but Robinson's new mastery is articulated as much by the mute human presence of what he is not, a slave, and human society is established by the fact of difference (206) [149].[1] At the same time, Friday, like Behn's Oroonoko, is a black man whose *"European"* beauty aids in the further differentiation of cultivated nature from the barbarian. He quickly learns to renounce his cannibalism, and when the master next confronts the savages, he enlists the aid of his civilized slave. Once again Robinson scruples at unsanctioned executions, and although in a "Fit of Fury" at their barbarity, he is if anything even more conscientious in his determination not to act without "a Call" (231–33) [167–68]. But the discovery that one of the cannibals' victims is a white European "fir'd all the very Soul within me," and his scruples are countermanded by a higher directive: "Are you ready, *Friday?* said I; yes, says he; let fly then, says I, in the name of God" (234) [169].

Defoe's aim here is not, of course, to suggest the religious hypocrisy of his protagonist—to make of Robinson what Bunyan makes of Mr. Mony-love—but rather to disclose the exquisitely subtle adjustments that comprise the process of arriving at a firm conviction of moral rectitude. The inescapable aura of irony that we sense in parts of Robinson's long passage out of sinfulness bespeaks the instability of ideas and institutions his author has tried to freeze in the midst of a secularization crisis. *Robinson Crusoe* at times emits the aura of irony because, like all ideology, it is dedicated to the instrumental disclosure—in De-

9. On Defoe's conception of natural law see Maximillian E. Novak, *Defoe and the Nature of Man* (Oxford: Oxford University Press, 1963), chap. 2.
1. The scene is prefigured in terms that are both more and less explicit when Robinson, having named and talked to his tame parrot, returns home after an unusually long absence and is startled to hear Poll repeat Robinson's own name back to him (*Robinson Crusoe*, 119, 142–43) [87, 104]. On the dialectical constitution of colonizer and colonized see Albert Memmi, *The Colonizer and the Colonized* (Boston: Beacon Press, 1967).

foe's case with unparalleled penetration and candor—of a complex of contradictions that it is simultaneously dedicated to mediating and rendering intelligible. The central and recurrent form of this contradiction can be expressed, as we have seen, in the notion of the human internalization of divinity, and it is precisely because Defoe "still" seeks to understand the problem of mediation in the awesome terms of a Christian culture that we, who have long since stopped trying, are sometimes distracted from the profundity to the absurdity of the effort.[2]

5

By now Robinson has become accomplished enough in that internalization to speak, without emotional repercussions, of having "an invincible Impression upon my Thoughts, that my Deliverance was at hand, and that I should not be another Year in this Place" (229) [166]. So when the arrival of the English mutineers is preceded by the counsel, "Let no Man despise the secret Hints and Notices of Danger, which sometimes are given him," we are prepared to be asked to view the sequel as a plain interposition of providence (250) [180]. Having masterfully trapped these "Brutes" as he once did his wild goats, Robinson remarks "that Providence had ensnar'd them in their own Ways," and he "fences" them in his island "Prison," as God first enclosed him there, on his final deliverance from it (255, 275–76, 269–70) [184, 198, 194]. Now Robinson has become, quite insistently, a "Deliverer." But he would not wish this furious activity in delivering others so as to help ensure his own escape to obscure his essential passivity: "For I saw my Deliverance indeed visibly put into my Hands," and "the whole Transaction seemed to be a Chain of Wonders; that such things as these were the Testimonies we had of a secret Hand of Providence governing the World" (273) [197]. But as this language of "governing" reminds us, *Robinson Crusoe* is an experiment in the internalization not only of divinity but of sociopolitical authority, and it is in this dimension of experience that Robinson's eventual deliverance from the island depends upon the progressive literalization of relationships that at first were only figurative.

For though he can never be said to "become" God, with the gradual population of his island Robinson does come to exercise absolute sovereignty. This is true not only of his paradigmatic colonial relationship with Friday but also of his rule over other human beings. Once again

2. For Defoe's reproof see *Serious Reflections*, 226; Gildon (*Adventures of Mr. D— De F—*, 8, 5) speaks of Robinson's "Coining of Providences," and points out that the adventures themselves commence with his "Secret Impulse to a Seafaring Life, to which Impulse you so often recommend a blind Obedience, whether grounded on Reason or not, and would perswade us that it proceeds from the secret Inspiration either of Providence, or some good Spirit" (see also ibid., 14, 37). For a useful formulation of *Robinson Crusoe's* ideological function see the comments in Richetti, *Defoe's Narratives*, 30–32; see also Reiss, *Discourse of Modernism*, 322. On the conventions of spiritual autobiography see, e.g., Starr, *Defoe and Spiritual Autobiography*, 123, 185–97.

he is initially inclined to express it as a diverting metaphor, a merely imaginative construct:

> My island was now peopled, and I thought my self very rich in Subjects; and it was a merry Reflection which I frequently made, How like a King I look'd. First of all, the whole Country was my own meer Property; so that I had an undoubted Right of Dominion. 2dly, My People were perfectly subjected: I was absolute Lord and Law-giver; they all owed their Lives to me, and were ready to lay down their Lives, *if there had been Occasion of it*, for me. It was remarkable too, we had but three Subjects, and they were of three different Religions . . . However, I allow'd Liberty of Conscience throughout my Dominions. (241) [174]

But so far from feeling guiltily impelled to an implicit retraction of the analogy, Robinson very soon has reason to insist upon its terms. Of the Spaniard he has saved he requires that his companions swear "upon their solemn Oath, That they should be absolutely under my Leading, as their Commander and Captain . . . and to be directed wholly and absolutely by my Orders . . . and that he would bring a Contract from them under their Hands for that Purpose" (245) [177]. Of the English captain he demands "that while you stay on this Island with me, you will not pretend to any Authority here; and . . . you will . . . be govern'd by my Orders" (256) [184]. And on the climactic victory over the mutineers he conceals his own presence "for Reasons of State" (268) [193]. On the basis of a legitimacy no greater than that of settlement and long possession, Robinson has truly come to exercise absolute sovereignty over his territory. [3]

Most important, Robinson is effectively socialized in these authoritative roles by the accreditation of his growing community. He is treated as the "*Generalissimo*" and the "Commander" of the island: "They all call'd me Governour," he says, and as in the case of Sancho Panza, we have good reason to attribute his dignified authority in these roles not simply to the "humoring" of a batty old hermit but to an experience that permits the manifestation of what in some sense was always there in potentiality (267–69) [192–94]. Robinson's consummate control of his environment persuades both the savages and the mutineers that his is an "enchanted Island," but they are degenerations of the race, and, like Sancho's, Robinson's governorship lays claim to being not an enchantment but a disenchantment of the world (243, 266) [176, 192]. We have watched him progress, like Bunyan's Christian, through a series of elevations to increasingly authoritative roles, and the end of the series— the reward toward which the progression has always been directed—is the long-awaited deliverance from captivity so as to assume the status of, not robe nobility but private citizen: the self-possessed and enlight-

3. Now Robinson extends to human malefactors the policy he earlier practiced on the thieving birds, by hanging the rebel captain as a sign to his confederates, cf. ibid., 117, 276 [85, 198]. On settlement and possession as criteria of sovereignty see my *The Origins of the English Novel*, chap. 5, n. 10.

ened capitalist entrepreneur of the modern age. The suspended time on the island has provided the laboratory conditions for acquiring, slowly and with relative impunity, the psychological equipment needed for possessive individualism. Now Robinson has internalized his utopia, and he is ready to return to society at large.[4]

For these reasons what remains is (as most readers feel) largely anti-climactic; nonetheless there are several points of interest. When Robinson first keeps the money that he ostentatiously scorns, we laugh at him; we know that he is in sin and that he is possessed of "a rash and immoderate desire of rising faster than the nature of the thing admitted" (57, 38) [43, 29]. But when, on his departure from the island, he takes with him the considerable store of money that he has accumulated over the years, he is implicitly in pursuit of his calling; his desire, and the nature of the thing, have become indistinguishable (278) [200]. What this means is that the imaginary value generated by exchange has become lawful because it has become real. Outwardly nothing has changed; the magical time on the island is immediately replaced by the bewildering but completely characteristic barrage of financial and legal quantifications by which Defoe generally tends to signify modern experience. But in another sense everything has changed. It is not only the old Portuguese captain who manifests his "honesty," "friendship," "honour," and "trust"; all the capitalists we now encounter are animated by these virtues, and the atmosphere is thick with fair dealing (280–84) [201–5].

This is also true of Robinson, who proceeds to exercise his charity not only on the captain (who had been so charitable years earlier) but on his two sisters, on the old widow in London, and on the Brazilian monastery and the poor (285–87) [206–7]. And despite Robinson's return to civilization, an air of enchantment lingers over Brazil, as though the magic of providence had effected a merger with that of capitalism. For although Robinson has become a wealthy man, neither he nor we have experienced any of the time and exploitation that were presumably expended in that laborious but invisible creation of exchange value. On the contrary, says Robinson, "I found all my Wealth about me," of which "I was now Master, all on a Sudden." Indeed, the event is in full accord with all his recent experiences, for it is an "Estate that Providence . . . put into my Hands" (284–86) [205–7]. Of course, this painless receipt of God's grace, this unrelieved honor among merchants, does not provide a "realistic" picture of capitalist activity, as Defoe well knew it would not. It may be plausible, however, to see him engaged here in the tangible externalization of Robinson's now securely inter-

4. Woodes Rogers reports that Alexander Selkirk's rescuers called him "Governour," and he himself refers to the castaway as "absolute Monarch" of the island; see Percy G. Adams, *Travel Literature and the Evolution of the Novel* (Lexington: University Press of Kentucky, 1983), 131. In *A Vision of the Angelick World*, 11 (in *Serious Reflections*, new pagination), Defoe admits that in the midst of one of his vapourish states "it had been easy to have possess'd me, if I had continued so much longer, that it was an enchanted Island, that there was a Million of evil Spirits in it, and that the Devil was Lord of the Manor."

nalized utopia, in the representation of the psychological state of being a principled possessive individualist, fully reconciled to the naturalness and morality of the pursuit of self-interest.

But in the crossing of the Pyrenees, Defoe clearly acknowledges that the world remains a treacherous place even for those whose minds are guided by providence. Robinson's desire to avoid a sea voyage is directly confirmed, in fact, by the familar signs: "But let no Man slight the strong Impulses of his own Thoughts in Cases of such Moment" (288; cf. 250) [208, 180]. Despite this, the crossing exposes his traveling party to as dangerous an assault of uncontrolled natural violence—the ravenous mountain wolves—as he has ever encountered, and he concludes that "I would much rather go a thousand Leagues by Sea, though I were sure to meet with a Storm once a Week" (302) [218]. Their mountain "Guide" had turned out to be "a Wretched faint-hearted Fellow" (297) [214]: had Robinson unaccountably been mistaken in his interpretation of God's secret hints? Defoe does not answer this question, but immediately after the close escape from the wolves we meet Robinson's "principle Guide . . . my good antient Widow" in London, a "good Gentlewoman" in whom he finds complete "Integrity" and "trust" in the management of his affairs; and the contrast at least confirms the relative moral safety of his financial dealings (303) [218].[5] Admitting with a clear conscience that "I was inur'd to a wandring Life," Robinson has now returned to his earliest scenes of prodigality. At this point, Defoe creates for him a wife, two sons, and a daughter, as though to give this long-lost younger son a second family from which to detach once again; but although we hear nothing more of them, Robinson adopts his two nephews. Between these stepsons he divides his own equivocation between assimilation and supersession, settlement and travel: "The eldest having something of his own, I bred up as a Gentleman, and gave him a Settlement of some addition to his Estate, after my Decease; the other I put out to a Captain of a Ship . . . And this young Fellow afterwards drew me in, as old as I was, to farther Adventures my self" (304–5) [219].

What is crucial about Robinson Crusoe's achievement of social success is not the degree of his elevation but his capacity to justify each station to which he attains as the way of nature and the will of God. As we have seen, this is a learned capacity. The product of his experience first in the society of God and then, gradually, among other people, it represents the hard-won lesson that the metaphysical realm of the Spirit may be accommodated and rendered accessible as the psychological realm of Mind. It is Defoe's remarkable achievement not simply to have provided this psychological access to spiritual crisis but to have specified it, with the mediating guidance of Puritan casuistry and soter-

5. Drawing on the conventions of Puritan metaphor, Hunter (*Reluctant Pilgrim*, 198–99) understands the episode of the wolves as Robinson's final allegorical victory over bestiality.

iology, to the concrete dimension of material and social ambition. * * *

In *Robinson Crusoe*, epistemology is so inextricably embedded in narrative substance that it may feel artificial to separate questions of truth from questions of virtue; but the distinction can be made. It is clear enough that Defoe's claim to historicity oversees the narrative's formal procedures. If it is complicated by the island, the journal, and the temporal dislocations of God's society and the power of imagination, that is because Defoe gives to the notion of the true history of the individual so intimate and introspective a form that it comes close to looking more like self-creation. This applies as well to the dominant, progressive ideology of the narrative, whose account of virtue delivered from early sin and then amply confirmed by the trials and rewards of providence is threatened repeatedly by the never-articulated insight that virtue is nothing but the ability to invoke providence with conviction.

* * *

CAROL HOULIHAN FLYNN

Consumptive Fictions: Cannibalism and Defoe†

In a Word, The Nature and Experience of Things dictated to me upon just Reflection, That all the good Things of this World, are no farther good to us, than they are for our Use.
                                                            Robinson Crusoe[1]

"If we were but seen by the people of any other country," Defoe complained, we would be taken for "if not cannibals, yet a sort of people that have a canine appetite."[2] While he insists upon a natural justice based upon utility, one that depends upon a "natural" restraint (that must be invented in conduct manuals), Defoe more often fleshes out the problematic aspects of modest economies. He insists in his explorations of physical economy that the cost of life may in fact be so dear that to survive we might find ourselves consuming one another. He uses the cannibal to explore the savage "other" that becomes incorporated into the civilized being, that part that exists "by necessity" in a consuming society grown complex and interdependent. Defoe demonstrates Crusoe "civilizing" his savage to make him part of a system he controls. But the savagery Crusoe combats turns out to be located as much within as without his own nature. He proves himself to be the most professionally savage inhabitant

† This essay has been revised by the author from chapter 7 in *The Body in Swift and Defoe* (Cambridge: Cambridge UP, 1990), 149–59. Reprinted with the permission of the Cambridge University Press.

1. *Robinson Crusoe*, ed. J. Donald Crowley (London: Oxford University Press, 1981), p. 129 [94]. [NCE page numbers appear in brackets.]

2. *Due Preparations for the Plague as well for Soul as Body*, ed. George Aitken (London, 1985), p. 37.

of his island as he feeds needs that grow increasingly complicated.

In his cannibal fictions, Defoe represents an imperialistic society that compromises his most compassionate instincts. He uses the cannibal as the emblem of a physical economy that requires an infusion of new blood to revitalize (and subsequently threaten) an ailing body politic. Just as "Moloch" London depended upon an influx of fresh bodies to grow faster than its death rate, England depended upon its colonized bodies to feed its "necessary" needs that resulted from its expansion. Defoe, ostensibly the professional booster of such a vigorous economy of expansion, points repeatedly to its cost, its dependence on slavery, upon violence, upon death. "To feed on Man's Flesh is lamentable, but not sinful," he observes, exposing in his charity the struggle implicit in the civilizing process.[3]

It is generally agreed, Defoe notwithstanding, that eating people is wrong. The cannibal provides a convenient benchmark of civilization, that place we more refined types depart from. Yet, at the same time, the cannibal has long been used as an index of the barbarity of its civilized observer. Montaigne offered the cannibal as a neutral moral model, arguing that "there is more barbarism in eating men alive, than to feed upon them being dead."[4] The idea of cannibalism can support a society's analysis of itself in complicated, often contradictory ways. The cannibal can be the neighboring enemy, the barbaric "other" that defines social worth. It can also serve as a mythic marker in the history of a civilization. We used to eat each other in the shadowy past before we knew better. Again, the cannibal may exist within the bounds of contemporary society as a reminder of that society's capacity for suffering.[5] And finally, the cannibal may stand as victim, visceral representative of larger and more powerful systems of consumption that mechanically reproduce its consumptive patterns.

Defoe employs the cannibal not just to explore a reprehensible

3. Cannibalism enters into Defoe's most vivid fantasies of a Hobbesian universe. Maximillian Novak, *Defoe and the Nature of Man*, Oxford, 1963, gives examples of Defoe's idea of "extreme of necessity." In *The Farther Adventures of Robinson Crusoe* a serving maid aboard a damaged ship is so hungry that she confesses herself "tempted to bite her own arm." "Had she been a mother she might have eaten her own child in her delerium . . . would have eaten her [mistress] with 'Relish'." Defoe, like Pufendorf, decided that to "feed on Man's Flesh in the desperate Extremity of Famine" is a lamentable "but not sinful Expedient," p. 71. Paula Backscheider, *A Being More Intense: A Study of the Prose Works of Bunyan, Swift, and Defoe*, New York, 1984, describes the "disastrous and perilous" state of a "mulatto" captured by Magadoxans so fierce in their hatred of white people that "they seize them, rip the flesh, and consider the chunks prizes to be exclaimed over or as tasty morsels to be savored," *The General History of the Pirates*, p. 49.
4. *The Essays of Montaigne Done into English by John Florio* (1615), 3 vols., ed. George Saintsbury, London, 1892, I, p. 226.
5. W. Arens, *The Man-Eating Myth: Anthroplogy and Anthropophagy*, Oxford and New York, 1980, considers the mythical implications of cannibalism, pp. 139–62. Arens is perhaps most extreme in his view that cannibalism itself is a fictional construct imposed upon civilization's "other" to enable the "civilized" people to subjugate their "cannibal" enemies and victims. Claude Rawson considers the theoretical implications of cannibalism in fiction in two long pieces in *Genre*: "Cannibalism and Fiction: Reflections on Narrative Form and 'Extreme' Situations," 10, 4 (1977); and "Cannibalism and Fiction," 11, 2 (1978). His reading of "A Modest Proposal," *Augustan Worlds*, ed. J. C. Hilson, M. M. B. Jones and J. R. Watson, Leicester and New York, 1978, pp. 29–50, reprinted in *Order from Confusion Sprung*, is also valuable.

"other," but to make that "other" part of the corporate sensibility that includes "ourselves." The process becomes by necessity complex. All the while Defoe yearns to annihilate the need that the denatured and cannibalized bodies of the poor represent, he immediately complicates his analysis in a most sentimental way. Ultimately, Defoe, for all of his allegiance to a well working economy, insists that his reader feel the pains of adjustment and acknowledge the cost of order. The desire to cleanse and rid the earth of its irritating and offensive burden is subsumed by a more basic need to incorporate the need that cannot be denied. In calling attention to the price of survival, in designing complex economies that depend upon the commercialization of human flesh, Defoe exposes a world of mutual dependency as he tells the cost that must be paid to sustain the fiction of a "Nature . . . very easily satisfied."

MY SAVAGE: DEFOE ORDERS HIS FICTIONAL WORLD

After his fourth year of confinement, Robinson Crusoe examines his insularity and finds it relatively good. The happiness he can manufacture depends upon his isolation. Removed from "all the Wickedness of the World," he is freed from "the *Lust of the Flesh, the Lust of the Eye, or the Pride of Life*," As Lord of his solitary manor, he becomes almost embarrassed by riches, "Tortoise or Turtles enough; but now and then one, was as much as I could put to any use." Pastoral circumstances protect him from the bustle and wickedness of a more complex economy, for although he has wood enough to build a fleet and grapes enough to have overloaded his ships with wine and raisins, Crusoe the speculator is prevented all too materially from carrying out visionary schemes of commerce. The mother of *Due Preparations* would have applauded his self-enforced austerity.

Sounding like Gulliver among the Houyhnhnms, Crusoe decides that nature is very easily satisfied as long as we temper our desires. "All I could make use of was All that was valuable," he muses as he contemplates the moldy parcel of money, that "nasty sorry useless Stuff." As often noted, the nasty stuff has its uses later on, but in the fourth year on the island, it remains hermetically sealed off from a world of consumption. "I had no room for desire," he decides, "except it was of Things which I had not, and they were but Trifles, though of great Use to me." Desire comes in the back door in this sequence, for while his circumstances do not allow the room for its presence, the absence of things of "great use" yet "trifling" conflate luxury and necessity, need and desire.[6] Without the "room" for desire, Defoe sets out to build traps of necessity. His Crusoe would give a handful of gold and silver for a

6. John Sekora argues that luxury "was probably an idea born of psychological necessity. . . . It provided its users with a powerful measure of self-worth, for it identified all they *were not*," *Luxury: The Concept in Western Thought* (Baltimore and London, 1977), p. 51. Just as significant, however, is the way luxury measured all that its critics could be, enlarging their sense of power while implicating them in a desire that needed to be curbed.

gross of tobacco pipes, "nay . . . all for a Handful of *Pease* and *Beans*, and a Bottle of ink." Enumerating the "things" wanting, Crusoe strips away a desire that nevertheless represents itself in his self-denying act of accountancy.

Crusoe's stoicism depends upon his confined state. Yet even secured on his island, kept from his desires, he still depends upon a complex physical economy outside the island. Crusoe spends "whole Days" contemplating the inevitability of a Hobbesian descent into "Nature" had God not provided him with a foundering boat to gut. Without the proper tools, had he killed a goat or bird, he would have had "no way to flea or open them, or part the Flesh from the Skin, and the Bowels, or to cut it up; but must gnaw it with my Teeth, and pull it with my Claws like a Beast" (pp. 128–30) [94–95]. Trapped in his simple pastoral, Crusoe is saved from his natural state by goods belonging to other "civilized" men providentially sacrificed for his sake. To protect himself from his "Claws like a Beast," Crusoe constructs his "necessary" umbrella and fashions jerkins from animal skins that must have rubbed his skin raw. Inevitably the skins connect him to the state he is trying to contain.

Even as he disguises his savagery with the skins of fellow creatures, Crusoe worries more about the savage without. The "idea" of the savage causes him to limit the size of his economy, for his physical safety depends upon his relative inivisibility. A larger physical plant would not only be unwieldy (remember his first attempt at boat building), but would call attention to itself. Greater visibility requires more bodies to defend against encroaching "enemies." Yet he cannot risk becoming too insular or he will become "swallowed up" by a self-enclosing, self-reflexive landscape.

Burrowed into his "delightful Cavity or Grotto," Crusoe imagines himself "one of the ancient Giants." In his womb-like cave, Crusoe can boast that "if five hundred Savages were to hunt me, they could never find me out" (p. 179) [130], but nursery fantasies of potency quickly turn into nightmares. Even in his cave, a maternal structure that punishes as it entices, Crusoe frightens himself with visions of a personal nature both savage and frail. The presence of a "monstrous, frightful old He-Goat" fills him with terror.[7] Sighing loudly, "like . . . a Man in some pain," the goat undercuts Crusoe's presumption of strength, for all the while the "ancient Giant" pretends power, the dying goat signifies solitary, self-enclosed frailty. Crusoe tries to rationalize the goat's condition, deciding that "could I have but enjoy'd the Certainty that no Savages would come to the Place to disturb me," he would happily lie down and die in the same fashion. But his fear, even here, of being "disturbed" by the savages complicates his stoicism (pp. 177–80) [128–30].

When Crusoe investigates his cave, a refuge for ancient giants and

---

7. Homer O. Brown, "The Displaced Self," *English Literary History*, 38 (1971), pp. 572–3, and John Richetti, *Defoe's Narratives*, p. 50, consider the significance of the goat as a version or reflection of Crusoe.

dying goats, he uses a candle made from goat tallow. The tallow might very well be a circumstantially realistic detail, but its presence jars a reader preparing to sympathize with the sighs of a fellow creature sounding like a "Man in some pain." Swift will more self-consciously elaborate upon this juxtaposition in *Gulliver's Travels* when he blandly reports Gulliver's expropriation of Yahoo hides. It is more shocking here in its relatively unironic state. While Gulliver hates the Yahoos he skins, Crusoe tends to identify with the animal. Traditionally associated with the unregenerate qualities of fallen man, restless, unruly, and "in some pain," the goats on Crusoe's island reflect his vulnerable condition. They are the first "poor Creatures" that he thinks of after he takes courage "to peep abroad" after hiding from the single footprint—he thinks of them "in great Pain" for want of milking—and they are the first "poor Creatures" he sacrifices to feed his colonized savage's "hankering" for human flesh. The immediate erosion of Crusoe's sympathy, once he fears being eaten, calls attention to the luxury of feeding in his precariously balanced physical economy. Fearing that the savages "would have seiz'd on me with the same View, as I did of a Goat, or a Turtle; and have thought it no more Crime to kill and devour me than I did of a Pidgeon or a Curlieu" (p. 197) [142], Crusoe demonstrates the compromises that become necessary to preserve life.

When he separates himself from the goats to save his own skin, he does so to remain intact, to preserve his own most vulnerable body from dismemberment. By insisting upon his relatively high position on the eating chain, he reveals a fear of disconnection all the more threatening in light of the cannibalistic threat, for the cannibal actually scatters the body itself into discrete parts. No wonder Crusoe feared that even dead, he would be "disturbed" by savages, for in his primal savage scene, he sees the shore "spread with Skulls, Hands, Feet, and other Bones of humane Bodies" (p. 165) [119–20]. Early illustrators of cannibalistic scenes exploited just this fear. The earliest known representation of American Indians "depicts one of the characters contentedly gnawing away on a human arm while other parts of the body are roasting over a fire." The seventeenth-century engraving of the natives of Española offers glimpses of an odd foot and hand waving from the mouth of a primitive kettle. Fundamental to the illustrations is the dismemberment made graphic, the limbs drying in sheds, the bones scattered across the page.[8] To separate himself from the vulnerable material condition that connects him to the threat of such disconnection, Crusoe must separate himself from the savage-animal world that can eat him up. If there is to be an eating chain, he must be the one ordering it. For not to order it is to become consumed.

Crusoe faces the same problem that shaped Moll's and Roxana's

---

8. Arens, *The Man-Eating Myth*, pp. 24, 27, 29, 52, provides fascinating illustrations of cannibals, viewed through colonizing eyes, severing and scattering limbs.

lives—how to exert control over a system that depends upon—even as it disavows—human consumption. Defoe's characters are not by nature ruthless, but when pressed to eat their neighbor, or even their child, they comply, balancing precariously acts of savagery and restraint in the name of civilization. In his attempts to master his physical circumstances, Crusoe more than compensates for his frailty by "seizing upon" others, notably Friday, a compliant savage ready to be colonized. His first description of Friday reveals the unstable, ambiguous nature of the savage "other" Crusoe is attempting to contain. However cannibalistic by habit, Friday demonstrates "all the Sweetness and Softness of a *European* in his Countenance . . . especially when he smil'd." Showing his savage teeth in a gesture of friendship, Friday proves through his geniality, his willingness to offer signs of "Subjection, Servitude and Submission," that he possesses a mild and affectionate nature. Yet he also eats people when he gets the chance. Just this juxtaposition of sweetness and savagery complicates his character, suggesting that Friday might be another victim of another, perhaps simpler, physical system that eats up its fellow creatures, no more or less guilty than Moll Flanders laying her snares (pp. 205–6) [148–49].[9]

The fact of the cannibal upsets the notion of order for Crusoe and his world. Montaigne could philosophically rationalize his presence, but even late in the Enlightenment, long after the Chain of Being had lost its organizational power, witnesses to cannibalism had difficulty fitting the man-eater into any proper system of physical economy.[1] Crusoe's attempt to curb his captive's appetite reveals the high cost that civilized restraint demands. When Crusoe confronts gentle Friday's "hankering Stomach" for "some of the Flesh" still scattered around the sacrificial ground, he expresses "Abhorrence at the very Thoughts of it." His abhorrence is so strong, in fact, that Crusoe lets Friday know "by some Means" that he "would kill him if he offer'd it" (p. 208) [150]. This is pure Defoe, for just as Moll abhors a sexuality she employs, so Crusoe threatens murder to make his savage civil. To separate his savage from his "nature," Crusoe "falls to work" to cover over Friday's nakedness. Stitching up a soul for his savage out of goat and hare skins, Crusoe works seriously here with materials that Swift parodies in both *Tale of a Tub* and *Gulliver's Travels*. Just as Gulliver skins Yahoos to cover over his own yahoo nature, Crusoe covers over Friday not only with skins taken from another version of himself,[2] but with linen drawers looted from a dead man's chest. His investment links his savage to the civilized

9. Peter Hulme argues that this description is a "classic case of negation," *Colonial Encounters: Europe and the Native Caribbean, 1492–1797* (London and New York, 1986), p. 205.
1. Joseph Banks, exploring and botanizing with Captain James Cook, describes the Maori people as creatures who by their abnormality put into question the notion of the chain of being. *The Endeavour Journal of Joseph Banks, 1768–1771*, 2 vols., ed. J. C. Beaglehole, Sydney, 1962, volumes I and II.
2. Homi Bhabha considers "the technique of camouflage" implicit in colonial discourse in "Of Mimicry and Man: The Ambivalence of Colonial Discourse," *October*, 28 (Spring 1984), pp. 125–33.

world of commercial consumption that the "poor Gunner" defended in life. Friday complies with this sacrifice awkwardly enough, for "the Sleeves of the Wastcoat gall'd his Shoulders, and the insides of his Arms," but in time, he accommodates himself "very well" to civilization and its discontents (p. 208) [150].

Although the denatured Friday no longer looks savage—and probably looks more than a little ridiculous—he still possesses the "Relish" of a cannibal stomach. To alter his savage's hankering, Crusoe displays his talent for fire power to impress the benefits of civilized virtue upon his savage.

Crusoe shoots down a goat to separate Friday from the savage nature that threatens Crusoe's physical economy. But in the action, he makes further connections between man and animal. In the goat stew episode, Defoe links together the "fellow Creatures," the goat that is eaten, the savage that will eat anything, and Crusoe, who must resist being "seized" upon. Perhaps it is simply the way Crusoe casually picks off his random goat, a young kid sitting next to the "She Goat lying down in the Shade," that jars. His action violates both pastoral expectations and sporting ethics. The sitting goat is not even the animal that Crusoe intended to kill, but a random creature made personal in its description.

Friday's response to the kill connects him to the sacrifice. It becomes difficult to separate "poor Creature" Friday from poor victim goat in the following passage:

> I presented my Piece, shot and kill'd one of the Kids. The poor Creature who had at a Distance seen me kill the Savage his Enemy, but did not know, or could imagine how it was done, was sensibly surpriz'd . . . He did not see the Kid I shot at, or perceive I had kill'd it, but ripp'd up his Wastcoat to feel if he was not wounded, and as I found, presently thought I was resolv'd to kill him. (p. 211) [152]

Friday's fears are not misplaced. When Crusoe recalls "the Savage his Enemy," he alludes not only to Friday's enemy, but to Friday himself, that natural savage that so disturbs Crusoe's sense of civilization. Wearing the "poor Gunner's drawers," Friday represents the consumption of not just one goat but an entire shipload of goods that preserves him and Crusoe from his "savagery." Friday even wears a "wastcoat" constructed from the skins of a goat, that version of Crusoe's other self. It is not surprising within such a tangled context that Friday tries to rip away his clothing to separate himself from that which is being destroyed "for his sake."

Crusoe destroys more than a goat for Friday's sake. To convince Friday of his benevolence, Crusoe continues the carnage in killing a parrot. Shooting the goat, no matter how flashy the display of powder and power, can be rationalized as a way to replace human with animal flesh. But killing the parrot is an act of luxury. Even Crusoe seems to recognize the gratuitous nature of his deed, for on Crusoe's island, parrots are made not to be eaten, but to speak. Crusoe's own Poll "would sit upon my Finger, and lay his Bill close to my Face, and cry, *Poor* Robin Crusoe, *Where are you? Where have you been?* (p. 143) [104]. Out shooting parrots, Crusoe would have to answer, for the edification of my savage.

The murder of the parrot seems almost accidental. His gun loaded, Crusoe sees a great fowl, alerts Friday, and discharges his weapon. Crusoe is guilty and not guilty of the action. After all, he mutters, it could have been a hawk. Crusoe might call upon dull organs to justify the killing of a fellow creature, but Defoe refuses easy absolution. For when Friday runs to fetch the parrot, we learn that the "Parrot not being quite dead, was flutter'd away a good way off from the Place where she fell" (p. 212) [153]. Pronouns tell. "She" fell. Verbs tell more. "Flutter" suggests a nervous presence, a tremulous emotion sympathetic in its neurological connections. Crusoe himself experienced "fluttering thoughts" (p. 154) [112] after viewing his primal footprint on his deserted shore. Insistent upon computing the cost of living, Defoe makes his readers know the creatures they consume: the idle kid sitting next to its mother in the shade, the sentient parrot picked out of the tree, beings sacrificed to make safer the idea of civilization.

To protect himself from savagery, Crusoe must repeat acts of mastery, colonizing more and more subjects to feed his growing needs. By the time he leaves his island, it contains a mixture of Spaniards and Mutineers. Their "story," filled with agreements and disagreements, union and separation, until "at last the *Spaniards* were oblig'd to use Violence" to subject and "use" the villains honestly, exaggerates Crusoe's own attempts to manage an island that depends upon interdependency and subjugation. In his discussion of "improvements," he records the "Attempt" his colonials made on the mainland, and how they "brought away eleven Men and five Women Prisoners, by which, at my coming, I found about twenty young Children on the Island." Crusoe does his part to stock the island with "Supplies" including "seven Women, being such as I found proper for Service, or for Wives to such as would take them: As to the *English* Men, I promis'd them to send them some women from *England*, with a good Cargoe of Necessaries" (pp. 305–6) [220].

Slavery—physical and sexual—becomes "Necessary" here, sustaining not just life, but Crusoe's jaunts around the world. While Defoe repeatedly presents the rigors of the slavery system—Crusoe, Colonel Jack, Roxana and Moll all endure some sort of literal or figurative forced labor—he remains oddly outside of his own analysis of the system. Peter Earle ruefully notes that Defoe "went so far as to hope that one day all Englishmen might be masters, wishing for his country's good 'that it might please God that all our people were masters and able to keep servants, tho' they were obliged to buy their servants, as other nations do'."[3] The contradictions of such a wish for an equality based upon a greater inequality is never entirely absent from Defoe's attempts to explore "mutual subordination." Wallowing in wealth, Crusoe reports that he is "in a Condition which I scarce knew how to understand, or how to compose my self for the Enjoyment of it" (p. 285) [205]. Just that lack of understanding allows him to continue his attempts to control that nature that threatens him.

Once composed, Crusoe sets out to commit his final act of mastery over the savage within and without. He takes part in the most unnecessary shooting of "a very nice Gentleman" (p. 293) [211], a bear. Circumstantially, Crusoe has all the right in the world to kill the bear. He and Friday are in the process of heroically holding off a pack of starving wolves that have attacked their band in the Pyrenees. Making connections between the "Kind of two-legged Wolves" that threaten travellers and the "Hellish Creatures" (p. 291) [209–10] that physically assault their party, Crusoe interrupts his narrative of the wolves to report "the greatest Diversion imaginable"—the story of Friday and the bear.

Crusoe describes the bear much as H. F. describes the plague victim who kissed his "poor unhappy gentlewoman" into the grave. For although the bear might be dangerous, he appears weak, the victim of his own weight. He is "a heavy, clumsey Creature, and does not gallop as the Wolf does." Men are not even "his proper Prey." If you meet him in the woods, and don't meddle with him, "he won't meddle with you; but then you must take Care to be very Civil to him." This cumbersome gentleman will, however take affront, and "will have Satisfaction in Point of Honour."

Friday takes on this gentlemanly prey with "Joy and Courage":

> O! O! O! Says *Friday* three Times, pointing to him; O Master! *You give me to Leave! Me shakee te Hand with him: Me make you good laugh.*
>
> I was surpriz'd to see the Fellow so pleas'd; *You Fool you,* says I, *he will eat you up: Eatee me up! Eatee me up!* Says *Friday,* twice over again; *Me eatee him up: Me make you good laugh: You all stay here, me show you good laugh.*

Friday's joy in mastering Mr. Bear has been interpreted to reflect Crusoe's own confidence in his ability to triumph over circumstances that had once threatened to swallow him up. While this is true, Crusoe's mastery is compromised by a disturbing sadism central to the encounter. For the bear "was walking softly on, and offer'd to meddle with no Body," the hapless victim of Friday's and Crusoe's need to assert domination to be "safe." Friday plays with the bear not to protect himself, but to "show us some Laugh as he call'd it."

Throughout the episode, the painfully human characteristics of the

3. Peter Earle, *The World of Defoe* (New York, 1977), p. 170.

animal confuse the purpose of the bear-baiting. At one point, pursuing what even Crusoe suspects to be "Folly," Friday lures the animal on to the large limb of a tree:

> *Ha*, says he to us, *now you see me teachee the Bear dance*; so he falls a jumping and shaking the Bough, at which the Bear began to totter, but stood still, and began to look behind him, to see how he should get back; then indeed we did laugh heartily. But *Friday* had not done with him by a great deal; when he sees him stand still, he calls out to him again, as if he had suppos'd the Bear could speak *English*; *What you no come farther, pray you come farther*; so he left jumping and shaking the Bough; and the Bear, just as if he had understood what he said, did come a little further, then he fell a jumping again, and the Bear stopp'd again.

A bear with a hand to shake, a bear who can learn how to dance on the shaking limb of a tree, a bear that appears to understand English, and not only totters, but consciously "look[s] behind him" for his bearings might make his immediate audience "laugh heartily," but his confusion reflects Defoe's less than hearty appreciation of Friday's play. "We could not imagine what would be the End of it, and where the Jest would be at last," Crusoe recalls uneasily, "But *Friday* put us out of doubt quickly."

Giving his audience *"one more laugh,"* Friday draws the bear into his immediate vicinity, creating in the shooting an intimacy between victim and victimizer difficult to "laugh" at. While the bear, thinking his enemy gone, comes back from the bough "mighty leisurely, looking behind him every Step," moving tenuously, "one Foot at a Time, very leisurely," before the animal can set his hind feet on the ground, *"Friday* stept up close to him, clapt the Muzzle of his Piece into his Ear, and shot him dead as a Stone" (pp. 293–6) [211–14].

"Mighty leisurely," tottering clumsily, betraying at the very worst a gentle curiosity towards Friday's strategies, the bear, like the parrot, falls victim to Crusoe's need for mastery. That Friday, first civilized victim to Crusoe's rage for order, who learned from his master how to shoot fluttering parrots out of the sky, expresses Crusoe's desire for mastery and demonstrates just how well Crusoe has established his "natural" physical economy. But Crusoe's complacency, his own pleasure in Friday's play, is not entirely Defoe's. For all his love of mastery, Defoe would not stop looking hard at what was being mastered, at the cost of life dearly maintained. Just as Moll and Roxana are compelled to assert their material presence over a system that in the end absorbs their desperate energies, Crusoe compulsively ranges about the world to order an economy bigger than himself, one that incorporates fear into its triumphs and demands that freedom depend upon slavery. It becomes indeed a place to run from.

Daniel Defoe: A Chronology

1660	Born Daniel Foe in London. Son of James, a tallow chandler, and Alice Foe.
1662	Act of Uniformity forces the family of James Foe and their pastor, Dr. Samuel Annesley, out of the Church of England to become Presbyterians, a dissenting sect.
1665–66	The Great Plague and the Great Fire of London.
c. 1668	Death of Alice Foe.
c. 1671–79	First educated at the Reverend James Fisher's school at Dorking, Surrey; then attended the academy for dissenters of the Reverend Charles Morton at Newington Green in preparation for a ministerial career.
1683	An established merchant living in Cornhill, near the Royal Exchange.
1684	Marries Mary Tuffley, who brings him a dowry of £3,700; together they would have seven children.
c. 1685–92	Prospering in business as a trader in hosiery, importer of wine and tobacco, and insurer of ships. Travels in England and Europe. Publishes political tracts.
1688–1702	Supports and serves in assorted offices William III.
1690–91	Contributor to the *Athenian Mercury* and member of the Athenian Society.
1692	Declared bankrupt for £17,000 and imprisoned for debt.
1695	Adds the prefix "De" to his name publicly for the first time as manager-trustee of royal lotteries; henceforth calls himself "De Foe."
1697	Publishes *An Essay on Projects*, which brings him to the attention of influential men.
1701	*The True-Born Englishman*, a poetic defense of King William and his Dutch ancestry; it outsells any previously published poem in the language.
1702	Death of William III and accession of Anne ends his hopes of preferment. Publishes *The Shortest Way with the Dissenters*, a satiric attack on High Church extremists.
1703	Arrested for writing *The Shortest Way*, charged with seditious libel by the Tory ministry, committed to Newgate, tried, convicted, and sentenced to stand in the pillory (July 29–31). Publishes *Hymn to the Pillory* and an authorized collected edition of his writings. The failure of his brick and tile works near Tilbury while in prison precipitates another bankruptcy.
1703–30	Secures his release from Newgate at the intercession of Robert Harley, who employs his services on behalf of the Tory ministry. Defoe serves successive administrations, Tory and Whig, as political journalist, adviser, and secret agent.

1704–13	Wrote and edited *The Review*, an influential journal appearing three times a week.
1707	Union of England and Scotland, which Defoe worked to promote.
1713–14	Arrested several times for debt and for political writings.
1715	*The Family Instructor*, a popular conduct manual.
1718	Second volume of *The Family Instructor*.
1719	*Robinson Crusoe; The Farther Adventures of Robinson Crusoe*.
1720	*Memoirs of a Cavalier; Captain Singleton; Serious Reflections . . . of Robinson Crusoe*.
1722	*Moll Flanders; Religious Courtship; A Journal of the Plague Year; Colonel Jack*.
1724	*The Fortunate Mistress (Roxana); A General History of the Pyrates; A Tour Thro' the Whole Island of Great Britain* (3 vols., 1724–26).
1725	*The Complete English Tradesman*; also pirate and criminal "lives."
1726	*The Political History of the Devil*.
1727	*Conjugal Lewdness (A Treatise Concerning the Use and Abuse of the Marrige Bed); An Essay on the History and Reality of Apparitions; A New Family Instructor*; second volume of *The Complete English Tradesman*.
1728	*Augusta Triumphans; A Plan of the English Commerce*.
1731	Dies "of a lethargy" (April 24) in Ropemaker's Alley, London; buried (April 26) in Bunhill Fields among Puritan Worthies like John Bunyan.

At the time of his death Defoe left incomplete manuscripts of two works that were published posthumously, *The Compleat English Gentleman* (1890) and *Of Royall Educacion* (1895). Defoe was one of the most prolific and versatile of English authors, whose publications in poetry and prose numbered in the hundreds and treated subjects as varied as economics, politics, religion, education, travel, and literature. As a journalist he was associated with more than two dozen periodicals.

Selected Bibliography

BIBLIOGRAPHICAL WORKS

The standard bibliographies of Defoe are:

Moore, John Robert. *A Checklist of the Writings of Daniel Defoe.* Bloomington: Indiana UP, 1960.

Novak, Maximillian E. "Daniel Defoe." *The New Cambridge Bibliography of English Literature: 1660–1800.* Ed. George Watson. Rev. ed., New York: Cambridge UP, 1971. 882–918.

For problems relating to the Defoe canon, see P. N. Furbank and W. R. Owens, *The Canonisation of Daniel Defoe* (New Haven: Yale UP, 1988).

The following bibliographical studies are useful for an understanding of the text and early editions of *Robinson Crusoe*:

Hubbard, Lucius L. "Text Changes in the Taylor Editions of *Robinson Crusoe* with Remarks on the Cox Edition." *Papers of the Bibliographical Society of America* 20 (1926): 1–76.

Hutchins, Henry Clinton. *Robinson Crusoe and Its Printing, 1719–1731.* New York: Columbia UP, 1925.

———. "Two Hitherto Unrecorded Editions of *Robinson Crusoe.*" *The Library* (1927): 58–72.

Maslen, Keith I. "The Printers of *Robinson Crusoe. The Library* 7 (1952): 124–31.

Maslen, K. I. D. "Edition Quantities for *Robinson Crusoe*, 1719." *The Library* 24 (1969): 145–50.

Useful reference books include John A. Stoler, *Daniel Defoe, An Annotated Bibliography of Modern Criticism, 1900–1980* (New York: Garland, 1984); Spiro Peterson, *Daniel Defoe: A Reference Guide, 1731–1924* (Boston: G. K. Hall, 1987); and I. J. Spackman, W. R. Owens, and P. N. Furbank, eds., *A KWIC Concordance to Daniel Defoe's Robinson Crusoe* (New York: Garland, 1987).

BIOGRAPHICAL WORKS

The authoritative modern biographies of Defoe are:

Backscheider, Paula. *Daniel Defoe: His Life.* Baltimore: Johns Hopkins UP, 1989.

Moore, John Robert. *Daniel Defoe: Citizen of the Modern World.* Chicago: U of Chicago, 1958.

Sutherland, James. *Defoe* 1937. 2nd ed. London: Methuen, 1950.

The Backscheider biography is the most current and comprehensive; the Moore is detailed yet idealized; the Sutherland is concise and insightful. See also F. Bastian, *Defoe's Early Life* (Totowa, N.J.: Barnes & Noble, 1981). Important earlier biographical studies include:

Chalmers, George. *The Life of Daniel De Foe.* London, 1790. (The first biography of Defoe, with a list of his writings.)

Lee, William, *Daniel Defoe: His Life and Recently Discovered Writings.* 3 vols. London: Hotten, 1869. (Volume I is biographical.)

Trent, W.P. *Daniel Defoe: How to Know Him.* Indianapolis: Bobbs-Merrill, 1916.

Wilson, Walter. *Memoirs of the Life and Times of Daniel De Foe.* 3 vols. London: Hurst, Chance, 1830.

For the standard edition of Defoe's letters, see George Harris Healey, ed., *The Letters of Daniel Defoe* (Oxford: Clarendon Press, 1955).

SELECTED CRITICAL STUDIES OF DEFOE AND HIS WRITINGS

Alkon, Paul K. *Defoe and Fictional Time.* Athens: U of Georgia P, 1979.

Backscheider, Paula. *Daniel Defoe: Ambition and Innovation.* Lexington: UP of Kentucky, 1986.

Baine, Rodney. *Daniel Defoe and the Supernatural*. Athens: U of Georgia P, 1979.

Bender, John. *Imagining the Penitentiary*. Chicago: U of Chicago P, 1987.

Blewett, David. *Defoe's Art of Fiction*. Toronto: U of Toronto P, 1979.

Bloom, Harold, ed. *Daniel Defoe: Modern Critical Views*. New York: Chelsea House, 1987.

Boardman, Michael M. *Defoe and the Uses of Narrative*. New Brunswick: Rutgers UP, 1983.

Brown, Homer O. "The Displaced Self in the Novels of Daniel Defoe." *Journal of English Literary History* 38 (1971): 562–90.

Byrd, Max, ed. *Daniel Defoe: A Collection of Critical Essays*. Englewood Cliffs, N.J.: Prentice Hall, 1976.

Earle, Peter. *The World of Defoe*. New York: Atheneum, 1977.

Novak, Maximillian E. *Economics and the Fiction of Daniel Defoe*. Berkeley: U of California P, 1962.

——. *Defoe and the Nature of Man*. Oxford: Oxford UP, 1963.

——. *Realism, Myth, and History in Defoe's Fiction*. Lincoln: U of Nebraska P, 1983.

Richetti, John J. *Defoe's Narratives*. Oxford: Oxford UP, 1975.

——. *Daniel Defoe*. Boston: G.K. Hall, 1987.

Shinagel, Michael. *Daniel Defoe and Middle-Class Gentility*. Cambridge, Mass.: Harvard UP, 1968.

Sill, Geoffrey M. *Defoe and the Idea of Fiction*. Newark: U of Delaware P, 1983.

Starr, George A. *Defoe and Spiritual Autobiography*. Princeton: Princeton U, 1965.

——. *Defoe and Casuistry*. Princeton: Princeton UP, 1971.

——. "Defoe's Prose Style: The Language of Interpretation," *Modern Philology* 71 (1964): 277–94.

Sutherland, James. *Daniel Defoe: A Critical Study*. Cambridge, Mass.: Harvard UP, 1971.

Zimmerman, Everett. *Defoe and the Novel*. Berkeley: U of California P, 1975.

SELECTED CRITICISM OF ROBINSON CRUSOE

Ayers, Robert W. "*Robinson Crusoe*: 'Allusive Allegorick History.' " *Publications of the Modern Language Association* 82 (1967): 399–407.

Baker, Ernest A., *The History of the English Novel*. 1929. Vol. 3. New York: Barnes & Noble, 1961. 130–74.

Damrosch, Leopold. *God's Plot & Man's Stories*. Chicago: U of Chicago P, 1985. 187–212.

Dottin, Paul, ed. *Robinson Crusoe Examin'd and Criticis'd*. London: Dent, 1923. (An annotated edition of Charles Gildon's *The Life and Strange Surprizing Adventurs of Mr. D. . . De F. . of London . . . , 1719*.)

Ellis, Frank, ed. *Twentieth Century Interpretations of Robinson Crusoe*. Englewood Cliffs, N.J.: Prentice-Hall, 1969.

Ganzel, Dewey, "Chronology in *Robinson Crusoe*." *Philological Quarterly* 40 (1961): 495–512.

Hunter, J. Paul. *The Reluctant Pilgrim: Defoe's Emblematic Method and Quest for Form in Robinson Cusoe*. Baltimore: Johns Hopkins UP, 1966.

Lannert, Gustav L. *An Investigation Into the Language of Robinson Crusoe*. Uppsala and Cambridge, 1910.

McKeon, Michael. *The Origins of the English Novel, 1600–1740*. Baltimore: Johns Hopkins UP, 1987. 315–37.

McKillop, Alan D. *The Early Masters of English Fiction*. Lawrence, Kans.: U of Kansas P, 1975. 20–25.

Novak, Maximillian E. "Crusoe the King and the Political Evolution of His Island." *Studies in English Literature* 2 (1962): 337–50.

Rogers, Pat. *Robinson Crusoe*. London: Allen & Unwin, 1979.

Schonhorn, Manuel. *Defoe's Politics*. Cambridge: Cambridge UP, 1991. 141–64.

Seidel, Michael. *Robinson Crusoe: Island Myths and the Novel*. Boston: G.K. Hall, 1991.

Tillyard, E. M. W. *The Epic Strain in the English Novel*. London: Chatto & Windus, 1958. 24–50.

Watt, Ian. *The Rise of the Novel*, Berkeley and Los Angeles: U of California P, 1957. 60–92.

For a suggestive fictive rendering of the Crusoe story, see J. M. Coetzee, *Foe* (London: Penguin Books, 1987).

ANDERSON *Winesburg, Ohio* edited by Charles E. Modlin and Ray Lewis White
AQUINAS *St. Thomas Aquinas on Politics and Ethics* translated and edited by
Paul E. Sigmund
AUSTEN *Emma* edited by Stephen M. Parrish *Second Edition*
AUSTEN *Mansfield Park* edited by Claudia L. Johnson
AUSTEN *Persuasion* edited by Patricia Meyer Spacks
AUSTEN *Pride and Prejudice* edited by Donald Gray *Second Edition*
BALZAC *Père Goriot* translated by Burton Raffel edited by Peter Brooks
BEHN *Oroonoko* edited by Joanna Lipking
Beowulf (the Donaldson translation) edited by Joseph F. Tuso
BLAKE *Blake's Poetry and Designs* selected and edited by Mary Lynn Johnson and
John E. Grant
BOCCACCIO *The Decameron* selected, translated, and edited by Mark Musa and
Peter E. Bondanella
BRONTË, CHARLOTTE *Jane Eyre* edited by Richard J. Dunn *Second Edition*
BRONTË, EMILY *Wuthering Heights* edited by William M. Sale, Jr., and Richard Dunn
Third Edition
BROWNING, ELIZABETH BARRETT *Aurora Leigh* edited by Margaret Reynolds
BROWNING, ROBERT *Browning's Poetry* selected and edited by James F. Loucks
BURNEY *Evelina* edited by Stewart J. Cooke
BYRON *Byron's Poetry* selected and edited by Frank D. McConnell
CARROLL *Alice in Wonderland* edited by Donald J. Gray *Second Edition*
CERVANTES *Don Quixote* (the Ormsby translation, revised) edited by Joseph R. Jones and
Kenneth Douglas
CHAUCER *The Canterbury Tales: Nine Tales and the General Prologue* edited by
V. A. Kolve and Glending Olson
CHEKHOV *Anton Chekhov's Plays* translated and edited by Eugene K. Bristow
CHEKHOV *Anton Chekhov's Short Stories* selected and edited by Ralph E. Matlaw
CHOPIN *The Awakening* edited by Margo Culley *Second Edition*
CLEMENS *Adventures of Huckleberry Finn* edited by Sculley Bradley,
Richmond Croom Beatty, E. Hudson Long, and Thomas Cooley *Second Edition*
CLEMENS *A Connecticut Yankee in King Arthur's Court* edited by Allison R. Ensor
CLEMENS *Pudd'nhead Wilson and Those Extraordinary Twins* edited by Sidney E. Berger
CONRAD *Heart of Darkness* edited by Robert Kimbrough *Third Edition*
CONRAD *Lord Jim* edited by Thomas C. Moser *Second Edition*
CONRAD *The Nigger of the "Narcissus"* edited by Robert Kimbrough
CRANE *Maggie: A Girl of the Streets* edited by Thomas A. Gullason
CRANE *The Red Badge of Courage* edited by Donald Pizer *Third Edition*
DARWIN *Darwin* selected and edited by Philip Appleman *Second Edition*
DEFOE *A Journal of the Plague Year* edited by Paula R. Backscheider
DEFOE *Moll Flanders* edited by Edward Kelly
DEFOE *Robinson Crusoe* edited by Michael Shinagel *Second Edition*
DE PIZAN *The Selected Writings of Christine de Pizan* translated by Renate
Blumenfeld-Kosinski and Kevin Brownlee edited by Renate Blumenfeld-Kosinski
DICKENS *Bleak House* edited by George Ford and Sylvère Monod
DICKENS *David Copperfield* edited by Jerome H. Buckley
DICKENS *Hard Times* edited by George Ford and Sylvère Monod *Second Edition*
DICKENS *Oliver Twist* edited by Fred Kaplan
DONNE *John Donne's Poetry* selected and edited by Arthur L. Clements *Second Edition*
DOSTOEVSKY *The Brothers Karamazov* (the Garnett translation) edited by Ralph E. Matlaw
DOSTOEVSKY *Crime and Punishment* (the Coulson translation) edited by George Gibian
Third Edition
DOSTOEVSKY *Notes from Underground* translated and edited by Michael R. Katz

DOUGLASS *Narrative of the Life of Frederick Douglass, an American Slave, Written by Himself* edited by William L. Andrews and William S. McFeely
DREISER *Sister Carrie* edited by Donald Pizer *Second Edition*
Eight Modern Plays edited by Anthony Caputi
ELIOT *Middlemarch* edited by Bert G. Hornback
ELIOT *The Mill on the Floss* edited by Carol T. Christ
ERASMUS *The Praise of Folly and Other Writings* translated and edited by Robert M. Adams
FAULKNER *The Sound and the Fury* edited by David Minter *Second Edition*
FIELDING *Joseph Andrews with Shamela and Related Writings* edited by Homer Goldberg
FIELDING *Tom Jones* edited by Sheridan Baker *Second Edition*
FLAUBERT *Madame Bovary* edited with a substantially new translation by Paul de Man
FORD *The Good Soldier* edited by Martin Stannard
FORSTER *Howards End* edited by Paul B. Armstrong
FRANKLIN *Benjamin Franklin's Autobiography* edited by J. A. Leo Lemay and P. M. Zall
FULLER *Woman in the Nineteenth Century* edited by Larry J. Reynolds
GOETHE *Faust* translated by Walter Arndt, edited by Cyrus Hamlin
GOGOL *Dead Souls* (the Reavey translation) edited by George Gibian
HARDY *Far from the Madding Crowd* edited by Robert C. Schweik
HARDY *Jude the Obscure* edited by Norman Page
HARDY *The Mayor of Casterbridge* edited by James K. Robinson
HARDY *The Return of the Native* edited by James Gindin
HARDY *Tess of the d'Urbervilles* edited by Scott Elledge *Third Edition*
HAWTHORNE *The Blithedale Romance* edited by Seymour Gross and Rosalie Murphy
HAWTHORNE *The House of the Seven Gables* edited by Seymour Gross
HAWTHORNE *Nathaniel Hawthorne's Tales* edited by James McIntosh
HAWTHORNE *The Scarlet Letter* edited by Seymour Gross, Sculley Bradley, Richmond Croom Beatty, and E. Hudson Long *Third Edition*
HERBERT *George Herbert and the Seventeenth-Century Religious Poets* selected and edited by Mario A. DiCesare
HERODOTUS *The Histories* translated and selected by Walter E. Blanco, edited by Walter E. Blanco and Jennifer Roberts
HOBBES *Leviathan* edited by Richard E. Flathman and David Johnston
HOMER *The Odyssey* translated and edited by Albert Cook *Second Edition*
HOWELLS *The Rise of Silas Lapham* edited by Don L. Cook
IBSEN *The Wild Duck* translated and edited by Dounia B. Christiani
JAMES *The Ambassadors* edited by S. P. Rosenbaum *Second Edition*
JAMES *The American* edited by James W. Tuttleton
JAMES *The Portrait of a Lady* edited by Robert D. Bamberg *Second Edition*
JAMES *Tales of Henry James* edited by Christof Wegelin
JAMES *The Turn of the Screw* edited by Robert Kimbrough
JAMES *The Wings of the Dove* edited by J. Donald Crowley and Richard A. Hocks
JONSON *Ben Jonson and the Cavalier Poets* selected and edited by Hugh Maclean
JONSON *Ben Jonson's Plays and Masques* selected and edited by Robert M. Adams
KAFKA *The Metamorphosis* translated and edited by Stanley Corngold
LAFAYETTE *The Princess of Clèves* edited and with a revised translation by John D. Lyons
MACHIAVELLI *The Prince* translated and edited by Robert M. Adams *Second Edition*
MALTHUS *An Essay on the Principle of Population* edited by Philip Appleman
MANN *Death in Venice* translated and edited by Clayton Koelb
MARX *The Communist Manifesto* edited by Frederic L. Bender
MELVILLE *The Confidence-Man* edited by Hershel Parker
MELVILLE *Moby-Dick* edited by Harrison Hayford and Hershel Parker
MEREDITH *The Egoist* edited by Robert M. Adams
Middle English Lyrics selected and edited by Maxwell S. Luria and Richard L. Hoffman
Middle English Romances selected and edited by Stephen H. A. Shepherd
MILL *Mill: The Spirit of the Age, On Liberty, The Subjection of Women* selected and edited by Alan Ryan

MILTON *Paradise Lost* edited by Scott Elledge *Second Edition*
Modern Irish Drama edited by John P. Harrington
MORE *Utopia* translated and edited by Robert M. Adams *Second Edition*
NEWMAN *Apologia Pro Vita Sua* edited by David J. DeLaura
NEWTON *Newton* edited by I. Bernard Cohen and Richard S. Westfall
NORRIS *McTeague* edited by Donald Pizer *Second Edition*
Restoration and Eighteenth-Century Comedy edited by Scott McMillin *Second Edition*
RICH *Adrienne Rich's Poetry and Prose* edited by Barbara Charlesworth Gelpi and
Albert Gelpi
ROUSSEAU *Rousseau's Political Writings* edited by Alan Ritter and translated by
Julia Conaway Bondanella
ST. PAUL *The Writings of St. Paul* edited by Wayne A. Meeks
SHAKESPEARE *Hamlet* edited by Cyrus Hoy *Second Edition*
SHAKESPEARE *Henry IV, Part I* edited by James L. Sanderson *Second Edition*
SHAW *Bernard Shaw's Plays* edited by Warren Sylvester Smith
SHELLEY *Frankenstein* edited by J. Paul Hunter
SHELLEY *Shelley's Poetry and Prose* selected and edited by Donald H. Reiman and
Sharon B. Powers
SMOLLETT *Humphry Clinker* edited by James L. Thorson
SOPHOCLES *Oedipus Tyrannus* translated and edited by Luci Berkowitz and
Theodore F. Brunner
SPENSER *Edmund Spenser's Poetry* selected and edited by Hugh Maclean and
Anne Lake Prescott *Third Edition*
STENDHAL *Red and Black* translated and edited by Robert M. Adams
STERNE *Tristram Shandy* edited by Howard Anderson
STOKER *Dracula* edited by Nina Auerbach and David Skal
STOWE *Uncle Tom's Cabin* edited by Elizabeth Ammons
SWIFT *Gulliver's Travels* edited by Robert A. Greenberg *Second Edition*
SWIFT *The Writings of Jonathan Swift* edited by Robert A. Greenberg and William B. Piper
TENNYSON *In Memoriam* edited by Robert H. Ross
TENNYSON *Tennyson's Poetry* selected and edited by Robert W. Hill, Jr.
THACKERAY *Vanity Fair* edited by Peter Shillingsburg
THOREAU *Walden and Resistance to Civil Government* edited by William Rossi
Second Edition
THUCYDIDES *The Peloponnesian War* translated by Walter Blanco edited by Walter Blanco
and Jennifer Tolbert Roberts
TOLSTOY *Anna Karenina* edited and with a revised translation by George Gibian
Second Edition
TOLSTOY *Tolstoy's Short Fiction* edited and with revised translations by Michael R. Katz
TOLSTOY *War and Peace* (the Maude translation) edited by George Gibian *Second Edition*
TOOMER *Cane* edited by Darwin T. Turner
TURGENEV *Fathers and Sons* translated and edited by Michael R. Katz
VOLTAIRE *Candide* translated and edited by Robert M. Adams *Second Edition*
WASHINGTON *Up from Slavery* edited by William L. Andrews
WATSON *The Double Helix: A Personal Account of the Discovery of the Structure of DNA*
edited by Gunther S. Stent
WHARTON *Ethan Frome* edited by Kristin O. Lauer and Cynthia Griffin Wolff
WHARTON *The House of Mirth* edited by Elizabeth Ammons
WHITMAN *Leaves of Grass* edited by Sculley Bradley and Harold W. Blodgett
WILDE *The Picture of Dorian Gray* edited by Donald L. Lawler
WOLLSTONECRAFT *A Vindication of the Rights of Woman* edited by Carol H. Poston
Second Edition
WORDSWORTH *The Prelude: 1799, 1805, 1850* edited by Jonathan Wordsworth,
M. H. Abrams, and Stephen Gill